A HISTORY OF ANCIENT SANSKRIT LITERATURE

A HISTORY
OF
ANCIENT SANSKRIT LITERATURE

SO FAR AS IT ILLUSTRATES
THE PRIMITIVE RELIGION OF THE BRAHMANS.

BY

MAX MÜLLER, M. A.

GYAN

Published by

Gyan Publishing House
5, Ansari Road
Daryaganj, New Delhi-110002
Phone: 011-47034999, 9811692060
E-mail: books@gyanbooks.com

Distribution Network
gyanbooks.com
India, USA, Canada, UK, Australia, France

ISBN: 978-81-212-8250-5 (PB)
First Published, 1859

2nd Impression 2023

Printed at: Gyan Press, Delhi.

A HISTORY OF ANCIENT SANSKRIT LITERATURE
Author: MAX MÜLLER

A HISTORY

OF

ANCIENT SANSKRIT LITERATURE

SO FAR AS IT ILLUSTRATES

THE PRIMITIVE RELIGION OF THE BRAHMANS.

BY

MAX MÜLLER, M.A.

Fellow of All Souls College, Oxford;
Correspondant de l'Institut de France; Foreign Member of the Royal Bavarian Academy;
Honorary Member of the Royal Society of Literature, of the Asiatic Society of Bengal,
and of the Société d'Ethnographie de France;
Corresponding Member of the Royal Sardinian Academy, and of the American Oriental Society;
Member of the Asiatic Society of Paris, and of the Oriental Society of Germany; and
Taylorian Professor in the University of Oxford.

Second Edition, Revised.

WILLIAMS AND NORGATE,

14 HENRIETTA STREET, COVENT GARDEN, LONDON;
AND
20 SOUTH FREDERICK STREET, EDINBURGH.

PARIS: B. DUPRAT. LEIPZIG: R. HARTMANN.

1860

TO

HORACE HAYMAN WILSON, ESQ.

BODEN PROFESSOR OF SANSKRIT, ASSOCIATE OF THE INSTITUTE OF FRANCE, ETC.

This Work is Inscribed

AS A TOKEN OF ADMIRATION AND GRATITUDE

BY HIS PUPIL AND FRIEND

MAX MÜLLER.

PREFACE

TO

THE FIRST EDITION.

A few words of personal explanation are due to those who may have seen, in the Preface to the First Volume of my edition of the Rig-Veda*, a note announcing as ready for publication an Introductory Memoir on the Literature of the Veda. Ten sheets of this Memoir were printed when, in the beginning of the year 1851, I was appointed Deputy Professor, and, after the death of my lamented friend, Francis Trithen, in the year 1854, Professor of Modern European Languages and Literature in the University of Oxford. In compliance with the statutes of the Foundation of Sir Robert Taylor, I had to write "Three Courses of Lectures in every year, on the Philology or Literature of some of the principal Languages of Europe." These new and unexpected duties rendered it necessary for me to discontinue for a time my favourite studies. And when, after the first years of my new office, I was able to employ again a greater amount of leisure on their prose-

* Rig-Veda-Sanhitâ, the sacred songs of the Brahmans, together with the Commentary of Sâyaṇâchârya, edited by Max Müller, Vol. I., 1849; Vol. II., 1854; Vol. III., 1856. There will be three more volumes, the first of which is to be published next year. The first volume of Professor Wilson's Translation was published 1850; the second, 1854; the third, 1857.

cution, I felt that I should better serve the interests of Sanskrit Philology by devoting all my spare time to editing the text and commentary of the Veda, than by publishing the results, more or less fragmentary, of my own researches into the language, literature, and religion of the ancient Brahmans.

In resuming now, after the lapse of nearly ten years, the publication of these Essays, I may regret that on many points I have been anticipated by others, who during the interval have made the Veda the special subject of their studies. But this regret is fully balanced by the satisfaction I feel in finding that, in the main, my original views on the literature and religion of the Vedic age have not been shaken, either by my own continued researches or by the researches of others; and that the greater part of this work could be printed, as it now stands, from the original manuscript. It will be seen, however, that in the notes, as well as in the body of the work, I have availed myself, to the best of my ability, of all the really important and solid information that could be gathered from the latest works of Sanskrit philologists. The frequent references to the works of Wilson, Burnouf, Lassen, Benfey, Roth, Boehtlingk, Kuhn, Regnier, Weber, Aufrecht, Whitney, and others, will show where I have either derived new light from the labours of these eminent scholars, or found my own conclusions confirmed by their independent testimony. Believing, as I do, that literary controversy is more apt to impede than to advance the cause of truth, I have throughout carefully abstained from it. Where it seemed necessary to controvert unfounded statements or hasty conclusions, I have endeavoured to do so by stating the true facts of the case, and the legitimate conclusions that may be drawn from these facts.

My readers have to thank Dr. Bühler, a pupil of Professor Benfey of Göttingen, for the alphabetical index at the end of this volume.

MAX MÜLLER

Ray Lodge, Maidenhead,
Aug. 3, 1859.

TABLE OF CONTENTS.

HISTORY OF VEDIC LITERATURE.

CHAPTER I.

THE SÛTRA PERIOD.

CHAPTER II.

THE BRÂHMAṆA PERIOD.

CHAPTER III.

THE MANTRA PERIOD.

CHAPTER IV.

THE CHHANDAS PERIOD.

INTRODUCTION.

FULL seventy years have passed since Sir William Jones published his translation of Śakuntala[1], a work which may fairly be considered as the starting-point of Sanskrit philology. The first appearance of this beautiful specimen of dramatic art created at the time a sensation throughout Europe, and the most rapturous praise was bestowed upon it by men of high authority in matters of taste.[2] At the same time the attention of the historian, the philologist, and the philosopher was roused to the fact that

[1] "Śacontala, or the Fatal Ring, an Indian drama, translated from the original Sanskrit and Prakrit. Calcutta, 1789." There have since appeared three editions of the Sanskrit text, and translations in French, German, Italian, Danish, and Swedish. A new and very elegant English version has lately been published by Professor Williams. Hertford, 1856.

[2] Goethe was one of the greatest admirers of Śakuntala, as may be seen from the lines written in his Italian Travels at Naples, and from his well-known Epigram:

"Willt Du die Blüthe des frühen, die Früchte des späteren Jahres,
Willt Du was reizt und entzückt, willt Du was sättigt und nährt,
Willt Du den Himmel, die Erde mit einem Namen begreifen,
Nenn ich, Sacontala, Dich, und so ist Alles gesagt."

"Wilt thou the blossoms of spring and the fruits that are later in season,
Wilt thou have charms and delights, wilt thou have strength and support,
Wilt thou with one short word encompass the earth and the heaven,
All is said if I name only, Sacontala, thee."

a complete literature had been preserved in India, which promised to open a new leaf in the ancient history of mankind, and deserved to become the object of serious study. And although the enthusiasm with which works like Śakuntala were at first received by all who took an interest in literary curiosities could scarcely be expected to last, the real and scientific interest excited by the language, the literature, the philosophy, and antiquities of India has lasted, and has been increasing ever since. England, France, Germany, Italy, Denmark, Sweden, Russia, and Greece have each contributed their share towards the advancement of Sanskrit philology, and names like those of Sir W. Jones, Colebrooke, Wilson, in England, Burnouf in France, the two Schlegels, W. von Humboldt, Bopp, and Lassen, in Germany, have secured to this branch of modern scholarship a firm standing and a universal reputation. The number of books that have been published by Sanskrit scholars in the course of the last seventy years is but small.[1] Those works, however, represent large and definite results, important not only in their bearing on Indian antiquities, but, as giving birth to a new system of Comparative Philology, of the highest possible importance to philology in general.[2] In little more than half a

[1] Professor Gildemeister, in his most laborious and accurate work, "Bibliothecæ Sanscritæ Specimen, Bonnæ, 1847," brings the number of books that have been published up to that time in Sanskrit philology to 603, exclusive of all works on Indian antiquities and Comparative Philology. During the last twelve years that number has been considerably raised.

[2] Professor Lassen, in his work on Indian Antiquities, now in course of publication, is giving a resumé of the combined labours of Indian philologists during the last seventy years, sifted critically

century, Sanskrit has gained its proper place in the republic of learning, side by side with Greek and Latin. The privileges which these two languages enjoy in the educational system of modern Europe will scarcely ever be shared by Sanskrit. But no one who wishes to acquire a thorough knowledge of these or any other of the Indo-European languages, — no one who takes an interest in the philosophy and the historical growth of human speech, — no one who desires to study the history of that branch of mankind to which we ourselves belong, and to discover in the first germs of the language, religion, and mythology of our forefathers, the wisdom of Him who is not the God of the Jews only, — can, for the future, dispense with some knowledge of the language and ancient literature of India.

And yet Indian philology is still in its infancy, and the difficulties with which it has had to contend have been great, much greater, indeed, than those which lay in the way of Greek philology after its revival in the fifteenth century. Seventy years after the fall of Constantinople, the classical works of Greek literature were not only studied from manuscripts : they had been edited and printed. There were men like Reuchlin, Erasmus, and Melanchthon, who had investigated the most important documents in the different periods of Greek literature, and possessed a general knowledge of the historical growth of the Greek

and arranged scientifically by a man of the most extensive learning, and of the soundest principles of criticism. His work may indeed be considered as bringing to its conclusion an important period of Sanskrit philology, which had taken its beginning with Sir W. Jones's translation of Śakuntala. Indische Alterthums-Kunde, von Christian Lassen. Bonn, 1847—1858.

mind. Learned Greeks who were taking refuge in the west of Europe, particularly in Italy, had brought with them a sufficient knowledge to teach their language and literature; and they were able and ready to guide the studies of those who were afterwards to contribute to the revival of classical learning in Europe. Men began where they ought to begin, namely, with Homer, Herodotus, and Thucydides, and not with Anacreontic poetry or Neo-Platonist philosophy. But when our earliest Sanskrit scholars directed their attention to Indian literature, the difficulties they had to struggle with were far greater. Not to mention the burning and enervating sky of India, and the burden of their official occupations, men like Halhed, Wilkins, and Sir W. Jones could hardly find a single Brahman who would undertake to teach them his sacred idiom. When, after some time, learned Pandits became more willing to impart their knowledge to Europeans, their own views of Indian history and literature were more apt to mislead their pupils than to guide them in a truly historical direction. Thus it happened that, at the beginning of Sanskrit philology, preference was given either to works which still enjoyed amongst the Hindus themselves a great, but frequently undeserved, popularity, or to those which by their poetical beauty attracted the attention of men of taste. Everything Indian, whether Manu's Code of Laws, the Bhagavadgîtâ, Śakuntala, or the Hitopadeśa, was at that time considered to be of great and extravagant antiquity, and it was extremely difficult for European scholars to form a right opinion on the real merits of Indian literature. The literary specimens received from India were generally fragments only of larger works:

or, if not, they had been chosen so indiscriminately from different and widely distant periods, that it was impossible to derive from them an adequate knowledge of the rise and fall of the national literature of India.

Herder, in other respects an excellent judge of ancient national poetry, committed himself to some extraordinary remarks on Indian literature. In his criticism on Śakuntala, written in the form of letters to a friend, he says: "Do you not wish with me, that instead of these endless religious books of the Vedas, Upavedas, and Upangas, they would give us the more useful and more agreeable works of the Indians, and especially their best poetry of every kind? It is here the mind and character of a nation is best brought to life before us, and I gladly admit, that I have received a truer and more real notion of the manner of thinking among the ancient Indians from this one Śakuntala, than from all their Upnekats and Bagavedams."[1] The fact is that at that time Herder's view on the endless religious books of the Vedas, could only have been formed from a wretched translation of the Bagavedam, as he calls it,—that is, the Bhâgavatapurâṇa,—a Sanskrit work composed as many centuries after as the Vedas were before Christ; or from the Ezour-vedam, a very coarse forgery, if, indeed, it was intended as such, written, as it appears, by a native servant, for the use of the famous Jesuit missionary in India, Roberto de Nobilibus.[2]

[1] Herder's Schriften, vol. ix. p. 226, Zur schönen Literatur und Kunst. Tübingen, 1807.

[2] Comp. Account of a discovery of a Modern Imitation of the

Even at a much later time, men who possessed the true tact of an historian, like Niebuhr, have abstained from passing sentence on the history of a nation whose literature had only just been recovered, and had not yet passed through the ordeal of philological criticism. In his Lectures on Ancient History, Niebuhr leaves a place open for India, to be filled up when the pure metal of history should have been extracted from the ore of Brahmanic exaggeration and superstition.

Other historians, however, thought they could do what Niebuhr had left undone; and after perusing some poems of Kâlidâsa, some fables of the Hitopadeśa, some verses of the Ânanda-lahari, or the mystic poetry of the Bhagavadgîtâ, they gave, with the aid of Megasthenes and Apollonius of Tyana, a so-called historical account of the Indian nation, without being aware that they were using as contemporary witnesses, authors as distant from each other as Dante and Virgil. No nation has, in this respect, been more unjustly treated than the Indian. Not only have general conclusions been drawn from the most scanty materials, but the most questionable and spurious authorities have been employed without the least historical investigation or the exercise of that critical ingenuity, which, from its peculiar character, Indian literature requires more than any other.[1]

Vedas, with Remarks on the genuine works, by Fr. Ellis; Asiatic Researches, xiv. p. 1—59: Calcutta, 1822.

[1] Professor H. H. Wilson, in the preface to his translation of the Vishṇu-Purâṇa, remarks: "It is the boast of inductive philosophy that it draws its conclusions from the careful observation and accumulation of facts; and it is equally the business of all philosophical research to determine its facts before it ventures

There is another circumstance which has retarded the progress of Sanskrit philology: an affectation of that learned pedantry which has done so much mischief to Greek and Latin scholarship. We have much to learn, no doubt, from classical scholars, and nothing can be a better preparation for a Sanskrit student than to have passed through the school of a Bentley or a Hermann. But in Greek and Latin scholarship the distinction between useful and useless knowledge has almost disappeared, and the real objects of the study of these ancient languages have been well nigh forgotten. More than half of the publications of classical scholars have tended only to impede our access to the master-works of the ancients; and a sanction has been given to a kind of learning, which, however creditable to the individual, is of no benefit to the public at large. A similar spirit has infected Sanskrit philology. Sanskrit texts have been edited on which no rational man ought to waste his time. Essays have been written on subjects on which it is folly to be wise. These remarks are not intended to disparage critical scholarship or to depreciate the results which have been obtained by minute and abstruse erudition. But scholars who devote all their time to critical niceties and recondite subtleties are apt to forget that these are but accessories. Knowledge which has no object beyond itself is, in most cases, but a pretext for vanity. It is so easy, even for the most superfi-

upon speculation. This procedure has not been observed in the investigation of the mythology and traditions of the Hindus. Impatience to generalise has availed itself greedily of whatever promised to afford materials for generalisation; and the most erroneous views have been confidently advocated, because the guides to which their authors trusted were ignorant or insufficient."

cial scholar, to bring together a vast mass of information, bearing more or less remotely on questions of no importance whatsoever. The test of a true scholar is to be able to find out what is really important, to state with precision and clearness the results of long and tedious researches, and to suppress altogether lucubrations, which, though they might display the laboriousness of the writer, would but encumber his subject with needless difficulty.

The object and aim of philology, in its highest sense, is but one,—to learn what man is, by learning what man has been. With this principle for our pole-star, we shall never lose ourselves, though engaged in the most minute and abstruse inquiries. Our own studies may seemingly refer to matters that are but secondary and preparatory, to the clearance, so to say, of the rubbish which passing ages have left on the monuments of the human mind. But we shall never mistake that rubbish for the monuments which it covers. And if, after years of tiresome labour, we do not arrive at the results which we expected, — if we find but spurious and unimportant fabrications of individuals, where we thought to place ourselves face to face with the heroes of an ancient world, and among ruins that should teach us the lessons of former ages, — we need not be discouraged nor ashamed, for in true science even a disappointment is a result.

If, then, it is the aim of Sanskrit philology to supply one of the earliest and most important links in the history of mankind, we must go to work historically; that is, we must begin, as far as we can, with the beginning, and then trace gradually the growth of the Indian mind, in its various manifestations, as far as the remaining literary monuments allow us to follow this course. What has been said with regard to philosophy, that "we must acquire a knowledge of the beginning and first principles, because then only can we say that we understand any thing when we believe we know its real beginning," applies with equal force to history. Now every one acquainted with Indian literature, must have observed how impossible it is to open any book on Indian subjects without being thrown back upon an earlier authority, which is generally acknowledged by the Indians as the basis of all their knowledge, whether sacred or profane. This earlier authority, which we find alluded to in theological and philosophical works, as well as in poetry, in codes of law, in astronomical, grammatical, metrical, and lexicographic compositions, is called by one comprehensive name, the *Veda*.

It is with the Veda, therefore, that Indian philology ought to begin, if it is to follow a natural and historical course. So great an influence has the Vedic age (the historical period to which we are justified in referring the formation of the sacred texts) exercised upon all succeeding periods of Indian history, so closely is every branch of literature connected with Vedic traditions, so deeply have the religious and moral ideas of that primitive era taken root in the mind of the Indian nation, so minutely has almost every private and public act of Indian life been regulated by old traditionary precepts, that it is impossible to find the right point of view for judging of Indian religion, morals, and literature without a knowledge of the literary remains of the Vedic age. No one could fairly say that those men who first began to study Sanskrit, now seventy years ago, ought to have begun with reading the Veda. The difficulties connected with the study of the Veda would have made such a course utterly impossible and useless. But since the combined labours of Sanskrit scholars have now rendered the study of that language of more easy access, since the terminology of Indian grammarians and commentators, which not long ago was considered unintelligible, has become more familiar to us, and manuscripts can be more readily procured at the principal public libraries of Europe, Sanskrit philology has no longer an excuse for ignoring the Vedic age.

It might be inferred from the very variety of subjects upon which, as has been just observed, the Veda is quoted as the last and highest authority, that by Veda must be understood something more than a single work. It would be, indeed, much nearer the truth to take "Veda" as a collective name for the sacred literature of the Vedic age, which forms, so to speak, the background of the whole Indian world. Many of the works which belonged to that period of literature have been irrecoverably lost. With regard to many of them, though their existence cannot be doubted, it is uncertain whether they were ever committed to writing. A large number, however, of Vedic works does still exist; and it will require many years before they can be edited together with their commentaries. Till then it will be impossible to arrive at definite results on many questions connected with Vedic literature, and it would not be safe to take a comprehensive view of the whole Vedic age before all the sources have been exhausted from which its history and character can be studied. Nothing could be farther from the purpose of this historical essay than to attempt anything of this kind at present. What I have to offer are but Prolegomena to the Veda, or treatises on some preliminary questions connected with the history of the Vedic age. There are points which can be settled with complete certainty, though it may be impossible to bring, as yet, the whole weight of evidence to bear upon them; and the general question as to the authenticity, the antiquity, and the different periods of Vedic literature, ought to be answered even before beginning an edition of Vedic works. Again, there are many questions of special interest for Sanskrit literature, in which even now, with the materials that have been published, and with the help of manuscripts that are accessible in the public libraries of Europe, it is possible to arrive at certain results; while other points are such that even after the complete publication of all Vedic texts and commentaries, they will remain open to different views, and will necessarily become the subject of literary discussions. The principal object of the following essays will be to put the antiquity of the Veda in its proper light. By antiquity, however, is meant, not only the chronological distance of the Vedic age from our own, measured by the revolutions and the progress of the heavenly bodies, but also and still more, the distance between the intellectual, moral, and religious state of men as represented to us during the Vedic age, compared with that of other periods of history, — a distance which can only be measured by the revolutions and the progress of the human mind.

No one who is at all acquainted with the position which India occupies in the history of the world, would expect to find many synchronisms between the history of the Brahmans and that of other nations before the date of the origin of Buddhism in India. Although the Brahmans of India belong to the same family, the Aryan or Indo-European family, which civilised the whole of Europe, the two great branches of that primitive race were kept asunder for centuries after their first separation. The main stream of the Aryan nations has always flowed towards the north-west. No historian can tell us by what impulse those adventurous Nomads were driven on through Asia towards the isles and shores of Europe. The first start of this world-wide migration belongs to a period far beyond the reach of documentary history; to times when the soil of Europe had not been trodden by either Celts, Germans, Slavonians, Romans, or Greeks. But whatever it was; the impulse was as irresistible as the spell which, in our own times, sends the Celtic tribes towards the prairies or the regions of gold across the Atlantic. It requires a strong will, or a great amount of inertness, to be able to withstand the impetus of such national, or rather ethnical movements. Few will stay behind when all are going. But to let one's friends depart, and then to set out ourselves—to take a road which, lead where it may, can never lead us to join those again who speak our language and worship our gods—is a course which only men of strong individuality and great self-dependence are capable of pursuing. It was the course adopted by the southern branch of the Aryan family, the Brahmanic Aryas of India and the Zoroastrians of Iran.

At the first dawn of traditional history we see these Aryan tribes migrating across the snow of the Himâlaya southward toward the "Seven Rivers" (the Indus, the five rivers of the Panjâb and the Sarasvatî), and ever since India has been called their home. That before that time they had been living in more northern regions, within the same precincts with the ancestors of the Greeks, the Italians, Slavonians, Germans, and Celts, is a fact as firmly established as that the Normans of William the Conqueror were the Northmen of Scandinavia. The evidence of language is irrefragable, and it is the only evidence worth listening to with regard to ante-historical periods. It would have been next to impossible to discover any traces of relationship between the swarthy natives of India and their conquerors, whether Alexander or Clive, but for the testimony borne by language. What other evidence could have reached back to times when Greece was not peopled by Greeks, nor India by Hindus? Yet these are the times of which we are speaking. What authority would have been strong enough to persuade the Grecian army, that their gods and their hero ancestors were the same as those of King Porus, or to convince the English soldier that the same blood was running in his veins and in the veins of the dark Bengalese? And yet there is not an English jury now a days, which, after examining the hoary documents of language, would reject the claim of a common descent and a legitimate relationship between Hindu, Greek, and Teuton. Many words still live in India and in England, that have witnessed the first separation of the northern and southern Aryans, and these are witnesses not to be shaken by cross-examination. The terms for God, for house, for father, mother, son, daughter, for dog and cow, for heart and tears, for axe and tree, identical in all the Indo-European idioms, are like the watchwords of soldiers. We challenge the seeming stranger; and whether he answer with the lips of a Greek, a German, or an Indian, we recognise him as one of ourselves. Though the historian may shake his head, though the physiologist may doubt, and the poet scorn the idea, all must yield before the facts furnished by language. There *was* a time when the ancestors of the Celts, the Germans, the Slavonians, the Greeks, and Italians, the Persians, and Hindus, were living together within the same fences, separate from the ancestors of the Semitic and Turanian races.

It is more difficult to prove that the Hindu was the last to leave this common home, that he saw his brothers all depart towards the setting sun, and that then, turning towards the south and the east, he started alone in search of a new world. But as in his language and in his grammar he has preserved something of what seems peculiar to each of the northern dialects singly, as he agrees with the Greek and the German where the Greek and the German seem to differ from all the rest, and as no other language has carried off so large a share of the common Aryan heirloom — whether roots, grammar, words, mythes, or legends—it is natural to suppose that, though perhaps the eldest brother, the Hindu was the last to leave the central home of the Aryan family.

The Aryan nations who pursued a north-westerly direction, stand before us in history as the principal nations of north-western Asia and Europe. They have been the prominent actors in the great drama of history, and have carried to their fullest growth all the elements of active life with which our nature is endowed. They have perfected society and morals, and we learn from their literature and works of art the elements of science, the laws of art, and the principles of philosophy. In continual struggle with each other and with Semitic and Turanian races, these Aryan nations have become the rulers of history, and it seems to be their mission to link all parts of the world together by the chains of civilisation, commerce, and religion. In a word they represent the Aryan man in his historical character.

But while most of the members of the Aryan family followed this glorious path, the southern tribes were slowly migrating towards the mountains which gird the north of India. After crossing the narrow passes of the Hindukush or the Himâlaya, they conquered or drove before them, as it seems without much effort, the aboriginal inhabitants of the Trans-Himalayan countries. They took for their guides the principal rivers of Northern India, and were led by them to new homes in their beautiful and fertile valleys. It seems as if the great mountains in the north had afterwards closed for centuries their Cyclopian gates against new immigrations, while, at the same time, the waves of the Indian Ocean kept watch over the southern borders of the peninsula. None of the great conquerors of antiquity—Sesostris, Semiramis, Nebuchadnezzar, or Cyrus, who waged a kind of half-nomadic warfare over Asia, Africa, and Europe, and whose names, traced in characters of blood, are still legible on the threshold of history[1], disturbed the

[1] Thus Strabo says, xv. I. 6.: Ἡμῖν δὲ τίς ἂν δικαία γένοιτο πίστις περὶ τῶν Ἰνδικῶν ἐκ τῆς τοιαύτης στρατείας τοῦ Κύρου ἢ τῆς Σεμιράμιδος; Συναποφαίνεται δέ πως καὶ Μεγασθένης τῷ λόγῳ τούτῳ, κελεύων ἀπιστεῖν ταῖς ἀρχαίαις περὶ Ἰνδῶν ἱστορίαις· οὔτε γὰρ παρ' Ἰνδῶν ἔξω σταλῆναί ποτε στρατιὰν οὔτ' ἐπελθεῖν ἔξωθεν καὶ κρατῆσαι, πλὴν τῆς μεθ' Ἡρακλέους καὶ Διονύσου, καὶ τῆς νῦν μετὰ Μακεδόνων.

peaceful seats of these Aryan settlers. Left to themselves in a world of their own, without a past, and without a future before them, they had nothing but themselves to ponder on. Struggles there must have been in India also. Old dynasties were destroyed, whole families annihilated, and new empires founded. Yet the inward life of the Hindu was not changed by these convulsions. His mind was like the lotus leaf after a shower of rain has passed over it; his character remained the same, passive, meditative, quiet, and full of faith.

The chief elements of discord amongst the peaceful inhabitants of this rich country were, the struggle for supremacy between the different classes of society, the subjugation of the uncivilised inhabitants, particularly in the south of India, and the pressure of the latest comers in the north upon the possessors of the more fertile countries in the south.

These three struggles took place in India at an early period, and were sufficiently important to have called forth the active faculties of any but the Indian

Καίτοι Σέσωστριν μὲν τὸν Αἰγύπτιον καὶ Τεάρκωνα τὸν Αἰθίοπα ἕως Εὐρώπης προελθεῖν. Ναβοκοδρόσορον δὲ τὸν παρὰ Χαλδαίοις εὐδοκιμήσαντα Ἡρακλέους μᾶλλον καὶ ἕως Στηλῶν ἐλάσαι· μέχρι μὲν δὴ δεῦρο καὶ Τεάρκωνα ἀφικέσθαι· ἐκεῖνον δὲ καὶ ἐκ τῆς Ἰβηρίας εἰς τὴν Θρᾴκην καὶ τὸν Πόντον ἀγαγεῖν τὴν στρατιάν. Ἰδάνθυρσον δὲ τὸν Σκύθην ἐπιδραμεῖν τῆς Ἀσίας μέχρι Αἰγύπτου· τῆς δὲ Ἰνδικῆς μηδένα τούτων ἅψασθαι. Καὶ Σεμίραμιν δ' ἀποθανεῖν πρὸ τῆς ἐπιχειρήσεως. Πέρσας δὲ μισθοφόρους μὲν ἐκ τῆς Ἰνδικῆς μεταπέμψασθαι Ὕδρακας· ἐκεῖ δὲ μὴ στρατεῦσαι, ἀλλ' ἐγγὺς ἐλθεῖν μόνον, ἡνίκα Κῦρος ἤλαυνεν ἐπὶ Μασσαγέτας. With regard to the expeditions of Herakles and Dionysos, Strabo adds: Καὶ τὰ περὶ Ἡρακλέους δὲ καὶ Διονύσου Μεγασθένης μὲν μετ' ὀλίγων πιστὰ ἡγεῖται· τῶν δ' ἄλλων οἱ πλείους, ὧν ἐστι καὶ Ἐρατοσθένης, ἄπιστα καὶ μυθώδη, καθάπερ καὶ τὰ παρὰ τοῖς Ἕλλησιν, κ. τ. λ. Cf. Megasthenis Indica, ed. Schwanbeck. Bonnæ, 1846.

nation. In these struggles we may recognise almost the same elements by which the Greek character was perfected and matured. But how different have been the results upon the Indian mind! The struggle for supremacy between the different classes, which in Greece ended with the downfall of the tyrannies and the rising of well-organised republics, has its counterpart in India in the extirpation of the Kshatriya race and the triumph of the Brahmans through Paraśu-Râma.[1]

The second struggle, or the war against the uncivilised inhabitants of the South, is represented by the Indian poet of the Râmâyaṇa as the battle of a divine hero against evil spirits and uncouth giants. What this is to India, the war of Persia was to Greece; the victory of patriotic valour over brute force. The Muses of Herodotus are the Râmâyaṇa of Hellas.

In the third of these parallel struggles the contrast is no less striking. We follow, with a mournful interest, the narrative of international jealousies between the different states of Greece; we see how one

[1] "Paraśu-Râma cleared the earth thrice seven times of the Kshatriya caste, and filled with their blood the five large lakes of Samanta-panchaka, from which he offered libations to the race of Bhṛigu. Offering a solemn sacrifice to the king of the gods, Paraśu-Râma presented the earth to the ministering priests. Having given the earth to Kaśyapa, the hero of immeasurable prowess retired to the Mahendra mountain, where he still resides; and in this manner was there enmity between him and the race of the Kshatriyas, and thus was the whole earth conquered by Paraśu-Râma." (Vishṇu-Purâṇa, p. 403.) In the Mahâbhârata the earth is made to say, "The fathers and grandfathers of these Kshatriyas have been killed by the remorseless Râma in warfare on my account."

tries to crush the power of the other, while all are preparing the common ruin of the country. But what characters are here presented to our analysis, what statesmanship, what eloquence, what bravery! In India the war of the Mahâbhârata was, perhaps, more bloody than the Peloponnesian war: but in the hands of the Brahmans the ancient epic has dwindled into a didactic legend.

Greece and India are, indeed, the two opposite poles in the historical development of the Aryan man. To the Greek, existence is full of life and reality; to the Hindu it is a dream, an illusion. The Greek is at home where he is born; all his energies belong to his country: he stands and falls with his party, and is ready to sacrifice even his life to the glory and independence of Hellas. The Hindu enters this world as a stranger; all his thoughts are directed to another world; he takes no part even where he is driven to act; and when he sacrifices his life, it is but to be delivered from it.

No wonder that a nation like the Indian cared so little for history; no wonder that social and political virtues were little cultivated, and the ideas of the Useful and the Beautiful scarcely known to them. With all this, however, they had what the Greek was as little capable of imagining as they were of realising the elements of Grecian life. They shut their eyes to this world of outward seeming and activity, to open them full on the world of thought and rest. Their life was a yearning after eternity; their activity a struggle to return into that divine essence from which this life seemed to have severed them. Believing as they did in a divine and really existing eternal Being (τὸ ὄντως ὄν), they could not believe in the existence of this passing world. If the one existed, the other could only seem to exist; if they lived in the one, they could not live in the other. Their existence on earth was to them a problem, their eternal life a certainty. The highest object of their religion was to restore that bond [1] by which their own self (âtman) was linked to the eternal Self (paramâtman); to recover that unity which had been clouded and obscured by the magical illusions of reality, by the so-called Mâyâ of creation. It scarcely entered their mind either to doubt or to affirm the immortality of the soul [2], except in later times, and then only for philosophical and controversial purposes.[3] Not only their religion and literature, but their very language, reminded them daily of that relation between the real

[1] In one of the old hymns of the Rig-veda this thought seems to weigh upon the mind of the poet, when he says:

सतो बंधुमसति निरविंदन् हृदि प्रतीष्य कवयो मनीषा ॥

"Poets discovered in their heart, through meditation, the bond of the existing in the non-existing." Rv. x. 129. 4.

[2] In the Veda life after death is not frequently alluded to, and it is more for the goods of this world, for strength, long life, a large family, food, and cattle, that the favour of the gods is implored. One of the rewards for a pious life, however, consists in being admitted after death to the seat of the gods. Thus Kakshîvat says, Rv. i. 125. 5: "He who gives alms goes and stands on the highest place in heaven, he goes to the gods." Thus Dîrghatamas (Rv. i. 150. 3), after having rebuked those who are rich, and do not give alms, nor worship the gods, exclaims, "The kind mortal, O Sage, is greater than the great in heaven; let us worship thee, O Agni, for ever and ever!"

[3] The technical term "pretyabhâva," which occurs so frequently in Indian philosophy, and has generally been rendered by "condition of the soul after death," means really the state in which we are while living on earth. Our present life, according to Indian notions, is "bhâva," birth and growth, "pretya," after a previous death.

and the seeming world. The word *âtman*, for instance, which in the Veda occurs often as *tman*, means life, particularly animal life. Thus we read, Rv. i. 63. 8., "Increase, O bright Indra! this our manifold food, like water all over the earth; by which, O Hero! thou givest us *life*, like sap, to move every where." Here *tman* means the vital principle, and is compared with the juice that circulates in plants. In another hymn, addressed to the horse which is to be sacrificed (Rv. i. 162. 20.), the poet says, "Mâ tvâ tapat priya âtmâ-piyantam," literally, "Let not thy dear self burn or afflict thee as thou approachest the sacrifice." Here *priya âtmâ* corresponds to the Greek φίλον ἦτορ. But we find *âtman* used in a higher sense also in the Veda. For instance, Rv. i. 115. 1., "Sûrya âtmâ jagatas tasthushaś cha:" "the sun is the soul of all that moves and rests."[1] Most frequently, however, *tman* and *âtman* are employed for self, just as we say, My soul praises, rejoices, for I praise, I myself rejoice. This is the most usual signification of *âtman* in the later Sanskrit, where it is used as a pronoun. Yet *âtman* means there also the soul of the universe, the highest soul or Self (paramâtman) of which all other

[1] In the same sense the sun is called jîvo asuḥ, "the vital spirit," cf. Rv. i. 113. 16.:

उदीर्ध्वं जीवो असुर्न आगादप प्रागात्तम आ ज्योतिरेति ॥

"Rise! our life, our spirit, came; the darkness went off; the light approaches!" Rv. ii. 3. 14.:

को ददर्श प्रथमं जायमानमस्थन्वंतं यदनस्था बिभर्ति ।
भूम्या असुरसृगात्मा क्व स्वित्को विद्वांसमुप गात्प्रष्टुमेतत् ॥

"Who has seen the first born, when he who has no bones (*i. e.* form) bore him who had bones? Where was the life, the blood, the soul (self) of the world? Who went to ask this from any that knew it?"

souls partake, from which all reality in this created world emanates, and into which every thing will return. Thus a Hindu speaking of himself (âtman) spoke also, though unconsciously, of the soul of the universe (âtman); and to know himself was to him to know both his own self and the universal Self, or to know himself in the divine Self. The Sanskrit, "âtmânam âtmanâ paśya," "see (thy) self by (thy) self," had a deeper signification than the Greek γνῶθι σεαυτόν[1], because it had not only a moral, but also a

[1] It is difficult to find a satisfactory etymology for *âtmâ* (nomin.), particularly in its older, and possibly more original, form, *tmâ*. Bopp (Comp. Grammar, i. § 140.) says, "if *âtmâ* stand for *âhmâ*, and be derived from a lost root, *âh*, to think (when it must be remembered that the root *nah* also changes its final *h* sometimes into *t*, upânah and upânat), it might be compared with the Gothic *ahma*, soul." This root, *âh*, is afterwards traced by Bopp in the Sanskrit *âha*, "he said;" and he observes that to speak and to think are in the Indo-European languages sometimes expressed by one and the same word. The last observation, however, is not quite proved by the example taken by Bopp from the Zend, *manthra*, speech. For although the Sanskrit *mantra* is derived from *man*, to think, it receives its causal meaning by the termination *tra*, and has therefore the signification of prayer, hymn, advice, speech (*i. e.* what makes us think). If *âtmâ* come from a root *ah*, the meaning of this root is more likely that of breathing, which would account for Gothic *ahma* (πνεῦμα), as well as for Sanskrit *âha*, Greek ἦ and ἠχώ, Latin *ajo* and *nego*, and similar words. If we derive *âtmâ*, spirit, soul, self, from this root *ah*, we may also derive from it *ah-am*, I (cuneiform inscript. *adam*, ego, ἐγώ, ich). But there always remains a difficulty as regards the elision of â in the old Vedic form *tmâ*, instead of *âtmâ*, and the Zend *thmanangh*, which, according to Burnouf's conjecture, is the Sansk. *tmanas* (Commentaire sur le Yaśna, p. 509.); a difficulty which neither European etymologists (Pott, Etymologische Forschungen, i. 196.; Benfey, Griechisches Wurzellexicon, i. 265.) nor Indian Auṇâdik scholars (Uṇâdi Sûtras, 4. 152.) have yet explained.

metaphysical meaning. How largely this idea of the Âtman, as the Divine Spirit, entered into the early religious and philosophical speculations of the Indians, may be seen from the following dialogue between Yâjnavalkya and Maitrêyî, which forms part of the Bṛihadâraṇyaka.

"Maitrêyî[1]," said Yâjnavalkya, "I am going away from this my house (into the forest). Forsooth, I must make a settlement between thee and my other wife Kâtyâyanî."

Maitrêyî said, "My Lord, if this whole earth full of wealth belonged to me, should I be immortal by it?"

"No," replied Yâjnavalkya; "like the happy life of rich people will be thy life. But there is no hope of immortality by wealth."

And Maitrêyî said, "What should I do with that by which I do not become immortal? What my Lord knoweth of (immortality) may he tell that to me."

Yâjnavalkya replied, "Thou, who art truly dear to me[2], thou speakest dear words. Sit down, I will explain it to thee, and listen well to what I say." And he said, "A husband is loved, not because you love the husband, but because you love (in him) the

[1] Bṛihadâraṇyaka, 2d Adhyâya, 4th Brâhmaṇa, p. 28. edit. Poley; 4th Prapâṭhaka, 4th Brâhmaṇa, p. 444. edit. Röer.

[2] Instead of प्रिचा वतारे नः सती Dr. Poley reads प्रियावतारे नः सती which he may have meant for "thou Avatâr, or incarnation of our love." Not to speak, however, of the grammatical difficulties of this construction, the Commentary leaves no doubt that we ought to read, प्रिया (इष्टा) वत (इत्यनुकंप्याह) अरे (मैत्रेयि).

Divine Spirit (âtman, the absolute Self). A wife is loved, not because we love the wife, but because we love (in her) the Divine Spirit. Children are loved not because we love the children, but because we love the Divine Spirit in them. This spirit it is which we love when we (seem to) love wealth, Brahmans, Kshatriyas, this world, the gods, all beings, this universe. The Divine Spirit, O beloved wife, is to be seen, to be heard, to be perceived, and to be meditated upon. If we see, hear, perceive, and know him, O Maitrêyî, then this whole universe is known to us."

"Whosoever looks for Brahmahood elsewhere than in the Divine Spirit, should be abandoned by the Brahmans. Whosoever looks for the Kshatra-power elsewhere than in the Divine Spirit, should be abandoned by the Kshatras. Whosoever looks for this world, for the gods, for all beings, for this universe, elsewhere than in the Divine Spirit, should be abandoned by them all. This Brahmahood, this Kshatra-power, this world, these gods, these beings, this universe, all is the Divine Spirit."

"Now, as we cannot seize the sounds of a drum externally by themselves, but seize the sound by seizing the drum, or the beating of it,—as we cannot seize the sounds of a conch-shell by themselves, but seize the sound by seizing the conch-shell, or the shell-blower,—as we cannot seize the sounds of a lute by themselves, but seize the sound by seizing the lute, or the lutanist,—so is it with the Divine Spirit."

"As clouds of smoke rise out of a fire kindled with dry fuel, thus, O Maitrêyî, have all the holy words been breathed out of that Great Being."

"As all the waters find their centre in the sea,

so all sensations find their centre in the skin, all tastes in the tongue, all smells in the nose, all colours in the eye, all sounds in the ear, all thoughts in the mind, all knowledge in the heart, all actions in the hands, and all the Holy Scriptures in speech."

"It is with us, when we enter into the Divine Spirit, as if a lump of salt was thrown into the sea; it becomes dissolved into the water (from which it was produced), and is not to be taken out again. But wherever you take the water and taste it, it is salt. Thus is this great, endless, and boundless Being but one mass of knowledge. As the water becomes salt, and the salt becomes water again, thus has the Divine Spirit appeared from out the elements and disappears again into them. When we have passed away, there is no longer any name. This, I tell thee, my wife," said Yâjnavalkya.

Maitrêyî said, "My Lord, here thou hast bewildered me, saying that there is no longer any name when we have passed away."

And Yâjnavalkya replied, "My wife, what I say is not bewildering, it is sufficient for the highest knowledge. For if there be as it were two beings, then the one sees the other, the one hears, perceives, and knows the other. But if the one Divine Self be the whole of all this, whom or through whom should he see, hear, perceive, or know? How should he know (himself), by whom he knows every thing (himself)? How, my wife, should he know (himself) the knower?[1] Thus thou hast been taught, Maitrêyî:

[1] This last sentence is taken from the fifth Brâhmaṇa of the fourth Adhyâya, where the same story is told again with slight modifications and additions.

this is immortality." Having said this Yâjnavalkya left his wife for ever, and went into the solitude of the forests.

It must be observed that the work from which this dialogue is taken belongs to a later period of Vedic literature. In the earlier times which are represented to us in the hymns of the Veda, these mystic tendencies are not yet so strongly developed. In the songs of the Rig-veda we find but little of philosophy, but we do occasionally meet with wars of kings, with rivalries of ministers, with triumphs and defeats, with war-songs and imprecations. The active side of life is still prominent in the genuine poetry of the Ṛishis, and there still exists a certain equilibrium between the two scales of human nature. It is only after the Aryan tribes had advanced southward, and taken quiet possession of the rich plains and beautiful groves of Central India, that they seem to have turned all their energies and thoughts from the world without them to that more wonderful nature which they perceived within.

Such was their state when the Greeks first became acquainted with them after the discovery of India by Alexander. What did these men, according to Megasthenes, most think and speak about? Their most frequent conversations, he says, were about life and death. This life they considered as the life of an embryo in the womb; but death as the birth to a real and happy life for those who had thought, and had prepared themselves to be ready to die.[1] Good and

[1] Strabo, xv. 59.: Πλείστους δ' αὐτοῖς εἶναι λόγους περὶ τοῦ θανάτου· νομίζειν γὰρ δὴ τὸν μὲν ἐνθάδε βίον ὡς ἂν ἀκμον κυομένων εἶναι· τὸν δὲ θάνατον γένεσιν εἰς τὸν ὄντως βίον καὶ τὸν εὐδαίμονα τοῖς φιλοσοφήσασι· διὸ τῇ ἀσκήσει πλείστῃ χρῆσθαι πρὸς τὸ ἑτοιμο-

bad was nothing to them; not that they denied the distinction between good and bad in a moral sense. They recognised law and virtue, as we see in their sacred poetry[1], as well as in their codes of law. But they denied that anything that happened to men in this life could be called either good or bad, and they maintained that philosophy consisted in removing the affections of pleasure as well as of pain. Liking pain and hating pleasure was what they considered the highest state of indifference that man could arrive at.[2]

θάνατον. "Nay, for aught we know of ourselves, of our present life, and of death; death may immediately, in the natural course of things, put us into a higher and more enlarged state of life, as our birth does."—*Bishop Butler.*

[1] The notion of sin is clearly expressed, for instance, in a song of Gṛitsamada's (Rv. ii. 28. 5.):

वि मच्छ्रथाय रशनामिवाग ऋध्याम ते वरुण खामृतस्य।
मा तंतुश्छेदि वयतो धियं मे मा मात्रा शार्यपसः पुर ऋतोः॥
अपो सु म्यक्ष वरुण भियसं मत्सम्राळृतावोऽनु मा गृभाय।
दामेव वत्साद्विमुमुग्ध्यंहो न हि त्वदारे निमिषश्चनेशे॥

"Deliver me from sin, as from a rope; let us obtain, O Varuṇa, thy path of righteousness. May the thread not be torn while I am weaving my prayer; may the form of my pious work not decay before its season.

"Varuṇa, take all fear away from me; be kind to me, O just king! Take away my sin like a rope from a calf; for afar from thee I am not the master even of a twinkling of the eye."

And again, Rv. ii. 29. 1.:

धृतव्रता आदित्या इषिरा आरे मत्कर्त रहसूरिवागः॥

"You quick Âdityas, ye who never fail in your works, carry away from me all sin, as a woman does who has given birth to a child in secret."

[2] Strabo, xv. 59.: Ἀγαθὸν δὲ, ἢ κακὸν, μηδὲν εἶναι τῶν συμβαι-

We are told by the same author that the Indians did not communicate their metaphysical doctrines to women; thinking that, if their wives understood these doctrines, and learned to be indifferent to pleasure and pain, and to consider life and death as the same, they would no longer continue to be the slaves of others: or, if they failed to understand them, they would be talkative, and communicate their knowledge to those who had no right to it. This statement of the Greek author is fully borne out by the later Sanskrit authorities. We find, for instance, in the ceremonial Sûtras (śrauta and gṛihya-sûtras), that women were not allowed to learn the sacred songs of the Vedas, the knowledge of which constituted one of the principal acquirements of a Brahman before he was admitted to the performance of the sacrifices. Indeed, the whole education of a Brahman consisted in learning the old sacred literature by heart, and many years were spent for this purpose by every Brahmachârin in the house and under the severe discipline of his Guru, or of an Âchârya. As it was necessary[1], however, for a husband to perform

νόντων ἀνθρώποις· οὐ γὰρ ἂν τοῖς αὐτοῖς τοὺς μὲν ἄχθεσθαι, τοὺς δὲ χαίρειν, ἐνυπνιώδεις ὑπολήψεις ἔχοντας, καὶ τοὺς αὐτοὺς τοῖς αὐτοῖς τότε μὲν ἄχθεσθαι, τότε δ' αὖ χαίρειν μεταβαλλομένους. Ibid. xv. 65.: Τὰ γοῦν λεχθέντα εἰς τοῦτ' ἔφη συντείνειν, ὡς εἴη λόγος ἄριστος ὃς ἡδονὴν καὶ λύπην ψυχῆς ἀφαιρήσεται· καὶ ὅτι λύπη καὶ πόνος διαφέρει· τὸ μὲν γὰρ πολέμιον, τὸ δὲ φίλον αὐτοῖς· τὰ δὲ σώματα ἀσκοῦσι πρὸς πόνον, ἵν' αἱ γνῶμαι ῥωννύοιντο, ἀφ' ὧν καὶ στάσεις παύοιεν, καὶ σύμβουλοι πᾶσιν ἀγαθῶν παρεῖεν, καὶ κοινῇ καὶ ἰδίᾳ.

[1] Sâyaṇa, in his commentary on the Rig-veda, i. 131. 3., explaining the words वि त्वा ततस्रे मिथुना अवस्यवः "Couples wishing for protection have magnified thee, O Indra!" quotes passages from the Brâhmaṇas, the Sûtras, and the Smṛitis, in

sacrifices together with his lawful wife, and as passages of the hymns[1], as well as of the Brâhmaṇas, speak clearly of man and wife as performing sacrifices in common, it was laid down in the Sûtras that the husband or the priest should, at the sacrifice itself, make his wife recite those hymns which were necessary for the ceremony. But although women were thus allowed to participate in the sacrifices of their husbands, they were not initiated, still less were they admitted to the highest knowledge, the knowledge of the Âtman or the Brahman.[2] Cases like that of Maitrêyî were exceptions, not the rule.

Thus the account which Megasthenes gives of the Indians shows us the same abstract and passive

support of the law laid down in the Pûrvamîmânsâ, that man and wife should perform sacrifices in common. From the Brâhmaṇas he quotes the beginning of the Agnyâdhâna, where it is said that man and wife are to place the sacred fire in common: जायापती अग्निमादधीयातां। From the Sûtras he quotes a rule, वेदं पत्न्यै प्रदाय वाचयेत्। This seems to mean, "Let him, after giving the Veda to his wife, make her recite it." The passage is taken from the Âśvalâyana Śrauta-sûtras, i. 11. If the word *veda*, used by Âśvalâyana, meant the Veda, this passage would be most important, as proving the existence of the Veda as a written book, at the time of Âśvalâyana. *Veda*, however, is used here in the sense of "a bundle of grass," and is connected with *vediḥ*, an altar made of grass (Root *ve*, Lat. viere). Lastly, Sâyaṇa quotes from the Smṛitis, Manu, v. 155., "Women cannot sacrifice without their husbands:" नास्ति स्त्रीणां पृथग्यज्ञः॥

[1] The piety and happiness of a married couple is well described in a hymn ascribed to Manu Vaivasvata, Rv. viii. 31. 5—9.

[2] Manu, ix. 18., translated by Sir W. Jones. "Women have no business with the texts of the Veda, thus is the law fully settled; having, therefore, no evidence of law, and no knowledge of expiatory texts, sinful women must be as foul as falsehood itself; and this is a fixed rule."

character which we find throughout the whole post-vedic literature of the Brahmans, and which, to a great extent, explains the absence of anything like historical literature among this nation of philosophers.

A people of this peculiar stamp of mind was never destined to act a prominent part in what is called the history of the world. This exhausting atmosphere of transcendental ideas could not but exercise a detrimental influence on the active and moral character of the Indians. But if we admire in classical history even those heroes in whom the love of country was driven to the highest pitch of fanaticism, we have scarcely a right to despise a nation, in whom the love of a purer and higher life degenerated sometimes into reckless self-sacrifice. No people certainly made a more favourable impression upon the Greeks than the Indians. And when we read the account of their moral and intellectual condition at the time of Alexander, we are obliged to admit that if some of their good qualities are no longer to be met with among the Indians of later times, this is owing, not entirely to an original defect of character, but to that continual system of oppression exercised upon them by foreign conquerors, to whose physical power they submitted, while they could not help despising their masters as barbarians. Of the demoralising influence of a foreign occupation we have an instance in the time of Alexander, in the story of Kalânas (Kalyâna), who yielded to the flattering offers of the European conqueror, and left his sacred home to follow his royal master as a piece of curiosity. But Megasthenes was afterwards informed that the behaviour of Kalânas was strongly disapproved of by his friends, as ambitious and servile; while Maṇdanis was praised for his manly answer to Alexander's messengers, not only by his countrymen, but by Alexander himself. It was not long before Kalânas repented his unworthy ambition, for he burnt himself soon after at Pasargada, in the same manner as the only other Brahman who reached Europe in ancient times, burned himself at Athens, to the astonishment of the Greeks, who erected a tomb to him, with the inscription, "Here lies the Indian Sarman Cheya (Śarman Âchârya ?), from Barygaza, who sought immortality after the old custom of the Indians."

The genius of the Greek nation owes its happy and healthy growth to liberty and national independence. The Homeric songs were addressed to a people, proud of its heroes, whether real or legendary. If Persia had crushed the chivalry of Greece, we should never have heard the names of Herodotus, Æschylus, Sophocles, Phidias, and Pericles. Where the feeling of nationality has been roused, the poet is proud to be listened to by his nation, and a nation is proud to listen to her poet. But in times of national degradation the genius of great men turns away from the realities of life, and finds its only consolation in the search after truth, in science and philosophy. Socrates, Plato, and Aristotle arose when the Greek nation began to decline; and, under the heavy grasp first of Macedonian sway, then of Roman tyranny, the life of the Greek genius ebbed away, while its immortal productions lived on in the memory of other and freer nations. The Indian never knew the feeling of nationality, and his heart never trembled in the expectation of national applause. There were no heroes to inspire a poet,—no history to call forth a historian. The only sphere where the Indian mind found itself at liberty to act, to create, and to worship, was the sphere of religion and philosophy; and nowhere have religious and metaphysical ideas struck roots so deep in the mind of a nation as in India. The Hindus were a nation of philosophers. Their struggles were the struggles of thought; their past, the problem of creation; their future, the problem of existence. The present alone, which is the real and living solution of the problems of the past and the future, seems never to have attracted their thoughts or to have called out their energies. The shape which metaphysical ideas take amongst the different classes of society, and at different periods of civilisation, naturally varies from coarse superstition to sublime spiritualism. But, taken as a whole, history supplies no second instance where the inward life of the soul has so completely absorbed all the practical faculties of a whole people, and, in fact, almost destroyed those qualities by which a nation gains its place in history.

It might therefore be justly said that India has no place in the political history of the world. While other nations, as the Egyptians, the Jews, the Babylonians, Assyrians, Persians, the Greeks, the Romans, and the Teutonic races, have, during certain periods, culminated on the political horizon of the world, India has moved in such a small and degraded circle of political existence that it remained almost invisible to the eyes of other nations. An expedition like that of Alexander could never have been conceived by an Indian king, and the ambition of native conquerors, in those few cases where it existed, never went beyond the limits of India itself.

But if India has no place in the political history of the world, it certainly has a right to claim its place in the intellectual history of mankind. The less the Indian nation has taken part in the political struggles of the world, and expended its energies in the exploits of war and the formation of empires, the more it has fitted itself and concentrated all its powers for the fulfilment of the important mission reserved to it in the history of the East. History seems to teach that the whole human race required a gradual education before, in the fulness of time, it could be admitted to the truths of Christianity. All the fallacies of human reason had to be exhausted, before the light of a higher truth could meet with ready acceptance. The ancient religions of the world were but the milk of nature, which was in due time to be succeeded by the bread of life. After the primeval physiolatry, which was common to all the members of the Aryan family, had, in the hands of a wily priesthood, been changed into an empty idolatry, the Indian alone, of all the Aryan nations, produced a new form of religion, which has well been called subjective, as opposed to the more objective worship of nature. That religion, the religion of Buddha, has spread, far beyond the limits of the Aryan world, and, to our limited vision, it may seem to have retarded the advent of Christianity among a large portion of the human race. But in the sight of Him with whom a thousand years are but as one day, that religion, like all the ancient religions of the world, may have but served to prepare the way of Christ, by helping, through its very errors, to strengthen and to deepen the ineradicable yearning of the human heart after the truth of God.

Though the religion of Buddha be of all religions the most hostile to the old belief of the Brahmans,—the Buddhists standing to the Brahmans in about the same relation as the early Protestants to the Church of Rome,—yet the very bitterness of this opposition proves that Buddhism is peculiarly Indian. Similar ideas to those proclaimed by Buddha were current long before his time, and traces of them may be found even in other countries. But for the impressive manner in which these ideas were first proclaimed and preached throughout India, for the hold which they took on the Indian mind, for the readiness with which they were received, particularly by the lower classes, till at last they were adopted by the sovereign as the religion of state,—in a word, for the historical and universal character which this doctrine there assumed, the cause must be sought in the previous history of the Indian nation. There is something in the doctrines of Buddhism that is common to all systems of philosophy or religion, which break with the traditions of an effete idol-worship and a tyrannical hierarchy. There is some truth in Buddhism as there is in every one of the false religions of the world. But it was only in India, where people had been prepared by centuries of thought and meditation, as well as by the very corruption of the old Brahmanical system to embrace and nurture the religious ideas of Buddha Śâkya Muni; it was only in India, that those new doctrines took an historical shape, and grew into a religion which, if truth depended on majorities, would be the truest of all forms of faith.

Up to the present day there is no religion of the world more extensively prevalent than the religion of Buddha[1]; and though it has been banished from

[1] M. Troyer, in his valuable edition of the Radjatarangini (ii. 399.), gives the following data as to the extent of the Buddhistic

the soil of India, and no living follower of this creed is now to be met with in that country[1], yet it has found a refuge and second home in Ceylon, Siam, Ava, Pegu, the Birman Empire, China, Tibet, Tatary, Mongolia and Siberia, and is, even in its present corruption, looked upon and practised as the only true system of faith and worship by many millions of human beings. Truly, then, the moment when this religious doctrine took its origin in India is an era in the intellectual history of the world; and, from an historical point of view, India may be considered, at that time, as passing through the meridian of history. The most accurate observers of the progress of the Indian mind have, therefore, chosen this moment as the most favourable for fixing, historically and chronologically, the position of India: Professor Wilson in his "Vishṇu-Purâṇa," Professor Burnouf in his "Introduction to the History of Buddhism," and Professor Lassen in his "Indian Antiquities."

It would be out of place to discuss at present all the arguments by which the historical origin of the Buddhistic religion has been fixed chronologically in the works here mentioned. The date of Buddha's

religion: "La population de la terre est évaluée par M. Hassel à 921 millions; par Malte-Brun, à 642 millions; par d'autres, à 737 millions d'habitants. Le Buddhisme est professé dans presque tout l'empire de la Chine, qui seul, d'après différents computs, contient de 184 à 300 millions d'habitants. Ajoutons-y les Buddhistes de plusieurs îles de l'Est, de la Cochinchine, du Siam, du pays des Birmans, de l'Inde, du Nepal, du Tibet, et de la majeure partie de la Tartarie, etc., et l'on trouvera que je n'exagère pas trop le nombre des Buddhistes actuels."

[1] See J. Bird, Historical Researches on the Origin and Principles of the Buddha and Jaina Religion. Bombay, 1847.

death, in the middle of the sixth century B.C., and the beginning of the Ceylonese era, 543 B.C., will have to be considered hereafter. For the present it will be sufficient to keep in mind that the Buddhistic era divides the whole history of India into two parts, in the same manner as the Christian era divides the history of the world. It is therefore of the greatest importance with regard to the history of Vedic literature. The rise of a new religion so hostile to the hierarchical system of the Brahmans is most likely to have produced a visible effect on their sacred and theological writings. If traces of this kind can be discovered in the ancient literature of India, an important point will be gained, and it will be possible perhaps to restore to this vast mass of Brahmanic lore a certain historical connection. After the rise of a new religious doctrine in the first centuries after Buddha, it could not be expected that the Brahmanic literature should cease at once. On the contrary, we should expect at first a powerful reaction and a last effort to counteract the influence of the rising doctrine. And, as in India the religion of Buddha addressed itself more especially to the lower classes of the people, and found its strongest support amongst those who had to suffer from the exclusiveness of the Brahmanic system, a period of transition would most likely be marked by a more popular style of literature,—by an attempt to simplify the old complicated system of the Brahmanic ceremonial, till at last the political ascendency, secured to the new doctrine through its adoption by the reigning princes, like Aśoka, would cause this effort also to slacken.

Before it can be shown, however, that this really

took place in India, and that traces of this religious crisis exist in the Vedic literature of the Brahmans, it seems necessary to point out what Sanskrit works can be included within that literature, and what other books are to be excluded altogether when we look for evidence with regard to the true history of the Vedic age.

Let us begin by the negative process, and endeavour to separate and reject those works which do not belong to the genuine Vedic cycle. If we examine the two epic poems of India, the Râmâyaṇa and Mahâbhâratâ, we shall find it impossible to use them as authorities for the Vedic age, because we are not yet able to decide critically which parts of these poems are ancient, and which are modern and post-Buddhistic, or at least retouched by the hands of late compilers and editors. There are certainly very ancient traditions and really Vedic legends in both of these poems. Some of their heroes are taken from the same epic cycle in which the Vedic poetry moves. These, however, only form subjects for episodes in the two poems, while their principal heroes are essentially different in their character and manners. In fact, though there are remains of the Vedic age to be found in the epic poems, like the stories of Urvaśî and Purûravas, of Śakuntalâ and Dushmanta, of Uddâlaka, Śunaḥśepha, Janaka Vaideha, and particularly of the Vedic Rishis, like Vasishṭha, Viśvâmitra, Yâjnavalkya, Dîrghatamas, Kakshîvat, Kavásha, and many others, yet this would only prove that the traditions of the Vedic age were still in the mouth of the people at the time when the epic poetry of the Hindus was first composed, or that they were not yet forgotten in after times, when the Brahmans began to collect all the remains of epic songs into one large body, called the Mahâbhârata. If we compare the same legends as exhibited in the hymns and Brâhmaṇas of the Veda, and as related in the Mahâbhârata, Râmâyaṇa, or the Purâṇas, the Vedic version of them will mostly be found to be more simple, more primitive, and more intelligible than those of the epic and paurâṇic poems. This is not meant as a denial that real epic poetry, that is to say, a mass of popular songs, celebrating the power and exploits of gods and heroes, existed at a very early period in India, as well as among the other Aryan nations; but it shows, that, if yet existing, it is not in the Mahâbhârata and Râmâyaṇa we have to look for these old songs. In the collection of the Vedic hymns, there are some which may be called epic, and may be compared with the short hymns ascribed to Homer. In the Brâhmaṇas passages occur, in prose and verse, celebrating the actions of old kings Other compositions of a similar character must have existed formerly, though they are now lost.

The following extract from the Śânkhâyana-sûtras (xvi. 1.), throws some light on the literature which the Brahmans possessed, in addition to what we are accustomed to call the Veda[1]:—

"At the Horse-sacrifice, the Adhvaryu calls upon singers who sing to the lute (vîṇâgaṇaginas), and invites them to celebrate the king, who then performs the sacrifice, together with other virtuous kings of old. On the first day of the sacrifice, the priest tells the story which begins with *Manu Vaivasvata*. As the people of Manu were men, and there are men pre-

[1] The same account is given in the Âśvalâyana-sûtras, x. 7, and in the Śatapatha-brâhmaṇa, xiii. 3, 1, 1.

sent at the sacrifice, the priest teaches these, the householders, by telling this story. He then says, 'The Rich verses are the Veda, this is the Veda,' and recites a hymn.

"On the second day he tells the story which begins with *Yama Vaivasvata* (from the Śatapatha). As the people of Yama were the fathers, and there are fathers present, he teaches the elders by this story. He then says, 'The Yajur-veda is the Veda; this is the Veda,' and recites an Anuvâka (âśvamedhika) of the Yajush.

"On the third day he tells the story which begins with *Varuṇa Âditya*. As the people of Varuṇa were the Gandharvas, and as they are present, he teaches the young and fair youths by this story. He then says, 'The Atharva-veda is the Veda; this is the Veda,' and recites the Bhishaja[1], a work on medicine.

"On the fourth day he tells the story which begins with *Soma Vaishṇava* (from the Śatapatha). As the people of Soma were the Apsaras, and as these are present, he teaches the young and fair maids by this story. He then says, 'The Ângirasa-veda is the Veda; this is the Veda,' and recites the Ghora[2], another work of the Âtharvaṇikas.

"On the fifth day he tells the story which begins

[1] The commentator insists on this being a distinct book of the Âtharvaṇikas, and not a hymn. या ओषधीरित्येतत्सूक्तं केचिदाहुः। तदयुक्तं। समाख्यानाद्भेषजग्रंथस्याथर्वणिकानां॥ The Śatapatha says अथर्वणामेकं पर्व॥ Âśvalâyana, यद्भेषजं निशांतं॥

[2] घोरमाथर्वणो ग्रंथः॥ The Śatapatha says अंगिरसामेकं पर्व॥

with *Arbuda Kâdraveya.* As the people of Arbuda were the Sarpas (snakes), and as these are present, he teaches the Sarpas, or the snake-charmers, by this story. He then says, 'The Sarpavidyâ is the Veda; this is the Veda,' and recites the Sarpavidyâ.[1]

"On the sixth day he tells the story which begins with *Kuvera Vaiśravaṇa.* As the people of Kuvera were Rakshas, and as these are present, he teaches Selagas, or evil-doers, by this story. He then says, 'The Rakshovidyâ is the Veda, this is the Veda,' and recites the Rakshovidyâ.[2]

"On the seventh day he tells the story which begins with *Asita Dhânvana.*[3] As his men were the Asuras, and as these are present, he teaches the usurers (Kusîdin) by this story. He then says, 'The Asuravidyâ is the Veda, this is the Veda,' and performs a trick by slight of hand.[4]

"On the eight day he tells the story which begins with *Matsya Sâmmada.* As his men were the creatures of the water, and as these are present, he teaches the Matsyas (fishes), or the fishermen by this

[1] गारुडां कंकनीयां वा॥ The Śatapatha: सर्पविद्याया एकं पर्व॥

[2] कुञ्जकुरूपा रक्षोविद्या॥ According to the Śatapatha देवजनविद्याया एकं पर्व॥ according to Âśvalâyana, पिशाचविद्या॥

[3] Asita Dhânva, Śatapatha and Âśvalâyana.

[4] असुरविद्येंद्रजालादिना तन्निर्देशान्मायामपि कांचित्कुर्यादंगुलिन्यासरूपां॥

story. He then says, 'The Itihâsa-veda is the Veda, this is the Veda,' and recites an Itihâsa.[1]

"On the ninth day he tells the story which begins with *Târkshya Vaipaśyata.*[2] As his men were the birds, and as these are present, he teaches the birds, or the young students (brahmachârin)[3], by this story. He then says, 'The Purâṇa-veda is the Veda, this is the Veda,' and recites the Purâṇa.[4]

"On the tenth day he tells the story which begins with *Dharma Indra* (from the Śatapatha). As his men were the gods and as these are present, he teaches the young, learned, and poor priests by this story.[5] He then says, 'The Sâma-veda is the Veda, this is the Veda,' and sings the Sâma."[6]

This extract shows that epic poetry, traditional as well as improvised on the spur of the moment, existed during the Vedic age, though it was lost afterwards.

In several parts of the Brâhmaṇas and Âraṇyakas, where an account is given of the literature known to the ancient Hindus, we meet with the names of Gâthâ, Nâraśansî, Itihâsa, and Âkhyâna[7] (songs, legends, epic poems, and stories) as parts

1 इतिहासवेदस्य पृथग्भावेन दर्शनात् ॥

2 Vaipaśchita, according to Âśvalâyana.

3 वायोविद्यिकाः ॥ Śatapatha.

4 पुराणं वायुप्रोक्तमत्राख्येयं ॥ The Vâyu-purâṇa has a more ancient appearance than the other Purâṇas.

5 यूनोऽप्रतिग्राहकाञ्छ्रोत्रियान् ॥

6 साम्नां दशतं ॥ Śatapatha.

7 Cf. Taittirîya-Âraṇyaka, ii. 9.: ब्राह्मणानीतिहासान्पुराणानि कल्पान् गाथा नाराशंसीः ॥ Bṛihadâraṇyaka, ii. 4. 10.:

of the Vedic literature. The occurrence of titles of literary works like these, has been made use of to prove the existence, at that early period, of the writings which afterwards were designated by the same names. But though the Mahâbhârata is called an *Itihâsa*, and the Râmâyaṇa an *Âkhyâna*, and though many works have in later times become famous under the name of *Purâṇas*, yet these enumerations of literary works in the Brâhmaṇas do not refer to them.[1] They contain only general names or

इतिहासः पुराणं विद्या उपनिषदः श्लोकाः सूत्राण्यनुव्याख्यानानि व्याख्यानानि॥ ibid. iv. 1, 2., iv. 5. 9.; Śatap. Brâhm. xi. 7. 1.; Âtharv. Sanhitâ, xv. 6: इतिहासश्च पुराणं च गाथाश्च नाराशंसीश्च॥ Cf. Aufrecht, Indische Studien, p. 133. Sâyaṇa himself is sometimes doubtful, and in his Commentary on the Taittirîya-âraṇyaka, for instance, he says that, by purâṇa might be meant the Brahmâṇḍa, &c.; and by itihâsa, the Mahâbhârata. This, however, is a mistake, and it would bring Sâyaṇa into contradiction with himself. He has fully proved in his Introduction to the Rig-veda that in this passage of the Taittirîyâraṇyaka, no works separate from the Veda could be understood. Cf. Rig-veda-sanhitâ, p. 23. Dr. Weber, in his extracts from Pâṇini (iv. 2. 60.), shows that vyâkhyâna, âkhyâna, kathâ, âkhyâyikâ, itihâsa, and purâṇa, were titles of literary works known at the time of Kâtyâyana. But he inclines to the opinion that Kâtyâyana did not mean the Mahâbhârata, Râmâyaṇa, and the Purâṇas, as we now possess them, by these general names. Cf. Indische Studien, I. p. 147.

[1] In the later literature also, names like Itihâsa, Âkhyâna, and Purâṇa are by no means restricted to the Mahâbhârata, Râmâyaṇa, and the Purâṇas. The Mahâbhârata is called Purâṇa, Âkhyâna, and Itihâsa. Cf. M. Bh. I. 17—19. Vyâsa himself calls his poem, the Mahâbhârata, a Kâvya; and Brahman sanctions this as its proper title. Cf. M. Bh. I. 72. This passage modifies Professor Lassen's opinion as to Kâvya being the distinctive title of the Râmâyaṇa. Cf. Indian Antiquities, I. 485. The Mahâbhârata

titles, which have been applied to certain parts of the sacred literature, containing either stories of gods or men, or cosmogonic traditions.[1] There is no allusion to any of the titles of the Purâṇas or to the Râmâyaṇa in Vedic works, whether Brâhmaṇas or Sûtras. But as in the Sûtras of Âśvalâyana[2] the name of the

is also called the fifth Veda, or the Kârshṇa-veda; that is, the Veda composed by Kṛishṇa Dvaipâyana Vyâsa. Cf. M. Bh. I. 2300 Burnouf. Bhâg. III. préf. XXI. Lassen. Ind. Antiq. I. 789.

[1] Cf. Sâyaṇa, Introduction to the Rig-veda-sanhitâ, p. 23.

[2] Gṛihya-Sûtras, iii. 4. MS. 1978, E. I. H., reads, भारतधर्माचार्याः instead of भारतमहाभारतधर्माचार्याः the reading adopted by Dr. Roth (Zur Literatur, p. 27). Unfortunately the Commentary to this passage is very scanty, which is so much the more to be regretted as the text itself seems to contain spurious additions. According to the MSS. the passage reads, अथ ऋषयः शतर्चिनो माध्यमा गृत्समदो विश्वामित्रो वामदेवोऽत्रिर्भरद्वाजो वसिष्ठः प्रगाथाः पावमान्यः क्षुद्रसूक्ता महासूक्ता इति। प्राचीनावीती सुमंतुजैमिनिवैशंपायनपैलसूत्रभाष्यभारतधर्माचार्या जानंतिबाहविगार्ग्यगौतमशाकल्यबाभ्रव्यमांडव्यमांडूकेया गार्गी वाचक्नवी वडवा प्रातीथेयी सुलभा मैत्रेयी कहोलं कौषीतकं महाकौषीतकं पैंग्यं महापैंग्यं सुयज्ञं शांखायनमैतरेयं महैतरेयं शाकलं बाष्कलं सुजातवक्त्रमौदवाहिं सौजामिं शौनकमाश्वलायनं ये चान्ये आचार्यास्ते सर्वे तृप्यंत्विति॥
According to the commentator we have first, 12 Ṛishis, who, as Ṛishis, are to be invoked, when the Brahmanical thread is suspended round the neck (nivîta). These are indeed the Ṛishis of the Rig-veda: first the Śatarchins, the common title of the poets of the first Maṇḍala; then Gṛitsamada (2d Maṇḍala), Viśvâmitra (3d M.), Vâmadeva (4th M.), Atri (5th M.), Bharadvâja (6th M.), Vasishṭha (7th M.); then follow the poets of the Pra-

Bhârata, and according to some MSS. even the name of the Mahâbhârata, is mentioned, this may be considered as the earliest trace, not merely of single epic poems, but of a collection of them. The age of Âśvalâyana, which will be approximately fixed afterwards, would, therefore, if we can rely on our MSS., furnish a limit below which the first attempt at a collection of a Bhârata or Mahâbhârata ought not to be placed. But there is no hope that we shall ever succeed by critical researches in restoring the Bhârata to that primitive form and shape in which it may have existed before or at the time of Âśvalâyana. Much has indeed been done by Professor Lassen, who, in his Indian Antiquities, has pointed out characteristic marks by which the modern parts of the Mahâbhârata can be distinguished from the more ancient; and we may soon expect to see his principles still farther carried out in a translation of the whole Mahâbhârata, which, with the help of all the Sanskrit commentaries, has been most carefully prepared by one of the most learned and laborious scholars of Germany. If it were possible to sift out from the huge mass of Indian epic poetry, as we now possess it in the Mahâbhârata and Râmâyaṇa, those old stories and songs

gâtha hymns (8th M.), the poets of the Pâvamânîs (9th M.), and finally, the authors of the 10th and last Maṇḍala, who are called Kshudrasûktas, and Mahâsûktas, authors of short and long hymns. The next class comprises twenty-three invocations, according to the Commentary, and they are to be made when the Brahmanical cord is suspended over the right shoulder (prâchînâvîtî). The text, however, contains more than twenty-three names, and it is likely that some of them have been added afterwards, while others are perhaps to be taken collectively. भारतधर्माचार्याः may also be taken as one word, in the sense of the legal authorities of the Bhâratas.

which must have been living for a long time in the mouth of the people before they were collected, enlarged, arranged, and dressed up by later hands, a rich mine of information would be opened for the ancient times of India, and very likely also for the Vedic age. But the whole frame of the two epic poems as they now stand, their language and metre, as well as the moral and religious system they contain, show that they were put together at a period when the world of the Veda was living by tradition only, and, moreover, partly misunderstood, and partly forgotten. The war between the Kurus and Pâṇḍavas, which forms the principal object of our Mahâbhârata, is unknown in the Veda. The names of the Kurus and Bhâratas are common in the Vedic literature, but the names of the Pâṇḍavas have never been met with. It has been observed [1], that even in Pâṇini's grammar the name Pâṇḍu or Pâṇḍava does not occur, while the Kurus and Bhâratas are frequently mentioned, particularly in rules treating of the formation of patronymics and similar words.[2] If, then, Âśvalâyana

[1] Dr. Weber, Indische Studien, I. p. 148. Kâtyâyana, however, the immediate successor of Pâṇini, knows not only Pâṇḍu, but also his descendants, the Pâṇḍyas.

[2] The names of the two wives of Pâṇḍu, *Kuntî* and *Mâdrî*, occur in the commentary on Pâṇini. (Cf. i. 2. 49., iv. 1. 65., iv. 1. 176. (text) for Kuntî, and iv. 1. 177. for Mădrî). But both these names are geographical appellatives, Kuntî signifying a woman for the country of the Kuntas, Mădrî, a Madra-woman. *Prithâ*, another name of Kuntî, stands in the Gaṇa śivâdi. As to the proper names of the Pâṇḍava princes, we find *Yudhishṭhira*, Pâṇ. vi. 1. 134., vi. 3. 9., viii. 3. 95. (text); *Arjuna*, Pâṇ. iii. 1. 119., iv. 3. 64., v. 4. 48., vi. 2. 131.; *Bhîma*, Pâṇ. vi. 1. 205.; *Năkula*, Pâṇ. vi. 3. 75. The name of *Sahadeva* does not occur; but his descendants, the Sâhadevas, are mentioned as belonging to the race of Kuru, together with the Nâkulas, Pâṇ. iv. 1. 114. In the same

can be shown to have been a contemporary, or at least an immediate successor, of Pâṇini, the Bhârata which he is speaking of must have been very different from the epic poem which is known to us

way we find the descendants of Yudhishṭhira and Arjuna mentioned as members of the eastern Bhâratas, Pâṇ. ii. 4. 66. *Draupadî's* name does not occur in Pâṇini, but *Subhadrâ*, the sister of Kṛishṇa and the wife of Arjuna, is distinctly mentioned, Pâṇ. iv. 2. 56. Another passage in the commentary on Pâṇini (iv. 3. 87.) proves even the existence of a poem in praise of Subhadrâ, which, if we remember the former mention of a war about Subhadrâ (iv. 2. 56.), seems most likely to have celebrated this very conquest of Subhadrâ by Arjuna. In the Mahâbhârata this story forms a separate chapter, the Subhadrâ-haraṇa-parva (Âdiparva, p. 288.) which may be the very work which Pâṇini, according to his commentator, is alluding to. That the chapter in the Mahâbhârata belongs to the oldest parts of this epic, may be seen from its being mentioned in the Anukramaṇî of Dhṛitarâshṭra (i. 149), "When I heard that Subhadrâ, of the race of Madhu, had been forcibly seized in the city of Dvarakâ, and carried away by Arjuna, and that the two heroes of the race of Vṛishṇi had repaired to Indraprastha, I then, O Sanjaya, had no hope of success." The Mahâbhâshya, however, does not explain the former Sûtra, (iv. 2. 56.), and for the latter it gives examples for the exceptions only, but not for the rule. The word *grantha*, used in the Sûtra, (iv. 3. 87.), is also somewhat suspicious. That some of the Sûtras which now form part of Pâṇini's grammar, did not proceed from him, is acknowledged by Kaiyyaṭa (cf. iv. 3. 131, 132.) अपाणिनीयः सूत्रेषु पाठ इत्याह इति कैय्यटः। कौपिंजल-हास्तिपादादित्यस्यापाणिनीयत्वात् इति कैय्यटः॥ *Kṛishṇa Vâsudeva*, who is considered as peculiarly connected with the tradition of the Pâṇḍavas, is quoted as *Vâsudeva*, of the race of Vṛishṇi (Pâṇ. iv. 1. 114.); as *Vâsudeva*, together with Śiva and Âditya (Pâṇ. v. 3. 99.); as *Vâsudeva*, together with Arjuna (iv. 3. 98. text). In the commentary to Pâṇ. iii. 3. 156., and ii. 3. 72., we have proof of *Kṛishṇa's* being worshipped as a god; in i. 4. 92. he is mentioned as a hero. His residence, *Dvâraka*, however, does not occur in Pâṇini.

under the name of the Mahâbhârata, celebrating the war of the Kurus and Pâṇḍavas.[1]

In the form in which we now possess the Mahâbhârata it shows clear traces that the poets who collected and finished it, breathed an intellectual and religious atmosphere, very different from that in which the heroes of the poem moved. The epic character of the story has throughout been changed and almost obliterated by the didactic tendencies of the latest editors, who were clearly Brahmans, brought up in the strict school of the Laws of Manu. But the original traditions of the Pâṇḍavas break through now and then, and we can clearly discern that the races among whom the five principal heroes of the Mahâbhârata were born and fostered, were by no means completely under the sway of the Brahmanical law. How is it, for instance, that the five Pâṇḍava princes, who are at first represented as receiving so strictly Brahmanic an education, — who, if we are to believe the poet, were versed in all the sacred literature, grammar, metre, astronomy, and law of the Brahmans, — could afterwards have been married to *one* wife? This is in

[1] That Pâṇini knew the war of the Bhâratas, has been rendered highly probable by Prof. Lassen (Ind. Alterthumskunde, i. 691. 837.). The words which called forth Pâṇini's special rule (iv. 2. 56), can scarcely be imagined to have been different from those in the Mahâbhâshya; viz., Bhâratah sangrâmah, saubhadrah sangrâmah. It was impossible to teach or to use Pâṇini's Sûtras without examples. These necessarily formed part of the traditional grammatical literature long before the great Commentary was written, and are, therefore, of a much higher historical value than is commonly supposed. The coincidences between the examples used in the Prâtiśâkhyas and in Pâṇini, show that these examples were by no means selected at random, but that they had long formed part of the traditional teaching. See also Pâṇ. vi. 2. 38., where the word "mahâbhârata" occurs, but not as the title of a poem.

plain opposition to the Brahmanic law, where it is said, "they are many wives of one man; not many husbands of one wife."[1] Such a contradiction can only be accounted for by the admission, that, in this case, epic tradition in the mouth of the people was too strong to allow this essential and curious feature in the life of its heroes to be changed. However, the Brahmanic editors of the Mahâbhârata, seeing that they could not alter tradition on this point, have at least endeavoured to excuse and mitigate it. Thus we are told in the poem itself, that at one time the five brothers came home, and informed their mother that they had found something extremely precious. Without listening further, their mother at once told them they ought to divide it as brothers. The command of a parent must always be literally obeyed; and as Draupadî was their newly discovered treasure, they were obliged, according to the views of the Brahmans, to obey, and to have her as their common wife. Indian lawgivers call this a knotty point[2]; they defend the fact, but refuse to regard it as a precedent.

[1] वेदेऽप्येवं श्रूयते एकस्य बह्व्यो जाया भवंति नैकस्या एव बहवः पतयः संति॥

[2] धर्मो द्विविधः स्थूलः सूक्ष्मश्च। मंदमतिभिरपि सुखेन बुध्यमानः स शौचाचमनसंध्यावंदनादिः स्थूलो धर्मः। शास्त्रपारंगतैः पंडितैरेव बोद्धुं योग्य इतरेषामधर्मभ्रांतिविषयो द्रौपदीविवाहादिः सूक्ष्मो धर्मः।
Cf. Sâyaṇa's Com. on Parâśara, MS. Bodl. 172, 173. Another explanation is given by Kumârila:
यौवनस्थैव कृष्णा हि वेदिमध्यात्समुत्थिता। सा च श्री श्रीश्च भूयोभिर्भुज्यमाना न दुष्यति॥

Neither does the fact that Pâṇḍu is lawfully married to two wives, harmonise with the Brahmanic law. That law does not prohibit polygamy, but it regards no second marriage as legal, and it reserves the privilege of being burnt together with the husband to the eldest and only lawful wife. Such passages in the ancient epics are of the greatest interest. We see in them the tradition of the people too far developed, to allow itself to be remodelled by Brahmanic Diaskeuastes. There can be little doubt that polygamy, as we find it among the early races in their transition from the pastoral to the agricultural life, was customary in India. We read in Herodotus (v. 5.), that amongst the Thracians it was usual, after the death of a man, to find out who had been the most beloved of his wives, and to sacrifice her upon his tomb. Mela (ii. 2.) gives the same as the general custom of the Getæ. Herodotus (iv. 71.) asserts a similar fact of the Scythians, and Pausanias (iv. 2.) of the Greeks, while our own Teutonic mythology is full of instances of the same feeling.[1] And thus the customs of these cognate nations explain what at first seemed to be anomalous in the epic tradition of the Mahâbhârata, that at the death of Pâṇḍu, it is not Kuntî, his lawful wife, but Mâdrî, his most beloved wife, in whose arms the old king dies, and who successfully claims the privilege of being burnt with him, and following her husband to another life.[2]

[1] Cf. Grimm, History of the German Language, p. 139.

[2] Other instances of Dharmavyatikrama are:

कृष्णद्वैपायनस्य गृहीतनैष्ठिकब्रह्मचर्यस्य विचित्रवीर्यदारेष्व-
पत्योत्पादनप्रसंगः॥ युधिष्ठिरस्य कनीयोनिर्जितभ्रातृजा-

The same remark applies to the Râmâyaṇa. In this second epic also, we see that the latest editors were shocked by the anomalies of the popular traditions, and endeavoured to impart a more Brahmanic polish to the materials handed down to them from an earlier age. Thus king Daśaratha kills the son of a Brahman, which would be a crime so horrible in the eyes of the Brahmans, that scarcely any penance could expiate it.[1] This is the reason why the young Brahman is represented as the son of a Śûdrâ woman, and tells the king so himself, in order to relieve him from the fear of having killed the son of a Brahman. The singular relation, too, between Râma and Paraśu-Râma, was probably remodelled by the influence of the Brahmans, who could not bear the idea of their great-hero, the destroyer of all the Kshatriyas, being in turn vanquished by Râma, who was himself a Kshatriya.

The Vedic literature, by the very sacredness of its character, has fortunately escaped from the remodelling puritanism of the later Brahmans. There must, from the first, have been as great a variety in the intellectual, religious, and moral character of the Indians, as there is in the geographical and physical character of India. If we look at Greece, and consider the immense diversity of local worship, tradition, and customs, which co-existed within that small tract of country, and then turn

यापरिणयनं॥ वासुदेवार्जुनयोर्निषिद्धमातुलदुहितृरुक्मिणी-
सुभद्रापरिणयनं॥—Kumârila Bhaṭṭa.

[1] Cf. Manu, viii. 381. "No greater crime is known on earth than slaying a Brahman, and the king, therefore, must not even form in his mind an idea of killing a priest."

our eyes to the map of India, barred as it is by mountain-ranges and rivers, it becomes clear that the past ages of such a country cannot be represented in their fulness and reality by the traditions of the later Brahmans, which as we now possess them in the epic and pauraṇic poetry of the Hindus, are all tinged with the same monotonous colouring. Such a uniformity is always the result of an artificial system, and not of a natural and unimpeded development. It is indeed acknowledged by the Brahmans themselves that different customs prevailed in different parts of India. Some were even sanctioned by them, notwithstanding their policy of monopolising or (so to speak) *brahmanising* the whole Indian mind. Although, for instance, in the liturgic works annexed to the Vedas (Śrauta-sûtras), an attempt was made to establish a certain unity in the sacrifices of the people all over India, yet in the performance of these sacrifices there existed certain discrepancies, based on the traditionary authority of the wise of old, between family and family. This is still more the case in the so-called domestic ceremonies of baptism, confirmation, marriage, &c., described in the Gṛihya-sûtras, which, connected as they were with the daily life of the people, give us much more real information on the ancient customs of India than those grand public or private sacrifices which are prescribed in the Śrauta-sûtras, and could only have been kept up by sacerdotal influence. In these domestic ceremonies everybody is allowed, as a general law, to follow the customs of the family[1] to which he belongs, or of

[1] Thus it is said, for instance, in the Commentary to Pâraskara's Gṛihya-sûtras, that it is wrong to give up the customs of one's own family and to adopt those of others :

his village and country, provided these customs do not too grossly insult the moral and religious feelings of the Brahmans.

Although these domestic ceremonies were fully sanctioned by the Brahmanic law, the authority upon

शाखांतरीयकर्मकरणे दोषमाह वसिष्ठः॥ न जातु परशाखोक्तं कर्म बुधः समाचरेत्। आचरन्परशाखोक्तं शाखारंडः स उच्यते॥ यः स्वशाखोक्तमुत्सृज्य परशाखोक्तमाचरेत्। अप्रमाणमृषिं कृत्वा सोऽंधे तमसि मज्जते॥ स्मृत्यंतरेऽपि॥ स्वकर्म पर्युत्सृज्य तु यदन्यत्कुरुते नरः। अज्ञानादथवा लोभात्स हतः पतितो भवेत्॥ छंदोगपरिशिष्टेऽपि॥ स्वशाखाश्रयमुत्सृज्य परशाखाश्रयं तु यः। कर्तुमिच्छति दुर्मेधा मोघं तस्य च यत्कृतं॥

"Vasishṭha declares that it is wrong to follow the rules of another Śâkhâ. He says, 'A wise person will certainly not perform the duties prescribed by another Śâkhâ; he that does is called a traitor to his Śâkhâ. Whosoever leaves the law of his Śâkhâ, and adopts that of another, he sinks into blind darkness, having degraded a sacred Ṛishi.' And in another law-book it is said: 'If a man gives up his own customs and performs others, whether out of ignorance or covetousness, he will fall and be destroyed.' And again, in the Pariśishṭa of the Chhandogas: 'A fool who ceases to follow his own Śâkhâ, wishing to adopt another one, his work will be in vain.'"

Only in case no special rule is laid down for certain observances in some Gṛihyas, it is lawful to adopt those of other families:

स्वशाखानुक्तमप्यविरुद्धं परशाखोक्तं ग्राह्यं॥ तथा च कात्यायनः॥ यन्नाम्नातं स्वशाखायां परोक्तमविरोधि च। विद्वद्भिस्तदनुष्ठेयमग्निहोत्रादिकर्मवत्॥ सूत्रांतरानुक्तमपि स्मृत्युक्तं ग्राह्यं॥

which they are founded does not lie directly in the sacred revelation of the Brahmans (Śruti), but in tradition (Smṛiti), a difference, the historical importance of which will have to be pointed out hereafter. As to the customs of countries and villages, there can be no doubt that in many cases they were not only not founded upon Brahmanic authority, but frequently decidedly against it. The Brahmanic law, however, is obliged to recognise and allow those customs, with the general reservation that they must not be in open opposition to the law. Thus Âśvalâyana in his Gṛihya-sûtras, says:—"Now the customs of countries and places are certainly manifold. One must know them as far as marriage is concerned. But we shall explain what is the general custom."[1]

Here the commentator adds:—"If there be contradiction between the customs of countries, &c., and those customs which we are going to describe, one must adopt the custom as laid down by us, not those of the country. What we shall say is the general law, this is our meaning. Amongst the Vaidehas, for instance, one sees at once that loose habits prevail. But in the domestic laws continence is prescribed; therefore there is no doubt that the domestic and not the national customs are to be observed."[2]

[1] Âśv. S. i. 7.,

अथ खलूच्चावचा जनपदधर्मा ग्रामधर्माश्च तान्विवाहे प्रतीयाद्यत्तु समानं तद्वक्ष्यामः॥

[2] जनपदादिधर्माणां वक्ष्यमाणानां धर्माणां च विरोधे सति वक्ष्यमानं धर्ममेव कुर्यान्न जनपदादिधर्ममिति। यद्वक्ष्यामस्तत्सर्वत्र समानमित्येवार्थः। वैदेहेषु सद्य एव व्यवायो

In the Sûtras of Gautama, too, a similar line of conduct is traced out. After it has been said that the highest authority by which a government ought to be guided consists in the Vedas, Vedângas, Śâstras, and old traditions, it is added (Adhy. 11. Sûtra 20.), that in cases where the customs of countries, classes, and families are not expressly founded upon a passage of the Veda, they are, notwithstanding, to be observed, if they are not clearly against the principles of the sacred writings, such as would be, for instance, marrying the daughter of a maternal uncle.[1]

There is an interesting passage in the Gṛihya-sangraha-pariśishṭa, composed by the son of Gobhila, which Dr. Roth quotes in his Essays on the Veda, p. 120. :—" The Vâsishṭhas wear a braid on the right side, the Âtrêyas wear three braids, the Angiras wear

दृष्टः। गृह्येषु तु ब्रह्मचर्यं विहितं। तत्र गृह्योक्तमेव कुर्यान्न देशधर्ममिति सिद्धं॥

[1] The commentator Haradatta here mentions the following as customs that prevailed in certain territories, and which had no sanction in the Veda :—When the sun stands in Aries (mesha), the young girls would paint the Sun with his retinue, on the soil, with coloured dust, and worship this in the morning and evening. And in the month Mârgaśîrshâ (November-December) they roam about the village, nicely dressed, and whatever they receive as presents they give to the god. When the sun stands in Cancer (karkaṭa) in Pûrvâ Phalgunî (February), they worship Umâ, and distribute sprouting kidney-beans and salt. When the sun stands in Aries in Uttarâ Phalgunî (?), they worship the goddess Śrî.

As customs of classes he mentions that at the marriage of Śûdras, they fix posts in the ground, put thousands of reflecting lamps upon them, and lead the bride round by the hand.

As customs of families, again, he remarks, that some wear the śikhâ (lock of hair) in front, some behind, and that passages of the Veda (pravachanas) allow both according to different times.

five locks, the Bhṛigus have their head quite shaved, others have a lock of hair on the top of the head." [1]

Another peculiarity ascribed to the Vâsishṭhas is that they exclude meat from their sacrifices.[2]

A similar notice of the customs of neighbouring nations, is found in Raghunandana's quotation from the Harivanśa, — that the Śakas (Scythians) have half their head shorn, the Yavanas (Greeks?) and Kambojâs the whole, that the Pâradas (inhabitants of Paradene) wear their hair free, and the Pahlavas (Persians) wear beards.[3]

In the same way, then, as different traditions were current in India relative to such observances, it is probable that different families had their own heroes, perhaps their own deities, and that they kept up the memory of them by their own poetic traditions. It is true that such a view is merely conjectural. But when we see that in some portions of the Veda, which are represented as belonging to different illustrious

[1] दक्षिणकपर्दा वासिष्ठा आत्रेयास्त्रिकपर्दिनः।
अंगिरसः पंचचूदा मुंडा भृगवः शिखिनोऽन्ये॥

[2] This we learn from the Karma-pradîpa, a supplement to the Sûtras of Gobhila, i. 18.: वसिष्ठोक्तो विधिः कृत्स्नो द्रष्टव्योऽत्र निरामिषः॥

[3] अर्द्धं शकानां शिरसो मुंडयित्वा व्यसर्जयत्
यवनानां शिरः सर्वं कंबोजानां तथैव च॥
पारदा मुक्तकेशाश्च पह्लवाः श्मश्रुधारिणः।
निःस्वाध्यायवषट्कारा: कृतास्तेन महात्मना॥
See also Pâṇ. gaṇa mayûravyansakâdi.

and noble families, certain gods are more exclusively celebrated[1]; that names which in Vedic poetry

[1] In later times, when the sects of Vishṇu and Śiva had sprung up, and the Indian world was divided between them, it seems as if different deities had been ascribed to different castes. Thus it is said in the first Adhyâya of the Vasishṭha-smṛiti :

चतुर्वेदी च यो विप्रो वासुदेवं न विंदति।
वेदभारभयाक्रांतः स वै ब्राह्मणगर्दभः॥
तस्माद्वैष्णवत्वेन ब्राह्मण्यादि विहीयते।
वैष्णवत्वेन संसिद्धिं लभते नात्र संशयः॥
नारायणं परं ब्रह्म ब्राह्मणानां हि दैवतं।
सोमसूर्यादयो देवाः क्षत्रियाणां विशामपि॥
शूद्रादीनां तु रुद्राद्या अर्चनीयाः प्रयत्नतः।
यत्र रुद्रार्चनं प्रोक्तं पुराणेषु स्मृतिष्वपि॥
तदब्राह्मण्यविषयमेवमाह प्रजापतिः।
रुद्रार्चनं त्रिपुंड्रं च पुराणेषु च गीयते॥
क्षत्रविट्शूद्रजातीनां नेतरेषां तदुच्यते।
तस्मात् त्रिपुंड्रं विप्राणां न धार्यं मुनिसत्तमाः॥

"A Brahman versed in the four Vedas, who does not find Vâsudeva, is a donkey of a Brahman, trembling for the heavy burden of the Veda. Therefore, unless a man be a Vaishṇava, his Brahmahood will be lost; by being a Vaishṇava one obtains perfection, there is no doubt. For Nârâyaṇa (Vishṇu) the highest Brahman, is the deity of the Brahmans; Soma, Sûrya, and the rest, are the gods of Kshatriyas and Vaiśyas; while Rudra and similar gods ought to be sedulously worshipped by the Śûdras. When the worship of Rudra is enjoined in the Purâṇas and law-books, it has no reference to Brahmans, as Prajâpati declared. The worship of Rudra and the Tripuṇḍra (the three horizontal marks across the forehead) are celebrated in the Purâṇas, but only

are known as those of heroes and poets (Purûravas, Kutsa) are afterwards considered as names of infidels and heretics, we have a right to infer that we have here the traces of a widely extended practice.

In the hymns of the Rig-veda we meet with allusions to several legendary stories—afterwards more fully developed by the Brahmans in their Brâhmaṇas—by which laws that were in later times acknowledged as generally binding, and as based upon the authority of the Veda, are manifestly violated. It is an essential doctrine of the Brahmans, that the religious education, and the administration of sacrifices, as well as the receiving of rewards for these offices, belong exclusively to their own caste. Kakshîvat, however, whose hymns are found in the first and ninth maṇḍalas of the Rig-veda, and who, whether on account of his name or for some better reason, is said to have been a Kshatriya, or of royal extraction, is represented as receiving from King Svanaya presents, which, according to Manu [1], it would have been unlawful for him to accept. In order to explain this

for the castes of the Kshatriyas, Vaiśyas, and Śûdras, and not for the others. Therefore, ye excellent Munis, the Tripuṇḍra must not be worn by Brahmans."

[1] Cf. Manu, x. 76.; and Rig-veda-bhâshya, ii. p. 30. Rosen, who has quoted this passage to Rv. i. 18. 1., reads याजनाध्यापने चैव विशुद्धाच्च प्रतिग्रहात् which he translates by "abstinere jubet a dirigendis sacrificiis, ab institutione sacra et ab impuris donis," referring to Manu, x. 103—110. विशुद्ध however, does not mean impure, but pure. The reading of the commentary ought to be विशुद्धाच्च प्रतिग्रहः for thus the very words of Manu, x. 76., are restored.

away, a story is told, that although Kakshîvat was the son of King Kalinga, yet his real father was the old Ṛishi Dîrghatamas, whose hymns have likewise been preserved in the first maṇḍala of the Rig-veda. This poet had been asked by the king to beget offspring for him, according to ancient Indian custom. The queen, however, refused to see the old sage, and sent her servant-maid instead. The son of this servant and the Ṛishi Dîrghatamas was Kakshîvat, and as the son of a Ṛishi he was allowed to perform sacrifices and to receive presents. This story shows its purpose very clearly, and there can be little doubt that it owes its origin to the tender conscience of the Brahmans, who could not bear to see their laws violated by one of their own sacred Ṛishis. It is a gratuitous assumption to suppose that the poets of the Veda should have been perfect in the observance of the Brahmanic law. That law did not exist when they lived and composed those very songs for which in later times they were raised to the rank of saints. Whether Kakshîvat was the son of a Brahman or a Kshatriya, of a servant-maid or of a queen, it is impossible to determine. But it is certain that in the times in which he lived, he would not have scrupled to act both as a warrior and priest, if circumstances required it. This becomes still more evident, if we accept Professor Lassen's view, who considers Dîrghatamas, the father of Kakshîvat, as one of the earliest Brahmanic missionaries in the southern parts of Bengal, among the Angas and Kalingas.[1]

[1] In this case, the name of the queen also, Sudeshṇâ, would be significant, for Sudeshṇa is the name of one of the nations in

Now, under circumstances of this kind, when the Brahmans were still labouring to establish their supremacy over different parts of India, it can hardly be believed that the different castes and their respective duties and privileges should have been established as strictly as in later times. In later times it is considered a grievous sin to recite the hymns of the Veda in places where a Śûdra might be able to hear them. In the Rig-veda we find hymns which the Brahmans themselves allow to be the compositions of the son of a slave. Kavasha Ailûsha is the author of several hymns in the tenth Book of the Rig-veda; yet this same Kavasha was expelled from the sacrifice as an impostor and as the son of a slave (dâsyâḥ putra), and he was readmitted only because the gods had shown him special favour. This is acknowledged by the Brâhmaṇas of the Aitareyins[1] and

Bengal. See Vishṇu-Purâṇa, p. 188. The word "godharma," which occurs in the story of Dîrghatamas, in the Mahâbhârata, i. 4195., and which Prof. Lassen translates by "pastoral law," must have an opprobious sense, and Indian Pandits explain it by "open and indiscriminate concupiscence."

[1] Aitareya-Brâhmaṇa, II. 19.:

ऋषयो वै सरस्वत्यां सत्रमासत। ते कवषमैलूषं सोमादनयन्दास्याः पुत्रः कितवो ब्राह्मणः कथं नो मध्ये दीक्षिष्टेति। तं बहिर्धन्वोदवहन्नत्रैनं पिपासा हंतु सरस्वत्या उदकं मा पादिति। स बहिर्धन्वोदूळ्हः पिपासयावित्त एतदपोनप्त्रीयमपश्यत्प्र देवत्रा ब्रह्मणे गातुरेत्विति। तेनापां प्रियं धामोपागच्छत्। तमापोऽनूदायंस्तं सरस्वती समंतं पर्यधावत्। तस्माद्धाप्येतर्हि परिसारमित्याचक्षते। यदेनं

Kaushîtakins, and in the Mahâbhârata also Kavasha is called a Nishâda.

The marked difference between the Vedic and epic poetry of India has been well pointed out by Professor Roth of Tübingen, who for many years has devoted much time and attention to the study of the Veda. According to him, the Mahâbhârata, even in its first elements, is later than the time of Buddha.[1] "In the epic poems," he says, "the

सरस्वती समंतं परिससार॥ ते वा ऋषयोऽब्रुवन् विदुर्वा इमं देवा उपेमं ह्वयामहा इति तथेति तमुपाह्वयंत। तमुपहूयैतदपोनप्त्रीयमकुर्वत प्र देवत्रा ब्रह्मणे गातुरेत्विति॥

Kaushîtaki-Brâhmaṇa, XI.:

माध्यमाः सरस्वत्यां सत्रमासत। तद्धापि कवषो मध्ये निषसाद। तं हेम उपोदुर्दास्या वै त्वं पुत्रोऽसि न वयं त्वया सह भक्षयिष्याम इति। स ह क्रुद्धः प्रद्रवंत्सरस्वतीमेतेन सूक्तेन तुष्टाव। तं हेयमन्वेयाय। तत उ हेमे निरागा इव मेनिरे। तं हान्वानृत्योचुर्ऋषे नमस्त अस्तु मा मा हिंसीस्त्वं वै नः श्रेष्ठोऽसि यं त्वेयमन्वेतीति। तं ह ज्ञापयां चक्रुस्तस्य ह क्रोधं विनिन्युः। स एष कवषस्यैव महिमा सूक्तस्य चानुवेदिता॥

Comment: उपोदुः परुषं वदितवंतः॥ निरागा निकृष्टो रागो येषां॥ अन्वानृत्य विनयेन नृतमनुसृता इव॥ ज्ञापयां चक्रुः संतोषयां चक्रुः॥

[1] Zur Litteratur und Geschichte des Veda. Drei Abhandlungen von R. Roth, Doctor der Philosophie. Stuttgart, 1846.

Veda is but imperfectly known; the ceremonial is no longer developing, it is complete. The Vedic legends have been plucked from their native soil, and the religion of Agni, Indra, Mitra, and Varuṇa has been replaced by an altogether different worship. The last fact," he says, "ought to be the most convincing. There is a contradiction running throughout the religious life of India, from the time of the Râmâyaṇa to the present day. The outer form of the worship is Vedic, and exclusively so[1]; but the eye of religious adoration is turned upon quite different regions.[2] The secondary formation, the religion of Vishṇu and Brahma, began with the epic poetry, and remained afterwards as the only living

[1] The worship of the Hindus at the present day cannot be called exclusively Vedic, though Vedic remains may be traced in it. In the Introduction to the edition of the Rig-veda, by the Tattvabodhinî-sabhâ, it is said, on the contrary,

আদ্য কালিক বৈদিক ধর্ম্মের সহিত ইদানীন্তন প্রচলিত ধর্ম্মের বি-ভিন্নতা উজ্জ্বল রূপে প্রতীত হইবেক॥

"the difference between the present received law and the early Vedic law, will clearly be perceived by this edition." And again,

পুরাণ বিহিত নর, পশু, পক্ষী সর্প, মৎস্যাদি নানা অবয়ব বিশিষ্ট দেবগণের পৌরাণিক অর্চ্চনা এবং লোক বিখ্যাত আধুনিকতম তান্ত্রিক ক্রিয়ার বিস্তারিত পদ্ধতির সহিত বেদ বিহিত যজ্ঞানুষ্ঠানের কি-পর্য্যন্ত ভিন্নতা তাহা সম্যক্ রূপে দৃষ্ট হইবেক॥

"It will be seen exactly what difference there is between the Paurâṇic worship of the gods, who, according to the Purâṇas, are exhibited with the different bodies of men, animals, birds, serpents, and fishes; the widely spread custom of tântric ceremonies, which are the most modern and famous on earth; and the performance of sacrifices as prescribed in the Veda."

[2] Professor Burnouf has treated the same subject in his Review of Prof. Wilson's Translation of the Vishṇu-purâṇa, Journal des Savants, 1840, May, p. 296.

one, but without having the power to break through the walls of the Vedic ceremonial, and take the place of the old ritual."

And if it be unsafe to use the epic poems as authorities for the Vedic age, it will readily be admitted that the same objection applies with still greater force to the Purâṇas. Although one only of the eighteen Purâṇas has as yet been completely published, enough is known of their character, partly by Professor Burnouf's edition of the Bhagavat-purâṇa, partly by extracts given from other Purâṇas by Professor Wilson, to justify our discarding their evidence with reference to the primitive period of Vedic literature. Even the Mânava-dharma-śâstra, the law-book of the Mânavas, a sub-division of the sect of the Taittirîyas, or, as it is commonly called, the Laws of Manu, cannot be used as an independent authority. It cannot be said that the compilers of these laws were ignorant of the traditions of the Vedic age. Many of their verses contain a mere paraphrase of passages from the hymns, Brâhmaṇas, and Sûtras; but they likewise admitted the rules and customs of later ages, and their authority is therefore valid only where it has been checked by more original and genuine texts.

The Code of Manu is almost the only work in Sanskrit literature which, as yet, has not been assailed by those who doubt the antiquity of everything Indian. No historian has disproved its claim to that early date which had, from the first, been assigned to it by Sir William Jones. It must be confessed, however, that Sir William Jones's proofs of the antiquity of this code cannot be considered as conclusive, and no sufficient arguments have been brought forward to substantiate any of the different dates ascribed to Manu, as the author of our Law-book, which vary, according to different writers, from 880 to 1280 B.C.

If the age of Manu or of the epic poems could be fixed, so as to exclude all possible doubt, our task of determining the age of the Veda would be an easy one. The Veda is demonstrably earlier than the epic poetry and the legal codes of India. We do not, however, advance one step by saying that the Veda is older than the author of the Mânava-dharma-śâstra, whose date is altogether unknown, or even than the Mahâbhârata, if it can be doubted whether that poem in its first elements be anterior to the Buddhistic religion or not; while it is said, at the same time, that the last elements which have been incorporated into this huge work allude to historical events later than the Christian era.[1] Here, then, we must adopt a new course of procedure. We must try to fix the age of the Veda, which forms the natural basis of Indian history; and we must derive our knowledge of the Vedic age from none but Vedic works, discarding altogether such additional evidence as might be obtained from the

[1] That the principal part of the Mahâbhârata belongs to a period previous to the political establishment of Buddhism, has been proved by Prof. Lassen, Ind. Ant. i. 489—491. Much has been said since to controvert his views with regard to the age of the Mahâbhârata, but nothing that is really valuable has been added to Prof. Lassen's facts or reasonings. "It is not at all difficult," as Prof. Lassen remarks, "to look at this question from one single point of view, and to start a confident assertion. But in doing this, many persons commit themselves to inconsiderate judgments, and show an ignorance of the very points which have to be considered."

later literature of India. Let some Vedic dates be once established, and it will probably be possible to draw lines of connection between the Vedic and the rest of the Indian literature. But the world of the Veda is a world by itself; and its relation to all the rest of Sanskrit literature is such, that the Veda ought not to receive, but to throw light over the whole historical development of the Indian mind.

The Veda has a two-fold interest: it belongs to the history of the world and to the history of India. In the history of the world the Veda fills a gap which no literary work in any other language could fill. It carries us back to times of which we have no records anywhere, and gives us the very words of a generation of men, of whom otherwise we could form but the vaguest estimate by means of conjectures and inferences. As long as man continues to take an interest in the history of his race, and as long as we collect in libraries and museums the relics of former ages, the first place in that long row of books which contains the records of the Aryan branch of mankind, will belong for ever to the *Rig-veda.*

But in the history of India, too, the Veda is of the greatest importance. It has been a standing reproach to our studies that it is impossible to find anything historical in Indian literature.[1] To a certain extent that reproach is well-founded; and this accounts no doubt for the indifference with which Sanskrit literature is regarded by the public at large.

We may admire the delicate poetry of Kâlidâsa, the

[1] See Burnouf, Introduction à l'Histoire de Buddhisme, p. iii.

philosophical vigour of Kapila, the voluptuous mysticism of Jayadeva, and the epic simplicity of Vyâsa and Vâlmîki, but as long as their works float before our eyes like the mirage of a desert, as long as we are unable to tell what real life, what period in the history of the nation they reflect, there is something wanting to engage our sympathies in the same manner as they are engaged by the tragedies of Æschylus, or the philosophical essays of Cicero. We value the most imperfect statues of Lycia and Ægina, because they throw light on the history of Greek art, but we should pass by unnoticed the most perfect mouldings of the human frame, if we could not tell whether they had been prepared in the studio of a Phidias, or in the dissecting-room of a London hospital.

In the following sketch of the history of Vedic literature, I cannot promise to give dates, such as we are accustomed to find in the literary histories of other nations. But I hope I shall be able to prove that there exist in that large mass of literature which belongs to the Vedic age, clear traces of an original historical articulation; and that it is possible to restore something like chronological continuity in the four periods of the Vedic literature. If this can be achieved, if we can discover different classes of literary works, and establish their chronological succession, the reproach, so often repeated, that there is nothing historical to be found in India will be removed, as far at least as the peculiar nature of that literature allows.

The modern literature of India, though not yet grouped in chronological order, will find in the literature of the Vedic age something like a past, some testimony to prove that it did not spring up in a day, but clings by its roots to the earliest strata of Indian thought. The Laws of the Mânavas, though no longer the composition of a primeval sage, will at least be safe against the charge of being the invention of some unemployed Indian lawgiver. Plays like Śakuntala and Urvaśî, though no longer regarded as the productions of a Periclean age, will be classed among the productions of what may properly be called the Alexandrian period of Sanskrit literature. But whatever we may have to surrender with regard to the antiquity claimed by these and other Sanskrit works, that portion of the literature of India which alone can claim a place in the history of the world, and which alone can command the attention of those who survey the summits of human intellect, not only in the East but over the whole civilised world, will, I hope, for the future, be safe against the doubts which I myself have shared for many years. It is difficult, no doubt, to believe that the most ancient literary work of the Aryan race, a work more ancient than the Zendavesta and Homer, should, after a lapse of at least three thousand years, have been discovered, and for the first time published in its entirety, not in one of the Parishads on the borders of the Ganges, but in one of the colleges of an English University. It is difficult to believe that sufficient MSS. should have been preserved, in spite of the perishable nature of the material on which they are written, to enable an editor to publish the collection of the Vedic hymns in exactly that form in which they existed at least 800 years before the Christian era; and, still more, that this collection, which was completed at the time of, Lycurgus, should contain the poetical relics of a pre-Homeric age; an age in which the names of the Greek gods and heroes had not yet lost their original sense, and in which the simple worship of the Divine powers of nature was not yet supplanted by a worship of personal gods. It is difficult to believe this; and we have a right to be sceptical. But it is likewise our duty to inquire into the value of what has been preserved for us in so extraordinary a manner, and to extract from it those lessons which the study of mankind was intended to teach to man.

HISTORY OF VEDIC LITERATURE.

In taking a survey of the works which belong to the Vedic literature of India, our task would be greatly facilitated if general and characteristic features could be pointed out by which Vedic and non-Vedic works might at once be distinguished. Without entering into a minute analysis of the individual character of a work,—a mode of criticism which, with our present knowledge of the earliest Indian literature, must be very uncertain,—it will often happen that some external mark presents itself, determining at once the age or class of writing to which it belongs. It is true that there are certain grammatical forms and orthographical peculiarities which Indian grammarians restrict to the Veda, and which, therefore, might be used as distinguishing marks of works belonging to that era. But Manu, or rather the author of the Mânava-dharma-śâstra, has also employed several Vedic forms; because in transforming Vedic verses into epic Ślokas, he was sometimes obliged to retain words and forms which are not in strict accordance with the general character of his language; a fact which accounts in some degree for the strange appearance of many of his verses, which are stiff and artificial, and very inferior in fluency to the older strains which they paraphrase.

There is a strongly marked character in Vedic prose, and no attempt has been made to imitate it in later times. But in order to distinguish Vedic from non-Vedic poetry, we must attend more closely to the metre. Several Vedic metres have been imitated by later poets, but there are metres which never occur in Vedic works, and which may be used as criteria for distinguishing ancient from more modern poetry.

That difference of metre should form a broad line of demarcation between two periods of literature, is not at all without analogy in the literary history of other nations, particularly in older times. If once a new form of metre begins to grow popular by the influence of a poet who succeeds in collecting a school of other poets around him, this new mode of utterance is very apt to supersede the other more ancient forms altogether. People become accustomed to the new rhythm sometimes to such a degree, that they lose entirely the taste for their old poetry on account of its obsolete measure. No poet, therefore, who writes for the people, would think of employing those old-fashioned metres; and we find that early popular poems have had to be transfused into modern verse in order to make them generally readable once more.

Now it seems that the regular and continuous Anushṭubh-śloka is a metre unknown during the Vedic age, and every work written in it may at once be put down as post-Vedic. It is no valid objection that this epic Śloka occurs also in Vedic hymns, that Anushṭubh verses are frequently quoted in the Brâhmaṇas, and that in some of the Sûtras the Anushṭubh-śloka occurs intermixed with Trishṭubhs, and is used for the purpose of recapitulating[1] what had been explained before in prose. For it is only the *uniform*

[1] Sangraha-ślokas. Cf. Weber, Indische Studien, i. p. 47.

employment of that metre[1] which constitutes the characteristic mark of a new period of literature. Thus rhyme occasionally occurs in English poetry before the Norman period; yet, when we find whole poems written in rhyme and without the old Teutonic system of alliteration, we are sure that they cannot have been composed in an Ante-Norman period. The elegiac measure seems to have been used before Callinus; yet Callinus and Archilochus are always mentioned as the inventors of it:—that is, they were the first to sanction the uniform employment of this metre for entire poetical compositions. Hence no elegiac poem can be previous to the close of the 8th century B.C. The same applies to the iambus, the invention of which is commonly ascribed to Archilochus; although iambics occur interspersed in the Margites, a poem ascribed to Homer by no less an authority than Aristotle.[2] In the history of German literature we have several instances where

[1] It is remarkable that in Pâṇini also, the word *śloka* is always used in opposition to Vedic literature (Pâṇ iv. 1. 66., iv. 3. 103. 1., iv. 3. 107.). *Ślokas*, even if ascribed by Indian tradition to the same author, who is considered as the Ṛishi of Vedic hymns or Brâhmaṇas, are quoted by a name different from that of his other works. The hymns or Brâhmaṇas ascribed to Kaṭha, for instance, are always to be quoted as "Kaṭhâḥ" (*οἱ περὶ Κάτθον*); an expression which could never apply to poetical compositions ascribed to the same Kaṭha, if written in Ślokas. Verses written in this modern style of poetry must be quoted as "Kaṭhic Ślokas" (Kâṭhâḥ ślokâḥ). The Brâhmaṇa promulgated by Tittiri, and kept up in the tradition of the Taittirîyas, is quoted by the name of "the Taittirîyas," but Ślokas composed by Tittiri are never included under this title. Vâlmîki ślokas are mentioned. Pâṇ. ii. 4. 21.

[2] See Mure's Critical History, vol. iii. ch. i.

poems of the 12th century [1] had to be recast as early as the 13th, on account of their metre and language, which, during this period of rapid transition, had already become obsolete and unreadable.

Excluding, then, from the Vedic period the Mahâbhârata, Râmâyaṇa, Manu, the Purâṇas, and all the Śâstras and Darśanas, we have now to see what remains of literary works belonging to the Vedic age.

There are in that age four distinct periods, which can be established with sufficient evidence. They may be called the *Chhandas period*, *Mantra period*, *Brâhmaṇa period*, and *Sûtra period*, according to the general form of the literary productions which give to each of them its peculiar historical character.

In order to prove that these four periods follow each other in historical order, it is necessary to show that the composition of Sûtra works presupposes the existence of a Brâhmaṇa literature; that the Brâhmaṇa literature again is only possible with the presupposition of a Mantra literature; and lastly, that the form in which we possess the Mantra literature presupposes a period of Vedic history preceding the collection and final arrangement of the ancient Mantras or hymns.

[1] For instance, "Reinhard the Fox," an old High-German poem of the 13th century, is a new edition of the same poem written in the 12th century, of which fragments have been found by Grimm. Other poems, which are supposed to have been remodelled in the 13th century are "Crescentia," "Duke Ernst," and the "Roland Song." Lachmann supposed the same to have taken place with the "Nibelungen Klage."

CHAPTER I.

THE SÛTRA PERIOD.

THE *Sûtra period*, with which we have to begin, is of peculiar importance to the history of Indian literature, inasmuch as it forms the connecting link between the Vedic and the later Sanskrit. While on the one hand we must place several works written in Sûtras under the head of the post-Vedic or modern Sanskrit, we shall also find others which, although written in continuous Anushṭubh-ślokas, or, more frequently, intermixed with Trishṭubh and other verses (as, for instance, some of the Prâtiśâkhyas and Anukramaṇîs, and the still more modern Pariśishṭas), must be considered as the last productions of the Vedic age, trespassing in a certain degree upon the frontiers of the later Sanskrit.

It is difficult to explain the peculiarities of the style of the Sûtra literature to any one who has not worked his way through the Sûtras themselves. It is impossible to give anything like a literal translation of these works, written as they are in the most artificial, elaborate, and enigmatical form. *Sûtra* means string; and all the works written in this style, on subjects the most various, are nothing but one uninterrupted string of short sentences, twisted together into the most concise form. Shortness is the great object of this style of composition, and it is a proverbial saying (taken from the Mahâbhâshya) amongst the Pandits[1], that "an author rejoiceth in the economising of half a short vowel as much as in the birth of a son." Every doctrine thus propounded, whether grammar, metre, law, or philosophy, is reduced to a mere skeleton. All the important points and joints of a system are laid open with the greatest precision and clearness, but there is nothing in these works like connection or development of ideas. "Even the apparent simplicity of the design vanishes," as Colebrooke remarks, "in the perplexity of the structure. The endless pursuit of exceptions and limitations so disjoins the general precepts, that the reader cannot keep in view their intended connection and mutual relation. He wanders in an intricate maze, and the clew of the labyrinth is continually slipping from his hands." There is no life or meaning in these Sûtras, except what either a teacher or a running commentary, by which these works are usually accompanied, may impart to them.

Many of these works go even further: they not only express their fundamental doctrines in this concise form of language, but they coin a new kind of language, if language it can be called, by which they succeed in reducing the whole system of their tenets to mere algebraic formulas. To understand these is quite impossible without finding first what each algebraic x, y, and z, is meant to represent, and without having the key to the whole system. This key is generally given in separate Sûtras, called *Paribhâshâ*, which a pupil must know by heart, or always have present before his eyes, if he is to advance one step in the reading of such works. But

[1] Benares Magazine, Oct. 1849.

even then it would be impossible to arrive at any real understanding of the subject, without being also in possession of the laws of the so-called *Anuvṛitti* and *Nirvṛitti*. To explain the meaning of these technical words, we must remember that the Sûtras generally begin by putting forward one proposition (Adhikâra), which is afterwards never repeated, but always to be understood, till a new subject of the same kind is introduced. After the statement of a subject, the author goes on by giving a first rule, which may extend its influence over the next following rules, whether these be restrictions or amplifications of it. These restrictive rules exercise again their influence to a certain extent over other rules, so that the whole becomes one continuous chain, each link held and modified by the others, and itself holding to and modifying the rest. The influence of one rule over the others is called *Anuvṛitti*, its cessation, *Nirvṛitti*. Without knowing the working of these two laws, which can only be learnt from commentaries, the Sûtras appear very much confused. This is particularly the case in those works where the so-called Mîmânsâ method of Pûrva-paksha (reasons contrà), Uttara-paksha (reasons pro), and Siddhânta (conclusion), is adopted. Here the concatenation of pros and cons is often so complicated, and the reasons on both sides defended by the same author with such seriousness, that we sometimes remain doubtful to which side the author himself leans, till we arrive at the end of the whole chapter. It is indeed one of the most curious kinds of literary composition that the human mind ever conceived; and though altogether worthless in an artistic point of view, it is wonderful that the Indians should have invented and mastered this difficult form, so as to have made it the vehicle of expression for every kind of learning. To introduce and to maintain such a species of literature was only possible with the Indian system of education, which consisted in little else except implanting these Sûtras and other works into the tender memory of children, and afterwards explaining them by commentaries and glosses. An Indian pupil learns these Sûtras of grammar, philosophy, or theology by the same mechanical method which fixes in our minds the alphabet and the multiplication-table; and those who enter into a learned career spend half their life in acquiring and practising them, until their memory is strengthened to such an unnatural degree, that they know by heart not only these Sûtras, but also their commentaries, and commentaries upon commentaries. Instances of this are found among the learned in India up to the present day.

These numerous Sûtra works which we still possess, contain the quintessence of all the knowledge which the Brahmans had accumulated during many centuries of study and meditation. Though they are the works of individuals, they owe to their authors little more than their form; and even that form was, most likely, the result of a long-continued system of traditional teaching, and not the invention of a few individuals.

There is a great difference, according to the notions of the Hindus themselves, between a work composed previous to the Sûtra period, and a Sûtra composition. The difference of style between a Brâhmaṇa and a Sûtra work (with the exception of some Kalpa-Sûtras, to be mentioned hereafter) would strike every body at first sight, although, as regards the grammatical forms, Vedic irregularities are, according to Sanskrit grammarians, allowed in Sûtras also.[1] But there is another, and more important difference. Literary works, belonging to the preceding periods, the Brâhmaṇas as well as the Mantras, are considered by Indian theologians as forming the Śruti, or divine revelation, in contradistinction to the Sûtras and all the rest of their literature. In the dogmatical language of orthodox Hindus, the works, which contain the Śruti, have not been composed, but have only been seen or perceived by men, *i.e.*, they have been revealed to men. The Sûtras, on the contrary, although based upon the Śruti, and therefore in some instances also called Śrauta Sûtras, are yet avowedly composed by human authors. Whenever they appear to be in contradiction with the Śruti, their authority is at once overruled, and only in cases where anterior evidence

[1] Vedic forms occur in the Prâtiśâkhya-Sûtras, and are pointed out as such by the commentators. For instance, I. Prâtiśâkhya, iv. 33. ता वशंगमानि instead of तानि वशंगमानि। The Commentator says तानिशब्दलोपो द्रष्टव्यः। छंदोवत्सूत्राणि भवंति। The same applies also to the Sâmayâchârika-Sûtras, for instance, those of Âpastamba, i. 53., where we read अधामनशायी। The Commentator explains this irregular form by अधःशब्दस्य सवर्णदीर्घश्छांदसोऽपपाठो वा। Again, i. 93. we find अग्लाँस्तु explained by the Commentary as तत्रानुस्वारपाठश्छांदसः। अपपाठो वा। Gautama-Sûtras, p. 40. l. 20. we read मकारांतपाठ आर्षः सुमेधसो दुर्मेधस इत्यादिषु दर्शनात्॥.

is wanting from the Śruti, can they have any claim to independent authority.

Now, even if we had no other means of proving that the Sûtras could have been composed only after the composition of the Brâhmaṇas, there would be no reason to consider this distinction, drawn by the Indians themselves between their sacred and profane literature, as altogether artificial and devoid of historical meaning, particularly if it can be shown how great an influence that very distinction has exercised on the religious struggles of India.

It is clear that this distinction has ever been the stronghold of the hierarchical pretensions of the Brahmans. We can understand how a nation might be led to ascribe a superhuman origin to their ancient national poetry, particularly if that poetry consisted chiefly of prayers and hymns addressed to their gods. But it is different with the prose compositions of the Brâhmaṇas. The reason why the Brâhmaṇas, which are evidently so much more modern than the Mantras, were allowed to participate in the name of Śruti, could only have been because it was from these theological compositions, and not from the simple old poetry of the hymns, that a supposed divine authority could be derived for the greater number of the ambitious claims of the Brahmans. But, although we need not ascribe any weight to the arguments by which the Brahmans endeavoured to establish the contemporaneous origin of the Mantras and Brâhmaṇas, there seems to be no reason why we should reject as equally worthless the general opinion with regard to the more ancient date of both the Brâhmaṇas and Mantras, if contrasted with the Sûtras and the profane literature of India. It may easily happen, where there is a canon of sacred books, that later compositions become incorporated together with more ancient works, as was the case with the Brâhmaṇas. But we can hardly imagine that old and genuine parts should ever have been excluded from a body of sacred writings, and a more modern date ascribed to them, unless it be in the interest of a party to deny the authority of certain doctrines contained in these rejected documents. There is nothing in the later literature of the Sûtras to warrant a supposition of this kind. We can find no reason why the Sûtras should not have been ranked as Śruti, except the lateness of their date, if compared with the Brâhmaṇas, and still more with the Mantras. Whether the Brahmans themselves were aware that ages must have elapsed between the period during which most of the poems of their Ṛishis were composed, and the times which gave rise to the Brâhmaṇas, is a question which we need hardly hesitate to answer in the affirmative. But the recklessness with which Indian theologians claim for these Brâhmaṇas the same title and the same age as for the Mantras, shows that the reasons must have been peculiarly strong which deterred them from claiming the same divine authority for the Sûtras.

To ascribe to literary compositions such as the Mantras and Brâhmaṇas a divine origin, and to claim for them a divine and absolute authority, is a step which can hardly pass unnoticed in the intellectual history of a nation, whether for the circumstances which led to it, or for the results which it produced. Now, in India the results of that fatal step are palpable. It may have been intended as a check on religious reforms, but it led to a religious revolution.

Buddhism would be unintelligible, unless as the overthrow of a system which had tried to maintain its position by an appeal to a divine revelation; and we may be certain that the distinction between Śruti and Smṛiti, between revealed and profane literature, was established by the Brahmans, previous to the schism of Buddha.

If the belief was once established, that not only the simple effusions of the Ṛishis, but the pointed doctrines of the Brâhmaṇas also, emanated from a divine source, and could not therefore be attacked by human reasoning, it is clear that every opposition to the privileges which the Brahmans claimed for themselves, on the sacred authority of the Veda, became heresy; and where the doctrines of the Brahmans were the religion of the people, or rather of the king, such opposition was amenable to the hierarchical laws of the state. The Brahmans themselves cared much more to see the divine authority of the Śruti as such, implicitly acknowledged, than to maintain the doctrines of the Ṛishis in their original simplicity and purity. In philosophical discussions, they allowed the greatest possible freedom; and, although at first three philosophical systems only were admitted as orthodox (the two Mîmânsâs and the Nyâya), their number was soon raised to six, so as to include the Vaiśeshika, Sânkhya, and Yoga-schools.[1] The most conflicting views on points of vital importance were tolerated as

[1] Kumârila quotes Sânkhya and Yoga, together with other heretical systems. सांख्ययोगपांचरात्रपाशुपतशाक्यनिर्ग्रंथ-परिगृहीतधर्माधर्मनिबंधनानि॥ As to the Vaiśeshikas, see page 84.

long as their advocates succeeded, no matter by what means, in bringing their doctrines into harmony with passages of the Veda, strained and twisted in every possible sense. If it was only admitted that, besides the perception of the senses and the induction of reason, revelation also, as contained in the Veda, furnished a true basis for human knowledge, all other points seemed to be of minor importance. Philosophical minds were allowed to exhaust all possible views on the relation between the real and transcendental world, the Creator and the created, the divine and the human nature. It was not from such lucubrations that danger was likely to accrue to the caste of the Brahmans. Nor was the heresy of Buddha Śâkya Muni found so much in his philosophical doctrines, many of which may be traced in the orthodox atheism of Kapila. His real crime lay in his opposition to the exclusive privileges and abuses of the Brahmans. These abuses were sanctioned by the divine authority of the Veda[1], and particularly of the Brâhmaṇas. In attacking these abuses, Buddha attacked the divine authority on which they were founded, and the argument was short: he is a heretic; anathema esto.

Buddha was a Kshatriya.[2] He was of princely

[1] The Buddhists say that the three Vedas were propounded originally by Maha Brahma, at which time they were perfect truth; but they have since been corrupted by the Brahmans and now contain many errors. Cf. R. Spence Hardy, Eastern Monachism, p. 185.

[2] Kumârila always speaks of Buddha as a Kshatriya who tried to become a Brahman. For instance,

स्वधर्मातिरेकेण च क्षत्रियेण सता प्रवक्तृत्वप्रतिग्रहौ प्रतिपन्नौ

And again, बुद्धादेः पुनरयमेवातिक्रमोऽलंकारबुद्धौ स्थितः

origin, and belonged to the nobility of the land. He was not the first of his caste who opposed the ambition of the Brahmans. Several centuries before Buddha, Viśvâmitra, who, like Buddha, was a member of the royal caste, had to struggle against the exclusiveness of the priests. At that early time, however, the position of the Brahmans was not yet impregnable; and Viśvâmitra, although a Kshatriya, succeeded in gaining for himself and his family the rights for which he struggled, and which the Brahmans had previously withheld from all but their own caste. King Janaka of Videha again, whose story is given in the Brâhmaṇas, refused to submit to the hierarchical pretensions of the Brahmans, and asserted his right of performing sacrifices without the intercession of priests. However great the difference may have been between the personal character of these two men and of Buddha,

येनैवमाह कलिकलुषकृतानि यानि लोके मयि निपतंतु विमुच्यतां तु लोक इति स किल लोकहितार्थं क्षत्रियधर्ममतिक्रम्य ब्राह्मणवृत्तिं प्रवक्तृत्वं प्रतिपद्य प्रतिषेधातिक्रमसमर्थैर्ब्राह्मणैरननुशिष्टं धर्मं बाह्यजनानुशास्तिं धर्मपीडामप्यात्मनोऽंगीकृत्य परानुग्रहं कृतवानित्येवंविधैरेव गुणैः स्तूयते॥

"And this very transgression of Buddha and his followers is represented as if it did him honour. For he is praised because he said, 'Let all the sins that have been committed in this world fall on me, that the world may be delivered.' It is said that if he thus transgressed the duty of a Kshatriya, and entered the life of a Brahman and preached, it was merely for the good of mankind; and that in adopting for the instruction of excluded people a law which had not been taught by the Brahmans, he took the sin upon himself and was benefitting others."

the first principle of their opposition was the same. All three were equally struggling against the overweening pretensions of a selfish priesthood.

But while Viśvâmitra contented himself with maintaining the rights of his tribe or family, and became reconciled as soon as he was allowed to share in the profits of the priestly power, — while King Janaka expressed himself satisfied with the homage paid to him by Yâjnavalkya and other Brahmans, — while, in short, successive reformers as they appeared were either defeated or gained over to the cause of the Brahmans, — the seeds of discontent were growing up in the minds of the people. There is a dark chapter in the history of India, the reported destruction of all the Kshatriyas by Paraśu-râma. It marks the beginning of the hierarchical supremacy of the Brahmans. Though the Brahmans seem never to have aspired to the royal power, their caste, as far as we know the history and traditions of India, has always been in reality the ruling caste. Their ministry was courted as the only means of winning divine favour, their doctrines were admitted as infallible, their gods were worshipped as the only true gods, and their voice was powerful enough to stamp not only the simple strains of the Ṛishis, but the absurd lucubrations of the authors of the Brâhmaṇas, with a divine authority. After this last step, however, the triumph of Brahmanism was preparing its fall. In India, less than in any other country, would people submit to a monopoly of truth; and the same millions who were patiently bearing the yoke of a political despotism threw off the fetters of an intellectual tyranny. In order to overthrow one of the oldest religions of the world, it was sufficient that one man should challenge the authority of the Brahmans, the gods of the earth, (bhûdeva), and preach among the scorned and degraded creatures of God, the simple truth that salvation was possible without the mediation of priests, and without a belief in books to which these very priests had given the title of revelation. This man was *Buddha Śâkya Muni.*

Now if we inquire how Buddha's doctrines were met by the Brahmans, it is true that here and there in their philosophical works they have endeavoured to overthrow some of his metaphysical axioms by an appeal to reason. An attempt of this kind we have, for instance, in Vâchaspati Miśra's commentary on the Vedânta Sûtras. In commenting on the tenet of Buddha, that "ideas like those of being, and not-being, &c., do not admit of discussion,"[1] Vâchaspati observes that the very fact of speaking of these ideas, includes the possibility of their conception; nay, that to affirm they do not admit of reasoning involves an actual reasoning on them, and proves that the mind can conceive the idea of being as different from that of not-being.

Such, however, were not the usual weapons with which Brahmanism fought against Buddhism. The principal objection has always been, that Buddha's teaching could not be true, because it did not derive its sanction from Śruti or revelation. The Brahmans, as a caste, would readily have allowed being and not-being, and the whole of Buddha's philosophy, as they did the Sânkhya philosophy, which

[1] सदादीनामन्यतमद्विचारं न सहते॥

on the most important points is in open opposition to the Vedânta. But while Kapila, the founder of the Sânkhya school, conformed to the Brahmanic test by openly proclaiming the authority of revelation as paramount to reasoning and experience, Buddha would not submit to this, either for his philosophical (abhidharma), or for his much more important moral and religious doctrines (vinaya). No doubt it would have been easy for him to show how some of his doctrines harmonised with passages of the Veda, as in the Veda all possible shades of the human mind have found their natural reflection. If he had done so only for some of his precepts, such, for instance, as, "Thou shalt not murder,"[1] "Thou shalt not drink,"[2] "Thou shalt eat standing,"[3] the Brahmans would readily have passed over other doctrines, even such as came into practice after Buddha's death, like "Who longs for heaven, shall worship the holy sepulchre,"[4] "He shall pull out his hair,"[5] &c. As he refused to do so, the line of argument taken by the Brahmans was simply confined to an appeal to revelation, in disproof of the possibility of the truth of Buddha's doctrines.

There must be something very tempting in this line of argument, for we see that in later times the

[1] न हन्यात्॥

[2] न पिबेत्। *i. e.* "thou shalt not drink intoxicating liquors."

[3] तिष्ठन्भुंजीत॥

[4] चैत्यं वंदेत स्वर्गकामः॥

[5] केशान् लुंचेत्॥

Buddhists also endeavoured to claim the same divine character for their sacred writings which the Brahmans had established for the Veda. A curious instance of this is given in the following discussion, from Kumârila's Tantra-vârttika. Here the opponent (pûrva-paksha) observes, that the same arguments which prove that the Veda is not the work of human authors, apply with equal force to Śâkya's teaching. His authority, he says, cannot be questioned, because his precepts are clear and intelligible; and as Śâkya is not the inventor, but only the teacher of these precepts, and no name of an author is given for Śâkya's doctrines, the frailties inherent in human authors affect them as little as the Veda.[1] Everything, in fact, he concludes, which has been brought forward by the Mîmânsakas to prove the authority of the Veda, proves in the same way the authority of Buddha's doctrine. Upon this, the orthodox Kumârila grows very wroth, and says: "These Śâkyas, Vaiśeshikas, and other heretics, who have been frightened out of their wits by the faithful Mîmânsakas, prattle away with our own words as if trying to lay hold of a shadow. They say that their sacred works are eternal; but they are of empty minds, and only out of hatred they wish to deny that the Veda is the most ancient book.

[1] अकर्तृकतया नापि कर्तृदोषेण दुष्यति।
वेदवद्बुद्धवाक्यादि कर्तृस्मरणवर्जणात्॥
बुद्धवाक्यसमाख्यापि प्रवक्तृत्वनिबंधना।
तद्दृष्टत्वनिमित्ता वा काठकांगिरसादिवत्॥
यावद्वेदोदितं किंचिद्वेदप्रामाण्यसिद्धये।
तत्सर्वं बुद्धवाक्यानामतिदशेन गम्यते॥

And these would-be logicians declare even that some of their precepts (which they have stolen from us), like that of universal benevolence, are not derived from the Veda, because most of Buddha's other sayings are altogether opposed to the Veda. Wishing, therefore, to keep true on this point also, and seeing that no merely human precept could have any authority on moral and supernatural subjects, they try to veil their difficulty by aping our own arguments for the eternal existence of the Veda. They know that the Mîmânsakas have proved that no sayings of men can have any authority on supernatural subjects; they know also that the authority of the Veda cannot be controverted, because they can bring forward nothing against the proofs adduced for its divine origin, by which all supposition of a human source has been removed. Therefore, their hearts being gnawed by their own words, which are like the smattering of children, and having themselves nothing to answer, because the deception of their illogical arguments has been destroyed, they begin to speak like a foolish suitor who came to ask for a bride, saying, 'My family is as good as your family.' In the same manner they now maintain the eternal existence of their books, aping the speeches of others. And if they are challenged and told that this is *our* argument, they brawl, and say that we, the Mîmânsakas, have heard and stolen it from them. For a man who has lost all shame, who can talk away without any sense, and tries to cheat his opponent, will never get tired, and will never be put down!" Towards the end of this harangue, Kumârila adds, what is more to the point, that the Bauddhas, who ascribe to everything a merely temporary existence, have no business to talk of an eternal revelation.

Now, it ought not to be overlooked, that in all these discussions the distinction between Śruti (Mantras and Brâhmaṇas) and Smṛiti (Sûtras) is always taken for granted. If, at the time of the first controversies between Bauddhas and Mîṃânsakas, the authors of the Mantras or Brâhmaṇas, and particularly the founders of the so-called ancient Brâhmaṇas, had still been alive, or their names generally known, even a Brahman could not have ventured to stand up for the divine and eternal origin of this part of the Śruti. On the other hand, nothing could have prevented the Brahmans from ascribing the same supernatural origin to the Sûtras, if at the time of the rising power of Buddhism their authors also had been lost in oblivion. The distinction, therefore, between Śruti (revelation) and Smṛiti (tradition) which is a point of such vital importance for the whole Brahmanic system, will also be found significant in an historical point of view.

It must be observed, however, before we proceed farther, that what is called Smṛiti includes not only Sûtras, but also Śloka works, such as the laws of Manu, Yâjnavalkya, and Parâśara (the Mânava, Yâjnavalkya, and Parâśara-dharma-śâstras), which sometimes are called *the* Smṛitis, in the plural. Most of these, if not all, are founded on Sûtras; but the texts of the Sûtras have mostly been superseded by these later metrical paraphrases.

How then did the Brahmans, after they had established the distinction between Śruti and Smṛiti, defend the authority of the Smṛiti, including the Sûtras and the later works in Ślokas?

That the Smṛiti has no claim to an independent authority, but derives its sanction from its intimate connection with the Śruti, is implied by its very name, which means recollection. For, as Kumârila remarks (in the pûrva-paksha), "Recollection is knowledge; the object of which is some previous knowledge; and if Manu and other authors of Smṛitis had not originally been in possession of an authoritative knowledge, it would be impossible to appeal to their recollection as an authority.[1] It would be as if a man, omitting his son or daughter, was to appeal to the son of a barren daughter. For the original knowledge of Manu might be compared to his son, but his recollection could only be like a grandson. Now as people, if they have reason to doubt the existence of a daughter, would disbelieve every mention of the son of a daughter, thus the recollection (smṛiti) of Manu would be futile, if he himself had not possessed some means of authoritative knowledge."

The following extracts from Sâyaṇa's Commentary on Parâśara's Code[2] will show the use which the

[1] पूर्वविज्ञानविषयं विज्ञानं स्मृतिरुच्यते। पूर्वज्ञानाद्विना तस्याः प्रामाण्यं नावधार्यते॥ And again, मन्वादीनामपि यदि प्रथमं किंचित्प्रमाणं संभाव्यते ततः स्मरणं भवेन्नान्यथा। कस्मात्पुनः पुत्रं दुहितरं चाधिक्रम्य वंध्यादौहित्रोदाहरणं कृतं। स्थानतुल्यत्वात्पुत्रस्थानीयं हि मन्वादेः पूर्वविज्ञानं। दौहित्रस्थानीयं स्मरणं। अतश्च यथा दुहितुरभावं परामृश्य दौहित्रस्मृतिं भ्रांतिं मन्यंते तथा मन्वादिभिः प्रत्यक्षाद्यसंभवपरामर्शादष्टकादिस्मरणं मिथ्येति मंतव्यं॥

[2] MS. Bodl. 172, 173.

Brahmans made of this argument, in order to substantiate the authority of their legal text-books.

"Does it not seem after all," he says, "as if this Smṛiti (containing as it does the laws of men) hardly deserved a commentary of its own, inasmuch as it is difficult to make out on what grounds it claims any authority? For if we appeal to a Sûtra of Jaimini's (the founder of the Pûrva-mîmânsâ) wherein he has proved that the Veda possesses an authority irrespective of anything else, these arguments can hardly apply to books which are evidently the works of men, and entirely dependent on the authority of their sources. These sources again, if they be considered as the life and strength of that authority, are often very indistinct. First, they could never fall under the cognizance of the senses, because the very nature of duty or law is transcendental. Nor can this ultimate reason or source be found in induction, inasmuch as induction is only possible after observation. Neither can it be looked for in the sayings of other men, because man is exposed to error, and cannot even express things as he has really perceived them. But even if man were free from error, there would always be room for doubt and opposition. And as to finding the authority for these laws in direct precepts of the Śruti (Mantras and Brâhmaṇas) this is out of the question, because such precepts are not to be found there. We have never seen a passage in the Veda where precepts like those of the Smṛiti, to keep the body clean, &c., are given. To admit the right of induction for laws of this kind would be most dangerous, for it would apply with equal force to the precepts of Buddha, to worship the holy sepulchre, &c.

"However, there is an answer to all these doubts.

A great difference exists between the Smṛitis of Manu and the Smṛitis of Buddha, because Manu's authority is asserted by the undeniable Veda itself. It is said in the Veda, 'Whatever Manu said, was medicine;' but there is no passage there in any way favourable to the Smṛiti of Buddha, and therefore the right of applying induction cannot be considered dangerous, because it never could be extended to Buddha's doctrines.

"Quod non," says the opponent. "This passage of the Veda, 'Whatever Manu said, was medicine,' is only an Arthavâda (an explanatory remark), and has no evidence by itself. It only serves to illustrate or recommend another precept, viz., that two verses of Manu's are to be used at a certain sacrifice.[1] Therefore, there is no passage in the Veda to warrant the authority of the Smṛiti; and if Śâkya's, *i.e.* Buddha's, Smṛiti be exceptional, the same applies to the Smṛiti of Manu. Thus it is said, 'As men speak often untruth and are exposed to error, as no divine precept is given, faith only can be authority.' But

[1] As dhayyâs at the Somâraudra Charu, in the middle of the Sâmidhênî, or fire-kindling hymns. The same argument occurs in Kumârila's Tantra-vârttika, i. 3.,

तथा च मनोर्ऋचः सामिधेन्यो भवंतीत्यस्य विधेर्वाक्यशेषे श्रूयते मनुर्वै यत्किंचिदेव वदेत्तद्भेषजं भेषजतायाा इति॥

Mahâdeva, in his Commentary on the Hiraṇyakeśi-sûtras, says that the Śruti bears witness to the authority of the Smṛitis by declaring that whatever Manu said was medicine.

श्रुतिरपि स्मृतीनां वेदमूलत्वमाह यद्वै किंच मनुरवदत्तद्भेषजमिति भेषजं यथा हितमेवं मनुवचनमपि प्रमाणत्वेन हितमित्यर्थः॥

further, even admitting that there was a shadow of authority for Manu, what could be said in favour of Parâśara's Smṛiti, which is now to be explained? For, although the Veda may praise Manu, it never does the same for Parâśara, and thus Parâśara's authority at least can hardly be defended.

"Against all this our answer is: the Smṛitis are an authority, because that they should have authority is understood by itself; and there is no reason why they should not be considered as having authority. Three reasons are given why Manu and the rest could not claim any authority, viz., 'that men speak untruth, that they are exposed to error, and that no divine precept is given.' These objections, however, are entirely out of order, because nobody would ever think that Manu and Parâśara, who have been perfect from their very birth, could have spoken untruth, and could have erred. So much for the first two objections. And who ever denied that these sages were perfect from their very birth, as Mantras, Arthavâdas, Itihâsas, and Purâṇas, prove distinctly not only the existence of Parâśara and others, but also their perfection? Nay, even if we had not the testimony of the Mantras, how could the perfection of Parâśara and others be denied, which is involved in their very existence? A difference of opinion is quite impossible. And has it not been proved in the chapter on the gods [1] in the Uttara-mîmânsâ, that the Mantras do not require

[1] If this refers to the Sankarshaṇakâṇḍa, which is ascribed to Jaimini, and forms an appendix to the Karmamîmânsâ-sûtras (cf. Prasthânabheda), we ought to read Pûrva-mîmânsâ instead of Uttara-mîmânsâ.

any further proof for what they say? It is true that in the chapter on the Arthavâdas it has been admitted that what the Arthavâdas contain is not always to be believed. But this is only on account of some impossible things which are occasionally mentioned therein. Therefore an Arthavâda like this 'Whatever Manu says is medicine,' although it only serves to recommend another rule, must yet be considered as true in itself. With regard to Śakya, nothing similar can be brought forward; and thus it is well said elsewhere, 'May a man scorn all the erroneous doctrines of Arhat, Chârvâka, and Buddha.' As regards Parâśara in particular, it is wrong to say that his fame is not equally founded on the Veda, for it is said in the Śruti, 'Thus spoke Vyâsa, the son of Parâśara.' If, therefore, the famous Veda-Vyâsa is praised as the son of Parâśara, how much more famous must not Parâśara, his father, have been! In the genealogical Brâhmaṇa of the Vâjasanêyi-śâkhâ, the son also and the grandson of Parâśara are mentioned in the succession of pupils and teachers who handed down the Veda[1], 'Ghṛitakauśika received from Pârâśaryâyaṇa, Pârâśaryâyaṇa from Pârâśarya, Pârâśarya from Jâtukarṇya, &c.' Therefore Parâśara stands quite on a level with Manu; and the same applies to all the other Ṛishis, like Vasishṭha and Yâjnavalkya, who are authors of Smṛitis, and are mentioned in the Śruti. Thus we read, 'The Ṛishis did not see Indra clearly, but Vasishṭha saw him clearly.'[2] 'Atri

[1] Bṛihadâraṇyaka, 5. 6. 3. See page 439.

[2] Taittirîya-Sanhitâ, 3. 5. 2.

ऋषयो वा इंद्रं प्रत्यक्षं नापश्यन् तं वसिष्ठः प्रत्यक्षमपश्यत्

gave his children to Aurva, who longed for a son.'[1] 'Yâjnavalkya had two wives.'[2] Therefore one must not think of attacking the Smṛitis of Manu and others by any means.

"The third reason also which was brought forward against the authority of the Smṛiti, viz. that the

सोऽब्रवीत् ब्राह्मणं ते वक्ष्यामि यथा त्वत्पुरोहिताः प्रजाः प्रजनिष्यंतेऽथ मेतरेभ्य ऋषिभ्यो मा प्रवोच इति। तस्मा एतान् स्तोमभागानब्रवीत् ततो वसिष्ठपुरोहिताः प्रजाः प्राजायंत तस्माद्वासिष्ठो ब्रह्मा कार्यः॥

"The Ṛishis did not see Indra clearly, but Vasishṭha saw him clearly. Indra said, 'I shall tell you a Brâhmaṇa, so that all men that are born will have thee for Purohita; but do not tell of me to the other Ṛishis.' Thus he told him these parts of the hymns; and ever since, men were born having Vasishṭha for their Purohita. Therefore a Vásishṭha is to be chosen as Brahman."

Cf. Tâṇḍya Brâhmaṇa, xv. 5., where it is said of the Bharatas that they will always have a Vasishṭha as Purohita. The Commentator there observes, that Bharata may either mean the kings of that name, or men in general.

[1] Taittirîya-Sanhitâ, 7. 1. 8:

अत्रिरददादौर्वाय प्रजां पुत्रकामाय स रिरिचानोऽमन्यत निर्वीर्यः शिथिलो यातयामा स एतं चतूरात्रमपश्यत्तमाहरत्तेनायजत ततो वै तस्य चत्वारो वीरा अजायंत सुहोता सूद्गाता स्वध्वर्युः सुसभेयः॥

"Atri gave his children to the son of Urva, who longed for a son. Then he felt lonely, and saw that he was without power, weak, and decrepit. He saw this Chatûrâtra; he took it and sacrificed with it. Four sons were born to him from it,—a good Hotṛi, a good Udgâtṛi, a good Adhvaryu, and a good Brahman."

[2] Śatapatha-brâhmaṇa, xvii. 4. 5.

precepts given there are not based upon passages of the Śruti, does not hold good, because passages are met with which are the source of all the laws given in the Smṛiti. Thus we read, 'These five great sacrifices are every day commenced and every day finished: the Devayajna (to the gods), the Pitṛiyajna (to the fathers, the manes), the Bhûtayajna (to all beings), the Manushyayajna (to men), the Brahmayajna (to Brahman, the divine Self).'[1] And although there is no distinct precept in the Veda for ablutions, &c., yet all this is implied. Thus the Bhaṭṭâchâryas say, 'It is right to respect the Smṛitis, because they are delivered by Vedic authors, because their origin is well established, and because they derive their authority from the Veda, if but rightly understood.' The Munis see the Śruti, and they deliver the Smṛiti; therefore the authority of both is proved on earth by full evidence. A man who despises these two, and adopts fallacious doctrines, is to be avoided by good men as a heretic and Veda-blasphemer.

"But one might object that if these precepts can be learnt from the Śruti, the Smṛiti would be unnecessary, because that only which cannot be learnt from other sources forms a fit object for a new work. Here then we say that these precepts, though they can be learnt from the Veda, are nevertheless put together in the Smṛitis for the purpose of making the order of their performance more easy, by leaving out the Arthavâdas, and by taking from some Śâkhâs of the Veda particular facts omitted in others. Now it might again be objected that this

[1] Taittirîya-âraṇyaka, ii. 10.

is done in the *Kalpa-sûtras*, and that therefore there was no necessity for the Smṛitis. But this is wrong, because there are two different kinds of duties to be performed, called *Śrauta* (based on Śruti) and *Smârta* (based on Smṛiti). The *Śrauta* ceremonies consist in sacrifices like the Darśa-pûrṇamâsa, &c., which can only be performed after the sacred fire has been placed in the house, and they are clearly based upon the Veda, as we read it. The *Smârta* sacraments and traditional customs, on the contrary, consist in ablutions, rinsing the mouth, &c., and they are to be considered as based upon a Śâkhâ of the Veda which is hidden, but the existence of which must be inferred. Although, therefore, those precepts which regard the placing of the sacred fire, &c., are put together in the Kalpa-sûtras, yet as other duties, such as ablutions, rinsing, &c., are not included in them, the Smṛitis have still their legitimate object."

This discussion has been given here at full length because it is a genuine specimen of Indian orthodox dialectics. Whatever may be thought of this style of argument, we see at all events how great an importance has always been attached by the Brahmans to the distinction between Śruti and Smṛiti.

It may also have been observed in this extract, that it is not quite in accordance with the language of Sâyaṇa to speak of Sûtra works as Smṛitis in the plural. He applies this term to metrical codes only, like those ascribed to Manu, Yâjnavalkya, and Parâśara, but not to Sûtras or Vedângas.[1] This, however,

[1] Kumârila remarks that, although the six Vedângas are not called by the name of Smṛiti, they are Smṛiti in the same sense

does not affect our present question, because even Sâyaṇa, though he does not call the Sûtras by the name of Smṛitis, places them notwithstanding in the same category with the codes of law, and separates them from the Śruti, upon which they are founded, but with which they are not to be confounded. The Kalpa-sûtras are called by him śrauta, *i. e.* based on revelation, but not Śruti (revelation), because although they treat of the same subjects as the Śruti, they are themselves extracts only from the sacred writings. They are arranged by authors whose names are given, while, according to Indian notions, Mantras and Brâhmaṇas were only seen by the Ṛishis, but neither composed nor arranged by them.[1]

That Sûtras, even where they contain Vedânga-doctrines, are distinctly excluded from the Śruti, may be seen from the following passage. In the Tantra-vârttika (1. 3.), Kumârila says, "There is a great

as the Dharma-sûtras, i. 3. 9. स्मृतित्वं त्वंगानां धर्मसूत्राणां चाविशिष्टं॥ यद्यपि स्मृतिशब्देन नांगानामभिधेयता। तथाप्येषां न शास्त्रत्वप्रमाणत्वनिराक्रिया॥ Mahâdeva, in his Commentary on the Hiraṇyakeśi-sûtras, says distinctly, सूत्रेषु स्मृतित्वं स्मृत्यधिकरणे स्थितं। तत्सूत्रकारेणैवोक्तं न्यायवित्समय इति मीमांसासिद्धांतस्वीकारदर्शनेन॥

[1] "When we spoke of this (the authorship of Madhuchhandas) to a learned Hindu friend, he exhibited very marked dissatisfaction and distress, begging us to write and tell Professor Wilson that the hymn had *no* author; that it had existed from everlasting; and that Madhuchhandas was only the fortunate seer to whom, on the last occasion of its revelation, it had been revealed."—*Benares Magazine for June*, 1851, "On Müller's Edition and Wilson's Version of the Rig-Veda."

difference between the Kalpa-sûtras, which teach the performance of sacrifices enjoined by the Vedas, such as we now possess them, and the Smṛitis, which derive their authority from parts of the Veda that have either disappeared or are dispersed, or the existence of which can be proved by induction only. It is easier, therefore, to establish the authority of the Kalpa-sûtras than that of the Smṛitis. The objections which have been raised against the authority of the Smṛitis, and which had to be removed by us before, cannot be thought of with regard to the Kalpa-sûtras, not even if it were only for argument's sake.[1] The question, therefore, is only this, whether the Kalpa-sûtras have the same authority as the Veda, or whether they merely derive their authority from it. As the Veda is called 'shaḍanga,' 'having six members,' these six members, and amongst them the Kalpa-sûtras, might seem to be implied by the common name of Veda. This, however, would be wrong[2]; for the Kalpa-sûtras, as is well-known, are composed by human authors like Maśaka, &c. They do not take their names, like the Kâṭhaka and other Śâkhâs of the Veda, from those by whom they were proclaimed, but from their real authors. It is true, no doubt, that the authors of the Kalpa-sûtras have the name of Ṛishis, and it might be said that as Śiśu

[1] अप्रमाण्यं स्मृतीनां च यदशब्दतयोदितं।
पूर्वपक्षे न तद्वक्तुं कल्पसूत्रेषु शक्यते॥
प्रत्यक्षवेदशब्दत्वात्तदुक्ता नापशब्दता।
न ह्यत्यंतानृतं वक्तुं शक्यते पूर्वपक्षिणा॥

[2] वेदत्वं कल्पसूत्राणां नो वक्तव्यं मनागपि॥

Ângirasa was not the author of the Śaiśava hymns in the Sâma-veda, the Kalpa-sûtras too were not composed, but only proclaimed, by those whose names they bear, particularly as there are even Brâhmaṇas, for instance those of the Aruṇa and Parâśara-śâkhâ, which have nearly the same form as the Kalpa-sûtras. Nevertheless, nothing can be more mistaken than the opinion of those who would put the Kalpa-sûtras on the same footing as the Veda, because people who teach and learn the Kalpa-sûtras know that there was a time when these works did not exist, and that they were composed by certain authors like Maśaka, Baudhâyana, Âpastamba, Âśvalâyana, Kâtyâyana, and others." [1] They are drawn, as he

[1] Kumârila expressly observes that these names signify certain individuals, and not Charaṇas (sects), like those of Kaṭha, by which certain Śâkhâs of the Veda were promulgated.

यथा च कठादिचरणैरनादिभिः प्रोच्यमानानामनादिवेदशाखानामनादिसमाख्यासंभवो नैवं नित्यावस्थितमशकादिगोत्रचरणप्रवचननिमित्तसमाख्योपपत्तिः। मशकबौधायनापस्तंबादिशब्दा ह्यादिमदेकद्रव्योपदेशिन इति न तेभ्यः प्रकृतिभूतेभ्योऽनादिग्रंथविषयसमाख्याव्युत्पादनसंभवः॥

"The branches of the Veda which were proclaimed by the sects of Kaṭha and others from all eternity, have a fair claim to be called eternal. But this does not apply to works handed down by the sects or families of Maśaka and others, however long they may have been established. For names like Maśaka, Baudhâyana, and Âpastamba, imply an individual being which had a beginning, and therefore it is impossible that a title derived from these names should ever belong to an eternal work."

And again:

यथैव हि कल्पसूत्रग्रंथानितरांगस्मृतिनिबंधनानि चाध्येत-

observes in another place, partly from the Veda, but partly also from other sources; and the same applies, according to him, to all the Vedâṅgas and Smṛitis; nay, even to later works, such as the epic and paurâṇic poems.[1]

ध्यापयितारः स्मरंति तथाश्वलायनबौधायनापस्तंबकात्यायनप्रभृतीन् ग्रंथकारत्वेन॥

"For teachers and pupils do not only know by heart the Kalpasûtra books, and the other Vedâṅga and Smṛiti compositions, but they also remember Âśvalâyana, Baudhâyana, Âpastamba, Kâtyâyana and others, as the authors of these books."

[1] तत्र यावद्धर्ममोक्षसंबंधि तद्वेदप्रभवं। यत्त्वर्थसुखविषयं तल्लोकव्यवहारपूर्वकमिति विवेक्तव्यं। एषैवेतिहासपुराणयोरप्युपदेशवाक्यानां गतिः॥

"All that has reference to virtue and final beatitude is taken from the Veda, while other matters, the purpose of which consists in pleasure and gain, are according to the customs of men. This distinction applies not only to the Vedâṅgas, but also to authoritative passages in the Purâṇas and Itihâsas."

Uvaṭa, in his commentary on the Śâkala-prâtiśâkhya, takes the same view. He says, "that as the Veda was too difficult to be used by itself, learned men have extracted from it different doctrines on the ceremonial, the metre, and grammar, and brought them into a more intelligible form in the Sûtras."

यस्मात्केवलवेदवाक्यैर्न शक्यतेऽनुष्ठातुं विच्छिन्नत्वाद्वेदवाक्यानां गूढार्थत्वाच्च अतः कविभिराचार्यैर्वेदार्थकुशलैर्वेदार्थेभ्यो निष्कृष्य कर्मार्थं सुखावबोधनानीमानि विद्यास्थानानि प्रवर्तितानि। शिक्षा कल्पो व्याकरणं निरुक्तं छंदो ज्योतिषमिति धर्मशास्त्रं पुराणं न्यायविस्तरो मीमांसादीनि॥

And again:

अत आचार्यो भगवान् शौनको वेदार्थवित् सुहृद्भूत्वा

It might therefore be best to distinguish between Smṛiti or tradition in general, and the Smṛitis or law-books in particular. We might then speak of *śrauta-* and *smârta*-sûtras, comprehending by the former name all Sûtras, the source of which can be traced in the Śruti; by the latter those of which no such source exists, or is at least, known to exist.[1] The title of Smṛitis in the plural (or Smṛiti-prabandhâs) might then be left, for convenience sake, to such works as Sâyaṇa is speaking of, which are composed not in Sûtras but in Ślokas. It ought to be remembered, however, that the same subjects which are treated in the metrical Smṛitis of Manu and others, had similarly been treated in Sûtras (śrauta, gṛihya, and sâmayâchârika), and that the principal difference between the two lies, not in their matter, but in their age, and their style.

ब्राह्मणेभ्योऽर्थवादानुत्सृज्य विधिं समाहृत्य पुरुषहितार्थ-मृग्वेदस्य शिक्षाशास्त्रं कृतवानिति॥

[1] Thus, *smârtam karma* is well defined by Shaḍguruśishya in the Sarvânukramaṇîbhâshya, as "nishekâdi śmaśânântam smṛiti-gṛihyavihitam karma." In the Commentary on Âśvalâyana's Śrauta-sûtras, it is said, that, if observances like rinsing the mouth, &c., are prescribed in the Śrauta-sûtras (as they are for instance Âśval. i. 1. 3.), this is only done in order to show that such observances are acknowledged and presupposed by the Śrauta-sûtras, though they belong to the province of the Gṛihya ceremonies.

स्मार्तानां स्नानाचमनयज्ञोपवीतादीनां श्रौतकर्माविरुद्धाना-मस्मिन् शास्त्रे प्राप्तिप्रदर्शनार्थमिदमाचमनं कर्मांगं विधीयते। शौचार्थस्य गृहप्रवेशात्प्रागेव कृतत्वात्। तदुक्तं। मनःप्रसा-दात्सत्योक्त्या तपसा स्नानकर्मणा। आचांत्या चात्मनः शुद्धिं कृत्वा कर्म समारभेदिति॥

An objection against this division and terminology, not unknown to the Brahmans themselves, is that it is difficult to say whether certain Smârta-sûtras may not be based upon some lost Śâkhâ of the Veda. The Śrauta portions of the Kalpa-sûtras, there can be no doubt, are founded on Śruti, if by this name we understand not only the hymns, but also the Brâhmaṇas of the Veda. But there are only few allusions, even in the Brâhmaṇas, to the ceremonies described in the Gṛihya-sûtras; and the few passages which are quoted from the Śruti in their support, are chiefly taken from the Âraṇyakas and Upanishads, the latest branches of Vedic literature. As to the Âchâras, or the established rules of conduct with regard to particular temporal duties, even Indian writers admit that there are only very vague allusions to them in the Śruti, and they try to prove that these laws are based on parts of the Veda which are now lost. This is a view which is taken, for instance, by Haradatta in his Commentary on Âpastamba's Sâmayâchârika-sûtras, and it deserves to be examined more closely. On the first Sûtra[1], "*Therefore let us now explain the Sâmayâchârika duties*," he makes the following observations:—

"The word '*therefore*' implies a reason, which is that as the *śrauta* (sacrificial) and *gârhya* (domestic) ceremonies have been explained, and as these ceremonies presuppose other observances, these other observances must now be explained too. For when it was said before (in the Śrauta and Gṛihya-sûtras), that such and such an act was to be performed by a man after

[1] अथातः सामयाचारिकान्धर्मान्व्याख्यास्यामः॥१॥

he had rinsed his mouth, by a man who is clean, who holds a pavitra in his hand, who is invested with the sacred thread, &c., an acquaintance with all these things, such as rinsing, &c., is presupposed. The twilight prayers, too, are referred to in the preceding Sûtras, when it is said, that a man who does not perform his twilight prayers is impure, and unworthy to perform any sacrifice. Several other instances occur; and it is therefore necessary to explain now immediately those other precepts called sâmayâchârika (temporal). *Sâmayâchârika* is derived from *samaya* (agreement) and *âchâra* (custom). *Samaya*, a human agreement, is of three kinds: *vidhi*, injunction; *niyama*, restriction; *pratishedha*, prohibition. Rules founded upon *samaya* are called *samayâchâras*, from which the adjective *sâmayâchârika*. *Dharma* (virtue) is the quality of the individual self, which arises from action, leads to happiness and final beatitude, and is called *apûrva* supernatural. But, in our Sûtra, *dharma* means law, and has for its object *dharma* as well as *adharma*: things to be done and things to be avoided.

"It might be said, however," continues the Commentator Haradatta, alluding to the same controversy which we saw before treated of by Sâyaṇa, "that if *samaya* (human agreement) be the authority for the law, it would be difficult to deny the same authority to the Bauddhas and their laws, to worship the holy sepulchre, &c.; and therefore Âpastamba has added the next Sûtra:[1]

[1] धर्मज्ञसमयः प्रमाणं॥२॥

"'*Those agreements are of authority which were made by men who knew the law.*'

"We do not say," Haradatta remarks, with regard to these words, "that every agreement becomes of authority, but those only made by men like Manu, &c., who knew the law. But then, it might be asked, how it can be found out that Manu knew the law, and Buddha did not? People answer, that Buddha could not have had a knowledge of the divine law. But the same might be said also of Manu; and if a knowledge of divine things be ascribed to Manu, on account of the excellence which he acquired by his virtue, then, again, it would be the same for Buddha. There is a known verse[1]: 'If Buddha know the law, and Kapila does not, what is truth? If they

[1] सुगतो यदि धर्मज्ञः कपिलो नेति का प्रमा।
तावुभौ यदि सर्वज्ञौ मतिभेदः कथं तयोः॥

Dr. Weber, in his dissertation on the Upanishads, thinks it is not impossible that Kapila, the founder of the Sânkhya, and Buddha were in fact one and the same person. (Indische Studien, i. 436.) He afterwards qualifies this conjecture, and calls it not very probable. It is true that the Indians themselves observed a certain similarity between the doctrines of Kapila and Buddha. But this would rather show that the two were different persons. Nor would the legend that Buddha was born at Kapila-vastu, the town of Kapila, or rather of the Kâpilas, seem to prove the identity of Kapila and Buddha. By another conjecture, the same ingenious scholar makes the founder of the Sânkhya (Panchaśikha Kâpileya) the same person with Kâpya Pâtanchala, who occurs in the Śatapatha-brâhmaṇa; while, in a former article (i. 84.), both Kapila and Patanchali together, the former as the founder of the Sânkhya, the latter as the author of the Yoga system, are merged into Kâpya Pâtanchala. Afterwards, however, this opinion also is retracted, because Dr. Weber thinks that the Yoga system might be a later development of the Sânkhya.

were both omniscient, how could there be difference of opinion between them?' If this be not so, a distinction must be made; and this has been done by Âpastamba in his next Sûtra: '*And the Vedas* (are of authority).'"[1]

This Sûtra is explained by Haradatta in the following manner:—"The Vedas are the highest authority for good and bad; and none of the objections made before could apply to the Vedas, which are faultless from all eternity, evident by themselves, and, as they were revealed, unaffected by the faults of human authors. Therefore, while to us those agreements are of authority which were made by men who knew the law, the Vedas, again, were the authority for those men themselves, like Manu, &c. And although we have not before our eyes a Veda, which is the source of these laws, we must still conclude that Manu and the rest had."[2]

[1] वेदाश्च॥२॥

[2] Someśvara, who calls himself a son of Mâdhava, and of whose work "Tantra-vârttikaṭîkâ" there is a manuscript at the E. I. H. (No. 1030.), dated Samvat, 1552, goes even a step farther, and says that, although rules of the Smṛitis may be against the sacred law, the Veda must notwithstanding be considered as their source, because the Smṛitis themselves maintain that the Veda is the highest authority, an admission which the followers of Buddha protest against. Cf. p. 80. ननु याज्ञवल्क्यादिभिरपि यदुच्यते द्विजातीनां शूद्राद्दारोपसंग्रहः न तन्मम मतं यस्मात्तत्रात्मा जायते स्वयं तेन पुनरित्यादिहेतुदर्शनपूर्वकं धर्माधर्मोपदेशनान्न तन्मात्रेण वेदमूलत्वनिराकरणं युक्तमित्याशंक्य वेद एव द्विजातीनां निःश्रेयसकरः पर इत्या-

It is a matter of considerable interest to know whether this opinion of Haradatta's, as to the previous existence of a larger number of Vedic works, deserves credit or not. The opponent of the orthodox Kumârila in the Tantra-vârttika remarks very truly, that to invoke the testimony of lost parts of the Veda is like calling a dead person as a witness.[1] And if we had no better authority for this opinion than so late a commentator as Haradatta, we should hardly be justified in mentioning it as an argument. Anybody, however, who is acquainted with the character of Indian commentators, will admit that they seldom

दिना तैः प्राधान्येन वेदमूलत्वाभिधानात्। &c. Cf. Yâjnavalkya, ed. Stenzler, i. 56., i. 40.; Manu, iii. 12, 13., where the Commentator mentions Vâsishṭha as having spoken of the marriage of a Brahman with a Śûdra, the ceremony not being accompanied by sacred hymns, as a kind of morganatic marriage, kâmato vivâhaḥ, वासिष्ठोऽपि शूद्रामप्येके मंत्रवर्जमिति मंत्रवर्जितं शूद्राविवाहमाह॥

[1] मृतसाक्षिकव्यवहारवच्च प्रलीनशाखामूलत्वकल्पनायां यस्मै यद्रोचते स तत्प्रमाणीकुर्यात्॥

"If a man maintain a lost tradition to have been a source, he may prove what he pleases, for it is like appealing to a dead witness." And again:

येन यत्नेन मन्वाद्यैरात्मवाक्यं प्रपाठितं कस्मात्तेनैव तन्मूलं चोदना न समर्पिता॥ यस्यैव यदभिप्रेतं स एव तत्प्रलीनशाखामस्तके निक्षिप्य प्रमाणीकुर्यात्॥

"Why has a divine precept not been established by Manu and the others as the source of their teaching, which would not have cost them more labour than to proclaim their own doctrine? Anybody may throw whatever he likes into the skull of a lost tradition, and then invoke it as an authority."

commit themselves to novel theories, but almost always repeat what existed before in the tradition of their schools; a fact which at once increases and diminishes the usefulness of their works. Thus we find in the case before us, that Âpastamba himself, whose Sûtras Haradatta explains, entertained a similar opinion on this subject. In the twelfth section of his Sûtras, when speaking of some rules on the Svâdhyâya (praying), he says [1], "that certain rules must be considered as given in Brâhmaṇas of which the tradition or reading has been destroyed. Their former existence," he says, "must be inferred from

[1] ब्राह्मणोक्ता विधयस्तेषामुत्सन्नाः पाठाः प्रयोगादनुमीयंते। यत्र तु प्रीत्युपलब्धितः प्रवृत्तिर्न तत्र शास्त्रमस्ति तदनुवर्तमानो नरकाय राध्यति॥

The Commentator says: उत्सन्नाः पाठा अध्येतृदौर्बल्यात्॥

"The original passages were lost by the negligence of the students."

Kumârila observes: शाखानां विप्रकीर्णत्वात्पुरुषाणां प्रमादतः। नानाप्रकरणस्थत्वात् स्मृतेर्मूलं न दृश्यते॥

"The original text from which the Smṛiti was derived cannot always be found, because the Śâkhâs are scattered about; students are negligent, and because these rules stand under different heads."

And again: दृश्यते ह्यद्यत्वेऽप्यर्थ(वि)स्मरणं ग्रंथनाशश्च॥

"As if we did not see in our own time that subjects are forgotten and works lost."

न च प्रलयो न संभाव्यते। दृश्यते हि प्रमादालस्यादिभिः पुरुषक्षयाच्च॥

"And it must not be said that their destruction is impossible, for we see it take place every day, whether by negligence, idleness, or by the death of men."

the simple fact, that these rules are still followed by men; the only exception being where customs can be proved to depend on selfish motives. In this case, a man who follows such unauthorised customs, shall go to hell."

With regard to the hymns, it is in itself very unlikely that no more should have existed than those which happen to bê collected in the Rig-veda; and even in the Rig-veda we see that the number of hymns varied in different communities. The ancient poetry of India, however, would hardly have furnished authoritative passages for legal and ceremonial questions; and there is no doubt that the lost tradition which is appealed to by later writers, refers only to Brâhmaṇas. A number of these dogmatic works are still in existence; but others, which are always quoted along with them, are now lost, or known by extracts only. There existed a considerable number of ancient sages who embodied their doctrines, whether on philosophical or ceremonial, on metrical or grammatical questions, in independent works, and these were handed down by tradition among their descendants. But, as Kumârila observes, through the carelessness and forgetfulness of men, and also by the extinction of families, these works were necessarily lost; and it is, indeed, less surprising that many of these Brâhmaṇas should have been lost, than that so many should still have been saved, if we remember for how long a time oral tradition was in India the only means of preserving them. Kumârila, however, was too keen-sighted not to perceive the danger of admitting lost Śâkhâs of the Veda as authorities, and he makes several reservations in order to guard against a promiscuous use of this argument. The Buddhists also might appeal to a lost Śâkhâ, and thus upset all the arguments of the orthodox philosophers. But in spite of the bug-bear of the Buddhists, the general fact that some Śâkhâs had perished was admitted by Kumârila, as well as by Âpastamba, both endeavouring to prop up the authority of the Smṛiti by the broken pillars of the Śruti.[1]

The evidence which has been brought together is sufficient to establish the fact, that the distinction between Śruti and Smṛiti, revelation and tradition, had been established by the Brahmans previous to the rise of Buddhism, or, at all events, previous to the time when the style of Sûtras began to be adopted in Indian literature. There existed, previous to the Sûtra period, a body of literary works propagated by oral tradition, which formed the basis of all later writings on sacred subjects, and which by the Brahmans was believed to be of divine origin. The idea expressed by the verb *sru*, to hear, *i. e.* to receive by inspiration, is known in the Brâhmaṇas. The name of Smṛiti seems to occur for the first time in the Taittirîya-âraṇyaka[2], though

[1] यैश्च मन्वादिस्मृतीनामप्युत्सन्नवेदशाखामूलमभ्युपगतं तान्प्रति सुतरां शाक्यादिभिरपि शक्यं तन्मूलत्वमेव वक्तुं। को हि शक्नुयादुत्सन्नानां वाक्यविषयेयत्तानियमं कर्तुं। ततश्च यावत्किंचित्कियंतमपि कालं कैश्चिदाद्रियमाणं प्रसिद्धिं गतं तत्प्रत्यक्षशाखाविसंवादे ऽप्युत्सन्नशाखामूलत्वावस्थामनुभवत्तुल्यकक्षतया प्रतिभायात्। अत एव विरोधे त्वनपेक्ष्यं स्यादिति॥

[2] Taitt. Âr. i. 1, 2.: स्मृतिः प्रत्यक्षमैतिह्यमनुमानश्चतुष्टयं॥ The Commentator explains Smṛiti by अनुमेयश्रुतिमूलं मन्वा-

it is said to be used there in the sense of Śruti. In the Sûtras, however, the distinction between Śruti and Smṛiti is distinctly stated. We find it in the Anupada-sûtras[1], which we have reason to reckon amongst the earliest specimens of this class of literature. In the Nidâna-sûtras also, ancient tradition is mentioned by the name of Smṛiti[2]; and although in Pâṇini the technical distinction between Śruti and Smṛiti is not mentioned, it would be wrong to draw any conclusions from this, as there can be little doubt that Pâṇini is later than the Anupada-sûtras.

The Six Vedângas.

We shall now proceed to an examination of the works which belong to the Sûtra-literature of India, so far as they have reference to the Veda.

दिशास्त्रं। "the laws of Manu and others whose source is a revelation the existence of which must be inferred." Pratyaksha (sensuous impression) is, according to Sâyaṇa, सर्वपुरुषाणां श्रोत्रिये ग्राह्यं वेदवाक्यं। "the word of the Veda which all men can perceive in their teacher." Aitihya (tradition) is explained by इतिहासपुराणमहाभारतब्राह्मणादिकं "legends, Purâṇas, the Mahâbhârata, and the Brâhmaṇas. Lastly, Anumâna, if we believe Sâyaṇa, does not here mean inference, but customs of good men, by which or from which the existence of an authority, that is, of Śruti and Smṛiti, as the source of these customs, is inferred. अनुमानः शिष्टाचारः। तेन हि मूलभूतं श्रुतिस्मृतिलक्षणं प्रमाणमनुमीयते॥

[1] Anupada-sûtra, ii. 4. श्रुतिस्मृतिदृष्टसंपन्नैः। Cf. Indische Studien, i. p. 44.

[2] Nidâna-sûtra, ii. 1. आचार्यस्मृतीनां। याज्ञिकाः स्मृतौ। Cf. Indische Studien, i. p. 45.

The Brahmans say that there are six members of the Veda, the six Vedângas. This name does not imply the existence of six distinct books or treatises intimately connected with their sacred writings, but merely the admission of six subjects, the study of which was necessary either for the reading, the understanding, or the proper sacrificial employment of the Veda. Manu calls the Vedângas by the name of Pravachanas[1], which is a title not unusually applied to the Brâhmaṇas.[2] And indeed, instead of looking

[1] Manu, iii. 184.: अग्र्याः सर्वेषु वेदेषु सर्वप्रवचनेषु च॥

"Those priests must be considered as the purifiers of a company who are most learned in all the Vedas and all their Angas."—Sir W. Jones.

Kullûka: प्रकर्षेणैवोच्यते वेदार्थ एभिरिति प्रवचनान्यंगानि॥

"Because the meaning of the Veda is proclaimed by them, therefore are the Angas called Pravachanas."

[2] कालबविनामपि प्रवचनविहितः स्वरः स्वाध्याये। Com. प्रवचनशब्देन ब्राह्मणमुच्यते। प्रोच्यत इति प्रवचनं॥

"Among the Kâlabavins also the accent exists in the perusal of the Veda enjoined by the Pravachanas. Com. By the word pravachana is meant the Brâhmaṇa, and it is called so because it is proclaimed"

There is a passage in the Prasthânabheda,

एवं प्रवचनभेदात्प्रतिवेदं भिन्ना भूयस्यः शाखाः॥

"For each Veda there are several Śâkhâs the difference of which arises from different Pravachanas."

Here pravachana means Brâhmaṇa, because the difference of the Brâhmaṇa-śâkhâs does arise from Brâhmaṇas peculiar to each. It is possible, however, that Madhusûdana used pravachana in the sense of pronunciation, the difference of pronunciation being the chief cause of the Sanhitâ-śâkhâs. Pravachana is used in the Kaṭhopanishad, ii. 23., in the sense of "reading."

for the Vedângas to those small and barren tracts which are now known by this name, it is in the Brâhmaṇas and Sûtras that we have to look for the Vedânga-doctrines in their original and authentic form. The short Vedângas which are generally added to the manuscripts of the Veda, and which by several scholars were mistaken for the real Vedângas, represent only the last unsuccessful attempts to bring the complicated and unintelligible doctrines of former sages into an easy and popular form, and to preserve at the same time the names which had been sanctioned by antiquity.

A very clear and rational statement as to the character of the Vedângas in early times, is given in the Bṛihadâraṇyaka and its commentary. According to them the different doctrines of the Vedângas are to be considered as integral parts of the Brâhmaṇas, in the same manner as the Purâṇas and Itihâsas. These, as we saw before, were to be taken in the sense of epic or paurâṇic stories, incorporated in the Brâhmaṇas, as illustrations of ceremonial questions. By Itihâsa, as the commentator says, (Bṛih. Âraṇy. ii. 4.) we have to understand stories like those of Urvaśî and Purûravas in the Śatapatha-brâhmaṇa; by *Purâṇa*, passages on creation and the like, for instance, "in the beginning there was nothing," &c. He then proceeds to quote passages from the Brâhmaṇas which he calls Upanishads (mysteries), Ślokas (verses), Sûtras (rules), Anuvyâkhyas (explanations), and Vyâkhyas (comments). It is under these heads that the Vedângas had their original place.

It is more difficult to determine where and when

the Vedângas were first mentioned as six. In the Muṇḍaka-upanishad the number of the Vedângas is given as six, but in a line which is not unlikely to have been interpolated. Yâska (Nir. i. 20.) quotes only the Vedângas, but not the six Vedângas. The number of six occurs in the Charaṇavyûha, where we meet with the well-known versus memorialis containing the titles of the six Vedângas.[1] The same number occurs in Manu (iii. 185). There is a passage in the Chhândogya-Upani-

[1] शिक्षा कल्पो व्याकरणं निरुक्तं छंदो ज्योतिषं॥ Âpastamba who occasionally quotes Ślokas in his Sûtras, does not seem to have known this verse. His words are (ii. 4. 8.), षडंगो वेदः छंदः कल्पो व्याकरणं ज्योतिषं निरुक्तं शिक्षा। What follows, in the only MS. I know, is eaten away by worms; but then comes the word छंदोविचिति, which was the title of a metrical treatise, and is quoted as such before Pingala, in the Śabda-Kalpa-druma, *s. v.* तस्य ग्रंथाः छंदोविचितिपिंगलछंदोमंजरीश्रुतबोधादयः संति॥ One of the Pariśishṭas of the Sâma-veda begins with the words अथातश्छंदसां विचयं व्याख्यास्यामः। The Pariśishṭas, however, are later than Âpastamba and Pingala; for the author of the Pariśishṭa declares that he made use of Pingala's work: ब्राह्मणात्तंडिनश्चैव पिंगलाच्च महात्मनः। निदानादुक्थशास्त्राच्च छंदसां ज्ञानमुद्धृतं॥ The title छंदोविचिति refers, therefore, most likely to the Nidâna-sûtra, which also begins with अथातश्छंदसां विचयं व्याख्यास्यामः। Cf. MS. Berol. 95. In the Commentary on the Śâkala-prâtiśâkhya, at the end of the 14th Book, the Vedângas are enumerated as follows:
कल्पो व्याकरणं निरुक्तं शिक्षा छंदोविचितिर्ज्योतिषामयनं॥

shad where a mention of the six Vedângas might be expected, at the beginning of the ninth Prapâṭhaka. The number six, however, does not occur there, although Vedânga doctrines are clearly implied under somewhat unusual names.[1] The earliest mention of the number six in reference to the Vedângas seems to be contained in one of the Brâhmaṇas of the Sâma-veda. But there again, though the number six is given, the titles of the several Vedângas are not mentioned. It is said there (Shaḍvinśa-Br. iv. 7.) of

[1] This passage has been pointed out and translated by Colebrooke (Miscellaneous Essays, i. 12). "Nârada, having solicited instruction from Sanatkumâra, and being interrogated by him as to the extent of his previous knowledge, says, 'I have learnt the Rig-veda, the Yajur-veda, the Sâma-veda, the Âtharvaṇa (which is) the fourth, the Itihâsa and Purâṇa (which are) a fifth, and (grammar, or) the Veda of Vedas, the obsequies of the manes (पित्र्यं), the art of computation (राशिं), the knowledge of omens (दैवं), the revolution of periods (निधिं, com. महाकालादिनिधिशास्त्रं), the intention of speech (or art of reasoning) (वाकोवाक्यं), the maxims of ethics (एकायनं), the divine science (or construction of scriptures) (देवविद्यां, com. निरुक्तं) the sciences appendant on holy writ (or accentuation, prosody, and religious rites) (ब्रह्मविद्यां), the adjuration of spirits (भूतविद्यां, com. भूततंत्रं), the art of the soldier (क्षत्रविद्यां, com. धनुर्वेदं), the science of astronomy, (नक्षत्रविद्यां) the charming of serpents (सर्पविद्यां), the science of demigods (or music and mechanical arts, गारुडं, see page 39.): all this I have studied; yet do I only know the text, and have no knowledge of the soul.

Svâhâ, that her body consists of the four Vedas, and that her limbs are the six Angas, or members of the Veda.[1] It is possible, however, that more ancient Brâhmaṇas allude to the number of six; at all events we see that it was sanctioned for the Vedângas before the end of the Brâhmaṇa period.

The six doctrines commonly comprehended under the title of Vedângas, are Śikshâ (pronunciation), Chhandas (metre), Vyâkaraṇa (grammar), Nirukta (explanation of words), Jyotisha (astronomy), and Kalpa (ceremonial). The first two are considered necessary for reading the Veda, the two next for understanding it, and the last two for employing it at sacrifices.

Śikshâ, or Phonetics.

Sâyaṇa, in his commentary on the Rig-veda, defines Śikshâ as the science of the pronunciation of letters, accents, &c.; and he quotes from a work of the Taittirîyas, who have devoted a chapter of their Âraṇyaka to this subject. Now in the seventh book of the Taittirîya-Âraṇyaka we still find the following headings: "Let us explain the Śîkshâ,"[2] "On Letters,"

[1] चत्वारोऽस्यै वेदाः शरीरं षडंगान्यंगानि। ओषधिवनस्पतयो लोमानि॥ "The four Vedas are her body; the six Angas her limbs; herbs and trees her hair." See also the text frequently quoted from the Veda, ब्राह्मणेन षडंगो वेदो निष्कारणोऽध्येयो ज्ञेयश्च॥ "The Veda; with its six members, ought to be known and understood by a Brahman without any further inducement."

[2] शीक्षां व्याख्यायामः The i in Śikshâ is short (hrasva), though it is strong (guru). It is only in the Âraṇyaka that Śîkshâ

"On Accents," "On Quantity," "On the Organs of Pronunciation," "On Delivery," "On Euphonic Laws."

Unless we admit that the rules on Śikshâ had formerly their place in this chapter of the Taittirîya-Âraṇyaka, it would be difficult to explain why all the principal subjects of the Śikshâ should be mentioned here, why the whole chapter should be called the Śikshâ chapter (ityuktaḥ śikshâdhyâyaḥ), and why it should begin with the words "Let us now explain the Śikshâ." Sâyaṇa, who was certainly acquainted with the Vedic tradition, takes the same view in his Commentary on the Sânhitî-upanishad.[1] He states that the Taittirîya-upanishad consists of three parts[2], of the Sânhitî, Yâjnikî, and Vâruṇî-upanishad. Of

occurs instead of Śikshâ. Śikshâ is derived from *śak* to be able, and means originally a desire to know. From the same root we have *śâkta*, a teacher (Rv. vii. 103. 5.); *śikshamaṇa*, a pupil (Rv. vii. 103. 5.). *Śishya*, a pupil, comes from a different root. Sâyaṇa says, शिक्ष्यंते वेदनार्थोपदिश्यंते स्वरवर्णादयो यत्रासौ शिक्षा। सैव शीक्षा॥ The other headings are, वर्णः। स्वरः। मात्रा। बलं। साम। संतानः॥

[1] I owe a copy of this Commentary of Sâyaṇa's to the kindness of Dr. Röer, at Calcutta. Seeing, in the catalogue of manuscripts published by the Asiatic Society of Calcutta, a work of Sâyaṇa's called Śikshâbhâshya, and imagining this to be a commentary on the Śikshâ-vedâṅga or one of the Prâtiśâkhyas, I wrote to Dr. Röer for a copy of it. Though I was ultimately disappointed when I found that it had nothing to do with the Prâtiśâkhyas, I still consider the Commentary of great interest, particularly Sâyaṇa's introduction to the Vedânta-system in it. Dr. Röer has since published the whole Taittirîya-upanishad, with the Commentaries of Śankara and Ânanda Giri, in No. 22. of the Bibliotheca Indica.

[2] सेयं तैत्तिरीयोपनिषत् त्रिविधा। सांहिती याज्ञिकी वारुणी चेति। तत्र प्रथमे प्रपाठके संहिताध्यानस्योक्तत्वात् जपोपनिषत्सांहिती। द्वितीयतृतीययोः प्रपाठकयोर्या ब्रह्म-

these the last is the most important, because it teaches the knowledge of the Divine Self. The first serves as an introduction or preparation, in order to bring the mind of the pupil into a proper state for receiving the doctrines on the highest subjects. Now immediately after the first invocation, the Upanishad begins with the Śikshâ chapter; and in order to explain this, Sâyaṇa remarks that this doctrine is necessary here, in order to enable the pupil to read and pronounce the sacred texts correctly, and thus to understand their real meaning.[1] It might be objected, Sâyaṇa remarks, that as a correct pronunciation is equally required for the earlier ceremonial portion of the Veda (Karma-kâṇḍa), the Śikshâ ought to have been inserted there. But then, he says, this chapter in its present place stands between the ceremonial and the philosophical portion of the Veda, like a lamp on the threshold of a door giving light to both. He adds, that a right pronunciation and understanding is of greater importance for the philosophical part; because mistakes in the sacrifices and the ceremonial can be made good by penance, while there is no penance for a wrong understanding of philosophical principles.

If then there is reason to believe that the doctrine

विद्या विहिता तस्यां। &c. तासां तिसृणां मध्ये वारुणी मुख्या।

[1] तस्माद्विद्यायामवैकल्याय यथाशास्त्रं बोद्धुमुपनिषत्पाठे प्रयत्नातिशयं विधातुमत्रैव शिक्षाध्यायोऽभिधीयते॥॥ तस्य च ग्रंथस्यार्थज्ञानप्रधानत्वात्पाठे मा भूदौदासीन्यमित्येतदर्थं द्वितीयानुवाके शिक्षाध्यायोऽभिधीयते॥

of the Śikshâ was formerly embodied in the Âraṇyakas, perhaps even in the Brâhmaṇas[1], the question is, why it afterwards lost this place. This can only be accounted for by the appearance of more scientific treatises, which embraced the same subjects, but in a much more systematic style than anything which we could expect to meet with in the Brâhmaṇas and Âraṇyakas.

These were the Prâtiśâkhyas, a branch of literature which will claim our particular attention for more than one reason. If we compare the Prâtiśâkhyas with Brâhmaṇas and Âraṇyakas, they evidently indicate a considerable progress of the Indian mind. They were written for practical purposes; their style is free from cumbrous ornaments, and unnecessary subtleties. It is their object to teach and not to edify; to explain, not to discuss. Where the Brâhmaṇas or Âraṇyakas allude to grammatical, metrical, or etymological questions, they give nothing but theological and mystical dreams. So far from receiving elucidation, the points in question generally become involved in still greater darkness. It is not unlikely that teachers appealed to these passages of the Brâhmaṇas in order to derive from them the highest possible sanction for their doctrines. But these doctrines, if they were intended for use and instruction, must have been delivered in a more homely and more intelligible form. The origin of the Prâtiśâkhyas may therefore

[1] The passage from the Pushpa-sûtras (viii. 8.) which was quoted before, कालबविनामपि प्रवचनविहितः स्वरः स्वाध्याये, does not prove that the rules on the accent were laid down in the Brâhmaṇa of the Kâlabavins, because it may also mean that the accented delivery of sacred texts was enjoined in the Brâhmaṇa.

be accounted for in the following manner:—During the Brâhmaṇa period the songs of the Veda were preserved by oral tradition only: and as the spoken language of India had advanced and left the idiom of the Veda behind as a kind of antique and sacred utterance, it was difficult to preserve the proper pronunciation of the sacred hymns without laying down a certain number of rules on metre, accent, and pronunciation in general. The necessity, however, of such a provision could hardly have been felt until certain differences had actually arisen in different seats of Brahmanic learning. Thus, when the attempt was made to prevent a further corruption, a certain number of local varieties in accent and pronunciation, and in the recital of the hymns, had actually crept in and become sanctioned by the tradition of different families or schools. These could not be given up, nor was there any means of determining which was the ancient and most correct way of reciting the sacred songs of the Veda. Discussions having arisen on this subject, we find in the Brâhmaṇas occasional mention of verses which, if improperly pronounced, become changed in their meaning. But even where the sense of the Veda was not affected, the respect paid by each teacher, by each family, and by each Brahmanic community to its own established oral tradition, was sufficient to give an imaginary value to the slightest peculiarities of pronunciation, accent, or metre.

A twofold advantage was gained when the rules and exceptions of the old sacred dialect were first reduced to a system. First, ancient dialectical differences, many of which are not so much attributable to corruptions as to the freedom of the old spoken language, were carefully preserved, and even apparent irregularities and exceptions were handed down as such, instead of being eliminated and forgotten. Secondly, a start was made towards a scientific study of language; by the collection of a large number of similar passages, general laws were elicited which afterwards served as the phonetic basis of a grammar like that of Pâṇini;—a work which, although ascribed to one author, must have required ages of observation and collection before its plan could be conceived or carried out by one individual. Even the Prâtiśâkhyas, though they do not refer to grammar properly so called, but principally to the phonetic laws of language, presuppose a long-continued study of grammatical subjects previous to the time of their composition. The best proof of this lies in the great number of authors quoted in the Prâtiśâkhyas, whose opinions are frequently at variance with the precepts contained in the Prâtiśâkhyas themselves. Though we are not now in possession of the works of these earlier authors, yet we have a right to assume that their doctrines existed formerly in the shape of Prâtiśâkhyas. In the same way as one only of the different Śâkhâs or recensions of the Rig-veda has been preserved to us in manuscript, the Śâkala-śâkhâ, which was followed by Śaunaka, we may understand how one only of the Prâtiśâkhyas of the Rig-veda has come down to us; particularly as its composition is ascribed to the same Śaunaka who is said to have united the Bâshkala and the Śâkala-śâkhâs, and who, as far as the Sanhitâ is concerned, was a follower of the Śaiśira-śâkhâ. Śaunaka's Prâtiśâkhya of the Śâkalas, being one of the latest compositions of this kind, was probably also the most perfect and complete. As Śaunaka states the different opinions of Śâkala grammarians on important points, where he himself differs from them, his work was the more likely to supersede previous Prâtiśâkhyas, particularly at the time when the Vedic religion was on its decline, and Brahmanic doctrines daily losing in influence. Though it is true that as yet only one Prâtiśâkhya belonging to each Veda has been found in manuscript, yet they all belong not to one of the four Vedas in general, but to one Śâkhâ of each of them. Prâtiśâkhya, therefore, does not mean, as has been supposed, a treatise on the phonetic peculiarities of each Veda, but a collection of phonetic rules peculiar to one of the different branches of the four Vedas, *i. e.* to one of those different texts in which each of the Vedas had been handed down for ages in different families and different parts of India. The differences between the Śâkhâs of the same Veda, as far as the words of the hymns are concerned, seem certainly not to have been very great, if we may judge from the few instances in which different Śâkhâs of the same Veda have been preserved in manuscripts. Most Śâkhâs do not differ in the general arrangement of the Sanhitâs, or collections of hymns, but merely in single words or verses. In a few cases only one Śâkhâ contains some hymns more than another. The Śâkhâs were not independent collections of the old hymns, but different editions of one and the same original collection, which in the course of a long-continued oral tradition had become modified by slight degrees. The texts of the Veda as they existed and lived in the oral tradition of various sects of people became Śâkhâs, differing from other Śâkhâs somewhat in the same way as the MSS. of the New Testament differ from each other. The Prâtiśâkhyas, besides giving general rules for the proper pronunciation of the Vedic language in general, were intended to record what was peculiar in the pronunciation of certain teachers and their schools. Even in cases where these schools had become extinct, we find the names of their founders, preserved as authorities on matters connected with the pronunciation of certain letters or words.

The real object of the Prâtiśâkhyas, as shown before, was not to teach the grammar of the old sacred language, to lay down the rules of declension and conjugation, or the principles of the formation of words. This is a doctrine which, though it could not have been unknown during the Vedic period, has not been embodied, as far as we know, in any ancient work. The Prâtiśâkhyas are never called Vyâkaraṇas, grammars [1], and it is only incidentally that they allude to strictly grammatical questions. The perfect phonetic system on which Pâṇini's grammar is built, is no doubt taken from the Prâtiśâkhyas; but the sources of Pâṇini's strictly grammatical doctrines must be looked for elsewhere.

Although, then, there is no necessity to suppose that every one of the numerous Vedic Śâkhâs possessed full and complete Prâtiśâkhyas, like that belonging

[1] According to the first Prâtiśâkhya, i. 58., पादवच्चैव प्रेषान् their rules would seem to affect passages of the Brâhmaṇas too, like होता यक्षत्, &c.: and the Commentator adds, ऋक्षु यल्लक्षणं तत्प्रैषेष्वपि। Most of these Praishas, however, are taken from the hymns; as, for instance, the words होता यक्षत्। Rv. i. 139. 10. This is different from the Yajur-veda where the general rules of the Prâtiśâkhya extend their influence to the sacrificial invocations.

to the Śâkala-śâkhâ, which was finally collected by Śaunaka, yet the great number of previous authorities quoted in our Prâtiśâkhyas makes it likely that a large number of similar works did actually exist for the principal Śâkhâs that are mentioned in earlier writings. In the Pratijnâpariśishṭa[1] it is stated that there were fifteen codes of law for the fifteen Śâkhâs of the Vâjasaneyins: and Kumârila says that the text of these Codes of law and of the Gṛihyas was peculiar in each Charaṇa, in the same manner as the formal rules of the Prâtiśâkhyas.[2] Madhusûdana Sarasvati's definition of Prâtiśâkhya is perfectly in accordance with this view of the subject. He says: —"The Veda[3] consists of two parts: one teaching the sacrifice, the other teaching Brahman, or the Su-

[1] MS. Bodl. W. 510.:

तेषां पंचदश यथास्वरं प्रतिष्ठाः प्रतिशाखं च कुलधर्माः।

The meaning of "Yathâsvaram pratishṭhâs" is doubtful. Should it mean "rules with reference to accents?" If so, they would be the rules of Prâtiśâkhyas. That the Śâkhâs differed about the accents is seen in the case of the Mâṇḍukeyas and Śâkalas. Prâtiśâkhya I. 200. Kâtyâyana, as the author of a Prâtiśâkhya is called

स्वरसंस्कारप्रतिष्ठापयिता॥

[2] Tantra V. I. 3. (MS. Bodl. W. 325. p. 15 b.)

धर्मशास्त्राणां गृह्यग्रंथानां च प्रातिशाख्यलक्षणवत्प्रतिचरणं पाठव्यवस्थोपलभ्यते॥

[3] Veda is taken here in the general sense of sacred literature, as Uvaṭa says,

सर्वकालं सर्वदेशेषु प्रतिचरणमविभागेनैकैको मंत्रराशिर्वेद इत्युच्यते॥

"Every single collection of hymns which existed at any time, and in any place, without reference to the divisions in each Charaṇa (sect), is called Veda."

preme Being. As there are three different branches of the ceremonial, the Veda is, for the better performance of the sacrifices, divided into three: the Rig-Veda, Yajur-Veda, and Sâma-Veda. The ceremonial of the Hotṛi priests is performed with the Rig-Veda; that of the Adhvaryu priests with the Yajur-Veda; that of the Udgâtṛi priests with the Sâma-Veda. The duties of the Brahman priests, and of him for whom the sacrifice is offered, are also contained in these three Vedas. The Atharva-Veda is not used for solemn sacrifices, and is very different from the others, as it teaches only expiatory, preservative, or imprecatory rites. For each Veda there are several Śâkhâs, and their differences arise from various readings."[1] Afterwards he goes on to observe that "the rules of pronunciation (śikshâ), which apply to all the Vedas in general, have been explained by Pâṇini, but that the same rules, as they apply to the Śâkhâs of each Veda, have been taught by other sages under the title of Prâtiśâkhyas."[2] If

[1] According to Madhusûdana, the Brahman part of the Veda, by which he can only mean the Upanishads, is not affected by the peculiarities of the Śâkhâs. If this were true, it would only prove the late origin of the Upanishads. Some Upanishads, however, show traces of various readings, which must properly be attributed to various Śâkhâs. This is admitted, for instance, by Sâyaṇa, in his Commentary on the Yâjnikî or Narâyaṇîyâ-upanishad. "Tadîyapâṭhasampradâyo deśaviśesheshu bahuvidho dṛiśyate; tatra yadyapi śâkhâbhedaḥ kâraṇam tathâpi Taittirîyâdhyâyakais tattaddeśanivâsibhiḥ śishṭair âdṛitatvât, sarvo'pi pâṭha upâdeya eva." Ind. Stud. i. 76.

[2] See also Someśvara's Tantra-vârttikaṭîkâ. (MS. E. I. H. 1030. p. 95.)
साधारणी विशेषविषया च द्विविधा शिक्षा। तत्र साधारणा

we here take the word śâkhâs (branches) in the sense of different traditionary texts of the four Vedas, Madhusûdana's words do not require any alteration; they would become obscure if, as has been proposed, we took śâkhâ either in the sense of "a school" or of "a portion of the Veda."

The word śâkhâ is used, however, by some writers in so vague a manner that we need not wonder if its meaning has sometimes been misapprehended. "Traditional text ('recension') of the Veda" is perhaps the nearest approach to its real meaning.

The word is sometimes applied to the three original Sanhitâs, the Rig-veda-sanhitâ, Yajur-veda-sanhitâ, and Sâma-veda-sanhitâ[1], in their relation to one another, and without any reference to subordinate śâkhâs

. वेदांगत्वेन धर्मप्रामाण्येऽपि कात्यायनादिप्रणीताया विशेषविषयायाः प्रतिवाक्यं प्रतिपदं चोच्चारणं नियच्छंत्या धर्मप्रमाणाभावाशंकानिराकरणार्थं पृथगुपादानेऽपि शिक्षात्वेनैक्यान्नातिरेकापत्तिः॥

"There are two kinds of Śikshâ, a general and one which has regard to particulars. It is true that the authority of the general Śikshâ is established, on account of its belonging to the Vedângas; but in order to remove all doubt as to the authority of the particular Śikshâs, published by Kâtyâyana and others, which determine the pronunciation of each sentence and each word, it is clear that it is not different from the other, inasmuch as both are one by their common character of Śikshâ, although they are spoken of separately."

[1] It is said of Sâyaṇa that he wrote commentaries on each of the Śâkhâs of the Ṛich, Yajush, and Sâma.

ऋग्यजुःसामशाखानामेकैका व्याकृता त्वया।
तावता तत्समानार्था ज्ञातुं शक्यास्ततः पराः॥

Ekaikâ could hardly mean "one from among the Śâkhâs of each Veda."

belonging to each of them. They may be called the original branches or the three stems of the Veda-tree, each of them branching off again in a number of other śâkhâs. The "branches," as Kumârila says, have all the same root, revelation (śruti), and they bear all the same fruit, the sacrifice (karman). If otherwise, they would be different trees, not different branches.[1] In the same acceptation the word is used for instance by Âpastamba, where he is giving rules as to the time and place where the Veda ought not to be read. He says there (Sâm. Sûtra, 3. 44, 45,) that it ought not to be rehearsed where music or Sâma-hymns are performed, and he adds, that Sâma-hymns ought not to be practised in the neighbourhood of another śâkhâ, that is, as the commentator observes, of another Veda.[2]

More frequently, however, śâkhâ is used to signify the various editions, or, more properly, the various traditions, that branched off from each of the three original branches of the Veda. In this latter sense śâkhâ seems sometimes synonymous with charaṇa. But there was originally an important difference in the meaning of these two terms.

[1] यदि प्रतिशाखं कर्मभेदः स्यात् तत एकमूलाभावादादित एवारभ्य भिद्यमानत्वात् समस्तकर्माख्यफलांतरत्वात् वृक्षांतरवद्वेदांतराण्येवोच्येरन् न शाखांतराणि॥

[2] गीतिशब्दाश्च सामशब्दाश्च एते श्रूयमाणा अनध्यायहेतवः॥ शाखांतरे च साम्नामनध्यायः॥ ४५॥ वेदांतरसकाशे साम नाध्येयं॥ The first Sûtra is paraphrased by the Mânavas, iv. 123., सामध्वनावृग्यजुषी नाधीयीत कदाचन॥

In order to appreciate the difference between śâkhâ and charaṇa, it need only be remembered that we find "śâkhâm adhîte," "he reads a certain edition of the Veda," but never "charaṇam adhîte," still less "parishadam adhîte," "he reads a charaṇa or a Parishad." Hence it is clear that śâkhâ means originally a literary work, and that Charaṇa does not. If śâkhâ is sometimes used in the sense of charaṇa or sect, this is because in India the śâkhâs existed in reality not as written books, but only in the tradition of the Charaṇas, each member of a Charaṇa representing and embodying what, in our modern times, we should call the copy of a book.

The Brahmans themselves were fully aware of this difference between śâkhâ and charaṇa. In a Vârttika to Pâṇini, iv. 1. 63., we find charaṇa explained by śâkhâdhyetṛi, &c., "the readers of a śâkhâ." In a passage of Jagaddhara's Commentary on Mâlatîmâdhava, Charaṇa is said to mean "a number of men who are pledged to the reading of a certain śâkhâ of the Veda, and who have in this manner become one body."[1] Pâṇini[2] speaks of Charaṇas as constituting a multitude, that is to say, as comprising a number of followers. In Âpastamba's Sâmayâchârika-sûtras, where rules are given as to the relative age of persons who ought to be saluted, the Châraṇas or members of the same Charaṇa are mentioned immediately after the Pauraśâkhyam, or town acquaintances; and in

[1] चरणशब्दः शाखाविशेषाध्ययनपरैकतापन्नजनसंघवाची। Cf. Zur Litteratur, p. 57.

[2] Pâṇ. iv. 2. 46. चरणेभ्यो धर्मवत् scil. समूहार्थे॥

the third place stand the Śrotriya-Brahmans.[1] Pâṇini speaks of the Kâṭhaka and Kalâpaka as works belonging to Charaṇas of the Kaṭhas and Kalâpas.[2] In a Vârttika to iv. 1. 63., women are mentioned as belonging to a Charaṇa; for Kaṭhî is the wife or daughter of a Brahman who belongs to the Charaṇa, or reads the Śâkhâ, of the Kaṭhas. A śâkhâ, which is always a portion of the Śruti, cannot properly include law books. But followers of certain Śâkhâs might well, in the course of time, adopt a code of laws, which, as it was binding on their Charaṇa only, would naturally go by the name of their Charaṇa. That this actually took place may be seen from a Vârttika to Pâṇ. iv. 3. 120., where it is said that Kâṭhaka may be used not only for the sacred traditions, but also for the laws of the Kaṭhas. Thus the Prâtiśâkhyas also were called by the name of the Charaṇas, because they were the exclusive property of the readers of certain śâkhâs, and even more so than the Kuladharmas or family-laws.

As a śâkhâ consisted of a Sanhitâ as well as a Brâhmaṇa, at all events in later times, differences in the text of the hymns, as well as discrepancies in the Brâhmaṇas, might lead to the establishment of new Charaṇas, founded as they were on sacred texts peculiar to themselves.[3] Śâkhâs of this kind, which

[1] Âp. i. 4. 4. The Commentator says that चारणशब्दः शाखाध्यायिषु रूढः। Châraṇa, therefore, means a member of a Charaṇa. Lassen (Ind. Alterthumsk. i. 640.) takes Châraṇa in the sense of wandering poets, so named still in Western India.

[2] Pâṇ. iv. 3. 126. गोत्रचरणाद्वुञ् scil. इदमर्थे॥

[3] Mahâdeva's Hiraṇyakeśibhâshya:

स्वाध्यायैकदेशो मंत्रब्राह्मणात्मकः शाखेत्युच्यते। तयोर्मंत्र-

differed through the various readings of the Śruti, were considered by the Brahmans as eternal śâkhâs, and the Charaṇas to which they belonged, were not supposed to have been founded by human authors.[1] It will be seen hereafter that the Brahmans admitted another class of śâkhâs, which were founded on Sûtras[2] and derived their names from historical personages. They were confessedly of a later date.

But although, after a careful examination of these passages, we cannot doubt that there was an original difference between śâkhâ and charaṇa, it is not less certain that these two words were frequently used synonymously[3]; in the same way as we may speak of the Jews when we mean the Old Testament, or of the Koran when we mean the Mohammedans.

ब्राह्मणयोरन्यतरभेदेन वेदेऽवांतरशाखाभेदः स्यादिति चेत् सत्यं॥

"Any portion of oral tradition consisting of Mantras and Brâhmaṇas is called a śâkhâ, and it is clear that differences of either the Mantras or Brâhmaṇas will necessarily lead, in the Veda, to a variety of subordinate śâkhâs."

[1] अध्ययनभेदाच्छाखाभेदोऽनादिः। "The various śâkhâs which arise from various readings are eternal."

[2] शाखाभेदे ऽध्ययनभेदाद्वा सूत्रभेदाद्वा। आश्वलायनीयं कात्यायनीयं च सूत्रं हि भिन्नाध्ययनयोर्द्वयोः शाखयोरैकैकमेव। तैत्तिरीयके समाम्नाये समानाध्ययने नाना सूत्राणि। Mahâdeva's Commentary on the Hiraṇyakeśi-sûtra.

[3] Cf. Nirukta, i. 17., where सर्वचरणानां is explained by सर्वशाखांतराणां। and Pâṇ. ii. 4. 3. चरणः शाखा। Pâṇ. vi. 3. 86.

After having established the difference between śâkhâ and charaṇa, we have still to inquire how both differ from parishad, in order to determine the meaning of Pârshada, another title which is frequently applied to the Prâtiśâkhyas. Here it is important to observe that although every Prâtiśâkhya may be called a Pârshada[1], *i. e.* a word belonging to a Parishad, not every Pârshada can be called a Prâtiśâkhya, but those only which contain the rules of pronunciation for a particular śâkhâ or text of the Vedic hymns, studied and taught in certain Parishads.[2] Amara explains parishad by sabhâ or goshṭhi, an assembly; but the codes of law lay down more accurately the number, age, and qualifications of the Brahmans, necessary to form such an assembly as should be competent to give decisions on all points on which the people, or, if we may say so, the parishioners, might demand advice. That such Parishads or Brahmanic settlements existed in old times, we see in the Bṛihadâraṇyaka[3], where it is said that Śvetaketu

[1] Pârshada, instead of Pârishada. Cf. Pân. iv. 3. 123.

[2] I doubt the existence of a word like माध्यंदिनपार्षदं, which Dr. Roth mentions (Zur Literatur, p. 16.). One may speak of पंचालानां परिषद् or वत्सानां परिषद् &c., and a Prâtiśâkhya current in one of these Parishads may, perhaps, be called वत्सपार्षदं. But माध्यंदिन is not the name of a Parishad, but of a Śâkhâ; and therefore the Commentary on Gobhila speaks of a माध्यंदिनशाखीयप्रातिशाख्यं। but could not well have spoken of a वत्सशाखीयप्रातिशाख्यं॥

[3] Bṛh. Âr. vi. 2. श्वेतकेतुर्ह वा आरुणेयः पंचालानां परिषदमाजगाम॥

went to the Parishad of the Panchâlas, and many similar passages. The character of a Parishad is described in Manu's Code of Laws, xii. 110—113., and by Yâjnavalkya, i. 9., where we have the contracted form Parshad instead of Parishad. According to the ideas of these modern writers a Parishad ought to consist of twenty-one Brahmans well versed in philosophy, theology, and law.[1] This number, however, can be reduced according to circumstances, as will be seen from passages of Parâśara's Dharmaśâstra. It must not be supposed that the rules laid down in these law-books have always been observed in the formation of a Parishad, particularly as regards the early times of India; yet we may be able to form some conception of their original character by seeing what has become of them in later times. Parâśara says[2]: "Four, or even three able men from amongst the Brahmans in a village, (grâmamadhye) who know the Veda, and keep the sacrificial fire, form a Parishad.

[1] एकविंशतिसंख्याकैर्मीमांसान्यायपारगैः। वेदांगकुशलैश्चैव परिषत्त्वं प्रकल्पयेत्॥

[2] चत्वारो वा त्रयो वापि वेदवंतोऽग्निहोत्रिणः।
ब्राह्मणानां समर्था ये परिषत्सा विधीयते॥
अनाहिताग्नयो येऽन्ये वेद`दांगपारगाः।
पंच त्रयो वा धर्मज्ञाः परिषत्सा प्रकीर्तिता॥
मुनीनामात्मविद्यानां द्विजानां यज्ञयाजिनां।
वेदव्रतेषु स्नातानामेकोऽपि परिषद्भवेत्॥
पंच पूर्वं मया प्रोक्तास्तेषां वासंभवे त्रयः।
स्ववृत्तिपरितुष्टा ये परिषत्सा प्रकीर्तिता॥

"Or, if they do not keep the sacrificial fire, five or three who have studied the Vedas and Vedângas, and know the law, may well form a Parishad.

"Of old sages who possess the highest knowledge of the Divine Self, who are twice-born, perform sacrifices, and have purified themselves in the duties of the Veda, one, also, may be considered as a Parishad.

"Thus, five kinds of Parishads have been described by me; but if they all fail, three independent men may form a Parishad."

Mâdhava, in his Commentary on Parâśara, quotes a similar passage[1] from Bṛihaspati's Code:—"Where seven, five, or three Brahmans, who know the customs of the world, the Vedângas (or the Vedas and the Angas), and the law, have settled, that assembly is like a sacrifice." The real difference, therefore, between a Charaṇa and a Parishad, seems to be that the former signifies an ideal succession of teachers and pupils who learn and teach a certain branch of the Veda; while the latter means a settlement of Brahmans, a community or college to which members of any Charaṇa might belong. Thus members of the same Charaṇa might be fellows of different Parishads, and fellows of the same Parishad might be members of different Charaṇas.[2]

[1] लोकवेदांगधर्मज्ञाः सप्त पंच त्रयोवापि।
यत्रोपविष्टा विप्राः स्युः सा यज्ञसादृशी सभा॥

[2] See Gobhilabhâshya, MS. W. 72. p. 71. a. आचार्यं सपरिषत्कं भोजयेत्सब्रह्मचारिणश्च॥ Com. सह परिषदा शिष्यगणेन वर्तत इति सपरिषत्कः तं। समानं तुल्यकालं ब्रह्मचारित्वं येषां त इमेऽन्यशाखिनोऽपि सब्रह्मचारिणः सवयसो

Now as Pârshada may be used as the title of any work that belonged to a Parishad, or formed, so to say, the traditional library of the Pârishadyas, it is clear that this title could not be confined to the Prâtiśâkhyas, though it would necessarily include them. If a follower of the Śâkala-charaṇa was a fellow of the Vatsa-parishad, the Śâkala-prâtiśâkhya would necessarily be one of the Pârshada works of the Vatsas, and the Parishad of the Vatsas would, through this fellow, be connected with the Śâkala-charaṇa. This is what Durga means when in the Commentary on the Nirukta[1] he says "that those Pârshadas only are called Prâtiśâkhyas which are adopted in a Parishad of one's own Charaṇa for teaching certain grammatical doctrines connected with the reading of the Veda according to one or the other Śâkhâ." The Prâtiśâkhyas are in fact a subdivision of the Pârshada books, and

ऽभिधीयंते॥ The expression इत्येके, "thus say some," which occurs frequently in the Sûtras, is stated to refer to different Śâkhâs, उत्तरामित्येके॥ Com. इत्येवमेके शाखिन आहुः। एक इति स्वमतव्युदासार्थं परशाखाप्रदर्शनार्थं च। एवमेके मन्यंते न गोभिल इत्यर्थः। Nârâyaṇa's Commentary on Gobhila, MS. W. 72. page 23. b.

[1] Nir. i. 17. किं पार्षदानि। स्वचरणपर्षद्येव यैः प्रतिशाखं नियतमेव पदावग्रहप्रगृह्यक्रमसंहितास्वरलक्षणमुच्यते तानीमानि पार्षदानि प्रातिशाख्यानीत्यर्थः॥

"Those Pârshada books by which in a Parishad (parish or college) of one's own Charaṇa (sect), the peculiarities of accent, Sanhitâ and Krama-reading, of Pragṛihya-vowels and separation of words, are laid down as enjoined for and restricted to, certain Śâkhâs (branches or recensions of the Veda), are called Prâtiśâkhyas."

in this sense it might well be said that Prâtiśâkhya is an adjective to Pârshada.[1]

After the true meaning of Śâkhâ, Charaṇa, and Parishad, of Prâtiśâkhya and Pârshada, has thus been determined, we have still to inquire about those other works, which together with the Prâtiśâkhyas were mentioned as the peculiar property of the Charaṇas. I mean the Kula-dharmas, or law books. They of course could not be called Prâtiśâkhyas, but they might claim the title of Châraṇas, (a name which has not been met with,) or Pârshadas. Now we saw before that Âpastamba actually refers to the Parishads in his Sâmayâchârika-sûtras (1. 11.), where, after having pointed out the days on which the Veda ought not to be repeated, he remarks, that further particulars on this point are to be found in the Parishads.[2] What does this mean? All that Haradatta has to say in the commentary on this very passage, is that by Parishads must here be understood the Mânava, Vâsishṭha, and other Dharmaśâstras.[3] These Dharmaśâstras, however, as we now possess them, betray their comparatively modern origin by their form and metre, and occasionally by their matter also. As many of them have been printed at Calcutta, it may be seen that the majority of these small Śloka works are utterly worthless. They were probably made up only

[1] See Dr. Roth, Zur Litteratur, p. 58.

[2] अन्यदतः परिषत्सु॥

[3] अत एतस्मादनध्यायप्रकरणादन्यदनध्यायनिमित्तं परिषत्सु मानवादिषु धर्मशास्त्रेषु यथोक्तं तथा द्रष्टव्यं। तत्र वासिष्ठः। &c.

in order to fill the gap which had been occasioned by the loss of ancient legal works. This loss was felt the more severely because the names of the old authors retained their celebrity, and were still quoted in common practice and courts of law. I have succeeded, however, in recovering in manuscript large portions of the Kula-dharmas, which are written in Sûtras, as might be expected in works contemporaneous with the Prâtiśâkhyas. It has been thought that the sources of Manu and other Dharmaśâstras must be looked for in the Gṛihya-sûtras. This is not quite correct. The Gṛihya-sûtras are concerned chiefly with the Sanskâras, or domestic sacraments, extending from the birth to the marriage of a man, and in so far only as these sacraments form a portion of the subjects treated in the Dharmaśâstras, the Gṛihya-sûtras might be considered as their original sources. But then the same might be said of the Śrauta-sûtras, because the solemn sacrifices prescribed by them are likewise alluded to in the Codes of Law. By far the greater portion, however, of these codes is taken up with Âchâra, *i. e.* laws, manners, and customs. The difference between these observances and the ceremonies laid down in the other two branches of Sûtras is this: the domestic sacraments (gṛihya), as well as the solemn sacrifices (śrauta), are administered by parents or priests for the good of their children and pupils, while the Âchâra comprises all the duties which are to be performed by an individual on his own behalf.[1] These duties refer to the different castes,

[1] The threefold division of Dharma is pointed out by the Prayogavaijayantî. (MS. Bodl. W. 68, p. 16. a.) तैः प्रत्येकं मितो धर्मस्त्रिविधः परिकीर्तितः॥४२॥ अनेनैवाभिप्रायेणाह बौधा-

and to the respective occupations of each. The rules of discipline for the young student, the occupations of the married man, the law of inheritance, the duties of the king, the administration of the law, are accurately detailed in these Sûtras. They are of great importance for forming a correct view of the old state of society in India, and the loss of the larger number of them is greatly to be regretted. Their general title is Sâmayâchârika-sûtras, or Dharmasûtras, and they form the third part to the Śrauta and Gṛihya-sûtras. Thus we have, besides the Śrauta and Gṛihya-sûtras of Âpastamba, a collection of Sâmayâchârika-sûtras belonging to the same Charaṇa of the Âpastambas, the members of which, as Kumârila tells us, followed one of the Śâkhâs of the Taittirîya-veda. Another collection of Dharmasûtras, which, however, is liable to critical doubts, belongs to the Gautamas, a Charaṇa of the Sâma-veda. It has been printed at Calcutta. A third one bears the name of Vishṇu, and has been printed at Calcutta, enlarged by modern additions written in Ślokas. The Vâsishṭha-dharma-śâstra, printed at Calcutta, belongs likewise, at least in part, to this class of Dharmasûtras. Whether we shall succeed in finding still more of these Sûtra works is questionable, though prose quotations from other Dharmaśâstras would justify this expectation. There can be no doubt, however, that all the genuine metrical Dharmaśâstras

यनः। उपदिष्टो धर्मः प्रतिवेदं तस्यानु व्याख्यास्यामः (sic)। स्मार्तो द्वितीयः। शिष्टाचारस्तृतीय इति॥

"Baudhâyana says, the highest law is that contained in each Veda, which we shall follow in our explanation; the second is the traditional law; the third, the customs of eminent sages."

which we possess now, are, without any exception, nothing but more modern texts of earlier Sûtra-works or Kula-dharmas belonging originally to certain Vedic Charaṇas.[1]

To return to those works of the Pârshada literature which are known by the name of Prâtiśâkhyas, I may refer for further particulars to Dr. Roth's valuable observations on this branch of literature. To him belongs the merit of having first pointed out in manuscript four of these works. The first is ascribed to Śaunaka, and belongs to the Śâkala-śâkhâ of the Rig-veda. I call it the Śâkala-prâtiśâkhya, not the Śaiśira-prâtiśâkhya, though it pretends to follow, like Śaunaka's Anukramaṇî, the Sanhitâ of the Śaiśirîya-śâkhâ, which is itself a subordinate branch of the Śâkala-śâkhâ.[2] Śiśira, however, is never mentioned in this or any other Prâtiśâkhya, as an authority on grammatical questions.

It is doubtful how far the rules given by Śaunaka

[1] See Prof. Stenzler's Introduction to his edition of Yâjnavalkya, and his remarks on Indian Law-books in Indische Studien, i. 232.

[2] इदं शास्त्रं पार्षदाख्यमखिलं संपूर्णमुत्तरत्र वक्ष्ये वक्ष्याम इत्यर्थः। शैशिरीये पारायणपाठ इति वाक्यशेषः। शैशिरीयायां संहितायामित्यर्थः। शैशिरी संहिता शिशिरदृष्टत्वात्। तथा पुराण उक्तं। मुद्गलो गोकुलो वात्स्यः शैशिरः शिशिरस्तथा। पंचैते शाकलाः शिष्याः शाखाभेदप्रवर्तका इति। तथा च ऋग्वेदे शैशिरीयायां संहितायामिति। यथा ऋग्वेदे पारायणाम्नाये शाकल्ये शैशिरीयकमिति वा। The verses to which the commentary refers are not in the MS. See also Vishṇu Purâṇa, p. 277. n. ऋग्वे - शैशिरीयायां संहितायां

in his Prâtiśâkhya, can be considered as representing the general opinion of the Śâkalas. Śaunaka, no doubt, wrote for the Śâkalas, to whom he likewise addresses his Anukramaṇî. But the author of the Prâtiśâkhya occasionally quotes the opinions of the Śâkalas, as different from his own, and speaks of them in the same manner as he alludes to the opinions of other grammarians. He mentions (i. 65.) the Śâkalas as observing a certain peculiar pronunciation out of respect for their master, who seems to have sanctioned it in his own rules. Who this master was is difficult to say. But it is most likely the same who (i. 52.) is called the Master, Vedamitra (friend of the Veda), and who (i. 223.) is called Śâkalyapitâ, the father of Śâkalya. His opinions, if we may judge by i. 232., differed from those of the younger Śâkalya. In i. 185. we meet with him again under the name of Śâkalya Sthavira, Śâkalya the elder, and he is there represented as advocating a pronunciation from which Śaunaka, the author of the Prâtiśâkhya, dissents. In i. 199. Śaunaka adopts the opinion of Śâkalya, and in i. 208. he likewise mentions him with approbation. But all this would only tend to show that Śaunaka does not consider himself bound to follow either Śâkalya or the father of Śâkalya, implicitly.[1]

There is not a single MS. at present existing of the Rig-veda in which the rules of our Prâtiśâkhya are uniformly observed, and the same applies to the MSS.

यथाक्रमं। प्रमाणमनुवाकानां सूक्तैः शृणुत शाकलाः॥ Com. शैशिरीयायां शिशिरनाममहर्षिप्रोक्तायां॥

[1] In xiii. 12. Śâkalya is mentioned as one of three Áchâryas, Vyâli, Śâkalya, Gârgya.

of the other Vedas. The rules of the Prâtiśâkhyas were not intended for written literature, they were only to serve as a guide in the instruction of pupils who had to learn the text of the Veda by heart, and to repeat it as part of their daily devotions. As Śaunaka was himself a member of the Śâkalas, we may quote his Prâtiśâkhya as the Śâkala-prâtiśâkhya. But strictly speaking it could only be called one of the Śâkala-prâtiśâkhyas, preserved by the pupils of Śaunaka, who, soon after, formed themselves into a new Charaṇa, under the name of Śaunakîyas.[1]

The second Prâtiśâkhya belongs to the ancient text of the Yajur-veda. There is only one MS. of it at the Bodleian Library, together with a considerable portion of the Commentary, the Tribhâshyaratna. Professor Wilson, in his catalogue of the Mackenzie Collection (i. 7, No. xxxiii.) mentions another MS., "The Prâtiśâkhya of the Yajur-veda, with a Bhâshya or comment, entitled Tribhâshyaratna, from its being said to be the substance of the works of three celebrated sages, Atreya, Mahisha, and Vararuchi." To what particular Śâkhâ of the Black Yajur-veda this Prâtiśâkhya belonged it is difficult to determine. It quotes several of the Charaṇas belonging to the Black Yajur-veda, such as Taittirîyakas, Âhvarakas, Ukhya, the founder of the Aukhîyas, and Bhâradvâja, the founder of the Bhâradvâjins. It also alludes to Mîmânsakas, a school of philosophers, mentioned in none of the other Prâtiśâkhyas. Until we receive some more complete MSS. of this work we can only say that it belongs to some Śâkhâ of the Taittirîya or Black Yajur-veda. Its grammatical termi-

[1] This Prâtiśâkhya has lately been edited by M. A. Regnier, in the "Journal Asiatique."

nology, as might be expected, is less advanced and less artificial than that of the Prâtiśâkhya of the modern or White Yajur-veda.

The third Prâtiśâkhya is ascribed to the Śâkhâ of the Mâdhyandinas, one of the subdivisions of the Vâjasaneyins[1]; though, perhaps, on the same grounds as those stated above with regard to the Śâkala-prâtiśâkhya, it might seem more correct to call it the Prâtiśâkhya of the Kâtyâyanîyas, a subdivision of the Mâdhyandinas. It was composed by Kâtyâyana, and shows a considerable advance in grammatical technicalities. There is nothing in its style that could be used as a tenable argument why Kâtyâyana, the author of the Prâtiśâkhya should not be the same as Kâtyâyana, the contemporary and critic of Pâṇini. It is true that Pâṇini's rules are intended for a language which was no longer the pure Sanskrit of the Vedas. The Vedic idiom is treated by him as an exception, whereas Kâtyâyana's Prâtiśâkhya seems to belong to a period when there existed but one recognised literature, that of the Ṛishis. This, however, is not quite the case. Kâtyâyana himself alludes to the fact that there were at least two languages. "There are two words," he says (i. 17.)[2], "*om* and *atha*, both used in the beginning of a chapter; but *om* is used in the Vedas, *atha* in the Bhâshyas." As Kâtyâyana himself writes in the Bhâshya or the common language, there is no reason why he should not have composed rules on the grammar of the profane Sanskrit, as well as on the pronunciation of the Vedic idiom.

Some of Kâtyâyana's Sûtras are now found re-

[1] It has been edited by Prof. Weber, Indische Studien, vol. iv.

[2] Indische Studien, iv. p. 103.

peated *ipsissimis verbis* in Pâṇini's grammar. This might seem strange; but we know that not all the Sûtras now incorporated in his grammar came from Pâṇini himself, and it is most likely that Kâtyâyana, in writing his supplementary notes to Pâṇini, simply repeated some of his Prâtiśâkhya-sûtras, and that, at a later time, some of these so-called Vârttikas became part of the text of Pâṇini.

The fourth Prâtiśâkhya belongs to the Atharva-veda. It is called Śaunakîyâ Châturâdhyâyikâ, and was, therefore, no doubt the property of the Śaunakîyas, a Charaṇa of the Atharva-veda. The name of the author is unknown, and we possess as yet but one MS., and that a very imperfect one, in the Royal Library at Berlin. That it belongs to a Śâkhâ of the Âtharvaṇa, is indicated by its very beginning[1], and one of its first rules is quoted by the commentator on the Śâkala-prâtiśâkhya as belonging to an Âtharvaṇa-prâtiśâkhya.[2] Besides, in the fourth chapter of the fourth and last book special reference is made to Âtharvaṇa sacrifices.[3] We can hardly suppose that Śaunaka, the author of the Prâtiśâkhya of the Rig-veda, was at the same time the author of this Śaunakîyâ Châturâdhyâyikâ. Śaunaka, whose name never occurs in the Śâkala-prâtiśâkhya[4], is quoted in

[1] नमो ब्रह्मवेदाय। अथांगिरसः॥

[2] तथा चाथर्वणप्रातिशाख्य इदमेव प्रयोजनमुक्तं। एवमिहेति च विभाषाप्राप्तं सामान्येन॥

[3] आथर्वणेषु च कर्मसु यागवर्जितेषु मणिबंधनादिषु॥

[4] I doubt the genuineness of the first verse of the Śâkala-prâtisâkhya where Śaunaka's name has been foisted in at the end. The emendation which I proposed in my edition of the Śâkala-prâtisâkhya, requires the admission of a so-called iyâdipûraṇa in *tvâdi.*

the Châturâdhyâyikâ, i. 1. 8.[1] The grammatical terminology of this little tract is far in advance of the technical terms used by Śaunaka. Yet there is a certain connection between the two books, and it is most likely that the author of the Châturâdhyâyikâ was a member of the Śaunakîya-charaṇa, founded by the author of the Śâkala-prâtiśâkhya. Nay, it seems as if its author had retained something of the allegiance which Śaunaka owed to Śâkalya and the Śâkalas. In one instance, when Pâṇini quotes the opinions of Śâkalya, the original is found in the Châturâdhyâyikâ, and not in the Śâkala-prâtiśâkhya. We are told by Pâṇini, that Śâkalya pronounced the *o* of the vocative to be unchangeable (pragṛihya), if followed by the particle *iti*.[2] Exactly the same rule, and in the very same words, is given in the Âtharvaṇa-prâtiśâkhya[3], whereas the Śâkala-prâtiśâkhya teaches first, that the *o* of the vocative is pragṛihya (i. 69)[4]; secondly, that it is liable to certain changes (i. 132, 135); and lastly, that all pragṛihya vowels are unchangeable, if followed by *iti* (i. 155). In none of these Sûtras do we find the exact words which Pâṇini quotes, and which are found in the Âtharvaṇa-prâtiśâkhya. Again, Pâṇini (viii. 3, 19.) ascribes the dropping of *y* and *v* in *vishṇa iha* instead of *vishṇav iha*, in *hara ehi* instead of *haray ehi*, to Śâkalya. Now it is true that this process is not unknown in the Śâkala-prâtiśâkhya, but it there assumes quite a dif-

[1] The quotation refers to Śâkala-pr. i. 114.

[2] 1. 1. 16. संबुद्धौ शाकल्यस्येतावनार्षे॥

[3] 1. 3. 19. आमंत्रितमितावनार्षे॥

[4] 1. 69. ओकार आमंत्रितजः प्रगृह्यः॥

ferent aspect (i. 129. 132. 135); whereas, in the Châturâdhyâyikâ the explanation is very mcuh the same as in Pâṇini.[1] Pâṇini quotes in the same place (viii. 3. 18.) the spelling adopted in these cases by Śâkaṭayana.[2] This is mentioned, in immediate connection with the rules which precede it likewise in the Âtharvaṇa-prâtiśâkhya; it is not mentioned at all in the Śâkala-prâtiśâkhya. It has been supposed[3] that a rule, which in Kâtyâyana's Prâtiśâkhya is ascribed to Śaunaka, was taken from the Châturâdhyâyikâ, and that therefore Kâtyâyana's Prâtiśâkhya was later than that of the Atharva-veda. But the rule ascribed to Śaunaka by Kâtyâyana is, that a final tenuis, if followed by a sibilant *of a different class*, is changed into the aspirate, whereas according to the Châturâdhyâyikâ (II. 1. 6.) a tenuis, followed by a sibilant *of its own class*, would have to be aspirated.[4] It must be admitted, however, that no such rule as that ascribed by Kâtyâyana to Śaunaka is found in the Śâkala-prâtiśâkhya, and, in other respects, the Prâtiśâkhya of Kâtyâyana shows traces of more modern origin than the Châturâdhyâyikâ.

[1] ii. 1 21. स्वराद्यवयोः पदांतयोः॥ ता इमा आपः॥ ii. 1. 22. नाकाराद्इकारस्य॥ उभाविदं॥ ii. 1. 23. गविष्टौ गवेषण इति च॥ Forms like ubhâ u, instead of ubhâv u, sanctioned by the Śâkala-pr. i. 129, would offend against the rule of the Âtharvaṇa-prâtiśâkhya.

[2] लेशवृत्तिरधिस्पर्शं शाकटायनस्य॥

[3] Indische Studien, iv. 249.

[4] Kâtyâyana would write दृषत् साये, विराट् षंडे। the Châturâdhyâyikâ, दृषथ् साये, विराठ् षंडे॥

The following list gives the names of the principal authorities quoted in the Śâkala-prâtiśâkhya, the Taittirîya-prâtiśâkhya, the Kâtyâyanîya-prâtiśâkhya, the Châturâdhyâyikâ, the Nirukta, and Pâṇini. I have availed myself of the lists given by Roth, Weber, and Böhtlingk; and though I do not pretend that my own list is complete, it will be sufficient to show the active interest which was taken in grammatical subjects at that early period:—

1. Âgniveśya. T.
2. Âgniveśyâyana. T.
3. Âgrâyaṇa. N.
4. Âtreya. T.
5. Ânyatareya. Ś. Ch.
6. Âpiśali. P.
7. Âhvarakas. T.
8. Ukhya. T.
9. Uttamottarîyas. (?) T.
10. Udîchyas. P.
11. Audumbarâyaṇa. N.
12. Aupamanyava. N.
13. Aupaśivi. K.
14. Aurṇavâbha. N.
15. Kâṇḍamâyana. T.
16. Kâṇva. K.
17. Kâtthakya. N.
18. Kâśyapa. K. P.
19. Kauṇḍinya. T.
20. Kautsa. N.
21. Kauhalîputra. T.
22. Kraushṭuki. N.
23. Gârgya. Ś. K. N. P.
24. Gâlava. N. P.
25. Gautama. T.
26. Charmaśiras. N.
27. Châkravarmaṇa. P.
28. Jâtukarṇya. K.
29. Taitîki. N.
30. Taittirîyakas. T.
31. Dalbhya. K.
32. Panchâlas. Ś.
33. Paushkarasâdi. T. P. (vârt.)
34. Prâchyas. Ś. P.
35. Plâkshi. T.
36. Plâkshâyaṇa. T.
37. Bâbhravya (Krama-kṛit). Ś.
38 Bhâradvâja. T. P.
39. Mâṇḍûkeya. Ś.
40. Mâśakîya. T.
41. Mîmânsakas. T.
42. Yâska. Ś.
43. Vâṭabhîkâra. T.
44. Vâtsapra. T.
45. Vâtsya. Ch. (?)
46. Vârshyâyaṇi. N.

47. Vâlmîki. T.
48. Vedamitra. Ś.
49. Vyâḷi. Ś.
50. Śatabalâksha Maudgalya. N.
51. Śâkaṭâyana. Ś. K. Ch. N. P.
52. Śâkapûṇi. N.
53. Śâkala (pâdakṛit). Ś.
54. Śâkalas. Ś.
55. Śâkalya. Ś. K. P.
56. Śâkalya-pitṛi (sthavira). Ś.
57. Śânkhâyana. T.
58. Śaityâyana. T.
59. Śaunaka. Ś (?). K. Ch.
60. Sânkṛitya. T.
61. Senaka. P.
62. Sthaulashṭhîvi. N.
63. Sphoṭâyana. P.
64. Hârîta. T.

For the Sâma-veda no Prâtiśâkhya has as yet been discovered, nor is it at all likely that such a work ever existed. The Sâma-veda was meant to be chanted, and the rules of chanting therefore, as contained in the Sâma-sûtras, naturally take the place of the rules of śikshâ or pronunciation. There is a small treatise in the same manuscript of the Bodleian Library which contains the Taittirîya-prâtiśâkhya, and which might be called a Prâtiśâkhya of the Sâma-veda. But it is so badly written, and so unintelligible without a commentary, that little use can be made of it at present. It is called Sâma-tantra[1],

[1] It begins (MS. Bodl. W. 505.) श्रीगणेशाय नमः॥ स्वरोऽनंत्यः। नीचानां। उपांत्यं। उपांत्ये। त्रिषु। आदिः। उपांत्यं च। द्वितीयं। अंतश्च। उपांत्ये॥१॥ आद्ये। अंत्ये। मध्यं। विपरीतस्वराणां। जारा। माहङ्। ग्म्ध्रु। ऊता। पारिव्रु। दि॥२॥ बि। पिबा। दधिविद्दपूर्वा। जरा परा च। स्त्रूव्वा। ईयाङ्। अंत्ये। ग्रता। तिपौगु॥ &c. From my notes taken in the Royal Library of Berlin, I see that the same work exists there with a commentary (?) in 13 Prapâṭhakas. समाप्तमिदं छंदोगसंबंधिकं सामतंत्राभिधानं व्याकरणं। The same work I find mentioned

and treats of subjects such as usually occur in the Prâtiśâkhyas. Its authenticity is supported by the Charanavyûha, where a Sâma-tantra is mentioned, but without any further particulars.

If it be asked now why all these works, so different in appearance, are to be ascribed to one period of literature, the Sûtra-period, the reasons for it are as follows: first, that the style of the majority of these works is the old Sûtra style, for instance, in the Taittirîya-prâtiśâkhya, the Kâtyâyanîya-prâtiśâkhya, and the Châturâdhyâyikâ[1]; secondly, that the manuscripts call these works Sûtras; thirdly that even works, written in mixed Ślokas, like those of Śaunaka, are quoted as Sûtras[2], a title which would never be given to works like the Mânava-dharma-śâstra, &c.; and fourthly, that the same men to whom these works are ascribed are known to have composed other works, generally written in the style of

in Dr. Weber's interesting article on the Sâma veda. (Indische Studien, i. 48.) It is curious that this Sâma-tantra is called Vyâkaraṇa, grammar. The same name is also given to the Rik-tantra, a small Śikshâ treatise, MS. Bodl. W. 375. This MS. contains several small treatises on Śikshâ matters connected with the Sâma-veda, but more in the form of Pariśishṭas: one on Avagraha, or division of words; another called Sâmasankhyâ; and a third called Stobhânusanhâra, beginning with the words अथातो ह्रस्वदीर्घप्लुतमात्राण्यक्षराणि व्याख्यास्यामः॥

[1] The title put at the end of the chapters of the Taittirîya-prâtiśâkhya is "iti prâtiśâkhya-sûtre prathamaḥ praśnaḥ samâptaḥ, &c."

[2] Shaḍguruśishya, in his Commentary on the Anukramaṇî, says that Śaunaka first composed a Kalpa-sûtra, consisting of 1000 parts and resembling a Brâhmaṇa. सहस्रखंडं स्वकृतं सूत्रं ब्राह्मणसंनिभं॥ This was afterwards destroyed by himself; but his few remaining works, which are written in verse, are equally called Sûtras, सूत्रदशकं॥

Sûtras. That the Prâtiśâkhya of the Śâkalas should be written in Ślokas and yet be ascribed to Śaunaka, the teacher of Kâtyâyana, is no objection. It would have to be excluded from the Sûtra period, if written in regular Anushṭubh-ślokas like those of Manu. But the mixture of the Śloka with other ancient metres indicates better than anything else the transition from one period to another, and is quite in accordance with that position which, as will be seen, Śaunaka occupies in the literary history of India.

By comparing Śaunaka's chapters on Śikshâ in his first Prâtiśâkhya with the small Śloka compilation which is generally quoted as *the* Vedânga, the difference of old and modern Ślokas will at once be perceived. This modern tract which has been printed in India, contains scarcely more than the matter of the Śiva or Śamkara-sûtras brought into Ślokas. It mentions the Prâkrit dialects, and represents itself as written after Pâṇini, but not, as Madhusûdana Sarasvati pretends, by Pâṇini.[1] Yet it is curious to see how great a reputation this small work must have gained, because Sâyaṇa, who knows the Prâtiśâkhyas, and quotes both from the Śâkala and Taittirîya-prâtiśâkhya, regards this small tract as the real Vedânga. In a Mîmânsâ work, which has been mentioned before, Someśvara's Tantra-

[1] अथ शिक्षां प्रवक्ष्यामि, पाणिनीयं मतं यथा।
and again:

शंकरः शांकरीं प्रादाद्दाक्षीपुत्राय धीमते।
वाङ्मयेभ्यः समाहृत्य देवीं वाचमिति स्थितिः॥
येनाक्षरसमाम्नायमधिगम्य महेश्वरात्।
कृत्स्नं व्याकरणं प्रोक्तं तस्मै पाणिनये नमः॥

vârttika-ṭîkâ, it seems even as if greater authority had been attributed to this short Śikshâ tract than to the more developed and evidently older works of Śaunaka, Kâtyâyana, and others.

Besides these works on Śikshâ which have been enumerated, from the Taittirîyâraṇyaka down to the so-called Vedânga, we possess another tract on Śikshâ, called the Mâṇḍûkî-śikshâ.[1] But this also is probably a production later than the Sûtra period, and it is important only in so far as it bears the name of another Charaṇa of the Rig-veda, the Mâṇḍûkâyanas[2], and thus confirms what was pointed out before, that each of the old Śâkhâs had originally its own Prâtiśâkhya, although the greater number of them, as well as

[1] Another work on Śikshâ is mentioned by Raja Râdhakânta in the article which he has dedicated to the Vedângas in his Śabda-kalpa-druma, and for which Amara and Bharata are quoted as authorities. तत्र अकरादिवर्णानां स्थानकरणप्रयत्नबोधिका अ कु ए ह विसर्जनीयाः कंठ्या इत्यादिका शिक्षा॥ The Commentary on the Śâkala-prâtiśâkhya also seems to speak of two Śikshâs. यथा तावच्छिक्षायां ऋुर्मूर्द्धन्या ऋटुरषाः सामान्येन सर्वशाखासु रेफो मूर्द्धन्य इत्युक्तः तथान्यस्यां शिक्षायां दंतमूलीय इति रेफो दंतमूलीय उक्तः। एवं सर्वा शिक्षा वर्णेषु स्थानकरणानुप्रदानादि सर्वासु शाखासु विदधाति। न तु नियतः कस्यां शाखायां रेफो मूर्द्धन्यः कस्यां दंतमूलीय इति। अत एव व्यवस्थापकमारभ्यते। दंतमूलीयस्तु तकारवर्गः सकाररेफलकारास्च रेफं वर्त्स्यमेके। शा० प्रा० १. ४५। ४६। ४७। एवमस्यां शाखायां दंतमूलीयो वा वर्त्स्यो वा रेफ इत्येतदवधारितं॥

[2] Mâṇḍukeya is quoted in the Śâkala-prâtiśâkhya, I. 200.

their Mantra texts, are now lost or preserved only under a more modern form, as in the case of this Mâṇḍûkî-śikshâ.

Chhandas, or Metre.

The second Vedânga doctrine, *Chhandas, or metre*, stands very much in the same position as the Śikshâ. Some names which have been afterwards adopted as the technical designations of metres, occur in some of the Mantras of the Rig-veda, and there are frequent allusions to metres in the Brâhmaṇas. What is said, however, in the Brâhmaṇas with reference to metres, is generally so full of dogmatic and mystical ingredients as to be of scarcely any practical use. In the Âraṇyakas and Upanishads whole chapters are devoted to this subject. Yet it is again in the Sûtras only that a real attempt has been made to arrange these archaic metres systematically. We have some chapters on metres at the end of the Śâkala-prâtiśâkhya, written in Śaunaka's usual style of mixed Ślokas. This treatise is anterior to that of Kâtyâyana, which we find in the introduction to his Sarvânukrama, because Kâtyâyana is the pupil of Śaunaka, as we shall see hereafter. For the metres of the Sâma-veda we have the Nidâna-sûtra in ten prapâṭhakas, which after explaining the nature and different names of all the Vedic metres, gives a kind of index (anukramaṇî) to the metres as they occur in the hymns employed at the Ekâha, Ahîna, and Sattra sacrifices. As to Pingalanâga's work on Chhandas, which is most frequently quoted under the title of Vedânga, it does not pretend to be of greater antiquity than the Mahâbhâshya, supposing it were admitted that Patanjali, the author of this famous commentary on Pâṇini, was the same as Pingala.[1] There would be nothing extraordinary in the fact that Pingala treats of Prâkrit as well as Sanskrit metres. For we have the instance of Kâtyâyana-Vararuchi, who wrote the Vârttikas on Pâṇini and lived before Patanjali, and is said to be the same who wrote a grammar of the Prâkrit dialects. It must be admitted, however, that Pingalanâga's Metric is one of the last works that could possibly be included in the Sûtra period; though there is no sufficient ground for excluding it from this period altogether, merely because those rules which refer to metres not yet employed in the Veda are ascribed to the same author. Besides, Pingala is quoted as an authority on metres in the Pariśishṭas[2], a class of literature which does not seem to be separated from the Sûtra period by a long interval.

To the same class of Chhandas works to which Pingala's treatise belongs, and which are not restricted to certain Śâkhâs, but are intended for the Veda in general, two other works are added by the commentator on the Śâkala-prâtiśâkhya, the one ascribed to Yâska, the other to Saitava.[3] Both these works, however, seem to be lost at present.

[1] Colebrooke, Miscellaneous Essays, ii. 63.

[2] MS. Bodl. W. 466. सामगानां छंदः। ब्राह्मणात्तंडिनश्चैव पिंगलाच्च महात्मनः। निदानादुक्थशास्त्राच्च छंदसां ज्ञानमुद्धृतं॥

[3] तथा सर्वैश्छंदश्चित्यादिभिः पिंगलयास्कसैतवप्रभृतिभिर्यत्सामान्येनोक्तं लक्षणं। See Dr. Roth's preface to the Nirukta,

The difference between a Chhandas work belonging to one of the Śâkhâs, and those treatises which are occupied with metre in general, may be seen from the following instance.

According to Pingala's Sûtras, a metre of seventy-six syllables is called Atidhṛiti, a metre of sixty-eight syllables Atyashṭi. Now Ṛv. i. 127, 6. a verse occurs of sixty-eight syllables which ought therefore to be called an Atyashṭi. According to Pingala himself, however, some syllables may be pronounced as two[1], and if we follow his rules on this point, the same verse consists of seventy-six instead of sixty-eight syllables. In order, therefore, to remove the uncertainty attached to the metre of this verse, the Chhandas chapter in the Śâkala-prâtiśâkhya (towards the end of the 16th Paṭala) declares that, according to the tradition of the Śâkala or Śaiśira-śâkhâ, this verse is to be pronounced as an Atidhṛiti, *i. e.* with seventy-six syllables. The same direction is given in Kâtyâyana's index to the Śâkala-sanhitâ.

p. 10.; and quære whether in the Śâkala-prâtiś. xvii. 25. one might read इति वै यास्कः instead of इति वैयास्कः as the commentator proposes. Saitava is the pupil of Pârâśarya and divided by thirteen teachers from Yâska. Cf. Bṛih. Âraṇy. Kâṇva. ii. 6. 2, 3.; Indische Studien, i. p. 156. n.

[1] Pingala, 3. 1. पाद इयादिपूरणः॥ इयादिः पूरणो यस्य (पादस्य) असावियादिपूरणः। आदिग्रहणे तु उवादयो गृह्यंते। तत्रायमर्थः। यत्र गायत्र्यादौ छंदसि पादस्याक्षरसंख्या न पूर्यते तत्रेयादिभिः पूरयितव्या। यथा तत्सवितुर्वरेणियमिति दिव्यं गच्छ सुवः पत इत्येवमादयः॥

Vyâkaraṇa, or Grammar.

The third Vedânga is *Vyâkaraṇa or Grammar.* According to the account which Indian authors give of their literature, this branch of Vedic learning would be represented by the Grammar of Pâṇini. Here the contradiction becomes even more glaring. In Pingala's Sûtras the Vedic metres were at least treated in the same way as the non-Vedic. But in Pâṇini, the rules which refer to Vedic grammar in particular, form only the exceptions to all the other rules which treat of the regular or classical language. Instead, therefore, of considering the third Vedânga doctrine as represented by the grammarians beginning with Pâṇini (Pâṇinyâdayaḥ), as Indian authors do, it would be more correct to say that it is represented by the grammarians ending with Pâṇini (Pâṇinyantâḥ). It unfortunately happened that Pâṇini's work acquired by its great merits such a celebrity as to supersede almost all that had been written on grammar before him, so that except the names and some particular rules of former grammarians, we have little left of this branch of literature, except what occurs occasionally in the Prâtiśâkhyas. That Pâṇini knew the Prâtiśâkhyas had been indicated long ago by Professor Böhtlingk; and it can be proved now by a comparison of Pâṇini's Sûtras with those of the Prâtiśâkhyas, that Pâṇini largely availed himself of the works of his predecessors, frequently adopting their very expressions, though he quotes their names only in cases where they have to serve as authorities for certain rules.

There are two separate treatises on grammatical

subjects, which belong to a period anterior to Pâṇini; the Sûtras on the Uṇâdi affixes, and the Sûtras of Śântanâchârya on accents. The Uṇâdi affixes are those by which nouns are formed from roots, the nouns being used in a conventional sense, and not in strict accordance with their radical meaning. They are called Uṇâdi, because, in the Sûtras as we now possess them, *uṇ* is the first-mentioned affix. That Pâṇini was acquainted with the same arrangement of these formative affixes cannot be doubted, because he uses the same technical name (uṇâdi) for them. We do not know by whom these Uṇâdi affixes were first collected, nor by whom the Uṇâdi-sûtras, as we now possess them, were first composed. All we can say is, that, as Pâṇini mentions them, and gives several general rules with regard to them, they must have existed before his time. But how many of the Sûtras existed before the time of Pâṇini, and how many were added afterwards, is a question that can hardly be solved. In their present form the Sûtras seem to treat the Vedic words as exceptions, at least they give now and then a hint that a certain derivation applies to the Chhandas only. Nevertheless it is curious to observe that the greater number of words, explained by the genuine Uṇâdi-sûtras, are Vedic, some of them exclusively so. If the author of the Sûtras had intended his rules for the Bhâshâ, there would have been no reason why he should have paid such prominent regard to words of a purely Vedic character. In fact, I believe, that originally the Uṇâdi-sûtras were intended for the Veda only, and that they were afterwards enlarged by adding rules on the formation of non-Vedic words. At last the non-Vedic or *laukika* words assumed such a preponderance that some rules, affecting Vedic words only, had actually to be inserted as exceptions. If a clear line could be drawn between words purely Vedic, and words never used in the Veda, and if the Sûtras referring to the former were separated from those of the latter class, we might perhaps arrive at the original text of this interesting work. This, however, is an undertaking which would require a more comprehensive and more critical knowledge of the history of the languages of India, than any scholar at present is likely to command.

As to Śântana's Phiṭsûtras, we know with less certainty to what period they belong. A knowledge of them is not presupposed by Pâṇini, and the grammatical terms used by Śântana are different from those employed by Pâṇini, — a fact from which Professor Böhtlingk has ingeniously concluded, that Śântana must have belonged to the eastern school of grammarians.[1] As, however, these Sûtras treat only of the accent, and the accent is used in the Vedic language only, the subject of Śântana's work would lead us to suppose that he was anterior to Pâṇini, though it would be unsafe to draw any further conclusions from this.

Nirukta, or Etymology.

The fourth Vedânga is *Nirukta or Etymology.* In the same way as, according to Indian authors, Grammar, as a Vedânga, was represented by Pâṇini's Grammar, we find Nirukta also represented by but one work, generally known by the name of Yâska's

[1] Cf. Böhtlingk, Ein erster Versuch über den Accent im Sanskrit, p. 64.; and Pâṇini, page xii.

Nirukta. Nirukta, however, has had this advantage over Vyâkaraṇa, that Yâska's work applies itself exclusively to Vedic etymologies. In the same way as we considered Pâṇini's Grammar as the work where Vyâkaraṇa, as a Vedâṅga, took its final shape, so Yâska also would seem to be one of the last authors who embodied the etymological lexicography of Vedic terms in one separate work. Niruktakâras, or authors of Niruktas, are mentioned by Yâska ; and some of them must have been as famous as Yâska himself, because we find that their merits in this respect were not forgotten even at the time of the compilation of the Purâṇas.[1] For explanations of old Vedic words, for etymologies and synonymous expressions, the Brâhmaṇas contain very rich materials, and, with the exception of the Kalpa, no other Vedâṅga has a better claim than the Nirukta to be considered as founded upon the Brâhmaṇas. Whole verses and hymns are shortly explained there; and the Âraṇyakas and Upanishads, if included, would furnish richer sources for Vedic etymologies than even the Nirukta itself. The beginning of the Aitareya-âraṇyaka is in fact a commentary on the

[1] Thus Śâkapûrṇi is mentioned as a Niruktakṛit in the Vishṇupurâṇa (p. 277. n. 9.); but this is no reason why Śâkapûrṇi should be the same as Yâska, as Colebrooke supposed. (Miscell. Essays, i. 15.) In fact Śâkapûṇi is quoted by Yâska himself, for there can be no doubt that Śâkapûrṇi is the same name as Śâkapûṇi. In later times, also, Yâska and Sâkapûṇi are regarded as distinct persons ; for instance, in a verse ascribed to Parâśara (Anukr. Bh. iv. 5. 7.), which occurs in the Bṛihaddevata, शुनासिरमिंद्रं यास्कस्तु मेने सूर्यैंद्रौ तु मन्यते शाकपूणिरिति पराशरः। Another Niruktakṛit mentioned by Sâyaṇa is the son of Sthûlashṭhîvi, or, as Yâska calls him, Sthaulashṭhîvi.

beginning of the Rig-veda; and if all the passages of the Brâhmaṇas were collected where one word is explained by another with which it is joined merely by the particle *vai*, they would even now give a rich harvest for a new Nirukta. It is important, however, not to confound Yâska's Nirukta with Yâska's Commentary on the Nirukta, although it has become usual, after the fashion of modern manuscripts, to call that commentary Nirukta, and to distinguish the text of the Nirukta by the name of Nighaṇṭu. The original Niruktas that formed an integral part of the Vedânga literature, known to Yâska himself, can have consisted only of lists of words arranged according to their meaning, like that upon which Yâska's Commentary is based. Whether the same Yâska who wrote the Commentary had some part in the arrangement of the lists of words, is unknown; probably these lists existed in his family long before his time, as Yâska implies himself (Nir. i. 20.). But, as he preserved them by his Commentary, it was natural that their authorship, too, should have been ascribed to him. Sâyaṇa gives the following account of this matter:—"Nirukta is a work where a number of words is given, without any intention to connect them in a sentence. In that book, where a traditional number of words is taught, which begin with Gauḥ, gmâ, and end with Vasavaḥ, Vâjinaḥ, Devapatnyaḥ, there is no intention to state things which are to be understood[1], because

[1] If Sâyaṇa means to give in these lines an etymology instead of a simple definition of Nirukta, the attempt would be very unsuccessful. Nirukta comes from *nirvach*, to explain. His definition, however, is right, in so far as the Nirukta does not

it is only said there that 'so many are the names of earth,' 'so many the names of gold,'" &c.

This Nirukta consists of three parts, as may be seen from the Commentary on the Anukramaṇikâ. Here we read:

"The first part is the Naighaṇṭuka, the second the Naigama, and the third the Daïvata, and thus must this traditional doctrine be considered as consisting of three parts.

"The Naighaṇṭuka begins with *Gauḥ*, and goes as far as *Apâre.*[1] The Naigama begins with *Jahâ*, and goes as far as *Ulbam Ribîsam.*[2] The third, or Deity-chapter, begins with Agni and ends with the Devapatnîs.[3] Here the gods from Agni to Devî Urjâhutî[4] are gods of the earth; from Vâyu to Bhaga[5], gods of the air; from Sûrya to the Devapatnîs[6], gods of

contain a connected string of ideas, but merely an enumeration of words. There is another definition of Nirukta, which is quoted by Râdhakant in his Śabdakalpadruma, and occurs as one of the Kârikâs in the Kâśikâvṛitti (Pân. vi. 3. 109.):

वर्णागमो वर्णविपर्ययश्च द्वौ चापरौ वर्णविकारनाशौ ।
धातोस्तदर्थातिशयेन योगस्तदुच्यते पंचविधं निरुक्तं ॥

"A Nirukta contains the doctrine of five things; of the addition, transposition, change, and dropping of letters, and of the use of one particular meaning of a root."

Instances of this are given in another verse;

भवेद्वर्णागमाद्धंसः सिंहो वर्णविपर्ययात् ।
गूढोत्मा वर्णविकृतेर्वर्णनाशात्पृषोदरं ॥

"*Hansa* is formed by an addition, *Sinha* by a transposition, *Gûḍhotmâ* by a change, *Pṛishodara* by a dropping of letters."

[1] 1—3 Adhyâya.
[2] 4 Adhyâya.
[3] 5 Adhyâya.
[4] §§ 1—3.
[5] §§ 4—6.
[6] § 6.

the sky. People learn the whole traditional number of words, from *Gauḥ* to *Devapatnyaḥ*.

"The word *Nighaṇṭu* applies to works where, for the most part, synonymous words are taught. Thus, ten Nighaṇṭus are usually mentioned; and this title has been applied to such works as Amarasinha, Vaijayantî, Halâyudha, &c. Therefore[1], the first part of this work also has been called *Naighaṇṭuka*, because synonymous words are taught there. In this part there are three lectures: in the first, we have words connected with things of time and space in this and the other worlds; in the second, we have words connected with men and human affairs; and, in the third, words expressing qualities of the preceding objects, such as thinness, multitude, shortness, &c.

"*Nigama* means Veda. As Yâska has quoted many passages from the Veda, which he usually introduces by the words, 'For this there is also a Nigama;' and as, in the second part, consisting of the fourth Adhyâya, words are taught which usually occur in the Veda only, this part is called *Naigama*.

"Why the third part, consisting of the fifth Adhyâya, is called *Daivata* is clear. The whole work, consisting of five Adhyâyas and three parts, is called Nirukta, because the meaning of words is given there irrespective of anything else. A commentary on this

[1] Sâyaṇa inverts here the historical order of things, because Yâska's Nighaṇṭu must have been called by this name before the time of Amara's Dictionary. Several Koshas are quoted which have not yet been met with in manuscript: Śarva Kosha, Ranti or Rantideva Kosha, Yâdava Kosha, Bhâguri Kosha, Bala Kosha, all of which must have been in existence as late as the Commentary on the Meghadûta.

has been composed by Yâska in twenty Adhyâyas. This also is called Nirukta, because the real meaning conveyed by each word is fully given therein."[1]

The Nirukta, together with the Prâtiśâkhyas and

[1] I have translated this passage of Sâyaṇa, because Dr. Roth has adopted a different division of the Nirukta in his edition, where he calls the first five books, containing the list of words, Naighaṇṭuka; the first six books of Yâska's Commentary, Naigama; and the rest Daivata. It would have been better to preserve the old divisions, which are based not only upon the authority of Yâska himself, but also of his commentators, with this exception, only that, according to them, the Naigama may also be called the Aikapadika. Thus Durga says,

एतावंतः समानकर्माणो धातवः एतावंत्यस्य सत्त्वस्य नामधेयानीति स एकः पदराशिर्नैघंटुकं नाम प्रकरणं। यत्र तावर्थौ प्रायेण चिंत्येते प्रसंगतोऽन्यत्किंचित्तदेतदेवंलक्षणं नैघंटुकं नाम प्रकरणं गवादि प्राग्जहाशब्दात्॥ अथ पुनर्यत्रैतावतामर्थानामिदमभिधानमित्यर्थः प्रायेण चिंत्यते अनवगतसंस्काराश्च निगमा जहादयः प्रायेण चिंत्यंतेऽनुषंगतोऽन्यत्किंचित्तदेतदेवंलक्षणमैकपदिकं नाम प्रकरणं जहादि प्रागग्निशब्दात्॥

Again, after having defined the third part, the Daivata, Durga goes on saying:

तान्येतानि त्रीणि प्रकरणानि नैघंटुकमैकपदिकं दैवतमिति। अनेन प्रकरणत्रयप्रपंचेनेदमवस्थितं नैरुक्तशास्त्रमिति॥

And further on:

यानि पुनर्नैघंटुकानि गवादीनि नैगमानि जहादीनि ..... प्रकरणद्वये नैघंटुके चैकपदिके च व्याख्यास्याम इत्येतदनुवर्तते॥

He afterwards seems to imply that the whole may also be called

Pâṇini's Grammar, supply the most interesting and important information on the growth of grammatical science in India. It would be out of place to enter here into this subject, but I cannot pass it over without at least pointing out the valuable materials preserved in these works, for tracing the origin of one of the most ancient branches of philosophy, *Grammar*.

There are only two nations in the whole history of the world which have conceived independently, and without any suggestions from others, the two sciences of Logic and Grammar, the Hindus and the Greeks. Although the Arabs and Jews, among the Semitic nations, have elaborated their own system of grammar, in accordance with the peculiar character of their language, they owe to the Greeks the broad outlines of grammatical science, and they received from Aristotle the primary impulse to a study of the categories

Nighaṇṭu, but there is no authority whatever for calling the first part of Yâska's Commentary, as Dr. Roth does, Naigama. Devarâja also takes the same view when he says,

भगवता यास्केन समाम्नायं नैघंटुकनैगमदेवताकांडरूपेण त्रिविधं गवादिदेवपत्न्यंतं निब्रुवता नैगमदेवताकांडपरिपठितानि पदानि प्रत्येकमुपादाय निरुक्तानि दर्शितानि निगमानि च। नैघंटुककांडपरिपठितानां तु गवाद्यपारेष्वंतानामेकचत्वारिंशच्छतत्रयाधिकं सहस्रं सामान्येन एतावंत्यस्य सत्त्वस्य नामधेयानीति व्याख्याय तत्र प्रदर्श्य कतिचिदेव निरुक्तानि तथापि कानिचिदेव दर्शितनिगमानि। अन्यानि तु ग्रंथविस्तरभीत्या सामान्येन निर्वचनलक्षणस्योक्तत्वाद्बुद्धिमद्भिर्निर्वक्तुं सुशक्यानीत्यभिप्रेत्य प्रायेण चोपेक्षितानि॥ &c.

of thought and speech. Our own grammatical terms came to us from the Greeks; and their history is curious enough, if we trace them back through the clumsy and frequently erroneous translations of the literary statesmen of Rome, to the scholars and critics of Alexandria, and finally to the early philosophers of Greece, the Stoics, Aristotle, Protagoras and Pythagoras. But it is still more instructive to compare this development of the grammatical categories in Greece with the parallel, yet quite independent, history of grammatical science in India. It is only by means of such a comparison that we can learn to understand what is organic, and what is merely accidental, in the growth of this science, and appreciate the real difficulties which had to be overcome in the classification of words and the arrangement of grammatical forms. The Greeks and Hindus started from opposite points. The Greeks began with philosophy, and endeavoured to transfer their philosophical terminology to the facts of language. The Hindus began with collecting the facts of language, and their generalisations never went beyond the external forms of speech. Thus the Hindus excel in accuracy, the Greeks in grasp. The grammar of the former has ended in a colossal pedantry; that of the latter still invigorates the mind of every rising generation throughout the civilised world.

Language had become with the Hindus an object of wonder and meditation at a very early period. In the hymns of the Veda we meet with poetical and philosophical speculations on speech, and Sarasvatî, the goddess of speech, is invoked as one of the most powerful deities. The scientific interest in language, however, dates from a later period. It was called forth, no doubt, by the careful study of a sacred literature, which in India, as elsewhere, called into life many an ancient science. In India the sacred strains of the Ṛishis were handed down with the greatest care, the knowledge of these songs constituted the only claim and hope of man for a higher life, and from a very early time they were looked upon with such a superstitious awe, that a mere error of pronunciation was supposed to mar their miraculous power.[1] We need not wonder, therefore, that the minutest rules were laid down as to the pronunciation of these hymns, and that the thoughts of the early teachers were led to dwell on the nature of language and its grammatical organisation. Where so much depended on letters, it was natural that words also and their grammatical variations should attract attention. A number of letters, or even a single letter, as Kâtyâyana says, may form a syllable (akshara), a number of syllables or even a single syllable may form a word (pada).[2] There are many lucubrations on letters, syllables, and words in the Brâhmaṇas and there are numerous expressions, occurring in the Brâhmaṇas, which mark a certain advance of grammatical knowledge.[3] In the Brâhmaṇa of the Vâjasaneyins (xiii. 5. 1. 18.) we meet with the names for Singular, Dual, and Plural. In the Chhândogya-upanishad (p. 135, ed. Roer) we find a classification of letters, and technical terms such as *sparśa*, consonants; *svara*, vowels; *ûshman*, sibilants. However, we must not expect in those sacred treatises anything sound and scientific. It is in the Sûtra lite-

[1] An analogous feeling among the Polynesians is mentioned in Sir G. Grey's Polynesian Mythology, p. 32.

[2] Kât.-pr. viii. 98.

[3] Ind. Studien, iv. p. 76.

rature that we meet with discussions on language of a purely scientific character; and what we do find in the Prâtiśâkhya, in the Nirukta and Pâṇini, is quite sufficient to show that at their time the science of language was not of recent origin. I can only touch upon one point. It is well known how long it took before the Greeks arrived at a complete nomenclature for the parts of speech. Plato knew only of Noun (ὄνομα) and Verb (ῥῆμα), as the two component parts of speech, and for philosophical purposes Aristotle too did not go beyond that number. It is only in discussing the rules of rhetoric that he is led to the admission of two more parts of speech, the σύνδεσμοι (conjunctions), and ἄρθρα (articles). The pronoun ἀντωνυμία does not come in before Zenodotos, and the preposition (πρόθεσις) occurs first in Aristarchos. In the Prâtiśâkhya, on the contrary, we meet at once with the following exhaustive classification of the parts of speech (xii. 5.)

"The noun (nâma), the verb (âkhyâta), the preposition (upasarga), and the particle (nipâta) are called by grammarians the four classes of words.[1] The

[1] नामाख्यातमुपसर्गो निपातश्चत्वार्याहुः पदजातानि शाब्दः।
तन्नाम येनाभिदधाति सत्त्वं तदाख्यातं येन भावं स धातुः॥
प्राभ्या परा निर्दुरनु व्युपाप सं परि प्रति न्यत्यधि सूदवापि।
उपसर्गा विंशतिरर्थवाचकाः सहेतराभ्यामितरे निपाताः॥
क्रियावाचकमाख्यातमुपसर्गो विशेषकृत्।
सत्त्वाभिधायकं नाम निपातः पादपूरणः॥
निपातानामर्थवशान्निपातनादनर्थकानामितरे च सार्थकाः।
नेयंत इत्यस्ति संख्येह वाङ्मये मिताक्षरे चाप्यमिताक्षरे च ये॥
(नेयंतः is न ईयंतः; it means तेषामियत्ता नास्ति॥)

noun is that by which we mark a being, a verb that by which we mark being; the latter is called a root (dhâtu). There are twenty prepositions, and these have a meaning, if joined with nouns or verbs. The rest of the words are called particles. The verb expresses an action; the preposition defines it; the noun marks a being; particles are but expletives. There are, however, besides the particles which have no meaning, others which have, for we see that some particles are used on account of their sense: but it is impossible to say how many there are of each class, whether they are used in measured or in prose diction."[1]

The same division is adopted by most grammarians, and it is more fully explained by the author of the Nirukta. After stating that there are four kinds of words, Yâska says that the verb is chiefly concerned with being, nouns with beings. He then brings in a new definition which reminds us of the first introduction of the προσηγορία, as distinct from the ὄνομα, by the Stoics. "The verb," he says, "when it expresses being, expresses a kind of being which lasts from an earlier to a later time, such as 'he walks,' 'he cooks'; the nouns, if they express being (and not a being), express a kind of being that has become embodied in one, from beginning to end, such as 'a walking,' 'a cooking.'" Here the chief difference between the verb and the noun appellative, is established on a similar ground to that on which Aristotle ascribes to the verb a temporal character, and denies it to the noun.[2]

[1] The name for pronoun, sarvanâman, occurs in the Nirukta, vii. 2, and in the Châturâdhyâyikâ.

[2] Poet. c. 20. ὄνομα δ' ἐστὶ φωνὴ συνθέτη, σημαντικὴ ἄνευ χρόνου,

The distinction of the numbers was first pointed out by Aristotle, but the technical terms for singular and plural (ἀριθμὸς ἑνικός, πληθυντικός) date from a later time. In India the terms for the three numbers, Singular, Plural, and Dual were known in the Brâhmaṇa period.

Aristotle had no clear conception of cases, in the grammatical sense of the word. *Ptosis*, with him, refers to verbs as well as nouns. The introduction of the five cases, in our sense of the word, is due to the Stoics. In the Prâtiśâkhyas we find not only a name for case, restricted to nouns (vibhakti, *i. e.* κλίσις) but the number of cases also is fixed at seven.

The distinction of the genders is the only point on which the Greeks may claim a priority to the Hindus. It was known in Greece to Protagoras; whereas in India the Prâtiśâkhyas seem to have passed it over, and it appears first in Pâṇini.[1]

There are some discussions in the beginning of the Nirukta which are of the highest interest with regard to etymology. While in Greece the notions of one of her greatest thinkers, as expressed in the Cratylus, represent the very infancy of etymological science, the Brahmans of India had treated some of the vital problems of etymology with the utmost sobriety. In the Prâtiśâkhya of Kâtyâyana we find, besides the philosophical division of speech into nouns, verbs, prepositions and particles, another division of a purely grammatical nature, and expressed in the most strictly technical language. "*Verbs* with their con-

ἧς μέρος οὐδέν ἐστι καθ' αὑτὸ σημαντικόν· ῥῆμα δε φωνὴ συνθέτη, σημαντικὴ μετὰ χρόνου, ἧς οὐδὲν μέρος σημαίνει καθ' αὑτό, ὥσπερ καὶ ἐπὶ τῶν ὀνομάτων.

[1] Kâtyâyanîya Prâtiśâkhya, iv. 170.

jugational terminations, *Nouns*, derived from verbs by means of kṛit-suffixes, *Nouns* derived from nouns by means of taddhita-suffixes, and four kinds of *Compounds*,—these constitute language."[1]

In the Nirukta this division is no longer considered sufficient. A new problem has been started, one of the most important problems in the philosophy of language, whether all nouns are derived from verbs? No one would deny that certain nouns, or the majority of nouns, were derived from verbs. The early grammarians of India were fully agreed that *kartṛi*, a doer, was derived from *kṛi*, to do; *pâchaka*, a cook, from *pach*, to cook. But did the same apply to all words? Śâkaṭâyana, an ancient grammarian and philosopher, answered the question boldly in the affirmative, and he became the founder of a large school, called the *Nairuktas* or (Etymologists), who made the verbal origin of all words the leading principle of all their researches. They were opposed, and not without violence, by another school, emphatically called the *Vaiyâkaraṇas* or Analysers, who, following the lead of Gârgya, the etymologist[2], admitted the verbal origin of those words only for which an adequate grammatical analysis could be given. The rest they left unexplained. Let us hear how Yâska states the arguments on both sides. After having explained the characteristics of the four classes of words, he says: "Śâkaṭâyana maintains that nouns are derived from verbs, and there is an universal agreement of all Etymologists (Nairukta) on this point. Gârgya, on the contrary, and some of the grammarians say, not all

[1] I. 27. तिङ्कृत्तद्धितचतुष्टयसमासाः शब्दमयं॥

[2] नैरुक्ताश्च गार्ग्यवर्जं। Durga.

(nouns are derived from verbs). For first, if the accent and formation were regular in all nouns and agreed entirely with the appellative power (of the root), nouns such as *go* (cow), *aśva* (horse), *purusha* (man), would be in themselves intelligible.[1] Secondly, if all nouns were derived from verbs, then if any one performed a certain action, he would, as a subject, be called in the same manner. For instance, if *aśva*, horse, were derived from *aś*, to get through, then any one who got through a certain distance, would have to be called *aśva*, horse. If *tṛiṇa*, grass, were derived from *tṛid*, to pierce, then whatever pierces would have to be called *tṛiṇa*. Thirdly, if all nouns were derived from verbs, then everything would take as many names as there are qualities belonging to it. A pillar, for instance, which is now called *sthûṇa*, might be called *dareśaya*, hole-rest, because it rests in a hole; or *sanjanî*, joiner, because there are beams joined to it. Fourthly, people would call things in such a manner that the meaning of nouns might be at least intelligible, whatever the regular formation may be by which the actions of these things are supposed to be expressed. Instead of *purusha*, man, which is supposed to be formed from *puriśaya*, dwelling in the body, they would say *puriśaya*, body-dweller; instead of *aśva*, horse, *ashṭṛi*, pervader; instead of *tṛiṇa*, grass, *tardana*, piercer. Fifthly, after a noun has been formed, these etymologists begin to discuss it, and say for instance that the earth is called *pṛithivî*, broad, from *prathana*, stretching. But, who stretched it, and what was his resting-place while he stretched

[1] This construction is against the Commentary, but, if the MS. such as we have it, is correct, it seems to me the only possible construction.

the earth? Sixthly, where the meaning cannot be discovered, no modification of the root yielding any proper signification, Śâkaṭâyana has actually taken whole verbs, and put together the halves of two distinct words. For instance, in order to form *satya*, true, he puts together the causal of *î*, to go, which begins with *ya*, as the latter half, and the participle of *as*, to be, which begins with *sa*. Lastly, it is well known, that beings come before being, and it is therefore impossible to derive the names of beings which come first, from being, which comes after.

"Now all this arguing," Yâska continues, "is totally wrong. For however all this may be, first, with regard to what was said, namely that, if Śâkaṭâyana's opinion were right, all words would be significative, this we consider no objection[1], because we shall show that they are all significative. With regard to the second point, our answer is, that we see as a matter of fact, that it is not so, but that of a number of people who perform the same action, some only take a certain name, and others do not. Not every one that shapes a thing is called *takshan*, a shaper, but only the carpenter. Not every one that walks about is called a *parivrâjaka*, but only a religious mendicant. Not everything that enlivens is called *jîvana*, but only the sap of the sugar-cane. Not everything that is born of Bhûmi (earth) is called *Bhûmija*, but only the planet Mars (an-gâraka).[2] And the same remark serves also as an

[1] The Commentator translates "even if it were so, even if some remained inexplicable, this would be no objection;" for, "boni grammatici est nonnulla etiam nescire."

[2] The remarks of the Commentator on this passage are so

answer to the third objection. With regard to the fourth objection, we reply, We did not make these words, we only have to explain them; and there are also some nouns of rare occurrence, which you grammarians derive by means of kṛit-suffixes, and which are liable to exactly the same objection. For who could tell, without some help from etymologists, that some of the words mentioned in the Aikapadika-chapter mean what they do mean? *Vratati* is derived by you from *vṛîṇâti*, he elects, but it signifies a garland. The same applies to your grammatical derivations of such words as *damûnas*, *jâṭya*, *âṭṇâra*,

curious, that they deserve to be copied. "You may well ask (he says) why this is so. But, my friend, go and ask the world. Quarrel with the world, for it is not I who made this law. For although all nouns are derived from verbs, yet the choice of one action (which is to be predicated in preference to others) is beyond any control. Or it may be that there is a certain law with regard to those who perform certain actions more exclusively. A man who performs one particular action more exclusively, whatever other actions he may perform, will have his name from that particular action. Nor do we say that he who at one time and in one place shapes things is a carpenter, but he who at any time or any place is a carpenter, him we always call carpenter. This is not a predicate restricted to one, it may freely be given to others. Now and then there may be other actions, more peculiar to such persons, and they may take other names accordingly, yet their proper name remains carpenter." And with regard to the next problem the Commentator says: "A carpenter may well perform other actions, but he need not therefore take his name from them. If it is said, several things might have one and the same name, and one and the same thing might have different names, all we can answer is, that this is not proved by the language such as it is. Words are fixed in the world we cannot say how (svabhâvataḥ, by nature)." This, together with the text, shows a clearer insight into the nature of Homonyma and Synonyma, or, as the Peripatetics called the latter, Polyonyma, than anything we find in Aristotle.

jâgarûka, darvihomin. In answer to the fifth objection we say, Of course we can discuss the etymological meaning of such words only as have been formed. And as to the questions, who stretched the earth, and what was his resting-place, all we can say is, that our eyes tell us that the earth is broad, and even though it has not been stretched out by others, yet all men speak as they see. With respect to the sixth objection, we admit, that he who combines words without thereby arriving at their proper meaning, is to be blamed. But this blame attaches to the individual etymologist, not to the science of etymology. As to the last objection, we must again appeal to the facts of the case. Some words are derived from qualities, though qualities may be later than subjects, others not."

I doubt whether even at present, with all the new light which Comparative Philology has shed on the origin of words, questions like these could be discussed more satisfactorily than they were by Yâska. Like Yâska, we maintain that all nouns have their derivation, but, like Yâska, we must confess that this is a matter of belief rather than of proof. We admit with Yâska that every noun was originally an appellative, and, in strict logic, we are bound to admit that language knows neither of homonymes nor synonymes. But granting that there are such words in the history of every language, granting that several objects, sharing in the same predicate, may be called by the same name, and that the same object, possessing various predicates, may be called by different names, we shall find it as impossible as Yâska to lay down any rule why one of the many appellatives became fixed in every dialect as the proper name of the sun, the moon, or any other object; or why generic words (homonymes) were founded on one predicate rather than another. All we can say is what Yâska says, it was so svabhâvataḥ, by itself, from accident, through the influence of individuals, of poets or law-givers. It is the very point in the history of language where languages are not amenable to organic laws, where the science of language ceases to be a strict science, and enters into the domain of history.

We leave this subject not without reluctance, and hope to return to it in some more appropriate place.

Kalpa, or the Ceremonial.

The most complete Vedânga is the fifth, the *Kalpa*, for which we have not only the Brâhmaṇas of the different Vedas, but also their respective Sûtras. The Sûtras contain the rules referring to the sacrifices[1], with the omission of all things which are not immediately connected with the performance of the ceremonial. They are more practical than the Brâhmaṇas, which for the most part are taken up with mystical, historical, mythological, etymological and

[1] Kumârila Tantravârttika, i. 3. 1.

एवं कल्पसूत्रेष्वर्थवादादिमिश्रशाखांतरविप्रकीर्णन्यायलभ्यवि-
ध्युपसंहारफलमर्थनिरूपणं तत्तत्प्रमाणमंगीकृत्य कृतं। लोक-
व्यवहारपूर्वकाश्च केचिदृत्विगादिव्यवहाराः सुखार्थहेतुत्वेना-
श्रिताः॥

"Thus the real sense has been ascertained in the Sûtras by means of collecting the commandments which were to be obtained systematically as they were dispersed in different Śâkhâs and mixed up with Arthavâdas, &c. One or the other authority was selected, and, to afford greater facility, some performances of the priests which are connected with worldly matters were also taken in."

theological discussions. Thus Sâyaṇa says, in his Commentary on the Baudhâyana-sûtras: "The whole mass of Vedic literature consists of three parts: Mantras, Vidhis, and Arthavâdas. The Vidhis enjoin an act, the Arthavâdas recommend it, the Mantras record it. In order to make the understanding of the prescribed ceremonies more easy, the Reverend Baudhâyana composed the Kalpa. For the Brâhmaṇas are endless, and difficult to understand, and therefore have old masters adopted the Kalpa-sûtras according to different Śâkhâs. These Kalpa-sûtras have the advantage of being clear, short, complete, and correct."[1]

[1] तत्र तावद्विध्यर्थवादमंत्रात्मना त्रिधा व्यवस्थितो वेदराशिः। विधिविहितमर्थवादप्ररोचितं मंत्रेण स्मृतमभ्युदयकारि भवतीति। ततश्च चोदितानां कर्मणां सुखावबोधाय भगवान् बौधायनः कल्पमकल्पयत्। यतो ब्राह्मणानामनंत्यं दुरवबोधतया - - - अतो न तैः सुखं कर्मावबोध इति कल्पसूत्राणीमानि प्रतिनियतशाखांतरानंगीचक्रुः पूर्वाचार्याः॥ कल्पस्य वैशद्यलाघवकात्स्न्र्यप्रकरणशुद्ध्यादिभिः प्रकर्षैर्युक्तस्य &c. MS. E.I.H. 104. In the beginning of the Commentary on Âpastamba's Sûtras, it is said that the author is going to explain the Yâjurvaidika performance of the whole vaitânika sacrifice, which is detached in many Śâkhâs and scattered in different parts of the Veda.

अत्र भगवानापस्तंबो वेदभागव्याकीर्णं विभक्तानेकशाखाव्यासक्तं च विश्वस्य वैतानिकस्य कर्मणो याजुर्वैदिकं प्रयोगं व्याचिख्यासुः। श्रुतौ संक्षिप्तयोर्दर्शपूर्णमासयोर्व्याकरणेन शाखांतरोपसंहारादिना च विस्पष्टीकरणं व्याख्यानं॥

"To explain means to separate, for instance, the new moon and the full moon sacrifices, which in the Veda are thrown together, and to make them intelligible by comprehending different Śâkhâs."

It is true that some of the Brâhmaṇas also have a more practical tendency, and might almost be taken for productions of the Sûtra period. We saw before that Kumârila in his Tantravârttika spoke of some Brâhmaṇas, for instance those of the Âruṇa and Parâśara-śâkhâs[1], as having the form of Kalpa works. Nay, there are passages in the Brâhmaṇas which, though properly they ought to be called Kalpa or vidhi, are quoted by the Commentators under the name of Sûtra.[2] The same name is used, in the late books of the Śatapatha-brâhmaṇa, as the title of literary compositions, which must then have formed part of the Brâhmaṇa literature.[3]

On the other hand, the Sûtras, composed by Śaunaka, were called Brâhmaṇa-sannibha, "having the appearance of a Brâhmaṇa," an assertion, which, to a certain extent, is true, as may be seen by comparing the Rigvidhâna, which is ascribed to Śaunaka, with the Sâmavidhâna-brâhmaṇa. The same might be said of the Śânkhâyana-sûtras, particularly of the last books, where we sometimes meet with considerable portions identically the same as in the Aitareya-brâhmaṇa. But no orthodox Brahman would for a moment admit that Brâhmaṇas and Sûtras belonged to the same class of literature. They fear the danger of such an ad-

[1] आरुणपराशरशाखाब्राह्मणस्य कल्परूपत्वं। See also Sâyaṇa's Introduction to the Aitareya-brâhmaṇa, where he says, कल्पस्त्वारुणकेतुकचयनप्रकरणे समाम्नायते। इति मंत्राः कल्पोऽत ऊर्द्ध्वं यदि बलिं हरेदिति। Might not the name आरुणपराजी, Pâṇ. iv. 3. 105., be meant for आरुणपराशरी?

[2] Indische Studien, i. 149. n.

[3] See Śatapatha-brâhmaṇa, xiv. 4. 4. 10. The word is not used in a similar passage, xi. 3. 8. 8. See page 40, note 7.

mission, because, as Kumârila says, If the name of Śruti were once granted to the Sûtras, it would with difficulty be denied to the sacred writings of Buddhists and other heretics. It would be, as he expresses himself in his graphic language, "Like letting in the heretics on the high road, after having driven them out of the village with sticks and fists."

Originally a Brâhmaṇa was a theological tract, and it was called brâhmaṇa, not because it treated of the Brahman, the Supreme Spirit, or of sacrificial prayers, sometimes called brahmâṇi, but because it was composed by and for Brahmans. These Brâhmaṇas or *dicta theologica*, were gradually collected in different families or Parishads, and gave rise to greater works, which were equally called by the name of Brâhmaṇa. Such a collection became a more or less comprehensive repository of theological lore, and no consideration as to practical usefulness seems to have influenced either the original contributors or the later collectors. In the course of time, however, and particularly during periods of theological controversy, these works began to assume a practical importance, and it was then that the want of proper arrangement was felt as a serious inconvenience. Hence, when new additions were made to the ancient stock of Brahmanic learning, or when, as in the case of a controversy or a schism, the founders of a new community were called upon to compose a Brahmanic code different from that which belonged to their adversaries, a more systematic and business-like spirit, such as afterwards led to the composition of Sûtras, began to show itself in the arrangement of these later Brâhmaṇas.

There was, however, a certain general system

which regulated the composition of the Brâhmaṇas from the very first. Long before the different Brâhmaṇas were composed, the sacrificial system, which they were chiefly intended to illustrate, had been definitely arranged, and the duties of the three or four classes of priests engaged at the great sacrifices, had been finally agreed upon. This division of priests and the general order of the sacrifices must have been settled previously even to the composition of the Sanhitâs of the Sâma and Yajur-vedas; for both follow the established order of the sacrifices, and are neither more nor less than collections, containing the verses which the second and third classes of priests, the Chhandogas and Adhvaryus, had to employ at various sacrifices. They are liturgical song-books, adapted to an already-existing sacrificial canon. The case is different with the Rig-veda. The Rig-veda-sanhitâ was collected without any reference to sacrificial purposes. The Brâhmaṇas, however, of all the three Vedas, the Rig-veda as well as the Sâma and Yajur-vedas, pre-suppose the final division of the three classes of priests. This division, to which we shall have to revert hereafter, may be shortly described as follows:—The chief part, or, as the Brahmans say, the body of each sacrifice, had to be performed by the Adhvaryu-priests. The preparing of the sacrificial ground, the adjustment of the vessels, the procuring of the animals, and other sacrificial oblations, the lighting of the fire, the killing of the animal, in short, all that required manual labour, was the province of the Adhvaryu priests. They stood lowest in the estimation of the Brahmans, and, as the proper pronunciation of the sacred texts required considerable study, they were allowed simply to mutter the verses which they used during the sacrifice. The recitation of Vedic verses was considered as so subordinate a part of their duty, that their Sanhitâ, at least the most ancient Sanhitâ[1] of the Adhvaryu-veda priests, is not a collection of hymns, but rather a complete description of the sacrifice, as performed by the Adhvaryus, interspersed with such verses and formulas as had to be muttered by the officiating priests. It was at a

[1] According to some commentaries, this ancient collection of the Adhvâryu priests was called *Kṛishṇa*, or the dark Yajur-veda, owing to its motley character, whereas the more recent version of the Yajur-veda was called *śukla* or bright, on account of the clear separation of hymns and rules, or, according to others, on account of its enabling the reader to distinguish clearly between the offices belonging to the Hotṛi and the Adhvaryu. A more popular explanation is given by Colebrooke from Mahîdhara's Commentary on the Vâjasaneyi-sanhitâ. It occurs also in the Purâṇas: "The *Yajush*, in its original form, was at first taught by *Vaiśampâyana* to twenty-seven pupils. At this time, having instructed *Yâjnavalkya*, he appointed him to teach the Veda to other disciples. Being afterwards offended by the refusal of *Yâjnavalkya* to take on himself a share of the sin incurred by *Vaiśampâyana*, who had unintentionally killed his own sister's son, the resentful preceptor bade *Yâjnavalkya* relinquish the science which he had learnt. He instantly disgorged it in a tangible form. The rest of *Vaiśampâyana's* disciples receiving his command to pick up the disgorged Veda, assumed the form of patridges, and swallowed the texts which were soiled, and for this reason termed 'black;' they are also denominated *Taittirîya*, from *tittiri* the name of a partridge. *Yâjnavalkya*, overwhelmed with sorrow, had recourse to the sun; and through the favour of that luminary, obtained a new revelation of the Yajush which is called 'white' or pure, in contradistinction to the other, and is likewise named *Vâjasaneyin*, from a patronymic, as it should seem, of *Yâjnavalkya* himself; for the Veda declares, 'these purer texts, revealed by the sun, are published by Yâjnavalkya, the offspring of *Vâjasani*.' But, according to the Vishṇu-purâṇa, the priests who studied the Yajush are called *Vâjins*, because the sun, who revealed it, assumed the form of a horse (vâjin)." It is

much later time, and probably in imitation of the Sâma-veda-sanhitâ, that a separate collection of the hymns of the Adhvaryu priests was made, and this we possess in the various Śâkhâs of the Vâjasaneyins, who have embodied the rules and the description of the sacrifice in a separate Brâhmaṇa, known by the name of the Śatapatha. According to the same metaphor, which assigns to the Adhvaryu priests the body of the sacrifice, its two most essential limbs fall to the lot of two other classes, the Hotṛi and Udgâtṛi priests; or, as Sâyaṇa says, in his introduction to the Taittirîya-sanhitâ: "The Rig-veda and Sâma-veda are like fresco-paintings whereas the Yajur-veda is the wall on which they stand." The Udgâtṛi priests have little to do with the actual performance of the sacrifice. Their chief duty is to chant their hymns in a loud melodious voice, and these hymns, in the order in which they had to be chanted, were collected in a book of songs, called the Sâma-veda-sanhitâ. The third class of priests, who were equally free from purely manual labour, had to recite the sacrificial hymns, according to the strict and difficult rules of the ancient pronunciation and accentuation, but without chanting. No collection, however, was made for them, containing the hymns in their sacrificial order; because the Hotṛi priests were supposed to be so thoroughly versed in the ancient Vedic poetry, as contained in the Rig-veda-sanhita, that they were

clear that these are nothing but late etymological legends. *Tittiri* and *Vajin* were proper names. *Tittiri* was the pupil of *Yâska* the pupil of *Vaiśampâyana,* and it is through them that the old or dark Yajur-veda was handed down. *Yâjnavalkya,* of the family of the *Vâjasaneyins,* was the founder of the more modern or bright Yajur-veda.

expected to know the whole of it, and to be able to repeat readily, without the help of a manual, whatever hymn was enjoined at any part of the sacrifice.

This distribution of the ceremonial between the three classes of priests, which, after the collection of the ancient Sanhitâ of the Rig-veda, called forth the two Sanhitâs of the Sâma- and Yajur-vedas, regulated from the first the composition of the Brâhmaṇas. Instead of one code of theology, we find three collections of Brâhmaṇas, treating respectively of the performance of those rites, which each of the three classes of priests was more particularly concerned with. The Adhvaryu priests had originally, as we saw, no Brâhmaṇa in the usual sense of the word, and what is called their Brâhmaṇa is in reality a mere supplement and continuation of their Sanhitâ; originally, therefore, neither of these names was correctly applicable to the Yajur-veda of the Charakas. In later times, however, the duties of the Adhvaryu were incorporated in a separate Brâhmaṇa, the Śatapatha, at the same time that their hymns were collected in a small manual, the later Sanhitâ of the Yajur-veda. In a similar manner the sacrificial duties of the Hotṛi priests were discussed in the Bahvṛicha-brâhmaṇas, and those of the Udgâtṛi priests, in the Chhandoga-brâhmaṇa.

Thus we see that the collection, if not the original composition, of the Brâhmaṇas, was not entirely without system; and that the remarks on certain parts of the sacrifice, although sometimes extremely diffuse, and mixed up with extraneous matter, were not thrown together at random. As most of the sacrifices were to be performed by two or three classes of priests in common, the same ceremony may be described in different Brâhmaṇas. The Agnishṭoma, for instance, begins with the ceremony of the Ṛitvig-varaṇa, the election of priests. This ceremony is performed by the Adhvaryu priests alone, and it was not necessary to explain it in the Brâhmaṇa of the Hotṛi priests. It is wanting therefore in the Bahvṛicha-brâhmaṇas. The next following ceremony, the Dîkshaṇîyeshṭi, is likewise performed by the Adhvaryus together with the Chhandoga priests; but as here the Hotṛi priests also have to take a part (the yâjyâs and anuvâkyâs), it is described in the beginning of the Aitareya-brâhmaṇa.[1]

The Kalpa-sûtras, with which we are at present concerned, follow the same system as the Brâhmaṇas. They presuppose, however, not only the existence of

[1] "The Aitareya-brâhmaṇa consists of forty Adhyâyas; the Âraṇyaka also is reckoned part of the Aitareya, and is equally ascribed to Mahidâsa, the son of Itarâ.

"In the Brâhmaṇa, the first subject is the Jyotishṭoma (chatuḥsamstha); then the Gavâm-ayana, the Âdityânâm-ayana, the Angirasâm-ayana, and the Dvâdaśâha. The Jyotishṭoma stands first among the Somayâgas (such as the Goshṭoma and Âyushṭoma), and it comprises seven sacrifices (saptasamstha.) Four of these are the Agnishṭoma, Ukthya, Shoḍaśin, and Atirâtra; and among these four the Agnishṭoma is the model, the whole ceremony being here fully detailed, while for the other sacrifices the peculiar rules only are given, the rest being supplied from the model. The Agnishṭoma ought therefore to be explained first. Now it is very true, that at the beginning of the Agnishṭoma the Ṛitvij priests are to be elected, for Âpastamba says in his Sûtras, 'he who is going to sacrifice with Soma, let him choose Ârsheya-brâhmans for Ṛitvij;' but as the Hotṛi priests have nothing to do in the ceremony of this election, and as the Rig-veda is only concerned with rules for the Hotṛi priests, the Dîkshaṇîyeshṭi is explained first. For although the Ishṭi, or the sacrifice itself, is performed by Adhvaryus, yet the Yâjyâs and Anuvâkyâs belong to the Hotṛi priests. In the Rig-veda we find the Yâjyâs, Puronuvâkyâs, &c.; in the Yajur-veda the Dohanas, Nirvâpas, &c.; in the Sâma-veda the Âjyastotras, Pṛishṭhastotras, &c."—*Sâyaṇa.*

three distinct collections of Brâhmaṇas, but of different Śâkhâs or recensions, which, in the course of time, had branched off from each of them.

It is a characteristic peculiarity of the Sûtras, that they were intended by their authors for more than one Charaṇa, or adapted to more than one Śâkhâ. This is remarked upon by Kumârila, when he says: "All authors of Kalpa-sûtras join with the rules of their own Śâkhâ, the optional commandments of other Śâkhâs, a proceeding approved of by Jaimini."[1] Or again, "Not one of the Sûtrakâras was satisfied with comprehending his own Śâkhâ only."[2] The same is maintained still more strongly by the author of the Hiraṇyakeśi-bhâshya. "No single Śâkhâ," he says, "contains a complete account of the ceremonial, and a reference to other Śâkhâs is absolutely necessary."[3] That this means a reference to other Śâkhâs of the same Veda, and not a reference to other Vedas, may be seen from a passage of Kauśika Râma[4], where he establishes the general principle,

[1] Kumârila, i. 3. स्वशाखाविहितैश्चापि शाखांतरगतान्विधीन्। कल्पकारा निबध्नंति सर्व एव विकल्पितान्॥ सर्वशाखोपसंहारो जैमिनेश्चापि संमतः॥

[2] Kumârila, ii. 4. 2. न च सूत्रकाराणामपि कश्चित् स्वशाखोपसंहारमात्रेणावस्थितः॥

[3] अवश्यं च शाखांतरोपसंहारो ऽपेक्षितः। न ह्येकस्यां शाखायां श्रौतस्मार्तकर्मानुष्ठानं साकल्येन विहितं तन्मंत्रा वा पठिताः किंतु किंचित् क्वचित्॥

[4] शाखासु विकल्पः वेदेषु समुच्चय इति न्यायाद्याजुर्वैदि

that in a Sûtra a quotation from a different Śâkhâ makes a rule optional, whereas a quotation from a different Veda confirms it as generally binding. It was not usual that a common Brahman knew more than one Śâkhâ. He might, if he liked, study each of the three Vedas, but, as Kumârila says: "It is not necessary that one man should read different Śâkhâs, because one Śâkhâ only is comprehended in that study of the sacred texts which every Brahman is bound to pass through. Therefore, if a very clever man should read different Śâkhâs of one Veda, he may do so, but he might as well, if very rich, sacrifice at the same time with rice and barley."[1] But, even if a Brahman had studied the Sanhitâs and Brâhmaṇas of the three Vedas, according to their various Śâkhâs, he would still have found it extremely difficult to learn from them the correct performance of every sacrifice. It was, therefore, in order to

कानामस्माकं छंदोगब्राह्मणस्य वेदांतरत्वादवश्यमुपसंहारः। अतो नित्यः प्रश्नः॥

[1] Kumârila, T. V. ii.; Jaimini Sûtra, ii. 4. 2. शाखांतराध्ययनं तावदेकस्य पुंसो नैवेष्यते। किं कारणं। स्वाध्यायग्रहणेनैका शाखा हि परिगृह्यते॥ ततश्च यो नामातिमेधावित्वादेकवेदे गतानि शाखांतराण्यप्यधीयीत स समृद्धः सन् व्रीहियवैरपि मिश्रैर्यजेत॥ This does not exclude, however, the obligation of reading different Vedas. न त्वेवं वेदांतरस्याध्ययनं न प्रसज्येत न वचनांतरेण प्रतिप्रसववात्। अनया त्रय्या विद्ययेति तथा वेदानधीत्य वेदौ वेति मानवं॥ See also Mitâkshara, p. 17. a. b. एकशाखाध्ययनक्षमो वेदपारगः॥

obviate this difficulty, that the Sûtras were called into existence, as a kind of grammar of the Vedic ceremonial, useful for members of all Charaṇas.

The Kalpa-sûtras for the Hotṛi priests, which were composed by Âśvalâyana, were intended both for the Śâkala- and Bâshkala-śâkhâs[1], and they contain occasional references to other Charaṇas also. Sâyaṇa, in his introduction to the Ṛig-veda (i. p. 34.) says distinctly, that Âśvalâyana teaches the employment of hymns, which do not occur in the Śâkala-śâkhâ. "These," he says, "have been taken from another Śâkhâ, and their employment, therefore, rests on the authority of a different Brâhmaṇa, although the sacrifice itself (karman) must be considered as one and the same for all Śâkhâs, in spite of some differences in its performance (prayoga)."[2]

There is a second, and more ancient, collection of Sûtras for the Hotṛi priests, written by Śânkhâyana. They were intended for members of the Kaushîtaki-śâkhâ, a Śâkhâ of which we still possess the Brâhmaṇa and the Âraṇyaka. The Brâhmaṇa is sometimes quoted under the name of the Śânkhâyana-brâhmaṇa, in the same manner as the Aitareya is sometimes

[1] निवित्प्रैषपुरोरुक्कुंतापवालखिल्यमहानाम्न्यैतरेयब्राह्मण-संहितस्य शाकलस्य बाष्कलस्य चाम्नायद्वयस्यैतदाश्वलायन-शास्त्रं नाम प्रयोगशास्त्रं। Nârâyaṇa Gârgya's Commentary on Âśvalâyana.

[2] Hiraṇyakeśi-bhâshya: सर्वशाखाप्रत्ययमेकं कर्मेति न्यायविदः॥ नास्ति कर्मभेदः। यथा नानाशाखाप्रत्ययमेकं कर्मेति न्यायशास्त्रनिर्णयेऽपि शाखापेक्षितानेव विधीन् न्यायांश्चोपसंहृत्य तत्तच्छाखिनः कर्माभेदेऽपि प्रयोगभेदं रचयंति। नहि शब्दांतरादिभिः प्रमाणैः कर्मभेदोऽस्ति॥

quoted as Âśvalâyana-brâhmaṇa. This Śânkhâyana text of the Kaushîtaki-brâhmaṇa may be more modern than the Aitareya-brâhmaṇa, but the Sûtras of Śânkhâyana are more ancient than the Sûtras of Âśvalâyana.

The Sûtras for the Adhvaryu priests were composed by Kâtyâyana, and adopted by the Kâṇva and Mâdhyandina-Śâkhâs.[1]

The ceremonial of the Udgâtṛi priests who followed the Sâma-veda, was likewise composed by authors who were free from the exclusive influence of one particular Śâkhâ. The Lâṭyâyana-sûtras were not originally the Sûtras of a Lâṭyâyana-śâkhâ, but they were written by Lâṭyâyana, and afterwards adopted by the numerous branches of the Kauthuma-śâkhâ. Another collection of Sûtras, almost identical with the former, was composed by Drâhyâyaṇa, and was adopted by the different Charaṇas of the Râṇâyanîyas.[2] Both Sûtras follow the same authority, the Tâṇḍya-brâhmaṇa, its old as well as its more modern portion, and they quote not only the traditional literature of various Charaṇas, such as the Śâṭyâyanins, Sâlankâyanins, but the works of individuals also, such as Śâṇḍilya, Śâṇḍilyâyana, Dhânanjayya, Kautsa, Kshairakalambhin, two Gautamas, Bhâṇḍitâyana, Râṇâyaniputra, Lâmakâyana, Śauchivṛikshi, &c.[3]

[1] आश्वलायनीयं कात्यायनीयं च सूत्रं हि भिन्नाध्ययनयोर्द्वयोर्द्वयोः शाखयोरेकमेव॥ Mahâdeva's Commentary on the Hiraṇyakeśi-sûtra.

[2] In a MS. of the Drâhyâyaṇa-sûtras, E. I. H. 363. they are called राणायनिशाखीयं द्राह्यायणसूत्रं॥

[3] See Weber, Vorlesungen, p. 74. The Kauthumas seem to be a later Charaṇa than the Râṇâyanîyas. Lâṭyâyana quotes a Râṇâyaniputra; Kauthumas are quoted in the Pushpa-sûtra.

But although the Sûtras were adopted by different Charaṇas existing previous to the composition of the Sûtras, and although the author of a new code of Sûtras might himself become the founder of a new Charaṇa or sect, the text of these short rules seems never to have changed. The text of the Âśvalâyana-sûtras was one and the same for a follower of the old Śâkala, Bâshkala or Aitareyi-śâkhâs. We meet with no authorized *variæ lectiones* as we do in the Brâhmaṇas. As late as the time of Sâyaṇa the various readings of the Brâhmaṇas were known, and he refers to them frequently in his Commentary on the Aitareyi-brâhmaṇa. Nothing of the kind ever occurs in the commentaries on the Sûtras; still less were the Sûtras liable to those more important changes which the Brâhmaṇas underwent, as they became the property of distinct Charaṇas or sects.

It would appear, therefore, that Kumârila's argument, by which he endeavoured to establish a distinction between the Brâhmaṇas and Sûtras[1], is fully confirmed by those traces which can still be discovered by philological criticism. We have only to translate what he calls śruti, or revelation, by "ancient literature handed down by oral tradition," and the distinction between Brâhmaṇas, as śruti, and Sûtras, as smṛiti, holds perfectly good. There is no doubt a distinction to be made between the manner in which the hymns and the Brâhmaṇas, both included under

[1] Kumârila i. 3. 7. अर्थैकत्वेन केषांचिदच्चराणां च साम्यतः। सादृश्याद्ब्राह्मणभ्रांतिर्जातैवमपनीयते॥ "The mistake of supposing the Sûtras to be Brâhmaṇas, which arose from their identity of object and occasional literal coincidences, has thus been removed.

the name of śruti, were preserved. But, in spite of Wolf's maxim, that prose literature marks everywhere the introduction of writing, we must claim for the Brâhmaṇas, as well as for the hymns, a certain period during which they were preserved by means of oral tradition only. Without the admission of an oral tradition, carried on for several generations and in several places by different families and Brahmanic colonies, it would seem impossible to account for the numerous recensions of the same Brâhmaṇa, and for the various readings of each recension. How the changes, the additions, the rearrangements of the original collections of the Brâhmaṇas were effected, we have no means of ascertaining; but we can see, that the Kâṇva and Mâdhyandina recensions of the Śatapatha-brâhmaṇa pre-suppose some point from whence they both started in common. The same applies to the Bahvṛicha-brâhmaṇa in the widely differing recensions of the Aitareyins, the Śânkhâyanins or the Kaushîtakins. There is a common stock in the Brâhmaṇas of each Veda. The same ceremonial is described, the same doubts are raised, similar solutions are proposed, and many chapters are repeated in the same words. Before each recension took its present shape — and few only of these numerous recensions have been preserved to us — they must have rolled from hand to hand, sometimes losing old, sometimes gathering new matter; now broken to pieces, now rearranged, till at last the name of their author became merged in the name of the Charaṇa that preserved his work. No traces of this kind can be discovered in the Sûtras. We probably read them in our MSS. exactly as they were written down at first by Kâtyâyana, Âśvalâyana and others. They are evidently the works of individual writers, the result of careful and systematic research. They presuppose the Sanhitâs and the Śâkhâs of the Sanhitâs; they presuppose the Brâhmaṇas and the Śâkhâs of the Brâhmaṇas. And they also refer to individual writers, whether they had become the founders of Charaṇas, or whether they enjoyed an authority as teachers of law and other subjects connected with the intellectual pursuits of the early Brahmans.

There is, however, one fact that seems to militate against the distinction between the Brâhmaṇas and Sûtras, in so far as it assigns a very early origin, and a traditionary character, to at least some works which were written in Sûtras. At the time of Kâtyâyana, if not at the time of Pâṇini, there existed Sûtras, which were not then considered as the works of modern or at least well-known authors, like Âśvalâyana or Kâtyâyana, but indicated by their very name, that they had formed, for a time, part of the traditional literary property of a Charaṇa, or of some learned school. Their titles are formed on the same principle as the titles of ancient Brâhmaṇas. The affix *in* (ṇini) is added to the names of their reputed authors, and this, as we know, is a mark that their authors were considered as Ṛishis or inspired writers.[1] Their works are not quoted in the singular, like all modern Sûtras (for instance, "this is the ceremonial of Âśmaratha," iti kalpa âśmarathaḥ), but,—and this is a characteristic feature of the ancient traditional literature of India—in the masculine plural, the literary works being supposed

[1] Cf. Pâṇ. iv. 3. 103—110. The Sûtras from 106 are not explained in the Mahâbhâshya according to the Calcutta edition.

to have their only substantial existence in the minds or memories of those persons who read or taught them. We find, for instance, "thus say the Pârâśarins, the Śailâlins, the Karmandins, the Kṛiśâśvins," whereas the work even of Pâṇini himself is quoted as "the Pâṇinîyam," as it were "Panineum," not as "the Pâṇineyins."[1] But although these quotations refer to Sûtras, it ought to be observed that not one of them refers to Kalpa, or ceremonial Sûtras. Where Pâṇini (iv. 3. 105.), or rather his commentator, quotes works on Kalpa in a similar, though not in exactly the same manner, we must bear in mind that expressions like "Paingî kalpaḥ," "the ceremonial taught by the old sage Pinga," "Kauśikî kalpaḥ," "the ceremonial taught by the old sage Kuśika," may refer to portions of the Brâhmaṇas which are called kalpa, ceremonial, in contradistinction to the brâhmaṇa or the purely theological discussions[2]; and it is nowhere said that these old Kalpas were written

[1] Kalpa-sûtras were composed contemporaneously with Pâṇini, and even after his time, as, for instance, the Sûtras of Âśvalâyana and Kâtyâyana, which we still possess, and those of Âśmarathya, which are lost. The last are quoted in the commentary to Pâṇini (iv. 3. 105.), as a modern work on Kalpa; yet Âśvalâyana in his Sûtras, v. 13., refers to Âśmarathya as an authority, whom he follows in opposition to other teachers whose opinion he rejects. Cf. Âśv. Sûtra, v. 13.; Indische Studien, i. 45.

[2] The wording of the Sûtra, "Purâṇaprokteshu brâhmaṇakalpeshu" seems to confirm this interpretation. The Paingins must be considered as a Brâhmaṇa-charaṇa, for there is a Paingyam, the work of a Paingin, quoted in the Kaushîtaki-brâhmaṇa, and in a doubtful passage of the Aitareya-brâhmaṇa. It is difficult to say anything equally positive about the Kauśikî kalpaḥ, an expression which may possibly refer to the Kauśika-sûtras of the Atharva-veda.

in Sûtras. Unless, therefore, a quotation can be brought forward previous to Kâtyâyana, and referring to a collection of Kalpa-sûtras, such quotation calling the Sûtras not by the name of their author, but by the name of a Charaṇa, not in the singular, but in the masculine plural, Kumârila's distinction between Brâhmaṇas and Sûtras remains unshaken, and we are justified in maintaining that the Kalpa-sûtras, in spite of some apparent similarity with the later Brâhmaṇas, belong to a period of literature different in form and character from that which preceded it, and which gave rise to the traditionary literature of the Brâhmaṇas.

The Kalpa-sûtras are important in the history of Vedic literature for more than one reason. They not only mark a new period of literature, and a new purpose in the literary and religious life of India, but they contributed to the gradual extinction of the numerous Brâhmaṇas, which to us are therefore only known by name. The introduction of a Kalpa-sûtra was the introduction of a new book of liturgy. If it was adopted by different Charaṇas, smaller differences in the ceremonial and its allegorical interpretation, which had been kept up by the Brâhmaṇas of each Charaṇa, would gradually be merged in one common ceremonial; or, if they were considered of sufficient importance, a short mention, such as we find here and there in the Sûtras, would suffice, and render the tedious discussions of the Brâhmaṇas on the same points, superfluous. If the Sûtras were once acknowledged as authoritative, they became the most important part of the sacred literature which a Brahman had to study. Those who had to perform the sacrifices might do so without the Veda, simply by means of the Kalpa-sûtras; but no one could learn the ceremonial from the hymns and Brâhmaṇas alone, without the help of the Sûtras.[1] There remained, indeed, the duty of every Brahman to learn his Svâdhyâya, which comprised the hymns and the Brâhmaṇas. But complaints were made, at least at a later time, that the hymns and the Brâhmaṇas were neglected on account of the Sûtras, and one of the reasons why the Hotṛi priests were never allowed to have a prayer-book, such as the hymn-books of the Yajur-veda and Sâma-veda, was the fear that they would then neglect their Svâdhyâya, and learn only those hymns which were enjoined for the sacrifices by the Kalpa-sûtras. We need not wonder, therefore, if, after a short time, the authors of Kalpa-sûtras became themselves the founders of new Charaṇas, in which the Sûtras were considered the most essential portion of the sacred literature; so that the hymns and Brâhmaṇas were either neglected, or kept up under the name of "the hymns and Brâhmaṇas of the new Charaṇa," having ceased to form by themselves the foundation of an independent tradition or school.

In order to make quite clear the influence which the Sûtras exercised on the final constitution of the Vedic Charaṇas we ought to distinguish between three classes of Charaṇas: 1. Those which originated with the texts of Sanhitâs; 2. Those which originated with the texts of Brâhmaṇas; 3. Those which originated with the Sûtras.

[1] वेदादृतेऽपि कुर्वंति कल्पैः कर्माणि याज्ञिकाः। न तु कल्पैर्विना केचिन्मंत्रब्राह्मणमात्रकात्॥ Kumârila.

We need not enter here into the question, whether originally there was but one Veda, and whether this original Veda became afterwards divided into three branches or Śâkhâs, the Rig-veda, Yajur-veda, and Sâma-veda. This is the view adopted by the Brahmans, and they consider these three divisions as the three most ancient Śâkhâs, and their propagators or pravartakas as the three most ancient Charaṇas. This is a natural mistake. It is the same mistake which leads to the assumption of a common literary language previous to the existence of the spoken dialects, whereas in fact the various dialects existed previous to the establishment of the classical language. The first collection of Vedic hymns is that which we have in the Rig-veda, a collection, not made with any reference to the threefold division of the later ceremonial, and therefore not one of three branches, but the original stock, to which the other two, the Yajur-veda and Sâma-veda, were added at a much later period.

The most ancient Śâkhâs and Charaṇas of which we have any knowledge are those which arose from differences in the text of the Ṛig-veda-sanhitâ, such as the Bâshkalas and Śâkalas. We never hear of either Brâhmaṇas or Sûtras peculiar to these śâkhâs, and the natural conclusion, confirmed besides by native authority, is that they diverged and became separated on the strength of various readings and other peculiarities, affecting the texts of their Sanhitâs. There is no evidence as to the existence of similar Sanhitâ-śâkhâs for the Yajur-veda or Sâma-veda. If we take the two śâkhâs of the Yajur-veda-sanhitâ, that of the Kâṇvas and that of the Mâdhyandinas, both presuppose the existence of a Vâjasaneyi-sanhitâ, and this Vâjasaneyi-sanhitâ would have been perfectly useless without a Brâhmaṇa. It was not the Sanhitâ, but the Brâhmaṇa of the Vâjasaneyins, handed down as it was in various texts, which gave rise to the fifteen Charaṇas of the Vâjasaneyins, and among them to the Kâṇva and Mâdhyandina-charaṇas. Their Sanhitâs were of secondary importance, and, startling as such an opinion might sound to an orthodox Brahman, were probably not put together till after the composition of the Vâjasaneyi-brâhmaṇa in its original and primitive form. The peculiar differences in the text of the Mantras of the Kâṇvas and Mâdhyandinas depend on the differences occurring in their respective Brâhmaṇas, and not *vice-versâ*. On the same ground we must doubt the existence of ancient Sanhitâ-śâkhâs for the Sâma-veda.

The next step which led to the formation of Charaṇas was the adoption of a Brâhmaṇa, and we therefore call this second class the Brâhmaṇa-charaṇas. When the growth of a more complicated ceremonial led to the establishment of three or four classes of priests, each performing peculiar duties, and requiring a special training for their sacerdotal office, there must have been a floating stock of Brâhmaṇas, *dicta theologica*, peculiar to each class of priests. They treated of the general arrangement of the sacrifice. They handed down the authoritative opinions of famous sages: they gave the objections raised against such opinions by other persons: and gradually they clothed these contradictory statements in the form of a logical argument. Occasionally an allegorical interpretation was given of the meaning of certain rites, the simple and natural import of which had been forgotten. Rewards were vouchsafed to the pious worshipper, and instances were recorded of such rewards having been obtained by the faithful of former ages. All these sayings and discussions were afterwards collected as three distinct Brâhmaṇas, belonging to the three classes of priests. We still meet with the general names of Bahvṛicha-brâhmaṇas for the Rig-veda, of Adhvaryu-brâhmaṇas for the Yajur-veda, and of Chhandoga-brâhmaṇas for the Sâma-veda, without any further reference to particular Charaṇas by which these Brâhmaṇas were collected or adopted. But those Brâhmaṇas are no longer met with in their original form. They have come down to us, without exception, as the Brâhmaṇas of certain Charaṇas of each Veda. Instead of one Bahvṛicha-brâhmaṇa of the Rig-veda, we only find the Bahvṛicha-brâhmaṇa of the Aitareyins, or the Kaushîtakins, or the Śânkhâyanins. Instead of one Chhandoga-brâhmaṇa or Chhândogyam, we have the Chhandoga-brâhmaṇa of the Tâṇḍins or the Tâṇḍya, and we find quotations from other Charaṇas, such as the Śâṭyâyanins[1] or the Kauthumas.

[1] In one of the most interesting Brâhmaṇas of the Chhandogas, the Sâmavidhâna-brâhmaṇa, we see how the two last, in a series of teachers, became the founders of a Charaṇa, by teaching this Brâhmaṇa, which had been handed down to them through a succession of nine or at least six masters, to a multitude of followers. अथास्य सामविधानस्य संप्रदायप्रवर्तकानाचार्याननुक्रमेण संकीर्तयति। सोऽयं प्राजापत्यो विधिः। तमिमं प्रजापतिर्बृहस्पतये प्रोवाच। बृहस्पतिर्नारदाय। नारदो विष्वक्सेनाय। विष्वक्सेनो व्यासाय पाराशर्याय। व्यासः पाराशर्यो जैमिनये। जैमिनिः पौष्पिंड्याय। पौष्पिंड्यः पाराशर्यायणाय। पाराशर्यायणो बादरायणाय। बादरायणस्तांडिशाट्याय-

Instead of one Adhvaryu-brâhmaṇa, we have the dark code of the old Charakas, or the Taittirîyas and the Kaṭhas, and the new Brâhmaṇa of the Vâjasaneyins, and their descendants, the Kâṇvas and Mâdhyandinas. We nowhere find the original collection from which the various recensions might be supposed to have branched off and deviated in time. In most cases, where we possess the texts of a Brâhmaṇa, preserved by different Śâkhâs, the variations are but small, and they point clearly to one and the same original from which they descended. Sometimes, however, the variations are of a different kind, so much so that we are inclined to admit several independent collections of that floating stock of Brahmanic lore, which went on accumulating in different places and through various generations. If we compare the Brâhmaṇas of the Aitareyins and the Kaushîtakins, we find their wording, even where they treat of the same matters, very different. The order in which the sacrifices are described is not always the same, nor are the ceremonial rules always identical. Illustrations and legends are interspersed in the Brâhmaṇa of the Kaushîtakins of which no trace can be found in the Brâhmaṇa of the Aitareyins. And yet, with all these differences, the literal coincidence of whole chapters, the frequent occurrence of the same sentences, the same comparisons and illustrations, render it impossible to ascribe to each of these Brâhmaṇas a perfectly independent origin. The two Brâhmaṇas of the Kâṇvas and Mâdhyandinas, in spite of their differences, in spite of

निभ्यां। तांडिभ्राव्यायनिनौ बह्वृभ्यः॥ On the Śâṭyâyanins and their relation to the Sâma-veda, see Indische Studien, i. 49.

additions and omissions that have been pointed out in either, compel us to admit that they had a common starting-point. To judge from frequent quotations, the number of Brâhmaṇas, differing from each other more or less considerably, and the number of Charaṇas founded on these Brâhmaṇas, must have been very large. We can easily imagine how this happened. The name of a famous teacher, who gathered a number of students around himself in a village, or who lived under the protection of some small Râja, was preserved by his pupils for generations. The sacred literature which he was, perhaps, the first to teach in a newly-founded colony, was afterwards handed down under the sanction of his name, though differing but slightly from the traditional texts kept up in the community from which he himself had started. He might, perhaps, add a few chapters of his own composition, a change quite sufficient, in the eyes of the Brahmans to constitute a new work, or at least to disqualify it for claiming any longer its original title. When these new Charaṇas had once been founded, it was but natural, though they originated chiefly with a Brâhmaṇa of their own, that the text of their Sanhitâs also should be slightly modified. This was not the case necessarily. The Aitareyins, for instance, and the Kaushîtakins, though they differed in their Brâhmaṇas, preserved, as far as we know, the same śâkhâ of the Sanhitâ, and preserved it each with the same minute accuracy. No Sanhitâ peculiar to the Kaushîtakins and Aitareyins is ever mentioned, and the points on which they differed were, from the very first, connected with the subject matter of the Brâhmaṇas. Students following different śâkhâs, as far as their Brâhmaṇa was concerned, might very well follow one and the same Śâkhâ of the Sanhitâ, though they would no longer call it by its own original name. In most cases, however, and particularly in the Charaṇas of the Yajur-veda, a difference in the Brâhmaṇas would necessitate, or, at least, naturally lead to, corresponding differences in the Sanhitâ, such as we find, for instance, in the hymns of the Kâṇvas and Mâdhyandinas.[1]

These Brâhmaṇa-charaṇas existed previous to the first composition of the Sûtras, and in the Sûtras belonging to the Sâma-veda, which are the earliest Sûtras we possess, they are quoted. No Sûtra is ever quoted in any of the Brâhmaṇas, but there is no collection of Sûtras in which the various Śâkhâs of the Brâhmaṇas are not referred to by name. The authorities quoted in the Sûtras on doubtful points of the Vedic ceremonial, are invariably taken from the Brâhmaṇa-charaṇas. In the commentary on Pâṇini, such names as "the Aitareyins, the Śâṭyâyanins, and Bhâllavins" are distinctly explained as supporters of ancient Brâhmaṇas; and the antiquity of the two last is still further confirmed by the fact of their being quoted as Brahmanic authorities in the Śatapatha-brâhmaṇa.[2]

The third and most modern class of Charaṇas consists of those which derive their origin from the introduction of a new body of Sûtras, such as the Âśvalâyanîyas, the Kâtyâyanîyas, and many of the subdivisions of the Taittirîyas. It is not always possible to determine with certainty whether a Charaṇa dates

[1] The differences of these schools may be seen in Weber's edition of the Yajur-veda at the end of each Adhyâya.

[2] See Weber's Indische Studien, ii. 44.

from the Brâhmaṇa period, or from the Sûtra period, because so many of the Brâhmaṇas and Sûtras have been lost, and some of the Brâhmaṇas have been handed down to us under the names of more modern Sûtra-charaṇas, by which they were adopted. It is easy to determine that the Kaushîtakins date from the Brâhmaṇa period, because there is neither a Kaushîtaki-sûtra nor a Kaushîtaki-sanhitâ, but only a Kaushîtaki-brâhmaṇa; but in other instances our knowledge of the ancient literature of India is too fragmentary to enable us to fix the age of the numerous Charaṇas which are quoted by later authorities. Some of the Sûtras again, as we saw before, are older than others, and seem almost to trespass on the frontiers of the Brâhmaṇa period. How are we to determine, for instance, whether the Śânkhâyanas were originally a Brâhmaṇa-charaṇa, and had their Sûtras written by one of their own sect, or whether the foundation of their Charaṇa rested on the text of the Sûtras [1], a new text of the original Brâhmaṇa of the Bahvṛichas being adopted by them in later times, and thenceforth quoted as the Śânkhâyana-brâhmaṇa? In some instances the relative age of certain Sûtras has been preserved by the tradition of the schools. Thus the most ancient Sûtra of the Taittirîyas is said to have been that of Baudhâyana, who was succeeded by Bhâradvâja, Âpastamba, Satyâshâḍha Hiraṇyakeśin, Vadhûna, and Vaikhânasa; all of whom, with the exception of the two last, have lent their names to different Charaṇas of the dark Yajur-veda.

[1] It should be observed, that in some MSS. of the Charaṇavyûha the two Charaṇas, which belong most likely to the Sautra period, those of Âśvalâyana and Śânkhâyana, are not mentioned.

Although none of the Sûtras seem to have been written with the distinct purpose of founding a new Charaṇa, it can easily be imagined how different communities, after adopting a collection of Sûtras as the highest authority for their ceremonial, became inclined to waive minor points of difference in the Sanhitâs and Brâhmaṇas, and thus coalesced into a new Charaṇa under the name and sanction of their Sûtrakâra. After these new Sautra-charaṇas had once been started, we find that the Sanhitâs and Brâhmaṇas, current among their members, were designated by the name of the new Charaṇas. Thus we may explain the title of Âśvalâyana-brâhmaṇa given to the Aitareya-brâhmaṇa in one of the MSS. of the Bodleian Library[1]; and we shall not hesitate to ascribe the same meaning to an Âśvalâyana-brâhmaṇa, said to be quoted by Yâjnikadeva in his commentary on Kâtyâyana.[2] Why such a Brâhmaṇa should not be quoted by early writers, such as the authors of Sûtras, is easily understood. Its title was necessarily of late origin, and it is important as marking the progressive changes in the nomenclature of Indian literature. We have a similar and still better authenticated instance in the so-called Âpastamba-brâhmaṇa, which is but a different title of the Taittirîya-brâhmaṇa, as adopted by the followers of the Âpastamba-sûtras. It is in this manner that the Sûtras may be said to have contributed partly to the formation of new Charaṇas, some of which are not mentioned in the ancient lists, as, for instance, the Kâtyâyanîyas; partly to the extinction

[1] MS. Wilson, 473. The title is आस्वलाएनक ब्राह्मण (sic); it contains the fifth Book of the Aitareya-brâhmaṇa.

[2] Kâtyâyana, ii. 5. 18.; vi. 6. 5. Indische Studien, i. 230.

of the more ancient Brâhmaṇa-charaṇas and Sanhitâ-charaṇas, many of which are now known to us by name only.

That the introduction of the Sûtras and the foundation of Sûtra-charaṇas was felt as an innovation by the Brahmans themselves, we perceive from the manner in which even modern writers speak of them; half objecting to their authority, yet glad to admit and even to defend what could no longer be prevented. The Sûtras were not, indeed, admitted as part of the Śruti, yet they were made part of the Svâdhyâya, and had to be learned by heart by the young student. They might, therefore, like the Sanhitâs and Brâhmaṇas, claim a kind of sacred character, and in time become the charter of a new Charaṇa. Thus we read in Mahâdeva's Commentary on the Hiraṇyakeśi-sûtras[1]: "The Kalpa-sûtra is sometimes different for different Śâkhâs, sometimes it is not. The difference of the Śâkhâs arises partly from a difference of the sacred texts (*adhyayana* being used in the sense of *svâdhyâya*, perhaps with reference to the peculiar pronunciation taught in the Prâtiśâkhyas), partly from a difference in the Sûtras. The Sûtras of Âśvalâyana and Kâtyâyana, for instance, are the same for

[1] तत्र कल्पसूत्रं प्रतिशाखं भिन्नमभिन्नमपि क्वचित् शाखाभेदेऽध्ययनभेदाद्वा सूत्रभेदाद्वा। आश्वलायनीयं कात्यायनीयं च सूत्रं हि भिन्नाध्ययनयोर्द्वयोर्द्वयोः शाखयोरेकैकमेव। तैत्तिरीयके च समाम्नाये समानाध्ययने नाना सूत्राणि। अनेन च सूत्रभेदे शाखाभेदः शाखाभेदे च सूत्रभेद इति परस्पराश्रय इति वाच्यं॥

two Śâkhâs whose respective texts are different, while in the Taittirîya-veda we find Śâkhâs with different Sûtras, but no differences in their sacred texts. Hence it may be said[1], that sometimes, where there is a difference in the Sûtras, there is also a difference of Śâkhâ; and, on the other hand, where there is a difference of Śâkhâ, there may be a difference in the Sûtras." Mahâdeva goes even further, and tries to show that, like all the revealed literature of the Brahmans, the Sûtras also existed previous to the beginning of time and had no historical origin.[2] "As the various Śâkhâs," he says, "which arise from various readings of the sacred texts are without a beginning, or eternal, so are also the various Śâkhâs which arise from different Sûtras. For the titles of certain Sûtras, derived from their authors, are not modern; but being eternal, as inherent in individual Ṛishis, whose names occur in certain Kalpas or ceremonials, and retaining the same character when applied to the Sûtras, which have been promulgated by the Ṛishis, they hold good as titles for

[1] Afterwards he says again: तथा चैकस्यां तैत्तिरीयशाखायां समानपाठायां सूत्रभेदादवांतरशाखाभेदश्चरणव्यूहशास्त्रे दर्शितः॥ "It has been shown in the Charaṇavyûha, that in the Taittirîya-śâkhâ, where there is but one and the same sacred text, subordinate Śâkhâs arise from different Sûtras."

[2] यथाध्ययनभेदाच्छाखाभेदोऽनादिरेवं सूत्रभेदादपि। न हि सूत्राणां कर्तृसंबंधिसंज्ञाद्यतनी किंतु नानाकल्पगतासु तत्तन्नामकर्षिव्यक्तिषु नित्या तत्प्रणीतसूत्रेषु च नित्यां जातिमवलंब्य तिष्ठति यथा पुरुषनामांकितशाखासु संज्ञा॥ "Nânâkalpa-gatâsu" cannot refer to the chronological Kalpas, because these are after the beginning of time.

Śâkhâs, which apparently are marked by the names of men."[1] We may now understand in what sense the same Mahâdeva gives to the word Charaṇa the meaning both of Śâkhâ and Sûtra. "It is true," he says, "that śâkhâ means a part of the sacred tradition, consisting of Mantras and Brâhmaṇas, and that the subordinate śâkhâs of the Veda owe their origin to the differences of either Mantras or Brâhmaṇas. Nevertheless, as Veda means the sacred tradition, together with the Angas or subsidiary doctrines, a śâkhâ may include the Angas and yet remain Veda, and as such become different from other śâkhâs, owing to a difference in the Angas. If, therefore, the Sûtra, which is an Anga, differs, there will be difference in the sacred tradition; and thus a difference in the Sûtras may well become the cause of a different name of a Śâkhâ."[2]

The following list, though far from being complete, contains some of the Kalpa-sûtras which are best known to us either from MSS. or otherwise: —

[1] Cf. p. 97, n.

[2] चरणव्यूहः। चरणाः शाखाः सूत्राणि च। व्यूहो वि-विच्य भेदः। न चात्राध्ययनभेदोऽस्ति तस्मात्सूत्रभेदादेव शाखाभेदः॥ ननु स्वाध्यायैकदेशो मंत्रब्राह्मणात्मकः शाखेत्युच्यते। तयोर्मंत्रब्राह्मणयोरन्यतरभेदेन वेदेऽवांतरशाखाभेदः स्यादिति चेत्। सत्यं। यथा सांगः स्वाध्यायो वेदशब्दवाच्य एवं शाखापि सांगैव वेदैकत्वेन शाखांतरत्वं लभते। तत्रांगस्य सूत्रस्य भेदाद्भिद्यत एव स्वाध्यायाध्ययनमिति भवतु चरणभेद एव शाखाभेदव्यवहारे हेतुः। तथा च यथा शाखाध्ययनं नियतं तथा सूत्राध्ययनमपि॥

I. Yajur-veda.

A. *Old, or Dark Text.*

1. Âpastamba, text and commentary existing.
2. Baudhâyana, text and commentary existing.
3. Satyâshâḍha Hiraṇyakeśin, text and commentary existing.
4. Mânava-sûtra, large fragments of text existing.
5. Bhâradvâja-sûtra, quoted.
6. Vâdhûna-sûtra, quoted.
7. Vaikhânasa-sûtra, quoted.
8. Laugâkshi-sûtra, quoted.
9. Maitra-sûtra, quoted.
10. Kaṭha-sûtra, quoted.
11. Vârâha-sûtra, quoted.

B. *New, or Bright Text.*

1. Kâtyâyana, text and commentary existing.

II. Sâma-veda.

1. Maśaka's Ârsheya-kalpa, text and commentary existing.
2. Lâṭyâyana-sûtra (Kauthuma), ditto.
3. Drâhyâyaṇa-sûtra (Râṇâyanîya), ditto.

III. Rig-veda.

1. Âśvalâyana-sûtra, text and commentary existing.
2. Śânkhâyana-sûtra, ditto.
3. Śaunaka-sûtra, quoted.

IV. Atharva-veda.

1. Kuśika-sûtra, text existing.

Two other classes of Sûtras have already been mentioned as belonging to the same branch of literature with the Śrauta-sûtras, viz. the Gṛihya, and Sâmayâchârika-sûtras. Both are included under the common title of Smârta-sûtras, in contradistinction to the Śrauta-sûtras; the latter deriving their authority from the Śruti (the Mantras and Brâhmaṇas), the former from Smṛiti, or immemorial tradition. The Gṛihya and Sâmayâchârika-sûtras have frequently been confounded by European scholars; but the Brahmans distinguish strictly between the Gṛihya ceremonies, performed by the married householder, chiefly for the benefit of his family, and the Sâmayâchârika rules, which are to be observed by the rising generation, and which regulate the various relations of every-day life. It is chiefly in the Sâmayâchârika, or, as they are sometimes called, Dharma-sûtras, that we have to look for the originals of the later metrical law-books, such as Manu, Yâjnavalkya, and the rest; and the statement of Megasthenes, that the Hindus at his time administered law from memory (*ἀπὸ μνήμης*)[1] can only refer to the Smârta-sûtras of the Charaṇas, and not to the modern Smṛiti-sanhitâs of Manu, Yâjnavalkya, Parâśara, &c.

[1] Strabo, xv. 1. 53, seq., quotes Megasthenes: *Γενομένους δ' οὖν ἐν τῷ Σανδροκύττου στρατοπέδῳ, φησὶν ὁ Μεγασθένης, τετταράκοντα μυριάδων πλήθους ἱδρυμένου, μηδεμίαν ἡμέραν ἰδεῖν ἀνηνεγμένα κλέμματα πλειόνων ἢ διακοσίων δραχμῶν ἄξια, ἀγράφοις καὶ ταῦτα νόμοις χρωμένοις. Οὐδὲ γὰρ γράμματα εἰδέναι αὐτούς, ἀλλ' ἀπὸ μνήμης ἕκαστα διοικεῖσθαι.* Schwanbeck suggests that only the last words *ἀπὸ μνήμης ἕκαστα διοικεῖσθαι* contain the truth, *μνήμη* being a vague interpretation of smṛiti, memory or tradition; and that the first part was a wrong conclusion of the Greeks. The question whether the Hindus possessed a knowledge of the art of writing during the Sûtra period, will have to be discussed hereafter.

The Gṛihya-sûtras, belonging to the old Yajur-veda, are numerous. Quotations have been met with from Baudhâyana, Bhâradvâja, Hiraṇyakesin, the Kâṭhaka[1], and the Maitrâyaṇîyas[2], all names connected with the Taittirîya-veda, and proving the existence of distinct collections of Gṛihya-sûtras. The number of similar Sûtras for the bright Yajur-veda seems to have been still more considerable. Every one of the fifteen Charaṇas of the Vâjasaneyins is said to have been possessed of Kula-dharmas, which may have been either Gṛihya or Dharma-sûtras.[3] The only collection, however, which has come down to us, is that of Pâraskara.[4] Another, ascribed to Vaijavâpin, is quoted, but has not yet been discovered in manuscript. Connected with the Sâma-veda, the Gṛihya-sûtras of Gobhila, adopted both by the Râṇâyanîyas and the Kauthumas, seem to have obtained the greatest celebrity, there being but one other collection, the Khâdira-gṛihya, which is sometimes quoted as a parallel authority of the Chhandogas.[5] The Gṛihya-sûtras of the Rig-veda or the Bahvṛichas were written by Śaunaka, and he is quoted as an authority on legal subjects by as late a writer as the author of the Mânava-dharma-śâstra (iii. 16.) The only two collections, however, which have been preserved in MS. are those of Âśvalâyana and Śânkhâyana.

[1] See Stenzler "On Indian Law Books," Ind. Stud. i. 232, and iii. 159.

[2] Weber, Vorlesungen, p. 97.

[3] See p. 121, n. 1.

[4] In a MS. (Wilson, 451.) Pâraskara's Gṛihya-sûtras are ascribed to the Mâdhyandinî-śâkhâ.

[5] See Âśâditya in his "Commentary on the Karma-pradîpa," Ind. Stud. i. 58. This Karma-pradîpa, a work ascribed to Kâtyâyana, is intended as a supplement to Gobhila.

Various opinions are expressed by the Brahmans themselves as to the meaning of gṛihya. Gṛiha, according to the commentary on Âśvalâyana, signifies not only *house*, but also *wife*. In support of the latter meaning he quotes a passage, *sagṛiho gṛiham âgataḥ*, "he is gone to the house with his wife." According to this derivation the gṛihya ceremonies would be those which are performed with the sacred fire, first lighted by a husband on the day of his marriage. This fire, or the altar on which it is kept, is called gṛihya, and the gṛihya sacrifices are all performed on that altar. But it is doubtful whether gṛiha can ever mean wife. In the passage quoted above, it rather means house or family. Besides, as the Hindus themselves admit, this domestic fire has sometimes to be lighted by a Brahman[1] before his marriage, in case his father should die prematurely.[2] Gṛihya, therefore, probably meant originally the house or the family-hearth, from gṛiha, house; and it was in opposition to the great sacrifices for which several hearths were required, and which were therefore called *vaitânika*[3], that the domestic ceremonies were

[1] भार्यादिरग्निर्दायादिर्वा तस्मिन्गृह्याणीति गौतमः। This is taken from Gautama, v. 1.

[2] A Brahmachârin who has not yet finished his religious education, possesses no sacred fires of his own, and if he is obliged to perform ceremonies with burnt-offerings, he must do so with common fire and without sacred vessels. Thus the Kâtyâyana-sûtra-paddhati says: गवेधुकचरुरवकीर्णिपशुश्च लौकिकेऽग्नौ भवति। तत्रावकीर्णिपशौ पुरोडाशश्रपणं भूमौ भवति न कपालेषु॥

[3] वितानोऽग्नीनां विस्तारः। तत्र भवानि वैतानिकानि

called *gṛihya*, as performed by means of the one domestic fire. It should be stated, however, in favour of the former interpretation, that in Gobhila's Sûtra these domestic ceremonies are not called gṛihya, but gṛihyâ-karmâṇi, and that here also the commentator admits gṛihyâ in the sense of housewife or tradition.[1]

The general name of the sacrifices performed, according to the Gṛihya-sûtras, is Pâkayajna, where *pâka* is not to be taken in the sense of cooking, but signifies, according to Indian authorities, either *small* or *good*. That *pâka* is used in the first sense appears from such expressions as "ŷo'smatpâkataraḥ," "he who is smaller than we." But the more likely meaning is *good* or *excellent* or *perfect;* because, as the commentators remark, these ceremonies impart to every man that peculiar fitness without which he would be excluded from the sacrifices, and from all the benefits of his religion. As it is necessary that the marriage ceremonies should be rightly performed, that the choice of the bride should be made according to sacred rules, prescribed in the Sûtras or established by independent tradition in various families and localities, the first ceremony described in

बह्वग्निसाध्यानि कर्माणीत्यर्थः॥ Nârâyaṇa on Âśv. Gṛihya-sûtra. The three fires are the Gârhapatya, Âhavanîya, and Dakshiṇa; the one fire is the Avasathya or Gṛihya.

[1] अथातो गृह्याकर्माण्युपदेक्ष्यामः॥१॥ गृह्यशब्देन स्मार्ताग्निरुच्यते। तस्मिन्यानि कर्माणि तानि गृह्याकर्माणि। दीर्घत्वं छांदसं॥ अथवा गृह्या स्मृतिः। तस्यां यानि कर्माणि॥ अथवा गृह्या पत्नी। तया सहितस्य यानि कर्माणि॥

the Gṛihya-sûtras is Marriage. Then follow the Sanskâras, the rites to be performed at the conception of a child, at various periods before his birth, at the time of his birth, the ceremony of naming the child, of carrying him out to see the sun, of feeding him, of cutting his hair, and lastly of investing him as a student, and handing him to a Guru, under whose care he is to study the sacred writings, that is to say, to learn them by heart, and to perform all the offices of a Brahmachârin, or religious student. It is only after he has served his apprenticeship and grown up to manhood, that he is allowed to marry, to light the sacrificial fire for himself, to choose his priests, and to perform year after year the solemn sacrifices, prescribed by the Śruti and the Smṛiti. The latter are described in the later books of the Gṛihya-sûtras, and the last book contains a full account of the funeral ceremonies and of the sacrifices offered to the spirits of the departed.

There is certainly more of human interest in these domestic rites than in the great sacrifices described in the Śrauta-sûtras. The offerings themselves are generally of a simple nature, and the ceremonial is such that it does not require the assistance of a large class of professional priests. A log of wood placed on the fire of the hearth, an oblation poured out to the gods, or alms given to the Brahmans, this is what constitutes a pâka-yajna. Âśvalâyana quotes several passages from the Veda, in order to show that the gods do not despise those simple offerings, nay, that a mere prayer will secure their favour, and that a hymn of praise is as good as bulls and cows. He quotes from Rv. viii. 19. 5. and 6.: "The mortal who sacrifices to Agni with a log of wood, with an oblation, with a bundle of grass[1], with a reverence, careful in his performance, his horses will press on quickly, his fame will be the brightest; nowhere will mischief, whether wrought by the gods or wrought by men, reach him." Another verse is quoted from Rv. viii. 24. 20., where men are called upon "to speak a mighty speech which is sweeter to Indra than milk (ghṛita, ghee) and honey." And lastly, reference is made to a passage (Rv. vi. 16. 47.) where the poet says: "With this hymn of praise, O Agni, we bring thee a sacrifice that is fashioned by the heart; may these be thy bulls, thy oxen, and thy cows." All these passages are more applicable to the Gṛihya than to the Śrauta ceremonies, and though the latter may seem of greater importance to the Brahmans, to us the former will be more deeply interesting, as disclosing that deep-rooted tendency in the heart of man to bring the chief events of human life in connection with a higher power, and to give to our joys and sufferings a deeper significance and a religious sanctification.[2]

[1] The Commentator explains *veda* as the sacred code. Such a code was not known to the authors of the hymns. On the meaning of *veda*, see page 27. note 1.

[2] In addition to a list of literary names quoted in the Gṛihya-sûtras of Âśvalâyana (see p. 42), I subjoin a larger list of a similar character from the Śânkhâyana-gṛihya-sûtras, of which a copy exists at Berlin. (Weber, "Catalogue of Sanskrit MSS." p. 33.) Sumantuḥ, Jaimini - Vaiśampâyana - Pailasûtrabhâshya - Gârgya-Babhru-Bâbhravya-Maṇḍu-Mâṇḍavyâḥ, Gârgî Vâchaknavî, Vaḍavâ Prâtitheyî, Sulabhâ Maitreyî; Kaholam, Kaushîtakim, Mahâkaushîtakim, Suyajnam, Śânkhâyanam, Âśvalâyanam, Aitareyam, Mahaitareyam, Bhâradvâjam, Jâtûkarṇyam, Paingyam, Mahâpaingyam, Bâshkalam, Gârgyam, Śâkalyam, Mâṇḍûkeyam, Mahâdamatram, Audavâhim, Mahaudavâhim, Sauyâmim, Śau-

The third class of the Sûtras, the Sâmayâchârika or Dharma-sûtras, are equally interesting on account of the light which they throw on the every-day life of the early Brahmans. According to the commentaries on these works, the existence of the Dharma-sûtras is presupposed by the Śrauta and Gṛihya-sûtras. It is said, for instance, in the former, that a certain act of the sacrifice is to be performed by a man, after he has adjusted his sacrificial cord (yajnopavîtin): but in what peculiar manner a man ought to adjust that cord is not stated, but is supposed to be known from the Dharma-sûtras. The same remark is made with reference to the exact manner of rinsing the mouth (âchânta), and of performing the morning and evening prayers (sandhyâvandana). These matters are spoken of as generally known from the Sûtras, and, according to Hindu commentators, they could only be known from the Dharma-sûtras. This argument, however, can hardly be considered conclusive as to the historical priority of the Dharma-sûtras. On the contrary, it seems more likely that these matters, such as adjusting the sacrificial cord, &c., were supposed to be so well known at the time when the Śrauta and Gṛihya-sûtras were first composed, that they required no elucidation. Instead, therefore, of considering the Dharma-sûtras as earlier in time, the evidence, as far as it is known at present, would rather point in the opposite direction, and make us look upon these Dharma-sûtras as the latest of the three branches of Sûtras. This impression is confirmed by other reflections. In neither of the other Sûtras is the position of the Śûdra so definitely

nakim, Gautamim, Śâkapûṇim, ye chânya âchâryâs, te sarve tṛipyantv iti. See also Karmapradîpa, MS. W. 465. p. 16. b.

marked as in the Dharma-sûtras. Âpastamba, in his Sâmayâchârika-sûtras, declares distinctly that there are four Varṇas, the Brâhmaṇa, the Kshatriya, the Vaiśya, the Śûdra, but that the initiatory rites, the Upanayana in particular, are only intended for the three first classes. The same is implied, no doubt, in the other Sûtras, which give the rules as to the proper time when a young Brahman, a young Kshatriya, or a young Vaiśya should be apprenticed with their spiritual tutors, but never say at what age this or similar ceremonies should be performed for one not belonging to these three Varṇas. Yet they never exclude the Śûdra expressly[1], nor do they represent him as the born slave or client of the other castes. In the Dharma-sûtras the social degradation of the Śûdra is as great as in the later Law-books, and the same crime, if committed by a Brahman and a Śûdra, is visited with very different punishments. Thus, if a member of the three Varṇas commits adultery with the wife of a Śûdra, he is to be banished; if a Śûdra commits adultery with the wife of a member of the three Varṇas, he is to be executed.[2] If a Śûdra

[1] Âpast. i. 6. अशूद्राणामदुष्टकर्मणामुपायनं वेदाध्ययनमग्न्याधेयं फलवंति च कर्माणि। शुश्रूषा शूद्रस्येतरेषां वर्णानां॥ In later works, such as the Sanṣkâra-gaṇapati, this Sûtra of Âpastamba, which excludes the Śûdras from initiation, has been so altered as to admit them. MS. E. I. H. 912, p. 16. अथ शूद्राणामुपनयनं। आपस्तंबः। शूद्राणामदुष्टकर्मणामुपनयनं। मद्यपानरहितानामिति कल्पतरुकरः॥

[2] MS. p. 163. b. नाश्य आर्यः शूद्रायां वध्यः शूद्र आर्यायां। (नाश्यो निर्वास्यः).

abuses an honest member of the three Varṇas, his tongue is to be cut out.[1] He is to be flogged for not keeping at a respectful distance. For murder, theft, and pillage the Śûdra is executed; the Brahman, if caught in the same offences, is only deprived of his eye-sight. This is the same iniquitous law, which we find in the later Law-books. But although the distinction between the Śûdras and the other Varṇas is so sharply drawn by Âpastamba, he admits that a Śûdra, if he obeys the law, may be born again as a Vaiśya, the Vaiśya as a Kshatriya, and the Kshatriya as a Brahman[2]; and that a Brahman, if he disregards the law, will be born again as a Kshatriya, the Kshatriya as a Vaiśya, and the Vaiśya as a Śûdra.

It might be supposed that the Dharma-sûtras formed merely an appendix to the Śrauta and Gṛihya-sûtras, and that they should be classed with the Pariśishṭa literature. But such a supposition is contradicted by the fact, that the Dharma-sûtras occasionally treat of the same subjects as the Gṛihya-sûtras, and employ almost the same words in explaining some of the initiatory rites, the Sanskâras. They must, therefore, be considered as independent collections of Sûtras, later perhaps than the Śrauta and

[1] MS. p. 164b. जिह्वाछेदनं शूद्रस्यार्यं धार्मिकमाक्रोशतो। वाचि पथि शय्यायामासन इति समीभवतो दंडताडनं॥ पुरुषवधे स्तेये भूम्यादान इति स्वान्यादाय वध्यश्चक्षुर्निरोधस्त्वेतेषु ब्राह्मणस्य॥

[2] MS. p. 125b. धर्मचर्यया जघन्यो वर्णः पूर्वंपूर्वं वर्णमापद्येत जातिपरिवृत्तौ अधर्मचर्यया पूर्वो वर्णो जघन्यं जघन्यं वर्णमापद्येत जातिपरिवृत्तौ॥

Gṛihya-sûtras, but enjoying the same authority on matters belonging to Smṛiti or tradition, as the Gṛihya-sûtras.

We have still to mention the Ten Sûtras of the Sâma-veda.[1] These Sûtras[2] do not all, strictly speaking, treat of the Kalpa, or the ceremonial. Some of them are little more than lists, such as we find in the Anukramaṇîs or Indices, appended to the other Vedas. Their style, however, approaches the style of the Sûtras; and, as they are quoted together as the Ten Sûtras, and as some of them belong decidedly to the earliest productions of the Sûtra literature, it will be more convenient to place them here, than to refer them to the Pariśishṭa literature, with which they have little or nothing in common. They are:

I. The Kalpa-sûtra, or Ârsheya-kalpa of Maśaka, an index of the hymns used by the Chhandoga priests, in the order in which the sacrifices are described in the Tâṇḍya-brâhmaṇa. Eleven Prapâṭhakas: 1—5, on the sacrifices called *Ekâha;* 6—9, on the sacri-

[1] The most important among them were first noticed and described by Dr. Weber, on whose authority some of our statements must rest.

[2] MS. Chamb. 100. लाट्यायनमनुपदं निदानं कल्पमेव च। उपग्रंथाश्च क्षुद्राश्च तंडालक्षणमेव च॥ सूत्रं पंचविधेयं च कल्पानुपदमेव च। अनुस्तोत्रं च विज्ञेयं दशसूत्रप्रकीर्त्तनं॥ Varadarâja, in his Commentary on Kâtyâyana's Pratihâra (MS. Bodl. W. 394.). वीक्ष्य ब्राह्मणसूत्रोपग्रंथनिदानतद्व्याख्याः। and again: इह खलु उपग्रंथकल्पब्राह्मणप्रोक्तानां ज्योतिष्टोमादिविश्वसृजामयनपर्यंतानामेकाहीनसत्राणां॥

fices called *Ahîna* ; 10—12, on the sacrifices called *Sattra*. Commentary by Varadarâja.

II. The Anupada-sûtra, a gloss to the Tâṇḍya-brâhmaṇa, in ten Prapâṭhakas.

III. The Kalpa-sûtra, already mentioned, either of Lâṭyâyana or Drâhyâyaṇa. Lâṭyâyana quotes Maśaka, and follows the order of the Tâṇḍya-brâhmaṇa.

IV. The Nidâna-sûtra, on Metres, in ten Prapâṭhakas.

V. The Upagrantha-sûtra, a treatise on the performance of some of the Sâma-veda sacrifices, commonly ascribed to Kâtyâyana.[1]

VI. The Kshudra-sûtra or Kshaudra, in three Prapâṭhakas, equally treating of the ceremonial of the Sâma-veda.[2]

VII. The Taṇḍâlakshaṇa-sûtra.

VIII. The Panchavidha-sûtra[3], in two Prapâṭhakas.

IX. The Kalpânupada, and

X. The Anustotra-sûtra[4], in two Prapâṭhakas.

We miss in this list the Pushpa-sûtra, ascribed to Gobhila, and containing rules on the adaptation of the text of the hymns to their musical performance.

Jyotisha, or Astronomy.

The last of the Vedângas is called *Jyotisha*, or

[1] Cf. Ind. Studien, i. 43. 54. 56. 58; MS. E. I. H. 121. सामवेद उपग्रंथसूत्रं, copied Samvat, 1586=1530 A.D. by Paṇḍita Śrî Lakshmîdhara, son of Śrî Bhîma, इत्युपग्रंथसूत्रे चतुर्थः प्रपाठकः॥

[2] MS. Bodl. W. 375.

[3] MS. Bodl. W. 375. Begins प्रस्तावोद्गीथप्रतिहारोपद्रवनिधनानि भक्तयः तत्पांचविध्यं स्मृतं व्याख्यास्यामः॥ One of these five Bhaktis, the Pratihâra, is described in the Pratihâra-sûtra, ascribed to Kâtyâyana, and explained by Varadarâja.

[4] MS. Bodl. W. 375.

Astronomy. Its literature is very scanty, and the small treatise, generally quoted as the Jyotisha, belongs to the same class of works as the Śikshâ. Colebrooke speaks of different Jyotishas for each Veda, and he calls one, which has a commentary, the Jyotisha of the Rig-veda. Among his MSS., however, which are now deposited at the East India House, there is but one work of this kind. It exists in various MSS. (Nos. 1378, 1743, 1520), and the differences between these MSS. are so small that we could hardly consider them as distinct works. This tract is later than the Sûtra period, and we possess as yet no work on ancient astronomy, composed in the style of the early Sûtras. Notwithstanding its modern form, however, the doctrines which are propounded in this small treatise represent the earliest stage of Hindu astronomy. The theories on which it is founded, and the rules which it lays down, are more simple, less scientific, than anything we find in other astronomical treatises. Nor is it the object of this small tract to teach astronomy. It has a practical object, which is to convey such knowledge of the heavenly bodies as is necessary for fixing the days and hours of the Vedic sacrifices. It was the establishment of a sacred Calendar, which in India, as elsewhere, gave the first impulse to astronomical studies. Thus we meet in the Brâhmaṇas and Âraṇyakas with frequent allusions to astronomical subjects, and even in the hymns we find traces which indicate a certain advance in the observation of the moon, as the measurer of time. The fact that the name of the moon is the same in Sanskrit, Greek, and German, and that it is derived from a root which originally means to measure, shows that even before the separation of the Indo-European family, the moon had been looked upon as the chief means of measuring time. And the close connection between the names of moon and month proves that a certain knowledge of lunar chronology existed during the same early period. In one passage of the Rig-veda[1] the moon is mentioned in connection with the Nakshatras, and we can hardly doubt that this is an allusion to the Nakshatras, the well-known name of the Lunar Mansions or the Lunar Zodiac. In the hymns[2] the phases of the moon have not only received proper names, but they have been personified, and are invoked as deities to grant progeny to their worshippers. Again, there is a passage in the first book of the Rig-veda, where, in addition to the twelve months, a thirteenth or intercalary month is mentioned. The poet says there (Rv. i. 25. 8.), "He (Varuṇa), firm in his work, knows the twelve months with their offspring, and knows the month which is produced in addition." It has been objected that the idea of an intercalary month was too scientific for the early poets of the Veda, and a different translation has been proposed: "Varuṇa, who knows the twelve months, and knows those which are to come." But the poet would not have used the singular of the verb, if he meant the plural. He could not have

[1] Rv. viii. 3. 20: "átho nákshatrâṇâm eshâ'm upásthe sóma â'hitaḥ," "Soma is placed in the lap of these Nakshatras."

[2] Rv. ii. 32. Râkâ, the full moon; Sinîvâli, the last day before the new moon; and Gungu, the new moon, are mentioned. Rv. v. 42. 12, Râkâ occurs again; and x. 48. 8. we read Gungubhyaḥ. In both these passages, however, the poet is speaking of rivers, and not of the moon.

said, "the twelve months and those which are to come," if he meant to say, "the past months and those which are to come." No doubt the acquaintance with an intercalary month presupposes a certain knowledge of lunar and solar astronomy, but not more than what a shepherd or a sailor might gain in the course of his life. The whole idea expressed by the poet is, that Varuṇa maintains the established order of the world, and therefore knows the twelve months and also the thirteenth. In the hymns of the Yajur-veda the thirteenth month is changed already into a deity. Oblations are offered (Vâjasan.-sanhitâ, vii. 30., xxii. 31.) to each of the twelve months, and at the end one oblation is made to Anhasaspati, the deity of the intercalary month. In the Brâhmaṇas[1] likewise the thirteenth month is mentioned, and in the Jyotisha the theory of intercalation is fully explained. Two names for "an astronomer," Nakshatra-darśa and Gaṇaka, occur as early as the Taittirîyaka and the Sanhitâ of the Yajur-veda[2]; and among the sciences of the early Brahmans, Nakshatra-vidyâ or Astronomy is mentioned in the Chhândogyopanishad. In the Gaṇapâṭha, appended to Pâṇini's Grammar[3], the title of Jyotisha occurs together with the titles of other Vedic works; and in the Charaṇavyûha we meet not only with the Jyotisha, but with an Upajyotisha, or a supplemen-

[1] Sâyaṇa, in his Commentary on Rv. ii. 40. 3, says, that the thirteenth month was called the seventh season, and he quotes from a Brâhmaṇa a passage: asti trayodaśo masa iti śruteḥ.

[2] Taitt.-brâhm. iv. 5; Vâj.-sanh. xxx. 10; 20.

[3] Gaṇa ukthâdi. Pâṇ. iii. 1. 143, graha, planet, is mentioned as different from grâha.

tary treatise on astronomy. This supplementary treatise is one of the Pariśishṭas, and in the same class of writings we meet with other tracts on astronomical subjects, such as the Gobhilîya Navagraha-śânti-pariśishṭa[1] belonging to the Sâma-veda, and several more belonging to the Atharva-veda.[2]

If now we take a comprehensive view of that class of literature which we have just examined, we find some characteristic features throughout. All these works were written with a practical object, quite a new phase in the literature of such a nation as the ancient Hindus. The only authority which the Sûtrakâras, the authors of the Sûtras, claimed for their works was the authority of that ancient, and, as it was then already considered, revealed literature on which their works were founded. These men claimed no inspiration for themselves. They had made a scientific study of the literature handed down to them by former generations, and they wished to make that study easier to their contemporaries and to future generations. The style which they adopted for that purpose was business-like in the extreme. It was the curt and dry style of the Sûtras, a style peculiar to India, which can only be compared with the elaborate tables of contents, or the marginal notes, of some of our own early writers. It has its first beginnings in the Brâhmaṇas, where some subjects, particularly those which had given rise to early controversy, are stated with all the conciseness and neatness of the Sûtra style. But whereas the authors

[1] MS. Chambers, 404.

[2] Nakshatrakalpa, Grahayuddha, Râhuchâra, Ketuchâra, Ṛitukctulakshaṇa, Nakshatragrahotpâtalakshaṇa. Weber, Ind. Stud. i. 87. 100.

of the Brâhmaṇas screened their poverty behind a constant display of the most inane verbosity, the writers of the Sûtras gloried in every word they could save without endangering the practical usefulness of their manuals. In some instances they adopted a poetical form, and they succeeded in combining the conciseness of their prose with the rhythm of their early metres, the mixed Ślokas. Thus their position is marked by the very form of their works, as intermediate between the antique style of the Brâhmaṇas, and the modern style of the metrical Śâstras. Their works form a distinct and compact class of literature, and if we succeed in fixing the relative age of any one of these Sûtrakâras or writers of Sûtras, we shall have fixed the age of a period of literature which forms a transition between the Vedic and the classical literature of India.

The Anukramaṇîs.

Several of the works mentioned before were ascribed to Śaunaka and his two pupils, Kâtyâyana and Âśvalâyana. But we have not yet mentioned a number of treatises, ascribed to the same authors, and belonging to the same sphere of literature as the Sûtras, which, however, on account of their technical character, could not lay claim to the title of Vedânga, or "member of the Veda." They are known by the name of the Anukramaṇîs, from *anu*, along, and *kram*, to step. They are systematic indices to various portions of the ancient Vedic literature.

The most perfect Anukramaṇî is that of the Sanhitâ of the Rig-veda. It is ascribed to Kâtyâyana, an author chiefly known by his works on the Yajur-veda and Sâma-veda. Its name is Sarvânukramaṇî or Sarvânukrama, *i. e.* the index of all things.[1] It gives the first words of each hymn, the number of verses, the name and family of the poets, the names of the deities, and the metres of every verse. Before the time of Kâtyâyana, there had been separate indices for each of these subjects, and it was with reference to them that Kâtyâyana called his own index the general or comprehensive index. Our authority for this is Shaḍguruśishya, the author of a commentary on the Index of Kâtyâyana; a man who like Devarâjayajvan, the author of a commentary on the Nighaṇṭu, was not without a certain appreciation of the historical progress of Indian literature. He tells us in his Vedârthadîpikâ, that before Kâtyâyana, there existed one index of the poets, one of the metres, one of the deities, one of the Anuvâkas, the old chapters of the Rig-veda, and one of the hymns;[2] and that these indices were composed by Śaunaka. Now we know the style of Śaunaka, and as by a happy accident some of these former indices have been preserved, some complete, others in fragments, we are able to test Shaḍguruśishya's accuracy.

We remarked before, as a distinctive peculiarity of the style of Śaunaka, as contrasted with that of Kâtyâyana, that the Prâtiśâkhya ascribed to the former is composed in mixed Ślokas, whereas the Prâtiśâkhya of Kâtyâyana is written in prose or in Sûtras. The same observation applies to the Anu-

[1] सर्वज्ञेयार्थवर्णनात्सर्वानुक्रमणीशब्दं निर्ब्रुवंति विपश्चितः॥

[2] आर्ष्यनुक्रमणीत्याद्या छांदसी दैवती तथा। अनुवाकानुक्रमणी सूक्तानुक्रमणी तथा॥

kramaṇîs. Those ascribed to Śaunaka are composed in mixed metres, as far as we can judge from quotations; the Anukramaṇî of his pupil Kâtyâyana is in prose, and exhibits all the artificial appliances of a Sûtra composition. There is one of Śaunaka's Anukramaṇîs, the Anuvâka-anukramaṇî, which can be restored completely from MSS.[1]; and this work bears the most manifest traces of Śaunaka's style, partly in the mixture, partly in a peculiar rudeness, of its metres. The other Anukramaṇîs ascribed to Śaunaka are lost to us, but they must have existed at the time of Shaḍguruśishya. He quotes not only from the Anuvâka-anukramaṇî (Bhâshya, viii. 1.), but also from the Deva-anukrama (Bhâshya, viii. 4.), and he distinguishes this work from the Bṛihaddevatâ, another work attributed to Śaunaka, of which there is one MS. in Europe at the Royal Library of Berlin.[2] Sâyaṇa also, though later than Shaḍguruśishya, was still in possession of Śaunaka's works, and he quotes particularly the Bṛi-

[1] Several MSS. contain portions of the Anuvâkânukramaṇî; and with the help of Shaḍguruśishya's Commentary, contained in the introduction to his commentary on Kâtyâyana's Sarvânukrama, (MS. Bodl. Wilson, 379.), the text might be published in a critical edition.

[2] Dr. Kuhn gives the following description of this MS. in Haupt's "Zeitschrift fur Deutsches Alterthum." The Bṛihaddevatâ (Chambers, 192.) composed in epical metre, is ascribed to Śaunaka, and contains an enumeration of the deities invoked in each hymn of the Rig-veda. It gives much mythological and other information as to the character of the gods of the Veda. The text of the MS. is so corrupt that we can scarcely think of restoring it without the help of other MSS." Another MS. has since been found in India, and a distinguished Sanskrit scholar is preparing an edition of it.

haddevatâ, in several of his own commentaries. Śaunaka's Ârsha-anukramaṇî is quoted by Sâyaṇa in his Commentary on the Rig-veda, i. 100. 1. If we add to these quotations a reference to Śaunaka's Chhando-'nukramaṇî, which is found in Shaḍgûruśishya's Vedârthadîpikâ (MS. E.I.H. 1823, p. 7. a.), we may consider the authenticity of these works sufficiently established; and it is hardly unreasonable to suppose that the fifth Anukramaṇî also, of which no quotations have as yet been met with, the Sûktânukramaṇî, was in existence as late as Sâyaṇa's time.[1]

This would give us for the Rig-veda five Anukramaṇîs by Śaunaka, one by Kâtyâyana, and one by an unknown author. The Bṛihaddevatâ is a work of too large a compass to be called an Anukramaṇî, and it is even doubtful whether we possess this work in the same form in which Śaunaka left it. To judge from Dr. Kuhn's extracts, the author of the Bṛihaddevatâ follows indeed the Śâkala-śâkhâ, but his text must have differed from that of our MSS. The author may have followed one of the subdivisions of the Śâkalas, the Śaiśira-śâkhâ, for instance, which we know was followed by Śaunaka. The division of the Sanhitâ which is adopted in the Bṛihaddevatâ, is that of Maṇḍalas, Anuvâkas, and Sûktas; but the other division into Ashṭakas is equally known, and even the Khilas are taken into account, whereas both Śaunaka and Kâtyâyana exclude these later hymns dis-

[1] Another Anukramaṇî, containing the last verses of each Maṇḍala, is quoted by Shaḍguruśishya (Anukr. Bh. viii. 1.). मंडलांतानामृचामनुक्रमणे प्रतिचक्ष्व विचक्ष्वेत्येष्वपि गृह्यते॥ Cf. Rv. Maṇḍ. vii. 6. 15; Ashṭ. v. 7. 9.

tinctly from their indices. Dr. Kuhn concludes from a passage in Shaḍguruśishya's Commentary, to which we shall revert hereafter, that not Śaunaka, but Âśvalâyana, was the author of our Bṛihaddevatâ. This conclusion, however, is not borne out by sufficient evidence, nor is the fact that Śaunaka is quoted by name in the work itself a sufficient argument against Śaunaka's authorship. According to the line of argument adopted by Dr. Kuhn, it would be equally objectionable to ascribe the Bṛihaddevatâ to Âśvalâyana; for in one passage, according to Dr. Kuhn's own emendations, the name of Âśvalâyana also occurs in it. Other authorities which are quoted in this curious work are the Aitareyaka, the Kaushîtakins the Bhâllavi-brâhmaṇa, the Nidâna (nidânasanjnake granthe), Śâkalas, Bâshkalas, Madhuka, Śvetaketu, Gâlava, Gârgya, Rathîtara, Râthantarin, Śâkaṭâyana, Śâṇḍilya, Romakâyana Sthavira, Kâṭhakya, Bhâgurin, Śâkapûni, Bhârmyaśva Mudgala, Aurṇavâbha, Kraushṭukin, Mâtrin, and Yâska. The last is most frequently mentioned, and the whole book is dedicated to him. To judge from the style of the Bṛihaddevatâ, the work, as we now possess it, though originally written by Śaunaka, seems to have been recast by a later writer.

The following figures, taken from Śaunaka's Anukramaṇîs, will serve to give an idea of the minuteness with which the Veda was studied at his time. According to Śaunaka, the Śâkala-śâkhâ of the Rig-veda-sanhitâ consists of 10 Maṇḍalas, or 64 Adhyâyas.

Maṇḍalas.		Anuvâkas.		Hymns.
The 1st	contains	24	and	191
2nd	,,	4	,,	43
3rd	,,	5	,,	62
4th	,,	5	,,	58
5th	,,	6	,,	87
6th	,,	6	,,	75
7th	,,	6	,,	104
8th	,,	10	,,	92(+11 Vâlakhilyas)
9th	,,	7	,,	114
10th	,,	12	,,	191
The 10 have		85	and	1017+11=1028.

The Bâshkala-śâkhâ had 8 hymns more=1025 hymns.

The 64 Adhyâyas have 2006 Vargas. These are arranged as follows:—

	Verses.		Vargas.		Verses.
Vargas consisting of	1	=	1	=	1
,,	2	=	2	=	4
,,	3	=	97	=	291
,,	4	=	174	=	696
,,	5	=	1207	=	6035
,,	6	=	346[1]	=	2076
,,	7	=	119	=	833
,,	8	=	59	=	472
,,	9	=	1	=	9
	64 Adhyâyas	=	2,006	=	10,417

Here we have to observe a difference between the number of verses, as deduced from the Vargas, and the number stated by Śaunaka. The latter gives the

[1] Trîṇi śatâni shaṭkânâm chatvârinśat shaṭ cha vargâḥ.

sum total of verses=10,580½, but, immediately afterwards, the sum total of half verses=21,232½=10,616 verses.

How this difference arose it is difficult to say; but it should be observed that, if we divide the sum total of half verses, 21,232, by 2, we get 10,616 verses, and this number comes very near to 10,622, which the Charaṇavyûha gives as the sum total of the verses of the Rig-veda. According to the Charaṇavyûha (MS. Ch. 785.) the 64 Adhyâyas of the Rig-veda have: —

	Verses.		Vargas.		Verses.
Vargas consisting of	1	=	1	=	1
"	2	=	2	=	4
"	3	=	93	=	279
"	4	=	176	=	704
"	5	=	1228	=	6140
"	6	=	357	=	2142
"	7	=	129	=	903
"	8	=	55	=	440
"	9	=	1	=	9
			2042		10,622

The number of padas or words in the Rig-veda-sanhitâ is stated as 153,826, which gives an average of between 14 to 15 words to each verse. Another computation brings the number of the charchâ-padas (*i. e.* words which are used in the Kramapâṭha, omitting the repeated passages or galitas) to 110,704, and the number of syllables to 432,000.

In another Anukramaṇî, Śaunaka gives a list of verses arranged according to the metres in which they are written; and at the end he states the sum total of verses as 10,402; but here again, if we cast up the number of verses in each metre, according to his own statement, we get 10,409 instead of 10,402. These differences are startling if we consider the general accuracy of the exegetical works of the Brahmans; but they may arise either from faults in the MSS. of the Anukramaṇîs, or from the fact that some of the Khilas were included, though, according to their own professions, both Śaunaka and Kâtyâyana would seem to exclude these later hymns from their Anukramaṇîs. The following table will show the distribution of metres according to Śaunaka: —

Gâyatrî	-	2,451	Brought forward	9793
Ushṇih	-	341	Ashṭi - -	6
Anushṭubh	-	855	Atyashṭi - -	84
Bṛihatî	-	181	Dhṛiti - -	2
Pankti	-	312	Atidhṛiti - -	1
Trishṭubh	-	4,253	Ekapadâ - -	6
Jagatî	-	1,348	Dvipadâ - -	17
Atijagatî	-	17	Pragâtha Bârhata	194
Śakvarî	-	26	Kâkubha - -	55
Atiśakvarî	-	9	Mahâbârhata -	251
Carried forward		9793		10,409

For the Yajur-veda we have three Anukramaṇîs, one for the Âtreyî-śâkhâ of the Taittirîyas, the other for the Śâkhâ of the Chârâyaṇîyas, the third for the Mâdhyandina-śâkhâ of the Vâjasaneyins. The former[1] differs from other Anukramaṇîs in so far as it contains an index not of the Sanhitâ only, but

[1] MS. E. I. H. 1623, 965.

also of the Brâhmaṇa and the Âraṇyaka. Its object is not simply to enumerate the Kâṇḍas (Ashṭakas), Praśnas, Anuvâkas, and Kâṇḍikâs as they follow in the text, but rather to indicate the chief subjects of this Veda, and to bring together the different passages where the same sacrifice with its supplements is treated. Though we do not possess a MS. of the Âtreyî-śâkhâ, it is possible to identify nearly the whole of the Index with the text of the Sanhitâ[1], the Brâhmaṇa[2], and the Âraṇyaka[3] which we possess. The Âtreyî-śâkhâ, though not mentioned in the Charaṇavyûha, must be considered as a subdivision of the Aukhîya-śâkhâ; and the Anukramaṇî says that Vaiśampâyana handed it down to Yâska Paingi, Yâska to Tittiri, Tittiri to Ukha, and Ukha to Âtreya, who was the author of a Pada-text[4], while Kuṇḍina composed a commentary (vṛitti) on the same Śâkhâ. The Âpastamba-śâkhâ, of which we possess the complete Brâhmaṇa, is a subdivision of the Khâṇḍikeyas.

There is a curious tradition, preserved in the Kâṇḍânukrama, that, although the greater portion of the Âtreyî-śâkhâ was originally taught by Tittiri, some chapters of it owed their origin to Kaṭha, the founder of the Kâṭhaka-śâkhâ. This assertion is confirmed by Sâyaṇa in his Commentary on the Taittirîyâraṇyaka. The chapters ascribed to Kaṭha and called the Kâṭhakam, are found at the end of the Brâhmaṇa and the beginning of the Âraṇyaka. They contain—

1 MS. E. I. H. 1701, 1702; name of Śâkhâ unknown.

2 MS. E. I. H. 293, containing the three books of the Âpastamba-brâhmaṇa.

3 MS. E. I. H. 1690, &c.

4 See MS. Bodl. Wilson, 361.

1. The Sâvitrâgnichayana with the Brâhmaṇa, Tait.-brâhm. iii. 10.

2. The Nâchiketachayana. Tait.-br. iii. 11.

3. Divaḥśyenaya ishṭayaḥ. Tait.-br. iii. 12. 1 & 2.

4. Apâdyâ ishṭayaḥ. Tait.-br. iii. 12. 3 & 4.

5. Châturhotrachiti. Tait. br. iii. 12. 5.

6. Vaiśvasṛijachiti. Tait.-br. iii. 12. 6—9, end of Brâhmaṇa.

7. Âruṇaketukachiti. Tait.-âraṇyaka, i. 1.

8. Svâdhyâya-brâhmaṇa. Tait.-âraṇyaka, i. 2.

They are given here as they follow one another in the text of the Âpastamba-śâkhâ, and this order is confirmed in every particular by Sâyaṇa's Commentary (MS. E. I. H. 1145), which is in fact a commentary intended for the Âpastamba-śâkhâ of the Taittirîya-brâhmaṇa. According to his introductory remarks prefixed to each Anuvâka, the Sâvitrachiti occupies the tenth, the Nâchiketachiti the eleventh Prapâṭhaka. In the twelfth Prapâṭhaka, he remarks, the Châturhotra and Vaiśvasṛija should be explained. But as the ishṭis, called the Divaḥśyenîs and Apâdyâs, form part of the complete Châturhotra (they stand either in the middle or at the end of it), they are explained first. Thus we find in the beginning of the twelfth Prapâṭhaka (iii. 12. 1.), the pratîkas of the Yâjyânuvâkyâs of the Divaḥśyenîs; in iii. 12. 2. the rules for the same ishṭis; and in the same manner, the Yâjyânuvâkyâs of the Apâdyâs in iii. 12. 3., and the rules in iii. 12. 4. Then follows the Châturhotra-chayana in iii. 12. 5., and in the last four Anuvâkas the Vaiśvasṛija-chayana.

A different order seems to have been observed in the Âtreyî-śâkhâ of the Taittirîya-brâhmaṇa, for, although the same chapters are here ascribed to

Kaṭha, their arrangement must have differed, unless we suppose that the author of the Kâṇḍânukrama introduced an alteration. He writes: "Tâvat Tittiriḥ provâcha. (Tittiris Taittirîyaśâkhâpravartako 'nyebhyo munibhyaḥ śishyebhyaḥ provâcha.) Athâshṭau Kâṭhakâni (athânantaram Kâṭhakaśâkhâpravartakena Kâṭhakamuninâ proktâny uchyante):

1. Sâvitra, Taittirîya-brâhmaṇa, iii. 10.
2. Nâchiketa " " iii. 11.
3. Châturhotra " " iii. 12. 5.
4. Vaiśvasṛija " " iii. 12. 6—9.
5. Âruṇa, Taittirîya-âraṇyaka, i. 1.
6. Divaḥśyenîs, Taittirîya-brâhmaṇa, iii. 12. 1—2.
7. Apâdyâs " " iii. 12. 3—4.
8. Svâdhyâya-brâhmaṇa, Taittirîya-âraṇyaka, i. 2."

The second Anukramaṇî of the Yajur-veda which we possess, belongs to the Chârâyaṇîya-śâkhâ, and is called the Mantrârshâdhyâya.[1] The only copy which we have of it is found in the same MS. which contains the Charaka-śâkhâ,[2] and it is evidently intended as an index to this śâkhâ. Nor is there anything anomalous in this, if we remember that the Chârâyaṇîya-śâkhâ is a subdivision of the Charaka-śâkhâ. But what is less intelligible is the title given to the text, which instead of Yajur-veda, is called in the MS. Yajur-veda-kâṭhaka. This title, Kâṭhaka, cannot well refer to the śâkhâ of the Kaṭhas, for this is itself a subdivision of the Charakas. It must most likely be taken in the same sense in which Kâṭhaka was explained before, *i. e.* "Kâṭhakamuninâ proktam;" though it is strange that the very chapters which in the Âpastamba-

[1] See Catalogue of the Berlin MSS., No. 142.

[2] The title is "Ekottaraśatâdhvaryuśâkhâprabhedabhinne Yajurvedakâṭhake Charakaśâkhâ."

śâkhâ of the Taittirîyaka are ascribed to Kaṭha, are wanting in our Śâkhâ, while all the other sacrifices which are described in the Taittirîya-sanhitâ and Brâhmaṇa, are laid down in very much the same order.

The third Anukramaṇî, that of the Mâdhyandina-śâkhâ of the Vâjasaneyaka, is ascribed to Kâtyâyana, who is mentioned also as the author of an Anuvâkânukramaṇî. It gives the names of the poets, the deities, and the metres, for all the verses of the Sanhitâ, including the Khila (Adhyâya 26—35.), and the Śukriya portions (Adhy. 36—40.).

For the Sâma-veda we have two classes of Anukramaṇîs, the former more ancient, the latter more modern than those of the other Vedas which we have hitherto examined. One index to the hymns of the Sâma-veda (following the order of the Veyagâna and Âraṇyagâna) has been preserved under the name of Ârsheya-brâhmaṇa [1], a title by which this work is admitted within the pale of the revealed literature of the Brahmans. Allusions to the names of poets and deities of different hymns occur in the Brâhmaṇas of other Vedas also; but in none, except the Sâma-veda, have these scattered observations been arranged into regular Anukramaṇîs before the beginning of the Sûtra period, or been incorporated in the body of their revealed literature. What the Brahmans call Śruti or revelation, signifies, as we saw, what is more ancient than the Sûtras; and that the Ârsheya-brâhmaṇa is earlier at least than Kâtyâyana, can be proved by the fact of Kâtyâyana's quoting passages from it.[2] It has been pointed out as a distinguishing mark of the Brâh-

[1] See Benfey, Sâma-veda, p. vii.

[2] In the first chapter of the Ârsheya-brâhmaṇa, we read: यो ह वा अविदितार्षेयच्छंदोदैवतब्राह्मणेन मंत्रेण या-

maṇas of the Sâma-veda that they are never accented, but it is doubtful whether any conclusion could be drawn from this as to their being of later origin than the Brâhmaṇas of the other Vedas.[1]

But while the existence of an Ârsheya-brâhmaṇa shows that the Chhandogas were the first to compose an index to their sacred literature, we find that their regular Anukramaṇîs are more modern than those of the Rig-veda, and must be referred to a class of works known by the name of Pariśishṭas. They are contained in MS. Bodl. Wilson 466, where they form the fifth and sixth of the twenty Pariśishṭas attached to the Sâma-veda. Their title is, "Naigeyânâm ṛikshv ârsham," and "Naigeyânâm ṛikshu daivatam," and they give respectively the names of the poets and the deities for the verses composing the Ârchika of the Chhandogas according to the Śâkhâ

जयति वाध्यापयति वा स्थाणुं वर्च्छति गर्तं वापद्यते (MS. 689. गर्तं वापद्यते) प्र वा मीयते पापीयान्भवति यातयामान्यस्य छंदांसि भवंति। This passage is referred to by Kâtyâyana, when he says: अनेवंविदो यातयामानि छंदांसि भवंति स्थाणुं वर्च्छति गर्तं वा पत्यते प्रमीयते वा पापीयान्भवतीति विज्ञायते॥ See also Kâtyâyana's Introduction to his Anukramaṇî of the Mâdhyandina-śâkhâ, and Rig-veda-bhâshya, p. 40.

[1] Kumârila says: यत्तु भाष्यकारेण स्वराभावादित्यसन्नियमार्थव्याख्यानं कृतं तन्मंत्रेष्वप्यवेदत्वं कल्पाधीतेषु साधयेत्। तथा गृह्योपदिष्टेषु छांदोग्यब्राह्मणेषु च। ब्राह्मणानि हि यान्यष्टौ सरहस्यान्यधीयते छंदोगास्तेषु सर्वेषु न कश्चिन्नियतः स्वरः। तेन तेष्वप्यवेदत्वं स्वराभावात्प्रसज्येत॥

of the Naigeyas, a subdivision of the Kauthumas. It agrees on the whole, but not in all particulars [1], with the Śâkhâ published by Stevenson and Benfey, and it has been supposed that their text is taken from MSS. belonging to the Râṇâyanîya Śâkhâ. The most characteristic difference between these Pariśishṭas and the Ârsheya-brâhmaṇa seems to lie in this, that the latter refers to the original prayer-books of the Chhandogas, the Veyagâna, and Âraṇyagâna, while the former follow the Sanhitâ, including Ârchika and Staubhika, or as they are also called, Pûrvârchika and Uttarârchika.

For the fourth Veda, the Âtharvaṇa, or Brahmaveda, an Anukramaṇî has been discovered by Professor Whitney in a MS. of the British Museum, prepared for Col. Polier. A copy of this MS. is found in MS. 2142 of the East India House. It is a complete index to the Sanhitâ in 10 Paṭalas, written in a simple and intelligible style. Its title is Bṛihatsarvânukramaṇî.

It is evident, that if it were possible to determine the age of the Anukramaṇîs, we should have a *terminus ad quem* for the Vedic age. The index of the Rig-veda enables us to check almost every syllable of the hymns; and we may safely say that we possess exactly the same number of verses, and words, and syllables in our MSS. of the Rig-veda as existed at the time of Kâtyâyana. The index of the Âtreyîśâkhâ (by Laugâkshi ?) authenticates our MSS. not only of the Sanhitâ, but also of the Brâhmaṇa and Âraṇyaka of the Taittirîya-veda, and the index to the Kâṭhaka refers to a work exactly the same as that of which we possess the text in MS. The Ârsheya-

[1] Cf. Sâma-veda, ed. Benfey, p. xx.

brâhmaṇa presupposes the existence of the Gânas of the Sâma-veda, and the Anukramaṇîs of the Naigeyas could only have been written after the text of the more modern Ârchika had branched off into different Śâkhâs.

The only Anukramaṇîs of which the authors are known are, the Anukramaṇîs of Śaunaka to the Rig-veda, and the two Sarvânukramas of Kâtyâyana, one to the Rig-veda, the other to the white Yajur-veda. We shall see whether it is possible to fix the age of these two writers.

We remarked before, that the Anukramaṇî of Kâtyâyana, if compared with the Anuvâkânukramaṇî of Śaunaka, shows the same progress in style which we may always observe between these two writers. Śaunaka writes in mixed Ślokas, and takes great liberties with the metre; Kâtyâyana writes in prose, and introduces the artificial contrivances of the later Sûtras. Again, Śaunaka's index follows the original division of the Rig-veda into Maṇḍalas, Anuvâkas, and Sûktas; Kâtyâyana has adopted the more practical and more modern division into Ashṭakas, Adhyâyas, and Vargas. The number of hymns is the same in Śaunaka and Kâtyâyana. They both follow the united Śâkhâ of the Śâkalas and Bâshkalas, and bring the number of hymns, exclusive of all Khilas, to 1017. Before this union took place, the Bâshkalas counted eight hymns more than the Śâkalas, *i. e.* 1025 instead of 1017; and they read some of the hymns in the first Maṇḍala in a different order.[1]

[1] In the Śâkala-śâkhâ, the hymns of Gotama are followed by those of Kutsa, Kakshîvat, Paruchchhepa, and Dîrghatamas; in the Bâshkala-śâkhâ their order was, Gotama, Kakshîvat, Paruchchhepa, Kutsa, Dîrghatamas.

The Khilas, or supplementary hymns, are omitted in the Anukramaṇîs of Śaunaka and Kâtyâyana, though they were known to both; Śaunaka, however, excludes them more strictly than Kâtyâyana.[1] The latter has admitted the eleven Vâlakhilya-hymns, and thus brings the total number of hymns to 1028.

From all these indications we should naturally be led to expect that the relation between Śaunaka and Kâtyâyana was very intimate, that both belonged to the same Śâkhâ, and that Śaunaka was anterior to Kâtyâyana. We know of only one other writer whose works are equally intended for the united Śâkhâ of the Śâkalas and Bâshkalas; this is Âśvalâyana, the author of twelve books of Śrauta-sûtras, of four books of Gṛihya-sûtras, and of some chapters in the Aitareyâraṇyaka.[2]

Let us see now, whether these indications can be supported by other evidence.

Shaḍguruśishya in his Commentary on Kâtyâyana's Sarvânukrama, says:—

"Śunahotra, the great Muni, was born of Bharadvâja, and of him was born Śauṇahotra, all the world being a witness. Indra himself went to the sacrifice of the Ṛishi in order to please him. The great Asuras, thinking that Indra was alone, and wishing

[1] खैलिकानामनादेशो ऽस्मिन्ग्रंथे ऽनुवाकानां; or, according to MS. 502., ऽनुवाकानामिह स्मृत:॥

[2] Thus it is said: एतस्य (समाम्नायस्य) इतिशब्दो निवित्प्रैषपुरोरुक्कुंतापवालखिल्यमहानाम्न्यैतरेयब्राह्मणसहितस्य शाकलस्य बाष्कलस्य चाम्नायद्वयस्यैतदाश्वलायनसूत्रं नाम प्रयोगशास्त्रमित्यध्येतृप्रसिद्धं संबंधविशेषं द्योतयति॥ Srauta-sûtra-bhâshya, i. 1.

to take him, surrounded the sacrificial inclosure. Indra, however, perceived it, and taking the guise of the Ṛishi, he went away. The Asuras seeing the sacrificer again, seized Śaunahotra, taking him for Indra. He saw the god that is to be worshipped, and saying, 'I am not Indra, there he is, ye fools, not I,' he was released by the Asuras. Indra called and spake to him: 'Because thou delightest in praising, therefore thou art called Gṛitsamada, O Ṛishi; thy hymn will be called by the name of *Indrasya indriyam*, the might of Indra. And thou, being born in the race of Bhṛigu, shalt be Śaunaka, the descendant of Śunaka, and thou shalt see again the second Maṇḍala, together with that hymn.' He, the Muni Gṛitsamada, was born again, as commanded by Indra. It was he who saw the great second Maṇḍala of the Rig-veda as it was revealed to him together with the hymn Sajanîya; it was he, the great Ṛishi, to whom at the twelve years' sacrifice, Ugraśravas, the son of Romaharshaṇa, the pupil of Vyâsa, recited, in the midst of the sacrifice, the story of the Mahâbhârata, together with the tale of the Harivanśa, a story to be learnt from Vyâsa alone, full of every kind of excellence, dear to Hari, sweet to hear, endowed with great blessing. It was he who was the lord of the sages, dwelling in the Naimishîya forest; he, who to the King Śatânîka, the son of Janamejaya, brought the laws of Vishṇu, which declare the powers of Hari. That Śaunaka, celebrated among the Ṛishis as the glorious, having seen the second Maṇḍala, and heard the collection of the Mahâbhârata, being also the propagator of the laws of Vishṇu, the great boat on the ocean of existence, was looked upon by the great Ṛishis as the only vessel in which worshippers might get over the Bahvṛicha, with its twenty-one Śâkhâs, like one who had crossed the Rig-veda. There was one Śâkhâ of Śâkala, another of Bâshkala: taking these two Sanhitâs, and the twenty-one Brâhmaṇas, the Aitareyaka, and completing it with others, Śaunaka, revered by numbers of great Ṛishis, composed the first Kalpa-sûtra."

It need hardly be pointed out that this passage contains a strange and startling mixture of legendary and historical matter, and that it is only the last portion which can be of interest to us. The story of Śaunahotra, the son of Śunahotra, and grandson of Bharadvâja, being born again as Gṛitsamada-Śaunaka, may have some historical foundation, and the only way in which it can be interpreted, is, that the second Maṇḍala, being originally seen by Gṛitsamada, of the family of Bhṛigu, was afterwards preserved by Śaunahotra, a descendant of Bharadvâja, of the race of Angiras, who entered the family of Bhṛigu, took the name of Śaunaka, and added one hymn, the twelfth, in praise of Indra. This is partly confirmed by Kâtyâyana's Anukramaṇî[1], and by the Ṛishyanukramaṇî of Śaunaka.[2] It would by no means follow that Śaunaka was the author of the hymns of the second Maṇḍala. The hymns of that Maṇḍala belong to Gṛitsamada of the Bhṛigu race. But Śaunaka may have adopted that Maṇḍala, and

[1] य आंगिरसः शौनहोत्रो भूत्वा भार्गवः शौनकोऽभवत्स गृत्समदो द्वितीयं मंडलमपश्यदिति॥

[2] तथा तस्यैव शौनकस्य ऋष्यनुक्रमणे। त्वमग्न इति गृत्समदः शौनको भृगुतां गतः। शौनहोत्रः प्रकृत्या तु य आंगिरस उच्यत इति॥

by adding one hymn, may have been said to have made it his own. Again, it does not concern us at present whether Śaunaka, the author of the Kalpa-sûtra, was the same as Śaunaka, the chief of the sages in the Naimishîya forest, to whom, during the great twelve-years' sacrifice, Ugraśravas related the Mahâbhârata, and who became the teacher of Śatânîka, the son of Janamejaya. If this identity could be established, a most important link would be gained, connecting Śaunaka and his literary activity with another period of Indian literature. This point must be reserved for further consideration. At present we are only concerned with Śaunaka, the author of the Kalpa-sûtras and other works composed with a view of facilitating the study of the Rig-veda.

Shadguruśishya continues:

"The pupil of Śaunaka was the Reverend Âśvalâyana. He, having learned from Śaunaka all sacred knowledge, made also a Sûtra and taught it, thinking it would improve the understanding and please Śaunaka. Then, in order to please his pupil, Śaunaka destroyed his own Sûtra[1], which consisted of a thousand parts and was more like a Brâhmaṇa. 'This Sûtra,' he said, 'which Âśvalâyana has made and taught, shall be the Sûtra for this Veda.' There are

[1] विपाटितं means "torn," and corresponds with Sûtra, "a thread." A similar expression is विच्छिन्नं, which is applied, for instance, to the Mahâbhâshya, when it fell into disuse in Kashmir. See Râjataranginî, Histoire des Rois du Kashmire, traduite et commentée par M. A. Troyer, iv. 487.; and Böhtlingk, Pâṇini, p. xvi. The true sense seems to be that in which Devarâjayajvan uses विच्छिन्न in such passages as तच्चाध्ययनं कलियुगे प्रायेण विच्छिन्नसंप्रदायमासीत् ॥ A work was lost when the chain of the oral tradition was broken.

altogether ten books of Śaunaka, written for the preservation of the Rig-veda; 1. The index of the Ṛishis; 2. The index of the Metres; 3. The index of the Deities; 4. The index of the Anuvâkas; 5. The index of the Sûktas; 6. The Vidhâna (employment) of the Ṛich-verses; 7. The employment of the Pâdas[1]; 8. The Bârhaddaivata; 9. The Prâtiśâkhya[2] of the Śaunakas; 10. His Smârta work on matters of law.[3] Âśvalâyana having learnt all these ten Sûtras, and knowing also the Gotras (genealogies[4]), became versed in all the sacrifices by the favour of Śaunaka. The sage Kâtyâyana had thirteen books before him: ten of Śaunaka and three of his pupil Âśvalâyana.[5] The latter consisted of the Sûtras in twelve chapters,

[1] I read विधाने च, because these must be two different works, the Rigvidhâna and Pâdavidhâna, in order to complete the number of ten. The Rigvidhâna exists in MS. (E. I. H. 1723), and is not only written in Śaunaka's mixed Ślokas, but distinctly ascribed to him in the second verse: कर्मणामृषिदृष्टानां विधिं प्रोवाच शौनकः। The book ends with the words शौनकाय नमः। Nevertheless, in the form in which we have it, it is later than Śaunaka. The term Rigvidhâna is mentioned in the Taittirîyâraṇyaka.

[2] This must be the Prâtiśâkhya of the Rig-veda, and not of the Atharva-veda, which is likewise ascribed to Śaunaka, the Châturâdhyâyikam Śaunakîyam.

[3] See Stenzler, Indische Studien, i. p. 243.

[4] साक्तगोत्रजः is unintelligible. Should it be व्याक्तगोत्रज्ञः?

[5] All the works of Âśvalâyana still exist, as Shaḍguruśishya describes them. Instead of चतुष्कगृह्यं, it would be better to read चतुष्कं गृह्यं॥

(Śrauta-sutra), the Gṛihya-sutras in four chapters, and the fourth Âraṇyaka (of the Aitareyâraṇyaka) by Âśvalâyana. The sage Kâtyâyana, having mastered the thirteen[1] books of Śaunaka and of his pupil, composed several works himself; the Sûtras of the Vâjins[2], the Upagrantha[3] of the Sâma-veda, the Ślokas[4] of the Smṛiti (the Karmapradîpa), the Brahma-Kârikâs of the Atharvans[5], and the Mahâvârttika[6], which was like a boat on the great ocean of Pâṇini's Grammar. The rules promulgated by him were explained by the Reverend Patanjali[7], the teacher of the Yoga-philosophy, himself the author of the Yoga-śâstra and the Nidâna, a man highly pleased by the great commentary, the work of the descendant of Śântanu. Now it was Kâtyâyana, the great sage, endowed with these numerous excellencies, who composed, by great exertion, this Sarvânukramaṇî. And because it gives the substance of all the works composed by Śaunaka and his pupils, therefore the chief among the Bahvṛichas have called it the General Index."

[1] If this number is right, Śaunaka's Śrauta-sûtra could not have been destroyed at the time of Kâtyâyana.

[2] The Kalpa-sûtras of the Yajur-veda. On the Vâjins or Vâjasaneyins, see Colebrooke, Essays, i. 61.

[3] See page 210. Upagrantha is not to be taken in the sense of Pariśishṭa.

[4] Bhrâjamâna, is unintelligible; it may be Pârshada.

[5] These Kârikâs have not yet been met with.

[6] The Vârttikâs to Pâṇini.

[7] Patanjali, the author of the Mahâbhâshya, according to tradition called by the name of Bhartṛihari also, was the reputed author of the Yoga-sûtras. On these a commentary was written by Vyâsa, who might be called a descendant of Śântanu. The reading may not be quite correct, and Mahâbhâshya is more likely to refer to Patanjali's own work; but the dental *n* of the MSS. speaks rather in favour of the reading mahâbhâgyena.

भरद्वाजसुतो जज्ञे शुनहोत्रो महामुनिः।
शौनहोत्रस्तस्य जज्ञे सर्वलोकस्य पश्यतः॥
इंद्रो जगाम प्रीत्यर्थमृषेर्यज्ञमपि स्वयं।
इंद्रमेकाकिनं मत्वा जिघृक्षंतो महासुराः॥
परिवव्रुर्यज्ञवाटं तदिंद्रोऽप्यन्वबुध्यत[1]।
इंद्रोऽपि यजमानस्य वेष[2]मास्थाय निर्गतः॥
यजमानं पुनर्दृष्ट्वा जगृहुस्ते महासुराः।
शौनहोत्रमिंद्रबुद्ध्या यजनीयं ददर्श सः॥
नाहमिंद्रः स एवाज्ञा नाहमित्यनुवर्णयन्।
मुक्तस्तैरसुरैरिंद्र आह्वयैवमुवाच ह॥
गृणन्मादयसे यस्मात्तस्माद्गृत्समद[3] ऋषे।
इंद्रस्येंद्रियमित्ये[4]तन्नाम्ना सूक्तं भविष्यति॥
त्वं तु भूत्वा भृगुकुले शुनकाच्छौनको भव।
एतत्सूक्तयुतं पश्य द्वितीयं मंडलं पुनः॥
स इंद्रचोदितो जातः पुनर्गृत्समदो मुनिः।
सजनीययु[5]तं यो वै द्वितीयं मंडलं महत्॥
ददर्श यस्मै चा[6]चष्टे सत्रे द्वादशवार्षिके।
वेदव्यासप्रसादेन रोमहर्षणनंदनः॥

---

[1] अवबुध्यत Ch. 192. Weber, Catalogue, p. 12.

[2] वेवं Ch. 192., W. 379. वेशं ?

[3] गृत्समदो Ch., W.

[4] त नाम्ना Ch., W.

[5] Rv. II. 12., the Sûkta with the refrain, "sa janâsa indraḥ."

[6] वाचस्ते Ch., W.

उग्रश्रवा व्यासशिष्यः कर्ममध्ये महर्षये।
महाभारतमाख्यानं हरिवंशकथान्वितं॥
वेदव्यासैक[1]विज्ञेयं महागुणगणान्वितं।
हरिप्रियं श्रुतिसुखं कर्ममध्ये महर्द्धिमत्॥
आसीद्गृहपतिर्यो वै नैमिषारण्यवासिनां।
शतानीकाय राज्ञे यो जनमेजयसूनवे॥
उपानयद्विष्णुधर्मान्[2] साक्षात्कारकरान्[3] हरेः।
स शौनको मुनिगतो श्रूयमाणो महायशाः॥
द्वितीयं मंडलं दृष्ट्वा[4] श्रुतभारतसंहितः[5]।
संसाराब्धिमहापोतविष्णुधर्मप्रवर्त्तकः॥
एकविंशतिशाखस्य[6] बह्वृचस्य महर्षिभिः।
कल्पितः[7] कल्पितारोऽभूदृग्वेद इव पारगः॥
शाकलस्य संहितैका बाष्कलस्य तथापरा।
ते संहिते समाश्रित्य ब्राह्मणान्येकविंशतिः॥
ऐतरेयकमाश्रित्य तदेवान्यैः प्रपूरयन्।
कल्पसूत्रं चकाराद्यं[8] महर्षिगण[9]पूजितः॥
शौनकस्य तु शिष्योऽभूद्भगवानाश्वलायनः।
स तस्माच्छ्रुतसर्वज्ञः सूत्रं कृत्वा न्यवेदयत्[10]॥

---

[1] से क Ch., W.

[2] द्धि धर्मात् W. द्द धर्मान् Ch.

[3] करां Ch., W.

[4] दृष्टा W.

[5] ता W., Ch.

[6] खास्य W., Ch.

[7] नः W.

[8] द्य Ch., W.

[9] गुण Ch., W.

[10] यन् Ch., W.

प्रबोधपरिशुद्ध्यर्थं शौनकस्य प्रियं त्विति।
सहस्रखंडं स्वकृतं सूत्रं ब्राह्मणसंनिभं॥
शिष्याश्वलायनप्रीत्यै शौनकेन विपाटितं।
उक्तं तत्तत्कृतं सूत्रमस्य वेदस्य चास्त्विति॥
शौनकीया दश ग्रंथास्तदा ऋग्वेदगुप्तये।
आर्ष्यनुक्रमणीत्याद्या छांदसी दैवती तथा॥
अनुवाकानुक्रमणी सूक्तानुक्रमणी तथा।
ऋक्पादयोर्विधाने च[1] बार्हद्दैवतमेव च॥
प्रातिशाख्यं शौनकीयं स्मार्तं दशममुच्यते।
स सूत्रदशकं ज्ञात्वा तथा[2] साकृतगोत्रज्ञः[3]॥
शौनकस्य प्रसादेन कर्मज्ञः समपद्यत।
कात्यायनमुनिर्मेने त्रयोदशकमत्र तु॥
शौनकीयं च दशकं तच्छिष्यस्य त्रिकं तथा।
द्वादशाध्यायकं सूत्रं चतुष्क[4]गृह्यमेव च॥
चतुर्थारण्यकं चेति ह्याश्वलायनसूत्रकं।
सशिष्यशौनकाचार्यत्रयोदशकविन्मुनिः॥
वाजिनां सूत्रकृत्साम्नामुपग्रंथस्य कारकः।
स्मृतेश्च कर्ता श्लोकानां भ्राजमानां च[5] कारकः॥
अथर्वणां निर्ममे यः सम्यग्वै ब्राह्मकारिकाः।
महावार्त्तिकनौकारः पाणिनीयमहार्णवे॥

---

[1] ने न W. Ch. [2] तया W. Ch.

[3] साकृतगोत्रजः W., साकृतगोत्रज Ch.

[4] चातुष्क W.

[5] पार्षदस्य?

यत्प्रणीतानि वाक्यानि भगवांस्तु पतंजलिः[1]।
व्याख्यच्छांतनवीयेन[2] महाभाष्येन[3] हर्षितः॥
योगाचार्यः स्वयं कर्ता योगशास्त्रनिदानयोः।
एवंगुणगणैर्युक्तः कात्यायनमहामुनिः॥
तपोयोगाग्निर्ममे यः सर्वानुक्रमणीमिमां।
सच्छिष्यशौनकाचार्यसर्वग्रंथार्थवर्तनात्॥
प्राक्त्रग्वेदसंहितास्तु सर्वानुक्रमणीमिमां। &c.

If we accept this statement of Shaḍguruśishya,—and it certainly seems to agree in the main with what we might have guessed from the character of the works, ascribed respectively to Śaunaka, Âśvalâyana and Kâtyâyana,— we should have to admit at least five generations of teachers and pupils: first Śaunaka; after him Âśvalâyana, in whose favour Śaunaka is said to have destroyed one of his works; thirdly, Kâtyâyana, who studied the works both of Śaunaka and Âśvalâyana; fourthly Patanjali, who wrote a commentary on one of Kâtyâyana's works; and lastly Vyâsa, who commented on a work of Patanjali. It does not follow that Kâtyâyana was a pupil of Âśvalâyana, or that Patanjali lived immediately after Kâtyâyana, but the smallest interval which we can admit between every two of these names is that between teacher and pupil, an interval as large as that between father and son, or rather larger. The question now arises: Can the date of any one of these authors be fixed chronologically?

Before we attempt to answer this question, it will be necessary to establish the identity of Kâtyâyana

[1] तदंजलिः Ch. W. [2] छांतयनीयेत W., छांतपनोयेन Ch.

[3] भाष्येण or भाग्येन?

and Vararuchi. Kâtyâyana was the author of the Sarvânukramaṇî, and the same work is quoted as the Sarvânukramaṇî of Vararuchi[1], the compiler of the doctrines of Śaunaka. In Professor Wilson's Catalogue of the Mackenzie Collection, a Prâtiśâkhya is ascribed to Vararuchi, and this can hardly be anything else but the Mâdhyandina-prâtiśâkhya of Kâtyâyana. Hemachandra in his Dictionary gives Vararuchi as a synonyme of Kâtyâyana without any further comment, just as he gives Śâlâturîya as a synonyme of Pâṇini.

Let us now consider the information which we receive about Kâtyâyana Vararuchi from Brahmanic sources. Somadevabhaṭṭa of Kashmir collected the popular stories current in his time, and published them towards the beginning of the twelfth century under the title of Kathâ-sarit-sâgara[2], the Ocean of the Rivers of Stories. Here we read that Kâtyâyana

[1] MS. E. I. H. 576. contains a commentary on the Rig-veda, where a passage from the Sarvânukramaṇî is quoted as अत्र शौनकादिमतसंग्रहीतुर्वररुचेरनुक्रमणिका ॥ This commentary of Âtmânanda seems anterior to Sâyaṇa. In the introduction different works and commentaries, connected with the Veda are quoted, but Mâdhava and Sâyaṇa are never mentioned. We find the Skândabhâshya, and commentators such as Udgîtha-bhâskara, mentioned (स्कांदभाष्यादिषु भाष्यकारैरुद्गीथभास्करादिभिः) by Âtmânanda, and the same works were known also to Devarâjayajvan. Devarâjayajvan, however, quotes not only Skandasvâmin and Bhaṭṭa-bhâskara-miśra, but also Mâdhava. He therefore was later than Mâdhava. Skandasvâmin, and Bhâskara, on the contrary, were anterior to Mâdhava, being quoted in his commentary. Âtmânanda, though not quoted by Mâdhava, seems anterior to Mâdhava, and the authorities which he quotes are such as Śaunaka, Vedamitra (Śâkalya), the Bṛihaddevatâ, Vishṇudharmottara, and Yâska.

[2] Kathâ-sarit-sâgara, edited by Dr. Hermann Brockhaus. Leipsig, 1839.

Vararuchi, being cursed by the wife of Śiva, was born at Kauśambî, the capital of Vatsa. He was a boy of great talent and extraordinary powers of memory. He was able to repeat to his mother an entire play, after hearing it once at the theatre; and before he was even initiated he was able to repeat the Prâtiśâkhya which he had heard from Vyâḷi. He was afterwards the pupil of Varsha, became proficient in all sacred knowledge, and actually defeated Pâṇini in a grammatical controversy. By the interference of Śiva, however, the final victory fell to Pâṇini. Kâtyâyana had to appease the anger of Śiva, became himself a student of Pâṇini's Grammar, and completed and corrected it. He afterwards is said to have become minister of King Nanda and his mysterious successor Yogananda at Pâṭaliputra.

We know that Kâtyâyana completed and corrected Pâṇini's Grammar, such as we now possess it.[1] His Vârttikas are supplementary rules, which show a more extensive and accurate knowledge of Sanskrit than even the work of Pâṇini. The story of the contest between them was most likely intended as a mythical way of explaining this fact. Again we know that Kâtyâyana was himself the author of one of the Prâtiśâkhyas, and Vyâḷi is quoted by the authors of the Prâtiśâkhyas as an earlier authority on the same subject.[2] So far the story of Somadeva agrees with the account of Shaḍguruśishya and with the facts as

[1] The same question with regard to the probable age of Pâṇini, has been discussed by Prof. Böhtlingk in his edition of Pâṇini. Objections to Prof. Böhtlingk's arguments have been raised by Prof. Weber in his Indische Studien. See also Rig-veda, Leipzig, 1857, Introduction.

[2] Cf. Rig-veda, Leipzig, 1857, p. lxvii.

we still find them in the works of Kâtyâyana. It would be wrong to expect in a work like that of Somadeva historical and chronological facts in the strict sense of the word ; yet the mention of King Nanda, who is an historical personage, in connection with our grammarian, may, if properly interpreted, help to fix approximately the date of Kâtyâyana and his predecessors, Śaunaka and Âśvalâyana. If Somadeva followed the same chronological system as his contemporary and countryman, Kalhaṇa Paṇḍita, the author of the Râjataranginî or History of Kashmir, he would, in calling Pâṇini and Kâtyâyana, the contemporaries of Nanda and Chandragupta, have placed them long before the times which we are wont to call historical.[1] But the name of Chandragupta fortunately enables us to check the extravagant systems of Indian chronology. Chandragupta, of Pâṭaliputra, the successor of the Nandas, is Sandrocottus, of Palibothra, to whom Megasthenes was sent as ambassador from Seleucus Nicator ; and, if our classical chronology is right, he must have been king at the turning point of the fourth and third centuries B.C. We shall have to examine hereafter the different accounts which the Buddhists and Brahmans give of Chandragupta and his relation to the preceding dynasty of the Nandas. Suffice it for the present that if Chandragupta was king in 315, Kâtyâyana may be placed, according to our interpretation of Somadeva's story, in the second half of the fourth century B.C. We may disregard the story of Somadeva, which actually makes Kâtyâyana himself minister of Nanda, and thus would make him an old man at the time of Chandragupta's accession to the throne. This is, according to its own

[1] Lassen, Indische Alterthumskunde, ii. 18.

showing, a mere episode in a ghost story[1], and had to be inserted in order to connect Kâtyâyana's story with other fables of the Kathâ-sarit-sâgara. But there still remains this one fact, however slender it may appear, that as late as the twelfth century A.D., the popular tradition of the Brahmans connected the famous grammarians Kâtyâyana and Pâṇini with that period of their history which immediately preceded the rise of Chandragupta and his Śûdra dynasty; and this, from an European point of view, we must place in the second half of the fourth century B.C.

The question now arises, can this conjectural date, assigned to Kâtyâyana, be strengthened by additional evidence? Professor Böhtlingk thought that this was possible; and he endeavoured to show that the great Commentary of Patanjali, which embraces both the Vârttikâs of Kâtyâyana and the Sûtras of Pâṇini, was known in the middle of the second century B.C. It is said in the history of Kashmir, that Abhimanyu, the king of Kashmir, sent for Brahmans to teach the Mahâbhâshya in his kingdom. Abhimanyu, it is true, did not reign, as Professor Böhtlingk supposed, in the second century B.C., but, as has been proved from coins by Professor Lassen, in the first century A.D. But even thus this argument is important. In the history of Indian literature dates are mostly so precarious that a confirmation even within a century or two is not to be despised. The fact that Patanjali's immense commentary on Pâṇini and Kâtyâyana had become so famous as to be imported by royal authority into Kashmir in the first half of the first century

[1] According to the southern Buddhists it was Chandragupta, and not Nanda, whose corpse was reanimated. As. Res. xx. p. 167.

A.D., shows at least that we cannot be very far wrong in placing the composition of the original grammar and of the supplementary rules of Kâtyâyana on the threshold of the third century B.C. At what time the Mahâbhâshya was first composed it is impossible to say. Patanjali, the author of the Great Commentary, is sometimes identified with Pingala; and on this view, as Pingala is called the younger brother, or at least the descendant of Pâṇini[1], it might be supposed that the original composition of the Mahâbhâshya belonged to the third century. But the identity of Pingala and Patanjali is far from probable, and it would be rash to use it as a foundation for other calculations.

It will readily be seen how entirely hypothetical all these arguments are. If they possess any force it is this, that in spite of the conflicting statements of Brahmanical, Buddhist, and European scholars, nothing has been brought forward as yet that would render the date here assigned to Kâtyâyana impossible. Nay more; — if we place Kâtyâyana in the second half of the fourth century, Âśvalâyana, the predecessor of Kâtyâyana, about 350, and Śaunaka, the teacher of Âśvalâyana, about 400; and if then, considering the writers of Sûtras anterior to Śaunaka and posterior to Kâtyâyana, we extend the limits of the Sautra period of literature from 600 to 200, we are still able to say, that there is no fact in history or literature that would interfere with such an arrangement. As an experiment, therefore, though as no more than an experiment, we propose to fix the years 600 and 200 B.C. as the limits of that age

[1] Shaḍguruśishya: तथा च स्मृयते हि भगवता पिंगलेन पाणिन्यनुजेन॥

during which the Brahmanic literature was carried on in the strange style of Sûtras.

In order to try the strength of our supposition we shall ourselves attempt the first attack upon it.

There is a work called the Uṇâdi-sûtras, which, as it is quoted under this name by Pâṇini, must have existed previous to his time. The author is not known. Among the words the formation of which is taught in the Uṇâdi-sûtras[1], we find (iii. 140) *dînâraḥ*, a golden ornament; (iii. 2) *Jinaḥ*, synonymous with Arhat, a Buddhist saint; (iv. 184) *tirîṭam*, a golden diadem; (iii. 25) *stûpaḥ*, a pile of earth.

The first of these words, *dînâra*, is derived by the author of the Uṇâdi-sûtras from a Sanskrit root, *dîñ*. By other grammarians it is derived from *dîna*, poor, and *ṛi*, to go, what goes or is given to the poor. It is used sometimes in the sense of ornaments and seals of gold. These derivations, however, are clearly fanciful, and the Sanskrit *dînâra* is in reality the Latin *denarius*.[2] Now, if Pâṇini lived in the middle of the fourth century B.C., and if the Uṇâdi-sûtras were anterior to Pâṇini, how could this Roman word have found its way into the Uṇâdi-sûtras? The word *de-*

[1] A new and more correct edition of the Uṇâdi-sûtras has lately been published by Dr. Aufrecht, Bonn, 1859.

[2] J. Prinsep says: "The Roman denarius, from which *Dinâr* was derived, was itself of silver, while the Persian *Dirhem* (a silver coin) represents the Drachma, or dram weight, of the Greeks. The weight allowed to the Dinar of 32 *ratis*, or 64 grains, agrees so closely with the Roman and Greek unit of 60 grains, that its identity cannot be doubted, especially when we have before us the actual gold coins of Chandragupta (?) (didrachmas), weighing from 120 to 130 grains, and indubitably copied from Greek originals, in device as well as weight."

narius is not of so late a date in India as is generally supposed. Yet the earliest document where it occurs is the Sanchi inscription No. I.[1] Burnouf remarked that he never found the word *dînâra* used in what he considered the ancient Buddhist Sûtras. It occurs in the Avadâna-śataka, and in the Divyâvadâna. It would seem to follow, therefore, either that the Uṇâdi-sûtras and Pâṇini must be placed later than Chandragupta, or that the Sûtra in which this word is explained is spurious. It would not be right to adopt the latter supposition without showing some cause for it. It is well known that in a literature which is chiefly preserved by oral tradition, corrections and additions are more easily admitted than in works existing in MS. The ancient literature of India was continually learnt by heart; and even at the present day, when MSS. have become so common, some of its more sacred portions must still be acquired by the pupil from the mouth of a teacher, and not from MSS. If new words, therefore, had been added to the language of India after the first composition of the Uṇâdi-sûtras, there would be nothing surprising in a Sûtra being added to explain such words. Happily, however, we are not left in this instance to mere hypothesis. Ujjvaladatta, the author of a commentary on the Uṇâdi-sûtras, forms a favourable exception to most Sanskrit commentators, in so far as he gives us in his Commentary some critical remarks on the readings of MSS. which he consulted. He states in his introduction that he had consulted old MSS. and commentaries, and he evidently feels conscious of the merit of his work, when

[1] Journal A. S. B., vol. vi. p. 455. Notes on the facsimiles of the inscriptions from Sanchi near Bhilsa, by James Prinsep.

he says, "If anybody, after having studied this commentary of mine, suppresses my name in order to put forth his own power, his virtuous deeds will perish."[1] Now in his remarks on our Sûtra, Ujjvaladatta says, "Dinâra means a gold ornament, but this Sûtra is not to be found in the Sûtîvṛitti and Devavṛitti."[2] If, therefore, the presence of this word in the Uṇâdi-sûtras would have overthrown our calculations as to the age of Pâṇini and his predecessor who wrote the Sûtras, the absence of it except in one Sûtra, which is proved to be of later date, must serve to confirm our opinion. Cosmas Indicopleustes remarked that the Roman denarius was received all over the world; and how the denarius came to mean in India a gold ornament we may learn from a passage in the "Life of Mahâvîra."[3] There it is said that a lady had around her neck a string of grains and golden dinars, and Stevenson adds that the custom of stringing coins together, and adorning with them children especially, is still very common in India.

That Ujjvaladatta may be depended upon when he makes such statements with regard to MSS. or commentaries, collated by himself, can be proved by another instance. In the Uṇâdi-sûtras IV. 184, we read: "kṛîtṛîkṛipibhyaḥ kîṭan." Out of the three words of which the etymology is given in this Sûtra, *kṛipîṭam*, water, and *kirîṭam*, a crest, are known as ancient words. The former occurs in the Gaṇa

[1] योऽमुं वृत्तिं समालोच्य स्वपौरुषसमीहया।
मन्नामाच्छादनं कुर्यात्सुकृतं तस्य नश्यति॥

[2] सूत्रमिदं सूतीवृत्तौ (सतीवृत्तौ ?) देववृत्तौ च न दृश्यते॥

[3] Kalpa-sûtra, translated by Stevenson, p. 45.

Kṛipaṇâdi (Pâṇ. VIII. 2. 18. 1.); the other in the Gaṇa arddharchâdi. The third word, however, *tirîṭa*, a tiara, has never been met with in works previous to Pâṇini. Now, with regard to this word, Ujjvaladatta observes that it is left out in the Nyâsa.[1] The authority of this work, a commentary by Jinendra on the Kâśikâvṛitti, would, by itself, be hardly of sufficient weight; but on referring to the MS. of Mahâbhâshya at the Bodleian Library, I find that there also the Sûtra is quoted exactly as Ujjvaladatta said, *i. e.* without the root from which *tirîṭa* is derived. Having thus found Ujjvaladatta trustworthy and accurate in his critical remarks, we feel inclined to accept his word, even where we cannot control him, or where the presence of certain words in the Sûtras might be explained without having recourse to later interpolations. Thus *stûpaḥ*, which occurs III. 25, might be explained as simply meaning a heap of earth. Nay, it is a word which, in its more general sense, is found in the Veda. Yet the most common meaning of *stûpa* is a Buddhist monument, and as we are told by Ujjvala, that this word does not occur in the Satîvṛitti, and that in the Sarvasva it is derived in a different manner, we can have little doubt that it was not added till after the general·

[1] कृपो रो लः (पा° ८. २. १८.) इत्यत्र न्यासे कृकपिभ्यां चेति सूत्रं दृश्यते। अतस्तरतिरत्र नास्तीति लक्ष्यते॥ Colebrooke, Miscellaneous Essays, ii. 40, mentions this work in his list of Sanskrit grammars: "Nyâsa or Kâśikâ vṛitti panjikâ by Jinendra: another exposition of the Kâśikâ vṛitti, with explanatory notes by Rakshita." He adds, however, with his usual caution: "I state this with some distrust, not having yet seen the book. The Nyâsa is universally cited; and the Bodhinyâsa is frequently so. Vopadeva's Kâvyakâmadhenu quotes the Nyâsa of Jinendra and that of Jinendrabuddhi."

spreading of Buddhism and the erection of Topes in India; a negative argument which gives additional strength to the supposition that the original Uṇâdi-sûtras were composed before that period.[1]

To add one more instance. In all the editions of the Uṇâdi-sûtras, Jina occurs as the name of the founder of a Bauddha sect. As many scholars have assigned to Jina and the Jains a very modern date, the presence of this name might seem to throw considerable doubt on the antiquity ascribed to the Uṇâdi-sûtras. In a passage of Sâyaṇa, however (Rv. i. 61. 4.), where he has occasion to quote the Sûtra containing, among other words, the etymology of Jina, all the MSS. omit the root *ji*, from which Jina is said to be derived. It is equally omitted in Nṛisinha's Svaramanjarî.

The test which has thus been applied to our chronological arrangement of the Sûtra literature in general, in the case of the Uṇâdi-sûtras, so far from invalidating, has rather strengthened our argument for placing the whole literature of the Sûtras, at least of those which are connected with the Vedas, between the years 600 and 200 B.C.

PARIŚISHṬAS.

her c is one class of works which must be mentioned before we leave the Sûtra period, the so-called *Pariśishṭas*. They are evidently later than the Sûtras, and their very name, Paralipomena, marks their secondary importance. They have, however, a character of their own, and they represent a distinct period of Hindu literature, which, though it is of

[1] The word stûpa does not occur in Pâṇini or the Gaṇapâṭha. Sâyaṇa to Rv. i. 24. 7. does not quote the Uṇâdi-sûtra, but derives stûpa from a root styai, affix pa.

less interest to the student, and though it shows clear traces of intellectual and literary degeneracy, is not on that account to be overlooked by the historian. Some of the more substantial Pariśishṭas profess to be composed by authors whose names belong to the Sûtra period. Thus Śaunaka is called the author of the Charaṇavyûha by the commentator of Pâraskara's Gṛihya-sûtras, Râma-kṛishṇa[1] (MS. E.I.H. 440. 577. 912.); a writer no doubt quite untrustworthy where he gives his own opinions, but yet of some importance where he quotes the opinions of others. Kâtyâyana is quoted as the author of the Chhandoga-pariśishṭa.[2] The same Kuśika, who is known as the author of the Sûtras for the Âtharvaṇa, is mentioned as the author of the Âtharvaṇa-pariśishṭas also. Other Pariśishṭas, though not ascribed to Kâtyâyana, are said to be composed in accordance with his opinions.[3] Again, while the Gṛihya-sûtras of the Chhandogas are acknowledged as the work of Gobhila, a Pariśishṭa on the same subject is ascribed to the son of Gobhila.[4] The names of Śaunaka and Kâtyâyana are frequently invoked at the beginning or end of these works, and though some of them appear to us simply useless and insipid, it is not to be

1 तन्निर्णयश्चरणव्यूहे शौनकेन दर्शितः॥

2 छंदोगपरिशिष्टं कात्यायनमुनिकृतं सामवेदिककर्मबोधकं गोभिलसूत्राणां परिशेषशास्त्रमिति स्मृतिः॥

3 MS. Bodl. W. 510. अष्टादश परिशिष्टानि तदादौ यूपलक्षणं। चातुर्ण्यं (चातुर्वर्ण्यं) प्रवक्ष्यामि वृत्ताणां पशुभिः सह॥ निंदाप्रशंसे वक्ष्यामः कात्यायनमतात्तथा॥

4 MS. Bodl. W. 504. गृह्यसंग्रहं नाम परिशिष्टं गोभिलपुत्रकृतं॥

denied that others contain information which we should look for in vain in the Sûtras. Their style is less concise than that of the Sûtras. The simple Anushṭubh Śloka preponderates, and the metre is more regular than that of the genuine Anushṭubh compositions of Śaunaka. Their style resembles that of the Bârhaddaivata and Rig-vidhâna, works originally composed by Śaunaka, but handed down to us, as it would seem, in a more modern form. But on the other side the Pariśishṭas have not yet fallen into that monotonous uniformity which we find in works like the Mânava-dharma-śâstra, the Paddhatis, or the later Purâṇas; and passages from them are literally quoted in the Purâṇas. The Pariśishṭas, therefore, may be considered the very last outskirts of Vedic literature, but they are Vedic in their character, and it would be difficult to account for their origin at any time except the expiring moments of the Vedic age.

The following argument may serve to confirm the favourable view which I take of some of the Pariśishṭas. Besides the MSS. of the Charaṇavyûha, there is a printed edition of it in Râja Râdhakânta Deva's Śabdakalpadruma. This printed text is evidently taken from more modern MSS. It quotes seventeen instead of fifteen Śâkhâs of the Vâjasaneyins; whereas the original number of fifteen is confirmed by our MSS. of the Charaṇavyûha, by the Pratijnâ-pariśishṭa, and even by so late a work as the Vishṇu-purâṇa (p. 281.). We may therefore suppose that at the time when the Pariśishṭa, called the Charaṇavyûha, was originally composed, these two additional Śâkhâs did not yet exist. Now one of them is the Śâkhâ of the Kâtyâyanîyas, a Śâkhâ like many of those mentioned in the Purâṇas, founded on Sûtras, not on

Brâhmaṇas. The fact, therefore, of this modern Śâkhâ not being mentioned in the original Charaṇavyûha serves as an indication that at the time of the original composition of that Pariśishṭa sufficient time had not yet elapsed to give to Kâtyâyana the celebrity of being the founder of a new Śâkhâ. On the other hand it should be stated that Pâṇini does not seem to have known literary works called Pariśishṭas.[1]

The number of Pariśishṭas is frequently stated at eighteen. This may have been their number at some time, or for one particular Veda, but it is now considerably exceeded. The Charaṇavyûha, itself a Pariśishṭa, gives the same number; but it seems to speak of the Pariśishṭas of the Yajur-veda only. There is a collection of Pariśishṭas for each Veda. Works, such as the Bahvṛicha-pariśishṭa, Śânkhâyana-pariśishṭa, Âśvalâyana-gṛihya-pariśishṭa, must be ascribed to the Rig-veda. One MS. (Bodl. 466.) contains a collection of Pariśishṭas which belong to the Sâma-veda. At the end of the first treatise it is said: "iti Sâmagânâm chhandaḥ samâptam," "here end the metres of the Sâma-singers."[2] Other treatises begin with the invocation, "Namaḥ Sâmavedâya." The second is called Kratu-sangraha[3], on sacrifices; the third, Viniyoga-sangraha, on the employment of hymns; the fourth, Somotpattiḥ, on the origin of Soma. The fifth and sixth treatises contain the index to the Ârchika of the Sâma-veda after the Naigeya-śâkhâ. As no pointed allusions to other Vedas occur

[1] Pariśishṭa occurs only as a pratyudâharaṇa in Pâṇ. iv. 1. 48, but it is used there as a feminine, and in quite a different sense.

[2] It is also called chhandasâm vichayaḥ, and contains quotations from the Tâṇḍya-brâhmaṇa, Pingala, the Nidâna, and Uktha-śâstra.

[3] The Kratu-sangraha and Viniyoga-sangraha are frequently quoted by Sâyaṇa in his commentary on the Tâṇḍyabrâhmaṇa in elucidation of obscure passages. (Bühler.)

in these tracts, the whole collection of these Pariśishṭas may be classed as Sâma-veda literature. The Chhandoga-pariśishṭa, however, which is commonly ascribed to Kâtyâyana, is not found in this MS. The Pariśishṭas of the Yajur-veda are enumerated in the Charaṇavyûha, and will have to be examined presently. Those of the Âtharvaṇa are estimated by Professor Weber at seventy-four[1], and are said to be written in the form of dialogues, in a style similar to that of the Purâṇas, and sometimes, we are told, agreeing literally with chapters of the astrological Sanhitâs.

According to the Charaṇavyûha[2] the following are the eighteen Pariśishṭas of the Yajur-veda :

1. The Yûpalakshaṇam ; according to Vyâsa's Charaṇavyûha, the Upajyotisham.
2. The Chhâgalakshaṇam ; Mângalalakshaṇam, (Vyâsa).
3. The Pratijnâ ; Pratijnânuvâkyam ? (Vyâsa).
4. The Anuvâkasankhyâ ; Parisankhyâ (Vyâsa).
5. The Charaṇavyûhaḥ ; Charaṇavyûhaḥ (Vyâsa).
6. The Śrâddhakalpaḥ ; Śrâddhakalpaḥ (Vyâsa).
7. The Śulvikâni or Śulvâni.
8. The Pârshadam.

[1] According to a passage in the Charaṇavyûha, belonging to the Âtharvaṇa, the number of the Kauśikoktâni Pariśishṭâni would amount to 70.

[2] Besides the MS. of the E. I. H., and collations of some of the MSS. at Berlin, I have used the printed edition of the Charaṇavyûha in Râdhakânta's Sanskrit Encyclopædia. The MSS. differ so much that it would be hazardous to correct the one by the other. They probably represent different versions of the same text. The name of the author varies likewise. Sometimes he is called Śaunaka, sometimes Kâtyâyana, and in Râdhakânta's edition, Vyâsa. The last is, perhaps, meant for the same whom we found mentioned before as the author of a Commentary on Patanjali's Yoga. The text has since been published by Prof. Weber.

9. The Ṛigyajûnshî.
10. The Ishṭakâpûraṇam.
11. The Pravarâdhyâyaḥ; Pravarâdhâyaḥ (Vyâsa, No. 7.)
12. The Uktha-śâstram; Śâstram (Vyâsa, No. 8.)
13. The Kratusankhyâ; Kratu (Vyâsa, No. 9).
14. The Nigamâḥ; Âgamaḥ (Vyâsa, No. 10).
15. The Yajnapârśve or pârśvam; Yajnam (Vyâsa, No. 11); Pârśvân (Vyâsa, No. 12).
16. The Hautrakam; Hautrakam (Vyâsa, No. 13).
17. The Prasavotthânam; Paśavaḥ (Vyâsa, No. 14); Ukthâni, (Vyâsa, No. 15).
18. The Kûrmalakshaṇam; Kûrmalakshaṇam, (Vyâsa, No. 16).

A similar order has evidently been followed in a collection of the Pariśishṭas, forming part of Professor Wilson's valuable collection of MSS., now deposited in the Bodleian Library. The MS., however, is incomplete, and seems to have been copied by a person ignorant of Sanskrit from another MS., the leaves of which had been in confusion. Most of the MSS. of these Pariśishṭas are carelessly copied, whereas the MSS. of the Sûtras are generally in excellent condition. The MSS. which Râja Râdhakântadeva used seem to have been in an equally bad state, if we may judge from the various readings which he occasionally mentions.[1] But although the Bodleian MS. leaves much to desire, it serves at least to support the authenticity of the titles given in the MS. of the Charaṇavyûha against the blunders of the printed text. We find there:

[1] For instance पारय्यानुह्रोत्रकमपि पाठः। instead of पार्श्वान्। हौत्रकं॥

1. The Yûpalakshaṇam[1], a short treatise on the manner of preparing the sacrificial post.

2. The Chhâgalakshaṇam[2], on animals fit for sacrifice.

3. The Pratijnâ.[3] It begins with giving some definitions of sacrificial terms, but breaks off with the fourth leaf, whereas the Pravarâdhyâya (No. 11) had already been commenced on the third, and is afterwards carried on on the fifth leaf. Thus we lose from the fourth to the eleventh Pariśishṭa, which formed part of the original MS. if we may judge from the fact that the Pravarâdhyâya is here also called the eleventh Pariśishṭa.

4. The Anuvâkasankhyâ exists in MS. E.I.H. 965.

5. The Charaṇavyûhaḥ is found in numerous copies.

6. The Śrâddhakalpaḥ exists in MS. E.I.H. 1201, and MS. Chambers 66. It is there ascribed to Kâtyâyana. There is also among the Chambers MSS. at Berlin (292—294) a Śrâddha-kalpa-bhâshya ascribed to Gobhila.

7. The Śulvikâni are found in MS. Chambers 66, and a Śulvadîpikâ, MS. E.I.H. 1678.

8. The Pârshadam. This must not be mistaken for a Prâtiśâkhya, nor would it be right to call the Prâtiśâkhyas Pariśishṭas. The Pârshada is a much smaller work, as may be seen from a MS. in the Royal Library at Berlin, Chambers 378.

9. The Ṛigyajûnshi is the only Pariśishṭa that cannot be verified in MS.; there is no reason for supposing that it was an Anukramaṇî either of the Yajur-veda or Ṛig-veda.

10. The Ishṭakâpûraṇam has been preserved in

[1] MS. Chambers, 66.

[2] MS. Chambers, 66.

[3] Called Prâtishṭhâlakshaṇam in MS. Chambers, 66.

MS. Chambers 389, with a commentary by Karka, and in MS. Chambers 392, with a commentary by Yâjnikadeva.

11. The Pravarâdhyâyaḥ is found again in our own MS., and is followed by a small tract, the Gotranirṇayaḥ. The seven principal Pravaras are those of the Bhṛigus, Angiras, Viśvâmitras, Vasishṭhas, Kaśyapas, Atris, and Agastis. The eight founders of Gotras or families are Jamadagni, Bharadvâja, Viśvâmitra, Atri, Gautama, Vasishṭha, Kaśyapa and Agastya.[1] The whole treatise, of which more hereafter, is ascribed to Kâtyâyana.[2]

12. The Uktha-śâstram is found in our MS. So is

13. The Kratusankhyâ, which gives an enumeration of the principal sacrifices.

14. The Nigama-pariśishṭa is the last in our MS. It contains a number of Vedic words with their explanations, and forms a useful appendix to Yâska's Nirukta. It alludes not only to the four castes, but the names of the mixed castes also, according to the Anuloma and Pratiloma order, are mentioned.

The four last Pariśishṭas are wanting in our MS.

The fifteenth, however, the Yajnapârśvam is found in MS. E.I.H. 1729, Chambers, 358; the sixteenth, the Hautrakam, exists with a commentary in MS. Chambers 669. The two last Pariśishṭas have not yet been met with in MS., but we may probably

[1] जमदग्निर्भरद्वाजो विश्वामित्रोऽत्रिगौतमौ।
वसिष्ठकश्यपागस्त्या मुनयो गोत्रकारिणः॥
एतेषां यान्यपत्यानि तानि गोत्राणि मन्यते॥

[2] कात्यायनविरचितो विप्राणां हितकाम्यया।
अध्यायः प्रवराख्योऽयं पुरा ब्रह्मविनिर्मितः॥

form some idea of the last, the Kûrmalakshaṇam, from some chapters of Varâhamihira's Bṛihatsanhitâ, where we find both a Kûrmavibhâgaḥ and a Kûrmalakshaṇam, the last being there followed by a chapter, called by the same name as the second Pariśishṭa, Chhâgalakshaṇam.

Although there is little of real importance to be learned from these Pariśishṭas, the fact of their existence is important in the history of the progress and decay of the Hindu mind. As in the first or Chhandas period, we see the Aryan settlers of India giving free utterance to their thoughts and feelings, and thus creating unconsciously a whole world of religious, moral, and political ideas; as we find them again during the second or Mantra period, carefully collecting their harvest; and during the third or Brâhmaṇa period busily occupied in systematising and interpreting the strains of their forefathers, which had already become unintelligible and sacred; as in the fourth or Sûtra period we see their whole energy employed in simplifying the complicated system of the theology and the ceremonial of the Brâhmaṇas; so we shall have to recognise in these Pariśishṭas a new phase of the Indian mind, marked by a distinct character, which must admit of historical explanation. The object of the Pariśishṭas is to supply information on theological or ceremonial points which had been passed over in the Sûtras, most likely because they were not deemed of sufficient importance, or because they were supposed to be well known to those more immediately concerned. But what most distinguishes the Pariśishṭas from the Sûtras is this, that they treat everything in a popular and superficial manner; as if the time was gone, when students would spend ten or twenty years of their lives in fathoming the mysteries and mastering the intricacies of the Brâhmaṇa literature. A party driven to such publications as the Pariśishṭas, is a party fighting a losing battle. We see no longer that self-complacent spirit which pervades the Brâhmaṇas. The authors of the Brâhmaṇas felt that whatever they said must be believed, whatever they ordained must be obeyed. They are frightened by no absurdity, and the word "impossible" seems to have been banished from their dictionary. In the Sûtras we see that a change has taken place. Their authors seem to feel that the public which they address will no longer listen to endless theological swaggering. There may have been deep wisdom in the Brâhmaṇas, and their authors may have sincerely believed in all they said; but they evidently calculated on a submissiveness on the part of their pupils or readers, which only exists in countries domineered over by priests or professors. The authors of the Sûtras have learned that people will not listen to wisdom unless it is clothed in a garb of clear argument and communicated in intelligible language. Their works contain all that is essential in the Brâhmaṇas, but they give it in a practical, concise and definite form. These works were written at a time when the Brahmans were fighting their first battles against the popular doctrines of Buddha. They were not yet afraid. Their language is firm, though it is no longer inflated. "Buddhism," as Burnouf says,[1] "soon grew into a system of easy devotion, and found numerous recruits among those who were frightened by the difficulties of Brahmanical science. At the same time that

[1] Burnouf, Introduction à l'Histoire du Buddhisme. Roth, Abhandlungen, p. 22.

Buddhism attracted the ignorant among the Brahmans, it received with open arms the poor and the miserable of all classes." It was to remove, or at least to simplify, the difficulties of their teaching, that men like Śaunaka and Kâtyâyana adopted the novel style of the Sûtras. Such changes in the sacred literature of a people are not made without an object, and the object of the Sûtras, as distinct from that of the Brâhmaṇas, could be no other than to offer practical manuals to those who were discouraged by too elaborate treatises, and who had found a shorter way to salvation opened to them by the heretical preaching of Buddha. After the Sûtras there is no literature of a purely Vedic character except the Pariśishṭas. They still presuppose the laws of the Sûtras and the faith of the Brâhmaṇas. There is as yet no trace of any definite supremacy being accorded to Śiva or Vishṇu or Brahman. New gods, however, are mentioned; vulgar or popular ceremonies are alluded to. The castes have become more marked and multiplied. The whole intellectual atmosphere is still Vedic, and the Vedic ceremonial, the Vedic theology, the Vedic language seem still to absorb the thoughts of the authors of the Pariśishṭas. Any small matter that had been overlooked by the authors of the Sûtras is noted down as a matter of grave importance. Subjects on which general instructions were formerly considered sufficient, are now treated in special treatises, intended for men who would no longer take the trouble of reading the whole system of the Brahmanic ceremonial. The technical and severe language of the Sûtras was exchanged for a free and easy style, whether in prose or metre; and however near in time the Brahmans may place the authors of the Sûtras and some of the Pariśishṭas, certain it is that no man who had mastered the Sûtra style would ever have condescended to employ the slovenly diction of the Pariśishṭas. The change in the position and the characters of the Brahmans, such as we find them in the Sûtras, and such as we find them again in the Pariśishṭas, has been rapid and decisive. The men who could write such works were aware of their own weakness, and had probably suffered many defeats. The world around them was moving in a new direction, and the old Vedic age died away in impotent twaddle.

Considerations like these, in addition to what we found before in inquiring into the age of Kâtyâyana, tend to fix the Sûtra period, as a phase in the literary history of India, as about contemporaneous with the first rise of Buddhism; and they would lead us to recognise in the Pariśishṭas the exponents of a later age, that had witnessed the triumphs of Buddhism and the temporary decay of Brahmanic learning and power. The real political triumph of Buddhism dates from Aśoka and his council, about the middle of the third century B.C., and while most of the Vedic Sûtras belong to this and the preceding centuries, none of the Pariśishṭas were probably written before that time.

Before the Council of Pâṭaliputra the Buddhists place, indeed, 300 years of Buddhist history, but that history was clearly supplied from their own heads and not from authentic documents. Buddhism, up to the time of Aśoka, was but one out of many sects established in India. There had been as yet no schism, but only controversy, such as we find in the Brâhmaṇas themselves between different schools and parties. There were as yet no Brahmans as opposed to

Buddhists, in the later sense of the word. No separation had as yet taken place, and the greatest reformers at the time of Buddha were reforming Brahmans. This is acknowledged in the Buddhist writings, though they probably were not written down before Aśoka's Council. But even then Buddha is represented as the pupil of the Brahmans, and no slur is cast on the gods and the songs of the Veda. Buddha, according to his own canonical biographer, learned the Rig-veda and was a proficient in all the branches of Brahmanic lore. His pupils were many of them Brahmans, and no hostile feeling against the Brahmans finds utterance in the Buddhist Canon. This forms a striking contrast with the sacred literature of the Jains. The Jains, though supposed to have made their peace with the Brahmans, yet in their sacred works, written towards the beginning of the fifth century A.D., treat their opponents with marked disrespect. Their great hero Mahâvîra, though at first conceived by a Brahman woman, is removed from her womb and transferred to the womb of a Kshatriya woman, for "surely," as Sakko (Indra) says[1], "such a thing as this has never happened in past, happens not in present, nor will happen in future time, that an Arhat, a Chakravarti, a Baladeva, or a Vasudeva should be born in a low caste family, a servile family, a degraded family, a poor family, a mean family, a beggar's family, or a Brahman's family; but, on the contrary, in all time, past, present, and to come, an Arhat, a Chakravarti, a Vasudeva, receives birth in a noble family, an honourable family, a royal family, a Kshatriya family, as in the family of Ikshvâku, or the Harivanśa, or some such family of pure descent."

[1] Kalpa-sutra, p. 35.

Now this is mere party insolence, intelligible in the fifth century A.D., when the Brahmans, as a party, were re-establishing their hierarchical sway. Nothing of the kind is to be found in the canonical books of the Buddhists. Buddha had his opponents, and among them chiefly the Tîrthakas; but so had all eminent sages of whom we read in the Brâhmaṇas. But Buddha had also his friends and followers, and they likewise were Brahmans and Ṛishis; some of them accepted his doctrines, not excluding the abolition of caste. Buddhism, in its original form, was only a modification of Brahmanism. It grew up slowly and imperceptibly, and its very founder could hardly have been aware of the final results of his doctrines. Before the time that Buddhism became a political power it had no history, no chronology, it hardly had a name. We hear nothing of Bauddhas in the Brâhmaṇas, though we meet there with doctrines decidedly Buddhistic. The historical existence of Buddhism begins with Aśoka, and the only way to fix the real date of Aśoka is by connecting him with Chandragupta, his second predecessor, the Sandrocottus of the Greeks. To try to fix it according to the early Buddhist chronology would be as hopeless as fixing the date of Alexander according to the chronology of the Purâṇas.

It is possible to discover in the decaying literature of Vedic Brahmanism the contemporaneous rise of a new religion, of Buddhism. Every attempt to go beyond, and to bring the chronology of the Buddhists and Brahmans into harmony has proved a failure. The reason, I believe, is obvious. The Brahmans had a kind of vague chronology in the different capitals of their country. They remembered the names of their kings, and they endeavoured to remember the years of their reigns. But to note the year in which an individual, such as Gautama Śâkyasinha, was born, however famous he may have been in his own neighbourhood or even in more distant Parishads, would have entered as little into their thoughts as the Romans, or even the Jews, thought of preserving the date of the birth of Jesus before he had become the founder of a religion. Buddha's immediate followers may have recollected and handed down, by oral communication, the age at which Buddha died; the age of his disciples too may have been recollected, together with the names of some local Râjas who patronised Buddha and his friends; but never, until the adoption of Buddhism as the state religion by Aśoka, could there have been any object in connecting the lives of Buddha and his disciples with the chronology of the Solar or Lunar Dynasties of India. When, at the time of Aśoka, it became necessary to give an account of the previous history of Buddhism, the chronology then adopted for the early centuries of that faith was necessarily of a purely theoretical kind. We possess more than one system of Buddhist chronology, but none of them can be considered authentic with regard to the times previous to Aśoka, the second successor of Chandragupta. There is the system of the Southern Buddhists, framed in Ceylon; there are the various systems of the Northern Buddhists, prevalent in Nepal, Tibet, and China; and the system of the Purâṇas, if system it can be called, in which Śâkya is made the father of his father, and grandfather of his son. To try to find out which of these chronological systems is the most plausible seems useless, and it can only make confusion worse confounded if we attempt a combination of the three. It has been usual to prefer the chronology of Ceylon, which places Buddha's death in 543 B.C. But the principal argument in favour of this date is extremely weak. It is said that the fact of the Ceylonese era being used as an era for practical purposes speaks in favour of its correctness. This may be true with regard to the times after the reign of Aśoka. In historical times any era, however fabulous its beginning, will be practically useful; but no conclusion can be drawn from this, its later use, as to the correctness of its beginning. As a conventional era, that of Ceylon may be retained, but until new evidence can be brought forward to substantiate the authenticity of the early history of Buddhism as told by the Ceylonese priests, it would be rash to use the dates of the Southern Buddhists as a corrective standard for those of the Northern Buddhists or of the Brahmans. Each of these chronological systems must be left to itself. They start from different premises, and necessarily arrive at different results. The Northern Buddhists founded their chronology on a reported prophecy of Buddha, that "a thousand years after his death his doctrines would reach the Northern countries."[1] Buddhism was definitely introduced into China in the year 61 A.D.; hence the Chinese fix the date of Buddha's death about one thousand years anterior to the Christian era. The variations of the date, according to different Chinese authorities, are not considerable, and may easily be explained by the uncertainty of the time at which Buddhism found its way successively into the various countries north of India, and at last into China.

[1] Lassen, Indian Antiquities, ii. p. 58. Schiefner, Mélanges Asiatiques, i. 436.

Besides 950 or 949 B.C.[1], which are the usual dates assigned to Buddha's death by Chinese authorities, we may mention the years 1130, 1045, 767, for each of which the same claim has been set up. The year 1130 rests on the authority of Tchao-chi, as quoted by Matouanlin in the annals of the Souï.[2] Fahian, also, seems to have known this date; for, according to his editor, he placed the death of Buddha towards the beginning of the dynasty Tcheu, and this, according to Chinese chronology, took place in 1122.[3] In another place, however, Fahian, speaking of the spreading of Buddhism towards the north, places this event 300 years after Buddha's Nirvâṇa, or in the reign of the Emperor Phing-Wang. As this emperor reigned 770—720, Fahian would seem to have dated the Nirvâṇa somewhere between 1070 and 1020. The date 767 rests on the authority of Matouanlin.[4] From Tibetan books no less than fourteen dates have been collected[5]; and the Chinese pilgrims who visited India found it impossible to fix on any one date as established on solid evidence. The list of the thirty-three Buddhist patriarchs, first published by Rémusat (Mélanges Asiatiques, i. p. 113), gives the date of their deaths from Chakia-mouni, who died 950 B.C., to Soui-neng, who died 713 A.D., and bears, like everything Chinese, the character of the most exact chronological accuracy. The first link,

[1] Lassen, ii. 52. Foucaux, Rgya Tcher Rol Pa, p. xi.

[2] Foucaux, l. c. note communicated by Stan. Julien.

[3] Neumann, Zeitschrift für die Kunde des Morgenlandes, ii. 117; Lassen, ii. 54.

[4] Foucaux, l. c. According to Klaproth Matouanlin places Buddha 688 to 609.

[5] Csoma, Tibetan Grammar, p. 199—201. They are: 2422, 2144, 2139, 2135, 1310, 1060, 884, 882, 880, 837, 752, 653, 576, 546.

however, in this long chain of patriarchs is of doubtful character, and the lifetime of Buddha, from 1029 to 950, rests only on his own prophecy, that a Millennium would elapse from his death to the conversion of China. If, therefore, Buddha was a true prophet he must have lived about 1000 B.C., and this date once established, everything else had to give way before it. Thus Nâgârjuna, called by the Chinese Nâga Koshuna, or Loung-chou, is placed in their own traditional chronology, which they borrowed from the Buddhists in Northern India, 400 years after the Nirvâṇa.[1] The Tibetans assign the same date to him.[2] In the list of the patriarchs, however, he occupies the fourteenth place, and dies 738 years after Buddha. The twelfth patriarch, Maning (Deva Bodhisatva), is traditionally placed by the Chinese 300 years after Buddha. In the list of the patriarchs he dies 618 years after the Nirvâṇa.

But if in this manner the starting-point of the Northern Buddhist chronology turns out to be merely hypothetical, based as it is on a prophecy of Buddha, it will be difficult to avoid the same conclusion with regard to the date assigned to Buddha's death by the Buddhists of Ceylon and of Burmah and other countries which received their canonical books from Ceylon. The Ceylonese possess a trustworthy and intelligible chronology beginning with the year 161 B.C.[3] Before that time their chronology is traditional, and full of absurdities. According to Professor Lassen, we ought to suppose that the Ceylonese, by some

[1] Lassen, ii. 58. Burnouf, Introduction, i. p. 350. n. 51.

[2] As they place Vasumitra more than 400 after Buddha, the date for Nágârjuna ought to be about 450.

[3] Turnour, Examination of the Pali Buddhistical Annals, Journal of the Asiatic Society of Bengal, vi. p. 721.

means or other, were in possession of the right date of Buddha's death; and as there was a prophecy of Buddha, that Vijaya should land in Ceylon on the same day on which he himself entered the Nirvâṇa,[1] we are further asked to believe that the Ceylonese historians placed the founder of the Vijayan dynasty of Ceylon in the year 543, in accordance with their sacred chronology. We are not told, however, through what channel the Ceylonese could have received their information as to the exact date of Buddha's death, and although Professor Lassen's hypothesis would be extremely convenient, and has been acquiesced in by most Sanskrit scholars, it would not be honest were we to conceal from ourselves or from others that the first and most important link in the Ceylonese, as well as in the Chinese chronology, is extremely weak. All we know for certain is, that the Ceylonese had an historical chro-

[1] Mahâvanso, p. 46. The Mahâvanśa was written in Pâli by Mahânâma. He was a priest and uncle of king Dasenkelleya or Dhâtusena, who reigned from A.D. 459 to 477. Mahânâma made use of earlier histories, and mentions among them the Dîpavanśa. This work, also called Mahâvanśa, and written in Pâli, is supposed to be still in existence, and carries the history to the reign of Mahâsena, who died A. D. 302. Mahânâma, though he lived more than a hundred years after Mahâsena's death, does not seem to have carried the history much further. His work ends with the account of Mahâsena's reign. It terminates with the 48th verse of the 37th chapter of what is now known as the Mahâvanśa, and it is only from conjecture that Turnour, the editor and translator of the first 38 chapters of the Mahâvanśa, ascribes the end of the 37th, and the whole of the 38th chapter, to the pen of Mahânâma. Mahânâma's work was afterwards continued by different writers. It now consists of 100 chapters, and carries the history of Ceylon to the middle of the 18th century. He is likewise the author of a commentary on his own work, which commentary ends at the 48th verse of the 37th chapter.

nology after the year 161 B.C., that is to say, long before the Brahmans or Buddhists of the North can show anything but tradition. If, then, the exact Ceylonese chronology begins with 161 B. C., it is but reasonable to suppose that there existed in Ceylon a traditional native chronology extending beyond that date; and that, at all events, the first conquest of Ceylon, the establishment of the first dynasty, had some date, whether true or false, assigned to it in the annals of the country. *Vijaya*, the founder of the first dynasty, means *Conquest*, and such a person most likely never existed. But his name and fame belong to Ceylon; and even the latest traditions have never connected him with the Buddhist dynasties of India. He is called in the Mahâvanśa, the son of Sinhabâhu, the sovereign of Lâla (supposed to be a subdivision of Magadha, near the Gandakî river), and he is connected by a miraculous genealogy with the kings of Banga (Bengal) and Kalinga (Northern Circars), but not with the Buddhist dynasties of Magadha. The only trace of Buddhism that can be discovered in the legends of Vijaya consists in the fact that his head, and the heads of his seven hundred companions, were shaved when they were sent adrift in a ship that was ultimately to bring them to Ceylon. But the author of the Mahâvanśa takes care to say that this shaving of their heads was part of the punishment inflicted on Vijaya by his father, who, when asked by the people to execute his own son for numberless acts of fraud and violence, preferred to send him and his companions adrift on the ocean, after their heads had been shaved. Supposing then that before Dushṭagâmani, *i. e.* before 161 B.C., the Ceylonese possessed a number of royal names, and that by assigning to each of them a more or less fabulous reign, they had arrived at the year 543 as the probable date of the Conquest, we can well understand how, under the influence of the later Buddhists, exactly the same thing took place in Ceylon which took place in China. Various temples in Ceylon had their legends, by which their first foundation was ascribed to Buddha himself. Hence the Mahâvanśa begins with relating three miraculous visits which Buddha, during his lifetime, paid to Ceylon. At that time, however, it is said that Ceylon was still inhabited by Yakshas. If thus the very earliest history of the island had been brought in connection with Buddha, it is but natural that some sanction of a similar kind should have been thought necessary with regard to the Conquest. A prophecy was, therefore, invented. "The ruler of the world, Buddha," so says the Mahâvanśa, "having conferred blessings on the whole world, and attained the exalted, unchangeable Nirvâṇa, seated on the throne on which Nirvâṇa is achieved, in the midst of a great assembly of devatâs, the great divine sage addressed this celebrated injunction to Śakra, who stood near him: 'One Vijaya, the son of Sinhabâhu, king of the land of Lâla, together with seven hundred officers of state, has landed on Lankâ. Lord of Devas! my religion will be established in Lankâ. On that account thoroughly protect, together with his retinue, him and Lankâ.' The devoted King of Devas having heard these injunctions of the successor (of former Buddhas), assigned the protection of Lankâ to the Deva Utpalavarṇa (Vishṇu). He, in conformity to the command of Śakra, instantly repaired to Lankâ, and in the character of a parivrâjaka (devotee) took his station at the foot of a tree.

"With Vijaya at their head the whole party approaching him, inquired, 'Pray, devotee, what land is this?' he replied, 'The land Lankâ.' Having thus spoken, he blessed them by sprinkling water on them out of his jug, and having tied (charmed) threads on their arms, departed through the air."

At the end of the preceding chapter, the date of the event is still more accurately fixed. "This prince named Vijaya," we read there, "who had then attained the wisdom of experience, landed in the division Tâmraparṇî of this land Lankâ, on the day that the successor of former Buddhas reclined in the arbour of the two delightful sal-trees, to attain Nirvâṇa." In this manner the conquest of Ceylon was invested with a religious character, and at the same time a connection was established between the traditional chronology of Ceylon and the sacred history of Buddha. If Buddha was a true prophet, the Ceylonese argue quite rightly that he must have died in the year of the Conquest, or 543 B.C.

This synchronism once established, it became necessary to accommodate to it, as well as possible, the rest of the legendary history of the Buddhists. It contained but few historical elements previous to Aśoka's Council, but that council had again to be connected with the history of Ceylon. Aśoka was the cotemporary of Devânâmpriya Tishya, King of Ceylon. This king adopted Buddhism, and made it, like Aśoka, the state religion of the island. Now, according to the traditional chronology of Ceylon, Devânâmpriya Tishya came to the throne 236 years after the landing of Vijaya[1], and he reigned forty years (307—267 B.C.) He was intimately connected with Aśoka, as we shall

[1] Mahâvanso, Pref. p. lii.

see, and it was necessary that the same interval which in the historical traditions of Ceylon separated Devânâmpriya Tishya from Vijaya should separate Aśoka from Buddha. This was achieved in the following manner: One Aśoka is supposed to have come to the throne ninety years after Buddha, and a council (the second, as it was called) is supposed to have taken place in the tenth year of his reign, or just one hundred years after Buddha. At that second council a prophecy was uttered that in 118 years a calamity would befall the Buddhist religion. This refers to the reign of the so-called second Aśoka, who was at first a great enemy to religion. Now the first Aśoka is represented to have reigned 18 years after the Council (100 anno Buddhæ), and if we cast up these 118 years, the 22 years of Aśoka's sons, the 22 years of the Nine, the 24 years[1] of Chandragupta, the 28 years of Bindusâra, and the 4 years which elapsed before Aśoka's inauguration[2], we find that Aśoka's inauguration would fall just 118 years after the second Council, 218 years after Buddha, or 325 B.C. The Council of this real Aśoka was held in the 17th year of his reign, or 235 after Buddha. Mahendra, the son of Aśoka, proceeded to Ceylon in the next year, or 236 years after Buddha; and in this manner the arrival of Mahendra in Ceylon, and the inauguration of Devânâmpriya Tishya as King of Ceylon, are brought together in the same year. It is true that in order to achieve this, it has become necessary to add a first Aśoka[3],

[1] Not thirty-four years, as printed in the Mahâvanso. See Lassen, ii. 62. n.

[2] As. Res. xx. p. 167.

[3] This first Aśoka is called Kâlâśoka, a name which it would be too bold to explain as the chronological Aśoka.

of whom the Northern Buddhists know nothing; it has become necessary to admit another Moggaliputto, and another Council, all equally unknown except in the traditional chronology of Ceylon. The Northern Buddhists know but one Aśoka, the grandson of Chandragupta; they know but one Council, besides the Assembly immediately following on the death of Buddha, viz. the Council of Pâṭaliputra under Dharmâśoka, and this they place 110 years after Buddha's Nirvâṇa.[1] Piṇḍola, a contemporary of Buddha, was seen as an old man by Aśoka. But who was to contradict the Ceylonese historians? They possessed, what the Buddhists of Magadha did not possess, a history of their island and their sovereigns. They valued historical chronology for its own sake, forming an exception in this respect to all other nations of India. They were a colony, and like most colonies, they valued the traditions of the past. The Buddhists of Magadha, as far as we are able to judge, preserved but a few historical recollections, frequently in the form of prophecies, which they afterwards forced into the loose frame of the Brahmanic chronology. The Buddhists of Ceylon did not borrow the outlines of their history either from the Brahmans or from the Buddhists of Magadha; and this is a point which has never been sufficiently considered. Their outlines of history were not constructed originally in order to hold the Buddhist traditions of the North. They may have been slightly modified, so as to avoid glaring inconsisten-

[1] In some instances that date is changed to 200 A.B., by means of a reaction exercised by the literature of Ceylon on the chronology of the Continental Buddhists. Burnouf, Introduction, p. 436. 578.

cies between the profane history of Ceylon and the sacred history of Buddhism. But there is evidence to show that, on the other hand, the historical legends of Magadha had to yield much more considerably,—the framers of the final chronology finding it impossible to ignore the annals of their island and the reigns of their ancient half-fabulous kings. The chronology of the Mahâvanśa is a compromise between the chronology of Ceylon and that of Magadha, but the latter was the more pliant of the two. There is nothing to prove that the *terminus à quo* of the chronology of Ceylon,—the date of Vijaya's landing—was borrowed from the North. There were Buddhist traditions connecting Vijaya's landing with the death of Buddha, but the date 543 B. C. is never found in the sacred chronology of Buddhism, before it was borrowed from the profane chronology of Ceylon. There were similar, and, as it would seem, better founded traditions, connecting Devânâmpriya Tishya with the great Aśoka; but the date of Devânâmpriya Tishya was not determined by the date of the great Aśoka, nor was the date of Aśoka's Council, as 110 after Buddha, accepted in Ceylon. On the contrary, the interval between Vijaya and Devânâmpriya Tishya was allowed to remain as it stood in the Ceylonese annals, and the Buddhist traditions were stretched in order to suit that interval. An intermediate Aśoka and an intermediate Council were admitted, which were unknown to the Northern Buddhists. The prophecy that Nâgârjuna should live 400 years after Buddha[1], had been altered by the Chinese so as to suit their chronology. They placed him 800 years after

[1] As. Res. xx. 513.

Buddha. In like manner the Ceylonese Buddhists, having fixed Buddha's death at 543 B.C., changed the traditional date of Nâgârjuna from 400 to 500 after Buddha.[1] All this is constructive chronology, and whether we follow the Chinese or Ceylonese date of Buddha, we must always remember that in both the *terminus à quo* is purely hypothetical. This does not interfere with the correctness of minor details, such as the number of years assigned to each king, and in particular the chronological distance between certain events. These may have formed part of popular tradition, long before any system of chronology was established. A very old man, Pindola, was represented in a popular legend to have been a contemporary both of Buddha and of Dharmâśoka. Hence the interval between the founder and the royal patron of Buddhism would naturally be fixed at about 100 years. This is a tradition which may be used for historical purposes. Again, when we see that a date like that of Nâgârjuna fixed in the North of India at 400 after Buddha, is altered to 800 and 500, so as to suit the requirements of two different systems of chronology, we may feel inclined to look upon the unsystematic date as the most plausible. But in order to make use of such indications we must first of all establish a ποῦ στῶ, and this can only be found in Chandragupta. Everything in Indian chronology depends on the date of Chandragupta. Chandragupta was the grandfather of Aśoka, and the contemporary of Seleucus Nicator. Now, according to Chinese chronology, Aśoka would have lived, to waive minor

[1] Turnour, Examination of some points of Buddhist Chronology, Journal of the As. S. B., v. 530. Lassen, ii. 58.

differences, 850 or 750 B.C., according to Ceylonese chronology, 315 B.C. Either of these dates is impossible, because it does not agree with the chronology of Greece, and hence both the Chinese and Ceylonese dates of Buddha's death must be given up as equally valueless for historical calculations.

There is but one means through which the history of India can be connected with that of Greece, and its chronology be reduced to its proper limits. Although we look in vain in the literature of the Brahmans or Buddhists for any allusion to Alexander's conquest, and although it is impossible to identify any of the historical events, related by Alexander's companions, with the historical traditions of India, one name has fortunately been preserved by classical writers who describe the events immediately following Alexander's conquest, to form a connecting link between the history of the East and the West. This is the name of Sandracottus or Sandrocyptus, the Sanskrit Chandragupta.

We learn from classical writers, Justin, Arrian, Diodorus Siculus, Strabo, Quintus Curtius and Plutarch, that in Alexander's time there was on the Ganges a powerful king of the name of Xandrames, and that soon after Alexander's invasion, a new empire was founded there by Sandracottus or Sandrocyptus. Justin says: "Sandracottus gave liberty to India after Alexander's retreat, but soon converted the name of liberty into servitude after his success, subjecting those whom he had rescued from foreign dominion to his own authority. This prince was of humble origin, but was called to royalty by the power of the gods; for, having offended Alexander by his impertinent language,[1] he was ordered to be put to death, and escaped only by flight. Fatigued with his journey he lay down to rest, when a lion of large size came and licked off the sweat that poured from him with his tongue, and retired without doing him any harm. The prodigy inspired him with ambitious hopes, and collecting bands of robbers he roused the Indians to rebellion. When he prepared for war against the captains of Alexander, a wild elephant of enormous size approached him, and received him on his back as if he had been tamed. He was a distinguished general and a brave soldier. Having thus acquired power, Sandracottus reigned over India at the time when Seleucus was laying the foundation of his greatness, and Seleucus entered into a treaty with him, and settling affairs on the side of India directed his march against Antigonus."[2]

Besides this we may gather from classical writers the following statements, bearing on Xandrames and Sandrocyptus: "When Alexander made inquiries about the interior of India, he was told that beyond the Indus there was a vast desert of 12 (or 11, according to Curtius,) days' journey, and that at the farthest borders thereof ran the Ganges. Beyond that river, he was told, the Prasii (Prâchyas) dwelt, and the Gangaridæ. Their king was named Xandrames, who could bring into the field 20,000 horse, 200,000 foot, 2,000 chariots, and 4,000 (or 3,000, Curtius,) elephants. Alexander who did not at first believe this, inquired from King Porus whether this account of the power

[1] Plutarch, Vita Alex. c. 62, says that Sandracottus saw Alexander when he was a μειράκιον.

[2] Justini Hist. Philipp. Lib. xv. cap. iv.

of Xandrames was true; and he was told by Porus that it was true, but that the king was but of mean and obscure extraction, accounted to be a barber's son; that the queen, however, had fallen in love with the barber, had murdered her husband, and that the kingdom had thus devolved upon Xandrames."[1] Quintus Curtius says[2], "that the father of Xandrames had murdered the king, and under pretence of acting as guardian to his sons, got them into his power and put them to death; that after their extermination he begot the son who was then king, and who, more worthy of his father's condition than his own, was odious and contemptible to his subjects." Strabo adds[3], "that the capital of the Prasii was called Palibothra, situated at the confluence of the Ganges and another river," which Arrian[4] specifies as the Erannoboas. Their king, besides his birth-name, had to take the name of the city, and was called the Palibothrian. This was the case with Sandracottus to whom Megasthenes was sent frequently. It was the same king with whom Seleucus Nicator contracted an alliance, ceding to him the country beyond the Indus, and receiving in its stead 500 elephants.[5] Megasthenes visited his court several times[6]; and the same king, as Plutarch says[7],

1 Diodorus Siculus, xvii. 93. The statement in Photii Biblioth. p. 1579, that Porus was the son of a barber, repeated by Libanius, tom. ii. 632., is evidently a mistake. Plutarch, Vita Alexandri, c. 62, speaks of 80,000 horse, 8,000 chariots, and 6,000 elephants.

2 Quintus Curtius, ix. 2.

3 Strabo, xv. 1. 36.

4 Arrian, Indica, x. 5.

5 Strabo, xv. 2. 9.

6 Arrian, Exped. v. 6, Indica, v. 3.

7 Plutarch, Vita Alexandri, c. 62.

"traversed India with an army of 600,000 men, and conquered the whole."

These accounts of the classical writers contain a number of distinct statements which could leave very little doubt as to the king to whom they referred. Indian historians, it is true, are generally so vague and so much given to exaggeration, that their kings are all very much alike, either all black or all bright. But nevertheless, if there ever was such a king as the king of the Prasii, an usurper, residing at Pâṭaliputra, called Sandrocyptus or Sandracottus, it is hardly possible that he should not be recognized in the historical traditions of India. There is in the lists of the kings of India the name of Chandragupta, and the resemblance of this name with the name of Sandracottus or Sandrocyptus was first, I believe, pointed out by Sir William Jones.[1] Wilford, Professor Wilson, and Professor Lassen have afterwards added further evidence in confirmation of Sir W. Jones's conjecture; and although other scholars, and particularly M. Troyer, in his edition of the Râjataranginî, have raised objections, we shall see that the evidence in favour of the identity of Chandragupta and Sandrocyptus is such as to admit of no reasonable doubt. It is objected that the Greeks called the king of the powerful empire beyond the Indus, *Xandrames*, or *Aggramen*. Now the last name is evidently a mere misspelling for Xandrames, and this Xandrames is not the same as Sandracottus. Xandrames, if we understand the Greek accounts rightly, is the predecessor of Chandragupta or rather the last king of the empire conquered by Sandracottus. If, however, it should be

[1] Asiatic Researches, vol. iv. p. 11.

maintained, that these two names were intended for one and the same king, the explanation would still be very easy. For Chandragupta (the protected of the moon), is also called Chandra[1], the Moon; and Chandramas, in Sanskrit, is a synonyme of Chandra. Xandrames, however, was no doubt intended as different from Chandragupta. Xandrames must have been king of the Prasii before Sandracottus, and during the time of Alexander's wars. If this Xandrames is the same as the last Nanda, the agreement between the Greek account of his mean extraction, and the Hindu account of Nanda being a Śûdra, would be very striking. It is not, however, quite clear whether the same person is meant in the Greek and Hindu accounts. At the time of Alexander's invasion Sandracottus was very young, and being obliged to fly before Alexander, whom he had offended, it is said that he collected bands of robbers, and with their help succeeded in establishing the freedom of India. Plutarch says distinctly that Sandracottus reigned soon after, that is, soon after Xandrames, and we know from Justin, that it was Sandracottus, and not Xandrames, who waged wars with the captains of Alexander. Another objection against the identification of Chandragupta and Sandracottus was the site of their respective capitals. The capital of Chandragupta, Pâṭaliputra, was no doubt the same as the Palibothra of Sandracottus, the modern Patna. But exception was taken on the ground that Patna is not situated near the confluence of the Ganges and the Sone or Erannoboas, where the ancient Palibothra stood. This, however, has been explained by a change

[1] See Wilson's notes on the Mudrâ Râkshasa, p. 132.

in the bed of the river Sone, which is established on the best geographical evidence.

There are several points on which the histories of Chandragupta and Sandracottus agree completely. Sandracottus founded a new empire at Palibothra. Chandragupta was the founder of a new dynasty, the Mauryas[1] at Pâṭaliputra. Sandracottus gained the throne by collecting bands of robbers. Chandragupta did the same. Sandracottus was called to royalty by the power of the gods and by prodigies. So was Chandragupta, although the prodigy related by Justin is not exactly the same as the prodigies related by Hindu authors. So far, therefore, there is nothing in the Greek accounts that is not confirmed by Hindu tradition. That there should be a great deal more in Hindu tradition than was known to the Greeks is but natural, particularly as many of the Hindu stories were evidently invented at a later time and with a certain object. As the grandson of Chandragupta was the great patron of the Buddhists, attempts were naturally made by Buddhist writers to prove that Chandragupta belonged to the same race as Buddha; while on the other hand the Brahmanic writers would be no less fertile in inventing fables that would throw discredit on the ancestor of the Buddhist sovereigns of India. Some extracts from the writings of these hostile parties will best show

[1] The name of Maurya seems to have been known to the Greeks. See Cunningham, Journal of the As. Soc. of Bengal, xxiii. p. 680.

The wooden houses in which the tribe of the Moricis are said to have lived, may refer to the story of the Mauryas living in a forest. See Mahâvanso, p. xxxix.

The statement of Wilford, that Maurya meant in Sanskrit the offspring of a barber and a Śûdra-woman, has never been authenticated.

how this was achieved. In the Mahâvanso[1] we read: "Kâlâsoko had ten sons: these brothers (conjointly) ruled the empire righteously for twenty-two years. Subsequently there were nine brothers: they also according to their seniority reigned for twenty-two years. Thereafter the Brahman Chânakko, in gratification of an implacable hatred borne towards the ninth surviving brother, called Dhana-nando, having put him to death, installed in the sovereignty over the whole of Jambudîpo, a descendant of the dynasty of Moriyan sovereigns, endowed with illustrious and beneficent attributes, and surnamed Chandagutto. He reigned 24 (not 34) years."

The commentary on this passage adds the following details[2]: "Subsequent to Kâlâsoko, who patronised those who held the second convocation, the royal line is stated to have consisted of twelve monarchs to the reign of Dhammâsoko, when they (the priests) held the third convocation. Kâlâsoko's own sons were ten brothers. Their names are specified in the Atthakathâ. The appellation of 'the nine Nandos' originates in nine of them bearing that patronymic title.

"The Atthakathâ of the Uttaravihâro priests sets forth that the eldest of these was of an extraction (maternally) not allied (inferior) to the royal family; and that he dwelt in one of the provinces[3]; it gives

[1] Mahâvanso, p. 21. The Pâli orthography has been preserved in the following extracts.

[2] Mahâv., p. 38.

[3] It would seem that the eldest son of Aśoka did not participate in the general government of the country, but received a provincial vice-royalty. But in the Burmese histories it is stated distinctly that the eldest son, named Bhadrasena, reigned with nine of his brothers during a period of twenty-two years.

also the history of the other nine. I also will give their history succinctly, but without prejudice to its perspicuity.

"In aforetime, during the conjoint administration of the (nine) sons of Kâlâśoko, a certain provincial person appeared in the character of a marauder, and raising a considerable force, was laying the country waste by pillage. His people, who committed these depredations on towns, whenever a town might be sacked, seized and compelled its own inhabitants to carry the spoil to a wilderness, and there securing the plunder, drove them away. On a certain day, the banditti who were leading this predatory life having employed a daring, powerful, and enterprizing individual to commit a robbery, were retreating to the wilderness, making him carry the plunder. He who was thus associated with them, inquired: 'By what means do you find your livelihood?' 'Thou slave' (they replied) 'we are not men who submit to the toils of tillage, or cattle tending. By a proceeding precisely like the present one, pillaging towns and villages, and laying up stores of riches and grain, and providing ourselves with fish and flesh, toddy and other beverage, we pass our lives jovially in feasting and drinking.' On being told this, he thought: 'This mode of life of these thieves is surely excellent; shall I, also, joining them, lead a similar life?' and then said, 'I also will join you, I will become a confederate of yours. Admitting me among you, take me (in your marauding excursions).' They replying 'sâdhu,' received him among them.

"On a subsequent occasion, they attacked a town which was defended by well armed and vigilant inhabitants. As soon as they entered the town the people rose upon and surrounded them, and seizing their leader, and hewing him with a sword, put him to death. The robbers dispersing in all directions repaired to, and reassembled in the wilderness. Discovering that he (their leader) had been slain; and saying, 'In his death the extinction of our prosperity is evident; having been deprived of him, under whose control can the sacking of villages be carried on? even to remain here is imprudent; thus our disunion and destruction are inevitable:' they resigned themselves to desponding grief. The individual above mentioned, approaching them, asked: 'What are ye weeping for?' On being answered by them, 'We are lamenting the want of a valiant leader, to direct us in the hour of attack and retreat in our village sacks.' 'In that case, my friends,' (said he) 'ye need not make yourselves unhappy; if there be no other person able to undertake that post, I can myself perform it for you: from henceforth give not a thought about the matter.' This and more he said to them. They, relieved from their perplexity by this speech, joyfully replied 'sâdhu,' and conferred on him the post of chief.

"From that period proclaiming himself to be Nando, and adopting the course followed formerly (by his predecessor), he wandered about, pillaging the country. Having induced his brothers also to co-operate with him, by them also he was supported in his marauding excursions. Subsequently assembling his gang, he thus addressed them: 'My men! this is not a career in which valiant men should be engaged; it is not worthy of such as we are; this course is only befitting base wretches. What advantage is there in persevering in this career, let us aim at supreme sovereignty?'

They assented. On having received their acquiescence, attended by his troops and equipped for war, he attacked a provincial town, calling upon (its inhabitants) either to acknowledge him as sovereign, or to give him battle. They on receiving this demand all assembled, and having duly weighed the message, by sending an appropriate answer, formed a treaty of alliance with them. By this means reducing under his authority the people of Jambudîpo in great numbers, he finally attacked Pâṭiliputta[1] (the capital of the Indian empire), and usurping the sovereignty, died there a short time afterwards, while governing the empire.

"His brothers next succeeded to the empire in the order of their seniority. They altogether reigned twenty-two years. It was on this account that (in the Mahâvanso) it is stated that there were nine Nandos.

"Their ninth youngest brother was called Dhananando, from his being addicted to hoarding treasure. As soon as he was inaugurated, actuated by miserly desires the most inveterate, he resolved within himself, 'It is proper that I should devote myself to hoarding treasure;' and collecting riches to the amount of eighty kotis, and superintending the transport thereof himself, and repairing to the banks of the Ganges, by means of a barrier constructed of branches and leaves interrupting the course of the main stream, and forming a canal, he diverted its waters into a different channel; and in a rock in the bed of the

[1] Pâṭaliputra was then governed by the youngest son of Aśoka, called Pinjamakh, and the robber-king, who first called himself Nanda, is said to have reigned a short time under the title of Ugrasena. As. Res. xx. p. 170.

river having caused a great excavation to be made, he buried the treasure there. Over this cave he laid a layer of stones, and to prevent the admission of water, poured molten lead on it. Over that again he laid another layer of stones, and passing a stream of molten lead (over it), which made it like a solid rock, he restored the river to its former course. Levying taxes even on skins, gums, trees, and stones, among other articles, he amassed further treasures, which he disposed of similarly. It is stated that he did so repeatedly. On this account we call this ninth brother of theirs, as he personally devoted himself to the hoarding of treasure, 'Dhana-nando.'

"The appellation of 'Moriyan sovereigns' is derived from the auspicious circumstances under which their capital, which obtained the name of Moriya, was called into existence.

"While Buddha yet lived, driven by the misfortunes produced by the war of (prince) Vidhudhabo, certain members of the Sâkya line retreating to Himavanto, discovered a delightful and beautiful location, well watered, and situated in the midst of a forest of lofty bo and other trees. Influenced by the desire of settling there, they founded a town at a place where several great roads met, surrounded by durable ramparts, having gates of defence therein, and embellished with delightful edifices and pleasure gardens. Moreover that (city), having a row of buildings covered with tiles, which were arranged in the pattern of the plumage of a peacock's neck, and as it resounded with the notes of flocks of 'konchos' and 'mayuros' (pea-fowls), was so called. From this circumstance these Sâkya lords of this town, and their children and descendants, were renowned throughout

Jambudîpo by the title of 'Moriya.' From this time that dynasty has been called the Moriyan dynasty."

After a few isolated remarks, the Tîkâ thus proceeds in its account of Chânakko and Chandagutto:

"It is proper that in this place a sketch of these two characters should be given. Of these, if I am asked in the first place, 'Where did this Chânakko dwell? Whose son was he?' I answer, 'He lived at the city of Takkasilâ. He was the son of a certain Brahman at that place, and a man who had achieved the knowledge of the three Vedas; could rehearse the mantos; skilful in stratagems; and dexterous in intrigue as well as policy. At the period of his father's death he was already well known as the dutiful maintainer of his mother, and as a highly gifted individual worthy of swaying the chhatta.

"On a certain occasion, approaching his mother, who was weeping, he inquired, 'My dear mother, why dost thou weep?' On being answered by her, 'My child, thou art gifted to sway a chhatta. Do not, my boy, endeavour by raising the chhatta, to become a sovereign. Princes everywhere are unstable in their attachments. Thou also, my child, wilt forget the affection thou owest me. In that case, I should be reduced to the deepest distress. I weep under these apprehensions.' He exclaimed: 'My mother, what is that gift that I possess? On what part of my person is it indicated?' and on her replying, 'My dear, on thy teeth,' smashing his own teeth, and becoming 'Kandhadatto' (a tooth-broken man) he devoted himself to the protection of his mother. Thus it was that he became celebrated as the filial protector of his mother. He was not only a tooth-broken man, but he was disfigured by a disgusting complexion, and by deformity of legs and other members prejudicial to manly comeliness.

"In his quest of disputation, repairing to Puppha-pura, the capital of the monarch Dhana-nando, (who, abandoning his passion for hoarding, becoming imbued with the desire of giving alms, relinquishing also his miserly habits, and delighting in hearing the fruits that resulted from benevolence, had built a hall of alms-offering in the midst of his palace, and was making an offering to the chief of the Brahmans worth a hundred kotis, and to the most junior Brahman an offering worth a lac,) this Brahman (Chânakko) entered the said apartment, and taking possession of the seat of the chief Brahman, sat himself down in that alms hall.

"At that instant Dhana-nando himself—decked in regal attire, and attended by many thousands of 'siwakâ' (state palanquins), glittering with their various ornaments, and escorted by a suite of a hundred royal personages, with their martial array of the four hosts, of cavalry, elephants, chariots, and infantry, and accompanied by dancing-girls, lovely as the attendants on the devos, himself a personification of majesty, and bearing the white parasol of dominion, having a golden staff and golden tassels, with this superb retinue repairing thither, and entering the hall of alms-offering, beheld the Brahman Chânakko seated. On seeing him, this thought occurred to him (Nando):- 'Surely it cannot be proper that he should assume the seat of the chief Brahman.' Becoming displeased with him, he thus evinced his displeasure. He inquired: 'Who art thou, that thou hast taken the seat of the chief Brahman?' and being answered (simply), 'It is I;'

'Cast from hence this cripple Brahman; allow him not to be seated,' exclaimed Nando; and although the courtiers again and again implored of him, saying, 'Dévo! let it not be so done by a person prepared to make offerings as thou art, extend thy forgiveness to this Brahman;' he insisted upon his ejection. On the courtiers approaching Chânakko, and saying, 'Achâriyo! we come, by the command of the râja, to remove thee from hence; but incapable of uttering the words, "Achâriyo, depart hence," we now stand before thee abashed.' Enraged against him (Nando), rising from his seat to depart, he snapt asunder his Brahmanical cord, and dashed down his jug on the threshold, and thus invoking malediction: 'Kings are impious: may this whole earth, bounded by the four oceans, withhold its gifts from Nando,' he departed. On his sallying out, the officers reported this proceeding to the râja. The king, furious with indignation, roared, 'Catch, catch, the slave.' The fugitive, stripping himself naked, and assuming the character of an ajîvako, and running into the centre of the palace, concealed himself in an unfrequented place, at the Sankhârathânan. The pursuers, not having discovered him, returned and reported that he was not to be found.

"In the night he repaired to a more frequented part of the palace, and meeting some of the suite of the royal Prince Pabbato, admitted them into his confidence. By their assistance he had an interview with the Prince. Gaining him over by holding out hopes of securing the sovereignty for him, and attaching him by that expedient, he began to search the means of getting out of the palace. Discovering that in a certain place there was a ladder leading to a secret passage, he consulted with the prince, and sent a message to his (the prince's) mother for the key of the passage. Opening the door with the utmost secrecy, he escaped with the prince, and they fled to the wilderness of Vinjjhâ (Vindhya).

"While dwelling there, with the view of raising resources, he converted (by recoining) each kahâpana into eight, and amassed eighty kotis of kahâpanas. Having buried this treasure, he commenced to search for a second individual entitled (by birth) to be raised to sovereign power, and met with the aforesaid prince of the Moriyan dynasty called Chandagutto.

"His mother, the queen consort of the monarch of Moriya-nagara, the city before mentioned, was pregnant at the time that a certain powerful provincial râja conquered that kingdom, and put the Moriyan king to death. In her anxiety to preserve the child in her womb, she departed for the capital of Pupphapura under the protection of her elder brothers, and under disguise she dwelt there. At the completion of the ordinary term of pregnancy she gave birth to a son, and relinquishing him to the protection of the devos, she placed him in a vase, and deposited him at the door of a cattle pen. A bull named Chando stationed himself by him, to protect him; in the same manner that Prince Ghoso, by the interposition of the devatâ, was watched over by a bull. In the same manner, also, that the herdsman in the instance of that Prince Ghoso repaired to the spot where that bull planted himself, a herdsman, on observing this prince, moved by affection, like that borne to his own child, took charge of and tenderly reared him; and in giving him a name, in reference to his having been watched by the bull Chando, he called him 'Chandagutto,' and brought him up. When he had attained an age to be able to tend cattle, a certain wild huntsman, a friend, of the herdsman, becoming acquainted with the boy, and attached to him, took him from (the herdsman) to his own dwelling, and established him there. He continued to dwell in that village.

"Subsequently, on a certain occasion, while tending cattle with other children in the village, he joined them in a game called 'the game of royalty.' He himself was named Râja; to others he gave the offices of sub-king, &c. Some being appointed judges, were placed in a judgment hall; some he made officers of the king's household; and others, outlaws or robbers. Having thus constituted a court of justice, he sat in judgment. On culprits being brought up, when they had been regularly impeached and tried, on their guilt being clearly proved to his satisfaction, according to the sentence awarded by his judicial ministers, he ordered the officers of the court to chop off their hands and feet. On their replying, 'Devo! we have no axes;' he answered: 'It is the order of Chandagutto that ye should chop off their hands and feet, making axes with the horns of goats for blades, and sticks for handles.' They acted accordingly; and on striking with the axe, their hands and feet were lopped off. On the same person commanding, 'Let them be reunited,' the hands and feet were restored to their former condition.

"Chânakko happening to come to that spot, was amazed at the proceeding he beheld. Accompanying (the boy) to the village, and presenting the huntsman with a thousand kahâpanas, he applied for him; saying, 'I will teach your son every accomplishment;

consign him to me.' Accordingly, conducting him to his own dwelling, he encircled his neck with a single fold of a woollen cord, twisted with gold thread, worth a lac.

"The discovery of this person is thus stated (in the former works): 'He discovered this prince descended from the Moriyan line.'

"He (Chânakko) invested Prince Pabbato, also, with a similar woollen cord. While these youths were living with him, each had a dream, which they separately imparted to him. As soon as he heard each (dream), he knew that of these Prince Pabbato would not attain royalty; and that Chandagutto would, without loss of time, become paramount monarch in Jambudîpo. Although he made this discovery, he disclosed nothing to them.

"On a certain occasion having partaken of some milk-rice prepared in butter, which had been received as an offering at a brahmanical disputation, they retired from the main road, and lying down in a shady place, protected by the deep foliage of trees, fell asleep. Among them the Achâriyo awakening first, rose, and for the purpose of putting Prince Pabbato's qualifications to the test, he gave him a sword, and telling him: 'Bring me the woollen thread on Chandagutto's neck, without either cutting or untying it,' sent him off. He started on the mission, and failing to accomplish it, he returned. On a subsequent day, he sent Chandagutto on a similar mission. He repairing to the spot where Pabbato was sleeping, and considering how it was to be effected, decided: 'There is no other way of doing it; it can only be got possession of, by cutting his head off.' Accordingly chopping his head off, and bringing away the woollen thread, he presented himself to the Brahman, who received him in profound silence. Pleased with him, however, on account of this (exploit), he rendered him in the course of six or seven years highly accomplished, and profoundly learned.

"Thereafter, on his attaining manhood, he decided: 'From henceforth this individual is capable of forming and controlling an army;' so he repaired to the spot where his treasure was buried, and took possession of it, and employed it, enlisting forces from all quarters, and distributing money among them; and having thus formed a powerful army, he entrusted it to him. From that time throwing off all disguise, and invading the inhabited parts of the country, he commenced his campaign by attacking towns and villages. In the course of their (Chânakko and Chandagutto's) warfare, the population rose to a man, and surrounding them, and hewing their army with their weapons, vanquished them. Dispersing, they re-united in the wilderness; and consulting together, they thus decided: 'As yet no advantage has resulted from war; relinquishing military operations, let us acquire a knowledge of the sentiments of the people.' Thenceforth, in disguise, they travelled about the country. While thus roaming about, after sunset retiring to some town or other, they were in the habit of attending to the conversation of the inhabitants of those places.

"In one of these villages, a woman having baked some 'appalapûva' (pancakes) was giving them to her child, who leaving the edges would only eat the centre. On his asking for another cake, she remarked: 'This boy's conduct is like Chandagutto's in his attempt to take possession of the kingdom.' On his inquiring: 'Mother, why, what am I doing; and what has Chandagutto done? 'Thou, my boy,' said she, 'throwing away the outside of the cake, eatest the middle only. Chandagutto also in his ambition to be a monarch, without subduing the frontiers, before he attacked the towns, invaded the heart of the country, and laid towns waste. On that account, both the inhabitants of the town and others, rising, closed in upon him, from the frontiers to the centre, and destroyed his army. *That* was *his* folly.'

"They, on hearing this story of hers, taking due notice thereof, from that time again raised an army. On resuming their attack on the provinces and towns, commencing from the frontiers, reducing towns, and stationing troops in the intervals, they proceeded in their invasion. After a respite, adopting the same system, and marshalling a great army, and in regular course reducing each kingdom and province, then assailing Pâtiliputta and putting Dhana-nando to death, they seized that sovereignty.

"Although this had been brought about, Chânakko did not at once raise Chandagutto to the throne; but for the purpose of discovering Dhana-nando's hidden treasure, sent for a certain fisherman (of the river); and after deluding him with the promise of raising the chhatta for him, and securing the hidden treasure, within a month from that date, put him also to death[1], and inaugurated Chandagutto monarch.

"Hence the expression (in the Mahâvanso) 'a descendant of the dynasty of Moriyan sovereigns;' as well as the expression 'installed in the sovereignty.' All the particulars connected with Chandagutto, both before his installation and after, are recorded in the

[1] This is probably the Kaivarta-nanda of the Râjaratnâkara.

Atthakathâ of the Uttaravihâro priests. Let that (work) be referred to, by those who are desirous of more detailed information. We compile this work in an abridged form, without prejudice however to its perspicuity.

"His (Chandagutto's) son was Bindusâro. After his father had assumed the administration, (the said father) sent for a former acquaintance of his, a Jatilian, named Maniyatappo, and conferred a commission on him. 'My friend, (said he) do thou restore order into the country ; suppressing the lawless proceedings that prevail.' He replying 'sâdhu,' and accepting the commission, by his judicious measures, reduced the country to order.

"Chânakko, determined that to Chandagutto—a monarch, who, by the instrumentality of him (the aforesaid Maniyatappo) had conferred the blessings of peace on the country, by extirpating marauders who were like unto thorns (in a cultivated land)—no calamity should befall from poison, decided on inuring his body to the effects of poison. Without imparting the secret to any one, commencing with the smallest particle possible, and gradually increasing the dose, by mixing poison in his food and beverage, he (at last) fed him on poison, at the same time taking steps to prevent any other person participating in his poisoned repast.

"At a subsequent period his queen consort was pronounced to be pregnant. Who was she? Whose daughter was she? 'She was the daughter of the eldest of the maternal uncles who accompanied the râja's mother to Pupphapura.'[1] Chandagutto wedding this daughter of his maternal uncle, raised her to the dignity of queen consort.

[1] See page 289.

"About this time, Chânakko, on a certain day having prepared the monarch's repast sent it to him, himself accidentally remaining behind for a moment. On recollecting himself, in an agony of distress, he exclaimed, 'I must hasten thither, short as the interval is, before he begins his meal;' and precipitately rushed into the king's apartment, at the instant that the queen who was within seven days of her confinement, was in the act, in the râja's presence, of placing the first handful of the repast in her mouth. On beholding this, and finding that there was not even time to ejaculate 'Don't swallow it,' with his sword he struck her head off; and then ripping open her womb, extricated the child with its caul, and placed it in the stomach of a goat. In this manner, by placing it for seven days in the stomach of seven different goats, having completed the full term of gestation, he delivered the infant over to the female slaves. He caused him to be reared by them, and when a name was conferred on him — in reference to a spot, (Bindu) which the blood of the goats had left — he was called Bindusâro."

This Bindusâra succeeded his father as king, and, after a reign of 28 years, he was succeeded by the great Aśoka. In this manner the Buddhists prove that through the Mauryas, Aśoka belonged to the same family as Buddha, to the royal family of the Śâkyas.

The Brahmans, on the contrary, endeavour to show that Chandragupta belonged to the same contemptible race as the Nandas. Thus we read in the Vishṇu-purâṇa[1]: —

"The last of the Bṛihadratha dynasty, Ripunjaya, will have a minister named Śunika (Śunaka, Bh. P.),

[1] Vishṇu-purâṇa, translated by H. H. Wilson, p. 466.

who having killed his sovereign, will place his son Pradyota upon the throne (for 23 years, Vâyu and Matsya P.). His son will be Pâlaka (14 years, V.; Tilaka or Bâlaka, 28 years, M.P.). His son will be Viśâkhayûpa (50 years, V.; 53, M.P.). His son will be Janaka (Ajaka, 21 years, V.; Sûryaka, 21 years, M.; Rajaka, Bh. P.). And his son will be Nandivardhana (20 years, V. and M.P.). These five kings of the house of Pradyota will reign over the earth for 138 years (the same number in V. and Bh. P.).

"The next prince will be Śiśunâga[1]; his son will be Kâkavarṇa (36 years, V. and M.); his son will be Kshemadharman (Kshemakarman, 20 years, V., Kshemadharman, 36 years, M.); his son will be Kshatraujas (40 years, V.; Kshemajit or Kshemarchis, 36 years, M.; Kshetrajna, Bh. P.); his son will be Vidmisâra (Vimbisâra, 28 years, V.; Vindusena or Vindhyasena, 28 years, M.; Vidhisâra, Bh.); his son will be Ajâtaśatru[2]; his son will be Dharbaka (Harshaka, 25 years, V.; Vanśaka, 24 years, M.); his son will be Udayâśva (33 years, V.; Udibhi or Udâsin, 33 years, M.)[3]; his son also will be Nandivardhana; and his son will be Mahânanda (42 and 43 years, V.; 40 and 43 years, M.). These ten Śaiśunâgas will be kings of the earth for 362 years.

"The son of Mahânanda will be born of a woman of the Śûdra-class; his name will be Nanda, called Mahâpadma, for he will be exceedingly avaricious.

[1] Śiśunâka, who, according to the Vâyu and Matsya Purâṇa, relinquished Benares to his son, and established himself at Girivraja or Râjagṛiha in Behar, reigned 40 years, V. and M.P.

[2] 25 years, V.; 27 years, M.: the latter inserts a Kaṇvâyana, 9 years, and Bhûmimitra or Bhûmiputra, 14 years, before him.

[3] According to the Vâyu, Udaya or Udayâśva founded Pâṭaliputra, on the southern angle of the Ganges.

Like another Paraśu-râma, he will be the annihilator of the Kshatriya race, for after him the kings of the earth will be Śûdras. He will bring the whole earth under one umbrella, he will have eight sons, Sumâlya, and others, who will reign after Mahâpadma; and he and his sons will govern for a hundred years. The Brahman Kauṭilya will root out the nine Nandas.

"Upon the cessation of the race of Nanda, the Mauryas will possess the earth. Kauṭilya will place Chandragupta[1] on the throne; his son will be Vindusâra[2]; his son will be Aśokavardhana; his son will be Suyaśas; his son will be Daśaratha; his son will be Sangata; his son will be Śâliśûka; his son will be Somaśarman; his son will be Śaśadharman, and his successor will be Vṛihadratha. These are the ten Mauryas who will reign over the earth for 137 years."

The title of Maurya, which by the Buddhists was used as a proof of Aśoka's royal descent, is explained by the Brahmans[3] as a metronymic, Murâ being given as the name of one of Nanda's wives.

If now, we survey the information here brought together from Buddhist, Brahmanic, and Greek sources, we shall feel bound to confess that all we really know is this:—

[1] The length of this monarch's reign is given uniformly by the Purâṇas and the Buddhist histories, as 24 years. The number is given by the Vâyu-Purâṇa, the Dîpavanśa, the Mahâvanśa (where 34 is a mistake for 24), and in Buddhaghosha's Arthakatha. Cf. Mahâv. p. lii.

[2] The Vâyu-Purâṇa calls him Bhadrasâra, and assigns 25 years to his reign.

[3] Vishṇu-purâṇa, p. 468. n. 21. This rests only on the authority of the commentator on the Vishṇu-purâṇa; but Chandragupta's relationship with Nanda is confirmed by the Mudrârâkshasa.

Chandragupta is the same person as Sandrocyptus, or Sandracottus. This Sandracottus, according to Justin (xv. 4.), had seized the throne of India after the prefects of Alexander had been murdered (317 B. C.). Seleucus found him as sovereign of India when, after the taking of Babylon and the conquest of the Bactrians, he passed on into India. Seleucus, however, did not conquer Sandracottus, but after concluding a league with him, marched on to make war against Antigonus. This must have taken place before 312, for in that year, the beginning of the Seleucidan era, Seleucus had returned to Babylon.

We may suppose that Chandragupta became king about 315, and as both the Buddhist and Brahmanic writers allow him a reign of 24 years, the reign of Bindusâra would begin 291 B.C. This Bindusâra again had according to both Brahmanic and Buddhistic authors, a long reign of either twenty-five or twenty-eight years. Taking the latter statement as the better authenticated, we find that the probable beginning of Aśoka's reign took place 263 B.C.; his inauguration 259 B.C.; his Council either 246 or 242 B.C. At the time of Aśoka's inauguration, 218 years had elapsed since the conventional date of the death of Buddha. Hence if we translate the language of Buddhist chronology into that of Greek chronology, Buddha was really supposed to have died 477 B.C., and not 543 B.C. Again, at the time of Chandragupta's accession, 162 years were believed to have elapsed since the conventional date of Buddha's death. Hence Buddha was supposed to have died 315+162=477 B.C. Or, to adopt a different line of argument, Kanishka, according to the evidence of coins[1], must have reigned before and after the Christian

[1] Lassen, Indische Alterthumskunde, ii. 413.

era. In the Stûpa of Manikyâla, which was built by Kanishka[1], Roman coins have been found of as late a date as 33 B.C. How long before that date this Turushka or Indoscythian king may have assumed the sovereignty of India it is difficult to determine. But under him the Northern Buddhists place a new Council which was presided over by Vasumitra[2], and the date of which is fixed at *more than* 400 after Buddha's Nirvâṇa.[3] If we add 400 and 33, and take into account that the Council took place *more* than 400 years after Buddha, and that Kanishka must have reigned some years before he built his Stûpa, we find again that 477 B. C. far more likely than 543, as the conventional date of Buddha's death. All the dates, however, before Chandragupta are to be considered only as hypothetical. The second council under Kâlâśoka is extremely problematical, and the date of Buddha's death, as 218 before Aśoka, is worth no more than the date of Vijaya's landing in Ceylon, fixed 218 before Devânâmpriya Tishya. Professor Lassen, in order to give an historical value to the date of 543 assigned to the death of Buddha, adds 66 years to the 22 years of the reign of the Nandas, and he quotes in support of this the authority of the Purâṇas, which ascribe 88 years to the first Nanda. The Purâṇas, however, if taken in their true meaning, are entirely at variance with the Buddhist chronology before Chandragupta, and it is not allowable to use them as a corrective. As to

[1] A. Cunningham in the Journal of the Asiatic Society of Bengal, xviii. p. 20.

[2] Asiatic Researches, xx. 297.

[3] Nâgârjuna, who must be somewhat later than Vasumitra, is roughly placed 400 years after Buddha by the Northern, 500 after Buddha by the Southern Buddhists.

the chronology of the Ceylonese Buddhists, so far from becoming more perfect by the addition of those sixty-six years, it would really lose all consistency. The most useful portions of that chronology are the prophecies of Buddha and others, as to the number of years intervening between certain events. All these dates would have to be surrendered if we adopted Professor Lassen's correction. The great Council would not fall 218 years after Buddha's death, Chandragupta would not come to the throne 162 years after the Nirvâṇa: Buddha, in fact, as well as his apostles, would be convicted as false prophets by their very disciples.

Whatever changes may have been introduced into the earlier chronology of India, nothing will ever shake the date of Chandragupta, the illegitimate successor of the Nandas, the ally of Seleucus, the grandfather of Aśoka. That date is the sheet-anchor of Indian chronology, and it is sufficient for the solution of the problem which occupies us at present. It enables us to place Kâtyâyana before Chandragupta, the successor of the Nandas, or, at all events, the founder of a new dynasty, subsequent to the collapse of Alexander's empire. It enables us to fix chronologically an important period in the literature of India, the Sûtra period, and to extend its limits to at least three generations after Kâtyâyana, to about 200 B. C. In doing so, I am far from maintaining that the evidence which connects the names of Kâtyâyana and Nanda is unexceptionable. Nowhere except in Indian history should we feel justified in ascribing any weight to the vague traditions contained in popular stories which were written down more than a thousand years after the event. The most that can be said in favour of these traditions is, first, that there was no object in inventing them; secondly, that they are not in contradiction with anything we know of the early history of India from other sources; and thirdly, that the date which from their suggestions we assign to the literary works of Kâtyâyana and his predecessors and successors, harmonises with the conclusions, derived from the literature of the Brahmans, as to the probable growth and decay of the Hindu mind previous to the beginning of our era.

Although these chronological discussions have occupied so much of our space, it is necessary to add a few words of explanation. It might seem as if, in bringing together all the evidence available for our purpose, certain authorities had been overlooked which might have confirmed our conclusions. Professor Böhtlingk, whose researches with regard to the age of Pâṇini deserve the highest credit, has endeavoured to fortify his conclusions by some additional evidence, derived from the works of Chinese travellers; and other writers on the same subject have followed his example, though they have given a different interpretation to the statements of those travellers, and have arrived at different results as to the probable date of Pâṇini. The evidence of these Buddhist pilgrims, however, yields no real results, either for or against the date assigned to Pâṇini and Kâtyâyana, and it is for this reason that it has been entirely discarded in the preceding pages. Professor Böhtlingk relied on the testimony of Hiouen-thsang, a Buddhist pilgrim who travelled through India in the years 629—645 after Christ, and whose travels have lately been translated by M. Stanislas Julien. There we read[1]:

[1] Mémoires sur les Contrées occidentales par Hiouen-thsang, liv. iv. p. 200.

"Après avoir fait environ cinq cent li, au sud-est de la capitale (de Chînapati), il arriva au couvent appelé Ta-mo-sou-fa-na-seng-kia-lan (Tâmasavana-sanghârâma), ou le couvent de la Forêt Sombre. On y comptait environ trois cent religieux qui suivaient les principes de l'école des Sarvâstivâdas. Ils avaient un extérieur grave et imposant, et se distinguaient par la pureté de leur vertu et l'élévation de leur caractère. Ils approfondissaient surtout l'étude du petit Véhicule. Les mille Buddhas du Kalpa des Sages (Bhadrakalpa) doivent, dans ce lieu, rassembler la multitude des Devas et leur expliquer la sublime loi. Dans la trois centième année après le Nirvâṇa de Śâkya Tathâgata, il y eut un maître des Śâstras, nommé *Kâtyâyana*, qui composa, dans ce couvent, le Fa-tchi-lun (Abhidharma-jnâna-prasthâna)."

At first sight this might seem a very definite statement as to the age of Kâtyâyana, placing him, if we accept the conventional date of Buddha's death, about 243 B.C. But how can we prove that Hiouen-thsang was speaking of Kâtyâyana Vararuchi? It might be said that the Kâtyâyana, so simply mentioned by Hiouen-thsang, must be a person of note. Hiouen-thsang does not mention ancient authors except men of note, and the Kâtyâyana whose dates he gives in this place, cannot be a chance person of that name, but must be some well-known author.[1] It could hardly be meant for Mahâkâtyâyana, because he was the pupil of Buddha, and could not be placed 300 years after his Nirvâṇa. Besides Mahâkâtyâyana there is certainly no person of the same name of greater

[1] Foucaux, Lalitavistara, pp. 3. 415. 417.

literary fame than Kâtyâyana Vararuchi. But the Kâtyâyana of whom Hiouen-thsang speaks was a Buddhist, and the author of a work on metaphysics, which Hiouen-thsang himself translated from Sanskrit into Chinese. Making all possible allowance for the tendency of later Buddhist writers to refer the authorship of certain works to names famous in ancient Brahmanic history, we can hardly build much on the supposition that the author meant by the Chinese traveller was the old Kâtyâyana Vararuchi, the contemporary of Pâṇini. But, even if all these objections could be removed, what use could we make of Hiouen-thsang's chronology, who follows the system of the Northern, and not of the Ceylonese, Buddhists, who makes Aśoka to reign 100 years after Buddha, Kanishka 400, the king of Himatala 600, and so on? We should first have to determine what, according to Hiouen-thsang, was the real date of Buddha's Nirvâṇa, and what was the era used at his time in the monasteries of Northern India; whether he altered the dates, assigned by the Buddhists of India to the various events of their traditional history, according to the standard of the Chinese Buddhist chronology, or whether he simply repeated the dates, such as they were communicated to him in the different places which he visited. All these questions would have to be answered, and if they could be answered, we should in the end only arrive at the date of a Kâtyâyana, but not of the Kâtyâyana with whom we are concerned.

There is another passage in Hiouen-thsang which has been frequently discussed, and according to which it would seem that we should have to place Pâṇini much later, and that Kâtyâyana, the critic of

Pâṇini, could not have lived before the first century after Christ.

M. Reinaud, in his excellent work, "Mémoire Géographique, Historique et Scientifique sur l'Inde, antérieurement au milieu du XIe siècle, d'après les écrivains arabes, persans et chinois (Paris, 1849)," was the first to call attention to this passage. He says (p. 88.): "Ainsi que pour plusieurs autres personnages notables du bouddhisme, Hiouen-thsang attribue à Pâṇini deux existences, la première à une epoque où la vie de l'homme était plus longue qu'à présent, et la seconde vers l'an 500 après la mort de Bouddha, c'est-à-dire au temps du second Vikramâditya, un siècle environ après le regne de Kanika. Dans sa première existence, Pâṇini professait le brahmanisme; mais dans la seconde il se convertit avec son père au bouddhisme." M. Reinaud pointed out with great sagacity the various consequences which would follow from such a statement, and he remarked besides that the fact of the Yavanânî (lipi), the writing of the Ionians or the Greeks, being mentioned in Pâṇini, would likewise tend to place that grammarian rather later than was commonly supposed.

The same legend, thus partially translated from Hiouen-thsang, was made by Professor Weber the key-stone of a new system of Indian chronology. Admitting the double existence of Pâṇini, he says that his second existence falls 500 years after Buddha, or 100 after Kanishka, whom Hiouen-thsang places 400 after Buddha. The date assigned by Hiouen-thsang to Kanishka is rejected by Professor Weber. He takes, however, the real date of Kanishka, as established on numismatic evidence, about 40 A. D.; he then adds to it the hundred years, which, according to the constructive chronology of the Northern Buddhists, elapsed between Kanishka and Pâṇini, and thus deduces 140 A.D. as a new date for Pâṇini.

Without entering into the merits of these calculations, we are enabled by the publication of the complete translation of Hiouen-thsang to show that, in reality, the Chinese pilgrim never placed Pâṇini so late as 500 after Buddha. On the contrary, he represents the reputation of that old grammarian as firmly established at that time, and his grammar as the grammar then taught to all children. I subjoin the extracts from Hiouen-thsang:—

"Après avoir fait environ vingt li au nord-ouest de la ville de *Ou-to-kia-han-t'cha* (Uḍakhâṇḍa ?), il arriva à la ville de *P'o-lo-tou-lo* (Śâlâtura) qui donna le jour au *Ṛishi Po-ni-ni* (Pâṇini), auteur du Traité *Ching-ming-lun* (Vyâkaraṇam).

"Dans la haute antiquité, les mots de la langue étaient extrêmement nombreux; mais quand le monde eut été détruit, l'univers se trouva vide et désert. Des dieux d'une longévité extraordinaire descendirent sur la terre pour servir de guides aux peuples. Telle fut l'origine des lettres et des livres. A partir de cette époque, leur source s'agrandit et dépassa les bornes. Le dieu *Fan* (Brahman) et le roi du ciel (Indra) établirent des règles et se conformèrent au temps. Des *Ṛishis* hérétiques composèrent chacun des mots. Les hommes les prirent pour modèles, continuèrent leur œuvre, et travaillèrent à l'envi pour en conserver la tradition; mais les étudiants faisaient de vains efforts, et il leur était difficile d'en approfondir le sens.

"A l'époque où la vie des hommes était réduite à cent ans, on vit paraître le *Ṛishi Po-ni-ni* (Pâṇini), qui était instruit dès sa naissance et possédait un vaste savoir. Affligé de l'ignorance du siècle, il voulut retrancher les notions vagues et fausses, débarrasser la langue des mots superflus et en fixer les lois. Comme il voyageait pour faire des recherches et s'instruire, il rencontra le dieu *Tseu-Thsaï* (Îśvara Deva), et lui exposa le plan de l'ouvrage qu'il méditait.

"'A merveille!' lui dit le dieu *Tseu-Thsaï* (Îśvara Deva); 'vous pouvez compter sur mon secours.'

"Après avoir reçu ses instructions, le *Ṛishi* se retira. Il se livra alors à des recherches profondes, et déploya toute la vigueur de son esprit. Il recueillit une multitude d'expressions, et composa un *livre de mots*[1] qui renfermait mille *ślokas;* chaque *śloka* était de trente-deux syllabes. Il sonda, jusqu'à leurs dernières limites, les connaissances anciennes et nouvelles, et ayant rassemblé, dans cet ouvrage, les lettres et les mots, il le mit sous une enveloppe cachetée et le présenta au roi, qui en conçut autant d'estime que d'admiration. Il rendit un décret qui ordonnait à tous ses sujets de l'étudier et de l'enseigner aux autres. Il ajouta que quiconque pourrait le réciter, d'un bout à l'autre, recevrait, pour récompense, mille pièces d'or. De là vient que, grâce aux leçons successives des maîtres, cet ouvrage est encore aujourd'hui en grand honneur. C'est pourquoi les Brâhmanes de cette ville ont une science solide et des talents élevés, et se distinguent à la fois par l'étendue

[1] "Livre de mots" is intended as the title of Pâṇini's grammar, which was "Śabdânuśâsanam." This title is left out in the Calcutta edition, and likewise in Professor Böhtlingk's edition of Pâṇini. See Zeitschrift der Deutschen Morgenländischen Gesellschaft, vii. 162.

de leurs connaissances et la richesse de leur mémoire.

"Dans la ville de *P'o-lo-tou-lo* (lisez *So-lo-tou-lo* — Śâlâtura), il y a un *Stûpa*. Ce fut en cet endroit qu'un *Lo-han* (un Arhat) convertit un disciple de *Po-ni-ni* (Pâṇini). Cinq cents ans après que *Jou-laï* (le Tathâgata) eut quitté le monde, il y eut un grand *'O-lo-han* (Arhat) qui, venant du royaume de *Kia-chi-mi-lo* (Cachemire), voyageait pour convertir les hommes. Quand il fut arrivé dans ce pays, il vit un *Fan-tchi* (un Brahmachârin) occupé à fouetter un petit garçon qu'il instruisait. 'Pourquoi maltraitez-vous cet enfant?' dit l'*Arhat* au *Fan-tchi* (Brahmachârin).

"'Je lui fais étudier,' répondit-il, 'le *Traité de la Science des Sons* (Ching-ming — Vyâkaraṇam), mais il ne fait aucun progrès.'

"L'*Arhat* se dérida et laissa échapper un sourire. Le vieux *Fan-tchi* (Brahmachârin) lui dit: 'Les *Cha-men* (Śramaṇas) ont un cœur affectueux et compatissant, et s'apitoient sur les créatures qui souffrent. L'homme plein d'humanité vient de sourire tout à l'heure; je désirerais en connaître la cause.'

"'Il n'est pas difficile de vous l'apprendre,' répondit l'Arhat, 'mais je crains de faire naître en vous un doute d'incrédulité. Vous avez, sans doute, entendu dire qu'un *Ṛishi*, nommé *Po-ni-ni* (Pâṇini) a composé le Traité *Ching-ming-lun* (Vyâkaraṇam), et qu'il l'a laissé, après lui, pour l'instruction du monde.' Le *Po-lo-men* (le Brâhmane) lui dit: 'Les enfants de cette ville, qui sont tous ses disciples, révèrent sa vertu, et la statue, élevée en son honneur, subsiste encore aujourd'hui.'

"'Eh bien!' repartit l'*Arhat*, 'cet enfant, à qui

vous avez donné le jour, est précisément ce *Ṛishi.* (Dans sa vie antérieure,) il employait sa forte mémoire à étudier les livres profanes ; il ne parlait que des traités hérétiques et ne cherchait point la vérité. Son esprit et sa science dépérirent, et il parcourut, sans s'arrêter, le cercle de la vie et de la mort. Grâce à un reste de vertu, il a obtenu de devenir votre fils bien-aimé. Mais les livres profanes et l'éloquence du siècle ne donnent que des peines inutiles. Pourrait-on les comparer aux saintes instructions de *Jou-laï* (du Tathâgata), qui, par une influence secrète procurent l'intelligence et le bonheur?

" 'Jadis, sur les bords de la mer du midi, il y avait un arbre desséché dont le tronc creux donnait asile à cinq cents chauves-souris. Des marchands s'arrêtèrent un jour au pied de cet arbre. Comme il régnait alors un vent glacial, ces hommes, qui étaient tourmentés par la faim et le froid, amassèrent du bois et des broussailles et allumèrent du feu au pied de l'arbre. La flamme s'accrut par degrés et embrasa bientôt l'arbre desséché.

" 'Dans ce moment, il y eut un des marchands qui, après le milieu de la nuit, se mit à lire, à haute voix, le Recueil de l'*O-pi-ta-mo* (de l'Abhidharma). Les chauves-souris, quoique tourmentées par l'ardeur du feu, écoutèrent avec amour les accents de la loi, supportèrent la douleur sans sortir de leur retraite, et y terminèrent leur vie. En conséquence de cette conduite vertueuse, elles obtinrent de renaître dans la classe des hommes. Elles quittèrent la famille, se livrèrent à l'étude, et, grâce aux accents de la loi, qu'elles avaient jadis entendus, elles acquirent une rare intelligence, obtinrent toutes ensemble la dignité d'*Arhat*, et cultivèrent, de siècle en siècle, le champ du bonheur. Dans ces derniers temps, le roi *Kia-ni-se-kia* (Kanishka) et l'honorable *Hie* (Ârya Pârśvika) convoquèrent cinq cents sages dans le royaume de *Kia-chi-mi-lo* (Cachemire), et composèrent le *Pi-po-cha-lun* (le Vibhâshâ-śâstra). Tous ces sages étaient les cinq cent chauves-souris qui habitaient jadis le creux de l'arbre desséché. Quoique j'aie un esprit borné, j'étais moi-même l'une d'elles. Mais les hommes diffèrent entre eux par la supériorité ou la médiocrité de leur esprit; les uns prennent leur essor, tandis que les autres rampent dans l'obscurité. Maintenant, ô homme plein d'humanité, il faut que vous permettiez à votre fils bien-aimé de quitter la famille. En quittant la famille (en embrassant la vie religieuse), on acquiert des mérites ineffables.'

"Lorsque l'*Arhat* eut achevé ces paroles, il donna une preuve de sa puissance divine en disparaissant à l'instant même.

"Le Brâhmane se sentit pénétré de foi et de respect, et après avoir fait éclater son admiration, il alla raconter cet événement dans tout le voisinage. Il permit aussitôt à son fils d'embrasser la vie religieuse et de se livrer à l'étude. Lui-même se convertit immédiatement, et montra la plus grande estime pour les *trois Précieux*. Les hommes de son village suivirent son example, et, aujourd'hui encore, les habitants s'affermissent de jour en jour dans la foi.

"En partant au nord de la ville de *Ou-to-kia-han-t'cha* (Uḍakhâṇḍa?), il franchit des montagnes, traversa des vallées, et, après avoir fait environ six cents li, il arriva au royaume de *Ou-tchang-na*[1] (Udyâna).[2]

[1] Inde du nord.

[2] Mémoires sur les contrées occidentales, traduits du Sanscrit

Whatever the historical value of this legend may be, it is quite clear that it lends no support of any kind to the opinion of those who would place the grammarian Pâṇini 500 years after Buddha, or 100 years after Kanishka.

It is possible that the inquiries into the ancient literature of Buddhism, particularly in China, may bring to light some new dates, and help us in unravelling the chronological traditions of the Brahmans of India. The services already rendered to Sanskrit archæology by the publications of M. Stanislas Julien are of the highest value, and they hold out the promise of a still larger harvest; but for the present we must be satisfied with what we possess, and we must guard most carefully against rash conclusions, derived from evidence that would break down under the slightest pressure. Even without the support which it was attempted to derive from Hiouen-thsang, Kâtyâyana's date is as safe as any date is likely to be in ancient Oriental chronology; and the connection between Kâtyâyana and his predecessors and successors, supported as it is not only by tradition but by the character of their works which we still possess, supplies the strongest confirmation of our chronological calculations. As to other works of the Sûtra period, there are no doubt many, the date of which cannot be fixed by any external evidence. Tradition is completely silent as to the age of many of their authors. With regard to them

en Chinois, en l'an 648, par Hiouen-thsang, et du Chinois en Français par M. Stanislas Julien, Membre de l'Institut; tome i. p. 125; Voyages des Pèlerins Bouddhistes, vol. ii. See also the author's edition of the Rig-veda and Prâtiśâkhya, Introduction, p. 12.

we must trust, at least for the present, to the similarity of their style and character with the writings of those authors whose age has been fixed. It is possible that the works of earlier authors quoted by Yâska and Pâṇini and others might still come to light, if any systematic search for ancient MSS. was made in different parts of India. Many works are quoted by Sâyaṇa, Devarâja, Ujjvaladatta, and other modern writers, which are not to be found in any European Library. Some of them may still be recovered.[1] We must not, however, expect too much. Vast as the ancient literature of India has been, we must bear in mind that part of it existed in oral tradition only, and was never consigned to writing. In India, where before the time of Pâṇini we have no evidence of any written literature, it by no means follows that, because an early Rishi is quoted in support of a theory, whether philosophical or grammatical, there ever existed a work written by him with pen and ink. His doctrines were handed down from generation to generation; but, once erased from the tablets of memory, they could never be recovered.

In the Sûtras which we still possess, it is most important to observe the gradual change of style. Śaunaka's style, when compared with that of his successors, is natural, both in prose and verse. His prose more particularly runs sometimes so easily and is so free from the artificial contrivances of the later Sûtras, that it seems a mistake to apply to it the

[1] According to the opinion of M. Fitz-Edward Hall, a scholar of the most extensive acquaintance with Sanskrit literature, the number of distinct Sanskrit works in existence is, probably, not less than ten thousand. (Journal of the Asiatic Society of Bengal, 1858, p. 305.)

name of Sûtra. It is not unlikely that this title was assigned to his works at a time when its meaning had not yet been restricted either to the long "yarns" of the Buddhists or to the compendious paragraphs of the Brahmans, and we may well believe the statement that Śaunaka's works on the ceremonial resembled more the Brâhmaṇas than the later Sûtras. Âśvalâyana's style is still intelligible, and less cramped by far than the style of the Nirukta, a work commonly ascribed to Yâska, the collector of the Nighaṇṭus. Pâṇini is more artificial. He is no longer writing and composing, but he squeezes and distils his thoughts, and puts them before us in a form which hardly deserves the name of style. Kâtyâyana is still more algebraic; but it is in Pingala that the absurdity of the Sûtras becomes complete. If any writers succeeded him, they could hardly have excelled him in enigmatic obscurity, and we may well believe that he was one of the last writers of Sûtras. The authors of the Pariśishṭas, unwilling to wear the strait-jacket of the Sûtrakâras, and unable to invent a more appropriate dress, adopted the slovenly metre of epic poetry, well adapted for legendary narration, but unfit for scientific discussion.

CHAPTER II.

THE BRÂHMAṆA PERIOD.

HAVING assigned to the Sûtra literature of India the wide limits of a period extending from 600 to 200 B.C., we have now to examine another and confessedly more ancient class of Vedic writings, differing in style both from the Sûtras, which are posterior, and from the Mantras, which are anterior to them. These are called by the comprehensive name of Brâhmaṇas. But as between the Sûtras and the later Sanskrit literature we discovered a connecting link in the writings known under the name of Pariśishṭas, so we meet on the frontier between the Brâhmaṇa and the Sûtra literature, with a class of works, intermediate between the Brâhmaṇas and Sûtras, which claim to be considered first. These are the Âraṇyakas, or "The Treatises of the Forest."

THE ÂRAṆYAKAS.

The Âraṇyakas are so called, as Sâyaṇa informs us, because they had to be read in the forest.[1] It

[1] Sâyaṇa on the Taittirîyâraṇyaka. अरण्याध्ययनादेतदारण्यकमितीर्यते। अरण्ये तदधीयीतेत्येवं वाक्यं प्रचक्ष्यते॥ And again, एतदारण्यकं सर्वं नाव्रती श्रोतुमर्हति॥ Parts of the Taittirîyâraṇyaka are exempted from the restriction that they

might almost seem as if they were intended for the *Vanaprasthas* only, people who, after having performed all the duties of a student and a householder, retire from the world to the forest to end their days in the contemplation of the deity. Thus it is said in the Âruṇikopanishad, that the *Sannyâsin*, the man who no longer recites the Mantras and no longer performs sacrifices, is bound to read, out of all the Vedas, only the Âraṇyaka or the Upanishad. In several instances the Âraṇyakas form part of the Brâhmaṇas, and they are thus made to share the authority of Śruti or revelation. We have seen, however, that part of an Âraṇyaka was ascribed to a human author, to Âśvalâyana. Another part is quoted by Sâyaṇa, in his Commentary on the Rigveda[1], as being a Sûtra work of Śaunaka's. Colebrooke found, in one transcript of this Âraṇyaka, that it was ascribed to Âśvalâyana; but he remarks, "probably by an error of the transcriber." This is not the case; and it is a good proof of a certain critical conscience even amongst the orthodox dog-

should be read in the forest only: नारण्याधीतिनियमः सावित्र्यादिचतुष्टये।; and hence they are ranged with the Brâhmaṇas, अतस्तद्ब्राह्मणग्रंथे श्रुतं व्याख्यातमप्यदः॥

[1] P. 112. पंचमारण्यक औष्णिहतृचाशीतिरिति खंडे शौनकेन सूत्रितं सुरूपकृत्नुमूतय इति त्रीण्यैंद्रं सानसिं रयिमिति द्वे इति। These words occur in the Aitareyâraṇyaka, v. 2. 11. सुरूपकृत्नुमूतय इति त्रीण्यैंद्रं सानसिं रयिमिति सूक्ते। Other passages quoted by Sâyaṇa from this Âraṇyaka can always be identified in the Aitareyâraṇyaka. Cf. Colebrooke, Misc. Essays, i. 46.

matists of the Hindus, that they acknowledged a certain difference between the Brâhmaṇas and Âraṇyakas, although it was of great importance to them, particularly in their orthodox philosophy, to be able to appeal to passages from the Âraṇyakas as invested with a sacred authority. The most important Upanishads, which are full of philosophy and theosophy, form part of the Âraṇyakas, and particularly in later times the Âraṇyaka was considered the quintessence of the Vedas.[1] Nevertheless it is acknowledged by Indian authors[2] that a mistake may be made, and the work of a human author may be erroneously received as a part of the sacred book by those who are unacquainted with its true origin. An instance, they say, occurs among those who use the Bahvṛich, a śâkhâ of the Rig-veda, by whom a ritual of Âśvalâyana has been admitted, under the title of the fifth Âraṇyaka, as a part of the Rig-veda.

That the Âraṇyakas presuppose the existence of the Brâhmaṇas may be clearly seen from the Bṛihadâraṇyaka, of which we possess now a complete edition by Dr. Röer, of Calcutta, together with two

[1] Mahâbhârata i. 258.: "This body of the Mahâbhârata (the index) is truth and immortality; it is like new butter from curds, like the Brahman among men, like the Âraṇyaka from the Vedas, like nectar from medicinal plants, like the sea, the best among lakes, like the cow, the highest among animals." Thus the Upanishad is called the essence of the Veda; Śatap.-brâhm. x. 3. 5. 12. तस्य वा एतस्य यजुषो रस एवोपनिषत्।

[2] This is taken from Colebrooke's extracts from the Pûrva-mîmânsâ; a system of philosophy of which it would be most desirable to have a complete edition. (Miscellaneous Essays, i. 307.) Dr. Goldstücker, of Königsberg, has collected large materials for such a work; and I trust he will shortly find an opportunity of publishing the important results of his studies.

Sanskrit commentaries. If we take for instance the story of Janaka, who promised a large prize to the wisest Brahman at his sacrifice, and compare this story, as it is given in the Śatapatha-brâhmaṇa (xi. 4. 6.) with the third Adhyâya of the Bṛihadâraṇyaka where the same subject occurs, we find in the Âraṇyaka all the details given almost in the same words as in the Brâhmaṇa, but enlarged with so many additions, particularly with respect to the philosophical disputations which take place between Yâjnavalkya and the other Brahmans, that we cannot hesitate for a moment to consider the Âraṇyaka as an enlargement upon the Brâhmaṇa.

The chief interest which the Âraṇyakas possess at the present moment consists in their philosophy. The philosophical chapters well known under the name of Upanishads are almost the only portion of Vedic literature which is extensively read to this day. They contain, or are supposed to contain, the highest authority on which the various systems of philosophy in India rest. Not only the Vedânta philosopher, who, by his very name, professes his faith in the ends and objects of the Veda[1], but the Sânkhya, the Vaiśeshika, the Nyâya, and Yoga philosophers, all pretend to find in the Upanishads some warranty for their tenets, however antagonistic in their bearing. The same applies to the numerous sects that have existed and still exist in India. Their founders, if they have

[1] Vedânta is used, but not yet in its technical sense, Taittirîya-âraṇyaka, x. 12.; a verse frequently repeated elsewhere.

वेदांतविज्ञानसुनिश्चितार्थाः संन्यासयोगाद्यतयः शुद्धसत्त्वाः।
ते ब्रह्मलोकेषु परांतकाले परामृताः परिमुच्यंति सर्वे॥

any pretentions to orthodoxy, invariably appeal to some passage in the Upanishads in order to substantiate their own reasonings. Now it is true that in the Upanishads themselves there is so much freedom and breadth of thought that it is not difficult to find in them some authority for almost any shade of philosophical opinion. The old Upanishads did not pretend to give more than "guesses at truth," and when, in course of time, they became invested with an inspired character, they allowed great latitude to those who professed to believe in them as revelation. Yet this was not sufficient for the rank growth of philosophical doctrines during the latter ages of Indian history; and when none of the ancient Upanishads could be found to suit the purpose, the founders of new sects had no scruple and no difficulty in composing new Upanishads of their own. This accounts for the large and ever growing number of these treatises. Every new collection of MSS., every new list of Upanishads given by native writers, adds to the number of those which were known before; and the most modern compilations seem now to enjoy the same authority as the really genuine treatises.

The original Upanishads had their place in the Âraṇyakas and Brâhmaṇas. There is only one instance of a Sanhitâ containing Upanishads — the Vâjasaneyi-sanhitâ, which comprises the Îśa-upanishad, forming the 40th book, and the Śivasankalpa, forming part of the 34th book. This, however, so far from proving the greater antiquity of that Upanishad, only serves to confirm the modern date of the whole collection known under the name of Vâjasaneyi-sanhitâ.[1] But though the proper place of the genuine Upanishads was in the Brâhmaṇas, and here chiefly in those secondary portions commonly called Âraṇyakas, yet in later times, the Upanishads obtained a more independent position, and though they still professed to belong more particularly to one or the other of the four Vedas, that relationship became very lax and changeable.

The true etymological meaning of the word Upanishad had been forgotten in India. It is generally explained by *rahasya*, or *guhyâ âdeśâḥ*, mystery; and an artificial etymology is given, according to which Upanishad would mean "destruction of passion or ignorance, by means of divine revelation."[2] The original signification of the word, however, must have been that of sitting down near somebody in order to listen, or in order to meditate and worship. Thus we find *up* + *sad* used in the sense of sitting and worshipping:

Rv. ix. 11. 6.—Námasâ ít úpa sîdata, "Approach him with praise."

Rv. x. 73. 11.—Váyaḥ suparṇâ'ḥ úpa sedur I'ndram priyámedhâḥ ríshayaḥ nâ'dhamânâḥ, "The poets with good thoughts have approached Indra begging, like birds with beautiful wings."

The root *âs*, which has the same meaning as *sad*, to sit, if joined with the preposition *upa*, expresses the same idea as *upa sad*, *i. e.* to approach respectfully, to worship (Rv. x. 153. 1). It is frequently used to express the position which the pupil occupies

[1] Mahîdhara maintains that some parts of the Upanishad were aimed at the Buddhists, who denied the existence of an intelligent Self, called life a water-bubble, and knowledge intoxication.

[2] Colebrooke, Essays, i. 92.

when listening to his teacher[1], and it clearly expresses a position of inferiority in such passages as, Śat.-brâhmaṇa, i. 3. 4. 15: "tasmâd uparyâsînam kshatriyam adhastâd imâḥ prajâ upâsate," "therefore those people below (the Viś or Vaiśyas) sit under, or pay respect to the Kshatriya who sits above." Still more decisive is another passage in the same work (ix. 4. 3. 3), where *upanishâdin* is used in the sense of subject: "kshatrâya tad viśam adhastâd upanishâdinîm karoti," "he thus makes the Viś below subject to the Kshatriya." There can be little doubt therefore that Upanishad meant originally the act of sitting down near a teacher[2], of submissively listening to him; and it is easy to trace the steps by which it came to mean implicit faith[3], and, at last, truth or divine revelation.

The songs of the Veda contained but little of philosophy or theosophy, and what the Brahmans call the higher knowledge is not to be sought for in the hymns of the Ṛishis. "What,"[4] says the author of the Śvetâśvatara-upanishad, "what shall a man do with the hymns, who does not know that eternal word of the hymns in the highest heaven, that in which all the gods are absorbed? Those who know it, they are blessed." The same sentiment is fre-

[1] Pân. iii. 4. 72. comment.: Upâsito gurum bhavân; and upâsito gurur bhavatâ.

[2] In this sense Upanishad is frequently used in the plural, and signifies sessions.

[3] Chhândogya-upanishad, i. 1. 9. यदेव विद्यया करोति श्रद्धयोपनिषदा तदेव वीर्यवत्तरं। "What a man performs with knowledge, trust, and faith, that is effectual."

[4] Śvetâśvatara-upanishad, ed. Röer, Bibliotheca Indica, vii. 339.

quently expressed, but nowhere with greater force than in a passage of the Kaṭha-upanishad[1], a passage most remarkable in many respects. "That divine Self," the poet says, "is not to be grasped by tradition[2], nor by understanding, nor by all revelation; by him whom He himself chooses, by him alone is He to be grasped; that Self chooses his body as his own." Rammohun Roy when he visited the British Museum and found the late Dr. Rosen engaged in preparing an edition of the hymns of the Veda, expressed his surprise at so useless an undertaking. But the same philosopher looked upon the Upanishads as worthy to become the foundation of a new religion, and he published several of them himself with notes and translations. "The adoration of the invisible Supreme Being," he writes, "is exclusively prescribed by the Upanishads or the *principal* parts of the Veda, and also by the Vedant," and if other portions of the Veda seem to be in contradiction with the pure doctrine of the Upanishads, he hints that the whole work must not only be stripped of its authority, but looked upon as altogether unintelligible.[3]

The early Hindus did not find any difficulty in reconciling the most different and sometimes contradictory opinions in their search after truth; and a most extraordinary medley of oracular sayings might be collected from the Upanishads, even from those which are genuine and comparatively ancient, all tending to elucidate the darkest points of philosophy and religion, the creation of the world, the nature of

[1] II. 23. It is also found in the Muṇḍaka.

[2] Pravachana, tradition, the Brâhmaṇas; see p. 109. Commentary: "ekavedasvîkaraṇena," "by learning one Veda."

[3] Translation of the Kena-upanishad by Rammohun Roy. Calcutta, 1816, p. 6.

God, the relation of man to God, and similar subjects. That one statement should be contradicted by another seems never to have been felt as any serious difficulty. Thus we read in the first verse of the Śvetâśvatara-upanishad: "Is Brahman the cause? Whence are we born? By what do we live? Whither do we go? At whose command do we walk after the Law, in happiness and misery? Is Time the cause, or Nature, or Law, or Chance, or the Elements? Is Man to be taken as the source of all? — Nor is it their union, because there must be an independent Self, and even that independent Self has no power over that which causes happiness and pain."[1] The answers returned to such questions are naturally vague and various. Thus Mâdhava in his Commentary on Parâśara, quotes first from the Bahvṛicha-upanishad. "In the beginning this (world) was Self alone, there was nothing else winking. He thought, Let me create the worlds, and he created these worlds." From this it would follow that the absolute Self was supposed to have created everything out of nothing. But immediately afterwards Mâdhava quotes from another Upanishad, the Śvetâśvatara (IV. 10.), where Mâyâ or delusion is called the principle, and the Great Lord himself, the deluded.[2] This is evidently an

[1] किं कारणं ब्रह्म कुतः स्म जाता जीवाम केन क्व च संप्रतिष्ठिताः।
अधिष्ठिताः केन सुखेतरेषु वर्तामहे ब्रह्मविदो व्यवस्थां॥
कालः स्वभावो नियतिर्यदृच्छा भूतानि योनिः पुरुष इति चिंत्या।
संयोग एषां न त्वात्मभावादात्माप्यनीशः सुखदुःखहेतोः॥

[2] मायां तु प्रकृतिं विद्यान्मायिनं तु महेश्वरं।
तस्यावयवभूतैस्तु व्याप्तं सर्वमिदं जगत्॥

allusion to Sânkhya doctrines, but Mâdhava explains it in a different sense. He maintains that here also the Divine Self is meant by the Great Lord, and that Delusion is only one of his powers, as heat is a power of fire.[1] And he appeals to another passage in the same Upanishad (I. 3.), where it is said "that sages endowed with meditation and intuition, saw the power of the Divine Self, concealed by his own qualities." This same interpretation is adopted in the Sûtras of the Vedânta-philosophy, but it by no means follows that therefore it is the true one. The principal interest of the older Upanishads consists in the absence of that systematic uniformity which we find in the later systems of philosophy, and it is to be regretted that nearly all scholars who have translated portions of the Upanishads have allowed themselves to be guided by the Brahmanic commentators. The commentators wrote all, more or less, under the influence of philosophical systems, and thought themselves justified in explaining the Upanishads in such a manner that they should agree, even in the most minute points, with the Sûtras of the philosophical schools. But the authors of the Upanishads were poets rather than philosophers. Truth itself assumed, in their eyes, an aspect varying ac-

[1] ननु श्वेताश्वतरोपनिषदि मायायाः प्रकृतित्वं परमात्मनस्तन्नियंतृत्वं श्रूयते मायां तु॰ इति। नायं दोषः। मायायाः परमात्मशक्तित्वेन शक्तिमतोऽप्यात्मनः प्रकृतित्वावश्यंभावात्। दहनशक्तियुक्तेऽग्नौ दाहकत्वे व्यवहारदर्शनात्। आत्मशक्तित्वं च मायायास्तस्यामेवोपनिषदि श्रुतं ते ध्यानयोगानुगता अपश्यन्देवात्मशक्तिं स्वगुणैर्निगूढामिति॥

cording to their own feelings and misgivings. We saw that the Bahvṛicha-upanishad placed Âtman or the Self at the beginning of all things. The Taittirîya-upanishad[1] speaks of Brahman the true, omniscient, and infinite, and derives from it the ether, the air, fire, water, earth, plants, food, seed, and body.[2] This, in the eyes of the later commentators, may appear substantially the same doctrine as that of the Bahvṛicha-upanishad. But to us it is of interest to mark the difference, and to watch the various attempts which were made to express the idea of a creator. The Bahvṛichas, by calling him Âtman in the masculine, showed that they were impressed more strongly with the idea of a personal Being; the Taittirîyas, speaking of Brahman as neuter, gave more prominence to the idea of a Power. It was an epoch in the history of the human mind when the identity of the masculine Self and the neutral Brahman was for the first time perceived, and the name of the discoverer has not been forgotten. It was Śâṇḍilya who declared that the Self within our heart is Brahman (Chhând.-up. iii. 4. 14. p. 208.), and this tenet, somewhat amplified, is quoted as "Śâṇḍilya's wisdom" by the author of the Śatapatha-brâhmaṇa (x. 6. 3.). Other sages among the Chhandogas[3] again

[1] Bibl. Ind. vii. 56.

[2] Purusha is body rather than man. Mâdhava says: तच्च पुरुषशब्देन शिरःपाण्याद्याकृतियुक्तो देहोऽभिधीयते। स च देहो ब्रह्मादिस्तंबांतो बहुप्रकारः॥

[3] Chhând.-up. vi. 2.; Bibl. Ind. iii. 394. सत्त्वेव सोम्येदमग्र आसीत् एकमद्वितीयं। तदैक्षत बहु स्यां प्रजायेयेति।

speak simply of a *Sat*, or a Being which desired to be many, and created the light, the light flowing into water, the water into food, and so on. The Âtharvaṇikas speak of the Creator as *Akshara*, and it must remain doubtful whether they connected with this word the idea of the Indestructible or of Element.[1] The term used by the Vâjasaneyins is *Avyâkṛita*, or the Undeveloped. Every one of these terms had originally a meaning of its own, and though in later times they may all be used synonymously, they ought to be kept distinct when we are tracing the history of the human mind. Some of the ancient sages, after having arrived at the idea of Avyâkṛita, Undeveloped, went even beyond, and instead of the *Sat* or τὸ ὄν, they postulated an *Asat*, τὸ μὴ ὄν, as the beginning of all things. Thus we read in the Chhândogya-upanishad[2]: "And some say, in the beginning there was Asat (not being), alone, without a second; and from this *Asat* might the *Sat* be born."

But in spite of the great variety of philosophical thought on this and similar subjects that was to be found in the Upanishads, the want of new Upanishads was felt by the sects which sprang up in every part of

तत्तेजऽसृजत। तत्तेज ऐक्षत बहु स्यां प्रजायेयेति तदपोऽसृजत॥

[1] See Goldstücker's Dictionary, s. v. Mâdhava says: अश्नुत इति वा न क्षरतीति वा परमात्मानमाचष्टे॥

[2] Chhând.-up. vi. 1. तद्धैक आहुरसदेवेदमग्र आसीदेकमेवाद्वितीयं तस्मादसतः सज्जायेत।

India.[1] The old Upanishads, however, were not rejected, and to the present day the ten which are chiefly studied in Bengal are the Bṛihadâraṇyaka, the Aitareya, Chhândogya, Taittirîya, Îśa, Kena, Kaṭha, Praśna, Muṇḍaka and Mâṇḍûkya-upanishads. Every one of these has been published, and we possess an excellent edition both of text and commentary by Dr. Röer in the volumes of the Bibliotheca Indica. The whole number of Upanishads, however, known to be or to have been in existence, is much larger. It was commonly stated at 62 [2], but it has lately been brought as high as 108 [3], and even higher. Some of the titles given in various lists belong most likely to smaller portions of certain Upanishads, and these extracts, adopted by some sect or other, were afterwards quoted as independent treatises.[4] Many are of very modern origin, and have no right to be mentioned in connection with Vedic literature. In order, however, to have this whole mass of literature together, every work that claims the title of Upanishad on any ground whatsoever, has been incorporated in an alphabetical list, which will be printed as an Appendix. There are several works which had to be consulted in drawing up this list. First, Anquetil Duperron's Oupnekhat [5], a

[1] Ward, A View of the History, Literature, and Mythology of the Hindus, ii. 61.

[2] Ward, loc. cit. p. 61.

[3] W. Elliot, Journal of the As. Soc. of Bengal, 1851, p. 607.

[4] The Maitreyî-upanishad (29. 89.) is probably meant for the dialogue between Yâjnavalkya and Maitreyî in the Bṛihadâraṇyaka. The Śâṇḍilya-upanishad (57. 105.) seems to be a portion of the Chhândogya-upanishad.

[5] Oupnekhat, id est, Secretum tegendum: opus ipsa in India rarissimum continens antiquam et arcanam, seu theologicam et philosophicam doctrinam, e quatuor sacris Indorum libris, Rak

work which contains the translation of fifty Upanishads from Persian into Latin. The author of this Persian translation is supposed to be *Dârâ Shakoh*, the eldest son of *Shah Jehan*, and pupil of Babu Lal; but in reality the work seems to have been performed by several Pandits, whom that enlightened prince called from Benares to Delhi, ordering them to translate some of their sacred works into Persian. Three years after the accomplishment of their work, their patron was put to death by his brother Aurung-

baid, Djedjer baid, Sam baid, Athrban baid, excerptam; ad verbum, e Persico idiomate, Samskreticis vocabulis intermixto, in Latinum conversum; Dissertationibus et Annotationibus difficiliora explanantibus, illustratum: studio et opera Anquetil Duperron, Indicopleustæ. Argentorati, typis et impensis fratrum Levrault, vol. i. 1801: vol. ii. 1802.

Duperron received a MS. of the Persian translation of the Upanishads from M. Gentil, the French resident at the court of Soudjaëddaulah. It was brought from Bengal to France by M. Bernier, in the year 1775. Duperron, after receiving another MS., collated the two, and translated the Persian into French (not published) and into literal Latin.

The Persian translation, of which several other MSS. exist, bears the following title in Duperron's translation: "Hanc interpretationem τῶν Oupnekhathai quorumvis quatuor librorum Beid, quod, designatum cum secreto magno (per secretum magnum) est, et integram cognitionem luminis luminum, hic Fakir sine tristitia (Sultan) Mohammed Dara Schakoh ipse, cum significatione recta, cum sinceritate, in tempore sex mensium, (postremo die, secundo τοῦ Schonbeh, vigesimo,) sexto mensis τοῦ Ramazzan, anno 1067 τοῦ Hedjri (Christi, 1657) in urbe Delhi, in mansione nakhe noudeh, cum absolutione ad finem fecit pervenire."

The MS. was copied by Atma Ram in the year 1767 A.D. Duperron adds: Absolutum est hoc Apographum versionis Latinæ τῶν quinquaginta Oupnekhatha, ad verbum, e Persico idiomate, Samscreticis vocabulis intermixto, factæ, die 9 Octobris, 1795, 18 Brumaire, anni 4. Reipubl. Gall. Parisiis.

zeb.[1] Secondly, there is Colebrooke's Essay on the Vedas, which gives a more complete enumeration of the Upanishads. Thirdly, Weber's Analysis of Duperron's translation of the Upanishads, in his "Indian Studies." Fourthly, an article by Mr. W. Elliot in the Journal of the Asiatic Society of Bengal, 1851, giving an account of Upanishads known in the South of India, among the Telugu Brahmans. Fifthly, Dr. Röer's introduction to the various Upanishads, edited and translated by him in the volumes of the Bibliotheca Indica. There are other works, the well-known pamphlets of Rammohun Roy, the Essays of Pauthier, Poley, d'Eckstein, Windischmann, and the publications of the Tattvabodhinî Society, all of which had to be consulted in drawing up our own alphabetical list.

The names of the authors of the principal Upanishads[2] are unknown. This is owing to the very character of these works. They contain authoritative statements on the highest questions, and such statements would lose all authority if they were represented to the people at large as the result of human reasoning and imagination. They, in a higher degree than any other part of the Vedas, must

[1] Elphinstone, History of India, ii. 446. An earlier instance of a translation of the Upanishads is mentioned in Elliot's Historians of India, i. 260. "Abdul Kâdir, author of the Tarikh-badaum, who died at the close of the 16th century, says that he was called upon to translate the Âtharvaṇa-veda from the Hindi, which he excused himself from doing on account of the exceeding difficulty of the style and abstruseness of meaning; upon which the task devolved on Hájí Ibrahim Sirhindi, who accomplished it satisfactorily."

[2] Some of the most modern Upanishads are confessedly the works of Gauḍapâda, Śankara, and other more recent philosophers.

have been considered from the very beginning as revelation, and as directly communicated to mankind by the Supreme Spirit. This sentiment is boldly expressed in the beginning of the Muṇḍaka-upanishad: "Brahman (masc.), the creator of the universe, the preserver of the world, appeared first among the gods. He taught the knowledge of Brahman (neuter), the foundation of all knowledge, to Atharvan, his eldest son. Atharvan long ago imparted the knowledge of Brahman, which Brahman had explained to him, to Angis: he told it to Satyavâha Bhâradvâja, Bhâradvâja in succession to Angiras. Śaunaka, the great lord, approached respectfully, and asked: 'What is it through which, if known, all this becomes known?'"[1]

It is stated that the text of the Upanishads, after it had once been revealed, was never affected by differences, arising from the oral tradition of various Śâkhâs; and in one instance where various texts of the same Upanishad have been noted by the Brahmans, they are ascribed to various localities, but not to various Śâkhâs. Each Śâkhâ, however, was supposed to be possessed of a Upanishad, and the Muktikâ states that, as there are 1180 Śâkhâs, there ought properly to be as many Upanishads.

Another reason why we never hear of the authors of Upanishads as we hear of the Ṛishis of hymns is that in many instances the Upanishads are mere compilations from other works. Verses from the hymns are incorporated into various Upanishads, and stories originally propounded in the Brâhmaṇas, are enlarged upon by the compilers of these philosophical tracts.

[1] See Muṇḍaka-up. ed. Röer.

In cases only where the Upanishads form part of an Âraṇyaka, the reputed authors of the larger works might likewise be considered as the authors of the Upanishads. This authorship, however, is different from the authorship of a Gauḍapâda and Śankara. As the Bṛihadâraṇyaka forms part of the Śatapatha-brâhmaṇa, Yâjnavalkya, the reputed author of the Brâhmaṇa, might well be considered as the author of the Upanishad known by the name of Bṛihadâraṇyaka. It forms the last five Prapâṭhakas of the 14th book of the Śatapatha-brâhmaṇa in the Mâdhyandina-śâkhâ, whereas in the Kâṇva-śâkhâ the whole of the 17th book is comprised under the name of Upanishad. Yâjnavalkya Vâjasaneya is mentioned towards the end of the Bṛihadâraṇyaka as the person who received the whole of the White Yajur-veda from Âditya or the Sun. His influential position at the court of Janaka, king of Videha, is alluded to several times, and one portion of the Bṛihadâraṇyaka is called the Yâjnavalkîyam Kâṇḍam, as specially celebrating the victories gained by that sage over all his rivals. But even if we accept the traditional opinion that Yâjnavalkya was the author of the Brâhmaṇa and the Âraṇyaka, such a supposition would be of very little help to us in determining the probable age of the Upanishad portion of the Śatapatha-brâhmaṇa. We need not enter at present into the question whether the supposed authorship of Yâjnavalkya implies that he actually composed, or only that he collected and arranged the sacred code of the Vâjasaneyins. That code is, no doubt, in some peculiar sense, considered as Yâjnavalkya's own work. At the time of Pâṇini it was called by a name which, by its very character, indicated that the

Śatapatha-brâhmaṇa was a work due to the exertion of *one* individual, and that it was not, like other Brâhmaṇas, simply proclaimed by him (prokta), or formed the traditional property of an ancient Vedic Śâkhâ bearing his name. This, together with a remark in the Vârttika to Pâṇini, iv. 3. 105., may be interpreted as indicating the more modern date of this Brâhmaṇa and its Âraṇyaka, as compared with the Brâhmaṇas and Âraṇyakas of other Vedas. But beyond this, the name of Vâjasaneya Yâjnavalkya, as the reputed author of these works, will not help us in fixing the age of the Vâjasaneyi-brâhmaṇa-upanishad.

Attempts have been made to fix the age of Yâjnavalkya, as the author of a Law-book, and to transfer this date to the author of the Vedic works, just mentioned. The versifier, however, of these laws is as distinct from the original Yâjnavalkya, as the poetical editor of the Laws of the Mânavas is from the mythic Manu, the founder of the Mânava-śâkhâ.

Although the poetical editor of this code of laws speaks of the Âraṇyaka[1] as his own work, nobody will be misled by an assertion of this kind.[2] But

[1] This can only mean the Bṛihadâraṇyaka, as the commentator also observes.

[2] Yâjn. Dh. iii. 110.

ज्ञेयं चारण्यकमहं यदादित्यादवाप्तवान्।
योगशास्त्रं च मत्प्रोक्तं ज्ञेयं योगमभीप्सता॥

"He who wishes to attain Yoga (union with the Divine Spirit) must know the Âraṇyaka, which I have received from Âditya, and the Yoga-śâstra, which I have taught." I thought, at first, that there might have been old Dharma-sûtras of Yâjnavalkya, and that the versifier of these Sûtras took this sentence simply

the age even of the versifier of the Yâjnavalkîya code of laws is difficult to determine. Professor Wilson, in his "Ariana Antiqua" (page 364), observes that the word Nâṇaka, a gold or silver coin having upon it the figure of Śiva, may be derived from Nâna, a term which occurs on the coins of Kanerki, and is supposed to be "the name of a goddess; probably the same as the Anaitis or Anahid of the Persians, or the tutelary goddess of Armenia, Anaia, or Nanaca." If so (and I think the explanation extremely doubtful) the age of Yâjnavalkya's legal dicta in which the word Nâṇaka occurs, would be subsequent to the era of Kanerki, and, as Professor Stenzler remarks in his edition of Yâjnavalkya, the second century after Christ would be the earliest date that could be assigned to Yâjnavalkya. Now the identification of Nâṇaka and Nâṇa (Nanaia, Nana Rao,) is a very ingenious conjecture, but no more. Even if admitted to be true, we should still have to prove that the same goddess did not occur in the same way on more ancient oriental coins. As the Hindus derived

from the Sûtras. I have not yet found, however, Yâjnavalkya-sûtras on Âchâra. The so-called Vaishṇava-dharma-śâstra, or Śrî-bhagavad-Vishṇu-sanhitâ, which has been printed at Calcutta, contains large portions of Sûtras which have been worked up in a very crude manner into a law treatise. The whole chapter on the anatomy of the human body, which in the Yâjnavalkîya Code precedes the verse in question (iii. 110.), a chapter which does not stand in the Mânava code, exists, still in prose, in the Vishṇu-sanhitâ (fol. 28. a. line 11.). The simile of the lamp, also, representing the mind in the middle of the body, is borrowed by the editor of the Yâjnavalkîya Code from the Vishṇa-sanhitâ (fol. 29. a. line 1.). Yet, although the Vishṇu-sanhitâ, like the Code of Yâjnavalkya, goes on describing the Yoga, no mention is made here of the Âraṇyaka, nor does the author speak of himself in the first person, as the author of the metrical Code does.

their knowledge of coined money from foreign nations, Nâṇakas may have been current in India long before the time of Kanerki, though the Nâṇakas of Kanerki may be the first known to us as coined in India. The occurrence of a word like Nâṇaka[1], therefore, is not sufficient by itself to prove that the second century after Christ is the earliest date of the Yâjnavalkîya Code, still less of Yâjnavalkya, as Professor Stenzler supposes. But whatever date may be assigned to this Śloka work, the date of Yâjnavalkya, the author of the Âraṇyaka and the Śatapatha-brâhmaṇa, would not be affected by it in any way, and

[1] In the same way it might be said that the Rig-veda-sanhitâ could not have been collected before the second century after Christ, because the word Nishka occurs in the hymns. Nishka is a weight of gold, or gold in general, and it certainly has no satisfactory etymology in Sanskrit. Nothing seems to be more likely than that it should be derived from Kanishka, the Sanskrit name of Kanerki, as we speak of a "Sovereign," the French of a "Louis." The first syllable Ka may be taken as the usual royal prefix, particularly as Fahian calls the same king Kanika and Nika. (Cf. Reinaud, Mémoire sur l'Inde, p. 76.) Yet nobody would draw from this the conclusion that the Veda was written after the time of Kanishka. If Nishka be really derived from the name of Ka-Nishka, Kanishka must have been the name or title of more ancient kings, whose money became known in India. But Nishka may have a very different etymology, and at all events it does not furnish any solid basis for chronological conclusions. Nishka does once occur in Pâṇini's Sûtras, v. 2. 119.; and it is frequently quoted as an example. Pâṇ. iv. 3. 156. निष्केण क्रीतं नैष्किकं। निष्कस्य विकारः नैष्किकः। द्विनिष्कः। द्विनैष्किकः। Pâṇ. i. 4. 87. उप निष्के कार्षापणं। v. 2. 119. नैष्कशतिकः। vi. 2. 55. निष्कमाला। iv. 3. 153. हाटको निष्कः। Cf. v. 1. 37.

the Śatapatha-brâhmaṇa is the only work from which we may expect information on this point.

Another attempt has been made to fix the age of Yâjnavâlkya, or, at least, to assign certain chronological limits to the first origin of the Śâkhâ of the Mâdhyandinas, a subdivision of the Vâjasaneyins. Arrian, when speaking of the course of the Ganges, mentions among the rivers falling into the Ganges, the "Andomatis, flowing from the country of the Mandiadini, an Indian people."[1] Lassen thought he discovered in this the Sanskrit word Mâdhyandina, meridional; and, as a mere conjecture, such a remark was valuable. Professor Weber, however, went beyond this, and, taking for granted the identity of Mandiadini and Mâdhyandina, taking for granted also the identity of this Indian people with the Mâdhyandina, a subdivision of the Śâkhâ of the Vâjasaneyins, he concluded that the text of this Śâkhâ, *i. e.* the Sanhitâ and Brâhmaṇa of the White Yajur-veda, published by himself, must have existed in the third century B. C. Such rapid conclusions are rarely safe. There may have been such a people as the Mâdhyandinas at any time before or after Christ, and there may have been such a Śâkhâ as that of the Mâdhyandinas at any time before or after Christ; but the people need not have had any connection with that Śâkhâ, as little as the Prâchyas or Prasii had anything in common with the Śâkhâ of the Prâchya-Kaṭhas, or the Καμβίσθολοι, another Indian people, mentioned by Greek writers, with the Śâkhâ of the Kapishṭhalas. Granted, however, that the Śâkhâ was formed in the country of the Mâdhyandinas, and derived its name

[1] Indische Alterthumskunde, i. 130. ; Schwanbeck, Megasthenis Indica, p. 106.

from it, nothing whatever would follow from this as to the exact date when this was effected.

A second Âraṇyaka is that of the Taittirîyas. As the Taittirîya-veda (or the Black Yajur-veda) is always represented as anterior to the White Yajur-veda, the Taittirîya-âraṇyaka also might be expected to be older than the Bṛihadâraṇyaka. It is more likely, however, that the Taittirîya-âraṇyaka did not yet exist at the time when Yâjnavalkya, after seceding from his master, founded a new school, and endowed it with a new Sanhitâ and Brâhmaṇa. The Âraṇyaka of the Taittirîyas may have been added to their Brâhmaṇas subsequently to this schism, in the same way as the Bṛihadâraṇyaka is certainly later than many portions of the Śatapatha-brâhmaṇa. At all events the Taittirîya-âraṇyaka represents the latest period in the development of the Vedic religion, and shows a strong admixture of post-vedic ideas and names. The same applies also to several parts of the Taittirîya-brâhmaṇa, the last part of which does not belong to Tittiri, but is ascribed to Kaṭha, the same Muni to whom the beginning of the Âraṇyaka is said to have been revealed.[1] There are some traces which would lead to the supposition that the Taittirîya-veda had been studied, particularly in the south of India, and even among people which are still considered as un-Aryan in the Brâhmaṇa of the Rig-veda. In the Taittirîya-âraṇyaka different readings are mentioned, which are no longer ascribed to different Śâkhâs but to certain countries in the south of India, like those of the Drâviḍas, Ândhras, and Karṇâṭakas. This fact by itself

[1] See page 224.

would throw some doubt on the antiquity and genuineness of this class of Vedic writings[1], at least in that form in which we now possess them.

The Taittirîya-âraṇyaka consists of ten books, of which the four last are devoted to Upanishad doctrines. No author is mentioned, and Tittiri, who might seem to hold the same position for the Taittirîyâraṇyaka which Yâjnavalkya holds for the Bṛihadâraṇyaka, is represented by the Brahmans themselves neither as the author nor as the first teacher. He received the tradition from Yâska Paingi, who received it from Vaiśampâyana. Tittiri himself handed it on to Ukha, and he to Âtreya. Tittiri, therefore, was believed to be the founder of a Śâkhâ, but not the author of the Âraṇyaka.

A third Âraṇyaka is the Aitareya-âraṇyaka, belonging to the Rig-veda. It forms a work by itself, and is not counted as part of the Aitareya-brâhmaṇa. This is an important point. The work consists of five books or Âraṇyakas[2], the second and third of which

[1] I find that Harisvâmin also, in his commentary on the Śatapatha-brâhmaṇa, quotes the Dâkshiṇâtyas and Saurâshṭras, together with the Kâṇvas, as authorities on Vedic subjects. See Dr. Weber's Ind. Studien, i. 77. In the same place Dr. Weber attempts to prove the late origin of this work by the contraction of sa indraḥ into sendraḥ. This contraction, however, occurs already in the Rig-veda-sanhitâ. See also Pâṇ. vi. 1. 134.

[2] The first Âraṇyaka consists of five Adhyâyas and twenty-two Khaṇḍas. The second Âraṇyaka consists of seven Adhyâyas and twenty-six Khaṇḍas. The Upanishad begins with the fourth Adhyâya and the twenty-first Khaṇḍa. The third Âraṇyaka consists of two Adhyâyas and twelve Khaṇḍas. The fourth Âraṇyaka consists of one Adhyâya and one Khaṇḍa (ascribed to Âśvalâyana in Shaḍguruśishya's commentary on the Sarvânukrama). The fifth Âraṇyaka consists of three Adhyâyas and fourteen Khaṇḍas (ascribed to Śaunaka).

form the Bahvṛicha-upanishad, if by this name we like to distinguish the complete Upanishad from a portion of it, viz.: Adhyâyas 4—6, of the second Âraṇyaka, commonly quoted as the Aitareyopanishad. If we ask for the name of the author, we find again the same uncertainty as in the Bṛihadâraṇyaka and the Taittirîyâraṇyaka. All we know for certain is that there was a Śâkhâ of the Aitareyins, which was in the possession of a Brâhmaṇa and an Âraṇyaka. Both these works were afterwards adopted by the later Śâkhâs of the Rig-veda, so that we actually hear of an Âśvalâyana text of the Aitareyakam. We also know from the Chhândogya-upanishad (iii. 16.) that there was a Mahidâsa Aitareya, who, by means of his sacred knowledge was supposed to have defied death for 1,600 years; and in the Aitareya-âraṇyaka, not in the Brâhmaṇa, he is several times quoted by the same name as an authority. In the later commentaries, a story is mentioned according to which the Brâhmaṇa and Âraṇyaka of the Rig-veda were originally revealed to one Aitareya, the son of Itarâ. The story, however, sounds very apocryphal, and had a merely etymological origin. Itarâ, in Sanskrit, means not only the other of two, but also low, rejected. Thus, if the patronymic Aitareya was to be accounted for, it was extremely easy to turn it into a metronymic, and to make Aitareya the son of an Itarâ, a rejected wife. Thus Sâyaṇa, in his introduction to the Aitareya-brâhmaṇa, tells us that there was once a great Ṛishi who had many wives. One of them was called Itarâ, and she had a son called Mahidâsa. His father preferred the sons of his other wives to Mahidâsa, and once he insulted him in the sacrificial hall, by placing all his other sons on his lap. Mahidâsa's mother, seeing her son with tears in his eyes, prayed to her own tutelary goddess, the Earth (svîyakuladevatâ Bhûmiḥ), and the goddess in her heavenly form appeared in the midst of the assembly, placed Mahidâsa on a throne, and gave him on account of his learning the gift of knowing the Brâhmaṇa, consisting of forty Adhyâyas, and, as Sâyaṇa calls it, another Brâhmaṇa, treating "of the Âraṇyaka duties."

This, and similar stories mentioned by Colebrooke[1], are not calculated to inspire much confidence. On the contrary we feel inclined to attach more value to the accidental admissions of the Brahmans who ascribe the later portions of the Aitareyâraṇyaka to such well known authors as Śaunaka and Âśvalâyana. There may have been an Aitareya, the founder of the Śâkhâ of the Aitareyins, and himself the expounder of those ceremonial, philological, and philosophical tracts which are incorporated in the Brâhmaṇa and the Âraṇyaka of the Aitareyins. He is quoted himself as an authority in those works. But nothing is said in them of his degrading descent, nor of the erudition granted to him by the goddess of the earth.

Another Âraṇyaka, belonging to another Śâkhâ of the Rig-veda, is the Kaushîtaki-âraṇyaka. Colebrooke stated in his Essay on the Veda that "the original of the Kaushîtakam was among the portions of the Veda which Sir Robert Chambers collected at Benares, according to a list which he sent to me some time before his departure from India." According to the catalogue of Sir Robert's MSS. which are now at the Royal Library at Berlin, there is in that col-

[1] Miscellaneous Essays, i. 46, n.

lection not only the text and commentary of the Kaushîtaki-brâhmaṇa, but likewise the Âraṇyaka, in three Adhyâyas, of which the third constitutes the Kaushîtaki-upanishad. Here again we know nothing as to the name of an author, Kaushîtakin being simply the name of that sect in which the text of these works was handed down from teacher to pupil.

There are no Âraṇyakas for the Sâma-veda, nor for the so-called fourth Veda, the Âtharvaṇa.

Traces of modern ideas are not wanting in the Âraṇyakas, and the very fact that they are destined for a class of men who had retired from the world in order to give themselves up to the contemplation of the highest problems, shows an advanced, and already declining and decaying society, not unlike the monastic age of the Christian world. The problems, indeed, which are discussed in the Âraṇyakas and the old Upanishads are not in themselves modern. They had formed the conversation of the old and the young, of warriors and poets, for ages. But in a healthy state of society these questions were discussed in courts and camps : priests were contradicted by kings, sages confounded by children, women were listened to when they were moved by an unknown spirit.[1] This time, which is represented to us by the early legends of the Âraṇyakas, was very different from that which gave rise to professional anchorites, and to a literature composed exclusively for their benefit. As sacrifices were performed long before a word of any Brâhmaṇa or Sûtra

[1] A Kumârî gandharvagṛihîtâ is quoted as an authority in the Kaushîtaki-brâhmaṇa, and it is explained by "viśeshâbhijnâ." Kaush.-br. ii. 9.; Ait.-br. v. 29. Ind. Studien, i. 84. 217.

had been uttered, so metaphysical speculations were carried on in the forests of India long before the names of Âraṇyaka or Upanishad were thought of. We must carefully distinguish between a period of growth, and a period which tried to reduce that growth to rules and formulas. In one sense the Âraṇyakas are old, for they reflect the very dawn of thought; in another, they are modern, for they speak of that dawn with all the experience of a past day. There are passages in these works, unequalled in any language for grandeur, boldness, and simplicity. These passages are the relics of a better age. But the generation which became the chronicler of those Titanic wars of thought, was a small race; they were dwarfs, measuring the footprints of departed giants.

Chronologically we can see with great clearness that the Âraṇyakas are anterior to the Sûtras. It is only in their latest portions that they show traces of the style of Sûtra compositions. We can likewise see that they are later than the Brâhmaṇas, to which they themselves, in several instances, form a kind of appendix. Beyond this we cannot go, but an impartial consideration of the arguments adduced in favour of a much earlier or a much later date for this class of Vedic literature, will show a complete absence of facts and arguments, such as are required for historical inductions. Whether Pâṇini knew the Âraṇyakas as a branch of sacred literature is uncertain. Although he mentions the word "âraṇyaka," he only uses it in the sense of "living in the forest;" and it is the author of the Vârttikas[1] who first remarks that the same word is also used in the

[1] IV. 2. 129.

sense of "read in the forest." The word *Upanishad*, besides being used in the Upanishads themselves[1], occurs in the Sûtras of Pâṇini (i. 4. 79.), but there is nothing to prove that Pâṇini knew Upanishad as the name of a class of sacred writings.

It is hardly necessary to remark that at the time when the Âraṇyakas were written, the hymns of the Sanhitâs were not only known, but known in the same form in which we now possess them.[2] The Rig-veda is quoted as a whole, and as consisting of ten Maṇḍalas. Though the name of Maṇḍala is not used, the names assigned to each of the ten books are the same as those used in the Anukramaṇîs, and they follow each other in the same succession. Nay, these names had evidently been current for some time before, for the author of the Âraṇyaka assigns the most extraordinary etymologies to them, and uses them in support of the wildest speculations. He first mentions the Śatarchins or the poets of the first Maṇḍala. He then comprehends the poets of Maṇḍala II. to IX. under the common name of the Mâdhyamas, assigning to the poets of the tenth and last Maṇḍala the name of Kshudrasûktas and Mahâsûktas. The middle books are related more in detail under their usual names, Gṛitsamada, (ii.), Viśvâmitra (iii.), Vâmadeva (iv.), the Atris (v.), Bharadvâja (vi.), Vaśishṭha (vii.), the Pragâthas (viii.), the Pâvamânîs (ix.) The names also of Rig-veda, Yajur-veda, and Sâma-veda occur as literary titles in this Âraṇyaka.[3]

[1] Ait.-âr. iii. 1.; ibid, i. 11. Upanishasâda.

[2] Ait.-âr. ii. 9.

[3] Ait.-âr. i. 10.: Bhûr bhuvaḥ svar ityetâ vâva vyâhṛitaya ime trayo vedâ, bhûr ityeva Ṛig-veda, bhuva iti Yajur-vedaḥ, svar iti Sâma-vedaḥ.

The etymologies assigned to these names are not perhaps more absurd than those which we find in the Brâhmaṇas. But there are other etymological explanations in the Âraṇyakas such as we scarcely find in any genuine Brâhmaṇa. Part of the first Âraṇyaka (i. 4.) reads almost like a commentary on the first hymns of the Rig-veda, and the short glosses scattered about in these books of the forest might well be considered as the first elements of a Nirukta.

The grammatical study of the hymns of the Veda was evidently far advanced, and scholastic pedantry had long taken the place of sound erudition, when the early portions of the Âraṇyaka were composed. Not only the ten books of the Rig-veda are mentioned, but likewise their subdivisions, the hymns (sûkta), verses (ṛich), half-verses (arddharcha), feet (pada), and syllables (akshara). Sometimes the syllables of certain hymns and classes of hymns are counted, and their number is supposed to possess a mysterious significance. In one passage (ii. 12.) speculations are propounded on the division of letters into consonants (vyanjana), vowels (ghosha), and sibilants (ûshman).

Admitting, therefore, that the Âraṇyakas represent the latest productions of the Brâhmaṇa period, and that in some cases the authors belong to the age of Śaunaka, in others even to a more modern age, we have now to consider the character of the genuine Brâhmaṇas, in order to point out the differences which distinguish the Brâhmaṇas from the Sûtras by which they are followed, and from the Mantras by which they are preceded.

THE BRÂHMAṆAS.

The difficulty of giving an exhaustive definition of what a Brâhmaṇa is, has been felt by the Brahmans themselves. The name given to this class of literature does not teach us more than that these works belonged to the Brahmans. They were Brahmanic, *i. e.* theological tracts, comprising the knowledge most valued by the Brahmans, bearing partly on their sacred hymns, partly on the traditions and customs of the people. They profess to teach the performance of the sacrifice; but for the greater part they are occupied with additional matter; with explanations and illustrations of things more or less distantly connected with their original faith and their ancient ceremonial.

Sâyaṇa, in his Introduction to the Rig-veda[1], has given such extracts from the Pûrva-mîmânsâ philosophy as may furnish a pretty correct idea of the Brâhmaṇas, and he has treated the same subject again in his Introduction to the Aitareya-brâhmaṇa. "A Brâhmaṇa," he says, "is twofold, containing either commandments (vidhi), or additional explanations (arthavâda). This is confirmed by Âpastamba, saying: 'The Brâhmaṇas are commandments for the sacrifices; all the rest consists of additional explanations.' The commandments, too, are of two kinds, either causing something to be done which was not done before, or making something known which was not known before. Of the former kind are all those commandments occurring in the prac-

[1] Rig-veda-bhâshya, p. 11.

tical part, such as, 'At the Dîkshaṇîyâ ceremony he presents a puroḍâśa oblation to Agni and Vishṇu.' Of the latter kind are all philosophical passages, such as, 'Self was all this alone in the beginning.'

"But how can it be said," Sâyaṇa goes on, "that the Veda consists of Mantras and Brâhmaṇas, as the essential qualities neither of the one nor of the other part can be satisfactorily defined? For if it be said that a Mantra alludes to those things which are commanded, this definition would not comprehend all Mantras, because there are some which are themselves commandments, as, for instance, 'He takes Kapinjalas for the Spring.' Again, if it be said that a Mantra is what makes one think (*man*, to think), this definition would comprehend the Brâhmaṇas also. Other definitions have been given, that a Mantra ends with the word 'thou art,' or that it ends with the first person plural; but none of these definitions can be considered as exhaustive. The only means, then, by which Mantras can be distinguished from Brâhmaṇas lies in their general sacrificial appellation, which comprehends the most different things under the one common name of Mantras. There are some recording the performance of sacrifices; some contain praises, some end with the word thee (tvâ), some are invocations, some are directions, some contain deliberations, some contain complaints, some are questions, some are answers, &c. All these attributes are so heterogeneous, that none of them can be used for a definition. Knowing, however, that the Veda consists only of two parts, we may say that whatever does not come under the name of Mantra is Brâhmaṇa, whether it contain reasons, explanations, censures, recommendations, doubts, commandments, relations, old stories, or particular determinations. Not one of these subjects belongs to the Brâhmaṇas exclusively, but they occur more or less frequently in the Mantras also, and could therefore not be used as definitions of the Brâhmaṇas. The same objection applies to all other definitions which have been attempted. Some have said that the frequent occurrence of the particle *iti* (thus) constitutes a Brâhmaṇa; others, that a Brâhmaṇa closes with the words *ityâha* (thus he said); others that a Brâhmaṇa contains stories, &c.; but all this would apply with equal force to some of the Mantras. The only division therefore of the Veda that holds good consists in comprehending one part under the old traditional appellation of Mantra, and considering all the rest as Brâhmaṇas.

"But it might be objected," Sâyaṇa continues, "that for instance in the chapter on the Brahmayajna, other parts of the Veda are mentioned besides the Brâhmaṇas and Mantras, under the title of Itihâsas, (epic stories) Purâṇas (cosmogonic stories), Kalpas (ceremonial rules), Gâthâs (songs), Nârâśansîs, (heroic poems). This, however, would be the same mistake as if we should place a Brahman coordinate with a Brahman who is a mendicant. For all these titles, like Itihâsa, &c., apply only to subdivisions of the Brâhmaṇas. Thus, passages from the Brâhmaṇas like 'The gods and the Asuras were fighting,' &c., would be called Itihâsas; other passages like 'In the beginning there was nothing,' would be called Purâṇas; therefore we may safely say, that the Veda consists of two parts only, of *Mantras* and *Brâhmaṇas*." [1]

[1] According to Madhusûdana's view, the Brâhmaṇas consist of three parts; of commandments, additional explanations, and Ve-

If after these not very satisfactory definitions of what a Brâhmaṇa is, and how it differs from a Mantra, we turn to the Brâhmaṇas themselves, such as we possess them in MS., we find that their number is much smaller than we should have expected.

If every Śâkhâ consisted of a Sanhitâ and a Brâhmaṇa, the number of the old Brâhmaṇas must have been very considerable. It must not be supposed, however, that the Brâhmaṇas which belonged to different Śâkhâs were works composed independently by different authors. On the contrary, as the Sanhitâs of different Śâkhâs were nothing but different recensions of one and the same original collection of hymns, and could be distinguished from each other only by a number of authorised *variæ lectiones* or by the addition and omission of certain hymns, the Brâhmaṇas also, which were adopted by different Charaṇas of the same Veda, must be considered not as so many independent works, but in most instances as different recensions of one and the same original. There was originally but one body of Brâhmaṇas for each of the three Vedas; for the Rig-veda, the Brâhmaṇas of the Bahvṛichas, for the Sâma-veda the Brâhmaṇas of the Chhandogas, and for the Yajur-veda in its two forms, the Brâhmaṇas of the Taittirîyas, and the Śatapatha-brâhmaṇa. These works were not composed in metre like the Sanhitâs, and were therefore more exposed to

dânta doctrines, the latter being more particularly represented by the Upanishads. The same author speaks of four classes of commandments. "A commandment may consist," he says, "either of a simple definition ('the oblation to Agni is given in eight cups'); or it may include the aim ('he who wishes for life in heaven may perform the sacrifices of the new and full moon'); or it may detail the means by which the sacrifice is performed ('let him sacrifice with rice'); or it may contain all this together."

alteration in the course of a long continued oral tradition.

We possess the Brâhmaṇa of the Bahvṛichas in the Śâkhâs of the Aitareyins and the Kaushîtakins. The various readings of other Śâkhâs, quoted by the commentator on the Aitareya-brâhmaṇa, show evidently that there were other Śâkhâs of the Bahvṛichas, which differed but little in the wording of their Brâhmaṇas. But even the Brâhmaṇa of the Kaushîtakins which has been preserved to us as a distinct work, different from the Brâhmaṇa of the Aitareyins, can only be considered as a branch of the original stock of Brâhmaṇa literature, current among the Bahvṛichas. Its arrangement differs considerably from that of the Aitareya-brâhmaṇa. The sacrifice described in the beginning of the Aitareya-brâhmaṇa forms the seventh Adhyâya of the Kaushîtaki-brâhmaṇa[1], and most of the other sacrifices are equally displaced. Others which are discussed in the Aitareya-brâhmaṇa are altogether wanting in the Kaushîtaki-brâhmaṇa, and must be supplied from the Sûtras of the Śânkhâyana-śâkhâ, a subdivision of the Kaushîtakins. But whenever parallel passages occur, it becomes clear that the coincidences in the description of sacrifices and the wording of legends cannot be accidental.

Most of the Brâhmaṇas which are left to us are collective works. A tradition has been preserved in confirmation of this fact. The Brâhmaṇa of the

[1] Aitareya-br. i. 1. अग्निर्वै देवानामवमो विष्णुः परमः, &c. Kaush.-br. vii. 1. अग्निर्वै देवानामवरार्द्ध्यो विष्णुः परार्द्ध्यः, &c. Ait.-brâhm. ii. 2.=Kaush.-br. x. 2.; ii. 6.=x. 4. (Śânkh.-sûtra, v. 17.); ii. 3.=xii. 1.

Taittirîyas, in the Śâkhâs both of the Âpastambîyas and the Âtreyas, contains some portions which bear the name of Kaṭha, and were formerly the property of his followers. The component parts are frequently called Brâhmaṇas instead of chapters or sections. The same applies to the Âraṇyakas and Upanishads. In some cases these smaller Brâhmaṇas are quoted by their special titles[1]; and in their collected form they are handed down, not always by the name of the Charaṇa by which they were adopted, but more frequently by that of the Charaṇa in which their original collection took place. Thus the Aitareya-brâhmaṇa, though adopted by the Âśvalâyanîyas, is more frequently quoted by its original name than by that of Âśvalâyana-brâhmaṇa.[2] The Brâhmaṇa of Kaushîtakin or the Kaushîtakins is more usually referred to by this name than by that of the later Charaṇa of the Śânkhâyanas.

In the Brâhmaṇa of the Chhandogas it is evident, that after the principal collection was finished (called the prauḍha or panchavinśa-brâhmaṇa, *i. e.* consisting of twenty-five sections), a twenty-sixth Brâhmaṇa was added which is known by the name of Shaḍvinśa-brâhmaṇa. This Brâhmaṇa together with the Adbhuta-brâhmaṇa must be of very modern date. It

[1] Maitreyî-brâhmaṇa is the title given to that portion of the Bṛihadâraṇyaka which contains the dialogue between Yâjnavalkya and Maitreyî. The Saulabhâni brâhmaṇâni, quoted by Âśvalâyana and Pâṇini as modern compositions, may refer to sections containing a dialogue similar to that between Janaka and Sulabhâ, which exists in the Mahâbhârata, III. v. 11,854. Cf. Lassen, Ind. Alterth. xv. note. According to Pâṇini, however, they ought to be taken as Brâhmaṇas composed by Sulabha.

[2] Quoted as such by Yâjnikadeva on Kâty. 2. 5. 18.; 6. 6. 25. Weber, Ind. Stud. i. 230.

mentions not only temples (Devâyatanâni), but images of gods (daivata-pratimâ) which are said to laugh, to cry, to sing, to dance, to burst, to sweat, and to twinkle. These two have long been supposed to be the only Brâhmaṇas of the Chhandogas, and they constitute, no doubt, the most important part of that class of literature. It is curious, however, that whenever the Brâhmaṇas of the Chhandogas are quoted, their number is invariably fixed at eight. Kumârila Bhaṭṭa, i. 3[1], says, "in the eight Brâhmaṇas, together with the Upanishads, which the Chhandogas read, no single accent is fixed." Still more explicit is a statement by Sâyaṇa which I quoted in the introduction to the first volume of my edition of the Rig-veda.[2] Here Sâyaṇa says: "There are eight Brâhmaṇas; the Prauḍha is the first (this means the large Brâhmaṇa, or the Panchavinśa); the one called Shaḍvinśa or Shaḍvinśad-brâhmaṇa, is the second; then follows the Sâmavidhi; then the Ârsheya-brâhmaṇa, the Devatâdhyâya-brâhmaṇa, and the Upanishad. These with the Sanhitopanishad and the Vanśa are called the eight books." Of these the Sâmavidhâna-brâhmaṇa was well known, the very quotation of Sâyaṇa being taken from his commentary on this very curious work. It might have been difficult, however, to identify the other five works if there had not been among the MSS. of Professor Wilson's collection at the Bodleian Library, one (No. 451) containing four of these small tracts, the Sanhitopanishadam-brâhmaṇam, the Devatâdhyâyaḥ, the Vanśa-brâhmaṇam, and the

[1] Brâhmaṇâni hi yâny ashṭau sarahasyâny adhîyate Chhandogâs teshu sarveshu na kaśchin niyataḥ svaraḥ.

[2] P. xxvii. note.

Ârsheya-brâhmaṇam.[1] The only Brâhmaṇa, therefore, on which any doubt could remain, was the Upanishad, and here we shall probably not be wrong if we adopt one of Professor Weber's less bold conjectures, that Sâyaṇa intended this for the Chhândogya-upanishad.[2] With the exception of this and the Sâmavidhâna, which contains most important information on questions connected with Âchâra or customs, all the other tracts are of comparatively small importance.

It is in the Śatapatha-brâhmaṇa, however, that we can best observe the gradual accumulation of various theological and ceremonial tracts which were to form the sacred code of a new Charaṇa. The text of this work has been edited by Professor Weber, and we can likewise avail ourselves of several essays on this branch of Vedic literature, published from time to time by that industrious scholar. According to Indian traditions, Yajnavalkya Vâjasaneya, the founder of the new Charaṇa of the Vâjasaneyins is himself, if not the author, at least the first who proclaimed the Sanhitâ and Brâhmaṇa of the Vâjasaneyins. We can see clearly that the composition of both the Sanhitâ and Brâhmaṇa was guided by the same spirit, and it is not at all unlikely that in this, the most modern of all Vedas, the final arrangement of the Sanhitâ may have been contemporaneous with, or even later than, the composition of the Brâhmaṇa.

First of all, it ought to be remarked that the story

[1] See also "A Catalogue Raisonée (sic) of Oriental Manuscripts in the Library of the late College Fort St. George," by the Rev. W. Taylor, Madras, 1857, p. 69.

[2] The Vanśa-brâhmaṇa has lately been printed, with some valuable remarks, by Prof. A. Weber, Ind. Stud. iv. 371.

which has been preserved by tradition of the schism introduced by Yâjnavalkya among the followers of the Adhvaryu or Yajur-veda is confirmed by internal evidence. The general name of the ancient Śâkhâs of the Yajur-veda is Charaka, and the Taittirîyas, therefore, together with the Kaṭhas, and others are called by a general name, Charaka-śâkhâs. This name Charaka is used in one of the Khilas of the Vâjasaneyi-sanhitâ as a term of reproach. In the 30th Adhyâya a list of people are given who are to be sacrificed at the Purushamedha, and among them we find the Charakâchârya, the teacher of the Charakas, as the proper victim to be offered to Dushkṛita or Sin. This passage, together with similar hostile expressions in the Śatapatha-brâhmaṇa, were evidently dictated by a feeling of animosity against the ancient schools of the Adhvaryus, whose sacred texts we possess in the Taittirîya-veda, and from whom Yâjnavalkya seceded in order to become himself the founder of the new Charaṇas of the Vâjasaneyins.

If we compare the Sanhitâ and Brâhmaṇa of the Vâjasaneyins with those of the Charakas, we see that the order of the sacrifices is on the whole the same, and that the chief difference between the two consists in the division of Mantras and Brâhmaṇas, which is carried out more strictly by Yâjnavalkya than in the ancient text of the Taittirîyas. This was most likely the reason why the text of Yâjnavalkya was called Śukla Yajur-veda, which is generally translated by the White Yajur-veda. But some commentators explain Śukla more correctly by śuddha[1], and translate

[1] Dvivedaganga explains शुक्लानि यजूंषि by शुद्धानि यद्वा ब्राह्मणेनामिश्रितमंत्रात्मकानि॥

it by "cleared," because in this new text the Mantras had been cleared and separated from the Brâhmaṇas, and thus the whole had been rendered more lucid and intelligible. In opposition to this they suppose that the old text was called Kṛishṇa or dark, because in it the verses and rules are mixed together, and less intelligible; or because, as Vidyâraṇya says, it contained the rules of the Hotṛi as well as of the Adhvaryu priests, and thus bewildered the mind of the student.[1]

It was in the nature of the duties which the Adhvaryus had to perform at the sacrifices, that their hymns and invocations could hardly be separated from the rules (vidhi) contained in the Brâhmaṇas. It was not a mere accident therefore that in the Veda of the ancient Adhvaryus the hymns and rules were mixed up, and it must be considered as a mere innovation if what is now called the Sanhitâ of the Black Yajur-veda is distinguished by this name from the Brâhmaṇa, which in reality is a continuation of the same work. It is not unlikely that it was the very wish to have, like the Bahvṛichas and Chhandogas, a Sanhitâ, *i. e.* a collection of hymns distinct from the ceremonial rules, which led to the secession of the Vâjasaneyins, and, by a kind of reaction, to the absurd adoption of the titles of Sanhitâ and Brâhmaṇa among the Taittirîyas. In the new code of the Vâjasaneyins the most important part was nevertheless the Brâhmaṇa, the Sanhitâ being a mere collection of verses,

[1] विद्यारण्यश्रीपादैर्व्याख्यातत्वेनाध्वर्यवं कचिद्धौत्रं कचिदित्यव्यवस्थया बुद्धिमालिन्यहेतुत्वात्तद्यजुः कृष्णमीर्यते॥ Râmakṛishṇa's Sanskâragaṇapati. Weber, Ind. Stud. i. 27. 84.

extracted and collected for the convenience of the officiating priest. The differences in the text of these verses and formulas would be marked in the Brâhmaṇa, and transferred from the Brâhmaṇa into the Sanhitâ. This is, therefore, the very opposite of what happened with the text of the Sanhitâ and Brâhmaṇa of the Bahvṛichas. Here the Sanhitâ existed long before the Brâhmaṇa, and it had diverged into different Śâkhâs, before the Brâhmaṇa of the Aitareyins was composed. The Vâjasaneyi-sanhitâ may possibly represent various readings which existed in the Śâkhâs of the Taittirîyas; but these verses were collected and formed into a Sanhitâ only as an appendix to the Śatapatha-brâhmaṇa, the real code of the Vâjasaneyins. Where the sacrificial invocations of the Vâjasaneyins differ from those of the Taittirîyas, we ought to recognise in those differences the last traces of Śâkhâs which existed previous to the establishment of the Vâjasaneyins. In the beginning, for instance, of the Darśa-pûrṇamâsa sacrifice, the Adhvaryu priest, having called the cows and calves together, has to touch the calves with a branch. This act of the sacrifice was originally accompanied by the words "vâyava stha, upâyava stha," "you are like the winds,"—and the whole ceremony, together with these invocations, is contained in the Taittirîya-sanhitâ. In the Mâdhyandina-śâkhâ, on the contrary, not only are the words "upâyava stha" omitted in the Sanhitâ, but a distinct warning is given in the Brâhmaṇa not to use these words, because they belong to a different Śâkhâ.[1]

[1] Cf. Sâyaṇa, Rig-veda-bhâshya, p. 12.; Śatapatha-brâhmaṇa, i. 7. 3. तस्मादाह वायव स्थेत्युपायव स्थेत्य हैक आहुरुप हि

A comparison of the texts of the Taittirîyas and Vâjasaneyins shows that it would be a mistake to call Yâjnavalkya the author, in our sense of the word, of the Vâjasaneyi-sanhitâ and the Śatapatha-brâhmaṇa. But we have no reason to doubt that it was Yâjnavalkya who brought the ancient Mantras and Brâhmaṇas into their present form, and, considering the differences between the old and new text, we must admit that he had a greater right to be called an author than the founders of the Charaṇas of other Vedas whose texts we possess. In this sense, Kâtyâyana says, in his Anukramaṇî, that Yâjnavalkya received the Yajur-veda from the Sun.[1] In the same sense the Śatapatha-brâhmaṇa ends with the assertion that the White Yajur-veda was proclaimed by Yâjnavalkya Vâjasaneya[2]; and in the same sense Pâṇini, or rather his editor, says in the first Vârttika to iv. 3. 105. that there were modern

द्वितीयोऽयतीति तदु तथा न ब्रूयात्॥ In the commentary on Baudhâyana's Sûtras, a passage from a Brâhmaṇa is quoted, which may have belonged to the Baudhâyanîya-śâkhâ. इषे त्वोर्जे त्वेति शाखामाच्छिनत्ति वायव स्थोपायव स्थेति वत्सानपाकरोति॥ The Baudhâyana-sûtras enjoin the first sentence for male calves, the second for females ones, वायव स्थेति पुंस उपायव स्थेति स्त्रियः॥

[1] शुक्लानि यजूंषि भगवान्याज्ञवल्क्यो यतः प्राप तं विवस्वंतं॥

[2] आदित्यानीमानि शुक्लानि यजूंषि वाजसनेयेन याज्ञवल्क्येनाख्यायंते॥

Brâhmaṇas proclaimed by Yâjnavalkya, and that their title differed by its formation from the title given to more ancient Brâhmaṇas. At the time when these titles were framed Yâjnavalkya was still alive; and his work, therefore, was not yet considered as one handed down by tradition through several generations. There might seem to be some difficulty in making Yâjnavalkya the author or editor of the whole Yajur-veda, because there are several portions of the Brâhmaṇa where Yâjnavalkya himself is introduced as one of the chief interlocutors, so much so that part of the Bṛihadâraṇyaka, the last book of the Śatapatha-brâhmaṇa, is designated by the name of Yâjnavalkîyam kâṇḍam. But similar instances occur in several of the traditional works of the Brahmans, and in this case the decided traces of a later origin which are to be found in the Bṛihadâraṇyaka, would justify us in supposing that these portions were added after Yâjnavalkya's decease, particularly as it is called Yâjnavalkîya, not Yâjnavalkya-kâṇḍa.[1]

That Yâjnavalkya, though deserting the Charakas, derived great advantage from their Veda, is seen at once by the whole arrangement of his work. I give a list of the various subjects treated in the Vâjasaneyi-sanhitâ, according to Mahîdhara. The Sanhitâ of the Vâjasaneyins begins with

The Darśapûrṇamâsamantras, Adhyâya, i.—ii. 28.

Then follow:—

Pitṛiyajnamantrâs, ii. 29—34.
Agnyâdheyamantrâs, iii. 1—8.
Agnihotram, iii. 9—10.
Agnyupasthânam, iii. 11—43.

[1] See Pân. v. 4. 105, on the purport of this difference.

Châturmâsyâni, iii. 44—63.
Soma. Agnishṭomas, iv. 1—viii. 23.
Śâlâpraveśas, iv. 1—37.
Âtithyeshṭau havirgrahaṇâdimantrâs, (yûpanirmâṇam), v. 1—fin.
Yûpasanskâra (âgnîshomîyapaśu) -somâbhishavamantrâs, vi. 1—fin.
Grahagrahaṇamantrâs (upânśvâdi-pradânânta), vii. 1—fin.
Tritîyasavanagatâ âdityagrahâdimantrâs, viii. 1—23.
Prâsangikâs, viii. 24—63.
Vâjapeyas, ix. 1—34.
Râjasûyas, ix. 35—40.
Râjasûya abhishekârthajalâdânâdirâjasûyaśeshas, Charakasautrâmaṇî cha, x. 1—fin.
Agnichayanam, xi.—xviii.
Ukhâsambharaṇâdimantrâs, xi.
Ukhâdhâraṇa, gârhapatyachayana, kshetrakarshaṇa, aushadhavapanâdi, xii.
Pushkaraparṇâdyupadhânamantrâs (prathamâ chitiḥ), xiii.
Dvitîyâdichititrayam, xiv.
Panchamachitiḥ, xv.
Śatarudriyâkhyahomamantrâs, xvi.
Chityaparishekâdimantrâs, xvii.
Vasordhârâdimantrâs, xviii.
Sautrâmaṇî, xix.—xxi.
Surâdîndrâbhishekântam, xix.
Sekâsandyâdi-hautrântam, xx.
Yâjyâdi-preshaṇântam, xxi.
Aśvamedhas, xxii.—xxv.
Homamantrâs, xxii.
Śishṭam âsvamedhikam, xxiii.[1]

[1] According to the forty-eighth Atharvapariśishṭa, the thirty-

Śrutirûpamantrâ âśvamedhikânâm paśûnâm, xxiv., xxv.

Khilâni, xxvi.—xxxv.

Anuktamantrakathanam, xxvi.

Panchachitikamantrâs, xxvii.

Sautrâmaṇîsambandhiprayâjânuyâjapraishanirûpaṇam, xxviii.

Śishṭâśvamedhamantrâs, xxix.

Purushamedhas, xxx., xxxi.

Sarvamedhas, xxxii.—xxxiii. 54.

Brahmayajnas, xxxiii. 55—xxxiv. fin.

Pitṛimedhas, xxxv.

Śukriyam (panchâdhyâyî), xxxvi.—xl.[1]

Pravargya Śântipâṭhas, xxxvi.

Abhryâdi-rauhiṇântam, xxxvii.

Mahâvîranirûpaṇam, xxxviii.

Gharmâdinishkṛitis, xxxix.

Jnânakâṇḍam, xl.

According to this list the Vâjasaneyi-sanhitâ may be divided into different sections. The first section comprises the Darśapûrṇamâsa, &c., i.—iii.; the second the Soma sacrifices, iv.—x.; the third the Agnichayanas, xi.—xviii.

These eighteen Adhyâyas, which correspond to the Taittirîya-sanhitâ, are explained in the first nine books of the Śatapatha-brâhmaṇa and the first eighteen chapters of Kâtyâyana's Sûtras. They form, no doubt, the most important part of the Adhvaryu-veda, but there is no evidence to show that they ever existed in a separate form. It has been well re-

second verse of the twenty-third Adhyâya would be the last verse of the Sanhitâ. See Weber, Ind. Stud. iv. p. 432.

[1] According to the Mitâkshara commentary on Yâjnavalkya's Dharma-śâstra, xxxvi. 1. forms the beginning of an Âraṇyaka. Weber, Vorlesungen, p. 103.

marked, however, by the editor of the Śatapatha-brâhmaṇa, that the first nine books consist altogether of sixty Adhyâyas[1], and that the name of Shashṭi-patha, the Sixty Paths, which is mentioned in the Vârttika to Pâṇ. iv. 2. 60., may refer to this portion, whereas the whole Brâhmaṇa, consisting of one hundred Adhyâyas, received the title of Śatapatha, the Hundred Paths.

The Sautrâmaṇî ceremony, which begins with the 19th Adhyâya, has nothing corresponding to it in the Taittirîya-sanhitâ, but, like the following sacrifices, it has been incorporated in the Taittirîya-brâhmaṇa. There is a difference also in the treatment which this sacrifice receives in the Śatapatha-brâhmaṇa. Adhyâya xix. and xx. are indeed explained there, in the 12th book, but they do not receive the same careful explanation which was given to the preceding sacrifices. The last Adhyâya, containing verses of the Hotṛi, is not explained at all. Kâtyâyana treats these three Adhyâyas in the 19th book of his Sûtras.

The Aśvamedha, which fills Books xxii.—xxv. of the Vâjasaneyi-sanhitâ, is but partially contained in the Taittirîya-sanhitâ; and the Śatapatha also, though it devotes to this ceremony a considerable part of the 13th book, treats it in a much more superficial manner than the former sacrifices. Kâtyâyana explains it in his 20th book.

[1] A similar ingenious remark has been made by the same *savant* with regard to the Aitareya and Kaushîtaki, or, as he calls it, Śâṅkhâyana-brâhmaṇa. The former consists of forty, the latter of thirty Adhyâyas, and it is not unlikely that the rule in Pâṇini, v. 1. 62, how to form the names of Brâhmaṇas, consisting of thirty and forty Adhyâyas, had special reference to these works. The names are "trainśâni" and "châtvârinśâni brâhmaṇâni;" the explanation, "trinśad adhyâyâḥ parimâṇam eshâm brâhmaṇânâm."

The Adhyâyas which follow the Aśvamedha are distinctly called Khilas or supplements by Kâtyâyana. They are relegated to the Brâhmaṇa by the Taittirîyas, and explained with less detail in the Śatapatha-brâhmaṇa. Adhyâya xxvi.—xxix. contain some hymns belonging to sacrifices previously explained, and they are passed over entirely by the Śatapatha-brâhmaṇa and by Kâtyâyana. Adhyâya xxx. and xxxi. contain the Purushamedha, which the Taittirîyas treat in their Brâhmaṇa. The Śatapatha-brâhmaṇa devotes but a short space to it in its 13th book, and Kâtyâyana explains Adhyâya xxxi. in his 21st book.

The ceremonies comprised in the three following Adhyâyas, xxxii. to xxxiv., Sarvamedha and Brahmayajna, are passed over by the Śatapatha-brâhmaṇa and Kâtyâyana. The Taittirîyas allow them no place in their Brâhmaṇa, but include them in their Âraṇyaka.

The Pitṛimedha which follows in the xxxvth Adhyâya, finds its place in the Brâhmaṇa of the Taittirîyas. The Śatapatha and Kâtyâyana explain it, the former in the 13th, the latter in the 21st book.

The Śukriya portion of the Vâjasaneyi-sanhitâ, xxxvii.—xl., is excluded from the Brâhmaṇa of the Taittirîyas, and treated in their Âraṇyaka. The Śatapatha-brâhmaṇa explains three of these Adhyâyas, xxxvii.—xxxix., in full detail in its 17th Kâṇḍa, and Kâtyâyana devotes to them the Sûtras of his last book.

Those who only take into account the general object of the Śatapatha-brâhmaṇa, have called it a running commentary on the Vâjasaneyi-sanhitâ. But this applies strictly to the first nine books only, and with the tenth book the Brâhmaṇa assumes a new and more independent character. The tenth book is called the Agnirahasyam, the mystery of fire, and it refers to no particular portion of the Sanhitâ, but enlarges on the ceremonies which have been described in the four preceding books. Towards the end (x. 4. 6.), it contains two chapters, which, in the Kâṇva-śâkhâ, form the beginning of the Bṛihadâraṇyaka-upanishad, and are there followed by the Madhu-kâṇḍa, the Yâjnavalkîya-kâṇḍa, and Khila-kâṇḍa of the 14th book of the Mâdhyandina-śâkhâ. The 10th book or Agnirahasyam closes with its own genealogy or Vanśa.

With the 11th book begins, according to Sâyaṇa, the second part of the Śatapatha-brâhmaṇa. It is called Ashṭâdhyâyî, and gives additional information on all the sacrifices mentioned before, beginning with the Agnyâdhâna.

The 12th book, which is called Sautrâmaṇî, treats of prayaśchitta, or penance in general, and it is only in its last portion that it refers to the text of the Sanhitâ, and to that ceremony in particular from which it has derived its name. Besides this name of Sautrâmaṇî, the 12th book is also known by the name of Madhyama or the middle book, and this title can only be explained if we begin the second part of the Śatapatha, not, as Sâyaṇa suggests, with the 11th, but with the 10th book.

The 13th book is chiefly concerned with the Aśvamedha, and its first three Adhyâyas may again be considered as a kind of commentary on the Sanhitâ. Towards the end some sacrifices, beginning with the Purushamedha, which the Sanhitâ treats in its Khila portion, are explained, but other ceremonies also are mentioned, for which there is no precedent in the Sanhitâ. The Bṛihadâraṇyaka, the last book of the

Śatapatha, contains in its first three Adhyâyas, a close commentary on the Pravargya of the Sanhitâ, but becomes quite independent afterwards. Its object is no longer the sacrifice, but the knowledge of Brahman, without any particular reference, however, to the last Adhyâya of the Sanhitâ, which, as we saw, was equally devoted to the doctrine of the Upanishads.

It is clear, therefore, that the Śatapatha-brâhmaṇa was not simply a running commentary on the Sanhitâ; nay there is nothing to prove that the hymn-book of the Vâjasaneyins existed previous to their Brâhmaṇa. The Śatapatha-brâhmaṇa may have been edited by Yâjnavalkya, but its component parts, like the component parts of the other Brâhmaṇas, must have been growing up during a long period of time in different localities before they were collected. The collection of ancient Brâhmaṇas must always have been the work of individual teachers, and their Brâhmaṇas, in their new and complete form, were at first the exclusive property of that one Charaṇa to which the collectors belonged, or of which they became the founders. Afterwards these collective Brâhmaṇas were adopted by the members of other Charaṇas, who either added some chapters of their own, or introduced certain modifications, by which we now find that different texts of one and the same Brâhmaṇa differ from one another. We must distinguish, therefore, between old and new Brâhmaṇas, the former being those which from time immemorial had been living in the oral tradition of various Charaṇas, the latter comprising the great collective works. Some of the latter vary slightly in the editions adopted in various Charaṇas; others, and these the most modern, show the distinct influence of individual editors. Pâṇini, whose views are not shackled by the inspiration-doctrine which blinded and misled all the followers of the orthodox Mimânsâ school, broadly states the fact that there are old and new Brâhmaṇas; whereas, according to the doctrine of later divines, the Brâhmaṇas are neither old nor new, but eternal, and of divine origin. Pâṇini, who is a grammarian, rests his opinion as to the different dates of the Brâhmaṇas on the evidence of language. "A book," he says, "composed by a certain author, may be called by an adjective derived from the author's name."[1] For instance, a book composed by Vararuchi may be called "Vâraruchо granthaḥ." A work, on the contrary, which has only been taught and promulgated[2] by a person, is not to be called his book (grantha), but bears its own title, such as "grammar," or, whatever else it may be, together with an adjective derived from the author's name. Pâṇini's grammar, for instance, is not to be called "Pâṇinîyo granthaḥ," but "Pâṇinîyam vyâkaraṇam"; because it is a canonical work, revealed to Pâṇini, but not invented by him. It may also be called "Pâṇinîyam," in the singular neuter; *i. e.* Pâṇineum.[3] In the same way it is perfectly correct to speak of an "Âpiśalam," a work composed by Apiśala, of a "Paingî Kalpaḥ," an old ceremonial of Pinga's, of a "Mâdhurî Vrittiḥ," a commentary of Madhura[4], and of "Chârakâḥ Ślokâḥ,"

[1] Pâṇ. iv. 3. 116. कृते ग्रंथे॥ Kaiyyaṭa says that this Sûtra does not belong to Pâṇini. See page 184.

[2] Pâṇ. iv. 3. 115. उपज्ञाते। Bhâshya: विनोपदेशेन ज्ञातं॥ iv. 3. 101. तेन प्रोक्तं॥ Bhâshya: यत्तेन प्रोक्तं न च तेन कृतं॥

[3] Cf. iv. 3. 101; iv. 2. 64.

[4] Cf. Pâṇ. iv. 3. 108.

verses composed by Charaka. "But," says Pâṇini, "if the work referred to consists either of Vedic hymns (Chhandas), or of old Brâhmaṇas (purâṇaprokteshu Brâhmaṇeshu), then it is not correct to use these derivative adjectives in the singular (unless we employ secondary derivatives, such as Taittirîyakam, Kâṭhakam), but it is necessary to use the masculine plural." It is wrong to use the word Kaṭham as an adjective from Kaṭha, in the sense of hymns promulgated by Kaṭha; or to use Taittirîyam (from Tittiri, like Pâṇinîyam from Pâṇini), or Taittirîyam Brâhmaṇam, in the sense of a Brâhmaṇa promulgated by Tittiri. Even Kalpas and Sûtras like the Kalpas of Kâśyapa, and Kauśika, or the Sûtras of Pârâśarya, Śilâla, Karmanda, and Kṛiśâśva, are better quoted as "the Kâśyapins" &c. if they are old works.[1] According to Pâṇini, we must speak of "the Kaṭhas," *i. e.* those who study and know the hymns promulgated by Kaṭha[2]; of "the Taittirîyas," those who study and know the Brâhmaṇa promulgated by Tittiri. This peculiarity of the Sanskrit language, which reminds us of the Greek expression of οἱ περὶ, admits of a very natural explanation, if we remember that in these old times literary works did not exist in writing, but were handed down by oral tradition in different communities, which represented, so to say, different works, or even different recensions of one and the same work, like so many manuscripts in

[1] Cf. Pâṇ. iv. 2. 66. छंदांसि ब्राह्मणानि च प्रोक्तप्रत्ययांतान्यध्येतृवेदितृप्रत्ययं विना न प्रयोक्तव्यानि॥

[2] That the Kaṭhas were an old Charaṇa, possessing their own tradition and laws, is seen from the 11th Vârttika to Pâṇ. iv. 3. 120. and from Pâṇ. iv. 3. 126.

later times. It was much more natural, therefore, to say, "the Taittirîyas relate," than to speak of a Taittirîyam, a work proclaimed by Tittiri, who was perhaps a merely nominal ancestor of the Taittirîyas, or to refer to a Taittirîya grantha, *i. e.* Tittiri's book, which in reality never existed. That this is the real ground for this Sanskrit idiom becomes more evident by the exceptions mentioned by Pâṇini himself. There are no exceptions with regard to the names of hymns, or rather of the supporters of their texts; but there are Brâhmaṇas, Kalpas, and Sûtras spoken of in the same way as Pâṇini's own work. It is wrong, for instance, to speak of the Yâjnavalkyâs in the same sense as we speak of the Taittirîyas, and the works promulgated by Yâjnavalkya, although they are Brâhmaṇas, are called Yâjnavalkyâni Brâhmaṇâni.[1] "And why?" says Kâtyâyana; "because they are of too recent an origin; that is to say, they are almost contemporaneous with ourselves." Here, then, we see that as early as Pâṇini and Kâtyâyana a distinction was made, not only by learned men, but in common language, between old and modern Brâhmaṇas. We see that the Brâhmaṇas of Yâjnavalkya, whose works, as those of a seceder, we had reason to consider as modern, are by their very name classed as modern. What other Brâhmaṇas belong to the same class it is not so easy to say[2], because the only other instan quoted, besides the Brâhmaṇas of Yâjnavalkya, the Saulabhâni Brâhmaṇâni, and they have r been met with. It is not unlikely, howe

[1] Pâṇ. iv. 3. 105. 1. याज्ञवल्क्यादिभ्यः प्रति त्वात्।

[2] There is no Gaṇa, Yâjnavalkyâdiḥ.

the so-called Anubrâhmaṇâni [1], or supplementary Brâhmaṇas, which we have, for instance, in the Sâma-veda [2], may come under this category.[3]

That different Brâhmaṇas existed at the time when the great collective Brâhmaṇas were composed, might be proved, even without the testimony of Pâṇini, by quotations occurring in the Brâhmaṇas themselves. The original Charaṇas were not all rival sects, and it was natural that one Charaṇa should be ready to accept Brâhmaṇas of another, if they contained any additional traditions or precepts which seemed to be valuable. Thus we find the Brâhmaṇas of the Kaṭhas added to the Brâhmaṇas of the Taittirîyas. In other cases we find that one Brâhmaṇa quotes the opinion of another Śâkhâ, not in support of its own doctrines, but in order to refute it. Thus the Kaushîtakins are frequently attacked in the Tâṇḍya-brâhmaṇa. Now, if these quotations of different authorities, which we meet with in Brâhmaṇas, alluded only to the opinions of certain individuals we might still be doubtful whether these opinions had formerly been laid down in separate Brâhmaṇa

[1] Cf. Pâṇ. iv. 2. 62.

[2] The Anubrâhmaṇinaḥ are mentioned in the Nidâna-sûtra belonging to the Sâma-veda. Cf. Ind. Stud. i. 45.

[3] Ancient Chhandas (Sanhitâ-śâkhâs) are those of the Kaṭhas, Charakas, Maudas, and Paippalâdas, Śaunakins, Vâjasaneyins, &c., iv. 2. 66. Ancient Brâhmaṇas are those of the Bhâllavins, Taittirîyas, Vâratantavîyas, Khâṇḍikîyas, Âukhîyas; the Âlambins, Pâlangins, Kâmalins, Ârchâbhins, Âruṇins, Tâṇḍins, Śyâmâyanins, Kaṭhas, and Kalâpas (these descended from the nine pupils of Vaiśampâyana); the Hâridrâviṇs, Taumburaviṇs, Aulapins, and Chhâgaleyins (these derived their origin from the four pupils of Kalâpin); the Śâṭyâyanins. Old Kalpas are those of the Kâśyapins, Kauśikins, the Paingî and Âruṇaparâjî Kalpaḥ. Old Sûtras those of the Pârâśarins, Śailâlins, Karmandins, and Kṛiśâśvins.

works. But when we see quotations like "iti Kaushîtakam," "iti Paingyam," "so says the work of the Kaushîtakins or Paingins," there can be little doubt that separate Brâhmaṇas, propagated by separate Charaṇas, are here intended, whatever commentators may say to the contrary.[1]

What became of these numerous Brâhmaṇa-charaṇas which are quoted both in the Brâhmaṇas and in the Sûtras, is not quite clear. Most likely they were absorbed or replaced by a more modern class of Charaṇas, the Sûtra-charaṇas. When the Sûtras once came to be regarded as part of the sacred canon, they gave rise to a large number of new Charaṇas.[2] Their members would preserve the text of the Sanhitâ and Brâhmaṇa of an earlier Charaṇa from which they originally branched off.[3] The ground of division being in the Sûtras, the minor differences between the texts of the Sanhitâs and

[1] Indische Studien, i. 393.

[2] Colebrooke has taken a different view with respect to the Sûtras. He says, "But those numerous Śâkhâs did not differ so widely from each other as might be inferred from the mention of an equal number of Sanhitâs, or distinct collections of texts. In general, the various schools of the same Veda seem to have used the same assemblage of prayers; they differed more in their copies of the precepts or Brâhmaṇas; and some received into their canon of scripture portions which do not appear to have been acknowledged by others. Yet the chief difference seems always to have been the use of particular rituals taught in aphorisms (sûtras) adopted by each school; and these do not constitute a portion of the Veda, but, like grammar and astronomy, are placed among its appendages." Misc. Essays, i. 18.

[3] तैत्तिरीयके समाम्नाये समानाध्ययने नाना सूत्राणि। तस्मादपि शाखाभेदः॥ तथा चैकस्यां तैत्तिरीयशाखायां समानपाठायां सूत्रभेदादवांतरशाखाभेदः॥

Brâhmaṇas might be waived in these modern Charaṇas, and this would gradually lead to the loss of many of the old Śâkhâs. We saw before, in the case of the Śâkalas and Bâshkalas, that at the time when Sûtras began to be composed there was a tendency to reunite different Śâkhâs into one. That the introduction of Sûtras encroached on the study of the Brâhmaṇas and Sanhitâs in the schools of the Brahmans, becomes evident from passages in which the custom of performing sacrifices after the prescriptions of Sûtras only is declared to be without merit and without effect. Kumârila in one passage simply states the fact that priests perform sacrifices by means of the Kalpa-sûtras only, and without the Veda, but that they could not do the same by means of the Mantras and Brâhmaṇas, and without the Kalpas.[1] In another place[2] he declares that the reason why the

[1] Kumârila, i. 3.

वेदादृतेऽपि कुर्वंति कल्पैः कर्माणि याज्ञिकाः।
न तु कल्पैर्विना केचिन्मंत्रब्राह्मणमात्रकात्॥

[2] Kumârila, i. 3. 1. यत्तु किमर्थं वेदवाक्यान्येव नोपसंगृहीतानीति। संप्रदायविनाशभीतेः। विशिष्टानुपूर्व्यव्यवस्थितो हि स्वाध्यायोऽध्येतव्यः श्रूयते। स्मार्तास्त्वाचाराः केचित्क्वचित्कस्यांचिच्छाखायां। तत्रापि तु केचित्पुरुषमेवाधिकृत्याम्नायंतेऽपरे क्रतुप्रकरणाम्नाताः केनचिन्निमित्तेनोत्कृष्यमाणाः पुरुषधर्मतां भजंते। यथा मलवद्वाससा सह न संवदेत्तस्मान्न ब्राह्मणायावगुरेदित्येवमादयः। तत्र यदि तावत्तान्येव वाक्यान्युद्धृत्याध्यापयेयुस्ततः क्रमान्यत्वात्स्वाध्यायविधिविरोधः स्यात्। अनेन च निदर्शनेनान्येऽप्यर्थवादोद्धारेण विधि-

Smṛitis or law-books, which he considers to be founded on the Veda, had not been made up of literal extracts, was because this would have endangered the sacred study of the whole Veda. The Veda would thus have been read in a different order, or small extracts only would have been studied instead of the whole Veda. Now this is what seems to have happened to a certain extent by the introduction of the Sûtras, and it would account for the loss of many of the old Śâkhâs, Sanhitâs as well as Brâhmaṇas.

In order to show more clearly to how great an extent the Vedic literature was fostered by means of the Charaṇas, I shall give a list from the Charaṇavyûha. This Pariśishṭa is a document of a comparatively late period, though it may be one of the oldest works belonging to this class of literature.[1] It is, therefore, no good authority as to the number of the old Sanhitâ-charaṇas and Brâhmaṇa-charaṇas, many of which were lost or merged into others during the Sûtra period; but it is of interest as the first attempt at a complete enumeration of all Charaṇas, and may be trusted particularly with regard to the Sûtra-charaṇas, which, at the time of its composition, were still of recent origin. The number of the old Charaṇas would, no doubt, have to be increased considerably, if the quotations of different Śâkhâs were

मात्रमधीयीरन् कर्मौपायिकमात्रं वा। तत्र वेदप्रलयः प्रसज्येत॥

[1] It has been printed by Prof. Weber in his Indische Studien. I possess the collation of some of the Berlin MSS., but not of all. In addition to the MSS. collated by Prof. Weber, I have used the text and various readings given in Râdhakântadeva's Śabdakalpadruma.

taken into account, which occur in the Brâhmaṇas as well as in the Sûtras. But at the same time we may conclude from the lists given in the Charaṇavyûha that most of these old Charaṇas were extinct shortly after the Sûtra-period, and that their works as well as their names, began to be forgotten.

Of the Rig-veda five Charaṇas are mentioned:

1. The Śâkalas.[1]
2. Bâshkalas.[2]
3. Âśvalâyanas.[3]
4. Śânkhâyanas.[4]
5. Mâṇḍukâyanas.[5]

We miss the names of several old Śâkhâs such as the Aitareyins, Śaiśiras[6], Kaushîtakins, Paingins,

[1] Pâṇ. iv. 3. 128.: iv. 2. 117.

[2] Bâshkala. Not mentioned in Pâṇini. As to its etymology, cf. Pâṇ. ii. 1. 65.

[3] Pâṇ. iv. 1. 99.: Gaṇa naḍadi.

[4] This Śâkhâ is spelt Sânkhyâyana, Śânkhyâyana, Sânkhâyana and Śânkhâyana. The last, however, is the most correct spelling. See Pâṇini, Gaṇapâṭha, aśvâdi, and kunjâdi. This Śâkhâ is omitted by accident in MS. E. I. H.

[5] Pâṇ. iv. 1. 19 (text). Mâṇḍûka; derivative, Mâṇḍûkâyana. See also Pâṇ. iv. 1. 119.

[6] The Śaiśira-śâkhâ, however, may perhaps be considered as a subdivision of the Śâkala-śâkhâ. Śaiśira, or Śiśira, is mentioned in the Purâṇas as one of the five Śâkala pupils, who propagated different Śâkhâs of the Rig-veda, all of them derived from the original recension of Śâkalya Vedamitra. In the Vishṇu-purâṇa these five pupils or descendants of Śâkalya Vedamitra are called Mudgala, Gosvalu, Vâtsya, Śâlîya, and Śiśira. (Vishṇu-pur. 277.) In the Vâyu-purâṇa their names are Mudgala, Goḷaka, Khâlîya, Mâtsya, Śaiśireya. In the commentary on the Śâkala-prâtiśâkhya they are called Mudgala, Gokula, Vâtsya, Śaiśira, and Śiśira, according to the Paris MS.; or Mudgala, Gokhula, Vâtsya, Śârîra, and Śaiśira, according to the MS. at the E. I. H.

इदं शास्त्रं पार्षदाख्यमखिलं संपूर्णमुत्तरच वक्ष्ये वक्ष्याम

while the Âśvalâyanas, who are mentioned, must be considered as the founders of one of the latest Śâkhâs of the Rig-veda.

The number of Śâkhâs of the Yajur-veda is stated at eighty-six. We have first the twelve Charaṇas comprehended under the common name of Charakas. They are, according to the MS. of the Charaṇavyûha:

1. Charakas.[1]
2. Âhvarakas.[2]
3. Kaṭhas.[3]
4. Prâchya-kaṭhas.[4]
5. Kapishṭhala-kaṭhas.[5]
6. Chârâyaṇîyas.[6]

इत्यर्थः। शैशिरीये पारायणपाठ इति वाक्यशेषः। शैशिरीयायां संहितायामित्यर्थः। शैशिरी संहिता शिशिरदृष्टत्वात्। तथा पुराण उक्तं। मुद्गलो गोकुलो वात्स्यः शैशिरः शिशिरस्तथा। पंचैते शाकलाः शिष्याः शाखाभेदप्रवर्तका इति। तथा च ऋग्वेदे शैशिरीयायां संहितायामिति। यथा ऋग्वेदे पारायणाम्नाये शाकल्ये शैशिरीयकमिति वा। The verses to which this commentary refers are not in the MS.

[1] Pâṇ. iv. 3. 107. text; v. 1. 11. text. Gaṇa Kshipakâdi.

[2] Âhvarakas, Ś. K. D. Âhûrakas, Sansk. G. P. Hvarakas, MS. Berol. 785. Cf. Pâṇ. ii. 4. 20.; vi. 2. 124.; iii. 2. 135. comment. Several of these names are very problematical.

[3] Pâṇ. iv. 3. 107. text; ii. 1. 65. com.; vii. 4. 38. text; vi. 3. 42. com.; ii. 4. 3. com.; i. 3. 49. com.; ii. 1. 163. com.

[4] Cf. Pâṇ. vi. 2. 10.

[5] Pâṇ. viii. 3. 91. Kapishṭhalaḥ and Kapisthalam. Gaṇa kraudyâdi and upakâdi. As to Καμβίσθολοι, see Megasthenes, edit. Schwanbeck, p. 33. note, and p. 108.

[6] Pâṇ. iv. 1. 89. com.; iv. 1. 63. com.; iv. 1. 99. com.; iv. 3. 80. com. Gaṇa naḍâdi.

7. Vâratantavîyas.[1]
8. Śvetâśvataras.[2]
9. Aupamanyavas.[3]
10. Pâtas.[4]
11. Aiṇḍineyas.[5]
12. Maitrâyaṇîyas.[6]

The Maitrâyaṇîyas are subdivided into seven Charaṇas: —

13. Mânavas.[7]
14. Vârâhas.[8]
15. Dundubhas.
16. Chhâgaleyas.[9]
17. Hâridravîyas.[10]
18. Śyâmas.[11]

[1] Vârtantavîya, MSS. See, however, Pâṇ. iv. 3. 102.

[2] A different reading is mentioned in the Ś. K. D., namely, Śvetâ Śvetatarâḥ. MS. Chamb. 785., has Śvetâḥ Śvetântarâḥ; 376. Śvetâ Aśvatarâḥ. Sansk. G. P., Śvetâḥ Śvetatarâḥ.

[3] See Gaṇa Vidâdi.

[4] Âshṭhalakaṭhas, Ś. K. D. Pâtâṇḍinîyas, Chamb. 785.

[5] Vârâyaṇîyas, Ś. K. D.

[6] See Gaṇapâṭha, arîhaṇâdi.

[7] Pâṇ. iv. 1. 105. Gaṇa Gargâdi, unless the reading be manutantu.

[8] Pâṇ. iv. 2. 80. Gaṇa Varâhâdi. Pâṇ. iv. 1. 78.

[9] Chaikeyas Ś. K. D. MSS. Chamb. 376. 785, have Chhâgeyas. MS. 785. places the Hâridravîyas at the end, adding five new divisions. तत्र हारिद्रवीया नाम पंच भेदा भवति। हारिद्रवमासुरं गार्ग्यं शार्कराक्षममाग्रावमवोयं पंचममेते हारिद्रवमंग्रहा:। Pâṇ. iv. 1. 117, Chhâgala, âtreyaś chet, chhâgalir anyaḥ; iv. 3. 109, Chhâgaleyinaḥ; vii. 1. 2, Gaṇa takshaśilâdi. Chhâgaleyaḥ, Pâṇ. iv. 2. 30, Gaṇa Sakhyâdi.

[10] Pâṇ. iv. 3. 104, Haridru and hâridraviṇaḥ; iv. 4. 53, Gaṇa kisarâdi.

[11] Gaṇa âśvadi.

19. Śyâmâyanîyas.[1]

Then follow

20. Taittirîyas, subdivided into
21. Aukhîyas[2] and
22. Khâṇḍikîyas.[3]

The Khâṇḍikîyas are again subdivided into: —

23. Kâleyas.[4]
24. Śâṭyâyanins.
25. Hiraṇyakeśins.
26. Bhâradvâjins.
27. Âpastambins.

This gives altogether twenty-seven Śâkhâs, the same number which is mentioned in the Vishṇu-purâṇa[5], although the manner of computing them is different.

Then follow the fifteen Śâkhâs of the Vâjasaneyins, a number which is confirmed by the Pratijnâ-pariśishṭa, and has also been preserved in the Vishṇu-purâṇa, while the Charaṇavyûha of the Śabda-kalpa-druma brings their number to seventeen. They are: —

28. Jâbâlas.[6]

[1] Pâṇ. iv. 3. 104.

[2] Aukshyas and Aukhyas, Ś. K. D.; Aukhîyas, Ch. 785.; Ausheyas, Ch. 376. Cf. Pâṇ. iv. 3. 102.

[3] Khâṇḍikîyas, Ch. 785.; Shâṇḍikeyas, Ch. 376.; Pâṇ. iv. 3. 102.

[4] The Charaṇavyûha of the Ś. K. D. has, — 23. Âpastambins; 24. Baudhâyanins; 25. Satyâshâḍhins; 26. Hiraṇyakeśins; 27. Aukheyas or Audheyins. MS. Ch. 785. has, — 23. Kâleyas (Kâleyâḥ, Pâṇ. iv. 2. 8.); 24. Śâṭyayanas (Pâṇ. iv. 3. 105.); 25. Hiraṇyakeśas; 26. Bhâradvâjas; 27. Âpastambîyas. MS. 376., Kaletas, Śâṭyâyinins, Hiraṇyakeśins, Bhâradvâjins, Âpastambins.

[5] P. 279. "Of the tree of the Yajur-veda there are twenty-seven branches, which Vaiśampâyana, the pupil of Vyâsa, compiled and taught to as many disciples."

[6] Pâṇ. vi. 2. 38. text; ii. 4. 58. 1.

29. Baudheyas.[1]
30. Kâṇvas.[2]
31. Mâdhyandinas.[3]
32. Śâpheyas.[4]
33. Tâpanîyas.[5]
34. Kapolas.[6]
35. Pauṇḍravatsas.[7]
36. Âvaṭikas.[8]
37. Paramâvaṭikas.[9]
38. Pârâśaryas.[10]
39. Vaineyas.[11]
40. Vaidheyas.[12]
41. Auḍheyas.[13]
42. Mauneyas.[14]

Though the number of the Śâkhâs of the Yajurveda is stated at eighty-six by the Charaṇavyûha,

[1] Baudheyas, P.-p. Ch. 785.; Augheyas, Ś. K. D.; Gaudheyas, S. G. P.; Baudhâyanas, Ch. 376. E. I. H.; Baudhiḥ, Pâṇ. ii. 4. 58. 1.

[2] Pâṇ. iv. 2. 111. text.

[3] Mâdhyandineyas, Ch. 376. See Gaṇa utsâdi.

[4] Śâpeyas, P. p.; Śâpîyas, Ś. K. D.; Śâpeya, Gaṇa śaunakâdi.

[5] Tâpâyanîyas, Ś. K. D.; Ch. 376.; Tâpâyanas, Ch. 785.

[6] Kalâpas, P.-p.; Kapâlas, Ś. K. D.; Ch. 785.; Kapolas, Ch. 376.

[7] Paundravachhas, P.-p.; Ch. 376. Cf. Pâṇ. vii. 3. 24.

[8] Cf. Gaṇa gargâdi, Pâṇ. iv. 1. 17.; iv. 1. 75, text.

[9] Pâmâvaṭikas or Paramâvaṭikas, Ś. K. D.

[10] Pârâśaras, P.-p.; Ch. 785. 376.; Pârâśarîyas, Ś. K. D.; Gaṇa kriśâśvâdi; gargâdi.

[11] Vaidheyas, Ch. 785.; Vaineyas, Ch. 376.

[12] Vaidheyas, Ch. 376.; Vaineyas, Ch. 785.

[13] Aukhyas, P.-p.; Addhas, Ch. 376.; Ugheyas, Ś. K. D.; See Pâṇ. ii. 4. 7.; Aukhîyas, Ch. 785.

[14] Baudhyaśvas, P.-p.; Mauneyas, Ch. 785.; Bodheyas, Ch. 376. The Ś. K. D. adds here,—42. Galavas; 43. Vaijaras; 44. Kâtyâyanîyas.

the names given, including the Vâjasaneyins, amount only to forty-three, exactly half the number expected.[1] It is difficult to account for this, for although some other names are mentioned, for instance the Prâchya, Udîchya and Nairṛitya Kaṭhas, yet this would not increase the number of Śâkhâs sufficiently.

The largest number of Śâkhâs is ascribed to the Sâma-veda. It is said to have been a thousand. The author of the Charaṇavyûha, however, confesses that the greater part of them no longer exist. Those remaining at the time when the Charaṇavyûha was composed were the seven Śâkhâs of the

1. Râṇâyanîyas.[2]
2. Sâtyamugryas.[3]
3. Kâlâpas.[4]
4. Mahâkalopas.[5]
5. Lângalâyanas.[6]
6. Śârdûlas.[7]
7. Kauthumas.[8]

The Kauthumas are again subdivided into the

8. Âśurâyaṇas.[9]
9. Vâtâyanas.[10]

[1] In a MS. of the Charaka-śâkhâ of the Kâṭhaka, 101 Śâkhâs of the Yajur-veda are mentioned. Catalogue of the Berlin MSS., p. 38. "Ekottaraśatâdhvaryuśâkhâprabhedabhinne yajurvedakâṭhake."

[2] Gaṇa pailâdi.

[3] Sâtyamurgyas and Śâṭyamurgryas, Ch. 785.; Śâṭyamurgryas, Ch. 376.; Pâṇ. iv. 1. 81.

[4] Kâlopas, Ch. 785. 376.; Pâṇ. iv. 3. 108.

[5] Mahâkâlopas, Ch. 785. 376.; probably Mahâkâlâpas.

[6] Lângalas, Ch. 785.

[7] Śârdûlas, Ch. 376.; wanting in Ch. 785.

[8] Gaṇa Kârtakaujapâdi.

[9] Kauthumas, Ch. 785.; Gaṇa taulvalyâdi.

[10] Sârdulas, Ch. 785.

10. Prânjalidvaitabhṛits.[1]
11. Prâchînayogyas.[2]
12. Naigeya-Kauthumas.[3]

The account given by the Ś. K. D. is very different and in many places corrupt. Here we have, 1. the Âsurâyaṇîyas or Surâyaṇîyas, 2. Vârtântaveyas, 3. Prânjalas, 4. Ṛigvarṇabhedas, 5. Prâchînayogyas, 6. Jnânayogyas, 7. Râṇâyaṇîyas. The Râṇâyaṇîyas are subdivided into nine; Râṇâyaṇîyas, 8. Śâṭhyâyanîyas (or Śârâyaṇîyas, Śâṭhyamugryas), 9. Śâtvalas (or Sâtyamudbhavas), 10. Maudgalas (not mentioned in the Bhâshya), 11. Khallalas, 12. Mahâkhallavas, 13. Lângalas, 14. Kauthumas, 15. Gautamas, 16. Jaiminîyas.

Of the Atharva-veda nine divisions are mentioned, but the names given are incomplete and corrupt. They are given here, with some conjectural emendations from the MSS.[4]

1. Paippalâdas.[5]

[1] Surâṇâyanîyas, Ch. 785.

[2] Prâjvalanâdvaitabhṛits, Ch. 785.; Prânjalidvenabhṛits, Ch. 376. Gaṇa Gargâdi.

[3] Prâchînayogyas and Naigeyas.

[4] The text in the Ś. K. D. has पैप्पलाः। दांताः। प्रदांताः। स्नाताः। स्नैता इति च पाठः। स्नैताः। ब्रह्मदावलाः। शौनकी। देविदर्शती। चरणविद्याश्चेति॥ दाता प्रदाता श्रोता ब्रह्मदीपशी वेदशी इति भाष्ये नामांतरं॥ MS. Ch. 785. reads शौनका दामोदा त्तोत्तायना जायला ब्रह्मपला शकुन खी देवदर्शी चारणविद्याश्चेति। MS. Ch. 376. reads, शौनका दामोदा तोत्तायना जाबाला ब्रह्मपलाशा शौनकी देवर्षि चारणविद्याश्चेति॥

[5] Pâṇ. iv. 2. 66.

2. Śaunakas.[1]
3. Dâmodas.
4. Tottâyanas.
5. Jayâlas.
6. Brâhmapalâśas.
7. Kaunakhins.
8. Devadarśanins.[2]
9. Chârаṇavidyas.

This list makes no distinction between old and new Charaṇas. If we had the whole Vedic literature before us, as it was living during ancient times in the tradition of numerous Brahmanic families, it would be possible to determine which of these Charaṇas owe their origin to Sûtras, which to Brâhmaṇas or Sanhitâs. As it is, we can only infer that some Charaṇas, like those of the Âśvalâyanas, Hiraṇyakeśins, Bhâradvâjins, Âpastambins, Baudhâyanas, Pârâśaryas, &c., are in all probability of modern origin, because the only works ascribed to their founders are Sûtra compilations. Their Sanhitâs and Brâhmaṇas, whenever they are mentioned, seem to be the same as those of older Charaṇas, with but slight modifications. Other Charaṇas, like those of the Paingins, Kaushîtakins, Aitareyins, Śâṭyâyanins, &c., are not mentioned in connection with any Sûtras composed by authors bearing these names; and it is most likely, therefore, that they derive their origin from authors whose names have been perpetuated in the titles of certain Brâhmaṇas. Whether these Charaṇas were in possession of Sûtras is doubtful, nor have we any means of determining whether, for instance, a member of the Aitareyi-charaṇa, after adopting the Kalpa-sûtras of

[1] Pâṇ. iv. 3. 106.

[2] Gaṇa Śaunakâdi.

Śaunaka, would retain his allegiance to the Aitareyins or not. The ancient Sanhitâs used in these Brâhmaṇa-charaṇas, and originally adopted from older Charaṇas, were not likely to be affected by considerable differences after their adoption. The fact that we never find a Kaushîtaki-sanhitâ or Paingi-sanhitâ quoted tends to show that the Charaṇas, which owe their independent constitution to the introduction of a Brâhmaṇa, retained in most instances the original text of their Sanhitâs. Charaṇas, lastly, like those of the Śâkalas, Bâshkalas, Śaiśiras, &c., whose names are connected neither with Sûtras nor Brâhmaṇas, but with Sanhitâs only, must be referred to the earliest period of the formation of Vedic communities, and must have existed, as the bearers of their own traditional collection of hymns, before the composition of either Brâhmaṇas or Sûtras. With regard to many Charaṇas, however, it will remain doubtful to which of these three classes they belong, until a larger number of Vedic works peculiar to each Charaṇa becomes available. Charaṇas like those of the Mâdhyandinas and Kâṇvas must be referred to the Brâhmaṇa period, because their Sanhitâs and Brâhmaṇas are ascribed to one and the same teacher. This teacher, Yâjnavalkya, is represented as the author of modern Brâhmaṇas, and we saw that, in all probability, his Sanhitâ was even more modern than his Brâhmaṇas. The fact, however, that the Sûtras adopted by the Mâdhyandina and Kâṇva-charaṇas are ascribed to Kâtyâyana, shows that these Charaṇas existed certainly previous to the Sûtra period. With regard to the Sanhitâ-charaṇas it will always be difficult to determine how far their differences were fixed, if not originally called forth by the introduction of the Brâhmaṇas. Most likely the Sanhitâ-charaṇas are restricted to the Rig-veda. It is certain, at least, that no Brâhmaṇas belonging to any Veda was composed before the division of priests into Hotṛis, Udgâtṛis, and Adhvaryus had taken place. Before that division there was but one collection of hymns, that of the Bahvṛichas, and it is among the Bahvṛichas only that we have any distinct traces of Sanhitâ-charaṇas.

It will always be very difficult to assign a distinct meaning to such terms of Charaṇa and Śâkhâ, because we have nothing that exactly corresponds to them in our own experience. Literary works, such as the Śâkhâs were, have assumed with us a much more tangible shape. They exist as books, and not merely as a body of thought handed down in schools, or in families. To read a śâkhâ meant not only to go over it (adhi-i), but to take possession of it, to guard it in the memory, and to enable others to read it by repeating it to them. A man who had read a book was himself the book: the song of the poet had no outward existence except through those who heard and remembered it. A work, once composed, might either wither for want of an audience, or grow, like a tree, of which every new listener would become a new branch. The idea of representing what we should call an edition of a hundred copies, by the simile of a branch, was a very natural one, and if we once adopt it and enter into the spirit of this Sanskrit idiom, we see that it is difficult to distinguish between the branch, as the book, and the branch, as the reader; between the trust, and the trustee. It would be well, however, to speak of the former only as śâkhâ, and of the latter as the reader of a śâkhâ, while we should reserve the name of Charaṇa for those ideal successions or fellowships to which all belonged who read the same śâkhâ.

If it is difficult to describe what a Śâkhâ and a Charaṇa were, it is all the more necessary to state what they were not. Now a Charaṇa was not the same as a Gotra or Kula. Gotra or Kula means a family, and the number of families that had a right to figure in the Brahmanic Peerage of India was very considerable. The Brahmans were proud of their ancestors, and preserved their memory with the most scrupulous care, as may be seen by the numerous treatises on the subject which are preserved to the present day. Mâdhava, for instance, after stating who his father, mother, and brothers were, what Śâkhâ he followed, what Sûtra he had adopted, adds at the end that his family was descended from Bhâradvâja.[1] Gotras or families existed among Kshatriyas and Vaiśyas as well as among Brahmans.[2] Charaṇas were confined to the priestly caste. Gotras depended on a real or imaginary community of blood, and thus correspond to what we call families. Charaṇas depended on the community of sacred texts. They were ideal fellowships, held together by ties, more sacred in the eyes of a Brahman than the mere ties of blood. They were the living depositaries of the most sacred heirlooms, and with the extinction of

[1] श्रीमती जननी यस्य सुकीर्तिर्मायणः पिता।
सायणो भोगनाथश्च मनोबुद्धी सहोदरौ॥
यस्य बौधायनं सूत्रं शाखा यस्य च याजुषी।
भारद्वाजं कुलं यस्य सर्वज्ञः स हि माधवः॥

[2] Baudhâyana-sûtra-bhâshya. MS. E. I. H. 104, p. 91.

a Charaṇa, the words which were believed to be the breath of God would have been lost without the hope of recovery. Members of different Gotras might belong to the same Charaṇa. Where the member of a Gotra became the founder of a new Charaṇa, the new Charaṇa might bear the name of its founder, and thus become synonymous, but not identical, with a Gotra.

The names of the Charaṇas were naturally preserved as long as the texts which they embodied continued to be studied. The names of the Gotras were liable to confusion, particularly in later times, when their number had become very considerable. But the respect which the Brahmans, from the very earliest time, paid to their ancestors, and the strictness with which they prohibited marriages between members of the same family, lead us to suppose that the genealogical lists, such as we find in the Brâhmaṇas, in the Sûtras, in the Mahâbhârata, in the Purâṇas, and even at the present day, present in their general outlines a correct account of the priestly families of India. All Brahmanic families who keep the sacred fires are supposed to descend from the Seven Ṛishis. These are:—*Bhṛigu*, *Angiras*, *Viśvâmitra*, *Vasishṭha*, *Kâśyapa*, *Atri*, *Agasti*. The real ancestors, however, are eight in number:—*Jamadagni*, *Gautama* and *Bharadvâja*, *Viśvâmitra*, *Vasishṭha*, *Kâśyapa*, *Atri*, *Agastya*. The eight Gotras, which descend from these Ṛishis, are again subdivided into forty-nine Gotras, and these forty-nine branch off into a still larger number of families. The names gotra, vanśa, varga, paksha, and gaṇa are all used in the same sense, to express the larger as well as the smaller families, descended from the eight ancestral Ṛishis.

A Brahman, who keeps the sacrificial fire, is obliged by law to know to which of the forty-nine Gotras his own family belongs, and in consecrating his own fire he must invoke the ancestors who founded the Gotra to which he belongs. Each of the forty-nine Gotras claims one, or two, or three, or five ancestors, and the names of these ancestors constitute the distinctive character of each Gotra.[1] A list of these forms part of most of the Kalpa-sûtras, and I here give one of them from the 12th Book of Âśvalâyana's Śrauta-sûtras.[2]

List of the Forty-nine Gotras, according to Âśvalâyana, xii. 10. seq.

1. The Bhṛigus.

Name of Gotra.	No. of Ancestors.	Invocation of Ancestors.
1. Jâmadagnâ Vatsâḥ	5	Bhârgava, Chyâvana, Âpnavâna, Aurva, Jamadagneti.
2. Jâmadagnyâḥ or Jâmadagnâḥ.	5	Bhârgava, Chyâvana, Âpnavâna, Ârshṭisheṇa, Anûpeti.

[1] सर्वगोत्राणि प्रवरगणायत्तानि। गोत्राणां तु सहस्राणि प्रयुतान्यर्बुदानि च। ऊनपंचाशदेतेषां प्रवरा ऋषिदर्शनात्॥

[2] These lists vary considerably in the different Sûtras. Purushottama, in his Pravaramanjarî, has made an attempt at collecting and explaining them. He uses the Kalpa-sûtras of Baudhâyana, Âpastamba, Satyâshâḍha, Kuṇḍina, Bharadvâja, Laugâkshi, Kâtyâyana, and Âśvalâyana; the Matsya-purâṇa, the Bhârata, Manu's Law-book and their commentaries. For Baudhâyana he quotes a commentary by Amala; for Âpastamba, Dhûrtasvamin, Kapardisvâmin, Gurudevasvâmin; for Âśvalâyana, Devasvâmin.

Name of Gotra.	No. of Ancestors.	Invocation of Ancestors.
3. Bidâḥ	5	Bhârgava, Chyâvana, Âpnavâna, Aurva, Baideti.
4. Yaska, Bâdhaula, Mauna, Mauka, Śârkarâkshi, Sârshṭi, Sâvarṇi, Śâlankâyana, Jaimini, Devantyâyanâḥ	3	Bhârgava, Vaitahavya, Sâvetaseti.
5. Śyaitâḥ	3	Bhârgava, Vainya, Pârtheti.
6. Mitrayuvaḥ	1 or 3	Bâdhryaśveti. or Bhârgava, Daivodâsa, Bâdhryaśveti.
7. Śunakâḥ	1 or 3	Gârtsamadeti. or Bhârgava, Śaunahotra, Gârtsamadeti.

II. The Ângirasas.

a. The Gotamas.

Name of Gotra.	No. of Ancestors.	Invocation of Ancestors.
8. Gotamâḥ	3	Ângirasa, Âyâsya, Gautameti.
9. Uchathyâḥ	3	Ângirasa, Auchathya, Gautameti.
10. Rahûgaṇâḥ	3	Ângirasa, Râhûgaṇya, Gautameti.
11. Somarâjakayaḥ	3	Ângirasa, Somarâjya, Gautameti.

Name of Gotra.	No. of Ancestors.	Invocation of Ancestors.
12. Vâmadevâḥ	3	Âṅgirasa, Vâmadevya, Gautameti.
13. Bṛihadukthâḥ	3	Âṅgirasa, Bârhadukthya, Gautameti.
14. Pṛishadaśvâḥ	3 or 3	Âṅgirasa, Pârshadaśva, Vairûpeti. Ashṭâdanshṭra, Pârshadaśva, Vairûpeti.
15. Rikshâḥ	5	Âṅgirasa, Bârhaspatya, Bhâradvâja, Vândana, Mâtavachaseti.
16. Kakshîvantaḥ	5	Âṅgirasa, Auchathya, Gautama, Auśija, Kâkshîvateti.
17. Dîrghatamasaḥ	3	Âṅgirasa, Auchathya, Dairghatamaseti.

b. The Bharadvâjas.

Name of Gotra.	No. of Ancestors.	Invocation of Ancestors.
18. Bharadvâjâgniveśyâḥ	3	Âṅgirasa, Bârhaspatya, Bhâradvâjeti.
19. Mudgalâḥ	3 or 3	Âṅgirasa, Bhârmyaśva, Maudgalyeti. Tarkshya, Bhârmyaśva, Maudgalyeti.
20. Vishṇuvṛiddhâḥ	3	Âṅgirasa, Paurukutsya, Trâsadasyaveti.
21. Gargâḥ	5 or 3	Âṅgirasa, Bârhaspatya, Bhâradvâja, Gârgya, Śainyeti. Âṅgirasa, Śainya, Gârgyeti.

Name of Gotra.	No. of Ancestors.	Invocation of Ancestors.
22. Harita Kutsa Pinga Śankha Darbhya Bhaimagavâḥ	3 or 3	Ângirasa, Âmbarîsha, Yauvanâśveti. Mândhâtra, Âmbarîsha, Yauvanâśveti.
23. Sankṛiti Putimâsha Taṇḍi Śambhu Śaivagavâḥ	3 or 3	Ângirasa, Gaurivîta, Sânkṛityeti. Śâktya, Gaurivîta, Sânkṛityeti.
24. Kaṇvâḥ	3 or 3	Ângirasa, Âjamîḷha, Kâṇveti. Ângirasa, Ghaura, Kâṇveti.
25. Kapayaḥ	3	Ângirasa, Mahîyava, Urukshayaseti.
26. Śaunga-Śaiśirayaḥ	5 or 3	Ângirasa, Bârhaspatya, Bhâradvâja, Kâtya, Atkîleti.

III. THE ATRIS.

Name of Gotra.	No. of Ancestors.	Invocation of Ancestors.
27. Atrayaḥ	3	Âtreya, Ârchanânasa, Śpâvâśveti.
28. Gavishṭhirâḥ	3	Âtreya, Gavishṭhira, Paurvâtitheti.

IV. THE VIŚVÂMITRAS.

Name of Gotra.	No. of Ancestors.	Invocation of Ancestors.
29. Chikita- Gâlava- Kâlabava- Manutantu- Kuśikâḥ	3	Vaiśvâmitra, Devarâta, Audaleti.

Name of Gotra.	No. of Ancestors.	Invocation of Ancestors.
30. Śraumata-kâmakâyânaḥ	3	Vaiśvâmitra, Devaśravasa, Daivataraseti.
31. Dhanañjayâḥ	3	Vaiśvâmitra, Mâdhuchhandasa, Dhânanjayyeti.
32. Ajâḥ	3	Vaiśvâmitra, Mâdhuchhandasa, Âjyeti.
33. Rohiṇâḥ	3	Vaiśvâmitra, Mâdhuchhandasa, Rauhiṇeti.
34. Ashṭakâḥ	3	Vaiśvâmitra, Mâdhuchhandasa, Âshṭaketi.
35. Pûraṇa-Vâridhâpayantâḥ	3	Vaiśvâmitra, Devarâta, Pauraṇeti.
36. Katâḥ	3	Vaiśvâmitra, Kâtya, Âtkîleti.
37 Aghamarshaṇâḥ	3	Vaiśvâmitra, Âghamarshaṇa, Kauśiketi.
38. Reṇavaḥ	3	Vaiśvâmitra, Gâthina, Raiṇaveti.
39. Veṇavaḥ	3	Vaiśvâmitra, Gâthina, Vaiṇaveti.
40. Śâlankâyana-Śâlâksha-Lohitâksha-Lohitajahnavaḥ	3	Vaiśvâmitra, Śâlankâyana, Kauśiketi.

V. The Kaśyapas.

41. Kaśyapâḥ	3	Kâśyapa, Âvatsâra, Âsiteti.
42. Nidhruvâḥ	3	Kâśyapa, Âvatsâra, Naidhruveti.
43. Rebhâḥ	3	Kâśyapa, Âvatsâra, Raibhyeti.

Name of Gotra.	No. of Ancestors.	Invocation of Ancestors.
44. Śaṇḍilâḥ	3	Śâṇḍila, Âsita, Daivaleti.
	or	
	3	Kâśyapa, Âsita, Daivaleti.

VI. The Vasishṭhas.

45. Vasishṭhâḥ	1	Vâsishṭheti.
46. Upamanyavaḥ	3	Vâsishṭha, Âbharadvasu, Indrapramadeti.
47. Parâśarâḥ	3	Vâsishṭha, Śâktya, Pârâśaryeti.
48. Kuṇḍinâḥ	3	Vâsishṭha, Maitrâvaruṇa, Kauṇḍinyeti.

VII. The Agastis.

49. Agastayaḥ	3	Âgastya, Dârḍhachyuta, Idhmavâheti.
	or	
	3	Âgastya, Dârḍhachyuta, Somavâheti.

There are other lists of much greater extent, which may become useful in time for chronological calculations. In them the first branch of the Bhṛigus, the Vatsas, count 73 names; among them such names as Śaunakâyanâḥ (8), Pailâḥ (13), Paingalâyanâḥ (14), Pâṇiniḥ (29), Vâlmîkayaḥ (30). The Vidas comprise 13, the Ârshṭishenas 8, the Yaskas 20, the Mitrayus 11, the Vainyas 3, and the Śunakas 9 names. It would occupy too much space to print these lists here.

In order to prove that these lists were not merely arbitrary compositions, their practical bearing on two very important acts of the ancient Brahmanic society, the consecrating of the sacrificial fires, and marriage, should be borne in mind.

When the fire is to be consecrated, Agni Havyavâhana, the god who carries the libations to heaven, must be invoked. This invocation or invitation of Agni, is called *pravara.*[1] Agni himself or the fire is called Ârsheya, the offspring of the Ṛishis, because the Ṛishis first lighted him at their sacrifices. He is the Hotṛi as well as the Adhvaryu among the gods. Like the Hotṛi and Adhvaryu priests, he is supposed to invite the gods to the sacrifice, and to carry himself the oblation to the seat of the immortals. When therefore a Brahman has his own fire consecrated, he wishes to declare that he is as worthy as his ancestors to offer sacrifices, and he invites Agni to carry his oblations to the gods as he did for his ancestors. The names of these ancestors must then be added to his invitation, and thus the invitation or invocation of the ancestors came to be called *pravara.* For instance, if a Brahman belongs to the family of the Mâṇḍûkeyas, he must know that the Mâṇḍûkeyas belong to the Vatsas, and that the Vatsas are descended from Bhṛigu, and invoke five ancestors. He must, therefore, like all members of the Vatsa-gotra, invoke Agni by the names of Bhârgava, Chyâvana, Âpnavâna, Aurva, and Jâmadgna. If he belong to the family of Yâjnavalkya, a branch of the Kuśikas, descendants of Viśvâmitra, he must invoke Agni by the name of Viśvâmitra, Devarâta and Udala. This, at least, is

[1] तस्य (अग्नेराहवनीयस्य) प्रकर्षेण प्रार्थनानि तैस्तैर्मंत्रदृग्भिरेकद्वित्रिपंचसंख्याकैर्विशिष्टानि एकार्षेया द्व्यार्षेयास्त्र्यार्षेयाः पंचार्षेयाः प्रवरा इत्युच्यंते॥

the rule laid down in the Baudhâyana-sûtra, with which the Âśvalâyana-sûtra coincides, except that he does not mention the Yâjnavalkyas as a subdivision of the Kuśikas. This custom was known at the time of the composition of the Brâhmaṇas, and we have no reason to doubt that ever since the first establishment of Vedic sacrifices, the forty-nine families preserved the tradition of their sacred pedigree, and that their genealogies possess a certain historical value.[1]

This is confirmed still further if we consider the ancient Brahmanic laws concerning marriage. To marry a woman belonging to the same Gotra, or having the same Pravara, was considered incest, and visited with severe penance. Âśvalâyana (xii. 15.) says: "Asamânapravarair vivâhaḥ." "Marriage takes place with persons who have not the same Pravara, *i. e.* who do not invoke the same Ṛishis as their ancestors." Âpastamba says: "Sagotrâya duhitaram na prayachchhet," "Thou shalt not give thy daughter to a man belonging to the same Gotra or family." Yâjnavalkya says: "Aroginîm bhrâtṛimatîm asamânârshagotrajâm udvahet." "Let a man marry a woman who is free from disease, who has brothers, and who is not the daughter of a man having the same ancestors and belonging to the same Gotra as himself." In each case severe punishments are threatened if a man

[1] Thus we read in the Śrauta-sûtras of the Mânavas, that the Dîkshita must say his name, the name of his Gotra, of his father, grandfather, and great grandfather; a custom which, if observed as a sacred law, must have preserved a genealogical knowledge for many generations. दीक्षितोऽयमसाविति नाम गृह्णाति। आमुष्यायणमिति गोत्रं। अमुष्य पुत्र इति पितुर्नाम्ना। अमुष्य पौत्रेति पितामहस्य। अमुष्य नप्त्रेति प्रपितामहस्य॥

transgress these rules knowingly, or even unknowingly. There are some special rules with regard to marriage, which differ again according to different Sûtras ; of which the following, taken from Âśvalâyana, may serve as a specimen :

1. Persons who have the same Pravara must not intermarry. Hence a Parâśara must not marry the daughter of a Parâśara.

2. Persons belonging to the same Gotra must not intermarry. Hence a Viśvâmitra must not marry the daughter of a Viśvâmitra.

3. There are exceptions to this rule among the Bhṛigus and Ângirasas. As a general rule, persons are called sagotra, if but one of the Ṛishis whom they invoke is the same. Hence an Upamanyu must not marry the daughter of a Parâśara, because the name of Vasishṭha occurs in the tryârsheya pravara of both. But the three Gotras of the Bhṛigus, from the Śyaitas to the Śunakas, may intermarry. The first four Gotras of the Bhṛigus must not, neither the six first Gotras of the Gotamas. The Pṛishadaśvas, Mudgalas, Vishṇuvṛiddhas, Kaṇvas, Agastyas, Haritas, Sankṛitis, Kapis and Yaskas may intermarry among themselves, and with the Jâmadagnyas, &c. Dhîrghatamas', on the contrary, Auchathyas and Kakshîvats are to be considered as members of one Gotra, nor are marriages allowed between the Bharadvâjâgniveśis, Ṛikshas, Śunga-Śaiśiris, (or Śungas, Śaiśiris), Katas, and, according to some, the Gargas.

It is clear from this that the science of genealogy, being so intimately connected with the social and ecclesiastical system of the Brahmans, must have been studied with great care in India, and that the genealogical lists which have been preserved to us in ancient works represent something real and historical.

After we have thus gained an insight into the system by which the Brâhmaṇas were handed down from generation to generation, we now return to a consideration of the literary merits of these works. The Brâhmaṇas represent no doubt a most interesting phase in the history of the Indian mind, but judged by themselves, as literary productions, they are most disappointing. No one would have supposed that at so early a period, and in so primitive a state of society, there could have risen a literature which for pedantry and downright absurdity can hardly be matched anywhere. There is no lack of striking thoughts, of bold expressions, of sound reasoning, and curious traditions in these collections. But these are only like the fragments of a *torso*, like precious gems set in brass and lead. The general character of these works is marked by shallow and insipid grandiloquence, by priestly conceit, and antiquarian pedantry. It is most important to the historian that he should know how soon the fresh and healthy growth of a nation can be blighted by priestcraft and superstition. It is most important that we should know that nations are liable to these epidemics in their youth as well as in their dotage. These works deserve to be studied as the physician studies the twaddle of idiots, and the raving of madmen. They will disclose to a thoughtful eye the ruins of faded grandeur, the memories of noble aspirations. But let us only try to translate these works into our own language, and we shall feel astonished that human language and human thought should ever have been used for such purposes. The following are a few specimens, and they have not been chosen to give an unfavourable idea of the Brâhmaṇas. The first is the beginning of the Aitareya-brâhmaṇa, and explains a sacrificial act in itself full of meaning. Originally the Dîkshaṇîyâ, as this ceremony is called, was meant to represent, by simple and natural emblems, the new birth (matriculation) through which a man, on his first admission to the sacrifice, was believed to enter a new life. Let us see what became of this act in the hands of the Brahmans.

Aitareya-brâhmaṇa.—Dîkshaṇîyâ.

Agni is the first among the Gods, Vishṇu the last.[1] Between them stand all the other deities.

They offer a Puroḷâśa to Agni and Vishṇu which has been prepared for the Dîkshaṇîyâ in eleven jars.[2]

[1] अग्निर्वै देवानामवमो विष्णुः परमस्तदंतरेण सर्वा अन्या देवताः॥

The Commentator says that the gods among whom Agni and Vishṇu are the first and last, are the gods to whom prayers are offered at the ceremonies belonging to the Agnishṭoma. There are 12 prayers (śastra), and the first is addressed to Agni (bhûr Agnir jyotiḥ); the last, which is an âgnimâruta, contains a verse in praise of Vishṇu (Vishṇor nu kam). See Kaushîtaki-brâhmaṇa, viii. 1. This passage proves nothing as to the relative dignity of Agni and Vishṇu. In the Kaush.-br. Agni is called avarârddhya, Vishṇu parârddhyas, and the Com. explains these terms as signifying the first in the former, and the first in the latter half.

[2] आग्नावैष्णवं पुरोळाशं निर्वपंति दीक्षणीयमेकादशकपालं॥

A puroḷâśa is a baked flour cake (pakvaḥ pishṭapiṇḍaḥ), and *nirvap*, to strew, means originally to take four handfuls of rice

They offer it indeed to all the deities of this ceremony, without any difference.[1]

For Agni is all the deities, Vishṇu is all the deities.[2]

They are the two extremities of the sacrifice, Agni and Vishṇu. Thus when men offer the Puroḷâśa to Agni and Vishṇu, they worship the deities at both ends.[3]

Here they say, if there be a Puroḷâśa prepared in eleven jars, and there be two gods, Agni and Vishṇu, what rule is there for the two, or what division?[4]

The Puroḷâśa of eight jars belongs to Agni, for the Gâyatrî verse consists of eight syllables, and the Gâyatri is Agni's metre. That of three jars belongs to Vishṇu, for Vishṇu strode thrice through this universe. This is their rule here, and this the division.[5]

from the cart and throw them into a winnowing basket. Here, however, it means the offering of the oblation which has been prepared in that manner. The original meaning of Dîkshâ is said to be "shaving or cleansing."

[1] सर्वाभ्य एवैनं तद्देवताभ्योऽनंतरायं निर्वपंति॥

[2] अग्निर्वै सर्वा देवता विष्णुः सर्वा देवताः॥

[3] एते वै यज्ञस्यांत्ये तन्वौ यदग्निश्च विष्णुश्च तद्यदाग्नावैष्णवं पुरोळाशं निर्वपंत्यंतत एव तद्देवानृध्नुवंति॥

[4] तदाहुर्यदेकादशकपालः पुरोळाशो द्वावग्नाविष्णू कैनयोस्तत्र क्लृप्तिः का विभक्तिरिति॥

[5] अष्टाकपाल आग्नेयोऽष्टाक्षरा वै गायत्री गायत्रमग्नेश्छंदस्त्रिकपालो वैष्णवस्त्रिर्हीदं विष्णुर्व्यचक्रमत सैनयोस्तत्र क्लृप्तिः सा विभक्तिः॥

He who thinks himself without wealth, may offer a Charu in ghee (clarified butter).[1]

On this earth no one succeeds who has no wealth.[2]

The ghee in the Charu is the milk of the woman, the grains belong to the man; both together are a pair. Thus the Charu increases him by this very pair with progeny and cattle, so that he may prosper.[3]

He who knows this is increased with progeny.[4]

He who performs the New-moon and Full-moon sacrifices, has commenced with the sacrifice and with the gods.[5] After having sacrificed with the new-moon or full-moon oblation, he may perform the Dîkshâ on the same oblation and the same sacrificial seat.[6]

[1] घृते चरुं निर्वपेत योऽप्रतिष्ठितो मन्येत॥

[2] अस्यां वाव स न प्रतितिष्ठति यो न प्रतितिष्ठति॥

[3] तद्यद्घृतं तत्स्त्रियै पयो ये तंडुलास्ते पुंसस्तन्मिथुनं मिथुनेनैवैनं तत्प्रजया पशुभिः प्रजनयति प्रजात्यै॥

[4] प्रजायते प्रजया पशुभिर्य एवं वेद॥

[5] आरब्धयज्ञो वा एष आरब्धदेवतो यो दर्शपूर्णमासाभ्यां यजत आमावास्येन वा हविषेष्ट्वा पौर्णमासेन वा तस्मिन्नेव हविषि तस्मिन्बर्हिषि दीक्षेतैषो एका दीक्षा॥

The commentator tries to show that the Darśa-pûrṇa-mâsa sacrifices are connected with all other rites. Although the Soma sacrifice is not a modification of the Darśa-pûrṇa-mâsa, still the Ishṭis, as, for instance, the Dîkshaṇîyâ and Prâyaṇîyâ, are, and they form part of the Soma sacrifice. The Agnihotra also, with all its parts, does not follow the rule of the D. P., but it has reference to the Âhavaṇîya and the other sacred fires, and these fires must be placed by means of the Pavamâna-ishṭi. Now, as all the Ishṭis are modifications of the D. P., the relation is established; and therefore the D. P. may be called the beginning of all sacrifices.

[6] The commentator says: *haviḥ* means the sacrifice, and *barhiḥ*

This is one Dîkshâ.[1]

The Hotṛi must recite seventeen Sâmidhenî verses.[2]

The Prajâpati, the Lord of the World, is seventeenfold, the months are twelve, and the seasons five, by putting the Hemanta and Śiśira seasons as one. So much is the year, and the year is Prajâpati.[3]

He who knows this prospers by those verses which reside in Prajâpati.[4]

The sacrifice went away from the gods. They wished to find it by means of the Ishṭis. The Ishṭis are called Ishṭis because with them they wished (*ish*, to wish) to find it.[5] They found it.[6]

means the same, and he takes the two locatives in the sense of "after this new moon and full moon sacrifice has been performed."

हविःशब्दवद्बर्हिःशब्दोऽपि यज्ञोपलक्षकः। तस्मिन्नामावास्याख्ये हविषि यज्ञे तस्मिन्पौर्णमासाख्ये बर्हिषि यज्ञेऽनुष्ठिते सति पश्चादेव दीक्षेत॥

[1] The last wards, "this is one Dîkshâ," indicate that there is another; that is to say, some allow the Soma sacrifice, which begins with the Dîkshâ, before the Darśa-pûrṇa-mâsa.

[2] सप्तदश सामिधेनीरनुब्रूयात्॥

The number is stated, because generally the Sâmidhenîs are only fifteen in number. These fifteen were originally but eleven verses, of which the first and last are repeated three times.

[3] सप्तदशो वै प्रजापतिर्द्वादश मासाः पंचर्तवो हेमंतशिशिरयोः समासेन तावान्त्संवत्सरः संवत्सरः प्रजापतिः॥

[4] प्रजापत्यायतनाभिरेनाभी राध्नोति य एवं वेद॥१॥

[5] The Brâhmaṇa gives here three fanciful etymologies, of *ishṭi*, the technical name of the sacrifice; of *âhuti*, the oblations enjoined at the sacrifice; and of *ûti*, another name for the same. The real etymology of *ishṭi* is not *ish*, to wish, but *yaj*, to sacrifice; of *âhuti*, not *hvayati*, to call, but *juhoti*, to offer; of *ûti*, not *âyâti*, to come, but *avati*, to protect.

[6] यज्ञो वै देवेभ्य उदक्रामत्तमिष्टिभिः प्रैषमैच्छन्यदिष्टिभिः

He who knows this prospers after having found the sacrifice.[1]

What are called oblations (âhŭti) are invocations (âhûti); with them the sacrificer calls the gods, this is why they are called âhŭtis.[2]

They are called Ûtis, for by their means the gods come to the calling of the sacrificer (*âyanti*, they come). Or because they are the paths and the ways, they are called ûtis; for they are the way to heaven for the sacrificer.[3]

There they say, as another priest makes the oblation (*scil.* the Adhvaryu), then why do they call him the Hotṛi (the offerer), who recites the prayers and formulas?[4]

Because he causes the deities to be brought near

प्रैषमैच्छंस्तदिष्टीनामिष्टित्वं तमन्वविंदन्॥

1 अनुवित्तयज्ञो राध्नोति य एवं वेद॥

2 आहुतयो वै नामैता यदाहुतय एताभिर्वै देवान्यजमानो ह्वयति तदाहुतीनामाहुतित्वं॥

3 ऊतयो खलु वै ता नाम याभिर्देवा यजमानस्य हवमायंति ये वै पंथानो याः स्रुतयस्ता वा ऊतयस्त उ एवैतत्स्वर्गयाणा यजमानस्य भवंति॥

4 तदाहुर्यदन्यो जुहोत्यथ योऽनुचाह यजति च कस्मात्तं होतेत्याचक्षत इति॥

The commentator says, that the proper name for the Hotṛi would seem to be Anuvaktṛi or Yashṭṛi, because पुरोनुवाक्यां चानुब्रूते याज्यां च पठति॥

according to their station, saying, "Bring him, bring him," this is the reason why he is called Hotṛi; he is a Hotṛi (from *âvah*, to bring near).[1]

He who knows this is called a Hotṛi.[2]

He whom the priests initiate (by means of the Dîkshâ ceremony), he is made again to be an embryo (he is born again).[3]

They sprinkle him with water.[4]

Water is seed; having thus given this to him, they initiate him.[5]

They anoint him with fresh butter (navanîta). Clarified butter for the gods is (called) Âjya; for men Surabhighṛita; for the manes Âyuta; for the embryos Navanîta. Therefore by anointing him with navanîta, they increase him with his own portion.[6]

1 यद्वाव स तत्र यथाभाजनं देवता अमुमावहामुमावहे-त्यावाहयति तदेव होतुर्होतृत्वं होता भवति॥

2 होतेत्येनमाचक्षते य एवं वेद॥२॥

3 पुनर्वा एतमृत्विजो गर्भं कुर्वंति यं दीक्षयंति॥

4 अद्भिरभिषिंचंति॥

5 रेतो वा आपः सरेतसमेवैनं तत्कृत्वा दीक्षयंति॥

6 नवनीतेनाभ्यंजंति॥

आज्यं वै देवानां सुरभिघृतं मनुष्याणामायुतं पितॄणां नवनीतं गर्भाणां तद्यन्नवनीतेनाभ्यंजंति स्वेनैवैनं तद्भागधेयेन समर्धयंति॥

The commentator quotes a verse to the effect that molten ghee is called *âjya*; hardened, it is called *ghṛita;* slightly molten, it is called *âyuta;* and well seasoned, it is called *surabhi.* But the Taittirîyas say, "*ghṛita* is for the gods, *astu* for the manes, *nishpakva* for men." *Astu* is here the same as *âyuta*, slightly molten, and *nishpakva*, quite liquid.

They anoint his eyes with a collyrium.[1]

Anointing is light for the eyes. Having thus imparted light to him, they initiate him.[2]

They rub him clean with twenty-one handfuls of Kuśa grass.[3]

Him who is pure and has thus been cleaned, they initiate.[4]

They take him to the hall.[5]

The hall is the womb for the pupil (dîkshita). By taking him to the hall they take him (who was before represented as an embryo) into his womb.[6]

In this true womb he sits, and hence he departs.[7]

Therefore the fruit is borne in the true womb and brought forth from it.[8]

Therefore let not the sun shine upon him in its

[1] आंजंत्येनं॥

[2] तेजो वा एतदक्ष्योर्यदांजनं सतेजसमेवैनं तत्कृत्वा दीक्षयंति॥

[3] एकविंशत्या दर्भपिंजूलैः पावयंति॥

[4] शुद्धमेवैनं तत्पूतं दीक्षयंति॥

[5] दीक्षितविमितं प्रपादयंति॥

The hall is called Dîkshita-vimita, because it was made (vimita) for the initiated (dîkshita). It is commonly called Prâchinavanśa.

[6] योनिर्वा एषा दीक्षितस्य यद्दीक्षितविमितं योनिमेवैनं तत्स्वां प्रपादयंति॥

[7] तस्माद्ध्रुवाद्योनेरास्ते च चरति च॥

[8] तस्माद्ध्रुवाद्योनेर्गर्भा धीयंते च प्र च जायंते॥

rising or setting away from the hall, nor let the priests speak to him.[1]

They cover him with a cloth.[2]

This cloth is the caul in which the pupil is to be born; thus they cover him with the caul.[3]

The skin of a black antelope is his next cloak.[4]

Next to the caul is the Jarâyu; thus they cover him with the Jarâyu.[5]

He closes his hands.[6]

With closed hands the embryo lies, with closed hands the child is born. As he closes his hands, he holds the sacrifice, and all its gods between his hands.[7]

They say, there is no confusion for him who has first finished his Dîkshâ; for his sacrifice is held fast (between his hands), and the gods are so likewise. Therefore there can be no loss for him, like that which falls on him whose Dîkshâ was finished later.[8]

[1] तस्माद्दीक्षितं नान्यत्र दीक्षितविमितादादित्योऽभ्युदियाद्वाभ्यस्तमियाद्वापि वाभ्याश्रावयेयुः॥

[2] वाससा प्रोर्णुवंति॥

[3] उल्बं वा एतद्दीक्षितस्य यद्वास उल्बेनैवैनं तत्प्रोर्णुवंति॥

[4] कृष्णाजिनमुत्तरं भवति॥

[5] उत्तरं वा उल्बाज्जरायु जरायुणैवैनं तत्प्रोर्णुवंति॥

[6] मुष्टी कुरुते॥

[7] मुष्टी वै कृत्वा गर्भोऽंतः शेते मुष्टी कृत्वा कुमारो जायते तद्यन्मुष्टी कुरुते यज्ञं चैव तत्सर्वाश्च देवता मुष्योः कुरुते॥

[8] तदाहुर्न पूर्वदीक्षिणः संसवोऽस्ति परिगृहीतो वा

After having put off his cloak, he descends to the bath. Therefore an embryo is born after he is separated from the Jarâyu.[1]

He descends together with his cloth—therefore a child is born together with the caul.[2]

For him who has not offered a sacrifice before, let (the Hotri) recite two puronuvâkyâs, "tvam agne saprathâ asi," (v. 13. 4.) for the first, "soma yâs te mayobhuvaḥ" (i. 91. 9.) for the second portion of the ghee.[3]

(The third line of the first verse is) "through thee they carry out the sacrifice;" and by reciting this line the Hotṛi carries out the sacrifice for the pupil.[4]

एतस्य यज्ञः परिगृहीता देवता नैतस्यार्त्तिरस्त्यपरदीक्षिण एव यथा तथेति॥

It is said by the commentator that if two or more Brahmans perform the Soma sacrifice on the same spot and at the same time, they commit a sin, which is called *sansava*, confusion of libations. They ought to be separated by a river or a mountain. He, however, who has finished his Dîkshâ first and holds the gods between his closed hands, is not exposed to the consequences of the sansava, because the gods will be with him and not with the other man whose Dîkshâ was finished later.

1 उन्मुच्य कृष्णाजिनमवभृथमभ्यवैति तस्मान्मुक्ता गर्भा जरायोर्जायंते॥

2 सहैव वाससाभ्यवैति तस्मात्सहैवोल्बेन कुमारो जायते॥ ३॥

3 त्वमग्ने सप्रथा असि सोम यास्ते मयोभुव इत्याज्यभागयोः पुरोनुवाक्ये अनुब्रूयाद्यः पूर्वमनीजानः स्यात्तस्मै॥

After the general remarks on the Dîkshaṇîyeshṭi which were given in the first three sections, without any particular regard to the offices of the Hotṛi, the fourth section begins with the ceremonial rules for the Hotṛi. The Hotṛi has to recite certain verses on being ordered to do so by the Adhvaryu.

4 त्वया यज्ञं वितन्वत इति यज्ञमेवास्मा एतद्वितनोति॥

For him who has offered a sacrifice before, let the Hotṛi recite instead "Agniḥ pratnena manmanâ," (viii. 44. 12.) and "soma gîrbhish ṭvâ vayam." (i. 91. 11.)[1]

By saying "pratnam" (former) a word which occurs in the first verse, he alludes to the former sacrifice.[2]

Both these rules (of using certain verses for a man who has not, and for a man who has, sacrificed before) are not to be observed.[3]

Let him rather use the two verses on the destruction of Vṛitra "Agnir vṛitrâṇi janghanat," (vi. 16. 24.) and "tvam Somâsi satpatiḥ" (i. 91. 5.)[4]

For he whom the sacrifice approaches destroys Vṛitra; therefore verses on the destruction of Vṛitra are to be used.[5]

Having enjoined these two verses for the introductory ceremony of the offering of ghee, the Brâhmaṇa now proceeds to detail the yâjyânuvâkyâs for the principal offering.

[1] अग्निः प्रत्नेन मन्मना सोम गीर्भिष्ट्वा वयमिति यः पूर्वमीजानः स्यात्तस्मै॥

[2] प्रत्नमिति पूर्वं कर्माभिवदति॥

[3] तत्तन्नादृत्यं॥

[4] अग्निर्वृत्राणि जंघनत्त्वं सोमासि सत्पतिरिति वार्त्रघ्नावेव कुर्यात्॥

[5] वृत्रं वा एष हंति यं यज्ञ उपनमति तस्माद्वार्त्रघ्नावेव कर्तव्याविति॥

The reason which the commentator gives for this extraordinary proceeding is, that in each of the two couples of verses which were first recommended, the first verse only contained an allusion to the peculiarities of the sacrifices, while the two verses now enjoined both treat of the destruction of Vṛitra.

"Agnir mukham prathamo devatânâm," &c., is the Puronuvâkyâ, "Agniś cha Vishṇo tapa uttamam mahaḥ," etc. the Yâjyâ verse. These two verses on Agni and Vishṇu are correct in form. The correctness of a sacrifice consists in its correctness of form; it consists in this that the verse recited alludes to the act performed.[1]

Agni and Vishṇu are the guardians of the Dîkshâ among the gods. They are the lords of the Dîkshâ. Therefore as the oblation is to Agni and Vishṇu, they who are the lords of the Dîkshâ are pleased and grant the Dîkshâ, saying, Let those who perform this rite be initiated.[2]

They are Trishṭubhs (by their metre), in order that they may give bodily strength.[3]

Having explained the verses used by the Hotṛi at the principal part of the sacrifice, the Brâhmaṇa adds some rules on the Svishṭakṛit verses.

[1] अग्निर्मुखं प्रथमो देवतानामग्निश्च विष्णो तप उत्तमं मह इत्याग्नावैष्णवस्य हविषो याज्यानुवाक्ये भवतः। आग्नावैष्णव्यौ रूपसमृद्धे एतद्वै यज्ञस्य समृद्धं यद्रूपसमृद्धं यत्कर्म क्रियमाणमृगभिवदति॥

Instead of saying "anuvâkyâyâjye," because the anuvâkyâ comes before the yâjyâ, the compound yâjyânuvâkye is formed, the shorter word, according to grammar, standing first in a Dvandva compound. The verses are not in the Śâkala-śâkhâ of the Rig-veda.

[2] अग्निश्च ह वै विष्णुश्च देवानां दीक्षापालौ तौ दीक्षाया ईशाते तद्यदाग्नावैष्णवं हविर्भवति यौ दीक्षाया ईशाते तौ प्रीतौ दीक्षां प्रयच्छतां यौ दीक्षयितारौ तौ दीक्षयेतामिति॥

[3] त्रिष्टुभौ भवतः सेन्द्रियत्वाय॥४॥

He who wishes for beauty and for wisdom, let him use the two Gâyatrî verses [1] of the Svishṭakṛit.[2]

The Gâyatrî is beauty, full of wisdom.[3]

He who knowing this uses the two Gâyatrîs becomes possessed of beauty and wisdom.[4]

He who desires long life, let him use two Ushṇih verses.[5]

Ushṇih is life.[6]

He who knowing this uses the two Ushṇihs, arrives at any age.[7]

He who desires heaven, let him use two Anushṭubhs.[8]

There are sixty-four syllables in the two Anushṭubhs, and three are these worlds (earth, sky and heaven), each of twenty-one parts. With each twenty-one syllables he ascends to these worlds, and with the sixty-fourth he stands firm in heaven.[9]

[1] They are "Sa havyavâḷ amartyaḥ," (iii. 11. 2.) and "Agnir hotâ purohitaḥ." (iii. 11. 1.)

[2] गायत्र्यौ स्विष्टकृतः संयाज्ये कुर्वीत तेजस्कामो ब्रह्मवर्चसकामः॥

[3] तेजो वै ब्रह्मवर्चसं गायत्री॥

[4] तेजस्वी ब्रह्मवर्चसी भवति य एवंविद्वान् गायत्र्यौ कुरुते॥

[5] उष्णिहावायुःकामः कुर्वीत॥
They are "Agne vâjasya gomataḥ," (i. 79. 4.) and "Sa idhâno vasush kaviḥ." (i. 79. 5.)

[6] आयुर्वा उष्णिक्॥

[7] सर्वमायुरेति य एवंविद्वानुष्णिहौ कुरुते॥

[8] अनुष्टुभौ स्वर्गकामः कुर्वीत॥
They are "Tvam Agne vasûn." (i. 45. 1.)

[9] द्वयोर्वा अनुष्टुभोश्चतुःषष्टिरक्षराणि त्रय इम ऊर्ध्वा एकविंशा लोका एकविंशत्यैकविंशत्यैवेमांल्लोकान्रोहति स्वर्ग एव लोके चतुःषष्टितमेन प्रतितिष्ठति॥

He who knowing this uses the two Auushṭubhs stands firm.[1]

He who desires wealth and glory, let him use two Bṛihatîs.[2]

The Bṛihatî is wealth and glory.[3]

He who knowing this uses two Bṛihatîs, gives himself wealth and glory.[4]

He who loves the sacrifice, let him use two Panktis.[5]

The sacrifice is like a Pankti.[6]

The sacrifice comes to him who, knowing this, uses two Panktis.[7]

Let him who desires strength use two Trishṭubhs.[8]

Trishṭubh is strength, which is vigour and power.[9]

He who knowing this uses two Trishṭubhs, becomes strong, vigorous and powerful.[10]

1 प्रतितिष्ठति य एवंविद्वाननुष्टुभौ कुरुते॥

2 बृहत्यौ श्रीकामो यशस्कामः कुर्वीत॥
They are "Enâ vo agnim" (vii. 16. 1.), and "Udasya śochiḥ" (vii. 16. 3.).

3 श्रीर्वै यशश्छंदसां बृहती॥

4 श्रियमेव यश आत्मन्धत्ते य एवंविद्वान्बृहत्यौ कुरुते॥

5 पंक्ती यज्ञकामः कुर्वीत॥
They are "Agnim tam manye" (v. 6. 1.).

6 पांक्तो वै यज्ञः॥

7 उपैनं यज्ञो नमति य एवंविद्वान् पंक्ती कुरुते॥

8 त्रिष्टुभौ वीर्यकामः कुर्वीत॥
They are "Dve virûpe charataḥ" (i. 95. 1.).

9 ओजो वा इंद्रियं वीर्यं त्रिष्टुप्॥

10 ओजस्वीद्रियवान् वीर्यवान्भवति य एवंविद्वाँस्त्रिष्टुभौ कुरुते॥

Let him who desires cattle, use two Jagatîs.[1]

Cattle is Jagatî-like.[2]

He who knowing this uses two Jagatîs, becomes rich in cattle.[3]

Let him who desires food, use two Virâj verses.[4]

Virâj is food.[5] (*virâj*, to shine.)

Therefore he who has the largest food here shines most on earth; this is the reason why it is called Virâj (shining).[6]

He who knows this shines forth among his own people; he is the best of his friends.[7]

All these are voluntary verses. We now come to those which are always to be used.

Now the metre Virâj possesses five powers.

Because it has three lines, therefore it is Gâyatrî and Ushṇih (which also have three lines.) Because its lines have each eleven syllables, therefore it is Trishṭubh. Because it has thirty-three syllables, therefore it is Anushṭubh. (If it be said that the two Virâj verses in question, *i. e.* "preddho agne," &c. and "imo agne," &c., have only thirty-one and thirty-

[1] जगत्यौ पशुकामः कुर्वीत॥

They are "Janasya gopâ" (v. 11. 1.).

[2] जागता वै पशवः॥

[3] पशुमान्भवति य एवंविद्वान् जगत्यौ कुरुते॥

[4] विराजावन्नाद्यकामः कुर्वीत॥

They are "Preddho agne" (vii. 1. 3.), "Imo agne" (vii. 1. 18.).

[5] अन्नं वै विराट्॥

[6] तस्माद्यस्यैवेह भूयिष्ठमन्नं भवति स एव भूयिष्ठं लोके विराजति तद्विराजो विराट्त्वं॥

[7] वि स्वेषु राजति श्रेष्ठः स्वानां भवति य एवं वेद॥५॥

two syllables, it must be remembered that) metres do not change by one syllable or by two. The fifth power is that it is Virâj (shining).[1]

He who knowing this uses the two Virâj verses, obtains the power of all metres, retains the power of all metres, obtains union, uniformity and unison with all metres, eats and has to eat, has food together with his family.[2]

Therefore the two Virâj verses are certainly to be used, those which begin with "Preddho agne" and "Imo agne."[3]

Dîkshâ is right, Dîkshâ is truth, therefore a man who performs the Dîkshâ must speak the truth.[4]

Now they say, what man can speak all truth? Gods are full of truth, men are full of falsehood.[5]

[1] अथो पंचवीर्यं वा एतच्छंदो यद्विराट्॥ यत् त्रिपदा तेनोष्णिहागायत्र्यौ यदस्या एकादशाक्षराणि पदानि तेन त्रिष्टुप् यत् त्रयस्त्रिंशदक्षरा तेनानुष्टुब्न वा एकेनाक्षरेण छंदांसि वियंति न द्वाभ्यां यद्विराट् तत्पंचमं॥

[2] सर्वेषां छंदसां वीर्यमवरुंद्धे सर्वेषां छंदसां वीर्यमश्नुते सर्वेषां छंदसां सायुज्यं सरूपतां सलोकतामश्नुतेऽन्नादोऽन्नपतिर्भवत्यश्नुते प्रजयान्नाद्यं य एवंविद्वान् विराजौ कुरुते॥

[3] तस्माद्विराजावेव कर्तव्ये। प्रेद्धो अग्न इमो अग्न इत्येते॥

[4] ऋतं वाव दीक्षा सत्यं दीक्षा तस्माद्दीक्षितेन सत्यमेव वदितव्यं।

Right (ṛita) and truth (satya) are said to differ, inasmuch as *ṛita* means a true conception, *satya*, a true speech.

[5] अथो खल्वाहुः कोऽर्हति मनुष्यः सर्वं सत्यं वदितुं सत्यसंहिता वै देवा अनृतसंहिता मनुष्या इति॥

Let him make each speech with the word "Vichakshaṇa" (which means, let him put "vichakshaṇa" at the end of the name of a person whom he addresses.)[1]

The eye is vichakshaṇa, for with it he sees clearly (*vi-chaksh*, to perceive).[2]

The eye is established as truth among men.[3]

Therefore people say to a man who tells something, "Hast thou seen it?" And if he says "I saw it," then they believe him. And if one sees a thing oneself, one does not believe others, even many.[4]

Therefore let a man make each speech with the word "Vichakshaṇa"; then his uttered speech becomes full of truth.[5]

---

[1] विचक्षणवतीं वाचं वदेत्॥

For instance, instead of saying, "Devadatta, bring the cow;" let him say, "Devadatta, vichakshaṇa, bring the cow." According to Âpastamba, vichakshaṇa ought to be used after the names of a Kshatriya and Vaiśya, but "chanasita" after the name of a Brahman.

[2] चक्षुर्वै विचक्षणं वि ह्येनेन पश्यतीति॥ Kaush.-br. चक्षुर्वै विचक्षणं चक्षुषा हि विपश्यति॥

[3] एतद्ध वै मनुष्येषु सत्यं निहितं यच्चक्षुः॥

[4] तस्मादाचक्षाणमाहुरद्रागिति स यद्यदर्शमित्याहाथास्य श्रद्दधति यद्यु वै स्वयं पश्यति न बहूनां चनान्येषां श्रद्दधाति॥

[5] तस्माद्विचक्षणवतीमेव वाचं वदेत्सत्योत्तरा हैवास्य वागुदिता भवति भवति॥ ६॥

The next extract is from the Kaushîtaki-brâhmaṇa (xxvi. 5.). It will show how completely the true character of the sacrifice had been forgotten, and how much importance was attached to mere trifles.[1] It is intelligible, wherever there is an established ceremonial, and priests appointed to watch over it, that certain rules should be laid down for remedying any mistake that may have occurred in the performance of a sacrifice. The chapter of accidents is a large one, and the Brahmans have spared no pains in laying down the most complicated rules, to counteract the consequences of a real mistake. The rules of pe-

[1] अथ ह स्माह दैवोदासिः प्रतर्दनो नैमिषीयाणां सत्रमुपगम्योपास्यन्व विचिकित्सां पप्रच्छ यद्यतिक्रांतमुल्बणं सदस्यो बोधयेतर्त्विजां वान्यतमो बुध्येत कथं वोऽनुल्बणं स्यादिति त उ ह तूष्णीमासुस्तेषामलीकयुर्वाचस्पतो ब्रह्मास स होवाच नाहमेतद्वेद हंत पूर्वेषामाचार्यं स्थविरं जातुकर्ण्यं पृच्छानीति तं ह पप्रच्छ यद्यतिक्रांतमुल्बणं कर्ता वा स्वयं बुध्येतान्यो वा बोधयेत कथं तदुल्बणमनुल्बणं भवेत्पुनर्वचनेन वा मंत्रस्य होमेन वेति पुनर्वाच्यो मंत्र इति ह स्माह जातुकर्ण्यस्तमलीकयुः पुनः पप्रच्छ शस्त्रं वानुवचनं वा निगदं वा याज्यां वा यद्वान्यत्सर्वं तत्पुनर्ब्रूयादिति यावन्मात्रमुल्बणं तावद्ब्रूयदृचं वार्द्धर्चं वा पादं वा पदं वा वर्णं वेति ह स्माह जातुकर्ण्योऽथ ह स्माह कौषीतकिर्न मंत्रं पुनर्ब्रूयान्नाहुतिं जुहुयादनुल्बणमेतदिति ह स्माह कौषीतकिर्यद्धि होतारो यज्ञस्य किंचिदुल्बणमबुध्यमानाः कुर्वंति सर्वं तदग्निर्दैवो होतानुल्बणं करोति तदेतदृचाभ्युदितं॥

nance or prâyaschitta occupy, in several instances, one third of the whole collections of ceremonial rules. But this was not enough. Discussions were raised, not only how to remedy mistakes, that had been observed at the time; but how to counteract the effects of mistakes unobserved during the performance of the sacrifice. To settle this question, the Kaushîtakins quote the following story:—

"And then Pratardana, the son of Divodâsa (a famous king) having gone to the sacrifice of the Ṛishis of Nimisha, sat down in their presence and asked the question: 'If the Sadasya (the superintending priest, according to the ceremonial of the Kaushîtakins) should make known a past blunder, or any one of the priests should observe it, how would you be free from sin?' The priests were silent. Their Brahman was Alîkayu, the descendant of Vâchaspati. He said, 'I do not know this, alas! Let us ask the teacher of our fathers, the elder Jâturkarṇya.' He asked him: 'If the performer himself should observe a past blunder, or some one else should make it known, how could that blunder become not a blunder? by saying the passage again, or by an offering?' Jâtukarṇya said, 'The passage must be said again.' Alîkayu asked him again: 'Should he say again the Śastra, the Anuvachana, the Nigada, the Yâjyâ, or whatever else it may be, from beginning to end?' Jâtukarṇya said: 'As far as the blunder extends, so far let him say it again, whether a verse, a half verse, a foot, a word, or a letter.' Then said Kaushîtaki: 'Let him not say the passage again, nor let him perform a penance offering (Kaush.-br. vi. 11.). It is not a blunder,' so said Kaushîtaki; 'for, whatever blunder the Hotṛis commit at the sacrifice without being aware of it, all that Agni, the divine Hotṛi, makes whole; and this is confirmed by a verse from the Rig-veda.'"

There are, however, numerous passages in the Brâhmaṇas full of genuine thought and feeling, and most valuable as pictures of life, and as records of early struggles, which have left no trace in the literature of other nations. The story of Śunaḥśepha, for instance, which we find in the Aitareya-brâhmaṇa, and in the Śânkhâyana-sûtras is interesting in many respects. It shows that, at that early time, the Brahmans were familiar with the idea of human sacrifices, and that men who were supposed to belong to the caste of the Brahmans were ready to sell their sons for that purpose. The text of this story, together with the various readings, as gathered from the Śânkhâyana-sûtras will be printed in the Appendix.[1]

"Hariśchandra[2], the son of Vedhas, of the family of the Ikshvâkus, was a king without a son. He had a hundred wives, but had no son by them. In his house lived Parvata and Nârada. He asked Nârada: 'Tell me, O Nârada, what do people gain by a son, whom they all wish for, as well those who reason as those who do not reason?'

Being asked by one verse, Nârada[3] replied in ten verses:

[1] See Professor Wilson's Essay on Human Sacrifices in the Veda, and Professor Roth, in Weber's Ind. Studien, i. p. 457.

[2] Hariśchandra was, according to the Purâṇas, the son of Triśanku, king of Ayodhyâ, whom Vasishṭha had cursed, and who made Viśvâmitra his Purohita. Viśvâmitra in the Brâhmaṇa is represented as one of Hariśchandra's priests, but the office of Brahman is held by Vasishṭha. In the Râmâyaṇa, the sacrifice of Śunaḥśepha takes place under King Ambarîsha.

[3] *Nârada* is known as a frequent interlocutor in the epic

'If a father sees the face of a son, born alive, he pays a debt in him, and goes to immortality.

'The pleasure which a father has in his son is greater than all the pleasures that are from the earth, from the fire, and from the waters.

'Always have the fathers overcome the great darkness by a son; for a Self is born from his Self; it (the new-born Self, the son) is like a ship, full of food, to carry him over.

'What is the flesh? What is the skin? What are the hairs? What the heat? Try to get a son, you Brahmans; he is undoubtedly the world.

'Food is life for men, clothing his protection, gold his beauty, cattle his strength. His wife is a friend, his daughter is a pity[1]; but the son is his light in the highest world.

'As husband he embraces a wife, who becomes

and puraṇic poetry, particularly in dialogues where moral and legal precepts are given. Cf. Burnouf, Bhagavat-purâṇa, vol. iii. preface.

[1] The commentator gives a very different version of this line. He takes *mala*, which usually means matter, or mud, to signify the state of life of a *Gṛihastha*, or householder. *Ajina*, the skin, particularly of the antelope (aja), he takes as a symbol of the *Brahmachârin* state, because the pupil wears a skin. *Śmaśrûṇi*, used in the singular for beard, he takes as a symbol for the *Vanaprastha*, because he does not shave any more; and *tapas* he explains to mean the penance practised by the *Parivrâjaka*.

Why the birth of a daughter was considered a pity we learn from the following verse (metre Rathoddhatâ):

संभवे स्वजनदुःखकारिका।
संप्रदानसमयेऽर्थहारिका।
यौवनेऽपि बहुदोषकारिका।
दारिका हृदयदारिका पितुः॥

his mother, when he becomes her child. Having been renewed in her, he is born in the tenth month.

'A wife is a wife (jâyâ) because man is born (jâyate) again in her. She is a mother (âbhûti) because she brings forth (âbhûti); a germ is hidden in her.

'The gods and the old ages brought great light unto her. The gods said to men: "In her you will be born again."

'There is no life for him who has no son, this the animals also know.

'The path which those follow who have sons and no sorrows, is widely praised and happy. Beasts and birds know it, and they have young ones everywhere.'

Having thus spoken, he said to him: 'Go to Varuṇa the king, and say: May a son be born to me, and I shall sacrifice him to you.' The king assented, he went to Varuṇa the king, and said: 'May a son be born to me and I shall sacrifice him to you.' Varuṇa said, 'Yes.' A son was born to him, called Rohita. Then Varuṇa said to Hariśchandra: 'A son is born to thee, sacrifice him to me.' Hariśchandra said: 'When an animal is more than ten days old, it can be sacrificed. May he be older than ten days and I shall sacrifice him to you.'

Varuṇa assented. The boy was more than ten days old, and Varuṇa said: 'He is older now than ten days, sacrifice him to me.' Hariśchandra said: 'When an animal's teeth come, then it can be sacrificed. May his teeth now come, and I shall sacrifice him to you.'

Varuṇa assented. His teeth came, and Varuṇa said: 'His teeth have come, sacrifice him to me.' Hariśchandra said: 'When an animal's teeth fall out, then it can be sacrificed. May his teeth fall out, and I shall sacrifice him to you.'

Varuṇa assented; his teeth fell out, and Varuṇa said: 'His teeth have fallen out, sacrifice him to me.' Hariśchandra replied: 'When an animal's teeth come again, then it can be sacrificed. May his teeth come again, and I shall sacrifice him to you.'

Varuṇa assented. His teeth came again, and Varuṇa said: "His teeth have come again, sacrifice him to me.' Hariśchandra said: 'When a warrior (kshatriya) is girt with his armour, then he can be sacrificed. May he be girt, and I shall sacrifice him to you.'

Varuṇa assented. He was girt, and Varuṇa said: 'He has been girt, let him be sacrificed to me.'

Hariśchandra assented. He addressed his son and said: "Child, he gave you to me; Death! that I sacrifice you to him.' The son said, 'No!,' took his bow, and went to the forest, and lived there for a year.

And Varuṇa seized Hariśchandra, and his belly swelled. This Rohita heard and went from the forest to the village (grâma). Indra, in the form of a man, went round him, and said: 'For a man who does not travel about there is no happiness, thus we have heard, O Rohita! A good man who stays at home is a bad man. Indra is the friend of him who travels. Travel!'

Rohita thought, a Brahman has told me to travel, and thus he travelled a second year in the forest. When he went from the forest to the village, Indra, in the form of a man, went round him, and said:

'A traveller's legs are like blossoming branches,

he himself grows and gathers the fruit. All his wrongs vanish, destroyed by his exertion on the road. Travel!'

Rohita thought, a Brahman has told me to travel, and thus he travelled a third year in the forest. When he went from the forest to the town, Indra, in the form of a man, went round him, and said:

'The fortune of a man who sits, sits also; it rises, when he rises; it sleeps, when he sleeps; it moves well when he moves. Travel!'

Rohita thought, a Brahman has told me to travel, and thus he travelled a fourth year in the forest. When he went from the forest to the town, Indra, in the form of a man, went round him, and said:

'A man who sleeps is like the Kali age[1]; a man who awakes is like the Dvâpara age; a man who rises is like the Tretâ age; a man who travels is like the Krita age. Travel!'

Rohita thought, a Brahman has told me to travel, and thus he travelled a fifth year in the forest. When he went from the forest to the town, Indra, in the form of a man, went round him, and said:

'A traveller finds honey, a traveller finds sweet figs. Look at the happiness of the sun, who travelling never tires. Travel!'

Rohita thought, a Brahman has told me to travel, and thus he travelled a sixth year. He met in the forest a starving Ṛishi, *Ajîgarta*, the son of *Sûyavasa*. He had three sons, *Śunaḥpuchha*, *Śunaḥśepha*, and *Śunolâṅgûla*. Rohita said to him: 'Ṛishi, I give you a hundred cows, I ransom myself with one

[1] This is one of the earliest allusions to the four ages of the world.

of these thy sons.' The father embraced the eldest son, and said: 'Not him.' 'Nor him,' said the mother, embracing the youngest. And the parents bargained to give Śunaḥśepha, the middle son. Rohita gave a hundred, took him, and went from the forest to the village. And he came to his father, and said: 'Father, Death! I ransom myself by him.' The father went to Varuṇa, and said: 'I shall sacrifice this man to you.' Varuṇa said, 'Yes, for a Brahman is better than a Kshatriya.' And he told him to perform a Râjasûya sacrifice. Hariśchandra took him to be the victim for the day, when the Soma is spent to the gods.

Viśvâmitra was his Hotṛi priest, *Jamadagni* his Adhvaryu priest, *Vasishṭha*, the Brahman, *Ayâsya*, the Udgâtṛi priest. When Śunaḥśepha had been prepared, they found nobody to bind him to the sacrificial post. And Ajîgarta, the son of Sûyavasa said: 'Give me another hundred, and I shall bind him.'[1] They gave him another hundred, and he bound him. When he had been prepared and bound, when the Âprî hymns had been sung, and he had been led round the fire, they found nobody to kill him. And Ajîgarta, the son of Sûyavasa said: 'Give me another hundred, and I shall kill him.' They gave him another hundred, and he came whetting his sword. Then Śunaḥśepha thought, 'They will really kill me, as if I was not a man.[2] Death! I shall pray

[1] Langlois, in his translation of the Harivanśa (i. 124.), takes a different view of this circumstance. According to his translation Śunaḥśepha "avait été, dans une autre existence, un des coursiers attelés au char du soleil." Langlois reads in the text Haridaśva, which he takes as a name of the sun with green horses.

[2] The commentator observes here, that although at a sacrifice men and wild beasts were bound to the post, yet both beasts

to the gods.' He went with a hymn to *Prajâpati* (Lord of the World), the first of gods. Prajâpati said to him: 'Agni (fire) is the nearest of gods, go to him.' He went with a hymn to Agni, and Agni said to him: '*Savitṛi* (the progenitor) rules all creatures, go to him.' He went with a hymn to Savitṛi, and Savitṛi said to him: 'Thou art bound for *Varuṇa* the king, go to him.' He went with a hymn to Varuṇa the king, and Varuṇa said to him: '*Agni* is the mouth of the gods, the kindest god, praise him, and we shall set thee free.' Thus he praised Agni, and Agni said to him: 'Praise the Viśve Devâḥ, and we shall set thee free.' Thus he praised the Viśve Devâḥ, and they said to him: 'Indra is the greatest, mightiest, strongest, and friendliest of the gods, praise him, and we shall set thee free.' Thus he praised Indra, and Indra was pleased, and gave him in his mind a golden car, which Śunaḥśepha acknowledged by another verse. Indra said to him: 'Praise the *Aśvinau*, and we shall set thee free.' Thus he praised the Aśvinau, and they said to him: 'Praise *Ushas* (dawn), and we shall set thee free.' Thus he praised Ushas with three verses. While each verse was delivered his fetters were loosed, and Hariśchandra's belly grew smaller, and when the last verse was said, his fetters were loosed, and Hariśchandra well again."

This story is chiefly interesting, as revealing to us three distinct elements in the early social life of India. These are represented by the royal or

and men were set free immediately after the *Paryagni-karaṇam* (purification by fire, carried round), and only animals like *sheep*, &c., were killed.

reigning family of the Ikshvâkus, by their priests or ministers belonging to several famous Brahmanical races, and by a third class of men, living in the forests, such as Ajîgarta, and his three sons. It is true that Ajîgarta is called a Ṛishi, and one of his sons a Brahman. But even if we accept the Aryan origin of Ajîgarta, the seller and butcher of his own son, it is important to remark how great a difference there must have been between the various Aryan settlers in India. Whether we ascribe this difference to a difference in the time of immigration, or whatever other reason we may assign to it, yet there remains the fact, that, with all the vaunted civilisation of the higher Aryan classes, there were Aryan people in India to whom not only a young prince could make the offer of buying their children, but where the father offered himself to bind and kill the son, whom he had sold for a hundred cows. This was a case so startling to the later Brahmans, that the author of the Laws of *Manu* was obliged to allude to it, in order to defend the dignity of his caste.[1] Manu says, that hunger is an excuse for many things, and that Ajîgarta, although he went to kill his own son, was not guilty of a crime, because he did so to appease his hunger. Now the author of the Aitareya-brâhmaṇa certainly does not adopt this view, for Ajîgarta is there, as we shall see, severely abused for his cruelty, so much so, that his son, whom he has sold, considers himself at liberty to leave the family of his parents, and to accept the offer made by Viśvâmitra of being adopted into his family. So revolting, indeed, is the description given of Ajîgarta's behaviour

[1] Manu, x. 105.

in the Brâhmaṇa, that we should rather recognise in him a specimen of the non-Aryan population of India. Such a supposition, however, would be in contradiction with several of the most essential points of the legend, particularly in what regards the adoption of Śunaḥśepha by Viśvâmitra. Viśvâmitra, though arrived at the dignity of a Brahman, clearly considers the adoption of Śunaḥśepha Devarâta, of the famous Brahmanic family of the Ângirasas, as an advantage to himself and to his descendants; and the Devarâtas are indeed mentioned as a famous branch of the Viśvâmitras. (V.-P. p. 405, 23.). Śunaḥśepha is made his eldest son, and the leader of his brothers, evidently as the defender and voucher of their Brahmahood, which must have been then of very recent date, because Viśvâmitra himself is still addressed by Śunaḥśepha as *Râja-putra*, and *Bharata-ṛishabha*.

The Aitareya-brâhmaṇa goes on to state that the priests asked Śunaḥśepha to perform the sacrifice of the day. Śunaḥśepha then invented the ceremony called *Añjaḥsava*, and prepared the Soma, accompanied by four verses.[1] He poured the Soma into the Droṇa-kalaśa vessel with one verse, and made the libations with the four first verses of the same hymn, accompanied by Svâhâ exclamations, as the sacrifice had been begun by Hariśchandra. Afterwards he carried out all the things belonging to the Avabhṛitha ceremony, employing two verses, and made Hariśchandra go to the Âhavanîya fire with another hymn.

"When the sacrifice had thus been performed Śunaḥśepha sat down on the lap of Viśvâmitra. Ajîgarta,

[1] These verses are to be found in the sixth Anuvâka of the first Maṇḍala of the Rig-veda.

the son of Sûyavasa, said: "Ṛishi, give me back my son." Viśvâmitra said, "No; for the gods have given him to me." He became Devarâta (Theodotus) the son of Viśvâmitra, and the members of the families of Kapila and Babhru became his relations. Ajîgarta the son of Sûyavasa said: "Come thou, O son, we, both I and thy mother call thee away." Ajîgarta the son of Sûyavasa said: "Thou art by birth an Âṅgirasa, the son of Ajîgarta, celebrated as a poet. O Ṛishi, go not away from the line of thy grandfather, come back to me." Śunaḥśepha replied: "They have seen thee with a knife in thy hand, a thing that men have never found even amongst Śûdras; thou hast taken three hundred cows for me, O Angiras." Ajîgarta the son of Sûyavasa said: "My old son, it grieves me for the wrong that I have done; I throw it away, may these hundred cows belong to thee." Śunaḥśepha replied: "Who once commits a sin will commit also another sin; thou wilt not abstain from the ways of Śûdras; what thou hast committed cannot be redressed." "Cannot be redressed," Viśvâmitra repeated. "Dreadful stood the son of Sûyavasa when he went to kill with his knife. Be not his son, come and be my son." Śunaḥśepha said: "Tell us thyself, O son of a king, thus as thou art known to us, how I, who am an Âṅgirasa, shall become thy son." Viśvâmitra replied: "Thou shalt be the eldest of my sons, thy offspring shall be the first, thou shalt receive the heritage which the gods have given me, thus I address thee." Śunaḥśepha replied: "May the leader of the Bharatas say so in the presence of his agreeing sons, for friendship's and happiness' sake, that I shall become thy son." Then Viśvâmitra addressed his sons: "Hear me, Madhuchhandas, Ṛishabha, Reṇu, Ashṭaka, and all ye brothers that you are, believe in his seniority."

This Viśvâmitra had a hundred sons, fifty older than Madhuchhandas, and fifty younger. The elder did not like this, and Viśvâmitra pronounced a curse upon them, that they should become outcasts. They became Andhras, Puṇḍras, Śabaras, Pulindas, Mûtibas, and many other outcast tribes, so that the descendants of Viśvâmitra became the worst of the Dasyus. But Madhuchhandas, together with the other fifty sons, said: "What our father tells us, in that we abide; we place thee before us and follow thee." When Viśvâmitra heard this, he praised his sons and said: "You sons will have good children and cattle, because you have accepted my will, and have made me rich in brave sons. You, descendants of Gâthin [1], are to be honoured by all, you brave sons, led by Devarâta; he will be to you good counsel. You, descendants of Kuśika, follow Devarâta, he is your hero, he will give you my riches, and whatever knowledge I possess. You are wise, all you sons of Viśvâmitra together; you are rich, you stood to uphold Devarâta, and to make him your eldest, descendants of Gâthin. Devarâta [2] (Śunaḥśepha) is mentioned as a

[1]
```
                     Purûravas
                     Jahnu
 . . . .   ×   Gâthin Kauśika (Bhṛigus)
   |              |            |
Viśvâmitra.   Satyavatî   ×  Ṛichîka  (Ikshvâkus)
                          |             |
                      Jamadagni   ×   Reṇukâ
                                |
                          Paraśu-râma.
```

[2] This last verse, which is also attributed to Viśvâmitra, ought

Ṛishi of both families, in the chiefdom of the Jahnus, and in the divine Veda of the Gâthins."

The same chapter of the Aitareya-brâhmaṇa, where this story of Śunaḥśepha is told, contains many curious details on the mutual relation of the Brahmans and the Kshatriyas. The story of Śunaḥśepha is said to form a part of the inauguration of a king, to whom it is related by the Hotṛi priest, the Adhvaryu priest acting the second part; perhaps an early attempt at dramatic representation.

It does not necessarily follow from this legend that the Ṛishis, the authors of the Vedic hymns, offered human sacrifices. No one would conclude from the willingness of Abraham to sacrifice his own son in obedience to a supposed command from Jehovah, that the Jews had been in the habit of offering their sons as victims. It is not, however, because human sacrifices seem to belong only to the most savage races of men, that we doubt the prevalence of this custom among the ancient Hindus. Human sacrifices are not incompatible with a higher state of civilisation, particularly among people who never doubted the immortality of the soul, and at the same time felt a craving to offer whatever seemed most valuable on earth to the gods in whom they believed. There are few nations in the history of the world whose early traditions do not exhibit some traces of human sacrifices. And though I doubt the continuance of that custom during the Chhandas period, I see no reason

to be taken rather as a recapitulation of the whole story. Jahnu is one of the ancestors of Viśvâmitra, belonging to the Lunar dynasty; Gâthin is considered as Viśvâmitra's father. The commentator gives Jahnu as a Ṛishi of the family of Ajîgartà, which seems better to agree with the Vedic story.

to doubt its previous existence. A passage from the Aitareya-brâhmaṇa offers a striking confirmation of this opinion. It is said there (Ait.-br. 6. 8.) that the gods took man for their victim. "As he was taken, medha (the sacrifice or the spirit) went out of him. It entered the horse. Therefore the horse became the sacrificial animal. Then the gods took the horse, but as it was taken, the medha went out of him. It entered the ox. Therefore the ox became the sacrificial animal. The same happened with the ox. Afterwards the sheep, then the goat, and at last the earth became the victim. From the earth rice was produced and rice was offered in the form of puroḷâśa, in lieu of the sacrificial animal. The other beings which had formerly been offered and then been dismissed, are supposed to have become changed into animals unfit for sacrifice: man into a savage, the horse into a Bos Gaurus, the ox into a Gayal ox, the sheep into a camel (ushṭra), the goaṭ into a śarabha. All these animals are amedhya or unclean, and should not be eaten."

The drift of this story seems to be that in former times all these victims had been offered. We know it for certain in the case of horses and oxen, though afterwards these sacrifices were discontinued. As to sheep and goats they were considered proper victims to a still later time. When vegetable offerings took the place of bloody victims, it was clearly the wish of the author of our passage to show that, for certain sacrifices, these rice-cakes were as efficient as the flesh of animals. He carries out his argument still further, and tries to show that in the rice the beard corresponds to the hair of animals; the husk to the skin; the phalîkaraṇas to the blood; the meal to the flesh; the straw to the bones.

The next story, from the Śatapatha-brâhmaṇa[1] serves to illustrate the relations between the priestly and royal families in the early history of India, and allows us an insight into the policy of the Brahmans in their struggle for political influence.

"Janaka of Videha once met with some Brahmans who had just arrived. They were Śvetaketu Âruṇeya, Somaśushma Sâtyayajni, and Yâjnavalkya. He said to them: 'How do you perform the Agnihotra?' Śvetaketu replied: 'O king, I sacrifice to two heats in one another, which are ever shining, and pervading the world with their splendour.' 'How is that?' said the king. Śvetaketu replied: 'Âditya (the sun) is heat; to him do I sacrifice in the evening in the fire (Agni). Agni is heat; to him do I sacrifice in the morning in the sun (Âditya).' 'What becomes of him who sacrifices thus?' said the king. The Brahman replied: 'He becomes evershining with happiness and splendour, and has his dwelling with these two gods and is one with them.'

"Then Somaśushma began: 'O king, I sacrifice to light in light.' 'How is that?' said the king. Somaśushma replied: 'Âditya is light, to him do I sacrifice in the evening in Agni. Agni is light, to him do I sacrifice in the morning in Âditya.' 'What becomes of him who sacrifices thus?' said the king. The Brahman replied: 'He becomes full of light and splendour in this life, and has his dwelling with these two gods and is one with them.'

[1] Śatapatha-brâhmaṇa, Mâdhyandina-śâkhâ, xi. 4. 5. The same story is alluded to in the Bṛihadâraṇyaka, iv. 3. 1.

"Then said Yâjnavalkya: 'I offer the Agnihotra in taking out the fire (from the house-altar); for when Âditya sets, all the gods follow him, and if they see that I take out the fire, they come back, and, after having cleaned the sacrificial vessels, having filled them again, and after having milked also the sacred cow, I shall delight them when I see them again, and they see me.'

"Janaka said: 'Thou, O Yâjnavalkya, hast come very near to the Agnihotra; I shall give thee a hundred cows. But thou dost not know what becomes afterwards of these two libations (in the morning and evening).' So he said, then mounted his car and went away.

"The priests said: 'This fellow of a Râjanya has insulted us; let us call him out for a Brahman-dispute.' Yâjnavalkya observed, 'We are Brahmans, he a fellow of a Râjanya. If we vanquished him, whom should we say we had vanquished? But if he vanquished us, people would say of us that a Râjanya had vanquished Brahmans. Do not think of this.' They allowed what he said, and Yâjnavalkya mounted his car and followed the king. He reached the king, and the king said to him, 'Yâjnavalkya, dost thou come to know the Agnihotra?' 'The Agnihotra, O king,' replied Yâjnavalkya."

Here the king begins to explain to Yâjnavalkya his own view of the two morning and evening libations, called Agnihotra. He says, that these two sacrifices rise into the air, and are there again performed; the wind being the fuel, and the rays the bright libation. Then he goes on explaining how these two sacrifices, after having delighted the air, enter the sky, where they are performed by sun and moon; how they come back to the earth, and are performed by fire (warmth) and plants; how they enter the man, and are performed by his tongue and food; how they enter the woman, and a son is born. "'This is the true Agnihotra, O Yâjnavalkya,' said the king; 'there is nothing higher than this.' Yâjnavalkya granted him a boon; and the king said, 'May I be allowed, Yâjnavalkya, to ask thee what I wish.' Since then Janaka became a Brahman."

The two following stories are of a more mythological character, and contain curious traditions about Manu, the supposed ancestor of mankind. The first is from the Aitareya-brâhmaṇa, v. 14.

"Nâbhânedishṭha, the son of Manu, had been deprived of his paternal share by his brothers, while he was pursuing his studies (in the house of his Guru). When he came home, he said, 'What is my share?' They replied (pointing to Manu), 'The father, who is our governor and arbitrator.' (Therefore sons call now their father, governor (nishṭhâva[1]) and arbitrator (avavaditṛi)). He went to his father, and said, 'Father, they have made thee to be my share.' The father replied, 'Do not believe it, my son, by

[1] The commentary explains निष्ठावः by धनविभागादेर्धर्मरहस्यं निःशेषेण स्थितिनिर्णयो निष्ठा। सा यस्मिन्नस्ति स निष्ठावः। तादृशं धर्मरहस्यनिर्णेतारमित्यर्थः॥ अववदितारं। ज्येष्ठपुत्रस्यैतावत् द्वितीयस्यैतावत् अन्यस्यैतावदित्यवच्छिद्य वेदितुं समर्थोऽववदिता। तादृशं॥ अयमर्थः। अयं मनुर्धर्मशास्त्रकर्तृत्वाद्धर्मरहस्यनिर्णयवान् पितृत्वेन तवैतावदित्यवच्छिद्य वक्तुं समर्थश्च॥

any means. The Angiras' there perform a sacrifice in order to go to heaven, but every time they come to the sixth day, they get confused. Let them recite these two hymns (of thine[1]) on the sixth day, and when they go to heaven they will give thee all the great riches which they have brought together for the sacrifice.' The son said, 'Yes;' went to them, and spoke: 'Ye sages, receive me, the son of Manu.'[2] They replied, 'What is thy wish that thou speakest thus?' He answered, 'I shall teach you this sixth day, and you shall give me, when you go to heaven, all these great riches which you have brought together for the sacrifice.' They agreed, and he recited for them these two hymns on the sixth day. Thus the Angiras' understood the sacrifice and the life in heaven. Therefore, when the Hotṛi priest recites these two hymns on the sixth day, it leads to an understanding of the sacrifice and of the life in heaven.

"When the Angiras' were going to heaven they said, 'All these great riches are thine, O Brahman.'[3] While he was putting them together, a man[4] in dark dress came up from the north, and said,

[1] Two hymns ascribed to Nâbhânedishṭha, occur in the Rig-veda, Maṇḍala x. 5. 1. & 2.

[2] These words are taken from the second hymn of Nâbhâ-nedishṭha.

[3] The text is एतत्ते ब्राह्मण सहस्रमिति। but the commentator says, it is to be understood of a thousand cows or animals, left on the spot of the sacrifice, and that in a different Śâkhâ of this Brâhmaṇa the text is ते सुवर्गं लोकं यंतो य एषां पशव आसन् तानस्मा अददुरिति॥

[4] The commentator says that this is Rudra, the lord of animals, and that this is clearly indicated in a different Śâkhâ, where the text is तं पशुभिश्चरंतं यज्ञवास्तौ रुद्र आगच्छदिति॥

'This is mine; mine is what is left on the sacred spot.' Nâbhânedishṭha replied, 'They gave it to me.' The man said, 'Then let us ask thy father about it.' He went to his father, and the father said, 'Have they given thee nothing, my son?' Nâbhânedishṭha replied, 'They gave me a portion, but then a man in dark dress came up from the north, and said, "This is mine; mine is what is left on the sacred spot," and took it.' The father said, 'It belongs to him, indeed, my son, but he will give it to thee.' Thereupon Nâbhânedishṭha went back and said, 'This is thine indeed, O reverend sir; thus spoke my father.' 'This I give to thee,' replied the man, 'who hast spoken the truth. Therefore the truth must be spoken by a man who knows it. These verses of Nâbhânedishṭha give great riches. They gave great riches; and he understands on the sixth day the life in heaven who knows this.'"

The next extract is taken from the Śatapatha-brâhmaṇa, i. 8. 1. 1. (Prap. vi. 3. 1.):—

"To Manu they brought in the morning water to wash. As they bring it with their hands for the washing, a fish comes into the hands of Manu as soon as he has washed himself.

He spoke to Manu the word:—'Keep me, I shall preserve thee.' Manu said, 'From what wilt thou preserve me?' The fish said, 'The flood will carry away all these creatures. I shall preserve thee from it.' 'How canst thou be kept?' said Manu.

The fish replied, 'As long as we are small there is much destruction for us; fish swallows fish. First, then, thou must keep me in a jar. If I outgrow it, dig a hole, and keep me in it. If I outgrow this, take me to the sea, and I shall be saved from destruction.'

He became soon a large fish. He said to Manu, 'When I am full-grown, in the same year the flood will come. Build a ship then, and worship me, and when the flood rises go into the ship, and I shall preserve thee from it.'

Manu brought the fish to the sea, after he had kept him thus. And in the year which the fish had pointed out Manu had built a ship, and worshipped the fish. Then when the flood had risen, he went into the ship. The fish came swimming to him, and Manu fastened the rope of the ship to a horn of the fish. The fish carried him by it over the northern mountain.

The fish said, 'I have preserved thee. Bind the ship to a tree. May the water not cut thee asunder while thou art on the mountain. As the water will sink, thou wilt slide down.' Manu slid down with the water; and this is called "the Slope of Manu" on the northern mountain. The flood had carried away all these creatures, and thus Manu was left there alone.

He went along meditating a hymn, and wishing for offspring. And he sacrificed there also (a pâkayajna). Taking clarified butter, coagulated milk, whey and curds, he made an offering to the waters. In a year a woman was brought forth from it. She rose unctuous and trickling; and where she stood there was clarified butter. Mitra and Varuṇa came to meet her.

They said to her, 'Who art thou?' She said, 'The daughter of Manu.' 'Say thou art ours,' they said. 'No,' said she; 'he who has begotten me to him I belong.' Then they asked her to be their sister, and she half agreed and half did not agree. She went off and came to Manu.

Manu said to her, 'Who art thou?' She said, 'I am thy daughter.' 'How art thou my daughter?' he asked. She replied, 'The oblations which thou hast thrown into the waters, clarified butter, coagulated milk, whey and curds, by them thou hast begotten me. I am a blessing. Praise me at the sacrifice. If thou praise me at the sacrifice, thou wilt be rich in offspring and cattle. Whatever blessing thou wilt ask by me, will all be given to thee.' Thus he praised her in the middle of this sacrifice; for the middle of the sacrifice is that which comes between the introductory and the final prayers (prayâjâs and anuyâjâs).

Manu went along with her, meditating a hymn, and wishing for offspring; and by her he begat this offspring, which is called the offspring of Manu, and whatever blessing he asked was all given to him.

She is indeed *Iḍâ.* Whoever knows this, and goes with Iḍâ, he begets the offspring which Manu begat; and whatever blessing he asks by her, is all given to him."

These extracts from the Brâhmaṇas will be sufficient to show that there is much curious information to be gathered from these compilations. In spite of their general dreariness, the Brâhmaṇas well deserve to be preserved from destruction, which can only be done by the help of European editors. It is true that the ceremonial, the vidhis, can be better studied in the Sûtras, but if we want to know what meaning was assigned to every act of the sacrifice, such as it had been handed down and become fixed in the Brahmanic society of India, long before the composition of any Brâhmaṇa, we must consult these works. Though their professed object is to teach the sacrifice, they allow a much larger space to dogmatical, exegetical, mystical and philosophical speculations, than to the ceremonial itself. They appeal continually to earlier authorities, and in some of them, particularly in the Kaushîtaki-brâhmaṇa, the conflicting opinions of ancient sages are so well confronted, and their respective merits so closely discussed, that we sometimes imagine ourselves reading the dogmatic philosophy of Jaimini. According to the views of native commentators, the characteristic feature of the Brâhmaṇas consists in doubt, deliberation, and discussion, and the word Mimânsâ, which afterwards became the title of Jaimini's philosophy, is frequently used in the Brâhmaṇas to introduce the very problems which occupy the attention of Jaimini and his followers. Of course the discussion is not a *bonâ fide* discussion. The two sides of every question are stated, but they only serve to lead us on to the conclusion which the author of the Brâhmaṇa considers in the light of a divine revelation. We are reminded of the disputations of two Doctors of Theology who defend for a time the most heretical propositions with the sharpest weapons of logic and rhetoric, though they would extremely regret the final victory of that cause which, for argument's sake, they are called upon to maintain. Never was dogmatism more successfully veiled under the mask of free discussion than in the Mimânsâ or discussion of the Brâhmaṇas.

The fact of so many authorities being quoted by

name in these works shows that the Brâhmaṇas exhibit the accumulated thoughts of a long succession of early theologians and philosophers. But the very earliest of these sages follow a train of thought which gives a clear evidence of a decaying religion. The Brâhmaṇas presuppose, not only a complete collection of the ten Maṇḍalas of the Rig-veda, not only the establishment of a most complicated ceremonial, not only the distribution of the ceremonial offices among three or four classes of priests, but a complete break in the primitive tradition of the Aryan settlers of India. At the time when the law was laid down about the employment of certain hymns at certain parts of the sacrifice, the original meaning of these hymns, and the true conception of the gods to whom they were addressed, had been lost. The meaning also of the old and sacred customs by which their forefathers had hallowed the most critical epochs of life and the principal divisions of the year, had faded away from the memory of those whose lucubrations on the purport of the sacrifices have been embalmed in the so-called Arthavâdas of the Brâhmaṇas. It is difficult to determine whether, before the beginning of the Brâhmaṇa period, there existed various Śâkhâs among the Bahvṛichas. The collection of the Rig-veda-sanhitâ must no doubt have been completed long before the age which led to the composition of Brâhmaṇas. Various readings also may have found their way into that collection before the Brâhmaṇa period. But the scrupulous preservation of such variations, which were the natural result of oral tradition, seems more akin to the spirit of the Brâhmaṇas than to that of an earlier age. There is less room for doubt as to the date of the Śâkhâs of the Âdhvaryus and Chhandogas. They do belong to the Brâhmaṇa period. What is called the Taittirîya-sanhitâ is no Sanhitâ, in the usual sense of the word, but was originally the Brâhmaṇa of the ancient Adhvaryus. It contains the description of the sacrifice, such as it would be required by the Adhvaryus. The composition of a separate Sanhitâ in their behalf, the so-called Sanhitâ of the White Yajurveda, is contemporaneous with, if not later than, the collection of the Śatapatha-Brâhmaṇa. We therefore consider all the Śâkhâs of the Adhvaryus, with the exception of their Sûtra-śâkhâs, as Brâhmaṇa-śâkhâs which had grown up during the Brâhmaṇa period. And if we feel more hesitation with regard to the Sanhitâ of the Chhandogas, it is not with reference to what is usually called the Sâma-veda-sanhitâ, but with regard to the Gânas. These collections of hymns, though they have a purely ceremonial object, have an air of antiquity, and we could hardly understand how the Tâṇḍya-brâhmaṇa, even in its original component parts, could have arisen, unless we suppose that there existed previously collections and groups of hymns, comprised under special names, such as we find in the Gânas. Without, therefore, pronouncing a definite opinion on the existence of any Śâkhâs of the two minor Vedas, previous to the first appearance of Brâhmaṇa literature, we confine ourselves to the assertion, that not one line of any of the Brâhmaṇas which we possess could have been composed, until after the complete collection of the Rig-veda, and after the threefold division of the ceremonial. Not one of the Brâhmaṇas was composed by a Brahman who was not either a Bahvṛicha, an Adhvaryu, or a Chhandoga.

There was a fourth class of superintending priests, who were supposed to be cognisant of the duties of all the three other classes: but there was, as we shall see, neither Brâhmaṇa nor Sanhitâ for their special benefit. According to the opinion of some, the superintendent or Brahman might indeed be an Adhvaryu, or even a Chhandoga, but the general rule is that he should be a Bahvṛicha[1], because the Bahvṛicha had the widest knowledge of Vedic hymns. There must have been a time when every Brahman who had to act as a priest, whatever offices he had to perform at the sacrifice, was acquainted with the complete body of the sacred hymns, collected in the Rig-veda. But of that time no traces are left in our Brâhmaṇas. Our Brâhmaṇas know of no hymns which are not the property of Hotṛi, Adhvaryu, or Udgâtṛi; they know of no priests, except the four classes which have divided between themselves all the sacrifices, and have distinct duties assigned to them, whether they officiate singly or jointly. Such a system could only have been carried out by a powerful and united priesthood; its origin and continuance can hardly be conceived without the admission of early councils and canons. Originally every sacrifice was a spontaneous act, and as such had a meaning. When the sacrifices fell into the hands of priests, the priest was at first the minister, afterwards the repre-

[1] Kaush.-br. vi. 11. तदाहुः किंविदं किंछंदसं ब्रह्माणं वृणीत इत्यध्वर्युमित्येके स परिक्रमाणां चेतज्ञो भवतीति छंदोगमित्येके तथा ह्यस्य त्रिभिर्वेदैर्हविर्यज्ञाः संस्क्रियंत इति बह्वृचमिति त्वेव स्थितं। Some allowance must be made for the fact that the Kaushîtakins are Bahvṛichas.

sentative, of those who offered the sacrifice. But it is only in the last stage of priestcraft that the spoils are divided, and certain acts made the monopoly of certain classes of priests. All this had taken place before the rising of what we call the Brâhmaṇa literature, and we may well conceive that but few traces are left in these works of the thoughts and feelings which had suggested the first spontaneous acts of the early worshippers of India.

The transition from a natural worship to an artificial ceremonial may take place gradually. It had taken place long before the beginning of the Brâhmaṇa period, and the process of corruption continued during this and the succeeding periods, till at last the very corruption became a principle of new life. But there is throughout the Brâhmaṇas such a complete misunderstanding of the original intention of the Vedic hymns, that we can hardly understand how such an estrangement could have taken place, unless there had been at some time or other a sudden and violent break in the chain of tradition. The author of the Brâhmaṇas evidently imagined that those ancient hymns were written simply for the sake of their sacrifices, and whatever interpretation they thought fit to assign to these acts, the same, they supposed, had to be borne out by the hymns. This idea has vitiated the whole system of Indian exegesis. It might be justified, perhaps, if it had only been applied to the purely sacrificial hymns, particularly to those which are found in the Sanhitâs of the Sâma-veda and Yajur-veda. But the Rig-veda too has experienced the same treatment at the hands of Indian commentators, and the stream of tradition, flowing from the fountain-head of the original poets, has, like the waters of the Sarasvatî, disappeared in the sands of a desert. Not only was the true nature of the gods, as conceived by the early poets, completely lost sight of, but new gods were actually created out of words which were never intended as names of divine beings. There are several hymns in the Rig-veda containing questions as to who is the true or the most powerful god. One in particular is well known, in which each verse ends with the inquiring exclamation of the poet; "Kasmai devâya havishâ vidhema?" "To which god shall we sacrifice with our offering?" This, and similar hymns, in which the interrogative pronoun occurred, were employed at various sacrifices. A rule had been laid down, that in every sacrificial hymn there must be a deity addressed by the poet. In order to discover a deity where no deity existed, the most extraordinary objects, such as a present, a drum, stones, plants, were raised to the artificial rank of deities. In accordance with the same system, we find that the authors of the Brâhmaṇas had so completely broken with the past, that, forgetful of the poetical character of the hymns, and the yearning of the poets after the unknown god, they exalted the interrogative pronoun itself into a deity, and acknowledged a god Ka or Who? In the Taittirîya-sanhitâ[1] (i. 7. 6. 6.), in the Kaushîtaki-brâhmaṇa (xxiv. 4.), in the Tâṇḍya-brâhmaṇa (xv. 10.), and in the Śatapatha-brâhmaṇa, whenever interrogative verses occur, the author states, that Ka is Prajâpati, or the Lord of Creatures (Prajâpatir vai Kaḥ). Nor did they stop here. Some of the hymns in which the inter-

[1] See Böhtlingk and Roth's Dictionary, s. v.

rogative pronoun occurred were called Kadvat, *i. e.* having *kad* or *quid*. But soon a new adjective was formed, and not only the hymns, but the sacrifice also, offered to the god, were called *Kâya*, or who-ish. This word, which is not to be identified with the Latin cujus, cuja, cujum, but is merely the artificial product of an effete mind, is found in the Taittirîya-sanhitâ (i. 8. 3. 1.), and in the Vâjasaneyi-sanhitâ (xxiv. 15.). At the time of Pâṇini this word had acquired such legitimacy as to call for a separate rule explaining its formation (Pâṇ. iv. 2. 25.). The Commentator here explains Ka by Brahman. After this, we can hardly wonder that in the later Sanskrit literature of the Purâṇas, Ka appears as a recognised god, as the supreme god, with a genealogy of his own, perhaps even with a wife; and that in the laws of Manu, one of the recognised forms of marriage, generally known by the name of the Prajâpati-marriage, occurs under the monstrous title of Kâya.

What is more natural than that the sun should be called in the hymns, golden-handed? The Brâhmaṇa, however, affected with a kind of voluntary blindness, must needs explain this simple epithet by a story of the sun having lost his hand, and having received instead a hand made of gold.

It would be useless to multiply these instances, as every page of the Brâhmaṇas contains the clearest proof that the spirit of the ancient Vedic poetry, and the purport of the original Vedic sacrifices, were both beyond the comprehension of the authors of the Brâhmaṇas. But although we thus perceive the wide chasm between the Brâhmaṇa period and that period by which it is preceded, we have still to answer the question whether any probable limits can be assigned to the duration of this literary period. The Brâhmaṇas are not the work of a few individuals. By whomsoever they were brought into that form in which we now possess them, no one can claim the sole authorship of the dogmas which are incorporated in each Brâhmaṇa. The Brâhmaṇas represent a complete period during which the whole stream of thought flowed in one channel, and took, at least in that class which alone sustained intellectual activity, the form of prose never before applied to literary productions. There are old and new Brâhmaṇas, but the most modern hardly differ in style and language from the most ancient. The old Brâhmaṇas passed through several changes, represented by the Brâhmaṇa-śâkhâs, and even the most modern were not exempt from these modifications. Considering, therefore, that the Brâhmaṇa period must comprehend the first establishment of the threefold ceremonial, the composition of separate Brâhmaṇas, the formation of Brâhmaṇa-charaṇas, and the schism between old and new Charaṇas, and their various collections, it would seem impossible to bring the whole within a shorter space than 200 years. Of course this is merely conjectural; but it would require a greater stretch of imagination to account for the production in a smaller number of years of that mass of Brâhmaṇic literature which still exists, or is known to have existed. Were we to follow the traditions of the Brâhmaṇas themselves, we should have much less difficulty in accounting for the great variety of authors quoted, and of opinions stated in the Brâhmaṇas. They contain lists of teachers through whom the Brâhmaṇas were handed down, which would extend the limits of this age to a very considerable degree. The Chhandogas have assigned a separate Brâhmaṇa to the list of their teachers, viz. the Vanśa-brâhmaṇa, a work the existence of which ought not to have been called into question, as a copy of it existed in the Bodleian Library.[1] In the Śatapatha-brâhmaṇa these lists are repeated at the end of various sections. There seems to be no imaginable object in inventing these long lists, as in the eyes of the Brahmans they would have been much too short for the extravagant antiquity assigned to their sacred books. With the exception of the highest links in each chain of teachers, the lists have an appearance of authenticity rarely to be met with in Indian compositions. The number of teachers in the Vanśa-brâhmaṇa amounts to 53, the last of them, Kaśyapa, the father, having received the tradition from Agni, or the god of fire. From Agni the tradition is further traced to Indra, Vâyu (wind), Mṛityu (death), Prajâpati (the Lord of Creation), and lastly to Brahman, the Self-existing. From Kaśyapa, down to Râdha Gautama, his 26th successor, the line of teachers seems to have been undivided. Râdha Gautama had two pupils, who apparently became the founders of different schools. One is called Anśu Dhânanjayya, who received instruction from Râdha Gautama and Amâvâsya Śâṇḍilyâyana; the other, Gobhila, had no teacher besides Râdha. The successors of Gobhila are eleven in number, while those of Anśu Dhânanjayya are twenty-five.

In the Śatapatha-brâhmaṇa we find four Vanśas.

[1] Prof. Weber's recent edition of this tract, is the best *amende* he could have made for his former scepticism with regard to the existence of this and other Brâhmaṇas of the Sâma-veda.

The most important of them stands at the end of the whole work, and consists of fifty-five names; the last of the human teachers being again Kaśyapa, who here is supposed to have received his revelation from Vâch, the goddess of speech. She received it through Ambhiṇî from Âditya, the sun. Among the successors of Kaśyapa we mark the 10th, Yâjnavalkya, the pupil of Uddâlaka and the teacher of Âsuri; and the 15th, Sânjîvîputra. Sânjîvîputra seems to have united two lines of teachers; he was the pupil of Kârśakeyîputra, and, according to the Vanśa of the 10th book, he was likewise the pupil of Mâṇḍûkâyani, the 9th successor of Tura Kâvasheya, who is fabled to have received his revelation, not through the agency of Vâch, Ambhiṇî, and Âditya, but direct from Prajâpati and the self-existing Brahman. There are two other Vanśas, one at the end of the Madhukâṇḍa, the other at the end of the Yâjnavalkîya-kâṇḍa. Both are, in reality, varieties of one and the same Vanśa, their differences arising from the confusion caused by the recurrence of similar names. That of the Madhukâṇḍa consists of sixty names, only forty-five or forty-six of which have an historical appearance. The principal divine teachers after Brahman, the Self-existing, are Parameshṭhin (Prajâpati?), Mṛityu (death), Dadhyach, Âtharvaṇa, and the two Aśvins.

At the end of the Khila-kâṇḍa a fifth list is found, not a Vanśa, but a list of teachers who handed down the Vanśa. This seems to be ascribed to Uddâlaka Âruṇeya, the teacher of Yâjnavalkya, as its original author.

Lists of Teachers from the Śatapatha-Brâhmaṇa.

	Madhukâṇḍa	Yâjnavalkîya-kâṇḍa.
1.	Śaurpaṇâyya.	The same as in the Madhukâṇḍa.
2.	Gautama.	
3.	Vâtsya.	
4.	Vâtsya and Pârâśarya.[1]	
5.	Sânkṛitya and Bhâradvâja.	
6.	Audavâhi and Śâṇḍilya.	
7.	Vaijavâpa and Gautama.	
8.	Vaijavâpâyana and Vaishṭapureya.	
9.	Śâṇḍilya and Rauhiṇâyana.	
10.	Śaunaka and Âtreya, and Raibhya.	Jaivantâyana instead of Âtreya.
11.	Pautimâshyâyaṇa and Kauṇḍinyâyana.	The same as in the Madhukâṇḍa.
		Kauṇḍinyau.
		Aurṇavâbhâḥ.
12.	Kauṇḍinya.	Kauṇḍinya.
13.	Kauṇḍinya.	Kauṇḍinya.
14.	Kauṇḍinya and Âgniveśya.	Kauṇḍinya and Âgniveśya.
15.	Saitava.	Saitava.
16.	Pârâśarya.	The same as in the Madhukâṇḍa.
17.	Jâtukarṇya.	

[1] When there are two teachers, it is always the second through whom the tradition was carried on, except in No. 28. where there has evidently been a great confusion.

Madhukâṇḍa.	Yâjnavâlkîyâ-kâṇḍa.
18. Bhâradvâja.	
19. Bhâradvâja and Âsurâyaṇa and Gautama.	
20. Bhâradvâja.	
21. Vaijavâpâyana.	Valâkâkauśika.
22. Kauśikâyani.	Kâshâyaṇa.
23. Ghṛitakauśika.	Saukarâyaṇa.
24. Pârâśaryâyaṇa.	
25. Pârâśarya.	desunt.
26. Jâtukarṇya.	desunt.
27. Bhâradvâja.	desunt.
28. Bhâradvâja and Âsurâyaṇa, and Yâska	desunt.
29. Traivaṇi.	Traivaṇi.
30. Aupajandhani.	Aupajandhani.[1]
31. Âsuri.	Âsuri.
32. Bhâradvâja.	
33. Âtreya.	
34. Mâṇṭi.	
35. Gautama.	
36. Gautama.	
37. Vâtsya.	

[1] The Yâjnavalkîya-kâṇḍa inserts here: Sâyakâyana.
Kauśikâyani (22).
Ghṛitakauśika (23).
Pârâśaryâyaṇa (24).
Pârâśarya (25).
Jâtukarṇya (26).
Bhâradvâja (27).
Bhâradvâja and
Âsurâyaṇa and Yâska (28).
Traivaṇi (29).
Aupajandhani (30).

Madhukâṇḍa.

38. Śâṇḍilya.
39. Kaiśorya Kâpya.
40. Kumârahârita.
41. Gâlava.
42. Vidarbhîkauṇḍinya.
43. Vatsanapât Bâbhrava.
44. Pathas Saubhara.
45. Ayâsya Âṅgirasa.
46. Âbhûti Tvâshṭra.
47. Viśvarûpa Tvâshṭra.
48. The two Aśvins.
49. Dadhyach Âtharvaṇa.
50. Atharvan Daiva.
51. Mṛityu Prâdhvansana.
52. Pradhvansana.
53. Ekarshi.
54. Viprajitti.
55. Vyashṭi.
56. Sanâru.
57. Sanâtana.
58. Sanaga.
59. Parameshṭhin.
60. Brahman Svayambhu.

Last Book.

1. Bhâradvâjî-putra.
2. Vâtsîmâṇḍavî-putra.
3. Pârâśarî-putra.
4. Gârgî-putra.
5. Pârâśarî-kauṇḍinî-putra.
6. Gârgî-putra.
7. Gârgî-putra.
8. Bâḍeyî-putra.

9. Maushikî-putra.
10. Hârikarnî-putra.
11. Bhâradvâjî-putra.
12. Paingî-putra.
13. Śaunakî-putra.
14. Kâśyapîvâlâkyâmâṭharî-putra.
15. Kautsî-putra.
16. Baudhî-putra.
17. Śâlankâyanî-putra.
18. Vârshaganî-putra.
19. Gautamî-putra.
20. Âtreyî-putra.
21. Gautamî-putra.
22. Vâtsî-putra.
23. Bhâradvâjî-putra.
24. Pârâśarî-putra.
25. Vârkârunî-putra.
26. Ârṭabhâgî-putra.
27. Śaungî-putra.
28. Sânkritî-putra.
29. Âlambî-putra.
30. Âlambâyanî-putra.
31. Jâyantî-putra.
32. Mâṇḍûkâyanî-putra.
33. Mâṇḍûkî-putra.
34. *Sâṇḍilî-putra.*
35. Râthîtarî-putra.
36. Kraunchikî-putrau.
37. Vaidabhritî-putra.
38. Bhâlukî-putra.
39. Prâchînayogî-putra. — Xth Book.
40. *Sânjîvî-putra.* — *Sânjîvî-putra.*
41. Kârśakeyî-putra. — Mâṇḍûkâyani.
42. Prâśnî-putra Âsurivâsin. — Mâṇḍavya.

43. Âśurâyaṇa.	Kautsa.
44. Âsuri.	Mâhitthi.
45. Yâjnavalkya. (Vâjasaneya Yâjnavalkya, Kh.)	Vâmakakshâyaṇa.
46. Uddâlaka. (Uddâlaka Âruṇeya, Kh.)	Vâtsya.
47. Aruṇa.	*Śâṇḍilya.*
48. Upaveśi.	Kuśri.
49. Kuśri.	Yajnavachas Râjastambâyâna.
50. Vâjaśravas.	*Tura Kâvasheya.*[1]
51. Jihvâvat Bâdhyoga.	Prajâpati.
52. Asita Vârshagaṇa.	Brahman Svayambhu.
53. Harita Kaśyapa.	
54. Śilpa Kaśyapa.	
55. Kaśyapa Naidhruvi.	
56. Vâch.	
57. Ambhiṇî.	
58. Âditya.	

Khila-kâṇḍa.

Satyakâma Jâbâla.
Jânaki Âyasthûṇa.
Chûḍa Bhâgavitti.
Madhuka Paingya.
Vâjasaneya Yâjnavalkya.
Uddâlaka Âruṇeya.

Vanśa of the Sâma-veda.

1. Śarvadatta Gârgya.
2. Rudrabhûti Drâhyâyaṇi.
3. Trâta Aishumata.

[1] The priest of Janamejaya Pârikshita, at his Abhisheka sacrifice, is called Tura Kâvasheya in the Ait.-br. viii. 21.

4. Nigada Pârṇavalki.
5. Giriśarman Kâṇṭheviddhi.
6. Brahmavṛiddhi Chhandogamâhaki.
7. Mitravarchas Sthairakâyana.
8. Supratîta Auluṇḍya.
9. Bṛihaspatigupta Śâyasthi.
10. Bhavatrâta Śâyasthi.
11. Kustuka Sârkarâksha.
12. Śravaṇadatta Kauhala.
13. Suśârada Śâlankâyana.
14. Ûrjayat Aupamanyava.

15. Bhânumat Aupamanyava.	Aryamabhûti Kâlabava.
16. Ânandaja Chândhanâyana.	Bhadraśarma Kauśika.
17. Sâmba Śârkarâksha, and Kâmboja Aupamanyava.	Pushyayaśas Audavraji.
18. Madragâra Śaungâyani.	Sankara Gautama.
19. Sâti Aushṭrâkshi.	Aryamarâdha Gobhila and Pûshamitra Gobhila.
20. Suśravas Vârshagaṇya.	Aśvamitra Gobhila.
21. Prâtarahna Kauhala.	Varuṇamitra Gobhila.
22. Ketu Vâjya.	Mûlamitra Gobhila.
23. Mitravinda Kauhala.	Vatsamitra Gobhila.
24. Sunîtha Kâpaṭâva.	Gaulgulavîputra Gobhila.
25. Sutemanas Śâṇḍilyâyana.	Bṛihadvasu Gobhila (pitâ).
26. Anśu Dhânanjâyya.	Gobhila.

27. Amâvâsya Śâṇḍilyâyana and Râdha Gautama.
28. Gâtṛi Gautama.

29. Samvargajit Lâmakâyana.
30. Śâkadâsa Bhâḍitâyana.
31. Vichakshaṇa Tâṇḍya.
32. Gardabhîmukha Śâṇḍilyâyana.
33. Udaraśaṇḍilya (the father).
34. Atidhanvan Śaunaka and Maśaka Gârgya.
35. Sthiraka Gârgya (the father).
36. Vâsishṭha Chaikitâneya.
37. Vâsishṭha Âraihaṇya (a prince).
38. Sumantra Bâbhrava Gautama.
39. Śûsha Vâhneya Bhâradvâja.
40. Arâla Dârteya Śaunaka.
41. Dṛiti Aindrota Śaunaka (the father).
42. Indrota Śaunaka (the father).[1]
43. Vṛishaśushṇa Vâtâvata.
44. Nikothaka Bhâyajâtya.
45. Pratithi Devataratha.
46. Devataras Śâvasâyana (the father).
47. Śavas (the father).
48. Agnibhû Kâśyapa.
49. Indrabhû Kâśyapa.
50. Mitrabhû Kâśyapa.
51. Vibhaṇḍaka Kâśyapa (the father).
52. Ṛishyaśṛinga Kâśyapa (the father).
53. Kaśyapa (the father).
54. Agni (fire).
55. Indra.
56. Vâyu (wind).
57. Mṛityu (death).
58. Prajâpati (Lord of Creation).
59 Brahman Svayambhu.

[1] The priest of Janamejaya Pârikshita, at his Horse sacrifice, is called Indrota (Daivâpa) Śaunaka in the Śatapatha, xiii. 5. 4. 1., and in the Mahâbh. xii. 5595. seq. Cf. Weber, Ind. Stud. i. pp. 203. 483.

It would be difficult to tell how these long strings of names are to be accounted for, whatever system of chronology we adopt. If we were in possession of the Vanśas of the Bahvṛichas and the ancient Adhvaryus, we might perhaps see more clearly. But it is important to observe that these two, which are decidedly the two most ancient Vedas, seem to have had no Vanśas at all. However this may be explained hereafter, certain it is,—and these long lists of names teach at least this one thing,—that the Brahmans themselves looked upon the Brâhmaṇa period as a long-continued succession of teachers, reaching from the time when these lists were made and recited to the most distant antiquity, back to the very dynasties of their gods. If, therefore, we limit the age of the Brâhmaṇas to the two centuries from 600 to 800 B.C., it is more likely that hereafter these limits will have to be extended than that they will prove too wide.

There is one work which ought to be mentioned before we leave the Brâhmaṇa period, the Gopatha-brâhmaṇa. It is the Brâhmaṇa of the Brahma-veda, the Veda of the Atharvângiras' or Bhṛigu-Angiras'. This Veda does not properly belong to the sacred literature of the Brahmans, and though in later times it obtained the title of the fourth Veda, there was originally a broad distinction between the magic formulas of the Atharvângiras' and the hymns of the Bahvṛichas, the Chhandogas, and the Adhvaryus. Madhusûdana states the case simply and clearly. "The Veda," he says, "is divided into Ṛich, Yajush and Sâman for the purpose of carrying out the sacrifice under its three different forms. The duties of the Hotṛi priests are performed with the Rig-veda, those of the Adhvaryu priests with the Yajur-veda, those of the Udgâtṛi priests with the Sâma-veda. The duties of the Brahman and the sacrificer are contained in all the three. The Atharva-veda, on the contrary, is totally different. It is not used for the sacrifice, but only teaches how too appease, to bless, to curse, &c." But although the hymns of the Atharvans were not from the first looked upon as part of the sacred literature of the Brahmans, the Brâhmaṇa of the Atharvans belongs clearly to the same literary period which saw the rise of the other Brâhmaṇas; and though it does not share the same authority as the Brâhmaṇas of the three great Vedas, it is written in the same language, and breathes the same spirit. The MSS. of this work are extremely scarce, and the copy which I use (E. I. H. 2142) is hardly legible. The remarks, therefore, which I have to offer on this work will necessarily be scanty and incomplete.

The original division of the Veda, and of the Vedic ceremonial, was, as we have seen, a threefold division. The Brahmans speak either of one Veda or of three; of one officiating priest, or of three. "Trayî vidyâ," the threefold knowledge, is constantly used in the Brâhmaṇas[1] with reference to their sacred literature. This, however, proves by no means that at the time when the Brâhmaṇas were composed the songs of the Atharvângiras' did not yet exist. It only shows that originally they formed no part of the sacred literature of the Brahmans. In some of the Brâhmaṇas, the Atharvângiras' are mentioned. The passage translated before (p. 38.) shows that at the time when the Śatapatha-brâhmaṇa was composed the songs of the Atharvângiras' were not only known, but had been collected, and had actually obtained the title of Veda. Their original title was the Atharvângiras' or the Bhṛigvangiras', or the Atharvans,

[1] Nirukta-pariśishṭa, i. 10.

and these very titles show that songs which could be quoted in such a manner[1], must have been of ancient date, and must have had a long life in the oral tradition of India. Their proper position with reference to the other Vedas is well marked in a passage of the Taittirîyâraṇyaka (viii. 3.), where the Yajush is called the head, the Ṛich the right, the Sâman the other side, the Âdeśa (the Upanishad) the vital breath, and the Atharvângiras' the tail.

The songs known under the name of the Atharvângiras' formed probably an additional part of the sacrifice from a very early time. They were chiefly intended to counteract the influence of any untoward event that might happen during the sacrifice. They also contained imprecations and blessings, and various formulas, such as popular superstition would be sure to sanction at all times and in all countries. If once sanctioned, however, these magic verses would soon grow in importance, nay, the knowledge of all the other Vedas would necessarily become useless without the power of remedying accidents, such as could hardly be avoided in so complicated a ceremonial as that of the Brahmans. As that power was believed to reside in the songs of the Atharvângiras', a knowledge of these songs became necessarily an essential part of the theological learning of ancient India.

According to the original distribution of the sacrificial offices among the four classes of priests, the supervision of the whole sacrifice, and the remedying of any mistake that might have happened belonged to the Brahman. He had to know the three Vedas, to follow in his mind the whole sacrifice, and to advise the other priests on all doubtful points.[2] If it was the office

[1] See page 362. [2] Sâyaṇa's Introduction to the Rig-veda, p. 3. l. 3.

of the Brahman to remedy mistakes in the performance of the sacrifice, and if, for that purpose, the formulas of the Atharvângiras' were considered of special efficacy, it follows that it was chiefly the Brahman who had to acquire a knowledge of these formulas. Now the office of the Brahman was contested by the other classes of priests. The Bahvṛichas maintain that the office of Brahman should be held by a Bahvṛicha (Hotṛi), the Adhvaryus maintain that it belongs to one of their own body, and the Chhandogas also preferred similar claims. It was evidently the most important office, and in many instances, though not always, it was held by the Purohita, the hereditary family priest. Certain families also claimed a peculiar fitness for the office of Brahman, such as the Vasishṭhas and Viśvâmitras. (See p. 92.)

Because a knowledge of the songs of the Atharvângiras' was most important to the Brahman or Purohita[1], these songs themselves, when once admitted to the rank of a Veda, were called the Veda of the Brahman, or the Brahma-veda. In the Gopatha-brâhmaṇa the title of Brahma-veda does not occur.[2] But the songs of the Atharvângiras' are mentioned there. They are called both Âtharvaṇa-veda (i. 5.), and Ângirasa-veda (i. 8.), and they are repeatedly represented as the proper Veda for the Brahman. Thus we read (iii. 1.): "Let a man elect a Hotṛi who knows the Ṛich, an Adhvaryu who knows the Yajush, an Udgâtṛi who knows the Sâman, a Brahman who knows the Atharvângiras'." It seems in fact the principal object of the Gopatha to show the necessity

[1] Yâjnavalkya's Law-book, i. 312.

[2] See, however, i. 22.

of four Vedas. A carriage, we are told, does not proceed with less than four wheels, an animal does not walk with less than four feet, nor will the sacrifice be perfect with less than four Vedas.[1] But although a knowledge of the fourth Veda is thus represented as essential to the Brahman, it is never maintained that such a knowledge would be sufficient by itself to enable a person to perform the offices of a Brahman. Like the Chhandogas (Rv. Bh. vol. i. page 3.), the Âtharvaṇikas also declare that the whole sacrifice is performed twice, once in words, and once in thought. It is performed in words by the Hotṛi, Udgâtṛi, and Adhvaryu separately; it is performed in thought by the Brahman alone (Gop. Br. vol. iii. 2.). The Brahman, therefore, had to know all the three Vedas and in addition the formulas of the Atharvângiras'. It is a common mistake in later writers to place the Âtharva-veda coordinate with the other Vedas, and to represent it as the Veda of the Brahman. The Gopatha-brâhmaṇa raises no such claims. When it describes the type of the sacrifice, it says:

Agni (fire) was the Hotṛi,
Vâyu (wind) the Adhvaryu,
Sûrya (sun) the Udgâtṛi,
Chandramas (moon) the Brahman,
Parjanya (rain) the Sadasya,
Oshadhi and Vanaspati (shrubs and trees) the Chamasâdhvaryus,

[1] At the end of the fifth Prapâṭhaka we read: ऋग्भिः पृथिवी यजुषांतरिक्षं साम्ना दिवं लोकजित्सोमजंभाः। अथर्वभिरंगिरोभिश्च गुप्तो यज्ञश्चतुष्पाद्दिव - - -॥

The Viśve Devas were the Hotrakas,
The Atharvângiras', the Goptṛis or protectors.

In another place (v. 24.) the persons engaged in the sacrifice are enumerated as follows:

Hotṛi, Maitrâvaruṇa, Achhâvâka, Grâvastut (Rig-veda), 1 — 4.

Adhvaryu, Pratiprasthâtṛi, Neshṭṛi, Unnetṛi (Yajur-veda), 5 — 8.

Udgâtṛi, Prastotṛi, Subrahmaṇya, Pratihartṛi (Sâma-veda), 9 — 12.

Brahman, Brâhmaṇâchhansin, Potṛi, Agnîdhra (Atharvângiras'), 13 — 16.

Sadasya, 17.

Patnî dîkshitâ (the wife), 18.

Śamitṛi (the immolator), 19.

Gṛihapati (the lord), 20.

Angiras, 21.

Here we see that besides the four Brahman-priests to whom a knowledge of the Atharvângiras' is recommended, there were other priests who are called Goptṛis, *i. e.* protectors or Angiras', and whose special office it was to protect the sacrifice by means of the magical formulas of the Atharvângiras', against the effects of any accidents that might have happened. Such was the original office of the Atharvans at the Vedic sacrifices, and a large portion of the Gopatha-brâhmaṇa (i. 13.; i. 22.) is taken up with what is called the Virishṭa, the Ûna, the Yâtayâma, or whatever else the defects in a sacrifice are called, which must be made good (sandhâna) by certain hymns, verses, formulas, or exclamations. There are long discussions on the proper way of pronouncing these salutary formulas, on their hidden meaning, and their miraculous power. The syllable Om, the so-called

Vyâhṛitis, and other strange sounds are recommended for various purposes, and works such as the Sarpa-veda, Piśâcha-veda, Asura-veda, Itihâsa-veda, Purâṇa-veda, are referred to as authorities (i. 10.).

Although, however, the Gopatha-brâhmaṇa is more explicit on the chapter of accidents than the Brâhmaṇas of the other Vedas, the subject itself is by no means peculiar to it. The question of expiation or penance (prâyaśchitta) is fully discussed in the other Vedas, and remedies are suggested for all kinds of mishaps. The ceremonial in general is discussed in the Gopatha in the same manner as in the other Brâhmaṇas. There is, in fact, very little, if any, difference between the Gopatha and the other Brâhmaṇas, and it is not easy to discover any traces of its more recent origin. It begins with a theory of the creation of the world, such as we find in many places of the other Brâhmaṇas. There is nothing remarkable in it except one idea, which I do not remember to have seen elsewhere. Brahman (neuter), the self-existing, burns with a desire to create, and by means of his heat, sweat is produced from his forehead, and from all the pores of his body. These streams of sweat are changed into water. In the water Brahman perceives his own shadow, and falls in love with it. This, however, is only one phase in the progress of creation, which is ultimately to lead to the birth of Bhṛigu and Atharvan. Atharvan is represented as the real Prajâpati, or Lord of Creation. From him twenty classes of poets, the same as those mentioned in the Anukramaṇî, are produced, and their poems are said to have formed the Âtharvaṇa-veda.

Then follows a new series of creation. Brahman creates the earth from his feet, the sky from his belly, heaven, from his skull. He then creates three gods: Agni (fire) for the earth, Vâyu (wind), for the sky, and Âditya (sun) for the heaven. Lastly, he creates the three Vedas: the Rig-veda proceeds from Agni, the Yajur-veda from Vâyu, the Sâma-veda from Âditya. The three Vyâhṛitis also, or sacred syllables (*bhûḥ*, *bhuvaḥ*, *svar*), are called into existence. It is important to remark, that nothing is here said of the fourth Veda; its origin is described separately, and its second name, Ângirasa, is explained in detail. We look in vain for any traces of more modern ideas in the Gopatha-brâhmaṇa, till we come to the end of the fifth Prapâṭhaka. This is the last Prapâṭhaka of the Gopatha-brâhmaṇa, properly so called. The text is very corrupt, but it seems to contain an admission that, besides the twenty-one sacrifices which are acknowledged in all the Vedic writings, the Angiras' had some new sacrifices of their own.[1] That the Gopatha-brâhmaṇa was composed after the schism of the Charakas and Vâjasaneyins, and after the completion of the Vâjasaneyi-sanhitâ, may be gathered from the fact that where the first lines of the other Vedas are quoted in the Gopatha, the first line of the

[1] सप्त सुत्याः सप्त च पाकयज्ञा हविर्यज्ञाः सप्त तथैकविंशतिः। सर्वे ते यज्ञा अंगिरसोऽपि यंति नूतना यानृषयो (?) सृजंति ये च सृष्टाः पुराणैः॥ And again यांश्च ग्रामे यांश्चारण्ये जपंति मंत्रान्नानार्थान्बहुधा जनासः। सर्वे ते यज्ञा अंगिरसोऽपि यंति नूतना सा हि गतिर्ब्रह्मणो यावरार्ध्या॥ त्रिविष्टपं त्रिदिवं नाकमुत्तमं तमेतया त्रय्या विद्ययैति। अत उत्तरे ब्रह्मलोका महांतोऽथर्वणामंगिरसां च सा गतिः॥

Yajur-veda is taken from the Vâjasaneyins, and not from the Taittirîyas.

The five Prapâṭhakas which we have hitherto discussed, form only the first part of the Gopatha-brâhmaṇa. There is a second part, called the Uttara-brâhmaṇa, which consists of more than five Prapâṭhakas. It is impossible to fix their exact numbers, as the MS. breaks off in the middle of the sixth book. It is likewise reckoned as belonging to the Atharva-veda, and quoted by the name of Gopatha. In this second part we meet repeatedly with long passages which are taken from other Brâhmaṇas. Sometimes they coincide literally, sometimes the differences are no greater than what we find in different Śâkhâs of the same Brâhmaṇa. Thus the legend of the sacrifice running away from the gods, which is told in the Aitareya-brâhmaṇa, i. 18, is repeated in the Uttara-brâhmaṇa, ii. 6. The story of Vasishṭha receiving a special revelation from Indra which is told in the Taittirîyaka[1] (iii. 5. 2.) is repeated in the Uttara-brâhmaṇa (ii. 13.). And here a difference occurs which is characteristic. The Taittirîyas relate that owing to this special revelation which Vasishṭha had received from Indra, the Vasishṭhas had always acted as Purohitas. So far both the Taittirîyas and the Atharvans agree. But when the Taittirîyas continue that therefore a Vasishṭha is to be chosen a Brahman, the Atharvans demur. The sentence is left out, and it is inculcated on the contrary that the office of Brahman belongs by right to a Bhṛigu, or to one cognisant of the songs of the Atharvângiras'.[2]

[1] See page 91, note.

[2] See also Uttara-brâhmaṇa, ii. 1. = Ait.-br. iii. 5.; Utt.-br.

If, as we have little reason to doubt, these passages in the second part of the Gopatha-brâhmaṇa were simply copied from other Brâhmaṇas, we should have to assign to the Uttara-brâhmaṇa a later date than to the Brâhmaṇas of the other Vedas. But this would in no way affect the age of the original Gopatha-brâhmaṇa. In it there is nothing to show that it was a more modern composition than, for instance, the Śatapatha-brâhmaṇa. In the Sanhitâ of the Atharva-veda we find something very similar.[1] Here also the last, if not the last two books, betray a more modern origin, and are full of passages taken from the Rig-veda. The Anukramaṇî calls the nineteenth book the Brahma-kaṇḍa, and the hymns of the last book yajnîyaśansanamantras, *i. e.* hymns for sacrificial recitations. The collection of the Sanhitâ was probably undertaken simultaneously with the composition of the Gopatha-brâhmaṇa, at a time when, through the influence of some of the families of the Bhṛigus and Angiras', the magic formulas of the Atharvans had been acknowledged as an essential part of the solemn ceremonial. With the means at present at our disposal it is impossible to trace the history of these verses back to the earlier period of Vedic literature, and I shall not return to them again. What is known of their origin and character has been stated by Professor Whitney in several very careful articles in the Journal of the American Oriental Society.[2] "The Âtharvaṇa," he says, "is, like the Ṛich, a his-

v. 14. = Ait.-br. vi. 17.; Utt.-br. vi. 1. = Ait.-br. vi. 18.; Utt.-br. vi. 3. = Ait.-br. vi. 21.

[1] Atharva-veda-sanhitâ, herausgegeben von Roth und Whitney. Berlin, 1855, and 1856.

[2] Journal of the American Oriental Society, iv. p. 254.

torical and not a liturgical collection. Its first eighteen books, of which alone it was originally composed, are arranged upon a like system throughout: the length of the hymns, and not either their subject or their alleged authorship, being the guiding principle: those of about the same number of verses are combined together into books, and the books made up of the shorter hymns stand first in order. A sixth of the mass, however, is not metrical, but consists of longer or shorter prose pieces, nearly akin in point of language and style to passages of the Brâhmaṇas. Of the remainder, or metrical portion, about one-sixth is also found among the hymns of the Ṛich, and mostly in the tenth book of the latter: the rest is peculiar to the Âtharvaṇa." And again[1], "The most prominent characteristic feature of the Âtharvaṇa is the multitude of incantations which it contains; these are pronounced either by the person who is himself to be benefitted, or, more often, by the sorcerer for him, and are directed to the procuring of the greatest variety of desirable ends; most frequently, perhaps, long life, or recovery from grievous sickness, is the object sought: then a talisman, such as a necklace, is sometimes given, or in very numerous cases some plant endowed with marvellous virtues is to be the immediate external means of the cure; further, the attainment of wealth or power is aimed at, the downfall of enemies, success in love or in play, the removal of petty pests, and so on, even down to the growth of hair on a bald pate."

[1] Loc. cit. iii. p. 308.

CHAPTER III.

MANTRA PERIOD.

HAVING ascribed to one period the first establishment of the three-fold ceremonial (trayî vidyâ), the composition and collection of the Brâhmaṇas, and the ramification of the Brâhmaṇa-charaṇas, we have now to see whether we can extend our view beyond the limits of this period and trace the stream of Vedic literature still further back to its source and its earliest diffusion. According to its general character, the Brâhmaṇa period must be called a secondary period. It exhibits a stratum of thought perfectly unintelligible without the admission of a preceding age, during which all that is misunderstood, perverted, and absurd in the Brâhmaṇas, had its natural growth, its meaning, and purpose. But can it be supposed that those who established the threefold ceremonial, and those who composed the threefold Brâhmaṇas, followed immediately upon an age which had known poets, but no priests, prayers, but no dogmas, worship, but no ceremonies? Or are there traces to show that, even previous to the composition of the Brâhmaṇas, a spirit was at work in the literature of India, no longer creative, free, and original, but living only on the heritage of a former age, collecting, classifying, and imitating? I believe we must decidedly adopt the latter view: The only document we have, in which we can study the character of the times, previous to the Brâhmaṇa period, is the Rig-veda-sanhitâ. The other two Sanhitâs were more likely the production of the Brâhmaṇa period. These two Vedas, the Yajur-veda and Sâma-veda, were, in truth, what they are called in the Kaushîtaki-brâhmaṇa, the attendants of the Rig-veda.[1] The Brâhmaṇas presuppose the Trayî vidyâ, the threefold knowledge, or the threefold Veda, but that Trayî vidyâ again presupposes one Veda, and that the Rig-veda. We cannot suppose that the hymns which are found in the Rig-veda, and in the Sanhitâs of the two supplementary Vedas, the Sâma and Yajur-veda, were collected three times by three independent collectors. If so, their differences would be much greater than they are. The differences which do exist between the same hymns and verses as given in the three Sanhitâs, are such as we should expect to find in different Śâkhâs, not such as would naturally arise in independent collections or Sanhitâs.

The principle on which the Sanhitâ of the Rig-veda was made is different from that which guided the compilers of the Sanhitâs of the Adhvaryus and Udgâtṛis. These two Sanhitâs follow the order of an established ceremonial. They presuppose a fixed order of sacrifices. This is not the case in the Sanhitâ of the Bahvṛichas. There is, as we shall see, a system in that Sanhitâ also, but it has no reference to the ceremonial.

The different character of the Rig-veda-sanhitâ, as compared with the Sanhitâs of the other two Vedas, has attracted the attention of the Brahmans, and we

[1] तत्परिचरणावितरौ वेदौ॥ vi. 11.

may quote on this subject the remarks of Sâyaṇa, in his Introduction to the Rig-veda.[1]

"Has Âśvalâyana," he says, "when composing his ceremonial Sûtras, followed the order of the Sanhitâ of the Rig-veda, or of the Brâhmaṇa? He could not have followed the order of the hymns, because he says at the beginning of his Sûtras, that first of all he is going to explain the new and full-moon sacrifices (Darśapûrṇamâsa), while the first hymns of the Rig-veda are never used at that sacrifice. Nor does he seem to have followed the Brâhmaṇa. For the Brâhmaṇa begins with the Dîkshaṇîyâ ceremony. Here then it must be observed that the collection of hymns follows the order which is observed at the Brahmayajna and on other occasions where prayers are to be recited. It does not follow the order in which hymns are employed at the different sacrifices. Brahmayajna is the name given to the act of repeating by heart one's own sacred text, or even a single verse of it, whether a Ṛich, Yajush or Sâman. This repeating of all the Ṛich, Yajush or Sâman verses is enjoined by many passages of the Brâhmaṇas, and whenever hymns are thus enjoined to be repeated, that order is to be observed in which they have been handed down by an uninterrupted tradition. But as Âśvalâyana teaches the particular employment of particular hymns, basing it upon the authority of what are termed indicative passages of the revelation, it is but natural that he cannot follow the order of the hymns of the Rig-veda. The texts of the Yajur-veda, however, are given, from the first beginning, according to their

[1] P. 34.

order at the performance of sacrifices, and thus have Âpastamba and others proceeded in the same order in the composition of their Sûtras. As this order has once been received, it is likewise adopted in the Brahmayajna. That Âśvalâyana should explain in the first place the Darśapûrṇamâsa sacrifice, while the Brâhmaṇa begins with the Dîkshaṇîyâ sacrifice, is no objection, because the Dîkshaṇîyâ is only a modification of the Darśapûrṇamâsa, and many of its rules must be supplied from the typical sacrifice. Thus the Kalpa-sûtra of Âśvalâyana assists in teaching the performance of the sacrifice by showing the employment of the hymns. That Âśvalâyana should teach the employment of passages which do not occur in the Sanhitâ of the Rig-veda[1], is no fault, because these

[1] Our MSS. represent, according to tradition, the text of the Śâkala-śâkhâ, and the same text is followed by Âśvalâyana in his Sûtras. Now, whenever Âśvalâyana quotes any verses which form part of the Śâkala-śâkhâ, he only quotes the first words. Every member of his Charaṇa was supposed to know the hymns of the Śâkala-śâkhâ by heart, and it was sufficient, therefore, to quote them in this manner. But when he has occasion to refer to the verses which are found in the Brâhmaṇa of the Aitareyins, without forming part of the Śâkala-sanhitâ, Âśvalâyana quotes them in full. As these verses are not quoted in full in the text of the Aitareya-brâhmaṇa, we may fairly suppose that the text of the Rig-veda-sanhitâ, current among the Aitareyins, was different from that of the Śâkala-śâkhâ, and contained the full text of these hymns. Sâyaṇa, in his Commentary, does not state that these additional verses belonged to the Śâkhâ of the Aitareyins, but there can be little doubt that at his time the text of their Sanhitâ was lost and forgotten. He says, however, that these verses belonged to a different Śâkhâ, and that they must be supplied from Âśvalâyana's Sûtras, where, for this very reason, they were given in full. At the time of Âśvalâyana, therefore, the text of the Sanhitâ of the Aitareyins was still in existence, and he likewise notices in his Sûtras peculiarities in the ceremonial of the

hymns occur in different Śâkhâs, and their employment is prescribed by a different Brâhmaṇa, so that their being mentioned can only increase the value of his Sûtras. Those who know the logic of this subject say, that there is but one sacrifice and that it is to be learnt from all the different Śâkhâs."

Here then we see that even so late a writer as Sâyaṇa is fully aware of the peculiar character of the Ṛig-veda, as compared with the other Vedas. In his eyes the collection of hymns, preserved in the Ṛig-veda, has evidently something anomalous. He, brought up in the system of a stiff liturgical religion, looks upon the Sanhitâs simply as prayer-books to be used at the sacrifices. The sacrifices as taught in the Brâhmaṇas and Sûtras, are to him a subject of far greater importance than the religious poetry of the Ṛishis. It is but natural, therefore, that he should ask, what is the use of this collection of hymns, in which there is no order or system, as in the hymn-books of the Yajur-veda and Sâma-veda? His answer, however, is most unsatisfactory. For if the other two collections of hymns can be used for private devotion although they follow the order of the sacrifices, why should not the same apply to the hymns of the Ṛig-veda?

Whenever we find in the ancient literature and

Aitareyins. Dr. Roth has pointed out one of these verses (Nirukta, xlv.) The passage in the Aitareya-brâhmaṇa from which the verse is taken, is, i. 4. 2.; and Sâyaṇa says there: ता एतास्त्वतस्त्र ऋचः शाखांतरगता आश्वलायनेन पठिता द्रष्टव्याः॥ In a similar manner the modern Sûtras of the Fratres Attidii (Tab. vi. vii.) contain the Mantras in full, which in the ancient statutes (Tab. i.) are only indicated as generally known. See Aufrecht und Kirchhoff, Die Umbrischen Sprachdenkmäler.

theology of the Brahmans anything that is contrary to their general rules, anything that seems anomalous to them and is yet allowed to exist, we may be sure that it contains some really historical elements, and that it was of too solid a nature to receive the smooth polish of the Brahmanic system. It is so with the Rig-veda-sanhitâ. It belongs to a period previous to the complete ascendancy of the Brahmans; it was finished before the threefold ceremonial had been worked out in all its details.

And yet there is some system, there is some priestly influence, clearly distinguishable in that collection also. It is true that the ten books of the Rig-veda stand before us as separate collections, each belonging to one of the ancient families of India; but were these collections undertaken independently in each of these families, at different times, and with different objects? I believe not. There are traces, however faint, of one superintending spirit.

Eight out of the ten Maṇḍalas begin with hymns addressed to Agni, and these hymns, with the exception of the tenth Maṇḍala, are invariably followed by hymns addressed to Indra.[1] After the hymns ad-

[1] First Maṇḍala, Anuvâka 1.=Agni.
Anuvâka 2. 3.=Indra.
Second Maṇḍala, Anuvâka 1.=Agni (—11).
Anuvâka 2.=Indra.
Third Maṇḍala, Anuvâka 1. 2.=Agni.
Anuvâka 3. 4.=Indra.
Fourth Maṇḍala, Anuvâka 1.—2. 5.=Agni.
Anuvâka 2. 3.=Indra.
Fifth Maṇḍala, Anuvâka 1.—2. 14.=Agni.
Anuvâka 2. 15.—3. 8.=Indra.
Sixth Maṇḍala, Anuvâka 1.—2. 1.=Agni.
Anuvâka 2. 1.—4. 4.=Indra.

dressed to these two deities we generally meet with hymns addressed to the Viśve Devâḥ. This cannot be the result of mere accident, nor is there anything in the character of the two gods, Agni and Indra, which would necessitate such an arrangement. Agni is indeed called the lowest of the gods, but this neither implies his inferiority nor his superiority.[1] It simply means that Agni, as the god of fire on the hearth, is the nearest god, who descends from his high station to befriend men, and who, in the form of the sacrificial fire, becomes the messenger and mediator between god and men.[2] This would not be sufficient to account for the place assigned to him at the beginning of eight out of the ten Maṇḍalas of the Rig-veda. Indra, again, is certainly the most powerful of the Vedic gods[3], but he never enjoys that supremacy which in Greece and Rome was allowed to Zeus and Jupiter. We can hardly doubt, therefore, that the place allowed to hymns addressed to Agni and Indra, at the beginning

Seventh Maṇḍala,	Anuvâka 1.=Agni.
	Anuvâka 2.=Indra.
Eighth Maṇḍala,	Pragâtha hymns.
Ninth Maṇḍala,	Soma hymns.
Tenth Maṇḍala,	Anuvâka 1=Agni.

[1] Schol. ad Pind. Nem. x. 59. Καὶ γὰρ τὸ πρῶτον ἔσχατον ποτὲ δύναται γενέσθαι, καὶ τὸ ἔσχατον πρῶτον· κέχρηται καὶ Σοφοκλῆς τῷ ἐσχάτῳ ἀντὶ τοῦ πρώτου, Ἤδη γὰρ ἕδρα Ζεὺς ἐν ἐσχάτῳ θεῶν (ἔχει γὰρ ἕδραν. Brunck.)

[2] Rv. iv. 1. 5. स त्वं नो अग्नेऽवमो भवोती नेदिष्ठो अस्या उषसो व्युष्टौ॥ "Come down to us, O Agni, with thy help, be thou most near to us to-day as the dawn flashes forth."

[3] इन्द्रो वै देवानामोजिष्ठो बलिष्ठः। Kaushîtaki-brâhmaṇa, vi. 14.

of the Maṇḍalas, was the result of a previous agreement, and that the Maṇḍalas themselves do not represent collections made independently by different families, but collections carried out simultaneously in different localities under the supervision of one central authority.

Another indication of the systematic arrangement of the Maṇḍalas, is contained in the Âprî hymns.

There are ten Aprî-sûktas in the Rig-veda: —

1. I. 13., by Medhâtithi, of the family of the Kâṇvas (ii. b.); 12 verses.

2. I. 142, by Dîrghatamas, son of Uchathya, of the family of the Ângirasas (ii. a.); 13 verses. (Indra.)

3. I. 188, by Agastya, of the family of the Agastis (vii.); 11 verses. (Tanûnapât.)

4. II. 3, by Gṛitsamada, son of Śunahotra, (Ângirasa), adopted by Śunaka (Bhârgava) (i. 7.); 11 verses. (Narâśansa.)

5. III. 4, by Viśvâmitra, son of Gâthin, of the family of the Viśvâmitras (iv.); 11 verses. (Tanûnapât.)

6. V. 5, by Vasuśruta, son of Atri, of the family of the Âtreyas (iii.); 11 verses. (Narâśansa.)

7. VII. 2, by Vasishṭha, son of Mitrâvaruṇau, of the family of the Vâsishṭhas (vi.); 11 verses. (Narâśansa.)

8. IX. 5, by Asita or Devala, of the family of the Kâśyapas (v.); 11 verses. (Tanûnapât.)

9. X. 70, by Sumitra, of the family of the Bâdhryaśvas i. (6.); 11 verses. (Narâśansa.)

10. X. 110, by Râma, the son of Jamadagni, or by Jamadagni, of the family of the Jâmadagnyas (i. 2.); 11 verses. (Tanûnapât.)

These hymns consist properly of 11 verses, each of

which is addressed to a separate deity. Their order is as follows: —

First verse, to Agni Idhma or Susamiddha, the lighted fire.

Second verse, to Tanûnapât, the sun hidden in the waters or the clouds, or to Narâśansa, the rising sun, praised by men.

Third verse, to the Iḷas, the heavenly gifts, or Îḷita, Agni, implored to bring them.

Fourth verse, to Barhish, the sacrificial pile of grass.

Fifth verse, to Devîr dvâraḥ, the gates of heaven.

Sixth verse, to Ushâsâ-naktau, dawn and night.

Seventh verse, to Daivyau hotârau prachetasau (*i. e.* Agni and Âditya, or Agni and Varuṇa, or Varuṇa and Âditya; Shaḍguruśishya).

Eighth verse, to the three goddesses Sarasvatî, Ilâ, Bhâratî.

Ninth verse, to Tvashṭṛi, the creator.

Tenth verse, to Vanaspati, the tree of the sacrifice.

Eleventh verse, to the Svâhâkṛitis. (Viśve Devâḥ; Shaḍguruśishya.)

The only differences in the ten Âprî hymns of the Rig-veda arise from the name by which the second deity is invoked. It is Tanûnapât in hymns 3, 5, 8, 10; Narâśansa in hymns 4, 6, 7, 9; whereas in hymns 1 and 2 the second deity is invoked under either name in two separate verses. This raises the number in these two hymns to twelve, and this number is again raised to thirteen in hymn 2, by the addition at the end of a separate invocation of Indra.

The whole construction of these hymns is clearly artificial. They share the character of the hymns which we find in the Sâma and Yajur-vedas, being evidently composed for sacrificial purposes. Nevertheless, we find these artificial hymns in seven out of the ten Maṇḍalas, in I., II., III., V., VII., IX., X. This proves a previous agreement among the collectors. For some reason or other, each family wished to have its own Âprî hymn, a hymn which had to be recited by the Hotṛi priest, previous to the immolation of certain victims [1], and such a hymn was inserted, not once for all in the Sanhitâ, but ten times over. Some of the verses in the Âprî hymns are mere repetitions, and even families so hostile to each other as the Vasishṭhas and Viśvâmitras have some verses in common in these Âprî hymns. But, if on one side the presence of the Âprî hymns in different Maṇḍalas proves a certain advance of the ceremonial system in the Mantra period, and the influence of a priestly society even in the first collection of the hymns; it proves likewise, that the traditional distribution of the Maṇḍalas among various Vedic families is not a merely arbitrary arrangement. These families insisted on having each their own Âprî hymn recorded, and whereas for the general ceremonial, as fixed in the Brâhmaṇas and Sûtras, the family of the poet of certain hymns employed at the sacrifices, is never taken into account, we find an exception made in favour of the Âprî hymns. If a verse of Viśvâmitra is once fixed by the Brâhmaṇas and Sûtras as part of any of the solemn sacrifices, no sacrificer, even if he were of the family of the Vasishṭhas, would have a right to replace that verse by another. But with regard to the Âprî hymns that liberty is conceded. The Aitareya-brâhmaṇa records

[1] Burnouf, Journal Asiatique, 1850, p. 249. Roth, Nirukta, p. xxxvi.

this fact in the most general form.[1] "Let the priest use the Âprîs according to the Ṛishi. If he uses the Âprîs according to the Ṛishi, he does not allow the sacrificer to escape from the relationship of that Ṛishi." Âśvalâyana enters more into details.[2] He says that those who belong to the Śunakas should use the hymn of Gṛitsamada; those who belong to the Vasishṭhas, that of Vasishṭha. The Âprî hymn of Râma or Jamadgni he allows to be used by all families (excepting the Śunakas and Vasishṭhas); but, he adds, that each family may choose the Âprî hymn of its own Ṛishi. How this is to be done is explained in a Śloka, ascribed to Śaunaka.[3] He ascribes the first Âprî hymn to the Kaṇvas; the second to the Angiras', with the exception of the Kaṇvas; the third to the Agastis; the fourth to the Śunakas; the fifth to the Viśvâmitras; the sixth to the Atris; the seventh to the Vasishṭhas; the eighth to the Kaśyapas; the ninth to the Badhryaśvas; the tenth to the Bhṛigus, with the exception of the Śunakas and Badhryaśvas.[4]

The original purpose of the Âprî hymns, and the

[1] यथऋष्याप्रीणीयात् यद्यथऋष्याप्रीणाति यजमानमेव तद्बंधुताया नोत्सृजति। Ait.-br. ii. 4.

[2] Âśv.-sûtra, iii. 2.

[3] तत्र भगवता शौनकेन यथर्षिपत्त आप्रीविवेकार्थमेव श्लोक उक्तः।

कण्वोऽंगिरोऽगस्त्यः शुनको विश्वामित्रोऽत्रिरेव च।
वसिष्टः कश्यपो बध्र्यश्वो जमदग्निरथोत्तमः॥

[4] सगोत्राणामपि भिन्नार्षेयत्वसंभवात् Nârâyaṇa on Âśv. Śrauta-sû. iv. 1.

motive for allowing the priest to choose among them according to the family to which his client belonged, are difficult to discover. An ancient author of the name of Gâṇagari[1], endeavoured to prove from the fact that one and the same Âprî hymn *may* be used by all, that all people belong really and truly to one family. It is possible, indeed, that the Âprî hymns may have been songs of reconciliation, and that they were called *âprî*, *i. e.* appeasing hymns, not from their appeasing the anger of the gods, but the enmities of members of the same or different families. However that may be, they certainly do prove that there had been an active intercourse between the ancient families of India long before the final collection of the ten books, and that these ten books were collected and arranged by men who took more than a merely poetical interest in the ancient sacred poetry of their country.

Although we see from these indications that the collection of the hymns which we possess in the Rig-veda took place during a period when the influence of the Brahmans, as a priestly caste, had made itself felt in India, we must claim, nevertheless, for this collection a character not yet exclusively ceremonial. Not only is the order of the hymns completely independent of the order of the sacrifices, but there are numerous hymns in our collection which could never have been used at any sacrifice. This is not

[1] सर्वे समानगोत्राः स्युरिति गाणगरिः कथं ह्याप्रीसूक्तानि भवेयुः। Âśv.-sûtras, xii. 10. See also Anuvâkânukramaṇî-bhâshya, śloka 7. हे शाकलाः। के ते। सर्वेषां शाकलत्वं आप्रीद्वारेण॥

the case with the other Vedas. Every hymn, every verse, every invocation in the Sanhitâs of the Sâma and Yajur-vedas are employed by the Udgâtṛis and Adhvaryus, whereas the hymns of the Rig-veda are by no means intended to be all employed by the Hotṛi priests. If we speak of the sacred poetry of the Brahmans, that of the Sâma and Yajur-vedas is sacred only because it is used for sacrificial purposes, that of the Rig-veda is sacred, because it had been handed down as a sacred heir-loom from the earliest times within the memory of man. The sacredness of the former is matter of system and design, that of the latter is a part of its origin.

There is an objection that might be raised against this view, and which deserves to be considered. No one acquainted with the ceremonial of the Brahmans could well maintain that, after the final division of that ceremonial among the three classes of priests, a collection like that of the Rig-veda could have been conceived. The Rig-veda is not a Veda for the Hotṛi priest, in the same sense in which the Sâma and Yajur-vedas are for the Udgâtṛi and Adhvaryu priests. But it might be said that there is a fourth class of priests, the Brahman class, and that the Rig-veda might have been collected for their special benefit. In order to answer this objection, we shall have to examine more closely the real character of the four classes of priests.

Âśvalâyana (iv. 1.), says that there are four priests, each having three men under him. These are:

I. Hotṛi, with Maitrâvaruṇa, Achhâvâka, Grâvastut.[1]

[1] This is not the order as given in Âśvalâyana; he places the Brahman and his three men before the Udgâtṛi and his attendants.

II. Adhvaryu, with Pratiprasthâtṛi, Neshṭṛi, Unnetṛi.

III. Udgâtṛi, with Prastotṛi, Âgnîdhra or Agnîdh, Potṛi.

IV. Brahman, with Brâhmaṇâchhansin, Pratihartṛi, Subrahmaṇya.

These sixteen priests are commonly called by the name of Ṛitvij, and are chosen by the man in whose favour the sacrifice is offered, the Yajamâna or Svâmin. There are other priests, such as the Śamitṛi, (the slayer,) the Vaikartas, (the butchers,) the Chamasâdhvaryus, (the assistants of the Adhvaryus,) but they do not rank as Ṛitvij. The Kaushîtakins admit a seventeenth Ṛitvij, the so-called Sadasya, who is to superintend the whole sacrifice.[1] This large array of

Some would seem to place the Brahman first of all, but Âśvalâyana (Gṛihya, i. 22.) remarks that the Brahman is first chosen when there is an election of four priests only. If all the sixteen are chosen, then the Hotri comes first, afterwards the Brahman, thirdly the Adhvaryu, and lastly the Udgâtṛi.

[1] Âśv.-Gṛihya, i. 22. सदस्यं सप्तदशं कौषीतकिनः समामनंति स कर्मणामुपद्रष्टा भवतीति। सप्तदशग्रहणमृत्विक्त्वधर्मो भवतीति ज्ञापनार्थं॥ This is confirmed by the Kaushîtaki-brâhmaṇa. Other authorities admit several Sadasyas. (शास्त्रांतरेऽनेके दृष्टाः) For the Sattra sacrifices a seventeenth priest, called the Gṛihapati, lord of the house, is admitted. He is not considered as the Yajamâna, but seems to be the actual sacrificer. (गृहपतिसंज्ञकेन केवलयजमानपदार्थकारिणा सप्तदशेन पुरुषेण सहिताः Nârâyaṇa on Âśv. Śrauta-sûtra, iv. 1.) In the Aitareya-brâhmaṇa (vii. 1.), where the division of the animal among the various priests is described, we have the sixteen Ṛitvij, and besides one Sadasya, three Gṛihapatis (probably the sacri-

priests was only wanted for certain grand sacrifices. In the Gautama-sûtra-bhashya (p. 30.) we are told that for the Agnihotra and Aupâsana one priest only, the Adhvaryu, was needed; for the Darśapûrṇamâsa, four; for the Châturmâsyas five; for the Paśubandha six; for the Jyotishṭoma sixteen. Âśvalâyana prescribes the sixteen priests for the sacrifices called Ahîna (sacrifices lasting from two to eleven days), and Ekâha (sacrifices of one day), and restricts the seventeen priests to the Sattras (sacrifices lasting from thirteen to one hundred days). Each of the four classes of these priests had peculiar duties to perform. These duties were prescribed in the Brâhmaṇas. The duties of the Hotṛi are laid down in the Brâhmaṇas of the Bahvṛichas, such as the Kaushîtaki and Aitareya-brâhmaṇas; those of the Adhvaryu in the Brâhmaṇas of the Charakas (the Taittirîyaka) and in the Brâhmaṇas of the Vâjasaneyins (the Śatapatha); those of the Udgâtṛi in the Brâhmaṇas of the Chhandogas (the Tâṇḍya.) Âpastamba, who describes the sacrifice in his Paribhâshâ-sûtras[1], says that it is prescribed by the three Vedas, the Rig-veda, Yajur-veda and Sâma-veda.[2] "The Hotṛi," he says,

ficer himself, one who acts for him, and one who acts for his wife), one Śamitṛi (a slayer, who need not be a Brahman), two Vaikartas (butchers), several Upagâtṛis (choristers), and an Âtreya, Other wives (patnîs), besides the bhâryâ, are mentioned as present. In the Tâṇḍya-brâhmaṇa (25. 15.) the Pratiprasthâtṛi is left out. but two Adhvaryus, two Unnetṛis, and two Abhigarâpagarau are mentioned.

[1] Translated by me in the ninth volume of the German Oriental Society.

[2] स त्रिभिर्वेदैर्विधीयते॥३॥

ऋग्वेदयजुर्वेदसामवेदैः॥४॥

"performs his duties with the Rig-veda, the Udgâtṛi with the Sâma-veda, the Adhvaryu with the Yajur-veda; the Brahman with all the three Vedas."

The Adhvaryus were the priests who were intrusted with the material performance of the sacrifice. They had to measure the ground, to build the altar (vedi), to prepare the sacrificial vessels, to fetch wood and water, to light the fire, to bring the animal and immolate it. They formed, as it would seem, the lowest class of priests, and their acquirements were more of a practical than an intellectual character. Some of the offices which would naturally fall to the lot of the Adhvaryus, were considered so degrading, that other persons besides the priests were frequently employed in them. The Śamitṛi, for instance, who had to slay the animal, was not a priest, he need not even be a Brahman[1], and the same applies to the Vaikartas, the butchers, and the so-called Chamasâdhvaryus. The number of hymns and invocations which they had to use at the sacrifices was smaller than that of the other priests. These, however, they had to learn by heart. But as the chief difficulty consisted in the exact recitation of hymns, and in the close observance of all the euphonic rules, as taught in the Prâtiśâkhyas, the Adhvaryus were allowed to mutter their hymns[2], so that no one at a distance could

ऋग्वेदेन होता करोति॥१६॥
सामवेदेनोद्गाता॥१७॥
यजुर्वेदेनाध्वर्युः॥१८॥
सर्वैर्ब्रह्मा॥१९॥

[1] Ait.-brâhmaṇa, vii. 1.

[2] उपांशु यजुर्वेदेन॥९॥ करणवदशब्दममनः प्रयोगमु-

either hear or understand them. Only in cases where the Adhvaryu had to speak to other officiating priests, commanding them to perform certain duties[1], he was of course obliged to speak with a loud and distinct voice. All these verses and all the invocations which the Adhvaryus had to use, were collected in the ancient liturgy of the Adhvaryus together with the rules of the sacrifice. In this mixed form they exist in the Taittirîyaka. Afterwards the hymns were collected by themselves, separated from the ceremonial rules, and this collection is what we call the *Yajurveda-sanhitâ*, or the prayer-book of the Adhvaryu priests.

There were some parts of the sacrifice, which according to ancient custom, had to be accompanied by songs, and hence another class of priests arose whose particular office it was to act as the chorus. This naturally took place at the most solemn sacrifices only. Though as yet we have no key as to the character

पांशु। अन्यत्राश्रुतप्रत्याश्रुतप्रवरसंवादसंप्रेषेभ्य॥१०॥ एतेषामुच्चारणस्य परार्थत्वादुच्चैष्ट्वमेव॥

[1] An instance of this occurs in a passage of the Aitareya-brâhmaṇa, translated by Prof. Roth. The first words (ii. 2.) अंज्मो यूपमनुब्रूहि are spoken by the Adhvaryu, and not, as Professor Roth supposes, by the Hotṛi. It is the Adhvaryu only who can say, "We anoint the sacrificial stake, do thou accompany us with the hymns." A passage like this, as it is addressed to another priest, the Adhvaryu would have to pronounce with a loud voice. The Brâhmaṇa itself says, इत्याहाध्वर्युः "so says the Adhvaryu." The presha, or command, "anubrûhi," can only be addressed to the Hotṛi, and there was no ground for placing the following verses in the mouth of the Adhvaryu. Roth, Nirukta, xxxiv.

of the music which the Udgâtṛis performed, we can see from the numerous and elaborate rules, however unintelligible, that their music was more than mere chanting. The words of their songs were collected in the order of the sacrifice, and this *libretto* is what we possess under the name of *Sâma-veda-sanhitâ*, or the prayer-book of the Udgâtṛi priests.[1]

Distinct from these two classes, we have a third class of priests, the Hotṛis, whose duty it was to recite certain hymns during the sacrifice in praise of the deities to whom any particular act of the sacrificer was addressed. Their recitation was loud and distinct, and required the most accurate knowledge of the rules of euphony or Śikshâ. The Hotṛis, as a class, were the most highly educated order of priests. They were supposed to know both the proper pronunciation and the meaning of their hymns, the order and employment of which was taught in the Brâhmaṇas of the Bahvṛichas. But while both the Adhvaryus and Udgâtṛis were confessedly unable to perform their duties without the help of their prayer-books, the Hotṛis were supposed to be so well versed in the ancient sacred poetry, as contained in the ten Maṇḍalas of the Rig-veda, that no separate prayer-book or Sanhitâ was ever arranged for their special benefit.

[1] The Sanhitâ consists of two parts; the Ârchika and Staubhika. The Ârchika, as adapted to the special use of the priests, exists in two forms, called Gânas, or Song-books, the Veyagâna and Âraṇyagâna. The Staubhika exists in the same manner as Ûhagâna and Uhyagâna. Cf. Benfey, Preface to his edition of the Sâma-veda-ârchika, Leipzig, 1848, and Weber, Ind. Studien, i. 30. The supposition that the modern origin of some of the hymns of the Rig-veda could be proved by their not occurring in the Sâma-veda, has been well refuted by Dr. Pertsch.

There is no Sanhitâ for the Hotṛis corresponding to the Sanhitâs of the Adhvaryus and Udgâtṛis. The Hotṛi learnt from the Brâhmaṇa, or in later times, from the Sûtra, what special duties he had to perform. He knew from those sources the beginnings or the names of the hymns which he had to recite at every part of the service. But in order to be able to use these indications, he had previously to know the whole body of Vedic poetry, so as to be ready to produce from the vast store of his memory whatever hymn or verse was called for at the sacrifice. There exists among the MSS. of Walker's Collection a work entitled, Âśvalâyana śâkhoktamantra-sanhitâ, a collection of hymns of the Âśvalâyana-śâkhâ, which contains the hymns as required according to the Gṛihya-sûtras of Âśvalâyana. It would have been easy to construct a similar collection for the Śrauta-sûtras, but such a collection was never made, and it is never alluded to in the ancient literature of the Brahmans.[1]

[1] Sâyaṇa (Rv. Bh. i. p. 23.) remarks that some verses of the Yajur-veda are called Ṛich in the Brâhmaṇas of the Adhvaryus. Thus the verse देवः सवितोत्पुनातु is called a Ṛich addressed to Savitṛi. Sâmans also are mentioned, as when it is said, "Singing the Sâman he sits down." In the Sâma-veda there are not only Ṛich verses, but also Yajush invocations, such as अच्चितमसि, अच्युतमसि, प्राणसंशितमसि। The Hotṛi priests have likewise to use invocations which would more properly be called Yajush, such as अवेरपोऽध्वर्या३उ "Adhvaryu, hast thou got the water?" to which the Adhvaryu replies: उतेमनंनमुः "Yes, it has come." Here the Commentator says, होतुर्यजुरात्मकं कंचिन्मंत्रं विधत्ते॥

If then the Rig-veda-sanhitâ was not composed for the special benefit of the Hotṛis, much less of the other two classes of priests, it might be supposed that it had nevertheless a sacrificial character, and was intended to assist the fourth class of priests or the Brahman, properly so called. The Brahman, as we saw, had to watch the three classes of priests and to correct any mistake they might commit. He was, therefore, supposed to know the whole ceremonial and all the hymns employed by the Hotṛi, Adhvaryu, and Udgâtṛi. Now the Rig-veda does contain most of the hymns of the other two Vedas[1], and in several places it is maintained that the Brahman ought properly to be a Hotṛi. All this would render it not improbable that the Rig-veda-sanhitâ belonged to the same age as the other two Sanhitâs, that its collection was suggested by the same idea which led to the collection of the hymns of the other two classes of priests, and that, for the special benefit of the Brahman, it comprehended in one body all the hymns which the Hotṛi, the Adhvaryu, and Udgâtṛi, were expected to know singly. In this case the Rig-veda-sanhitâ,

[1] The invocations, properly called Yajush, are of course not to be found in the Rig-veda. Some of the hymns of the Sâma and Yajur-vedas, which have a more modern appearance, are to be found in the tenth Maṇḍala of the Rig-veda, or among the latest additions, such as the Vâlakhilyas. There are, however, some, which, though they occur in the Sâma and Yajur-vedas, are not to be found in the Rig-veda. This may possibly be accounted for by the fact that we do not possess all the Śâkhâs of the Rig-veda. The differences also in the text of hymns, as read in the three Vedas, must be ascribed to the influence of early Śâkhâs, and cannot be used as an argument for determining the more or less ancient date of the three Vedas.

instead of being more ancient, would in fact represent the latest collection of a sacred poetry.

It would be of no avail to appeal to the testimony of later authorities, such as the Purâṇas, in order to refute this theory. The Vishṇu-purâṇa (p. 276), for instance, has the following remark on this subject: "Vyâsa," it is said, "divided the one sacrificial Veda into four parts, and instituted the sacrificial rite administered by the four kinds of priests, in which it was the duty of the Adhvaryu to recite the Yajush verses or direct the ceremony; of the Hotṛi to repeat the Ṛich; of the Udgâtṛi to chaunt the Sâman; and of the Brahman, to pronounce the formula called Atharvan. Then the Muni, having collected together the hymns called Ṛich, composed the Rig-veda, &c., and, with the Atharvaṇs, he composed the rules of all the ceremonies suited to kings, and the function of the Brahman agreeably to practice." This passage only serves to show that the authors of the Purâṇas were entirely ignorant of the tone and character of the Vedic literature. For although the Brahman priest was the only Ṛitvij who had occasionally to use passages from the Atharva-veda, blessings, imprecations, etc.; yet the so-called Atharva-veda had nothing in common with the three ancient Vedas, and contained no information on the general features of the great sacrifices, such as would have been indispensable to the superintendent of the other priests.[1]

[1] Prasthâna-bheda, p. 16. l. 10. अथर्ववेदस्तु यज्ञानुपयुक्तः शांतिपौष्टिकाभिचारादिकर्मप्रतिपादकत्वेनात्यंतविलक्षण एव। Against this statement that of Kumârila should be taken into

The real answer to a supposition which would assign the Rig-veda-sanhitâ to the Brahman is, that to him also that collection of hymns would have been of no practical utility. He would have learnt from it many a hymn never called for, never used at any sacrifice; and he would have had to unlearn the order both of hymns and verses whenever he wished to utilise his knowledge for the practical objects of his station.

We may, therefore, safely ascribe the collection of the Rig-veda, or, as Professor Roth calls it, the historical Veda, to a less practical age than that of the Brâhmaṇa period; to an age, not entirely free from the trammels of a ceremonial, yet not completely enslaved by a system of mere formalities; to an age no longer creative and impulsive, yet not without some power of upholding the traditions of a past that spoke to a later generation of men through the very poems which they were collecting with so much zeal and accuracy.

The work of the Mantra period is not entirely represented by the collection of the ancient hymns. Such a work would be sufficient in itself to give a character to an age, and we might appeal, in the history of ancient Greek literature, to the age of the Diaskeuasts. A generation which begins to collect has entered into a new phase of life. Nations, like individuals, become conservative when they cease to trust implicitly in themselves, and have learnt from experience that they are not better than their

account: (i. 3.) शांतिपुष्ट्यभिचारार्था ह्येकब्रह्मलिंगाश्रिताः क्रियास्तत्र प्रमीयंतेऽत्राप्येवात्मीयगोचराः॥

fathers. But though the distinctive feature of the Mantra period consisted in gathering the fruits of a bye-gone spring, this was not the only work which occupied the Brahmans of that age. Where poems have to be collected from the mouth of the people, they have likewise to be arranged. Corrections are supposed to be necessary; whole verses may have to be supplied. After collecting and correcting a large number of poems, many a man would feel disposed to try his own poetical powers; and if new songs were wanted, it did not require great talent to imitate the simple strains of the ancient Ṛishis. Thus we find in the Rig-veda, that, after the collection of the ten Maṇḍalas was finished, some few hymns were added, generally at the end of a chapter, which are known by the name of Khilas. We can hardly call them successful imitations of the genuine songs; but in India they seem to have soon acquired a certain reputation. They found their way into the Sanhitâs of the other Vedas; they are referred to in the Brâhmaṇas, and though they are not counted in the Anukramaṇîs, together with the original hymns, they are there also mentioned as recognized additions.

Besides these hymns, which were added after the collection of the ten books had been completed, there is another class of hymns, actually incorporated in the sacred Decads, but which nevertheless must be ascribed to poets who were imitators of earlier poets, and whose activity, whether somewhat anterior to, or contemporaneous with the final edition of the Rig-veda-sanhitâ, must be referred to the same Mantra period. We need not appeal to the tradition of the Brahmans, who, in matters of this kind, are extremely untrustworthy. They place a very small interval between the latest poets of the hymns and the final collection of the ten books. The latter they ascribe to Kṛishṇa Dvaipâyana Vyâsa, the embodiment of the Indian διασκευή, whereas one of the poets whose hymns form part of the Sanhitâ, is Parâśara, the reputed father of Vyâsa.

But we have better evidence in the hymns themselves, that some of their authors belonged to a later generation than that of the most famous Ṛishis. The most celebrated poets of the Veda are those who are now called the Mâdhyamas [1], from the fact of their hymns standing between the first and the last books of our collection. They are Gṛitsamada, (2d Maṇḍala), Viśvâmitra (3d Maṇḍala), Vâmadeva (4th Maṇḍala), Atri (5th Maṇḍala), Bharadvâja (6th Maṇḍala), and Vasishṭha (7th Maṇḍala). Added to these are, in the beginning, the hymns of various poets, collected in the first Maṇḍala, called the book of the Śatarchins, from the fact that each poet contributed about a hundred verses; and at the end, the book of the Pragâtha hymns (8th Maṇḍala), the book of the Soma hymns (9th Maṇḍala), and the book of long and short hymns, ascribed to the Kshudrasûkta and Mahâsûkta poets, which, in accordance with its very name, is a miscellaneous collection.

It by no means follows that all the hymns of the seven middle Ṛishis are more ancient than those of the first and the last books; or that these books contain nothing but modern hymns. But the very name of *Mâdhyama*, given to the poets of the books from the second to the seventh, shows that they were considered, even by the Brahmans, as dis-

[1] See page 42, note 2, and page 59.

tinct from the first and the three last books. They are not the middle books numerically, but they are called so because they stand by themselves, in the midst of other books of a more miscellaneous character.

Traces, however, of earlier and later poems are to be found through the whole collection of the Rig-veda; and many hymns have been singled out by different scholars as betraying a later origin than the rest. All such hymns I refer to the Mantra period, to an age which, though chiefly occupied in collecting and arranging, possessed likewise the power of imitating, and carrying on the traditions of a former age.

It is extremely difficult to prove the modern origin of certain hymns, and I feel by no means convinced by the arguments which have been used for this purpose. At present, however, I need not enter into the minutiæ of this critical separation of ancient and modern poetry. It is not my object to prove that this or that hymn is more modern than the rest; but I only wish to establish the general fact that, taken as a whole, the hymns do contain evidence of having been composed at various periods.

In order to guard against misconceptions, it should be understood that, if we call a hymn modern, all that can be meant is that it was composed during the period which succeeded the first spring of Vedic poetry, *i. e.* during the Mantra period. There is not a single hymn in the Rig-veda that could be ascribed to the Brâhmaṇa period. Even a few of the *Khilas*, modern as they appear to us, are presupposed by the Brâhmaṇas and quoted, together with other more ancient hymns. The most modern hymns in the Rig-veda-sanhitâ if our calculations are right, must have been composed previous to 800 B.C., previous to the first introduction of prose composition.

In order to prove that the hymns which are now thrown together into one body of sacred poetry, were not the harvest of one single generation of poets, we have only to appeal to the testimony of the poets themselves, who distinguish between ancient and modern hymns. Not only has the tradition of the Brahmans, which is embodied in the Anukramaṇîs, assigned certain hymns to Ṛishis, who stand to each other in the relation of father and son, and grandson, but the hymns themselves allude to earlier poets, and events which in some are represented as present, are mentioned in others as belonging to the past. The argument which Dr. Roth[1] has used in order to prove the comparatively modern date of the Âtharvaṇa, applies with equal force to some of the hymns of the Rig-veda. Here, also, the names of Purumîḷha, Vasishṭha, Jamadagni, and others, who are known as the authors of certain hymns, are mentioned in other hymns as sages, who in former times enjoyed the favour of the gods.

"As our ancestors have praised thee, we will praise thee," is a very frequent sentiment of the Vedic poets. A new song was considered a special honour to the gods. The first hymn of the Rig-veda gives utterance to this sentiment. "Agni," says Madhuchhandas, "thou who art worthy of the praises of ancient, and also of living poets, bring hither thou the gods."

Viśvâmitra, the father of Madhuchhandas, and

[1] Abhandlungen, p. 43.

himself one of the ancient Ṛishis, concludes his first hymn[1] with the words, "I have proclaimed, O Agni, these thy ancient songs[2], and new songs for thee who art old. These great libations have been made to him who showers benefits upon us: the sacred fire has been kept from generation to generation."

In another hymn[3], Viśvâmitra distinguishes between three classes of hymns, and speaks of Indra as having been magnified by ancient, middle, and modern songs.

The sacrifice itself is sometimes represented as a thread which unites the living with the departed, and through them, with the first ancestors of man, the gods.[4] The son carries on the weaving which was interrupted by the death of his father[5], and the poet, at the beginning of a sacred rite[6], exclaims, "I believe I see, with the eye of the mind, those who in byegone days performed this sacrifice." With a similar feeling, Viśvâmitra, in his morning prayer, looks back to his fathers, who have gazed on the rising sun before him, and have exalted the power of the gods:[7]

"To Indra goes my thought, spoken out from the heart, to him, the Lord, it goes, fashioned by the bard. It awakes thee when it is recited at the sa-

[1] Rv. iii. 1. 20.

[2] Janimâ, originally creations, ποιήματα; it is likewise explained as works. Cf. iii. 39. 1.

[3] Rv. iii. 32. 13.

[4] See my Essay on the Funeral Ceremonies, p. xxii. note.

[5] Rv. x. 130. 1.

[6] Rv. x. 130. 7.

[7] Rv. iii. 39.

crifice; Indra, take heed of that which is made for thee!

"Rising even before the day, awakening thee when recited at the sacrifice, clothed in sacred white raiments[1], this is our prayer, *the old*, *the prayer of our fathers*.

"The Dawn, the mother of the twins, has given birth to the twins (*i. e.* Day and Night)—the top of my tongue fell, for he (the Sun) came. The twins, who have come near the root of the Sun, assume their bodies as they are born together, the destroyers of darkness.

"Amongst men there is no one to scoff at them who were our fathers, who fought among the cattle. Indra, the mighty and powerful, has stretched out their firm folds."[2]

Vasishṭha, another of the ancient Ṛishis, speaks likewise of ancient and modern hymns by which others, besides his own family, secured the favour of the gods.[3] "Whatever poets, ancient or modern, wise men, made prayers to thee, O Indra, ours may be thy propitious friendship: protect us, O gods, always with your blessings!"

One of the greatest events in the life of Vasishṭha, was the victory which King Sudâs achieved under his guidance. But in the Maṇḍala of the Vasishṭhas, the same event is sometimes alluded to as belonging

[1] The Viśvâmitras wore white raiments. Their colour, called arjuna, can hardly be distinguished, however, from the colour of the dress of the Vasishṭhas, which is called śveta.

[2] Gotra, originally a hurdle, then those who live within the same hurdles or walls; a family, a race.

[3] Rv. vii. 23. 9.

to the past, and in one of the hymns ascribed to the same Vasishṭha we read: "Committing our sons and offspring to the same good protection which Aditi, Mitra, and Varuṇa, like guardians, give to Sudâs, let us not make our gods angry."

These passages, which might be greatly increased, will be sufficient to show that there were various generations of Vedic poets. The traces of actual imitations are less considerable than we might expect under such circumstances; and where we do meet with stereotyped phrases, it is often difficult to say which poet used them for the first time. When we find Dîrghatamas Auchathya, beginning a hymn to Vishṇu with the words, "Let me now proclaim the manly deeds of Vishṇu;" and another hymn of Hiraṇyastûpa Ângirasa to Indra, beginning with, "Let me now proclaim the manly deeds of Indra," we may suppose that the one hymn was composed with a pointed reference to the other; but we cannot tell which of the two was the original, and which the copy.

The fact, however, of ancient and modern hymns being once admitted, we may hope to arrive gradually at some criteria by which to fix the relative age of single hymns. Some of the hymns betray their comparatively modern origin by frequent allusion to ceremonial subjects. I do not mean to say that the sacrifice as such, was not as old and primitive an institution as sacred poetry itself. Most of the hymns owe their origin to sacrifices, to public or domestic holy-days. But those sacrifices were of a much more simple nature than the later Vedic ceremonial. When the father of a family was priest, poet, and king, in one person, there was no thought as yet of distributing the ceremonial duties among sixteen priests, each performing his own peculiar office, or of measuring the length of every log that should be put on the fire, and determining the shape of every vessel in which the libations should be offered. It was only after a long succession of sacrifices that the spontaneous acts and observances of former generations would be treasured up, and established as generally binding. It was only after the true meaning of the sacrifice was lost, that unmeaning ceremonies could gain that importance which they have in the eyes of priests. If a hymn addressed to the gods had been heard, if a famine had ceased after a prayer, an illness been cured with a charm, an enemy been vanquished with war songs; not only would these songs, however poor, be kept and handed down in a family as the most precious heirloom, but the position in which the poet recited them, the time of the day, the most minute circumstances of every act, would be superstitiously preserved, in order to insure the future efficiency of the prayer. This was the origin of a ceremonial so complicated as that of the Brahmans. Now, we find in some of the hymns allusions which refer, not to a naturally growing, but to an artificial and a decaying ceremonial.

The most ancient name for a priest by profession was *Purohita*, which only means *præpositus* or *præses*. The Purohita, however, was more than a priest. He was the friend and counsellor of a chief, the minister of a king, and his companion in peace and war. Vasishṭha and Viśvâmitra, who with their families have both been the Purohitas of King Sudâs, did more for the king than chanting hymns to implore the aid of their gods. Vasishṭha was with the army of Sudâs when that king conquered the ten kings who had crossed the Parushṇî (Hydraotis, Rawi); Viśvâmitra, when Sudâs himself crossed the Vipaś (Hyphasis, Beyah) and the Śatadru (Hesudrus, Sutlej).[1] The importance of their office is best shown by the violent contest which these two families of the Vasishṭhas and Viśvâmitras carried on, in order to secure for themselves the hereditary dignity of Purohita. There was a similar contest between the priests at the Court of Asamâti, and descendant of Ikshvâku. He, not satisfied with his four Purohitas, Bandhu, Subandhu, Śrutabandhu, and Viprabandhu, who were brothers and belonged to the family of the Gaupâyanas, dismissed them, and appointed two new priests (mâyâvinau). These new Purohitas, seeing that the Gaupâyanas used incantations against the life of King Asamâti, retaliated, and caused by their charms, the death of one of them, Subandhu. Thereupon the other three brothers composed a song to appease the wrath of the two priests, and to save their own lives. This song and some others connected with the same contest, form part of the 8th Ashṭaka of the Rig-veda.

The very fact of the office of Purohita being hereditary shows that it partook of a political character. It seems to have been so at an early time. In a hymn of the Rig-veda, i. 94. 6, where Agni is invoked under several priestly names, he is called, Janushâ Purohita or Purohita by birth. Cf. i. 102. 8. And we find several instances where priests, if once employed by a royal family, claim to be employed always. When Janamejaya Pârikshita ventured to perform a sacrifice

[1] See Prof. Roth's excellent essay on Vasishṭha and Viśvâmitra, in his work, "Zur Literatur und Geschichte des Veda," published as early as 1846.

without the Kaśyapas, he was forced by the Asita-mṛigas, a family of the Kaśyapas to employ them again. When Visvântara Saushadmana drove away the Syâparṇas from his sacrifice, he was prevailed upon by Râma Mârgaveya to call them back.[1] All this shows that the priestly office was of great importance in the ancient times of India.

The original occupation of the Purohita may simply have been to perform the usual sacrifices; but, with the ambitious policy of the Brahmans, it soon became a stepping-stone to political power. Thus we read in the Aitareya-brâhmaṇa: "Breath does not leave him before time; he lives to an old age; he goes to his full time, and does not die again, who has a Brahman as guardian of his land, as Purohita. He conquers power by power; obtains strength by strength; the people obey him, peaceful and of one mind."

Vâmadeva, in one of his hymns[2], expresses the same sentiment; and though he does not use the word Purohita, there can be little doubt that the Aitareya-brâhmaṇa is right in explaining the words Bṛihaspati and Brahman by Purohita.

"That king withstands his enemies with strong power who supports a Bṛihaspati[3] in comfort, praises him, and honours him as the first.

[1] Aitareya-br. vii. 27. Roth, Abhandlungen, p. 118. Weber, Ind. Studien, i. 39. Mârgaveya is a difficult name. It may be simply, as Sâyaṇa says, the son of his mother Mṛigû; but Mṛigû may be a variety of Bhṛigu, and thus confirm Lassen's conjecture that this Râma is Râma, the son of Jamadagni, of the race of Bhṛigu, commonly called Paraśu-râma. Cf. Weber, Ind. Stud. i. 216. Marghu is the name of Margiana in the Cuneiform Inscriptions.

[2] Rv. iv. 50. 7.

[3] "Bṛihaspati," says the Aitareya-brâhmaṇa, "was the Purohita of the gods, and the Purohitas of human kings are his successors."

"The king before whom there walks a priest, lives well established in his own house; to him the earth yields for ever, and before him the people bow of their own accord.

"Unopposed he conquers treasures, those of his enemies and his friends, himself a king, who makes presents to a Brahman: the gods protect him."

This shows that the position of the Brahmans at the courts of the Kshatriya kings was more influential than that of mere chaplains. They walked before the king, and considered themselves superior to him. In later times, when the performance of the ceremonies no longer devolved on the Purohita, the chief priest took the place of the so-called Brahman priest, who was the *episcopos* of the whole, though he himself took little active part in it. Thus at the sacrifice of Hariśchandra, described in the Aitareya-brâhmaṇa (vii. 16.), Ayâsya acts as Udgâtṛi, Jamadagni as Adhvaryu, Viśvâmitra as Hotṛi, and Vasishṭha, who is known as the Purohita of the Ikshvâku dynasty, as Brahman. In the Taittirîya-sanhitâ (iii. 5. 2.), we read: "Men were born, having a Vasishṭha for Purohita, and therefore a Vasishṭha is to be chosen as Brahman." In the Aitareya-brâhmaṇa again the Brahman is identified with Bṛihaspati, who was the Purohita, or pura-etṛi of the gods.

The original institution of a Purohita, as the spiritual adviser of a king or a chief, need not be regarded as the sign of a far advanced hierarchical system. The position of the Brahmans must have been a peculiar one in India from the very beginning. They appear from the very first as a class of men of higher intellectual power than the rest of the Aryan colonists; and their general position, if at all recognised, could hardly have been different from that of Vasishṭha in the camp of Sudâs. The hymns, therefore, which only allude to a Purohita, or priest in general, need not be ascribed to a late age. But when we meet in certain hymns, not only with these, but with various grades of priests, we may be sure that such hymns belong to the Mantra period, and not to the age of primitive Vedic poetry.

This is a question of degree. If we find such verses as "the singers sing thee, the chanters chant thee[1]," where the singers are called not by their technical name of Udgâtṛi, but Gâyatrins, and the chanters not by their technical name of Hotṛi, but Arkins, all we can say is that the later division of the sacrifice between Hotṛi and Udgâtṛi priests is here found in its first elements. It does not follow that there existed at that time two recognised classes of priests, still less that the Udgâtṛis were then in possession of their own Sanhitâ. But in Rv. v. 44. 14. we read:

"The Ṛich verses long for the god who watches; the Sâman verses go to him who watches; this Soma libation calls for him that watches: I, O Agni, am at home in thy friendship."[2]

Here it is clear that the distinction between Ṛich verses, that were recited, and Sâman verses, that were

[1] Rv. i. 10. गायंति त्वा गायत्रिणोऽर्चंत्यर्कमर्किणः।

[2] यो जगार तमृचः कामयंते यो जगार तमु सामानि यंति।
यो जगार तमयं सोम आह तवाहमस्मि सख्ये न्योकाः॥

Rv. viii. 3. 22. ऋक्सामाभ्यां॥

sung, must have been established, though again we need not go so far as to maintain the actual existence of a prayer-book for the Udgâtṛi priests.

The third class of priests, the Adhvaryus, who performed the principal acts of the sacrifice, are likewise alluded to in the hymns. We read Rv. iii. 36. 10: "Accept, O Indra, what is offered thee from the hand of the Adhvaryu, or the sacrifice of the libation of the Hotṛi."

There are several hymns which contain allusions to the Darśapûrṇamâsa, the famous New and Full Moon sacrifices. These sacrifices in themselves may have been of the greatest antiquity, as old as any attempt at a regulated worship of the gods. Passages, therefore, where we only meet with allusions to the phases of the moon, and their recurrent appeal to the human heart to render thanks to the unknown Powers that rule the changes of nature, and the chances of human life, prove by no means, as the Indian commentators suppose, that at the time of the ancient Vedic poets the lunar ceremonies were of the same solemn and complicated nature as in later times. We read, Rv. i. 194. 4: "Let us bring fuel, let us prepare oblations remembering thee at each conjunction of the moon.[1]

[1] I translate parva by conjunction, because parvaṇî, the dual, is used for the full and new moon; Âśvalâyana-sûtras, i. 3. 12. Mr. Weigle, in his interesting article on Canarese literature (Zeitschrift der Deutschen Morgenländischen Gesellschaft), states that *habba* or *pabba* means a festival in Canarese, whereas in Sanskrit its usual signification is a chapter of a book. Mr. Weigle therefore refers *pabba* to a class of words, which, in being transferred from the Sanskrit into the Dravidian languages, have changed their meaning. We see, however, that the old meaning of *parva* new and full moon, would account very well for the meaning attached to *pabba* in Canarese, a festival.

Do thou perfect our sacred acts that we may live long. Let us not fail in thy friendship, O Agni."[1] Passages like this do not necessitate the admission of a full-grown ceremonial, they only point to its natural beginnings. The same remark applies to the three daily prayers, at sun-rise, noon, and sun-set. Nature herself suggests these three periods as the most appropriate for rendering thanks to the heavenly givers of light and life. Thus Manu Vaivasvata[2] alludes several times to the three periods of the day which the gods themselves have fixed for their sacrifice, sun-rise (sûrya udyati, or sûra udite), mid-day (madhyandine divaḥ, or madhyandine), and sun-set (nimruchi, or âtuchi), and he calls this established order of the sacrifice *ṛita*, the law or the truth.

But when these sacrifices are mentioned with their technical names, when the morning, and noon, and evening prayers are spoken of as first, second, and third libation, we feel that we move in a different at-

[1] भरामेध्मं कृणवाम हवींषि ते चितयंतः पर्वणा पर्वणा वयं।
जीवातवे प्रतरं साधया धियोऽग्ने सख्ये मा रिषामा वयं तव॥

[2] Rv. viii. 27. 19:—

यदद्य सूर्य उद्यति प्रियक्षत्रा ऋतं दध।
यन्निम्रुचि प्रबुधि विश्ववेदसो यद्वा मध्यंदिने दिवः॥१९॥
यद्वाभिपित्वे असुरा ऋतं यते छर्दिर्येम वि दाशुषे।
वयं तद्वो वसवो विश्ववेदस उप स्थेयाम मध्य आ॥२०॥
यदद्य सूर उदिते यन्मध्यंदिन आतुचि।
वामं धत्थ मनवे विश्ववेदसो जुह्वानाय प्रचेतसे॥२१॥
वयं तद्वः सम्राज आ वृणीमहे पुत्रो न बहुपाय्यं।
अश्याम तदादित्या जुह्वतो हविर्येन वस्योऽनशामहै॥२२॥

mosphere, and that we are listening to priests rather than to poets. Thus Rv. iii. 28. 1:

"Agni, accept our offering, the cake, O Jâtavedas, at the *morning libation*, thou rich in prayer.

"The baked cake, O Agni, is prepared for thee alone indeed; accept it, O youngest of all the gods.

"Agni, eat the cake, offered to thee *when the day is over*, thou art the son of strength, stationed at the sacrifice.

"At the *mid day libation*, O Jâtavedas, accept here the cake, O sage! Agni, the wise do not diminish at the sacrifices the share of thee, who art great.

"Agni, as thou lovest at *the third libation* the cake, O son of strength, that is offered to thee, therefore, moved by our praise, take this precious oblation to the immortal gods to rouse them.

"Agni, thou who art growing, accept, O Jâtavedas, the offering, the cake, at the *close of day*."

This hymn contains in reality nothing but a set of invocations for the three daily libations; it uses the very words used in the ceremonial, and it would hardly have been written except by some pious priest brought up under the system of the Brahmanic ceremonial.

The technical names of the priests are of frequent occurrence. The name of *Ṛitvij* would not prove a great development of the ceremonial. It would only mean the priest who officiates at the various seasons. It was then that the sacred fire was kindled by friction. It was lighted in the morning day after day (dive dive), it was lighted at the full and new moon, and it was lighted likewise at each of the great natural divisions of the year. Thus it is said, Rv.

iii. 29. 10: "This wood is thy mother every season, born from which thou shonest. Do thou sit there, as thou knowest it, and make our prayers prosper."

There is nothing artificial in this. But when we meet with the names of the Ṛitvij priests, such as Potṛi, Âgnîdhra, Praśâstṛi, Neshṭṛi, Hotṛi, Adhvaryu, Brahman[1], we can no longer doubt that here we have to deal with late and artificial poetry. These names of priests are afterwards still further generalised, and transferred to Agni, who, as the god of fire, is supposed to carry the offerings of men to the seats of the gods. He is called the Purohita, or high-priest. Sapta-hotṛi also, and sapta-mânusha, acting as seven priests[2], are names applied to the god of the sacrificial flame.

There is a whole class of hymns commonly called *dânastutis*, or praises of gifts. They are the thanksgivings of certain priests for presents received from their royal patrons. All of these, like the Latin panegyrics, betray a modern character, and must be referred to the Mantra period. In the Brâhmaṇa period, however, not only are these panegyrics known, but the liberality of these royal patrons is held up to the admiration and imitation of later generations by stories which had to be repeated at the sacrifices. In the Śânkhâyana-sûtras (xvi. 11.), the following stories called Nârâśansa (neuter), are mentioned as fit for such occasions. The story of Śunaḥśepha; of Kakshîvat Auśija who received gifts from Svanaya Bhâvyaya; of Śyâvâśva Ârchanânasa who received gifts from Vaidadaśvi; of Bharadvâja who received gifts

[1] Rv. ii. 36.; ii. 37.

[2] These seven priests seem to be Hotṛi, Potṛi, Neshṭṛi, Agnîdh, Praśâstṛi, Adhvaryu and Brahmaṇ.

from Bṛibu the carpenter, and Prastoka Sârnjaya; of Vasishṭha who was Purohita of King Sudâs Paijavana; of Medhâthi, and how Âsanga Plâyogi having been a woman became a man; of Vatsa Kâṇva who received gifts from Tirindira Pâraśavyaya; of Vaśa Aśvya who received gifts from Pṛithuśravas Kânîna; of Praskaṇva who received gifts from Pṛishadhra Medhya Mâtariśva (sic); of Nâbhânedishṭha Mânava, who received gifts from the Angiras'." All these acts of royal liberality are recorded in the hymns of the Rig-veda, but the hymns themselves may safely be referred to the second age of Vedic poetry.

Another and most convincing proof that some of our hymns belong to a secondary period of Vedic poetry, is contained in a song, ascribed to Vasishṭha, in which the elaborate ceremonial of the Brahmans is actually turned into ridicule. The 103rd hymn in the 7th Maṇḍala, which is called a panegyric of the frogs, is clearly a satire on the priests; and it is curious to observe that the same animal should have been chosen by the Vedic satirist to represent the priests, which by the earliest satirist of Greece was selected as the representative of the Homeric heroes.

"After lying prostrate for a year, like Brahmans performing a vow, the frogs have emitted their voice, roused by the showers of heaven. When the heavenly waters fell upon them as upon a dry fish lying in a pond, the music of the frogs comes together, like the lowing of cows with their calves.

"When, at the approach of the rainy season, the rain has wetted them, as they were longing and thirsting, one goes to the other while he talks, like a son to his father, saying, akkhala (βρεκεκέξ κοάξκοάξ.)

"One of them embraces the other, when they revel in the shower of water, and the brown frog jumping after he has been ducked, joins his speech with the green one.

"As one of them repeats the speech of the other, like a pupil and his teacher, every limb of them is as it were in growth, when they converse eloquently on the surface of the water.

"One of them is Cow-noise, the other Goat-noise, one is brown, the other green; they are different though they bear the same name, and modulate their voices in many ways as they speak.

"Like Brahmans at the Soma sacrifice of Atirâtra, sitting round a full pond and talking, you, O frogs, celebrate this day of the year when the rainy season begins.

"These Brahmans with their Soma have had their say, performing the annual rite. These Adhvaryus, sweating whilst they carry the hot pots, pop out like hermits.

"They have always observed the order of the gods as they are to be worshipped in the twelvemonth; these men do not neglect their season; the frogs who had been like hot pots themselves are now released when the rainy season of the year sets in.

"Cow-noise gave, Goat-noise gave, the Brown gave, and the Green gave us treasures. The frogs who give us hundreds of cows, lengthen our life in the rich autumn."

There seems thus to be little room for doubt, if we consider the character of this and similar hymns, that we must make a distinction between two periods in the history of Vedic poetry, the one primitive, the other secondary. Poems, like those which we have just examined, are not the result of an original, free, and unconscious inspiration. They belong to an imitative, reflecting, and criticising age. An exact division between the ancient and the modern portions of the Rig-veda will propably be impossible even after these ancient relics have been studied with a much more searching accuracy than hitherto. The language, which might be expected to contain the safest indications of the more ancient or more modern date of certain hymns, has, owing to the influence of oral tradition, assumed an uniformity which baffles the most careful analysis. Nor would it be safe to trust to our preconceived notions as to the peculiar character of genuine and of artificial poetry. Some of the very latest poets may have been endowed with a truly poetical genius, when the originality and freshness of their thoughts would seem to place them in a better age. Nor is the fact that the ancient poets enunciate thoughts entirely their own, and with the full consciousness that what they say has never been said before, sufficient to give to all their productions so deep a stamp of truth and faith that our weakened eyes should always discern it. But although we may hesitate about single hymns, whether they are the productions of ancient or modern Ṛishis, we cannot hesitate as to the general fact that the ten books of the Rig-veda at the time they were finally collected, comprised the poetry of two different periods. This is the only important point for our purpose. We ascribe the later poets of the Veda to the Mantra period, so that we comprise within that period two apparently distinct, yet, in reality, very cognate tendencies. We suppose that the

Mantra period was an age of Epigonoi, occupied at first in imitating the works of their fathers, and towards the end engaged in the more useful employment of collecting all that was within reach, modern as well as ancient, and handing it down to the careful guardianship of later generations. Two hundred years will not be too long a time for the gradual progress of this work. There are several generations of modern poets, and probably two classes of collectors to be accommodated, and the work of the last collectors, the collectors of the Maṇḍalas, could not have commenced before the last line of every poem which now forms part of the ten Maṇḍalas was written. I therefore fix the probable chronological limits of the Mantra period between 800 and 1000 B.C.

Before we leave the Mantra period there is one question which, if it cannot be fully answered, requires at least to be carefully discussed. Was the collection of the ten books of Vedic hymns the work of persons cognisant of the art of writing or not? Were the 1017 hymns of the Rig-veda, after they had been gathered into one body, preserved by memory or on paper?

We can hardly expect to find an answer to this question in the hymns themselves. Most persons acquainted with the history of popular poetry among the principal nations of antiquity would be ready to admit that the original composition and preservation of truly national poetry were everywhere due to the unaided efforts of memory. Where writing is known, it is almost impossible to compose a thousand hymns without bringing in some such words as, writing, reading, paper, or pen. Yet there is not one single allusion in these hymns to anything connected with writing.

Let us consider the Old Testament.

The Ten Commandments were not only proclaimed by the voice of God, but Moses "went down from the mount, and the two tables of the testimony were in his hand: the tables were written on both their sides; on the one side and on the other were they written. And the tables were the work of God, and the writing was the writing of God, graven upon the tables." (Exodus xxxii. 15, 16.) Here we can have no doubt that the author of the Book of Exodus, and the people to whom it was addressed, were acquainted with the art of writing. Again we read (Exodus xxiv. 7.), that "Moses took the book of the covenant, and read in the audience of the people;" and (Exodus xxv. 16.), the Lord commanded Moses, saying, "Thou shalt put into the ark the testimony which I shall give thee." The covenant here spoken of must have existed as a book, or, at least, in some tangible form.

A nation so early acquainted with letters and books as the Jews would naturally employ some of the terms connected with writing in a metaphorical sense. Thus we read in the Psalms (lvi. 8.), "Put thou my tears into thy bottle: are they not in thy book?"

lxix. 28. "Let them be blotted out of the book of the living, and not be written with the righteous."

xl. 7. "Then said I, Lo I come: in the volume of the book it is written of me."

xlv. 1. "My tongue is the pen of a ready writer."

In the Book of Job (xix. 23.), we actually read, "Oh that my words were now written! oh that they were printed in a book! That they were graven with an iron pen and lead in the rock for ever!" "Printed" here can only mean "written."

Proverbs iii. 3. "Write them upon the table of thine heart."

In the Homeric poems, on the contrary, where the whole Grecian life lies before us in marvellous completeness and distinctness, there is not a single mention of writing. The σήματα λυγρὰ, carried by Bellerophon instead of a letter, are the best proof that, even for such purposes, not to speak of literary composition, the use of letters was unknown to the Homeric age. The art of writing, when it is not only applied to short inscriptions but to literature, forms such a complete revolution in the history of a nation, and in all the relations of society, both civil and political, that, in any class of ancient literature, the total absence of any allusion to writing, may safely be supposed to prove the absence of the art at the time when that literature arose. We know the complete regeneration of modern Europe which was wrought by the invention of printing. Every page of the literature of the sixteenth century, every pamphlet or fly-sheet of the Reformation, tells us that printing had been invented. The discovery of writing, and more especially the application of writing to literary purposes, was a discovery infinitely more important than that of printing. And yet we are asked to believe that Homer has hidden his light under a bushel, and erased every expression connected with writing from his poetical dictionary!

But though it is certain that the Homeric poets did not write, or, if we are to adopt the legendary language of certain critics, though it is certain that blind Homer did not keep a private secretary, there is no doubt that, at the time of Peisistratos, when the final collection of the Homeric poems took place, this collection was a collection of written poems. Peisistratos possessed a large library, and, though books were not so common in his time as they were in the time of Alcibiades, when every schoolmaster had his Iliad[1], yet, ever since the importation of paper into Greece, writing was a common acquirement of the educated classes of Greeks. The whole civilisation of Greece, and the rapid growth of Greek literature, has been ascribed to the free trade between Egypt and Greece, beginning with the Saidic dynasty.[2] Greece imported all its paper from Egypt; and without paper no Greek literature would have been possible. The skins of animals were too rare, and their preparation too expensive, to permit the growth of a popular literature. Herodotus mentions it as a peculiarity of the barbarians, that at his time some of them still wrote on skins only. Paper (papyrus or byblus) was evidently to Greece what linen paper was to Europe in the middle ages.[3]

Now, if we look for any similar traces in the history of Indian literature, our search is completely disappointed. There is no mention of writing-materials, whether paper, bark, or skins, at the time when the Indian Diaskeuasts collected the songs of their Ṛishis; nor is there any allusion to writing during the whole of the Brâhmaṇa period. This upsets the common theories about the origin of prose literature. According to Wolf[4], prose composition is a safe sign of a written literature. It is not so in

[1] Plutarch, Alcibiades, c. vii.

[2] See Grote, History of Greece, ii. p. 201.

[3] Plin. Hist. Nat. xiii. 13. § 27.: "Cum chartæ usu maxime humanitas vitæ constet et memoria."

[4] Wolf, Prolegomena, lxx—lxxiii.: "Scripturam tentare et communi usui aptare plane idem videtur fuisse atque prosam tentare et in eâ excolendâ se ponere."

India. The whole of the Brâhmaṇa literature, however incredible it may seem, shows not a single vestige of the art of writing. Nay, more than this, even during the Sûtra period all the evidence we can get would lead us to suppose that even then, though the art of writing began to be known, the whole literature of India was preserved by oral tradition only.

It is of little avail in researches of this kind to say that such a thing is impossible. We can form no opinion of the powers of memory in a state of society so different from ours as the Indian Parishads are from our universities. Feats of memory, such as we hear of now and then, show that our notions of the limits of that faculty are quite arbitrary. Our own memory has been systematically undermined for many generations. To speak of nothing else, one sheet of the "Times" newspaper every morning is quite sufficient to distract and unsettle the healthiest memory. The remnants of our own debilitated memory cannot furnish us with the right measure of the primitive powers of that faculty. The Guaranies, who are represented by Missionaries as the lowest specimens of humanity, evinced such powers of memory when they were once taught to listen and to reason, that it became a custom to make the chief Indian of the town, or one of the magistrates, repeat the sermon just delivered from the pulpit before the people in the street, or in the court-yard of a house; and they almost all did it with the utmost fidelity, without missing a sentence.[1] Even at the present day, when MSS. are neither scarce nor expensive, the young Brahmans who learn the songs of the Veda and the

[1] Dobrizhoffer's Account of the Abipones, vol. ii. p. 63.

Brâhmaṇas, and the Sûtras, invariably learn them from oral tradition, and know them by heart. They spend year after year under the guidance of their teacher, learning a little, day after day, repeating what they have learnt as part of their daily devotion, until at last they have mastered their subject, and are able to become teachers in turn. The ambition to master more than one subject is hardly known in India. This system of education has been going on ever since the Brâhmaṇa period, and as early as the Prâtiśâkhyas we find the most minute rules on the mnemonic system to be followed by every teacher. The only difference in modern times, after the invention of writing, is that a Brahman is not only commanded to pass his apprenticeship at the house of his Guru, and to learn from his mouth all that a Brahman is bound to know, but the fiercest imprecations are uttered against all who would presume to acquire their knowledge from written sources. In the Mahâbhârata we read, "Those who sell the Vedas, and even those who write them, those also who defile them, they shall go to hell."[1] Kumârila says, "That knowledge of the truth is worthless which has been acquired from the Veda, if the Veda has not been rightly comprehended, if it has been learnt from writing, or been received from a Śûdra."[2]

[1] वेदविक्रयिणश्चैव वेदानां चैव लेखकाः। वेदानां दूषकाश्चैव ते वै निरयगामिनः॥

[2] Kumârila, Tantra-Vârttika, i. 3. p. 86.:
यच्चैवान्यायविज्ञाताद्वेदाल्लेख्यादिपूर्वकात्। शूद्रेणाधिगताद्वापि धर्मज्ञानं न संमतं॥

How then was the Veda learnt? It was learnt by every Brahman during twelve years of his studentship or Brahmacharyâ. This, according to Gautama, was the shortest period, sanctioned only for men who wanted to marry, and to become Gṛihasthas. Brahmans who did not wish to marry were allowed to spend forty-eight years as students. The Prâtiśâkhya gives us a glimpse into the lecture-rooms of the Brahmanic colleges. "The Guru," it is said[1], "who has himself formerly been a student, should make his pupils read. He himself takes his seat either to the east, or the north, or the north-east. If he has no more than one or two pupils, they sit at his right hand. If he has more, they place themselves according as there is room. They then embrace their master, and say, 'Sir, read!' The master gravely says 'Om,' *i. e.* 'Yes.' He then begins to say a praśna (a question), which consists of three verses.[2] In order that no word may escape the attention of his pupils, he pronounces all with the high accent[3],

[1] Prâtiśâkhya du Rig-veda, par A. Regnier, Journal Asiatique, 1856. Chapitre XV.

[2] If the metre is pankti, the praśna may consist of two or three verses; if the metre is longer than pankti, two verses only constitute a praśna; if a hymn consists of one verse, that by itself forms a praśna. Samayas, *i. e.* passages which have occurred before (and are sometimes left out in the MSS.), are counted, if they consist of a complete verse. Two Dvipadâs are counted as one verse, and, as the Commentator adds (v. 12.), the two half-verses of each Dvipadâ-line are to be joined in recitation, and only if there is one odd Dvipadâ-line remaining, a pause is to be made at the end of the first half-verse. If there are some verses remaining at the end of a hymn, they may be joined to the last praśna; if there are more than two verses, this is optional.

[3] The only words which, in the Sanhitâ-pâṭha, would be likely to escape the pupil's attention are monosyllables consisting of

and repeats certain words twice, or he says 'so' (iti) after these words."

The chief difficulties in the pronunciation of the Veda are the changes of the final and initial letters.[1] The pupils are instructed in these euphonic rules independently (the Sikshâ), but whenever a difficult case of sandhi occurs, the Guru examines his audience and explains the difficulties. And here the method followed is this. After the Guru has pronounced a group of words, consisting of three or sometimes (in long compounds) of more words, the first pupil repeats the first word, and when anything is to be explained, the teacher stops him, and says, "Sir."[2] After it has been explained by the pupil who is at the head of the class, the permission to continue is given with the

one vowel only, and that a vowel not changed into a semi-vowel, in which form it would be more audible. This would restrict the rule regarding repetition to the two words *â* and *u*. Thus for *prâ*, which is *pra* + *â*, the Guru would have to say *prâ â*, or *prâ â iti*. Instead of *ud u shya deva, ud u u shya deva*. This repetition would not take place in *udv eti*, because *u* is changed into *v*. If sarvodâtta could mean a word being wholly udâtta, then *u* would be excluded, and the rule would refer to *â* only. But sarvodâtta means recitation when the accent is disregarded, and all syllables are pronounced with a high tone. The Commentary construes the rule differently. I construe इह प्रवचने सर्वोदात्तत्वं। तस्मिन् सर्वोदात्तप्रयुक्ते प्रवचने ऽपृक्तं तच्चाचैप्रयुक्तं द्विः प्रोक्तव्यं अथवेतिकरणांतं॥

[1] These are chiefly the change of a final m into Anusvâra before r and the ûshmans; the common sandhi of the ûshmans; the suppression of a final n; its transition into r; its transition into a sibilant; the absence of sandhi where ṛi follows; the sandhi of r, and the hiatus.

[2] The text is निर्वाच्ये तु &c.

words, "Well, Sir." After the words of the teacher have thus been repeated by one, the next pupil has to apply to him with the word, "Sir."[1] When there is no difficulty, the rule seems to be that the Guru says two words at a time, which are then repeated by the pupil. If it is a compound, one word only is to be pronounced by the Guru, and to be repeated by the pupil. After a section of three verses has thus been gone through, all the pupils have to rehearse it again and again. When they have mastered it, they have to recite the whole without any break, with an even voice, observing all the rules of sandhi, marking slightly the division in the middle of compounds, and pronouncing every syllable with the high accent.[2] It does not seem as if several pupils were allowed to recite together, for it is stated distinctly that the Guru first tells the verses to his pupil on the right, and that every pupil, after his task is finished, turns to the right, and walks round the tutor. This must occupy a long time every day, considering that a lecture consists of sixty and more praśnas, or of about 180 verses. The pupils are not dismissed till the lecture is finished. At the end of the lecture, the tutor, after the last half-verse is finished, says, "Sir,"

[1] Here again I differ from the Commentator, who takes parasya as an adjective referring to etad, *i. e.* guroḥ. At the end of a half-verse, this address, bho! is to be dropped; at the end of an Adhyâya it is optional.

[2] According to some Śâkhâs, (not the Śâkalas,) certain words (prepositions) are, in this final recitation also, to be followed by the particle *iti*; *abhi* is even, in some cases, to be pronounced *abhîtyabhi*. Some other rules are given, all of which are optional. The text of the Veda, as repeated in the lecture-room, is neither Sanhitâ, Pada, nor Krama-text. Some few Śâkhâs only maintain that the Sanhitâ-text should be used *pure et simple*.

the pupil replies, "Yes, Sir." He then repeats the proper verses and formulas, which have to be repeated at the end of every reading, embraces his tutor, and is allowed to withdraw.

These rules speak for themselves. They show that at the time when such rules were necessary, and when young Brahmans had to spend from twelve to forty-eight years of their life in doing nothing but learning and rehearsing the Veda[1], such a system must have had an object worthy of such efforts. Such an object existed, if, in the absence of writing, the sacred songs, which were believed to be the only means to salvation were to be preserved and guarded against loss and corruption. If, at the time of the Prâtisâkhyas, writing had been known, some mention of a book as a sacred object would surely have occurred somewhere. We know from the Gṛihya-sûtras every event in the life of a Brahman, from his birth to his death. Not a word is ever said about his learning to write.

The earliest allusion to this system of oral teaching occurs in a hymn of the Rig-veda which must be ascribed to the Mantra period. In the primitive poetry of the Chhandas period there is no mention either of writing or teaching. But in a satirical hymn of the Vasishṭhas (vii. 103. 5), in which the frogs are compared with Brahmans teaching their pupils, it is said: "One frog repeats the words of another, like a pupil who repeats the words of his teacher." (See p. 495.) No similar allusion to writing is to be found even in the latest hymns, the so-called Khilas. If writ-

[1] Cæsar (de Bello Gallico, vi. 14), speaking of the Druids says: "Magnum ibi numerum versuum ediscere dicuntur, itaque nonnulli annos vicenos in disciplina permanent, neque fas esse existimant ea literis mandare."

ing had been known during the Brâhmaṇa period, is it likely that these works, which are full of all kinds of mystic lucubrations on the origin of all things, should never with a single word have alluded to the art of writing, an art so wonderful that the Greeks would fain ascribe its discovery to one of the wisest gods of the wisest nation on earth? If letters had been known during the period when men in India were still able to create gods, the god of letters would have found his place in the Vedic pantheon side by side with Sarasvâtî, the goddess of speech, and Pûshan, the god of agriculture. No such god is to be found in India, or in any of the genuine mythologies of the Aryan world.

But there are stronger arguments than these to prove that, before the time of Pâṇini, and before the first spreading of Buddhism in India, writing for literary purposes was absolutely unknown.

If writing had been known to Pâṇini, some of his grammatical terms would surely point to the graphical appearance of words. I maintain that there is not a single word in Pâṇini's terminology which presupposes the existence of writing. The general name for letters is *varṇa*. This does not mean colour in the sense of a painted letter, but the colouring or modulation of the voice.[1] *Akshara*, which is used for letter and syllable, means what is indestructible, radical, or an element. We speak of stops as signs of interpunction; Pâṇini only speaks of *virâmas*, stoppages of the voice. The names of the letters are not derived from their shape, as in the Semitic names of Alpha, Beta, Gamma. With the exception of the r,

[1] Aristotle, Probl. x. 39.; τὰ δὲ γράμματα πάθη ἐστὶ τῆς φωνῆς.

their names are their sounds. The name for r, *Repha*, does not occur in Pâṇini. Kâtyâyana, however (iii. 3, 108, 4), explains the derivation of *Repha*, and in iv. 4, 128, 2, he uses it for *ra*. In the Prâtiśâkhyas likewise, the word is well known, and as the participle *riphita* is used in the same works, there can be little doubt that Repha is derived from a root *riph*, to snarl or hiss.

The terms for the three accents show no traces of writing, such as the Latin word "circumflexus."

What would have been more natural, if writing had been known in Pâṇini's time, than that he should have called the dot of the Anusvâra, *vindu*, *i. e.* dot, and the Visarga, *dvivindu*, the double dot? Let us take a later grammarian, Vopadeva, and we find such words at once. In Vopadeva, the Anusvâra is called *vindu*, the Visarga, *dvivindu*. What the Prâtiśâkhyas and Pâṇini called the *Jihvâmûlîya*, the sibilant formed near the base of the tongue, and *Upadhmânîya*, the labial flatus, Vopadeva calls *Vajrâkṛiti*, having the shape of the thunderbolt (×), and *Gajakumbhâkṛiti*, having the shape of an elephant's two frontal bones (ᨀ). The term *arddhachandra*, or half-moon, belongs to the same class of grammatical terms. Why should these words occur in later grammarians, and not one of them be found in the Prâtiśâkhyas or Pâṇini?

Another class of words which would be sure to betray the existence of writing where writing was known, are the words expressive of reading, composing, book, chapter, paragraph, &c. The most usual word for reading in Sanskrit is *adhyeti* or *adhîte*, and at first sight the very existence of such a word might seem to prove the existence of books that could be read. But we have seen in the Prâtiśâkhyas what was meant when the pupils asked their tutor to make them read. *Adhyeti* and *adhîte*, from *adhi*, over, and *i*, to go, mean "he goes over a thing, he conquers it, acquires it;" and the very expression "to read a work from the mouth of the tutor," would be sufficient to show that the wôrk existed, not as a book, but in men's memory. Another expression of the same kind is found in Manu (x. 1): "All the three castes may read the Veda, but the Brahman alone is allowed to proclaim, *i. e.* to teach it (prabrûyat)." To teach is expressed by the causative of the verb *adhyeti*, *adhyâpayati*, he makes read, *i. e.* he teaches.[1] The ancient Hindus distinguish between two kinds of reading, the *grahaṇâdhyayana*, the acquisitive reading, and the *dhâraṇâdhyayana*, the conservative reading; the former being the first acquisition of a work, the latter its rehearsing in order not to lose a volume that once belonged to one's mental library. This rehearsing, or *svâdhyâya*, self-reading, was as sacred a duty as the first acquisition. It was by means of this svâdhyâya alone that works could be said to live. We meet with similar expressions in other literatures of the ancient world. Ahura masdâ, when he wishes his law to live among men, requires Jima to be not only the "rememberer" (mĕrĕtâ), but the bearer and preserver (bhĕrĕtâ), of the Zarathustrian revelation. And many centuries later, Mahâvîra[2], the founder of the Jaina religion, is called *sâraê*, *vâraê*, and *dhâraê* of sacred knowledge, *i. e. smâraka*, a rememberer, *vâraka*, a guardian who keeps it from profane eyes, and *dhâraka*, a holder

1 Âpastamba, Dharma-sûtra, iii. 86.

2 Kalpa-sûtra, ed. Stevenson, p. 29.

who does not forget the knowledge which he once acquired.

Even so late a writer as Kumârila, when he speaks of the material existence of the Veda, can only conceive of it as existing in the minds of men. "The Veda," he says, "is distinctly to be perceived by means of the senses. It exists, like a pot or any other object, in man. Perceiving it in another man, people learn it and remember it. Then others again perceiving it, as it is remembered by these, learn it and remember it, and thus hand it on to others. Therefore, the theologian concludes, the Veda is without a beginning."[1] These theological arguments may be passed over: but immediately afterwards, in order to show that the Veda has a material existence, Kumârila uses another curious expression, which shows again that to him the Veda existed only in the memory of men. "Before we hear the word Veda," he says, "we perceive, as different from all other objects, and as different from other Vedas, something in the form of the Rig-veda that exists within the readers, and things in the form of Mantras and Brâhmaṇas, different from

[1] वेदः पुनः सविशेषः प्रत्यक्षगम्यः। तत्र घटादिवदेव पुरुषांतरस्थमुपलभ्य स्मरंति। तैरपि स्मृतमुपलभ्यान्येऽपि स्मरंतोऽन्येभ्यस्तथैव समर्थयंतीत्यनादिता॥ सर्वस्य चात्मीयस्मरणात्पूर्वमुपलब्धिः संभवतीति निर्मूलता॥ शब्दसंबंधव्युत्पत्तिमात्रमेव चेह वृद्धव्यवहाराधीनं॥ प्रागपि हि वेदशब्दादन्यवस्तुविलक्षणं वेदांतरविलक्षणं चाध्येतृस्थमृग्वेदादिरूपं मंत्रब्राह्मणादिरूपाणि चान्यविलक्षणान्युपलभ्यंते सर्वेषां चानादयः संज्ञाः॥

others." Such arguments would not occur to people who were accustomed from time immemorial to appeal to a book as the sacred authority of their faith. When contemporaneously with our Reformation Nanak founded the religion of the Sikhs, we find in India, as well as elsewhere, that a book, a real book, was considered as the firmest foundation of a new faith. "At their assemblies, when the chiefs and principal leaders are seated, the Âdi-Granth (the first book) and Daśama Pádshábka Granth are placed before them; they all bend their heads before these scriptures, and exclaim, 'Wa! Gurujika Khálsa! Wa! Gurujiki Fateh!' A great quantity of cakes, made of wheat, butter, and sugar, are then placed before the volumes of their sacred writings, and covered with a cloth. These holy cakes, which are in commemoration of the injunction of Nanak, to eat and to give to others to eat, next receive the salutation of the assembly, who then rise, and the Acalis pray aloud, while the musicians play. The Acalis, when the prayers are finished, desire the council to be seated. They sit down, and the cakes being uncovered are eaten of by all classes of Sikhs; those distinctions of original tribes, which are on other occasions kept up, being on this occasion laid aside, in token of their general and complete union in one cause. The Acalis then exclaim, 'Sirdars! (chiefs) this is a Gurumatâ' (a great assembly); on which prayers are again said aloud. The chiefs, after this, sit closer, and say to each other: 'The sacred Granth (book) is betwixt us, let us swear by our scriptures to forget all external disputes, and to be united.'"[1]

[1] Asiatic Researches, xi. 255.

Such a scene would be impossible among pure Brahmans. They never speak of their *granthas* or books. They speak of their *Veda*, which means "knowledge." They speak of their *Śruti*, which means what they have heard with their ears. They speak of *Smṛiti*, which means what their fathers have declared unto them. We meet with *Brâhmaṇas*, *i. e.* the sayings of Brahmans; with *Sûtras*, *i. e.* the strings of rules; with *Vedângas*, *i. e.* the members of the Veda; with *Pravachanas*, *i. e.* preachings; with *Śâstras*, *i. e.* teachings; with *Darśanas*, *i. e.* demonstrations; but we never meet with a book, or a volume, or a page.

If we take the ordinary modern words for book, paper, ink, writing, &c., not one of them has as yet been discovered in any Sanskrit work of genuine antiquity. Book, in modern Sanskrit, is *pustam* or *pustakam*, a word most likely of foreign origin.[1] It occurs in such works as the Hitopadeśa, where we read of a person, "neither read in books nor taught by a tutor." The Hitopadeśa itself is said to be written (likhyate) as an extract from the Panchatantra and another book.[2]

To write is *likh* and *lip*, the former originally used in the sense of scratching, whether on stone or leaves, the latter, in the sense of covering a surface with ink. Thus in Śakuntalâ, the chief heroine, when advised to write a love-letter (*madanalekha*), complains that she has no writing-materials (*lekhanasâdhanâni*), and her friend tells her to take a lotus-leaf as smooth as the breast of a parrot, and with her

[1] Could it be *apestak*, originally the Sanskrit *avasthâna?* See Spiegel, Grammar of the Parsi Language, p. 204.

[2] पंचतंत्रात्तथान्यस्माद्ग्रंथादाकृष्य लिख्यते॥

nails to scratch the letters on it. This is clearly writing. In the Vikramorvaśî, again, Urvaśî, not daring to face her lover, writes a letter (*lekha*) on a birch-leaf (*bhûrjapatra*). The king, who sees it, calls it *bhûrjagato aksharavinyâsa*, "letters put down on a birch leaf;" and when he reads it, he is said to make the leaf speak (*vâchayati*). The leaf (*patra*) is used here not in the sense in which we found it in the Śakuntalâ, as the leaf of a tree, but as a leaf or sheet of paper. This paper was made of the bark of the birch-tree; and hence, when the queen picks up the love-letter, she thinks "it is a strip of fresh bark which the south wind has blown thither."[1]

Passages like these, to which we might add the well-known introduction to the Mahâbhârata, leave little doubt that, at the time when these modern plays were composed, writing was generally practised by women as well as men. Why should there be no such passage in any of the genuine early Sanskrit works, if writing had then been equally known?

In Manu's Code of Laws we read (viii. 168.): "What is given by force, what is by force enjoyed, by force caused *to be written* (*lekhita*), and all other things done by force, Manu has pronounced void." Here again we have clearly writing. But this is only another proof that this metrical paraphrase of the laws of the Mânavas is later than the Vedic age.

In the Laws of Yâjnavalkya also written documents are mentioned; and the Commentator (ii. 22.) quotes Nârada and other authorities, all in Ślokas, on

[1] There are, I believe, but two Sanskrit MSS. in Europe which are written on birch bark; one in the Royal Library of Berlin, the other in the Library of All Souls College, Oxford.

several minor points connected with the signing (*chihnita*) of papers, and the treatment of witnesses who cannot write (*alipijna*). But I have found no such traces of written documents in any of the ancient Dharmasûtras.

The words for ink (*masi*,[1] *kâlî*, *mela*,[2] *golâ*) and pen (*kalama*)[3], have all a modern appearance; and, as to *Kâyastha*, the name of the writer-caste, proceeding from a Kshatriya father and a Śûdra mother, it does not even occur in Manu.

Another class of words which would be likely to contain allusions to writing are those used for the various subdivisions of literary compositions: but these too point to a literature kept up by oral tradition only. We observed before that a lecture (*adhyâya*) consisted of sixty questions or *praśnas*. We find these very words used instead of chapters and paragraphs in the Sanhitâs, Brâhmaṇas, and Sûtras. In the Rig-veda we have the ancient division into *sûktas*, hymns; *anuvâkas*, chapters (*i. e.* repetition); and *maṇḍalas*, books (*i.e.* cycles): and the later division into *vargas*, classes; *adhyâyas*, lectures; and *Ashṭakas*, Ogdoads. In the Taittirîyaka, the division is into *Kaṇḍikâs* (sections), *anuvâkas*, *praśnas*, and *ashṭakas*. In the Kâṭhaka we have *granthas*, compositions, and *sthânakas*, places. The name of the *Śatapatha-brâhmaṇa* is derived from its 100 *pathas* or walks; and *Shashṭipatha* is used for a work consisting of sixty walks or chapters. Other words of the same kind are *prapâṭhaka*, a reading, a lecture; *âhnika*, a day's work; *parvan*, a joint, &c. We look in vain for such words

[1] Lalita Vistara, adhyâya ix. p. 139. l. 17.

[2] The Greek μέλα; See Dr. Hincks' Review in the Dublin University Magazine, April, 1860.

[3] Uṇâdi-sûtras, iv. 84. calamus, reed.

as *volumen*, a volume, *liber*, *i. e.* the inner bark of a tree; or βίβλος, *i. e.* βύβλος, the inner bark of the papyrus; or *book*, *i. e.* beech-wood.

It is clear, from the evidence which we have examined, that it is far easier to prove the absence of writing during the early period of Sanskrit literature, than to discover any traces of writing even at the time when we are inclined to suppose that it was known in India. Writing was practised in India before the time of Alexander's conquest; and, though it may not have been used for literary purposes, we can hardly doubt that a written alphabet was known during the greater part of the Sûtra period. The Greek writers tell us exactly what we should expect under these circumstances. Megasthenes declared that the Indians did not know letters, that their laws were not written, and that they administered justice from memory.[1] This is perfectly true, if, as has been pointed out[2], we restrict their ignorance of letters to the fact that they did not employ them for literary purposes. Strabo himself, when quoting the statement of Nearchus that the Indians wrote letters on cotton that had been well beaten together, points out the contradiction between this author and others (*i. e.* Megasthenes), who declared that the Indians used no letters at all.[3] There is, however, no real contradiction between these two statements, if we only distinguish between the knowledge of letters and their use as a vehicle of literature. Nearchus fully agrees

[1] Strabo, xv. 53.: . . . . Ἀγράφοις καὶ ταῦτα νόμοις χρωμένοις. Οὐδὲ γὰρ γράμματα εἰδέναι αὐτοὺς, ἀλλ' ἀπὸ μνήμης ἕκαστα διοικεῖσθαι.

[2] Schwanbeck, Megasthenis Fragmenta, p. 50.

[3] Strabo, xv. 67.: Ἐπιστολὰς δὲ γράφειν ἐν σινδόσι λίαν κεκροτημέναις, τῶν ἄλλων γράμμασιν αὐτοὺς μὴ χρῆσθαι φαμένων.

with Megasthenes; for he also states that the laws of the Indians were not reduced to writing.[1] And Megasthenes agrees with Nearchus; for he also shows himself perfectly acquainted with the fact that the Indians used letters for inscriptions on milestones, indicating the resting-places and distances.[2] Nothing could offer a stronger confirmation of our opinion that the Indians had become acquainted with the art of writing during the Sûtra period and before the conquest of Alexander, but that they abstained from using it for literary purposes, than this apparent contradiction in the accounts of Nearchus and Megasthenes. Curtius, differing from Nearchus, maintains that they wrote on the soft rind of trees[3], a custom which we saw preserved in the play of Urvaśî. We can hardly believe that the Indians could have used skins for writing. And, though Nicolaus Damascenus declares that he saw the ambassadors of Porus presented to Cæsar Augustus in Antiochia, and that they brought a letter written ἐν διφθέρᾳ, we must remember that this letter was written in Greek[4], and that the word διφθέρα may have been used for paper in general.[5]

We shall not be able to trace the Indian alphabet back much beyond Alexander's invasion. It existed, however, before Alexander. This we know from

[1] Strabo, xv. 66.: Νέαρχος δὲ περὶ τῶν σοφιστῶν οὕτω λέγει· τοὺς μὲν νόμους ἀγράφους εἶναι.

[2] Οἱ ἀγορανόμοι . . . ὁδοποιοῦσι, καὶ κατὰ δέκα στάδια στήλας τιθέασι τὰς ἐκτροπὰς καὶ τὰ διαστήματα δηλούσας. Megasthenes, fragm. xxxiv.

[3] Curtius, 8, 9.: "Libri arborum teneri, haud secus quam chartæ literarum notas capiunt."

[4] Strabo, xv. 73.: Τὴν δὲ ἐπιστολὴν ἑλληνίζειν ἐν διφθέρᾳ γεγραμμένην.

[5] Herodotus, v. 58.

Nearchus himself, who ascribes to the Indians the art of making paper from cotton. Now, in looking for traces of writing before Alexander's time, we find in the Lalita-vistara, which contains the life of Buddha, that the young Śâkya is represented as learning to write. Though the Lalita-vistara cannot be regarded as a contemporaneous witness, it is nevertheless a canonical book of the Buddhists, and, as such, must be ascribed to the third council. It was translated into Chinese 76 A.D. As we have seen, before, the system of instruction practised in the lecture-rooms of the Brahmans, it will perhaps be of interest to glance at the schools in which Buddha was educated, or supposed to have been educated.

"When the young prince had grown, he was led to the writing-school (lipiśâlâ)."[1] We may leave out all the wonderful things that happened on this occasion, how he received a hundred thousand blessings, how he was surrounded by ten thousand children, preceded by ten thousand chariots full of sweetmeats, of silver and gold; how the town of Kapilavastu was cleansed, how music sounded everywhere, and showers of flowers were poured from the roofs, windows, and balconies; how, not satisfied with this, celestial ladies walked before him to clear the road, and the daughters of the wind scattered celestial flowers, besides other fabulous beings who all came to honour the Bodhisatva as he went to school. These marginal illustrations may be dropped in all Buddhist books, though they leave but little room for the text. When

[1] Lalita-Vistara, Adhyâya x. This work has lately been edited and partially translated by Babu Rajendralal Mitra, one of the most distinguished Sanskrit scholars in India.

Buddha entered the school, Viśvâmitra, the schoolm ter (dârakâchârya), unable to bear the majesty of the Bodhisatva's presence, fell to the ground, and had to be lifted up by an angel, named Śubhânga. After the king Śuddhodana and his suite had left, the nurses and attendants sat down, and the Bodhisatva took a leaf to write on (lipiphalaka) made of sandal-wood (uragasârachandana-mayam). He then asked Viśvâmitra what writing he was going to teach him. Here follow sixty-four names, apparently names of alphabets[1], all of which the Bodhisatva is acquainted with, whereas Viśvâmitra is obliged to confess his ignorance. Nevertheless the Bodhisatva stays at school, and learns to write, together with ten thousand boys.[2]

[1] The most interesting names are Anga (Bhagalpur), Banga (Bengal), Magadha, Drâviḍa, Dakshiṇa (Dekhan), Darada, Khâsya (Cassia hills), Chîna (Chinese), Hûṇa, Deva (Devanâgarî), Bhaumadeva (Brahman), Uttarakurus, anudruta (cursive).

[2] The following passage from the Evangelium Infantiæ (ed. Sike, p. 143.) offers a curious parallel: "Erat porro Hierosolymis quidam Zachæus nomine, qui juventutem erudiebat. Dicebat hic Josepho: Quare non mittis ad me Jesum, ut literas discat? Annuebat illi Josephus, et ad Divam Mariam hoc referebat. Ad magistrum itaque illum ducebant; qui simulatque eum conspexerat Alphabetum ipsi conscripsit, utque Aleph diceret præcepit. Et cum dixisset Aleph, magister ipsum Beth pronunciare jubebat. Cui Dominus Jesus: Dic mihi prius significationem literæ Aleph, et tum Beth pronunciabo. Cumque magister verbera ipsi intentaret, exponebat illi Dominus Jesus significationes literarum Aleph et Beth; item, quænam literarum figuræ essent rectæ, quænam obliquæ, quænam duplicatæ, quæ punctis insignitæ, quæ iisdem carentes; quare una litera aliam precederet; aliaque plurima enarrare cœpit et elucidare, quæ magister ipse nec audiverat unquam nec in libro ullo legerat. Dixit porro magistro Dominus Jesus: Attende, ut dicam tibi, cœpitque clare et distincte recitare, Aleph, Beth, Gimel, Daleth, usque ad finem Alphabeti. Quod miratus magister, Hunc, inquit, puerum ante Noachum

The alphabet which he learns is the common Sanskrit alphabet, with the omission of the letters l, ṛi, and ṛî. It consists of 45 letters, and, as in our own primers, every letter is followed by a word containing that letter at the beginning or in the middle. These words in the Lalita-vistara are so chosen as to illustrate some of the chief points of Buddha's own doctrines. The alphabet is: — a, â, i, î, u, û, e, ai, o, au, am̃, aḥ; k, kh, g, gh, ñ; ch, chh, j, jh, ñ; ṭ, ṭh, ḍ, ḍh, ṇ; t, th, d, dh, n; p, ph, b, bh, m; y, r, v; ś, sh, s, h, ksh.

Though the further education of Buddha is not fully described, we see him soon afterwards, in a general competition, the most distinguished scholar, arithmetician, musician, and everything else.[1] This comprehensive system of education, through which Buddha is here represented to have passed, is the very opposite of that followed by the Brahmans. We nowhere meet in the Buddhist literature with those strong imprecations against book-learning which we found among the Brahmans, and which may be heard, I believe, even at the present day.

If, thus, the first, though rather legendary, trace of writing, as a part of the elementary education in India, is[2] discovered in the life of Buddha, it is curious to

natum esse existimo; conversusque ad Josephum, Adduxisti, ait, ad me erudiendum puerum, magistris omnibus doctiorem. Divæ quoque Mariæ inquit: Filio tuo nulla doctrina opus est." The Gospel of Thomas the Israelite, or the Book of Thomas the Israelite, the philosopher, concerning the acts which the Lord did, when a child, was most popular in the east.

[1] Among the subjects in which he shows his learning, figure Nirghaṇṭu, Nigama, Purâṇa, Itihâsa, Veda, Vyâkaraṇa, Nirukta, Śikshâ, Chhandas, Kalpa, Jyotisha, Sânkhya, Yoga, Vaiśeshika.

[2] In an ancient inscription of Khandgiri (Journal of the Asiat.

observe that the first actual writing, the first well authenticated inscription in India, is likewise of Buddhist origin. There are no Brahmanic inscriptions earlier than the Buddhist inscriptions of Aśoka on the rocks of Kapurdigiri, Dhauli, and Girnar. They belong to the third century before Christ. They call themselves *lipi*, a writing[1], or *dharmalipi*[2], a sacred writing; and they mention the writer or engraver by the name of *lipikara*.[3] This last word *lipikara* is an important word, for it is the only word in the Sûtras of Pâṇini which can be legitimately adduced to prove that Pâṇini was acquainted with the art of writing. He teaches the formation of this word, iii. 2, 21. There is indeed another passage, which has frequently been quoted, where Pâṇini teaches the formation of the adjective *yavanânî*. This is simply the feminine of *yavana*, as *Indrâṇî* is of *Indra*. Kâtyâyana, however, and the Commentator, both maintain that *yavanânî* is used as a name of *lipi*, and that it meant the writing of the Yavanas. I see no reason to doubt that most of the examples which we find in the Commentaries go back to the very time of Pâṇini, and I am quite willing to admit that Pâṇini gave his rule on *yavanânî* simply in order to explain this word as the name of a certain alphabet. But I must demur to

Soc. of Bengal, vi. 318.), a king is mentioned who in his youth learned to write, and was taught, besides, arithmetic, navigation, commerce, and law ("tato likharûpagaṇa nâva vyapâra viḍhi viśâradena").

[1] Etâya athâya iyam lipi likhitâ; for this purpose was the writing written.

[2] Iyam dhammalipî Devânâm piyena piyadasinâ rânâ likhâpitâ asti eva. (p. 752.)

[3] Burnouf, Lotus, p. 752.

any further conclusions. Yavana is by no means the exclusive name of the Greeks or Ionians. Professor Lassen has proved that it had a much wider meaning, and that it was even used of Semitic nations. There is nothing to prove that Pâṇini was later than Alexander, or that he was acquainted with Greek literature. In the Lalita-vistara, where all possible alphabets are mentioned, nothing is said of a Yavanânî or a Greek alphabet. The Sanskrit alphabet, though it has always been suspected to be derived from a Semitic source, has not certainly been traced back to a Greek source. It shows more similarity with the Aramæan than with any other variety of the Phœnician alphabet.[1] Yavanânî lipi most likely means that variety of the Semitic alphabet which, previous to Alexander, and previous to Pâṇini, became the type of the Indian alphabet. But all this is merely conjectural. It is impossible to arrive at any certain interpretation of Yavanânî, as used by Pâṇini; and it is much better to confess this, than to force the word into an argument for any preconceived notions as to the origin of the Indian alphabet.

There is another word in Pâṇini which might seem to prove that, not only the art of writing, but written books were known at his time. This is *grantha*. *Grantha* occurs four times in our texts of Pâṇini.[2] In I. 3.

[1] Lepsius, Zwei sprachvergleichende Abhandlungen, p. 78., Schulze's conjecture about *Mesnud*. Weber, Indische Skizzen.

[2] समुदाङ्भ्यो यमोऽग्रंथे॥ १. ३. ७५॥

अधिकृत्य कृते ग्रंथे॥ ४. ३. ८७॥

कृते ग्रंथे॥ ४. ३. ११६॥

ग्रंथांताधिके च॥ ६. ३. ७९॥

75. it is so used as to apply to the Veda. In IV. 3. 87. it may refer to any work. In IV. 3. 116. it is applied to the work of any individual author. In VI. 3. 79. it may refer to any work that is studied. I do not attribute much importance to the fact that I. 3. 75. and IV. 3. 116. are marked as not explained in the Commentaries; for I confess that in none of these four passages can I discover anything to prove that *grantha* must mean a written or a bound book. Grantha is derived from a root *grath*, which means *nectere*, *serere*. Grantha, therefore, like the later *sandarbha*, would simply mean a composition.[1] It corresponds etymologically with the Latin *textus*. Thus it is used by the Commentator to Nir. I. 20., where he says that former teachers handed down the hymns *granthato 'rthataścha*, "according to their text and according to their meaning." In the later literature of India *grantha* was used for a volume, and in *granthakuṭî*, a library, we see clearly that it has that meaning. But in the early literature *grantha* does not mean *pustaka*, or book; it means simply a composition, as opposed to a traditional work.

This distinction between traditional works and works composed by individual authors is of frequent occurrence in Pâṇini, and we attempted, in a former part of this work, to draw some historical conclusions from this distinction. From IV. 3. 101. to 111. the grammarian gives rules how to derive the titles of works from the names of those by whom they were proclaimed (tena proktam). But in most cases these derivations are used by Pâṇini as intermediate links

[1] Thus the Commentator to the Rig-veda, i. 67. 4. explains chṛitanti by agnim uddiśya stutîr grathnanti, kurvantîtyarthaḥ.

only, in order to form the names of Charaṇas who read and preserve these works. Never, he says (IV. 2. 66.), use the derivative, which would be the title of a work, in the case of hymns (chhandas) or Brâhmaṇas. Do not call a work proclaimed by Kaṭha, Kaṭham, but only speak of Kaṭhas, *i. e.* those who hand down the works proclaimed by Kaṭha. Another still more significant restriction is made by Pâṇini. With reference to modern works, he says, you may use the neuter in the singular or plural, instead of the plural of the masculine. The Brâhmaṇas taught by Yâjnavalkya may be spoken of as such. But the ancient Brâhmaṇas, first proclaimed by Bhallava &c., can only be spoken of as "the Bhâllavins" (Bhallavidæ), because it is only in the tradition of his descendants that the works of Bhallava and other ancient sages may be said to live.

However we examine the ancient Sanskrit phraseology with regard to books and their authors, we invariably arrive at the same results. In the most ancient literature, the idea even of authorship is excluded. Works are spoken of as revealed to and communicated by certain sages, but not as composed by them. In the later literature of the Brâhmaṇa and Sûtra period the idea of authorship is admitted, but no trace is to be found anywhere of any books being committed to writing. It is possible I may have overlooked some words in the Brâhmaṇas and Sûtras, which would prove the existence of written books previous to Pâṇini. If so, it is not from any wish to suppress them. I believe, indeed, that the Brâhmaṇas were preserved by oral tradition only, but I should feel inclined to claim an acquaintance with the art of writing for the authors of the Sûtras. And there is one word which seems to strengthen such a supposition. We find that several of the Sûtras are divided into chapters called *paṭalas.* This is a word never used for the subdivisions of the Brâhmaṇas. Its meaning is a covering, the surrounding skin or membrane; it is also used for a tree. If so, it would seem to be almost synonymous with *liber* and *βίβλος*, and it would mean *book*, after meaning originally a sheet of paper made of the surrounding bark of trees. If writing came in towards the latter half of the Sûtra period, it would no doubt be applied at the same time to reducing the hymns and Brâhmaṇas to a written form. Previously to that time, however, we are bound to maintain that the collection of the hymns, and the immense mass of the Brâhmaṇa literature, were preserved by means of oral tradition only.[1]

[1] See Boehtlingk, Ein Paar Worte zur Frage über das Alter der Schrift in Indien. Bulletin, T. I. p. 347—353.

CHAPTER IV.

THE CHHANDAS PERIOD.

THE three periods of Vedic literature which we have examined, the Sûtra, Brâhmaṇa, and Mantra periods, all point to some earlier age which gave birth to the poetry of the early Ṛishis. There was a time, doubtless, when the songs which were collected with such careful zeal in the Mantra period, commented upon with such elaborate pedantry during the Brâhmaṇa period, and examined and analysed with such minute exactness during the Sûtra period, lived and were understood without any effort by a simple and pious race. There was a time when the sacrifices, which afterwards became so bewildering a system of ceremonies, were dictated by the free impulse of the human heart, by a yearning to render thanks to some Unknown Being, and to repay, in words or deeds, a debt of gratitude, accumulated from the first breath of life. There was a time when the poet was the leader, the king, and priest of his family or tribe, when his songs and sayings were listened to in anxious silence and with implicit faith, when his prayers were repeated by crowds who looked up to their kings and priests, their leaders and judges, as men better, nobler, wiser than the rest, as beings nearer to the gods in proportion as they were raised above the common level of mankind. These men themselves living a life of perfect freedom, speaking a language not yet broken by literary usage, and thinking thoughts unfettered as yet by traditional chains, were at once teachers, lawgivers, poets, and priests. There is no very deep wisdom in their teaching, their laws are simple, their poetry shows no very high flights of fancy, and their religion might be told in a few words. But what there is of their language, poetry, and religion has a charm which no other period of Indian literature possesses: it is spontaneous, original, and truthful.

We cannot say this of all the hymns: nay, the greater portion of what we now possess of Vedic poetry must, no doubt, be ascribed to a secondary period, the so-called Mantra period. But after we have discarded what bears the stamp of a later age, there remains enough to give us an idea of an earlier race of Vedic poets. It is true, no doubt, in one sense, that even those earliest specimens of Vedic poetry belong, as has been said by Bunsen, to the modern history of the human race. Ages must have passed before the grammatical texture of the Vedic Sanskrit could have assumed the consistency and regularity which it shows throughout. Every tense, every mood, every number and person of the verb is fixed, and all the terminations of the cases are firmly established. Every one of these terminations was originally an independent word with an independent meaning. Their first selection was more or less the result of individual choice, their technical character the result of long usage. There was more than one word for *I*, and more than one expression for the verb *to be*. The selection of *mi*, as the termination of the first person singular, the selection of *as* in the sense of *to be*, and the joining of the two so as to produce the auxiliary verb *asmi*, I am, all this was a conventional act, the act of one or two individuals, fixed by circumstances which were more or less accidental. If, then, we find the same combination in the ancient Greek ἐσμί, and the modern Lithuanian *esmi*, it is clear that the origin of that form goes back to times long anterior to the separate existence of Sanskrit, Greek, and Lithuanian. As *soy*, *suis*, and *sono* are modern modifications that point back to an earlier type, the Latin *sum*, the Sanskrit *asmi*, Greek ἐσμί, Lithuanian *esmi*, are likewise but the modern representatives of some earlier typical form, which existed in the undivided language of the Aryan race.

The same applies to the religion of the Veda. Words like *deva* for 'god' mark a more than secondary stage in the grammar of the Aryan religion. To use the root *div*, 'to shine,' with reference to the heavenly bodies, was the result of a free choice. There were other roots which might have been used instead. Nor was it by any means a necessity that the presence of a Divine Power should be felt exclusively in the bright manifestations of nature. All this was the result of a historical growth; and the early periods of that growth had passed away long before the Ṛishis of India could have worshipped their *Devas* or their bright beings, with sacred hymns and invocations.

From this point of view the Vedic language and poetry may be ascribed to a modern or secondary period in the history of the world, if only it be understood that what preceded that period in India, or in any other part of the Aryan world, is lost to us beyond the hope of recovery, and that, therefore, to us the

Veda represents the most ancient chapter in the history of the human intellect. We find no traces in the Veda, or in any Aryan work, of a growing language, growing in the sense in which some of the Turanian languages may be said to be still growing at the present day.[1] The whole grammatical mechanism is finished, the most complicated forms are sanctioned, and the only changes of which the Aryan speech, arrived at the point where we find it in the Veda, admits, are those of gradual decay and recomposition. Nor do we find any traces, in the Veda, of a growing religion. We look in vain for the effect produced on the human mind by the first rising of the idea of God. To the poets of the Veda that idea is an old and familiar idea: it is understood, never questioned, never denied. We shall never hear what was felt by man when the image of God arose in all its majesty before his eyes, assuming a reality before which all other realities faded away into a mere shadow. No whisper will ever reach us of that sacred colloquy when God for the first time spoke to man, and man to God; when man within his own heart heard that still small voice through which the father of mankind revealed himself to all his children, to the Jew first, and also to the Gentile; and when God received the first response from human lips: "Who art thou, Lord?" That first recognition of God, that first perception of the real presence of God — a perception without which no religion, whether natural or revealed, can exist or grow, — belonged to the past when the songs of the Veda were written. The idea of God,

[1] See my Letter on the Classification of the Turanian languages, p. 30.

though never entirely lost, had been clouded over by errors. The names given to God had been changed to gods, and their real meaning had faded away from the memory of man. Even the earliest hymns of the Veda are not free from mythological phraseology. How far the poets retained a vague consciousness of the original purport of the names of the gods is difficult to say. To our eyes the science of language has disclosed the smallest fibres in the tissue of these names, and allowed us an insight into the darkest secrets of their growth. We can see *nomina*, where even the most keen-sighted native could discover nothing but *numina*. Sometimes, however, we feel surprised at the precision with which even such modern writers as Kumârila are able to read the true meaning of their mythology. When Kumârila is hard pressed by his opponents about the immoralities of his gods, he answers with all the freedom of a comparative mythologist[1]: "It is fabled that Prajâpati, the Lord of Creation, did violence to his daughter. But what does it mean? Prajâpati, the Lord of Creation, is a name of the sun; and he is called so, because he pro-

[1] प्रजापतिस्तावत्प्रजापालनाधिकारादादित्य एवोच्यते। स चारुणोदयवेलायामुषसमुद्यन्नभ्येति सा तदागमनादेवोपजायत इति तद्दुहितृत्वेन व्यपदिश्यते। तस्यां चारुणकिरणाख्यबीजनिक्षेपात् स्त्रीपुरुषसंयोगवदुपचारः। एवं समस्ततेजाः परमेश्वरत्वनिमित्तेंद्रशब्दवाच्यः सवितैवाहनि लीयमानतया रात्रेरहल्याशब्दवाच्यायाः क्षयात्मकजरणहेतुत्वाज्जीर्यत्यस्मादनेन वोदितेन वेत्यहल्याजार इत्युच्यते न परस्त्रीव्यभिचारात्॥

tects all creatures. His daughter Ushas is the dawn. And when it is said that he was in love with her, this only means that, at sunrise, the sun runs after the dawn, the dawn being at the same time called the daughter of the sun, because she rises when he approaches. In the same manner, if it is said that Indra was the seducer of Ahalyâ, this does not imply that the god Indra committed such a crime; but Indra means the sun, and Ahalyâ (from ahan and lî) the night; and, as the night is seduced and ruined by the sun of the morning, therefore is Indra called the paramour of Ahalyâ."

But in spite of the mythological character which the religion of India has assumed in the Veda, in spite of other traces which show that even its most primitive hymns rest on numerous underlying strata of more primitive thoughts and feelings, we should look in vain, in any other literature of the Aryan nations, to Greece or Rome, for documents from which to study that important chapter in the history of mankind which we can study in the Veda,—the transition from a natural into an artificial religion.

In a history of Sanskrit literature the Chhandas period, though the most interesting from a philosophical point of view, can occupy but a small place. It is represented by a very limited literature, by those few hymns which show none of the signs of a more modern origin which we discussed when treating on the Mantra period. Their number will necessarily vary according to the rules which critics follow in testing the age and character of earlier and later hymns. This critical separation can be carried out successfully only after a comprehensive examination of the leading ideas of the whole Vedic poetry, and it could not be attempted within the small compass of this work. All I can do in this place is to give a few hymns which in thought and language represent the general character of genuine Vedic poetry, and to contrast them with some other hymns which decidedly belong to a later period.

The following hymn is ascribed to Manu Vaivasvata: viii. 30.

1. Among you, O gods, there is none that is small, none that is young: you all are great indeed.

2. Be thus praised, ye destroyers of foes, you who are thirty and three, you the sacred gods of Manu.

3. Defend us, help us, bless us! do not lead us far away from the path of our fathers, from the path of Manu!

4. You who are here, O gods, all of you, and worshipped by all men, give us your broad protection, give it to cow and horse.

. There is nothing striking, nothing that displays any warmth of feeling or power of expression in this hymn. The number of thirty-three, assigned to the gods of Manu, would rather tend to refer its composition to a time when the gods of old had been gathered up and had been subjected to a strict census. Nevertheless, the hymn is simple and primitive in thought and language; and the fact of its being ascribed to Manu Vaivasvata shows that the Brahmans themselves looked upon it as a relic of one of their earliest sages. That Manu himself should be mentioned in the hymn seems to have caused no scruple to the Brahmans; nor is it any real difficulty from our own point of view. No man of the name of

Manu ever existed. Manu was never more than a name —one of the oldest names for man; and it was given in India, as elsewhere, to the supposed ancestor or ancestors of the human race. The Brahmans, however, like most Aryan nations; changed the appellative into a proper name. They believed in a real Manu, or in several real Manus, to whom they assigned various cognomina, such as Vaivasvata, Âpsava (Rv. ix. 7. 3), Sâmvaraṇa (Rv. ix. 6. 5). All of these they naturally counted as among the earliest of human Rishis; and the hymns which they ascribed to them must have belonged in their eyes to the earliest and most important class.

In one sense it is true, no doubt, that invocations of all the gods, the Viśve Devas[1] as they are called, represent a later phase of thought than invocations of single deities. Nevertheless, there is nothing to show that this comprehensive view of all the deities belongs to an age later than that which gave rise to the most ancient hymns which we possess, and which celebrate the power and majesty of individual deities, such as Varuṇa, Indra, Agni (fire), the Maruts (the winds), Ushas (dawn), &c. When these individual gods are invoked, they are not conceived as limited by the power of others, as superior or inferior in rank. Each god is to the mind of the supplicant as good as all the gods. He is felt, at the time, as a real divinity—as supreme and absolute, in spite of the necessary limitations which, to our mind, a plurality of gods must entail on every single god. All the rest disappear for a moment from the vision of

[1] Viśve Devâḥ, though treated as a plural, has sometimes the meaning of a *pluralis majestaticus*. See Ewald, Ausführliches Lehrbuch, § 178, b.

the poet, and he only who is to fulfil their desires stands in full light before the eyes of the worshippers. "Among you, O gods, there is none that is small, none that is young; you are all great indeed," is a sentiment which, though, perhaps, not so distinctly expressed as by Manu Vaivasvata, nevertheless, underlies all the poetry of the Veda. Although the gods are sometimes distinctly invoked as the great and the small, the young and the old (Rv. i. 27. 13), this is only an attempt to find the most comprehensive expression for the divine powers, and nowhere is any of the gods represented as the slave of others. It would be easy to find, in the numerous hymns of the Veda, passages in which almost every single god is represented as supreme and absolute. In the first hymn of the second Maṇḍala, Agni is called the ruler of the universe[1], the lord of men, the wise king, the father, the brother, the son, the friend of men[2]; nay, all the powers and names of the others are distinctly ascribed to Agni. The hymn belongs, no doubt, to the modern compositions; yet, though Agni is thus highly exalted in it, nothing is said to disparage the divine character of the other gods. Indra is celebrated as the strongest god in the hymns as well as in the Brâhmaṇas, and the burden of one of the songs of the tenth book[3] is "Viśvasmâd Indra uttaraḥ," "Indra is greater than all." Of Soma it is said that he was born great, and that he conquers every one.[4] He is called the king of the world[5], he has the power to prolong the life of men[6],

[1] त्वं विश्वानि स्वनीक पत्यसे। ii. 1. 8. See Nirukta-pariśishṭa, i.

[2] ii. 1. 9.

[3] x. 86.

[4] ix. 59.

[5] ix. 96. 10., bhuvanasya râjâ.

[6] ix. 96. 14.

and in one sense he is called the king of heaven and earth, of Agni, of Sûrya, of Indra, and of Vishṇu.[1]

If we read the next hymn, which is addressed to Varuṇa (οὐρανός), we perceive that the god here invoked is, to the mind of the poet, supreme and almighty. Nevertheless, he is one of the gods who is almost always represented in fellowship with another, Mitra; and even in our hymn there is one verse, the sixth, in which Varuṇa and Mitra are invoked in the dual. Yet what more could human language achieve, in trying to express the idea of a divine and supreme power, than what our poet says of Varuṇa; — "Thou art lord of all, of heaven and earth." Or, as is said in another hymn (ii. 27. 10.), "Thou art the king of all; of those who are gods, and of those who are men." Nor is Varuṇa represented as the Lord of nature only. He knows the order of nature, and upholds it; for this is what is meant by dhṛitavrata.[2] Varuṇa, therefore, knows the twelve months, and even the thirteenth; he knows the course of the wind, the birds in the air, and the ships of the sea. He knows all the wondrous works of nature, and he looks not only into the past but into the future also. But, more than all this, Varuṇa watches over the order of the moral world. The poet begins with a confession that he has neglected the works of Varuṇa, that he has offended against his laws. He craves his pardon; he appeals in self-defence to the weakness of human nature; he deprecates death as the reward of sin. His devotion is all

[1] ix. 96. 5.

[2] Vrata means what must be done, and these Vratas or laws are not to be shaken (aprachyuta) because "they rest on Varuṇa as on a rock." (Rv. ii. 28. 8.)

he has wherewith to appease the anger of his god; and how natural the feeling, when he hopes to soothe the god by his prayers as a horse is soothed by kind words. The poet has evidently felt the anger of Varuṇa. His friends, wishing for booty elsewhere, have left him, and he knows not how to bring back Varuṇa, who is the only giver of victory. He describes the power of his god, and he praises him chiefly as the guardian of law and order. Like a true child of nature, he offers honey, sweet things, which the god is sure to like, and then appeals to him as to a friend: "Now be good, and let us speak together again." This may seem childish, but there is a real and childish faith in it; and, like all childish faith, it is rewarded by some kind of response. For, at that very moment, the poet takes a higher tone. He fancies he sees the god and his chariot passing by; he feels that his prayer has been heard. True, there is much that is human, earthly, coarse, and false in the language applied to the deity as here invoked under the name of Varuṇa. Yet there is something also in these ancient strains of thought and faith which moves and cheers our hearts even at this great distance of time; and a wise man will pause before he ascribes to purely evil sources what may be, for all we know, the working of a love and wisdom beyond our own.

The hymn is ascribed to Śunaḥśepha, according to the legend of the later Brâhmaṇas, the victim offered to Varuṇa by his own father Ajîgarta Sauyavasi. (See p. 413.)

1. However we break thy laws from day to day, men as we are, O god, Varuṇa,

2. Do not deliver us unto death, nor to the blow of the furious; nor to the anger of the spiteful!

3. To propitiate thee, O Varuṇa, we bind thy mind with songs, as the charioteer a weary steed.

4. Away from me they flee dispirited, intent only on gaining wealth; as birds to their nests.

5. When shall we bring hither the man who is victory to the warriors, when shall we bring Varuṇa, the wide-seeing, to be propitiated?

[6. This they take in common with delight, Mitra and Varuṇa; they never fail the faithful giver.]

7. He who knows the place of the birds that fly through the sky, who, on the waters knows the ships,—

8. He, the upholder of order, who knows the twelve months with the offspring of each, and knows the month[1] that is engendered afterwards,—

9. He who knows the track of the wind[2], of the wide, the bright, and mighty; and knows those who reside on high[3],—

10. He, the upholder of order, Varuṇa sits down among his people; he, the wise, sits there to govern.

11. From thence perceiving all wondrous things, he sees what has been and what will be done.

12. May he, the wise son of time (âditya), make our paths straight all our days; may he prolong our lives!

13. Varuṇa, wearing golden mail, has put on his shining cloak; the spies[4] sat down around him.

[1] The thirteenth or intercalary month; see page 212.

[2] Rv. vii. 87. 2., the wind is called the breath of Varuṇa.

[3] The gods.

[4] These spies or watchers are most likely the other Âdityas, of whom it is said (ii. 27. 3.) that "they see into what is evil and what is good, and that everything, even at the greatest distance, is

14. The god, whom the scoffers do not provoke, nor the tormentors of men, nor the plotters of mischief, —

15. He, who gives to men glory, and not half glory, who gives it even to our own bodies, —

16. Yearning for him, the far-seeing, my thoughts move onwards, as kine move to their pastures.

17. Let us speak together again, because my honey has been brought: thou eatest what thou likest, like a friend.[1]

18. Now I saw the god who is to be seen by all, I saw the chariot above the earth: he must have accepted my prayers.

19. O hear this my calling, Varuṇa, be gracious now; longing for help, I have called upon thee.

20. Thou, O wise god, art lord of all, of heaven and earth: listen on thy way.

21. That I may live, take from me the upper rope, loose the middle, and remove the lowest!

This one hymn to Varuṇa would be sufficient to show the mistake of those who deny the presence of moral truths in the ancient religions of the world and, more particularly, in the so-called nature-worship of the Aryans. On the contrary, whatever we find of moral sentiments in those ancient hymns is generally as true to-day as it was thousands of years ago; while what is false and perishable in them

near to them." "With them the right is not distinguished from the left, nor the east, nor the west." (Rv. ii. 27. 11.) See Roth, Zeitschrift der Deutschen Morgenländischen Gesellschaft, vi. 72.

[1] Hotṛi does not mean friend, but the priest who is chosen to invite the gods. Perhaps it means poet and priest in a more general sense than in the later hymns.

has reference to the external aspects of the deity, and to his supposed working in nature. The key-note of all religion, natural as well as revealed, is present in the hymns of the Veda, and never completely drowned by the strange music which generally deafens our ears when we first listen to the wild echoes of the heathen worship. There is the belief in God, the perception of the difference between good and evil, the conviction that God hates sin, and loves the righteous. We can hardly speak with sufficient reverence of the discovery of these truths, however trite they may appear to ourselves; and, if the name of revelation seems too sacred a name to be applied to them, that of discovery is too profane, for it would throw the vital truths of all religion, both ancient and modern, into the same category as the discoveries of a Galileo or a Newton. Theologians may agree in denying that any man in possession of his reason can, without a crime, remain ignorant of God for any length of time. Missionaries, however, who held and defended this opinion, have been led to very different convictions after some intercourse with savage tribes. Dobrizhoffer[1], who was for eighteen years a Missionary in Paraguay, states that the language of the Abipones does not contain a single word which expresses God or a divinity. Penafiel, a Jesuit theologian, declared that there were many Indians who, on being asked whether, during the whole course of their lives they ever thought of God, replied, *no*, *never*. Dobrizhoffer says, "Travelling with fourteen Abipones, I sat down by the fire in the open air, as usual on the high shore of the River

[1] Dobrizhoffer, Account of the Abipones, vol. ii. p. 58.

Plata. The sky, which was perfectly serene, delighted our eyes with its twinkling stars. I began a conversation with the Cacique Ychoalay, the most intelligent of all the Abipones I have been acquainted with, as well as the most famous in war. 'Do you behold,' said I, 'the splendour of Heaven, with its magnificent arrangement of stars? Who can suppose that all this is produced by chance? Whom do you suppose to be their creator and governor? What were the opinions of your ancestors on the subject?' 'My father,' replied Ychoalay, readily and frankly, 'our grandfathers and great-grandfathers, were wont to contemplate the earth alone, solicitous only to see whether the plain afforded grass and water for their horses. They never troubled themselves about what went on in the Heavens, and who was the creator and governor of the stars.'" The Guaranies, who had an expression for the supreme Deity whom they call *tupa*, a word composed of two particles—*tu*, a word of admiration, and *pa*, of interrogation, nevertheless worshipped only an evil spirit. Let us turn our eyes from the Indians of America to the Indians of India, and we shall perceive the immense distance by which these noble races are separated from the savage tribes to whom our Missionaries are still trying, and trying in vain, to impart the first principles of religion. The language of their simple prayers is more intelligible to us than anything we find in the literature of Greece and Rome, and there are, here and there, short expressions of faith and devotion in which even a Christian can join without irreverence. If the following were not addressed to Varuṇa, one of the many names of the deity, it would seem to contain nothing strange or offensive to our ears:

1. Let me not yet, O Varuṇa, enter into the house of clay; have mercy, almighty, have mercy!

2. If I go along trembling, like a cloud driven by the wind; have mercy, almighty, have mercy!

3. Through want of strength, thou strong and bright god, have I gone to the wrong shore; have mercy, almighty, have mercy!

4. Thirst came upon the worshipper, though he stood in the midst of the waters; have mercy, almighty, have mercy!

5. Whenever we men, O Varuṇa, commit an offence before the heavenly host; whenever we break thy law through thoughtlessness; have mercy, almighty, have mercy!

Here we have the two ideas, so contradictory to the human understanding, and yet so easily reconciled in every human heart: God has established the eternal laws of the moral world, and yet he is willing to forgive those who offend against them; just, yet merciful; a judge, and yet a father. "He is merciful even to him who has committed sin."[1]

The next hymn allows us a still deeper insight into the strange ideas which the Ṛishis had formed to themselves as to the nature of sin. (Rv. vii. 86.)

1. Wise and mighty are the works of him who stemmed asunder the wide firmaments. He lifted on high the bright and glorious heaven; he stretched out apart the starry sky and the earth.

[1] Rv. vii. 87. 7. yaḥ mṛiḷayâti chakrushe chit âgaḥ.

2. Do I say this to my own soul? How can I get unto Varuṇa? Will he accept my offering without displeasure? When shall I, with a quiet mind, see him propitiated?

3. I ask, O Varuṇa, wishing to know this my sin. I go to ask the wise. The sages all tell me the same: Varuṇa it is who is angry with thee.

4. Was it an old sin, O Varuṇa, that thou wishest to destroy thy friend, who always praises thee? Tell me, thou unconquerable lord, and I will quickly turn to thee with praise, freed from sin.

7. Absolve us from the sins of our fathers, and from those which we committed with our own bodies. Release Vasishṭha[1], O king, like a thief who has feasted on stolen cattle; release him like a calf from the rope.

6. It was not our own doing, O Varuṇa, it was necessity, an intoxicating draught, passion, dice, thoughtlessness. The old is near to mislead the young; even sleep brings unrighteousness.

7. Let me without sin give satisfaction, like a slave to the bounteous lord, the god, our support. The lord god enlightened the foolish; he, the wisest, leads his worshipper to wealth.

8. O lord, Varuṇa, may this song go well to thy heart! May we prosper in keeping and acquiring! Protect us, O gods, always with your blessings!

These ideas preponderate in hymns addressed to Varuṇa, but they likewise occur in the prayers to the other gods. Varuṇa is one of the Âdityas, the sons of time, the Kroniones, the heavenly gods. The hymns addressed to these Âdityas in general are full

[1] Name of the poet.

of moral sentiments, because these gods are believed to protect men, not only against the assaults of nature, against disease and suffering, but also against the temptations of sin.

Rv. viii. 13. 14. "May evil betide him, the cursing mortal, the enemy who, double-tongued, would deal us a felon's blow.

15. You gods are with the righteous; you know men in their hearts. Come to the true man, and to the false, ye Vasus!

16. We implore the protection of the mountains, and the protection of the waters.[1] Heaven and earth, remove from us all evil.

17. Carry us, O Vasus, by your blessed protection, as it were in your ship, across all dangers.

18. To our offspring, to our race, and thus to ourselves, make life longer to live, ye valiant Âdityas!

21. O Mitra, Aryaman, Varuṇa, and ye Winds, grant us an abode free from sin, full of men, glorious, with three bars.

22. We, who are but men, the bondsmen of death, prolong our time well, O Âdityas, that we may live!

Indra, one of the principal gods of the Veda, is likewise invoked, together with the Âdityas, as a god who may pardon sin. "Whatever sin we have committed against you[2]," the poet says, "let us obtain, O Indra, the broad safe light of day; let not the long darkness come upon us!" Indra is clearly conceived as a moral being in the following verse (Rv. viii. 21. 14.):

"Thou never findest a rich man to be thy friend;

[1] Rv. viii. 31. 10. [2] Rv. ii. 27. 14.

wine-swillers despise thee. But when thou thunderest, when thou gatherest (the clouds), then thou art called like a father."

Out of a large number of hymns addressed to the same god, we select one that is ascribed to Vasishṭha. (Rv. vii. 32.)

1. Let no one, not even those who worship thee, delay thee far from us! Even from afar come to our feast! Or, if thou art here, listen to us!

2. For these who here make prayers for thee, sit together near the libation, like flies round the honey. The worshippers, anxious for wealth, have placed their desire upon Indra, as we put our foot upon a chariot.

3. Desirous of riches, I call him who holds the thunderbolt with his arm, and who is a good giver, like as a son calls his father.

4. These libations of Soma, mixed with milk, have been prepared for Indra: thou, armed with the thunderbolt, come with the steeds to drink of them for thy delight; come to the house!

5. May he hear us, for he has ears to hear. He is asked for riches; will he despise our prayers? He could soon give hundreds and thousands;—no one could check him if he wishes to give.

6. He who prepares for thee, O Vṛitra-killer, deep libations, and pours them out[1] before thee, that hero thrives with Indra, never scorned of men.

[1] *Dhâvati* is explained as a neuter verb by the commentary, "he who runs towards thee." Dhâvati, however, is a technical term, applied to the libations of the Soma-juice, as may be seen, Rv. viii. 1. 17. "Sota hi somam adribhiḥ â îm enam apsu dhâvata," "Press the Soma with stones, make it run into the water."

7. Be thou, O mighty, the shield of the mighty (Vasishṭhas) when thou drivest together the fighting men. Let us share the wealth of him whom thou hast slain; bring us the household of him who is hard to vanquish.

8. Offer Soma to the drinker of Soma, to Indra, the lord of the thunderbolt; roast roasts; make him to protect us: Indra, the giver, is a blessing to him who gives oblations.

9. Do not grudge, ye givers of Soma; give strength[1] to the great god, make him to give wealth! He alone who perseveres, conquers, abides, and flourishes: the gods are not to be trifled with.

10. No one surrounds the chariot of the liberal worshipper, no one stops it. He whom Indra protects and the Maruts, he will come into stables full of cattle.

11. He will, when fighting, obtain spoil[2], O Indra, the mortal, whose protection thou shouldst be. O hero, be thou the protection of our chariots, and of our men!

12. His share is exceeding great, like the wealth of a winner. He who is Indra with his steeds, him no enemies can subdue; may he give strength to the sacrificer!

13. Make for the sacred gods a hymn that is not small, that is well set and beautiful! Many snares pass by him who abides with Indra through his sacrifice.

[1] Dakshata is construed with the dative, and the cæsura forbids to join mahe with râye. A similar construction occurs vii. 97. 8., Dakshâyyâya dakshata, where the commentator explains it rightly.

[2] This verse shows signs of a later origin; the ideas are taken from the preceding verse.

14. What mortal dares to attack him who is rich in thee? Through faith in thee, O mighty, the strong acquires spoil in the day of battle.

15. Stir us mighty Vasishṭhas in the slaughter of the enemies, stir us who give their dearest treasures. Under thy guidance, O Haryaśva, we shall with our wise counsellors overcome all hardships.

16. To thee belongs the lowest treasure; thou rearest the middle treasure; thou art king always of all the highest treasure; no one withstands thee in the flock.

17. Thou art well known as the benefactor of every one, whatever battles there be. Every one of these kings of the earth implores thy name, when wishing for help.

18. If I were lord of as much as thou, I should support the sacred bard, thou scatterer of wealth, I should not abandon him to misery.

19. I should award wealth day by day to him who magnifies, I should award it to whosoever it be.[1] We have no other friend but thee, no other happiness, no other father, O mighty!

20. He who perseveres acquires spoil with his wife as his mate; I bend Indra, who is invoked by many, for you, as a wheelwright bends a wheel made of strong wood.

21. A mortal does not get riches by scant praise: no wealth comes to the grudger. The strong man it is, O mighty, who in the day of battle is a precious gift to thee like as to me.

22. We call for thee, O hero, like cows that have

[1] According to the commentator *Kuhachidvid* means "wherever he be." It may perhaps mean the ignorant.

not been milked; we praise thee as ruler of all that moves, O Indra, as ruler of all that is immovable.

23. There is no one like thee in heaven or earth; he is not born, and will not be born. O mighty Indra, we call upon thee as we go fighting for cows and horses.

24. Bring all this to those who are good, O Indra, be they old or young[1]; for thou, O mighty, art the rich of old, and to be called in every battle.

25. Push away the unfriendly, O mighty, make us treasures easy to get! Be the protector of ourselves in the fight, be the cherisher of our friends!

26. Indra, give wisdom to us, as a father to his sons. Teach us in this path, let us living see the sun!

27. Let not unknown wretches, evil-disposed and unhallowed, tread us down. Through thy help, O hero, let us step over the rushing eternal waters!

In this hymn Indra is clearly conceived as the supreme god, and we can hardly understand how a people who had formed so exalted a notion of the deity and embodied it in the person of Indra, could, at the same sacrifice, invoke other gods with equal praise. When Agni, the lord of fire, is addressed by the poet, he is spoken of as the first god, not inferior even to Indra. While Agni is invoked, Indra is forgotten; there is no competition between the two, nor any rivalry between them or other gods. This is a most important feature in the religion of the Veda, and has never been taken into consideration by those who have written on the history of ancient polytheism.

[1] Jyâyaḥ stands for jyâyasaḥ.

There are other hymns, again, in which the notion of a deity is much less prominent. Indra is there represented like a hero fighting against enemies. He is liable to defeat, his heart fails him in the combat, and though at last he invariably conquers, he does so rather by an effort than by the mere assertion of his power. Agni, again, in many hymns, is simply described as a power of nature, as the fire such as it is seen in heaven and on earth. Many things that have become to us familiar, struck the poets of the Veda as wonderful and mysterious. They describe the power of the fire with an awe which, to the natural philosopher of the present day, must appear childish. The production of fire by the friction of wood, or its sudden descent from the sky in the form of lightning, is to them as marvellous as the birth of a child. They feel their dependence on fire; they have experienced what it is to be without it. They were not yet acquainted with lucifer-matches, and hence, when describing the simple phenomena of fire, they do it naturally with a kind of religious reverence. The following verses, taken from a hymn of Vasishṭha (vii. 3.) may serve as a specimen:

"Neighing like a horse that is greedy for food, when it steps out from the strong prison;—then the wind blows after his blast; thy path, O Agni, is dark at once.[1]

[1] The construction of this verse is very abrupt, particularly the transition from the simile of the horse, which is put in the third person, to the address to Agni in the second person. The idea, however, is clear. Agni, the fire, when first lighted, is compared with a neighing horse, on account of the crackling noise. He is greedy for food as soon as he steps out of his prison, viz., from the wood from which fire is produced by friction, like a horse stepping

O Agni, thou from whom, as a new-born male, undying flames proceed, the brilliant smoke goes towards the sky, for as messenger thou art sent to the gods.

Thou whose power spreads over the earth in a moment when thou hast grasped food with thy jaws,—like a dashing army thy blast goes forth; with thy lambent flame thou seemest to tear up the grass.

Him alone, the ever-youthful Agni, men groom, like a horse in the evening and at dawn; they bed him as a stranger in his couch; the light of Agni, the worshipped[1] male, is lighted.

Thy appearance is fair to behold, thou brightfaced Agni, when like gold thou shinest at hand; thy brightness comes like the lightning of heaven; thou showest splendour like the bright sun."

The human, and afterwards divine qualities ascribed to Agni arise chiefly from his character as messenger between gods and men, or, as high-priest, when he is supposed to carry the oblation to the gods. It is one of the most favourite themes of the Vedic poets, though perhaps of the modern rather than of the ancient, to celebrate Agni as a priest, as endowed with all priestly powers, and enjoying all the honorific titles given to the various persons who minister at the great sacrifices. The following hymns, one of Vatsa (Rv. viii. 11.), the other of Gotama (Rv. i. 74.), are rather simple as compared with others of the same class, though there are ex-

out of his stable. Then the wind is supposed to kindle the blaze of the fire, and as the path of the horse is darkened by dust, the path of Agni is darkened by smoke.

[1] Âhuta is used in the general sense of worshipped, well attended, with special reference to a guest. Cf. Rv. i. 44. 4.

pressions in both which indicate their more modern character.

1. Thou, Agni, art the guardian of sacred rites: thou art a god among mortals[1]; thou art to be praised at the sacrifices.

2. Thou strong Agni, art to be praised at the festivals, thou who like a charioteer carriest the offerings to the gods.

3. Fight and drive thou away from us the fiends, O Jâtavedas, the ungodly enemies, O Agni!

4. Thou, Jâtavedas, desirest not the offering of a hostile man, be it ever so nigh to thee.

5. We mortals and sages worship the great name of thee, the immortal Jâtavedas.

6. We sages call the sage to help, we mortals call on the god for protection, we call on Agni with songs.

7. May the poet draw thy mind even from the most distant abode with the song that longs for thee, O Agni.

8. Thou art the same in many places, a lord among all people: we call upon thee in battles.

9. In battles we call upon thee, Agni, for help when we want strength; we call in struggles upon the giver of precious gifts.

10. Thou art ancient, to be praised at the sacrifices; thou sittest as priest from of old and to-day. Replenish thy own body, O Agni, and grant happiness to us!

1. As we go to the sacrifice let us say a song to Agni, to him who hears us even from afar.

[1] Might it be "deveshv â martyeshv â," "among gods and among men"?

2. He who, existing from of old, defended the house for the sacrificer when hostile tribes were gathering together.

3. Let even the nations confess, "Agni was born, the slayer of the enemy, the winner of booty in every battle."

4. He whose messenger thou art in the house, whose offerings thou art pleased to accept, and whose sacrifice thou renderest efficient,

5. Of him indeed, O Angiras, son of strength, people say that his offerings are good, his gods are good and his altar is good.

6. Bring hither, O serene Agni, these gods, bring them that they may be praised, that they may accept the offerings.

7. When thou, O Agni, goest on a mission, the sound of the horses of thy moving chariot is never heard.

8. If protected by thee, the warrior is unabashed. Onward he goes, one after another, forward he steps, O Agni, who offers oblations.

9. Thou, O bright god, bestowest with increase a brilliant array of heroes upon him who offers oblations to the bright gods.[1]

It is curious to watch the almost imperceptible transition by which the phenomena of nature, if re-

[1] Every word of this verse baffles translation. Vivâsasi is not simply "thou bestowest," but "thou spreadest out as the sun spreads out his rays." Suvîrya is not "an array of heroes," but an abstract, signifying the possession of good strength, only that this good strength means "the chief of all their strength," and has special reference to the sons and all the males born in the house. Dyumad, brilliant, corresponds with the verb vivâsasi. Brihat should be taken as an adverb, signifying the ever increasing nature of the gift bestowed by Agni.

flected in the mind of the poet, assume the character of divine beings. The dawn is frequently described in the Veda as it might be described by a modern poet. She is the friend of men, she smiles like a young wife, she is the daughter of the sky. She goes to every house, (i. 123. 4.); she thinks of the dwellings of men (i. 123. 1.); she does not despise the small or the great (i. 124. 6.); she brings wealth (i. 48. 1.); she is always the same, immortal, divine (i. 124. 4.; i. 123. 8.); age cannot touch her (i. 113. 15.); she is the young goddess, but she makes men grow old (i. 92. 11.). All this may be simply allegorical language. But the transition from *devî*, the bright, to *devî*, the goddess, is so easy; the daughter of the sky assumes so readily the same personality which is given to the sky, Dyaus, her father, that we can only guess whether in every passage the poet is speaking of a bright apparition, or of a bright goddess; of a natural vision, or of a visible deity. The following hymn of Vasishṭha (vii. 77.), will serve as an instance:—

"She shines upon us, like a young wife, rousing every living being to go to his work. The fire had to be kindled by men[1]; she brought light by striking down darkness.

She rose up, spreading far and wide, and moving towards every one. She grew in brightness, wearing her brilliant garment. The mother of the cows (of the morning clouds), the leader of the days, she shone gold-coloured, lovely to behold.

She, the fortunate, who brings the eye of the god, who leads the white and lovely steed (of the

[1] The fire of the altar for the morning prayers.

sun), the Dawn was seen, revealed by her rays, with brilliant treasures she follows every one.

Thou, who art a blessing where thou art near, drive far away the unfriendly; make the pastures wide, give us safety! Remove the haters, bring treasures! Raise up wealth to the worshipper, thou mighty Dawn.

Shine for us with thy best rays, thou bright Dawn, thou who lengthenest our life, thou the love of all, who givest us food, who givest us wealth in cows, horses, and chariots.

Thou, daughter of the sky, thou high-born Dawn, whom the Vasishṭhas magnify with songs, give us riches high and wide: all ye gods, protect us always with your blessings!"

This hymn addressed to the Dawn is a fair specimen of the original simple poetry of the Veda. It has no reference to any special sacrifice, it contains no technical expressions, it can hardly be called a hymn, in our sense of the word. It is simply a poem expressing, without any effort, without any display of far-fetched thought or brilliant imagery, the feelings of a man who has watched the approach of the dawn with mingled delight and awe, and who was moved to give utterance to what he felt, in measured language. We have heard the same thoughts and feelings expressed by so many poets, that we can hardly enter into the pleasure with which those early singers spoke their hearts out for the first time. We have become so accustomed to the rules of the most complicated metres that we hardly consider how mysterious is that instinct which suggested to the first poets the extraordinary variety of rhythm which we find in the Veda. But there is a charm in these primitive strains discoverable in no other class of poetry. Every word retains something of its radical meaning, every epithet tells, every thought, in spite of the most intricate and abrupt expressions, is, if we once disentangle it, true, correct, and complete. But this is not the case with all the poems of the Veda. It would be tedious to translate many specimens of what I consider the poetry of the secondary age, the Mantra period. These songs are generally intended for sacrificial purposes, they are loaded with technicalities, their imagery is sometimes more brilliant, but always less perspicuous, and many thoughts and expressions are clearly borrowed from earlier hymns. One specimen may suffice, a hymn describing the sacrifice of the horse with the full detail of a superstitious ceremonial. (Ṛv. i. 162.)

"May Mitra, Varuṇa, Aryaman, Âyu, Indra, the Lord of the Ṛibhus, and the Maruts not rebuke us because we shall proclaim at the sacrifice the virtues of the swift horse sprung from the gods.

When they lead before the horse, which is decked with pure gold ornaments, the offering, firmly grasped, the spotted goat[1] bleats while walking onward; it goes the path beloved by Indra and Pûshan.

This goat, destined for all the gods, is led first with the quick horse, as Pûshan's share; for Tvashṭṛi himself raises to glory this pleasant offering which is brought with the horse.

When thrice at the proper seasons men lead around the sacrificial horse which goes to the gods, Pûshan's

[1] The goat is the victim or the offering which is led before the horse, and sacrificed to Indra and Pûshan.

share comes first, the goat, which announces the sacrifice to the gods.

Hotṛi, Adhvaryu, Âvayaj (Pratiprasthâtṛi), Agnimindha (Agnîdhra), Grâvagrâbha (Grâvastut), and the wise Śanstṛi (Prasâstṛi)[1], may you fill the streams (round the altar) with a sacrifice which is well prepared and well accomplished.

They who cut the sacrificial post, and they who carry it, they who make the ring for the post of the horse, and even they who bring together what is cooked for the horse, may their work be with us.

He came on — (my prayer has been well performed), — the bright-backed horse goes[2] to the regions of the gods. Wise poets celebrate him, and we have won a good friend for the love of the gods.

The halter of the swift one, the heel-ropes of the horse, the head-ropes, the girths, the bridle, and even the grass that has been put into his mouth, may all these which belong to thee be with the gods![3]

What the fly eats of the flesh, what adheres to the stick, or to the axe, or to the hands of the immolator and his nails, may all these which belong to thee be with the gods!

The ordure that runs from the belly, and the smallest particle of raw flesh, may the immolators well prepare all this, and dress the sacrifice till it is well cooked.

The juice that flows from thy roasted limb on the spit after thou hast been killed, may it not run on

[1] All names of priests.

[2] In these hymns it is sometimes difficult to say whether the horse be meant, or the sun, of which it is the emblem.

[3] The verb in the singular (astu) with the substantive in the plural (sarvâ) finds an analogy in Greek.

the earth or the grass; may it be given to the gods who desire it.

They who examine the horse when it is roasted, they who say "it smells well, take it away," they who serve the distribution of the meat, may their work also be with us.

The ladle of the pot where the meat is cooked, and the vessels for sprinkling the juice, the vessels to keep off the heat, the covers of the vessels, the skewers, and the knives, they adorn the horse.

Where he walks, where he sits, where he stirs, the foot-fastening of the horse, what he drinks, and what food he eats, may all these which belong to thee be with the gods!

May not the fire with smoky smell make thee hiss, may not the glowing cauldron smell and burst. The gods accept the horse if it is offered to them in due form.

The cover which they stretch over the horse, and the golden ornaments, the head-ropes of the horse, and the foot-ropes, all these which are dear to the gods, they offer to them.

If some one strike thee with the heel or the whip that thou mayest lie down, and thou art snorting with all thy might, then I purify all this with my prayer, as with a spoon of clarified butter at the sacrifices.

The axe approaches the thirty-four ribs of the quick horse, beloved of the gods. Do you wisely keep the limbs whole, find out each joint and strike.

One strikes the brilliant horse, two hold it, thus is the custom. Those of thy limbs which I have seasonably prepared, I sacrifice in the fire as balls offered to the gods.

May not thy dear soul burn thee while thou art coming near, may the axe not stick to thy body. May no greedy and unskilful immolator, missing with the sword, throw thy mangled limbs together.

Indeed thou diest not thus, thou sufferest not; thou goest to the gods on easy paths. The two horses of Indra, the two deer of the Maruts have been yoked, and the horse come to the shaft of the ass (of the Aśvins.)

May this horse give us cattle and horses, men, progeny, and all-sustaining wealth. May Aditi keep us free from sin; may the horse of this sacrifice give us strength!

A comparison of the general tone of this hymn with that of the hymns to Varuṇa, Indra, and Ushas, translated before, can leave little doubt in the mind of critical historians as to its more modern character. We must be careful, however, not to judge the poetry of the ancient bards of India according to our own standard of what is simple and natural and what is not. The great importance attached to what to us seem mere trifles in the performance of a sacrifice would not be sufficient to stamp this hymn as modern. The superstitious feeling about ceremonial minutiæ is natural in a primitive state of civilisation, and there are numerous hymns in the Veda which must be adjudged to the earliest period, and where, nevertheless, we meet with sentiments worthy of the most advanced ceremonialists.

The same caution is still more necessary with regard to another criterion which has been used to establish the modern date of certain hymns, the presence of philosophical ideas. It has been the custom to regard any hymn in which the nature of the deity, the problems of existence, the hope of immortality are expressed, as decidedly modern. The whole tenth Maṇḍala has been assigned to a later period, chiefly because it contains many hymns the language of which approaches the philosophical diction of the Upanishads and of the still later systems of philosophy. This is a mistake.

There is very little to guide us in forming a judgment of what is genuine and primitive in the ancient poetry of so peculiar a race as the Aryans of India. We have nothing to compare with the poetical relics of the Vedic age. Because we find in some hymns ideas or expressions which, in the literatures of other nations, such as the Jews, or Greeks and Romans, we have accustomed ourselves to regard as of comparatively modern growth, we have no right to conclude that they are equally modern in the history of the Indian mind. The Veda opens to us a chamber in the labyrinth of the human mind through which the other Aryan nations had passed long before they become visible to us by the light of history. Whatever the age of the Veda may be, in one sense it is the oldest book in existence. If this collection had been written but fifty years ago, in some distant part of the world untouched by the general stream of civilisation, we should still call it more ancient than the Homeric poems, because it represents an earlier phase of human thought and feeling. Names[1] which in Homer have become petrified and mythological, are to be found in the Veda as it were in a

[1] See Essai de Mythologie Comparée, traduit de l'Anglais de Max Müller, Paris, 1859, p. 47.

still fluid state. They next appear as appellatives, not yet as proper names; they are organic, not yet broken and smoothed down. Nor can we compare that earlier, lower, and more savage phase of thought which we find in the Veda, with what we know of really barbarous tribes, such as the Negroes of Africa or the Indians of America. For, however inferior to the Greeks of Homer and the Jews of Moses, the Aryas of the Seven Rivers are far above those races, and had long crossed the bounds of an unconscious barbarism, when they worshipped Dyaus and the other bright gods of nature.

Let us consider but a single point. We have accustomed ourselves to regard a belief in the unity of God as one of the last stages to which the Greek mind ascended from the depths of a polytheistic faith. The one unknown God was the final result which the pupils of Plato and Aristotle had arrived at when they came to listen to the strange teaching of St. Paul at Athens. But how can we tell that the course of thought was the same in India? By what right do we mark all hymns as modern in which the idea of one God breaks through the clouds of a polytheistic phraseology? The belief in a Supreme God, in a God above all gods, may in the abstract seem later than the belief in many gods. Yet let one poet but once perceive how he is drawn towards the Divine by the same feelings that draw him towards his father, let such a poet in his simple prayer but once utter, though it be thoughtlessly, the words, "My father," and the dreary desert through which philosophy marches step by step, is crossed at a single bound. We must not compare the Aryan and the Semitic races. Whereas the Semitic nations relapsed from time to time into polytheism, the Aryans of India seem to have relapsed into Monotheism. In both cases these changes were not the result of a gradual and regular progress, but of individual impulses and peculiar influences. I do not think, therefore, that the mere occurrence of monotheistic ideas, and of other large philosophical conceptions, is sufficient to stamp any class of hymns as of modern date. A decided preponderance of such ideas, coupled with other indications in the character of the language, might make us hesitate before we used such as witnesses for the Chhandas period. But there is a monotheism that precedes the polytheism of the Veda, and even in the invocations of their innumerable gods the remembrance of a God, one and infinite, breaks through the mist of an idolatrous phraseology, like the blue sky that is hidden by passing clouds.

There is a hymn of peculiar interest in the tenth Maṇḍala, full of ideas which to many would seem to necessitate the admission of a long antecedent period of philosophical thought. There we find the conception of a beginning of all things, and of a state previous even to all existence. "Nothing that is, was then," the poet says; and he adds, with a boldness matched only by the Eleatic thinkers of Greece, or by Hegel's philosophy, "even what is not (τὸ μὴ ὄν), did not exist then." He then proceeds to deny the existence of the sky and of the firmament, and yet, unable to bear the idea of an unlimited nothing, he exclaims, "What was it that hid or covered the existing?" Thus driven on, and asking two questions at once, with a rapidity of thought which the Greek and the Sanskrit languages only can follow, he says, "What was the refuge of what?" After this metaphysical flight, the poet returns to the more substantive realities of thought, and, throwing out a doubt, he continues, "Was water the deep abyss, the chaos, which swallowed everything?" Then his mind, turning away from nature, dwells upon man and the problem of human life. "There was no death," he says, and, with a logic which perhaps has never been equalled, he subjoins, "therefore was there nothing immortal." Death, to his mind, becomes the proof of immortality. One more negation, and he has done. "There was no space, no life, and lastly, there was no time, no difference between day and night, no solar torch by which morning might have been told from evening." All these ideas lie imbedded in the simple words, "Na râtryâ ahna âsît praketaḥ." Now follows his first assertion: "That One," he says, and he uses no other epithet or qualification—"That One breathed breathless by itself: other than it nothing since has been." This expression, "it breathed breathless" seems to me one of the happiest attempts at making language reflect the colourless abstractions of the mind. "That One," the poet says, "breathed, and lived; it enjoyed more than mere existence; yet its life was not dependent on anything else, as our life depends on the air which we breathe. It breathed breathless." Language blushes at such expressions, but her blush is a blush of triumph.

After this the poet plunges into imagery. "Darkness there was, and all at first was veiled in gloom profound, as ocean without light." No one has ever found a truer expression of the Infinite, breathing and heaving within itself, than the ocean in a dark night, without a star, without a torch. It would have been easy to fill out the picture, and a modern writer would have filled it out. The true poet, however, says but a single word, and, at his spell, pictures arise within our own mind, full of a reality beyond the reach of any art.

But now this One had to be represented as growing—as entering into reality—and here again nature must supply a similitude to the poet. As yet, the real world existed only as a germ, hidden in a husky shell; now, the poet represents the one substance as borne into life by its own innate heat. The beginning of the world was conceived like the spring of nature; one miracle was explained by another. But, even then, this Being, or this nature, as conceived by the poet, was only an unconscious substance, without will and without change. The question how there was generation in nature, was still unanswered. Another miracle had to be appealed to, in order to explain the conscious act of creation: this miracle was Love, as perceived in the heart of man. "Then first came love upon it," the poet continues, and he defines love, not only as a natural, but as a mental impulse. Though he cannot say what love is, yet he knows that all will recognise what he means by love,—a power which arises from the unsearchable depths of our nature,—making us feel our own incompleteness, and drawing us, half-conscious, half-unconscious, towards that far off and desired something, through which alone our life seems to become a reality. This is the analogy which was wanted to explain the life of nature, which he knew was more than mere existence. The One Being which the poet had postulated was neither self-sufficient nor dead: a desire fell upon it,—a spring of life, manifested in growth of every kind. After the manifestation of this desire or will, all previous existence seemed to be unreal, a mere nothing as compared with the fulness of genuine life. A substance without this life, without that infinite desire of production and reproduction, could hardly be said to exist. It was a bare abstract conception. Here, then, the poet imagines he has discovered the secret of creation,—the transition of the nothing into the something,—the change of the abstract into the concrete. Love was to him the beginning of real reality, and he appeals to the wise of old, who discovered in love, "the bond between created things and uncreated." What follows is more difficult to understand. We hardly know into what new sphere of thought the poet enters. The growth of nature has commenced, but where was it? Did the piercing ray of light come from below, or from above? This is the question which the poet asks, but to which he returns no answer, for he proceeds at once to describe the presence of male and female powers, nor is it likely that what follows, "svadhâ avastât, prayatiḥ parastât," is meant as an answer to the preceding enquiry. The figure which represents the creation as a ray entering the realm of darkness from the realm of light, occurs again at a much later time in the system of Manichaeism[1], but like all attempts at clothing transcendental ideas in the imagery of human thought, it fails to convey any tangible or intelligible impression. This our poet also seems to have felt, for he exclaims, "Who indeed knows? Who proclaimed it here, whence, whence this creation was produced? The gods were later than its production, therefore who knows whence it came?" And now a

[1] Lassen, Indische Alterthumskunde, iii. p. 409.

new thought dawns in the mind of the Ṛishi, a thought for which we were not prepared, and which apparently contradicts the whole train of argument or meditation that preceded. Whereas hitherto the problem of existence was conceived as a mere evolution of one substance, postulated by human reasoning, the poet now speaks of an Adhyaksha, an overseer, a contemplator, who resides in the highest heavens. He, he says, knows it. And why? Because this creation came from him, whether he made it or not. The poet asserts the fact that this overseer is the source of creation, though he shrinks from determining the exact process, whether he created from himself, or from nothing, or from matter existing by itself. Here the poet might have stopped; but there are yet four more words of extreme perplexity which close the poem. They may be interpreted in two ways. They either mean "Or does he not know?" and this would be a question of defiance addressed to all who might doubt his former assertion; or they mean "Or he knows not," and this would be a confession of doubt on the part of the poet startling perhaps after the firm assertion of his belief in this one overseer and creator, yet not irreconcileable with that spirit of timidity displayed in the words, "whether he made it himself or not," which skrinks from asserting anything on a point where human reason, left to herself, can only guess and hope, and if it venture on words, say in last resort, "Behold, we know not anything."

I subjoin a metrical translation of this hymn, which I owe to the kindness of a friend:—

"Nor aught nor naught existed; yon bright sky
Was not, nor heaven's broad woof outstretched above.
What covered all? what sheltered? what concealed?
Was it the water's fathomless abyss?
There was not death—hence was there naught immortal,
There was no confine betwixt day and night;
The only One breathed breathless in itself,
Other than it there nothing since has been.
Darkness there was, and all at first was veiled
In gloom profound,—an ocean without light.—
The germ that still lay covered in the husk
Burst forth, one nature, from the fervent heat.
Then first came Love upon it, the new spring
Of mind—yea, poets in their hearts discerned,
Pondering, this bond between created things
And uncreated. Comes this spark from earth,
Piercing and all-pervading, or from heaven?
Then seeds were sown, and mighty power arose—
Nature below, and Power and Will above.
Who knows the secret? who proclaimed it here,
Whence, whence this manifold creation sprang?—
The gods themselves came later into being.—
Who knows from whence this great creation sprang?—
He from whom all this great creation came.
Whether his will created or was mute,
The Most High seer that is in highest heaven,
He knows it,—or perchance e'en He knows not."

Many of the thoughts expressed in this hymn will, to most readers, appear to proceed rather from a school of mystic philosophers than from a simple and primitive clan of shepherds and colonists. Meditations on the mysteries of creation are generally considered a luxury which no society can indulge in before ample provision has been made for the lower cravings of human nature; such is no doubt the case in modern times. Philosophers arise after the security of a state has been established, after wealth has been acquired and accumulated in certain families, after schools and universities have been founded, and a taste created for those literary pursuits which, even in the most advanced state of civilisation, must necessarily be confined to but a small portion of our ever-toiling community. Metaphysics, whether in the form of poetry or prose, are, and always have been, the privilege of a limited number of independent thinkers, and thoughts like those which we find in this ancient hymn, though clothed in a form of argument more in accordance with the requirements of our age, would fail to excite any interest except among the few who have learnt to delight in the speculations of a Plato, a Tauler, or a Coleridge. But it would be false to transfer our ideas to the early periods of oriental life. First of all, the merely physical wants of a people living in the rich plains of India were satisfied without great exertions. Secondly, such was the simplicity of their life, that nothing existed that could absorb the energies of the most highly gifted among them. Neither war, nor politics, nor arts, opened a field for the exercise of genius, and for the satisfaction of a legitimate ambition. Nor should it be forgotten that, in the natural course of human life, there is after all nothing that appeals with greater force to our deepest interests than the problem of our existence, of our beginning and our end, of our dependence on a Higher Power, and of our yearnings for a better life. With us these key-notes of human thought are drowned in the din of our busy society. Artificial interests have supplanted the natural desires of the human heart. Nor less should we forget how, in these later ages, most of us have learnt from the history of the past that our reason, in spite of her unextinguishable aspirations, consumes this life in a prison the walls of which she cannot pierce, and where we only see light by lifting our eyes on high. All this was different in ancient times, and particularly among a people so remarkably gifted for philosophical abstraction as the Hindus. Long before they began to care for the laws of nature, the return of the seasons, the course of the stars, or any other scientific or practical subject, their thoughts were fixed on the one great and ever recurring question, What am I? What does all this world around me mean? Is there a cause, is there a creator—a God? or is it all an illusion, chance, or fate? Again and again the Rishis express their doubts, and the one knowledge which they value as wonderful and excellent is the knowledge of τὰ μέγιστα. It cannot be right to class every poem and every verse in which mystic or metaphysical speculations occur as modern, simply because they resemble the language of the Upanishads. These Upanishads did not spring into existence on a sudden: like a stream which has received many a mountain torrent, and is fed by many a rivulet, the literature of the Upanishads proves, better than anything else, that the elements of their philosophical poetry came from a more distant fountain. The evidence of language is the most decisive for settling the relative age of Vedic hymns; and the occurrence of such a word as *tadânîm*, then, is more calculated to rouse doubts as to the early date of this hymn than the most abstruse metaphysical ideas which may be discovered in it. Hymns like that ascribed to Dîrghatamas (i. 164.) contain, no doubt, many verses full of the most artificial conceptions, the lucubrations rather of conceited dreamers than of simple and original thinkers. But even in those large collective poems there are lines which look like relics of a better age, and bear the stamp of true and genuine feeling. Thus we read in the 37th verse:—"I know not what this is that I am like; turned inward I walk, chained in my mind. When the first-born of time comes near me, then I obtain the portion of this speech."

In the 30th verse of the same hymn we read: "Breathing lies the quick-moving life, heaving, yet firm, in the midst of its abodes. The living one walks through the powers of the dead: the immortal is the brother of the mortal." Sometimes when these oracular sayings have been pronounced, the poet claims his due. "One who had eyes," he says, "saw it; the blind will not understand it. A poet, who is a boy, he has perceived it; he who understands it will be the father of his father."

In the same hymn one verse occurs which boldly declares the existence of but one Divine Being, though invoked under different names. (Rv. i. 164. 46.) "They call (him) Indra, Mitra, Varuṇa, Agni; then he is the well-winged heavenly Garutmat; that which is One the wise call it many ways; they call it Agni, Yama, Mâtariśvan." Many of these verses have been incorporated in the Upanishads, and are there explained by later sophists who wish to represent them as a guarantee for the scholastic doctrines of the Vedânta philosophy. It was in the Upanishads and in the Sûtras of Vyâsa that most Sanskrit scholars became first acquainted with these quotations from the Veda, and hence, even after they had been discovered in their original place in the hymns of the Rig-veda-sanhitâ, a prejudice remained against their antiquity. The ideas which they expressed were supposed to be of too abstract a nature for the uneducated poets of the Vedic age. I am far from defending the opinion of those who maintained the existence of a school of priests and philosophers in the remotest ages of the world, and who discovered the deepest wisdom in the religious mysteries and mythological traditions of the East. But the reaction which these extravagant theories has produced goes too far, if every thought which touches on the problems of philosophy is to be marked indiscriminately as a modern forgery, if every conception which reminds us of Moses, Plato, or the Apostles, is to be put down as necessarily borrowed from Jewish, Greek or Christian sources, and foisted thence into the collections of the ancient poetry of the Hindus.

There is what Leibnitz called *perennis quædam philosophia*, a search after truth which was not confined to the schools of priests or philosophers. Its language, no doubt, is less exact than that of an Aristotle, its tenets are vague, and the light which it sheds on the dark depths of human thought resembles more the sheet-lightning of a sombre evening, than the bright rays of a cloudless sunrise. Yet there is much to be learnt by the historian and the philosopher from these ancient guesses at truth; and we should not deprive ourselves of the new sources which have so unexpectedly been opened for studying the history of man, fearful and wonderful as his structure, by casting wanton doubts on all that conflicts with our own previous conclusions. I add only one more hymn, in which the idea of one God is expressed with such power and decision, that it will make us hesitate before we deny to the Aryan nations an instinctive Monotheism. (Ṛv. x. 121.)

"In the beginning there arose the Source of golden light—He was the only born lord of all that is. He stablished the earth, and this sky;—Who is the God to whom we shall offer our sacrifice?

He who gives life, He who gives strength; whose blessing all the bright gods desire; whose shadow is immortality; whose shadow is death;—Who is the God to whom we shall offer our sacrifice?

He who through His power is the only King of the breathing and awakening world;—He who governs all, man and beast;—Who is the God to whom we shall offer our sacrifice?

He whose power these snowy mountains, whose power the sea proclaims, with the distant river—He whose these regions are as it were His two arms;—Who is the God to whom we shall offer our sacrifice?

He through whom the sky is bright and the earth firm—He through whom the heaven was stablished—nay, the highest heaven—He who measured out the light in the air;—Who is the God to whom we shall offer our sacrifice?

He to whom heaven and earth, standing firm by His will, look up, trembling inwardly—He over whom the rising sun shines forth;—Who is the God to whom we shall offer our sacrifice?

Wherever the mighty water-clouds went, where they placed the seed and lit the fire, thence arose He who is the only life of the bright gods;—Who is the God to whom we shall offer our sacrifice?

He who by His might looked even over the water-clouds, the clouds which gave strength and lit the sacrifice, He *who is God above all gods*;—Who is the God to whom we shall offer our sacrifice?

May He not destroy us—He the creator of the

earth; or He, the righteous, who created the heaven; He who also created the bright and mighty waters;—Who is the God to whom we shall offer our sacrifice?"

There is nothing to prove that this hymn is of a particularly ancient date. On the contrary, there are expressions in it, especially the name of Hiraṇyagarbha, which seem to belong to a later age. But even if we assign the lowest possible date to this and similar hymns, certain it is that they existed during the Mantra period, and before the composition of the Brâhmaṇas; certain it is that every verse and every syllable was counted in the Anukramaṇîs of the Sûtra period. With our received notions on the history of the human mind it may be difficult to account for facts like these; but facts must not be made to evaporate in order to maintain a theory. The difficulty, such as it is, will be felt by all who think seriously and honestly on these problems. But it is better to state this difficulty than to conceal it. Even if we assign all philosophical hymns to the last years of the Mantra period, we have to account, in the 9th century B.C., for thoughts which, like the stems of forest trees, disclose circles within circles, almost impossible to count. There are hymns which are decidedly modern if compared with others: but if the most modern be ascribed to the Mantra period, what must be the date of the earliest relics of the Chhandas age? There can be little doubt, for instance, that the 90th hymn [1] of the 10th book, a hymn which is likewise found in the 31st

[1] A very careful discussion on this hymn, together with its text, translation, various readings and notes, is to be found in Dr. J. Muir's "Original Sanskrit Texts," pp. 6—11.

book of the Vâjasaneyi-sanhitâ, and in the 19th book of the Atharva-veda, is modern both in its character and in its diction. It is full of allusions to the sacrificial ceremonials, it uses technical philosophical terms, it mentions the three seasons in the order of Vasanta, spring, Grîshma, summer, and Śarad, autumn; it contains the only passage in the Rig-veda where the four castes are enumerated. The evidence of language for the modern date of this composition is equally strong. Grîshma, for instance, the name for the hot season, does not occur in any other hymn of the Rig-veda; and Vasanta also, the name of spring, does not belong to the earliest vocabulary of the Vedic poets. It occurs but once more in the Rig-veda, x. 161. 4., in a passage where the three seasons are mentioned in the order of Śarad, autumn, Hemanta, winter, and Vasanta, spring. But in spite of all the indications of a modern date, this hymn, if our argument holds good, must have existed before the beginning of the Brâhmaṇa period. I see no possibility how we could account for the allusions to it which occur in the Brâhmaṇas, or for its presence in the Sanhitâs of the Vâjesaneyins and Atharvans, unless we admit that this poem formed part of the final collection of the Rig-veda-sanhitâ, the work of the Mantra period. There are no traces anywhere of hymns having been added after that collection was closed, except in the case of the Khilas, and no secret is ever made as to their spurious character. Oriental scholars are frequently suspected of a desire to make the literature of the eastern nations appear more ancient than it is. As to myself, I can truly say that nothing would be to me a more welcome discovery, nothing would remove so many doubts and difficulties, as some suggestion as to the manner in which certain of the Vedic hymns could have been added to the original collection during the Brâhmaṇa or Sûtra periods, or, if possible, by the writers of our MSS., of which most are not older than the 15th century. But these MSS., though so modern, are checked by the Anukramaṇîs. Every hymn which stands in our MSS. is counted in the Index of Śaunaka, who is anterior to the invasion of Alexander. The Sûtras, belonging to the same period as Śaunaka, prove the previous existence of every chapter of the Brâhmaṇas: and I doubt whether there is a single hymn in the Sanhitâ of the Rig-veda which could not be checked by some passage of the Brâhmaṇas and Sûtras. The chronological limits assigned to the Sûtra and Brâhmaṇa periods will seem to most Sanskrit scholars too narrow rather than too wide, and if we assign but 200 years to the Mantra period, from 800 to 1000 B.C., and an equal number to the Chhandas period, from 1000 to 1200 B.C., we can do so only under the supposition that during the early periods of history the growth of the human mind was more luxuriant than in later times, and that the layers of thought were formed less slowly in the primary than in the tertiary ages of the world.

APPENDIX.

THE STORY OF ŚUNAḤŚEPHA, ACCORDING TO THE ŚÂKHÂ OF THE AITAREYINS, COLLATED WITH THE TEXT IN THE ŚÂNKHÂYANA-ŚÂKHÂ.

The upper line shows the various readings of the Śânkhâyana-sûtras.

हरिश्चंद्रो
हरिश्चंद्रो ह वैधस ऐक्ष्वाको राजापुत्र आस तस्य ह शतं
ह
जाया बभूवुस्तासु पुत्रं न लेभे तस्य ह पर्वतनारदौ गृह

ऊषतुः स ह नारदं पप्रच्छ॥
च
यन्न्विमं पुत्रमिच्छंति ये विजानंति ये च न।
तन्नः प्रब्रुहि
किंस्वित्पुत्रेण विंदते तन्म आचक्ष्व नारदेति॥१॥ [1]

[1] Some MSS. accent these verses. There are no types to render these accents in print.

स एकया पृष्टो दशभिः प्रत्युवाच॥

विंदते

ऋणमस्मिन्त्संनयत्यमृतत्वं च गच्छति।

पिता पुत्रस्य जातस्य पश्येच्चेज्जीवतो मुखं॥२॥

यावंतः पृथिव्यां भोगा यावंतो जातवेदसि।

यावंतो अप्सु प्राणिनां भूयान्पुत्रे पितुस्ततः॥३॥

शश्वत्पुत्रेण पितरोऽत्यायन्बहुलं तमः।

यज्ञ[1]

आत्मा हि जज्ञ आत्मनः स इरावत्यतितारिणी॥४॥

किं नु मलं किमजिनं किमु श्मश्रूणि किं तपः।

पुत्रं ब्रह्माण इच्छध्वं स वै लोको वदावदः॥५॥

अन्नं ह प्राणः शरणं ह वासो रूपं हिरण्यं पशवो विवाहाः।

सखा ह जाया कृपणं ह दुहिता ज्योतिर्ह पुत्रः परमे व्योमन्॥६॥

[1] Mitâksharâ I. p. 6^b. l. 6. has यज्ञ.

त्वाथ

पतिर्जायां प्रविशति गर्भो भूत्वा स मातरं।

तस्यां पुनर्नवो भूत्वा दशमे मासि जायते॥ ७॥

तज्जाया जाया भवति यदस्यां जायते पुनः।

आभूतिरेषाभूतिर्बीजमेतन्निधीयते॥ ८॥

देवाश्चैतामृषयश्च तेजः समभरन्महत्।

देवा मनुष्यानब्रुवन्नेषा वो जननी पुनः॥ ९॥

नापुत्रस्य लोकोऽस्तीति तत्सर्वे पशवो विदुः।

तीति॥ १७॥

तस्मात्तु पुत्रो मातरं स्वसारं चाधिरोहति॥ १०॥ [1]

विततो देवयानो येनाक्रमंते पुत्रिणो ये विशोकाः।

एष पंथा उरुगायः सुशेवो यं पुत्रिण आक्रमंते विशोकाः।

तर्यपि मिथुनं चरंति॥

deest.

तं पश्यंति पशवो वयांसि च तस्मात्ते मात्रापि मिथुनीभवंति॥ ११॥

deest———————

इति ह स्मा आख्याय॥ १२॥

[1] The Śânkhâyana-sûtras place verse 11 before verse 10.

स होवाच स वै मे ब्रूहि यथा मे पुत्रो जायेतेति तं

———————————————————— अथैन-

होवाच वरुणं

मुवाच वरुणं राजानमुपधाव पुत्रो मे जायतां तेन त्वा

यजा इति तथेति स वरुणं राजानमुपससार पुत्रो मे

जायतां तेन त्वा यजा इति तथेति तस्य ह पुत्रो जज्ञे

वरुण उवाचाज-

रोहितो नाम तं होवाचाजनि वै ते पुत्रो यजस्व मानेनेति

स होवाच यदा वै पशुर्निर्दशो भवत्यथ स मेध्यो भवति

निर्दशो न्वस्त्वथ त्वा यजा इति तथेति स ह निर्दश आस

वा अभू

तं होवाच निर्दशो न्वभूद्यजस्व मानेनेति स होवाच यदा

वै पशोर्दंता जायंतेऽथ स मेध्यो भवति दंता न्वस्य जायं-

तामथ त्वा यजा इति तथेति तस्य ह दंता जज्ञिरे तं

होवाचाज्ञत वा अस्य दंता यजस्व मानेनेति स होवाच

यदा वै पशोर्दंताः पद्यंतेऽथ स मेध्यो भवति दंता न्वस्य

पद्यंतामथ त्वा यजा इति तथेति तस्य ह दंताः पेदिरे तं
होवाचापत्सत वा अस्य दंता यजस्व मानेनेति स होवाच
यदा वै पशोर्दंताः पुनर्जायंतेऽथ स मेध्यो भवति दंता न्वस्य
पुनर्जायंतामथ त्वा यजा इति तथेति तस्य ह दंताः पुनर्ज-
ज्ञिरे तं होवाचाज्ञत वा अस्य पुनर्दंता यजस्व मानेनेति
संनाहं प्राप्नोत्य
स होवाच यदा वै क्षत्रियः सांनाहुको भवत्यथ स मेध्यो
भवति संनाहं नु प्राप्नोत्वथ त्वा यजा इति तथेति स ह
प्रापद्ध संनाहं
संनाहं प्रापत्तं होवाच सन्नाहं नु प्राप्नोद्यजस्व मानेनेति
यां चक्रे
स तथेत्युक्त्वा पुत्रमामंत्रयामास ततायं वै मह्यं त्वामद-
स ने
दाद्धंत त्वयाहमिमं यजा इति स ह नेत्युक्त्वा धनुरादा-
मु राय
यारण्यमपातस्थौ स संवत्सरमरण्ये चचार॥१४॥
कं राजानं व-
अथ हैक्ष्वाकं वरुणो जग्राह तस्य होदरं जज्ञे तदु ह

रोहितः शुश्राव सोऽरण्याद्ग्राममेयाय तमिंद्रः पुरुषरूपेण

पर्येत्योवाच॥१८॥

श्रू

नानाश्रांताय श्रीरस्तीति रोहित शुश्रुम।

निषद्वरो चरैव रोहितेति

पापो नृषद्वरो जन इंद्र इच्चरतः सखा चरैवेति॥१॥ [1]

चरै स

चरैवेति वै मा ब्राह्मणोऽवोचदिति ह द्वितीयं संवत्सरमरण्ये

चचार। सोऽरण्याद्ग्राममेयाय तमिंद्रः पुरुषरूपेण पर्ये-

त्योवाच॥

ले

पुष्पिण्यौ चरतो जंघे भूष्णुरात्मा फलग्रहिः।

शेरते श्चरैव रो°

शेरेऽस्य सर्वे पाप्मानः श्रमेण प्रपथे हताश्चरैवेति॥२॥

स

चरैवेति वै मा ब्राह्मणोऽवोचदिति ह तृतीयं संवत्सरमरण्ये

चचार सोऽरण्याद्ग्राममेयाय तमिंद्रः पुरुषरूपेण पर्येत्योवाच॥

[1] The Sânkhâyana-sûtras place the verses of Indra in a different order: 1, 3, 4, 2, 5, and add a sixth verse at the end.

आस्ते भग आसीनस्योर्द्ध्वस्तिष्ठति तिष्ठतः।

व रो°

शेते निपद्यमानस्य चराति चरतो भगश्चरैवेति॥३॥

स

चरैवेति वै मा ब्राह्मणोऽवोचदिति ह चतुर्थं संवत्सरमरण्ये

चचार सोऽरण्याद्ग्राममेयाय तमिंद्रः पुरुषरूपेण पर्येत्योवाच॥

नः पुरुषः

कलिः शयानो भवति संजिहानस्तु द्वापरः।

उत्थित व रो°

उत्तिष्ठंस्त्रेता भवति कृतं संपद्यते चरंश्चरैवेति॥४॥

स

चरैवेति वै मा ब्राह्मणोऽवोचदिति ह पंचमं संवत्सरमरण्ये

चचार सोऽरण्याद्ग्राममेयाय तमिंद्रः पुरुषरूपेण पर्येत्योवाच॥

र पक्वमुदुं

चरन्वै मधु विंदति चरन्स्वादुमुदुंबरं।

श्रयमाणं चरैव°

सूर्यस्य पश्य श्रेमाणं यो न तंद्रयते चरंश्चरैवेति॥५॥

स र° च°

चरैवेति वै मा ब्राह्मणोऽवोचदिति ह षष्ठं संवत्सरमरण्ये

चरन्वै मधु विंदत्यपजिन्वन्परूषकं। उत्तिष्ठन्विंदते श्रियं न

निषत्किंच नावति। चरैव° स सप्तमं संव° चचार सोऽजीगर्तं

———————————————— चचार सोऽजीगर्तं

नाया परीतं पुत्रं भक्ष्यमाणमरण्य[1] ॥१९॥

सौयवसिमृषिमशनया परीतमरण्य——— उपेयाय———

तस्य ह त्रयः पुत्रा आसुः शुनःपुच्छः शुनःशेपः शु-

न्हषे हंताहमेषामेकेना—

नोलांगूल इति तं होवाच न्हषेऽहं ते शतं ददा-

——————— णा अहं ते गवां शतं ददानीति

म्यहमेषामेकेनात्मानं निष्क्रीणा——————— इति

स ज्येष्ठं deest.

स ज्येष्ठं पुत्रं निगृह्णान उवाच न्विममिति नो एवेममिति

deest.

कनिष्ठं माता तौ ह मध्यमे संपादयां चक्रतुः शुनःशेपे

deest. deest.

तस्य ह शतं दत्वा स तमादाय सोऽरण्याद्ग्राममेयाय स

पितरमेत्योवाच तत हंताहमनेनात्मानं निष्क्रीणा इति

स तथेत्युक्त्वा वरु° मामंत्रयां चक्रेऽनेन

स वरुणं राजानमुपससारानेन त्वा यजा इति तथेति

श्रेया deest————

भूयान्वै ब्राह्मणः क्षत्रियादिति वरुण उवाच तस्मा एतं

[1] The statement that Ajîgarta intended to devour his son is clearly a modern addition of the Śânkhâyanas.

स एतं राजसूये पुरुषपशुमा-
राजसूयं यज्ञक्रतुं प्रोवाच तमेतमभिषेचनीये पुरुषं पशु-
लेभे॥२०॥
मालेभे॥१९॥

तामायास्य उद्गाता जम°
तस्य ह विश्वामित्रो होतासीज्जमदग्निरध्वर्युर्वसिष्ठो ब्रह्मा-

deest————
यास्य उद्गाता। तस्मा उपाकृताय नियोक्तारं न विविदुः।

त्वा
स होवाचाजीगर्तः सौयवसिर्मह्यमपरं शतं दत्ताहमेनं

नियुयोज
नियोक्ष्यामीति तस्मा अपरं शतं ददुस्तं स निनियोज।

य पर्यग्नि———— शास्तारं
तस्मा उपाकृताय नियुक्तायाप्रीताय पर्यग्निकृताय विशसितारं

न विविदुः। स होवाचाजीगर्तः सौयवसिर्मह्यमपरं शतं

त्वा
दत्ताहमेनं विशसिष्यामीति तस्मा अपरं शतं ददुः सोऽसिं

निश्शान इच्छामासा मा
निःशान एयायाथ ह शुनःशेप ईक्षां चक्रे मानुषमिव वै

हंत दे नीति॥२१॥
मा विशसिष्यंति हंताहं देवता उपधावामीति स प्रजापतिमेव

प्रथमं देवतानामुपससार कस्य नूनं कतमस्यामृतानामित्येत-

ग्नैर्वै नेदिष्ठो ऽसि तमे

यर्चा तं प्रजापतिरुवाचाग्निर्वै देवानां नेदिष्ठस्तमेवोपधावेति

सोऽग्निमुपससाराग्नेर्वयं प्रथमस्यामृतानामित्येतयर्चा। तम-

ग्निरुवाच सविता वै प्रसवानामीशे तमेवोपधावेति स सवि-

तारमुपससाराभि त्वा देव सवितरित्येतेन तृचेन तं सवि-

तोवाच वरुणाय वै राज्ञे नियुक्तोऽसि तमेवोपधावेति। स

वरुणं राजानमुपससारात उत्तराभिरेकत्रिंशता तं वरुण

यं स्त नु

उवाचाग्निर्वै देवानां मुखं सुहृदयतमस्तं नु स्तुह्यथ त्वो-

त्स्रक्ष्यामीति भिरेव द्वा

त्स्रक्ष्याम इति सोऽग्निं तुष्टावात उत्तराभिर्द्वाविंशत्या।

वां स्तु त्स्रक्ष्यामीति

तमग्निरुवाच विश्वान्नु देवान्स्तुह्यथ त्वोत्स्रक्ष्याम इति स

श्वान्नु देवांस्तु

विश्वान्देवांस्तुष्टाव नमो महद्भ्यो नमो अर्भकेभ्य इत्येतयर्चा।

रिंद्रं नु स्तुह्य

तं विश्वे देवा ऊचुरिंद्रो वै देवानामोजिष्ठो बलिष्ठः सहिष्ठः

त्स्र

सत्तमः पारयिष्णुतमस्तं नु स्तुह्यथ त्वोत्स्रक्ष्याम इति स

इत्येतेन—

इंद्रं तुष्टाव यच्चिद्धि सत्य सोमपा इति चैतेन सूक्तेनोत्त-

नो मनसा——

रस्य च पंचदशभिस्तस्मा इंद्र स्तूयमानः प्रीतो मनसा

यर्चा

हिरण्यरथं ददौ तमेतया प्रतीयाय शश्वदिंद्र इति तमिंद्र

त्सृच्छामीति

उवाचाश्विनौ नु स्तुह्यथ त्वोत्स्रक्ष्याम इति सोऽश्विनौ तुष्टा-

वात उत्तरेण तृचेन तमश्विना ऊचतुरुषसं नु स्तुह्यथ

त्सृच्छाव इति णैव

त्वोत्स्रक्ष्याम इति स उषसं तुष्टावात उत्तरेण तृचेन

नितरां पाशो

तस्य ह स्मर्च्युक्तायां विपाशो मुमुचे कनीय ऐक्ष्वाकस्योदरं

बभूवोत्तमायां ह स्मर्च्यु

भवत्युक्तमस्यामेवर्च्युक्तायां विपाशो मुमुचेऽगद ऐक्ष्वाक

बभूवाथा हैनम् मेवैतस्याह्नः

आस॥१९॥ तमृत्विज ऊचुस्त्वमेव नोऽस्याह्नः संस्थामधि-

गच्छेः॥२२॥ अथ हैनमंजःसवं शुनःशेपो ददर्श यच्चि——

गच्छेत्यथ हैतं शुनःशेपोऽंजःसवं ददर्श। तमेताभिस्तस्र-

———— इति तमेताभिस्तस्र-

भिरभिसुषाव यच्चिद्धि त्वं गृहे गृह इत्यथैनं द्रोणकलश-

भिरभिषुत्योच्छिष्टं रेति द्रोणकलशे समवनिनाया-

मभ्यवनिनायोच्छिष्टं चम्वोर्भरेत्यतयर्चाथ हा——

थास्मिन्नन्वारब्धा एतस्यैव सूक्तस्य पू भिर्जु___
__स्मिन्नन्वारब्धे_______________पूर्वाभिःश्चतसृभिः सखा-
________ थ है स त्वं
हाकाराभिर्जुहवां चकाराथैनमवभृथमभ्यवनिनाय त्वं नो
अग्नेऽवमस्त्वं नो अग्ने मृग्भ्यामथ हैनमग्निमुप_____
अग्ने वरुणस्य विद्वानित्येताभ्यामथैनमत ऊर्ध्वमग्निमाहवनी-
___ यामास स शु त्येत-
यमुपस्थापयां चकार शुनश्चिच्छेपं निदितं सहस्रादित्यथ ह
यर्चा॥२३॥ अथ ह स्योपस्थमाससाद रतं
_______________शुनःशेपो विश्वामित्रस्यांकमाससाद। स
हो सिः पुन
होवाचाजीगर्तः सौयवसिर्ऋषे पुनर्मे पुत्रं देहीति नेति होवाच

विश्वामित्रो देवा वा इमं मह्यमरासतेति स ह देवरातो
आस तं होवाचाजीवगर्तः_______________
वैश्वामित्र आस तस्यैते कापिलेयबाभ्रवाः स होवाचाजीगर्तः
वै वि मह्रा इति तथेत्यांगि_________
सौयवसिस्त्वं वेहि विक्रयावहा इति स होवाचाजीगर्तः सौ-
________ र्तः
यवसिरांगिरसो जन्मनास्याजीगर्तिः श्रुतः कविः। ऋषे पैता-

महात्तंतोर्मापगाः पुनरेहि मामिति॥ स होवाच शुनःशेपोऽ
द्राचु लि
दर्शुस्त्वा शासहस्तं न यच्छूद्रेष्वलप्सत। गवां त्रीणि शतानि

तं
त्वमवृणीथा मदंगिर इति स होवाचाजीगर्तः सौयवसिस्तद्वै
कृ
मा तात तपति पापं कर्म मया कृतं। तदहं निह्नवे तुभ्यं
ती
प्रतियंतु शता गवामिति। स होवाच शुनःशेपो यः स-
तकं स्त मापगा कौद्राण्यायाद
कृत्पापकं कुर्यात्कुर्यादेनत्ततोऽपरं। नापागाः शौद्रान्न्यायाद-
वा अवोचदिति ह वि
संधेयं त्वया कृतमित्यसंधेयमिति ह विश्वामित्र उपपपाद
॥२४॥ भीम________
स होवाच विश्वामित्रो भीम एव सायवसिः शासेन विशि-
शिषत्।
शासिषुः। अस्थान्मेतस्य पुत्रो भूर्ममैवोपेहि पुत्रतामिति स
य त्रं
होवाच शुनःशेपः स वै यथा नो ज्ञपया राजपुत्र तथा
तं
वद। यथैवांगिरसः सन्नुपेयां तव पुत्रतामिति। स होवाच
विश्वामित्रो ज्येष्ठो मे त्वं पुत्राणां स्यास्तव श्रेष्ठा प्रजा
दु ने
स्यात्। उपेयादेवं मे दायं तेन वै त्वोपमंत्रय इति स
दे
होवाच शुनःशेपः संज्ञानानेषु वै ब्रूयात्सौहार्दाय मे श्रि-

ये। यथाहं भरतऋषभोपेयां तव पुत्रतामित्यथ ह वि-
यां चक्रे॥२५॥

श्वामित्रः पुत्रानामंत्रयामास मधुच्छंदाः शृणोतन ऋषभो रे-
ज्येष्ठाय तिष्ठध्वमिति

णुरष्टकः। ये केच भ्रातरः स्थनास्मै ज्यैष्ठ्याय कल्पध्वमिति॥१७॥
हैक____

तस्य ह विश्वामित्रस्यैकशतं पुत्रा आसुः पंचाशदेव ज्यायांसो

मधुच्छंदसः पंचाशत्कनीयांसस्तद्ये ज्यायांसो न ते कुशलं
रांतं वः ते
मेनिरेताननुव्याजहारांतान्वः प्रजा भक्षीष्टेति त एते
अंध्राः पुंड्राः रा deest. मूचिपा दंचो वङ्गद-
ऽध्राः पुंड्राः शबराः पुलिंदा मूतिबा इत्युदंत्या बहवो
स्यवो deest. यिष्ठा इत्युदाहरंत्यथ ये मधुच्छं-
——भवंति वैश्वामित्रा दस्यूनां भूयिष्ठाः। स होवाच मधुच्छंदाः
दःप्रभृतयः कनीयांसस्ते कुशलं मेनिरे स ह जगौ मधु-
पंचाशता सार्धं यन्नः पिता____
च्छंदा यन्नः पिता संजानीते स्तात्
____ संजानीते तस्मिंस्तिष्ठामहे वयं। पुरस्त्वा

सर्वे कुर्महे त्वामन्वंचो वयं स्मसीत्यथ ह विश्वामित्रः प्रतीतः
व॥२६॥ ते वै प्रजा
पुत्रांस्तुष्टाव ते व पुत्राः पशुमंतो वीरवंतो भविष्यथ। ये

मानं मेऽनुगृह्णंतो वीरवंतमकर्त मा॥ पुरएत्रा वीरवंतो
वसुद्धि वा-
देवरातेन गाथिनाः। सर्वे राध्या स्थ पुत्रा एष वः सद्विवा-
चकः।
चनं॥ एष वः कुशिका वीरो देवरातस्तमन्वित। युष्मांश्च
वोपेतां चामुत
दायं म उपेता विद्यां यामु च विद्मसि॥ ते सम्यंचो
ज्यैष्ठे
वैश्वामित्राः सर्वे साकं सरातयः। देवरातायं तस्थिरे धृत्यै
श्रैष्ठे च
श्रैष्ठ्याय गाथिनाः॥ अधीयत देवरातो रिक्थयोरुभयोर्ऋषिः।
तस्थिरे नाः॥ च्छौनःशे-
जह्नूनां चाधिपत्ये दैवे वेदे च गाथिनां॥ तदेतत्परऋक्श-
पमाख्यानं परशतगाथमपरिमितं तद्धोताभि
तगाथं शौनःशेपमाख्यानं______तद्धोता राज्ञेऽभिषिक्ता-

याचष्टे हिरण्यकशिपावासीन आचष्टे हिरण्यकशिपावासीनः
णात्योमि______
प्रतिगृणाति यशो वै हिरण्यं यशसै वैनं तत्समर्धयत्योमित्यृचः

प्रतिगर एवं तथेति गाथाया ओमिति वै दैवं तथेति मानुषं
सर्वस्मादेनसः संप्रमुच्येते
दैवेन चैवैनं तन्मानुषेण च पापादेनसः प्रमुंचति तस्माद्यो

जी

राजा विजिती स्यादप्ययजमान आख्यापयेतैवैतच्छौनःशेप-

माख्यानं न ह्यस्मिन्नल्पं चनैनः परिशिष्यते सहस्रमाख्यात्रे

शतं_____ पुत्रकामा ह्याप्याख्या-

दद्याच्छतं पतिगरित्र एते चैवासने श्वेतश्चाश्वतरो रथो

पयंते लभंते ह____________________

होतुः पुत्रकामा ह्याप्याख्यापयेरँल्लभंते ह पुत्राँल्लभंते ह

पुत्रान् ॥१८॥

INDEX.

A.

B.

C.

N.

T.

THE END.